New Online Biographical Resource from African American Publications

We're pleased to introduce the *Reference Library of American Men* and a wonderful, new online biographical resource. This online Web enhancement brings you extended coverage of notable individuals featured in the *Reference Library of American Men*, as well as coverage of other prominent male figures not found in the print publication.

We're pleased to remind you that you have been **automatically authorized** to access the site. Just follow these simple instructions:

• Locate the Web address card in the front matter of Volume I of this publication

• Go to **www.americanmenpubs.com** and simply access the Registration page

• When registering, be sure to include your invoice/access number

Your students are sure to enjoy these easy-to-read online essays that offer extensive insight into the lives of *hundreds* of fascinating American men.

Thank you for your interest and enjoy this terrific online biographical resource!

www.americanmenpubs.com

African American Publications
Phone: 215-321-7742
Fax: 215-321-9568
E-mail: afriampub@aol.com

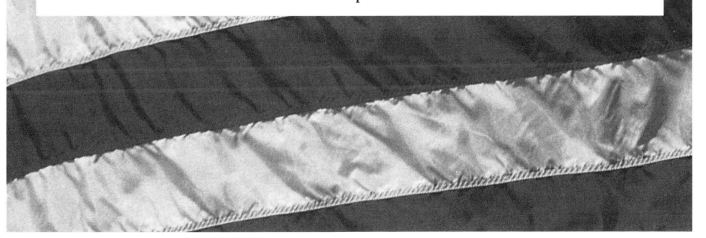

Reference
Library of

AMERICAN

MEN

Reference Library of

AMERICAN

MEN

VOLUME **I**

A-D

REFERENCE LIBRARY OF AMERICAN MEN

Staff

Editor: Jennifer Mossman
Managing Editor: Bridget Travers

Permissions Manager: Maria L. Franklin
Permissions Associate: Shalice Shah-Caldwell

Manufacturing Manager: Dorothy Maki
Production Manager: Evi Seoud
Buyer: Rita Wimberley

Product Design Manager: Kenn Zorn
Graphic Artist: Mike Logusz

Copyright © 2002
Gale Group, Inc.
27500 Drake Rd.
Farmington Hills, MI 48331-3535

ISBN 0-7876-6259-3 (4-volume set)
ISBN 0-7876-6260-7 (Volume 1)
ISBN 0-7876-6261-5 (Volume 2)
ISBN 0-7876-6262-3 (Volume 3)
ISBN 0-7876-6263-1 (Volume 4)

Printed in the United States of America

10 9 8 7 6 5 4 3 2 1

CONTENTS

INTRODUCTION

The *Reference Library of American Men* provides a unique, comprehensive source for biographical information on 650 men who have gained international recognition for their enduring contributions to human culture and society. Entries in this four-volume set have been culled from Gale's extensive biographical database. Both contemporary and historic figures covering a wide range of occupations or fields of endeavor can be found. Featured are such renowned contemporary personalities as Muhammad Ali, Woody Allen, Bob Dylan, Bill Gates, Steven Spielberg, and Tiger Woods. Important historic figures include presidents George Washington, Thomas Jefferson, Abraham Lincoln, and Franklin Roosevelt; writers William Faulkner, Ernest Hemingway, Herman Melville, Edgar Allan Poe and Mark Twain; industrialists Andrew Carnegie, Thomas Edison, William Randolph Hearst, Henry Ford, and John D. Rockefeller; and musicians Louis Armstrong, Duke Ellington, Elvis Presley, and Frank Sinatra. Biographical information can be found for the many social or political activists who have organized movements to demand equal rights for all American citizens, such as Martin Luther King Jr., Malcolm X, and Cesar Chavez. Others have made major contributions to the arts, business, education, journalism, religion, or science.

Format

Arranged alphabetically, each authoritative article begins with a brief descriptive paragraph that provides a capsule identification and a statement of the man's significance. Birth and death years are included. Often this is all the information required. This useful feature allows you to determine at a glance whether you need to read further. For example:

> The second president of the United States, John Adams (1735–1826) played a major role in the colonial movement toward independence. He wrote the Massachusetts Constitution of 1780 and served as a diplomatic representative of Congress in the 1780s.

The essays that follow are generally about 800 words in length and offer a substantial treatment of the men's lives. Some proceed chronologically, while others confine biographical data to a few paragraphs and then move on to a consideration of the subject's life work. When very few biographical facts are known, the article is necessarily devoted to an analysis of the subject's contribution to society and culture.

Following the essay is a "Further Reading" section and, when applicable, a list of additional sources providing more recent biographical works. Bibliographic citations include books, periodicals, and Internet addresses for World Wide Web pages. This feature will be especially helpful to students, who are frequently required to consult multiple sources when compiling a report or preparing a classroom presentation.

Additional Features

Images. Portraits accompany many of the articles and provide an authentic likeness or representation of the biographee. For historic figures, there are depictions from coins, engravings, and sculptures; for the moderns there are many photographs.

Indexes. Two indexes have been included to help researchers identify the men by name and occupation.

A Valuable Resource

Biographical information on internationally renowned men is always in high demand. The *Reference Library of American Men* can meet this need by presenting lively and informative essays on 650 men whose contributions have earned them a place in the annals of human history.

ACKNOWLEDGMENTS

Photographs and illustrations that appear in *Reference Library of American Men* were received from the following sources:

Aaron, Hank, photograph. National Archives and Records Administration.

Abernathy, Ralph, photograph. The Library of Congress.

Acheson, Dean, photograph. Archive Photos, Inc. Reproduced by permission.

Adams, Ansel, photograph. AP/Wide World Photos. Reproduced by permission.

Adams, Hank, photograph. AP/Wide World Photos. Reproduced by permission.

Adams, John, painting by C. W. Peale. National Archives and Records Administration.

Adams, Samuel, portrait by John S. Copley. National Archives and Records Administration.

Aiken, Conrad, photograph. The Library of Congress.

Ailey, Alvin, photograph. The Library of Congress

Ali, Muhammad, photograph. UPI/Corbis-Bettmann. Reproduced by permission.

Allen, Woody, photograph. United Artists.

Alvarez, Luis, photograph. The Library of Congress.

Armstrong, Edwin Howard, photograph. The Library of Congress.

Armstrong, Louis, photograph. AP/Wide World Photos, Inc. Reproduced by permission.

Armstrong, Neil A., photograph. U.S. National Aeronautics and Space Administration (NASA).

Arnold, Benedict, painting. The Library of Congress.

Arthur, Chester A., photograph. The Library of Congress.

Ashe, Arthur, photograph. AP/Wide World Photos. Reproduced by permission.

Asimov, Isaac, photograph. The Library of Congress.

Astaire, Fred, photograph. AP/Wide World Photos. Reproduced by permission.

Astor, John Jacob, painting. The Library of Congress.

Audubon, John James, engraving. The Library of Congress.

Balanchine, George, photograph. Archive Photos, Inc. Reproduced by permission.

Baltimore, David, 1975, photograph. AP/Wide World Photos, Inc. Reproduced by permission.

Banneker, Benjamin, engraving.

Baraka, Amiri, 1994, photograph by Christopher Felver. Archive Photos, Inc. Reproduced by permission.

Barnum, P. T., photograph. Archive Photos, Inc. Reproduced by permission.

Barthe, Richmond, photograph by Betsy G. Reyneau. National Archives and Records Administration.

Basie, Count, photograph. The Library of Congress.

Beadle, George W., Chicago, 1965, photograph. The Library of Congress.

Bell, Alexander Graham, photograph. U. S. National Aeronautics and Space Administration.

Bellow, Saul, photograph. The Library of Congress.

Bennett, William, photograph by Ira Schwarz. Archive Photos. Reproduced by permission.

Berg, Paul, photograph. The Library of Congress.

Berlin, Irving, photograph. The Library of Congress.

Bernardin, Joseph Cardinal, photograph. The Library of Congress.

Berry, Chuck, photograph. The Library of Congress.

Bieber, Owen, photograph. UPI/Bettmann Newsphotos. Reproduced by permission.

Bird, Larry, photograph. AP/Wide World Photos. Reproduced by permission.

Blanc, Mel, 1980, photograph. AP/Wide World Photos. Reproduced by permission.

Bluford, Guion, S. Jr., photograph. U.S. National Aeronautics and Space Administration (NASA).

Boeing, William E, photograph. AP/Wide World Photos. Reproduced by permission.

Bogart, Humphrey, photograph. Springer/Corbis-Bettmann. Reproduced by permission.

Bond, Julian, photograph. The Library of Congress

Boone, Daniel, photograph. The Library of Congress.

Bradbury, Ray, photograph. The Library of Congress.

Bradley, Ed, photograph. AP/Wide World Photos. Reproduced by permission.

Brady, Mathew B., photograph. The Library of Congress.

Brandeis, Louis, photograph . The Library of Congress.

Brown, James, photograph. The Library of Congress.

Brown, John, illustration. National Archives and Records Administration.

Bruce, Blanche Kelso, photograph. U.S. Senate Historical Office.

Bryant, William Cullen, photograph. The Library of Congress.

Buchanan, James, painting. The Library of Congress.

Buchanan, Patrick J., photograph. The Library of Congress.

Buffett, Warren E., photograph. AP/Wide World Photos. Reproduced by permission.

Burbank, Luther, photograph. The Library of Congress.

Burger, Warren E., photograph. The Library of Congress.

Burns, George, photograph. The Library of Congress.

Burroughs, William S., photograph. AP/Wide World Photos. Reproduced by permission.

Bush, George, photograph. The Library of Congress.

Bush, George W, photograph by Adrees Latif. Reuters/Archive Photos. Reproduced by permission.

Bush, Vannevar, photograph. The Library of Congress.

Byrd, Richard Evelyn, photograph by Underwood and Underwood. The Library of Congress.

Calder, Alexander S., photograph. The Library of Congress.

Calhoun, John Caldwell, photograph. The Library of Congress

Calvin, Melvin, photograph. The Library of Congress.

Campbell, Ben Nighthorse, photograph. AP/Wide World Photos. Reproduced by permission.

Capone, Al, photograph. Archive Photos, Inc. Reproduced by permission.

Capote, Truman, photograph. The Library of Congress.

Carmichael, Stokely, photograph. The Library of Congress.

Carson, Johnny, photograph. The Library of Congress.

Carson, Kit, painting. The Library of Congress.

Carter, Jimmy, photograph. The Library of Congress.

Carver, George Washington, photograph. The Library of Congress.

Cash, Johnny, photograph. The Library of Congress.

Chamberlain, Wilt, 1991, photograph. AP/Wide World Photos. Reproduced by permission.

Charles, Ray, photograph. The Library of Congress.

Chavez, Cesar, photograph. The Library of Congress.

Chavez, Dennis, photograph. Library of Congress.

Chavis, Benjamin Franklin, Jr., photograph. AP/Wide World. Reproduced by permission.

Chief Seattle, photograph. The Library of Congress.

Chomsky, Noam, photograph. Archive Photos. Reproduced by permission.

Christopher, Warren, photograph. Archive Photo/Popperfoto. Reproduced by permission.

Cisneros, Henry, photograph. AP/Wide World Photos. Reproduced by permission.

Clancy, Tom, photograph. AP/Wide World Photos. Reproduced by permission.

Cleaver, Eldridge, New York City, 1968, photograph. AP/Wide World Photos. Reproduced by permission.

Cleveland, Grover, photograph. The Library of Congress.

Cleveland, James, photograph. AP/Wide World Photos. Reproduced by permission.

Clinton, George, painting . The Library of Congress.

Clinton, Bill, flanked by Vice-President Gore and Attorney General Janet Reno, 1993 95, photograph. The Library of Congress.

Cole, Nat King, photograph. The Library of Congress.

Colt, Samuel, illustration.

Coltrane, John, photograph. The Library of Congress.

Compton, Arthur Holly, photograph. The Library of Congress.

Coolidge, Calvin, photograph. The Library of Congress.

Cooper, James Fenimore, drawing by C. L. Elliot. Source unknown.

Copland, Aaron, photograph.

Coppola, Francis Ford, photograph by Frank Capri. Archive Photos, Inc. Reproduced by permission.

Cosby, (Bill) William Henry, Jr., photograph. The Library of Congress.

Coughlin, Charles E., photograph. AP/Wide World Photos, Inc. Reproduced by permission.

Crane, Stephen, photograph. The Library of Congress.

Cray, Seymour, photograph. AP/Wide World Photos, Inc. Reproduced by permission.

Crazy Horse, photograph. The Library of Congress.

Crichton, Michael, photograph. AP/Wide World Photos, Inc. Reproduced by permission.

Cronkite, Walter L., Jr., photograph. The Library of Congress.

Cummings, E. E., photograph. The Library of Congress.

Cuomo, Mario, photograph. Archive Photos, Inc. Reproduced by permission.

Cushing, Harvey Williams, photograph. The Library of Congress.

Custer, George Armstrong, photograph. The Library of Congress.

Darrow, Clarence Seward, photograph. The Library of Congress.

Davis, Jefferson, photograph by Mathew Brady. National Archives and Records Administration.

Davis, Miles, photograph. The Library of Congress.

Davis, Richard Harding, photograph. The Library of Congress

Davis, Sammy Jr., photograph. The Library of Congress.

de Forest, Lee, photograph. The Library of Congress.

Dean, James B., photograph. The Library of Congress.

Debs, Eugene V., photograph. The Library of Congress

Dees, Morris, 1996, photograph by Laurence Agron. Archive Photos, Inc. Reproduced by permission.

Delany, Martin Robinson (holding sword in right hand to the ground), painting. Archive Photos. Reproduced by permission.

Delbruck, Max, photograph. The Library of Congress.

Deloria, Vine, Jr. (seated at desk, head tilted, right hand extended out), photograph. The Library of Congress.

Dewey, John, painting. Columbiana Collection, Columbia University Libraries.

Dinkins, David, photograph. Archive Photos. Reproduced by permissions.

Disney, Walt, photograph. UPI/Corbis-Bettmann. Reproduced by permission.

Dole, Robert, photograph. The Library of Congress.

Dos Passos, John, photograph. The Library of Congress.

Douglas, Stephen A., photograph. The Library of Congress.

Douglas, William Orville, photograph. Archive Photos, Inc. Reproduced by permission.

Douglass, Frederick, photograph. The Library of Congress.

Dreiser, Theodore, photograph by Pirie MacDonald. The Library of Congress.

Drew, Charles Richard, photograph. AP/Wide World Photos. Reproduced by permission.

DuBois, Dr. William E., Paris, 1949, photograph. AP/Wide World Photos, Inc. Reproduced by permission.

Dulles, John Foster, photograph.

Dunbar, Paul Laurence, photograph. The Library of Congress.

Durant, William Crapo, photograph, The Library of Congress.

Dylan, Bob, 1979, photograph by Joseph Sia. Archive Photos, Inc. Reproduced by permission.

Eastman, Charles J., drawing. Archive Photos, Inc. Reproduced by permission.

Eastman, George, photograph. The Library of Congress.

Eastwood, Clint, photograph. The Library of Congress.

Edison, Thomas Alva, photograph. The Library of Congress.

Eisenhower, Dwight D., photograph. The Library of Congress.

Eliot, T.S., photograph. The Library of Congress.

Ellington, Duke, New York, 1943, photographed by Gordon Parks. The Library of Congress.

Ellison, Ralph, photograph. AP/Wide World Photos. Reproduced by permission.

Ellsworth, Lincoln, photograph. The Library of Congress.

Emerson, Ralph Waldo, engraving by S.A. Choff. The Library of Congress.

Enders, John F., photograph. The Library of Congress.

Erving, Julius, photograph. AP/Wide World Photos. Reproduced by permission.

Evers, Medgar W., photograph. The Library of Congress.

Farmer, James, photograph. The Library of Congress.

Farragut, D.G., photograph. The Library of Congress.

Farrakhan, Louis, photograph. AP/Wide World Photos. Reproduced by permission.

Father Divine, photograph. The Library of Congress.

Feynman, Richard P., photograph. The Library of Congress.

Fillmore, Millard, photograph. The Library of Congress.

Fitzgerald, F. Scott, photograph.

Flory, Paul J., photograph. AP/Wide World Photos. Reproduced by permission.

Forbes, Malcolm, photograph. The Library of Congress.

Ford, Gerald R., photograph. The Library of Congress.

Ford, Henry, photograph.

Forman, James, photograph. The Library of Congress.

Fosse, Bob, photograph. The Library of Congress.

Frankfurter, Felix, photograph. The Library of Congress.

Franklin, Benjamin, painting. The Library of Congress.

Fremont, John Charles, photograph of engraving. The Library of Congress

Frost, Robert, photograph. The Library of Congress.

Fuller, Richard Buckminster, photograph. Archive Photos. Reproduced by permission.

Fulton, Robert, painting. The Library of Congress.

Gallup, George, photograph. The Library of Congress.

Garfield, James, illustration. The Library of Congress.

Garrison, William Lloyd, photograph. The Library of Congress.

Gates, Bill, photograph. AP/Wide World Photos. Reproduced by permission.

Geisel, Theodor (Dr. Seuss), photograph. The Library of Congress.

Gell-Mann, Murray, 1969, photograph. AP/Wide World Photos. Reproduced by permission.

Gephardt, Richard A., photograph. The Library of Congress.

Geronimo, photograph by Ben Wittick. The Library of Congress.

Getty, J. Paul, Sr., photograph. Archive Photos, Inc./ Express Newspapers. Reproduced by permission.

Ginsberg, Allen, photograph.The Library of Congress.

Giuliani, Rudolf, photograph. Archive Photo/Malafronte. Reproduced by permission.

Glenn, John, photograph. U.S. National Aeronautics and Space Administration (NASA).

Goddard, Robert H., photograph. The Library of Congress.

Goldwater, Barry, photograph. UPI/Corbis-Bettmann. Reproduced by permission.

Gompers, Samuel, photograph. The Library of Congress.

Goodman, Benny, photograph. Archive Photos, Inc. Reproduced by permission.

Goodyear, Charles, sketch. The Library of Congress.

Gordy, Berry, Jr., photograph. AP/Wide World Photos. Reproduced by permission.

Gorgas, William Crawford, photograph.

Gould, Stephen Jay, photograph. AP/Wide World Photos. Reproduced by permission.

Graham, Billy, photograph. The Library of Congress.

Grant, Ulysses Simpson, photograph. The Library of Congress.

Greeley, Reverand Andrew, photograph. AP/Wide World Photos, Inc. Reproduced by permission.

Greenspan, Alan, photograph.The Library of Congress.

Gregory, Dick, photograph. The Library of Congress.

Griffith, David Lewelyn Wark, photograph. Archive Photos, Inc. Reproduced by permission.

Grisham, John, photograph by Capri. Archive. Reproduced by permission.

Grove, Andrew, 1997, photograph by Russell Boyce. Reuters/Archive Photos, Inc. Reproduced by permission.

Guthrie, Woodrow W., photograph. The Library of Congress.

Halberstam, David, photograph by Bernard Gotfryd. Archive Photos, Inc. Reproduced by permission.

Haley, Alex, photograph. AP/Wide World Photos, Inc. Reproduced by permission.

Hamilton, Alexander, portrait by John Trumbull. National Archives and Records Administration.

Hammer, Armand, photograph. The Library of Congress.

Hancock, John, painting by John Singleton Copley. National Archives and Records Administration.

Handsome Lake, drawing by Jesse Cornplanter. The Library of Congress.

Handy, W.C., photograph. The Library of Congress.

Harding, Warren G., photograph. The Library of Congress.

Haring, Keith, photograph. Archive Photos, Inc. Reproduced by permission.

Harris, Joel Chandler, photograph. The Library of Congress.

Harrison, Benjamin, photograph. The Library of Congress.

Harte, Bret, engraving. The Library of Congress.

Hawthorne, Nathaniel, photograph.

Hay, John Milton, photograph. The Library of Congress.

Hayes, Rutherford B., photograph. The Library of Congress.

Hearst, William Randolph, photograph. The Library of Congress.

Heller, Joseph, photograph. AP/Wide World Photos. Reproduced by permission.

Hemingway, Ernest and Elizabeth Hadley, photograph.

Hendrix, Jimi, photograph. AP/Wide World Photos. Reproduced by permission.

Henry, Joseph, photograph. Corbis-Bettmann. Reproduced by permission.

Henson, Matthew A., illustration. The Library of Congress.

Hershey, Alfred D., photograph. The Library of Congress.

Heschel, Abraham J., photograph. The Library of Congress.

Hickok, Wild Bill, photograph. National Archives and Records Administration.

Hiss, Alger, photograph. The Library of Congress.

Hoffa, Jimmy, photograph. Archive Photos, Inc. Reproduced by permission.

Hoffman, Abbie, photograph. The Library of Congress.

Holmes, Oliver Wendall Jr., photograph. The Library of Congress.

Holmes, Oliver Wendell, photograph. The Library of Congress.

Hooks, Benjamin L., photograph. The Library of Congress.

Hoover, Herbert, photograph. The Library of Congress.

Hoover, J. Edgar, photograph. The Library of Congress.

Hope, Bob, photograph. UPI/Bettmann. Reproduced by permission.

Hopper, Edward, photograph. AP/Wide World Photos. Reproduced by permission.

Horowitz, Vladimir, photograph. The Library of Congress.

Houdini, Harry, photograph. Archive Photos, Inc. Reproduced by permission.

Houston, Charles H., photograph. UPI/Corbis-Bettmann. Reproduced by permission.

Houston, Samuel, drawing. The Library of Congress.

Howe, Elias, photograph. Archive Photos, Inc. Reproduced by permission.

Hubble, Edwin, photograph. The Library of Congress.

Hughes, Howard, photograph. The Library of Congress.

Humphrey, Hubert H., Jr., photograph. The Library of Congress.

Iacocca, Lee, photograph. The Library of Congress.

Irving, Washington, painting. The Library of Congress.

Jackson, Andrew, drawing. The Library of Congress.

Jackson, Jesse L., photograph. The Library of Congress.

Jackson, Michael, photograph. AP/Wide World Photos. Reproduced by permission.

Jackson, Reggie, photograph. AP/Wide World Photos. Reproduced by permission.

Jackson, T.J. (Stonewall), print.

James, Henry, photograph. The Library of Congress.

Jefferson, Thomas, engraving. The Library of Congress.

Jobs, Steven, photograph. Archive Photos/Reuters/Sell. Reproduced by permission.

Joffrey, Robert, photograph. AP/Wide World Photos. Reproduced by permissions.

Johns, Jasper, photograph. Corbis-Bettmann. Reproduced by permission.

Johnson, Andrew, photograph. The Library of Congress.

Johnson, Earvin "Magic", photograph. AP/Wide World Photos. Reproduced by permission.

Johnson, Jack, photograph. The Library of Congress.

Johnson, James Weldon, photograph. The Library of Congress.

Johnson, John H., photograph. The Library of Congress.

Johnson, Lyndon B., photograph. LBJ Library Collections.

Jolson, Al, photograph. The Library of Congress.

Jones, James Earl, photograph. The Library of Congress.

Jones, Quincy, photograph. The Library of Congress.

Jones, Robert T., photograph. The Library of Congress.

Joplin, Scott, illustration. Corbis-Bettmann. Reproduced by permission.

Jordan, Louis, photograph. The Library of Congress.

Jordan, Michael, photograph. Reuters/Corbis-Bettmann. Reproduced by permission.

Julian, Percy Lavon, photograph. The Library of Congress.

Kahn, Louis, photograph. AP/Wide World Photos. Reproduced by permission.

Kelly, Gene, photograph. The Library of Congress.

Kemp, Jack French Jr., photograph. The Library of Congress.

Kendall, Edward C., photograph. The Library of Congress.

Kennedy, John F., photograph. The Library of Congress.

Kennedy, Robert, photograph. John F. Kennedy Library.

Kerouac, Jack, photograph. Archive Photos. Reproduced by permission.

Kessler, David A., photograph by Dennis Cook. AP/Wide World Photos. Reproduced by permission.

Kettering, Charles Franklin, photograph. The Library of Congress

King, B.B., photograph. AP/Wide World Photos. Reproduced by permission.

King, Dr. Martin Luther, Jr., painting by Betsy G. Reyneau. National Archives and Records Administration.

King, Stephen, photograph. Archive Photos, Inc. Reproduced by permission.

Kinsey, Alfred, photograph. The Library of Congress.

Klein, Calvin, photograph. AP/Wide World Photos. Reproduced by permission.

Koop, C. Everett, photograph. Archive Photos. Reproduced by permission.

Kornberg, Arthur, portrait. The Library of Congress.

Kroc, Ray, photograph. The Library of Congress.

Kubrick, Stanley, photograph. Archive Photos. Reproduced by permission.

LaFlesche, Francis, photograph. The Library of Congress.

Land, Edwin H., photograph. The Library of Congress.

Langmuir, Irving, photograph. The Library of Congress.

Langston, John Mercer, photograph. The Library of Congress.

Lardner, Ring, photograph. The Library of Congress.

Lauren, Ralph, photograph. Archive Photos, Inc. Reproduced by permission.

Leary, Timothy, photograph. Archive Photos, Inc. Reproduced by permission.

Lederberg, Joshua, photograph. The Library of Congress.

Lee, Bruce, photograph. Archive Photos. Reproduced by permission.

Lee, Robert E., photograph by Mathew Brady. National Archives and Records Administration.

Lee, Spike, photograph by Chrystyna Czajkowsky. AP/Wide World Photos. Reproduced by permission.

Lee, Tsung-Dao, photograph. The Library of Congress.

Lewis, Carl, photograph. AP/Wide World Photos. Reproduced by permission.

Lewis, John L., photograph. The Library of Congress.

Lewis, John Robert, photograph.

Lewis, Meriwether, painting. The Library of Congress.

Lewis, Sinclair, photograph. The Library of Congress.

Libby, Willard F., photograph. The Library of Congress.

Lichtenstein, Roy, photograph. AP/Wide World Photos. Reproduced by permission.

Lincoln, Abraham, postcard. The Library of Congress.

Lindberg, Charles A., photograph. The Library of Congress.

Lipman, Fritz, photograph. The Library of Congress.

Lippmann, Walter, photograph. The Library of Congress.

Little Richard, photograph. AP/Wide World Photos. Reproduced by permission.

Little Wolf, photograph. The Library of Congress.

Locke, Dr, Alain, photograph. The Library of Congress.

London, Jack, photograph. The Library of Congress.

Long, Huey, photograph. Archive Photos, Inc. Reproduced by permission.

Longfellow, Henry Wadsworth, photograph. AP/Wide World Photos. Reproduced by permission.

Love, Nat, photograph. Denver Public Library.

Luce, Henry R., photograph. The Library of Congress.

Madison, James, portrait by Stuart Gilbert. National Archives and Records Administration.

Mahan, Alfred Thayer, photograph. The Library of Congress.

Malamud, Bernard, photograph. The Library of Congress.

Malcolm X, photograph. AP/Wide World Photos. Reproduced by permission.

Mamet, David Alam, Rebecca Pidgeon, photograph by Jose Goitia. AP/Wide World Photos. Reproduced by permission.

Marshall, George C., photograph.

Marshall, John, illustration. Source unknown.

Marshall, Thurgood, photograph. The Library of Congress.

Massasoit, engraving. The Library of Congress.

Masters, William, photograph. AP/Wide World Photos. Reproduced by permission.

Mather, Cotton, drawing. The Library of Congress.

Mather, Increase, engraving. The Library of Congress.

Maury, Matthew Fontain, photograph of engraving. The Library of Congress.

Mayo, Charles Horace, photograph.

Mays, Benjamin E., President John F. Kennedy, photograph. John F. Kennedy Library.

Mays, Willie, photograph. Archive Photos, Inc. Reproduced by permission.

McArthur, Douglas, photograph. National Archives and Records Administration.

McCarthy, Senator Joseph, photograph. Archive Photos. Reproduced by permisssion.

McCormick, Cyrus H., engraving. The Library of Congress.

McKinley, William, photograph. The Library of Congress.

McNamara, Robert and John F. Kennedy, photograph. Photograph No. ST-A26-23-62 in the John F. Kennedy Library.

McNickle, D'Arcy, illustration by Francisca Bollez. The Library of Congress.

Means, Russell, photograph. AP/Wide World Photos. Reproduced by permission.

Melville, Herman, photograph. The Library of Congress.

Mencken, Henry Louis, photograph. The Library of Congress.

Meredith, James, photograph. The Library of Congress.

Merrill, James, photograph. AP/Wide World Photos. Reproduced by permission.

Metacom, engraving. Archive Photos, Inc. Reproduced by permission.

Mfume, Kweisi, photograph. AP/Wide World Photos. Reproduced by permission.

Michelson, Albert, photograph. The Library of Congress.

Milk, Harvey, photograph. AP/Wide World Photos. Reproduced by permission.

Miller, Arthur, photograph. The Library of Congress.

Miller, Henry, photograph. The Library of Congress.

Millikan, Robert A., photograph. The Library of Congress.

Mills, Charles Wright, photograph. The Library of Congress.

Momaday, N. Scott, photograph. AP/Wide World Photos. Reproduced by permission.

Monk, Thelonius S., photograph. The Library of Congress.

Monroe, James, drawing. The Library of Congress.

Montana, Joe, Tim Grunhard and Glenn Montgomery, photograph. AP/Wide World Photos. Reproduced by permission.

Montezuma, Carlos, photogrraph. Source unknown.

Morgan, Garrett A., photograph. AP/Wide World Photos. Reproduced by permission.

Morgan, J. P, photograph. Archive Photos. Reproduced by permission.

Morgan, Thomas Hunt, photograph. The Library of Congress.

Morse, Samuel Finley Breese, painting. The Library of Congress.

Muhammed, Elijah, photograph. Archive Photos. Reproduced by permission.

Muller, Hermann Joseph, photograph. The Library of Congress.

Murrow, Edward R., photograph. The Library of Congress.

Nader, Ralph, photograph. The Library of Congress.

Nash, Ogden, photograph. AP/Wide World Photos. Reproduced by permission.

Newman, Paul, photograph. Archive Photos. Reproduced by permission.

Newton, Huey, photograph. AP/Wide World Photos, Inc. Reproduced by permission.

Niebuhr, Reinhold, photograph. The Library of Congress.

Nirenberg, Marshall Warren, photograph. The Library of Congress.

Nixon, Richard M., photograph. The Library of Congress.

Noguchi, Isamu, photograph. AP/Wide World Photos. Reproduced by permission.

Norris, George W., photograph. The Library of Congress.

Noyce, Robert, photograph. AP/Wide World Photos, Inc. Reproduced by permission.

O'Neill, Eugene G., photograph. The Library of Congress.

Onsager, Lars, photograph. Archive Photo/Express News. Reproduced by permission.

Oppenheimer, J. Robert, photograph. The Library of Congress.

Osceola, a Seminole chief, photograph. National Archives and Records Administration.

Parker, Charlie, photograph. Archive Photos, Inc. Reproduced by permission.

Parker, Quanah,, photograph by Lanney. National Archives and Records Administration.

Patton, George Smith, Tunisia, 1943, photograph. The Library of Congress.

Pauling, Linus, photograph. The Library of Congress.

Peary, Robert Edwin, photograph. AP/Wide World Photos. Reproduced by permission.

Peltier, Leonard, photograph. AP/Wide World Photos. Reproduced by permission.

Perot, Ross, photograph. Archive Photos, Inc. Reproduced by permission.

Perry, Bishop Harold, photograph.The Library of Congress.

Perry, Matthew Calbraith, engraving. The Library of Congress.

Pershing, John J., photograph. The Library of Congress.

Pierce, Franklin, photograph. The Library of Congress.

Pike, Zebulon M., illustration. U.S. Army Photographs

Pinchback, Pinckney Benton Stewart, photograph. The Library of Congress.

Pincus, Gregory, photograph. AP/Wide World Photos. Reproduced by permission.

Plenty Coups, photograph by Edward S. Curtis. The Library of Congress.

Poe, Edgar Allen, photograph.

Poitier, Sidney, photograph. The Library of Congress.

Polk, James Knox, photograph. The Library of Congress.

Pontiac, painting.

Porter, Cole, photograph. The Library of Congress.

Pound, Ezra, photograph. The Library of Congress.

Powell, Adam Clayton, photograph. The Library of Congress.

Powell, Colin L., photograph. AP/Wide World Photos. Reproduced by permission.

Powhatan, engraving. The Library of Congress.

Presley, Elvis, photograph. AP/Wide World Photos. Reproduced by permission.

Puente, Tito, photograph by Bruno Bernard. NYWTS/ The Library of Congress.

Pynchon, Thomas R., photograph. UPI/Corbis-Bettmann. Reproduced by permission.

Quayle, Dan, photograph. The Library of Congress.

Randolph, Asa P., photograph. The Library of Congress.

Rauschenberg, Robert, photograph by Felveregi. C. Archive Photos, Inc. Reproduced by permission.

Reagan, Ronald, photograph. The Library of Congress.

Red Cloud, photograph. National Archives and Records Administration.

Red Jacket, engraving. Archive Photos, Inc. Reproduced by permission.

Reed, Walter, photograph. AP/Wide World Photos. Reproduced by permission.

Reeve, Christopher, photograph by Gary Hershorn. Reuters/Archive Photos, Inc. Reproduced by permission

Remington, Frederic, photograph. The Library of Congress.

Revels, Hiram R., drawing. Harper's Weekly.

Revere, Paul, illustration. National Archives and Records Administration.

Richards, Theodore William, photograph. The Library of Congress.

Richter, Charles, Clarence Allen, photograph. AP/Wide World Photos, Inc. Reproduced by permission.

Riordan, Richard, photograph. AP/Wide World Photos. Reproduced by permission.

Ripken, Cal, Jr., photograph. Archive Photos, Inc. Re-

produced by permission.

Robertson, Pat, photograph by Steve Jaffe. Reuters/ Archive Photos, Inc. Reproduced by permission.

Robinson, Frank, photograph. Archive Photos. Reproduced by permission.

Robinson, Max, photograph. AP/Wide World Photos. Reproduced by permission.

Robinson, Smokey, photograph. AP/Wide World Photos. Reproduced by permission.

Rockefeller, John D., photograph. The Library of Congress.

Rockwell, Norman, photograph by Underwood & Underwood. The Library of Congress.

Rodgers, Richard, photograph. The Library of Congress.

Roebling, John Augustus, photograph. The Library of Congress.

Rogers, Will, photograph. The Library of Congress.

Roosevelt, Franklin D., photograph. Franklin D. Roosevelt Library.

Roosevelt, Theodore, photograph. The Library of Congress.

Ross, John, lithograph. The Library of Congress.

Rowan, Carl T., photograph. The Library of Congress.

Rustin, Bayard, photograph. A. Philip Randolph Institute.

Ruth, Babe, photograph. The Library of Congress.

Ryan, Nolan, photograph. UPI/Corbis-Bettmann. Reproduced by permission.

Sabin, Albert, photograph. The Library of Congress.

Sagan, Carl, photograph. The Library of Congress

Salinger, J.D., photograph. The Library of Congress.

Salk, Jonas, photograph. The Library of Congress.

Sandburg, Carl, photograph. The Library of Congress.

Schlesinger, Arthur, Jr., photograph. Corbis-Bettmann. Reproduced by permission.

Schulz, Charles M., photograph. The Library of Congress.

Schwarzkopf, Norman, Colin Powell, photograph by John Gaps. AP/Wide World Photos. Reproduced by permission.

Scorsese, Martin, photograph. Archive Photos/Popperfoto. Reproduced by permission.

Scott, Dred, illustration. The Library of Congress.

Scott, Winfield, photograph. The Library of Congress.

Seaborg, Glenn T., photograph. The Library of Congress.

Sequoyah, painting. The Library of Congress.

Seward, William H., bust. National Archives and Records Administration.

Shapley, Harlow, photograph. The Library of Congress.

Sharpton, Al, photograph. Archive Photos, Inc. Reproduced by permission.

Sheen, Fulton J., photograph by Louis Fabian Bachrach. The Library of Congress.

Shepard, Alan, photograph. The Library of Congress.

Shockley, William, photograph. The Library of Congress.

Siegel, Benjamin, photograph. AP/Wide World Photos.

Reproduced by permission.

Simon, Neil, photograph. AP/Wide World Photos. Reproduced by permission.

Simon, Paul, photograph. The Library of Congress.

Simpson, George Gaylord, photograph The Library of Congress.

Sinatra, Frank, photograph. AP/Wide World Photos, Inc. Reproduced by permission.

Sinclair, Upton, photograph. AP/Wide World Photos, Inc. Reproduced by permission.

Singer, Isaac Bashevis, photograph. UPI/Corbis-Bettmann. Reproduced by permission.

Singer, Isaac Merritt, illustration.

Sitting Bull, photograph. National Archives and Records Administration.

Slater, Samuel, engraving The Library of Congress.

Smith, Joseph, illustration. The Library of Congress.

Smohalla, photograph. The Library of Congress.

Sondheim, Stephen and Richard Rodgers, photograph.The Library of Congress.

Spielberg, Steven, photograph. Archive Photos, Inc. Reproduced by permission.

Spock, Benjamin, photograph.The Library of Congress.

Stanley, Wendell Meredith, photograph. The Library of Congress.

Steinbeck, John, photograph. The Library of Congress.

Steinmetz, Charles P., photograph. The Library of Congress

Stone, Oliver, photograph. AP/Wide World Photos. Reproduced by permission.

Stuart, Gilbert, engraving. The Library of Congress.

Sullivan, Leon Howard, photograph. The Library of Congress.

Sullivan, Louis Henry, photograph.

Sutter, John Augustus, photograph. The Library of Congress.

Taft, William Howard, photograph. The Library of Congress.

Tanner, Henry O., photograph. UPI/Corbis-Bettmann. Reproduced by permission.

Taylor, Zachary, photograph. The Library of Congress.

Teller, Edward, photograph. The Library of Congress.

Theiler, Max, photograph. The Library of Congress.

Thoreau, Henry David, drawing. The Library of Congress.

Thorpe, Jim, photograph. National Archives and Records Administration.

Thurber, James, photograph by Fred Palumbo. NYWTS/The Library of Congress.

Townes, Charles H., photograph. NYWTS/The Library of Congress.

Trudeau, Garry, photograph. The Library of Congress.

Truman, Harry S., photograph. The Library of Congress.

Trump, Donald, photograph. Archive Photos, Inc. Reproduced by permission.

Turner, Henry McNeal, engraving.

Turner, Nat, engraving. Corbis-Bettmann. Reproduced by permission.

Turner, Ted, photograph. Archive Photo/Malafronte. Reproduced by permission.

Twain, Mark, photograph. The Library of Congress.

Tyler, John, daguerrotype by Mathew Brady. The Library of Congress.

Updike, John, photograph by Wyatt Counts. AP/Wide World Photos. Reproduced by permission.

Urey, Harold, photograph. The Library of Congress.

Van Buren, Martin, photograph. The Library of Congress.

Von Neumann, John,, photograph. AP/Wide World Photos. Reproduced by permission.

Vonnegut, Kurt, photograph. AP/Wide World Photos. Reproduced by permission.

Waksman, Selman A., photograph. The Library of Congress.

Wallace, George, photograph. The Library of Congress.

Wang, An, photograph. AP/Wide World Photos. Reproduced by permission.

Warhol, Andy, photograph. The Library of Congress.

Warren, Earl, photograph. The Library of Congress.

Warren, Robert Penn, photograph. The library of Congress.

Washakie, photograph. National Archives and Records Administration.

Washington, Booker T., photograph. The Library of Congress.

Washington, George, painting by Stuart Gilbert. The Library of Congress

Waters, Muddy, photograph. Archive Photos. Reproduced by permission.

Watson, James Dewey, photograph. The Library of Congress.

Webster, Daniel, painting. The Library of Congress.

Webster, Noah, engraving. The Library of Congress.

Westinghouse, George, portrait. The Library of Congress.

Westmoreland, William, photograph. AP/Wide World Photos. Reproduced by permission.

Whipple, George Hoyt, photograph. The Library of Congress.

Whistler, James McNeill, drawing. The Library of Congress.

White, E.B., photograph. Corbis-Bettmann. Reproduced by permission.

White, Walter Francis, photograph. The Library of Congress.

Whitney, Eli, engravings. The Library of Congress.

Wiener, Norbert, photograph. The Library of Congress.

Wiesel, Elie, photograph. AP/Wide World Photos. Reproduced by permission.

Wilder, L. Douglas, photograph. AP/Wide World Photos. Reproduced by permission.

Wilkes, Charles, engraving. The Library of Congress.

Williams, Roger, photograph. Archive Photos, Inc. Reproduced by permission.

Williams, Tennessee, photograph. The Library of Congress.

Wilson, August, photograph. AP/Wide World Photos. Reproduced by permission.

Wilson, Woodrow, photograph. The Library of Congress.

Wolfe, Thomas, painting. The Library of Congress.

Woods, Tiger, photograph. AP/Wide World Photos. Reproduced by permission.

Woodson, Carter Goodwin, photograph. AP/Wide World Photos. Reproduced by permission.

Wyeth, Andrew, photograph. The Library of Congress.

Yeager, Charles E., photograph. The Library of Congress.

Young, Andrew, photograph. The Library of Congress.

Young, Brigham, photograph. The Library of Congress.

Zah, Peterson, photograph. UPI/Corbis-Bettmann. Reproduced by permission.

Zindel, Paul, photograph. AP/Wide World Photos. Reproduced by permission.

Henry Louis (Hank) Aaron

Henry Louis (Hank) Aaron (born 1934) was major league baseball's leading homerun hitter with a career total of 755 upon his retirement in 1976. He broke ground for the participation of African Americans in professional sports.

Henry (Hank) Aaron was born in Mobile, Alabama, in the midst of the Great Depression on February 5, 1934. He was the son of an African American shipyard worker and had seven brothers and sisters. Although times were economically difficult, Aaron took an early interest in sports and began playing sandlot baseball at a neighborhood park. In his junior year he transferred out of a segregated high school to attend the Allen Institute in Mobile, which had an organized baseball program. He played on amateur and semi-pro teams like the Pritchett Athletics and the Mobile Black Bears, where he began to make a name for himself. At this time Jackie Robinson, the first African American player in the major leagues, was breaking the baseball color barrier. Gaining immediate success as a hard-hitting infielder, the 17-year-old Aaron was playing semi-professional baseball in the summer of 1951 when the owner of the Indianapolis Clowns, part of the professional Negro American League, signed him as the Clown's shortstop for the 1952 season.

Record Breaker

Being almost entirely self-trained, Aaron in his early years batted cross-handed, ''. . . because no one had told him not to,'' according to one of his biographers. Nevertheless, Aaron's sensational hitting with the Clowns prompted a Boston Braves scout to purchase his contract in 1952. Assigned to Eau Claire, Wisconsin, in the minor Northern League (where coaching corrected his batting style), Aaron

batted .336 and won the league's rookie-of-the-year award. The following year he was assigned to the Braves' Jacksonville, Florida team, in the South Atlantic (Sally) League. Enduring the taunting of fans and racial slurs from fellow players in the segregated south, he went on to bat .362 with 22 homers and 125 runs batted in (RBIs). This achievement won him the title of the League Most Valuable Player in 1953.

During the winter of 1953-1954 Aaron played in Puerto Rico where he began playing positions in the outfield. In the spring of 1954 he trained with the major league Boston Braves (later the Milwaukee Braves) and won a starting position when the regular right-fielder suffered an injury. Although Aaron was sidelined late in the campaign with a broken ankle, he batted .280 as a rookie that year. Over the next 22 seasons, this quiet, six-foot, right-handed batting champion established himself as one of the most durable and versatile hitters in major league history.

In 14 seasons playing for the Braves Hank Aaron batted .300 or more; in 15 seasons he hit 30 or more homers, scored 100 or more runs, and drove in 100 or more runs. In his long career Aaron led all major league players in runs batted in with 2,297. He played in 3,298 games, which ranked him third among players of all time. Aaron twice led the National League in batting and four times led the league in homers. His consistent hitting produced a career total of 3,771 hits, ranking him third behind Pete Rose and Ty Cobb. When Aaron recorded his 3,000th hit on May 7, 1970, he was the youngest player (at 36) since Cobb to join the exclusive 3,000 hit club. Aaron played in 24 All-Star games, a record shared with Willie Mays and Stan Musial. Aaron's lifetime batting average was .305, and in his two World Series encounters he batted .364. Aaron also held the record of hitting homeruns in three consecutive National League

playoff games, a feat he accomplished in 1969 against the New York Mets.

A Quiet Superstar

Although Aaron's prodigious batting ranked him among baseball's superstars, he received less publicity than such contemporaries as Willie Mays. In part this was due to Aaron's quiet personality and to lingering prejudice against African American players in the majors. Moreover, playing with the Milwaukee Braves (which became the Atlanta Braves in 1966) denied Aaron the high level of publicity afforded major league players in cities like New York or Los Angeles. During Aaron's long career the Braves won only two National League pennants, although in 1957, the year Aaron's 44 homers helped him win his only Most Valuable Player Award, the Braves won the World Series. The following year Milwaukee repeated as National League champions, but lost the World Series.

Aaron perennially ranked among the National League's leading homerun hitters, but only four times did he win the annual homer title. It wasn't until 1970 that Aaron's challenge to Babe Ruth's record total of 714 homers was seriously considered by sportswriters and fans. By 1972 Aaron's assault on the all-time homer record was big news and his $200,000 annual salary was the highest in the league. The following year Aaron hit 40 homers, falling one short of tying the mark. Early into the 1974 season Aaron hit the tying homer in Cincinnati. Then on the night of April 8, 1974, before a large crowd at Atlanta and with a nationwide television audience looking on, Aaron hit his 715th homer

off pitcher Al Downing of the Dodgers to break Ruth's record. It was the peak moment of Aaron's career, although it was tempered by an increasing incidence of death threats and racist hate mail which made Aaron fear for the safety of his family.

A New Career

In the Fall of 1974 Aaron left the Braves and went on to play for the Milwaukee Brewers until his retirement in 1976. At the time of his retirement as a player, the 42-year-old veteran had raised his all-time homer output to 755. When he left the Brewers he became a vice president and Director of Player Development for the Braves, where he scouted new team prospects and oversaw the coaching of minor leaguers. His efforts contributed toward making the Braves, now of Atlanta, one of the strongest teams in the National League, and he has since become a senior vice president for that team. In 1982 Aaron was voted into the Baseball Hall of Fame at Cooperstown, New York, and in 1997 Hank Aaron Stadium in Mobile, Alabama, was dedicated to him.

Further Reading

Begin with Hank Aaron's autobiography, *I Had A Hammer: The Hank Aaron Story* (1992). Available biographies of Hank Aaron include Rick Rennert, Richard Zennert, *Henry Aaron (Black Americans of Achievement)* (1993), and James Tackach, *Hank Aaron (Baseball Legends Series)* (1991). A good book for younger readers is Jacob Margolies, *Home Run King (Full-Color First Books)* (1992). Other books that look at Aaron's place in baseball history are Clare Gault, Frank Gault, *Home Run Kings: Babe Ruth, Henry Aaron* (1994) and James Hahn and Lynn Hahn, *Henry Aaron* (1981). Joseph Reichler, *Baseball's Great Moments* (1985) covers the two highlights of Aaron's career—when he struck his 3,000th hit and when he broke the homer record in 1974. Recent published articles include Hank Aaron, "When Baseball Mattered," *The New York Times* (5/03/97, Vol. 146), "Aaron Still Chasing Ball No. 755," *The New York Times* (8/27/96, Vol. 145), and "Aaron honored With New Stadium," *The New York Times* (8/27/96, Vol. 145). Jules Tygiel, in *Baseball's Great Experiment* (1984), gives an excellent historical account of black players seeking admission into major league baseball. Art Rust, Jr., in *Get That Nigger Off the Field* (1976), furnishes sketches of black players who entered the majors during Aaron's time. David Q. Voigt, in *American Baseball: From Postwar Expansion to the Electronic Age* (1983), treats the black experience within the context of major league history since World War II. □

Ralph David Abernathy

Civil rights leader Ralph David Abernathy (1926–1990) was the best friend and trusted assistant of Martin Luther King, Jr., whom he succeeded as president of the Southern Christian Leadership Conference, a nonviolent civil rights organization.

Ralph David Abernathy, one of 12 children, was born in Marengo County, Alabama, about 90 miles outside of Montgomery. Originally named David, he was nicknamed Ralph by one of his sisters after a favorite teacher. His father William, the son of a slave, supported his family as a sharecropper until he saved enough money to

buy 500 acres of his own, upon which he built a prosperous self-sufficient farm. He eventually emerged as one of the leading African Americans in the county, serving as a deacon in his church and on the board of the local African American high school and becoming the first African American there who voted and served on the grand jury. Ralph aspired early on to become a preacher and was encouraged by his mother to pursue that ambition. Although Abernathy's father died when he was 16 years old, the young man was able to obtain a Bachelor of Science degree in mathematics from Alabama State University and a Master's degree in sociology from Atlanta University in 1951. During this time he worked as the first African American DJ at a white Montgomery radio station. While attending college he was elected president of the student council and led successful protests for better cafeteria conditions and living quarters. He earned the respect of both students and administrators, and he was later hired as the school's dean of men.

Montgomery Bus Boycott

Before obtaining his first degree, Abernathy was ordained as a Baptist minister and, after completing his education, served as minister at the Eastern star Baptist church in Demopolis, near his home town of Linden. When he was 26 he accepted a position as full time minister at the First Baptist Church in Montgomery, Alabama. Three years later, Martin Luther King accepted a call to another of Montgomery's leading African American churches, Dexter Avenue Baptist. During this time King and Abernathy became close friends.

In 1955 an African American seamstress from Montgomery named Rosa Parks refused to relinquish her bus seat to a white passenger and she was arrested and later fined. This began an important historic phase of the civil rights movement. Through hurried meetings in their churches ministers, along with the National Association for the Advancement of Colored People (NAACP), began a boycott of the city busses until all African Americans were assured better treatment. The ministers formed the Montgomery Improvement Association (MIA)—a name suggested by Abernathy—to coordinate the boycott and voted a young minister named Dr. Martin Luther King, Jr. their president.

The MIA convinced African American taxi-cab drivers to take African American workers to their jobs for a ten cent fare. When the city government declared that practice illegal, those with cars formed carpools so that the boycotters wouldn't have to return to the busses. After 381 days, the boycott was over and the busses were completely desegregated, a decision enforced by a United States district court. During 1956 Abernathy and King had been in and out of jail and court, and toward the end of the boycott on January 10, 1957, Abernathy's home and church were bombed. By the time the boycott was over it had attracted national and international attention, and televised reports of the activities of the MIA encouraged African American protesters all over the South.

Nonviolent Civil Rights Movement

King and Abernathy's work together in the MIA commenced their career as partners in the civil rights struggle and sealed their close friendship, which lasted until King's assassination in 1968. Soon after the boycott they met with other African American clergymen in Atlanta to form the Southern Christian Leadership Conference (SCLC) and press for civil rights in all areas of life. King was elected president and Abernathy the secretary-treasurer. This group began to plan for a coordinated nonviolent civil rights movement throughout the South, the ultimate purpose of which would be to end segregation and to hasten the enactment of effective federal civil rights legislation. In the early 1960s when the civil rights movement began to intensify because of student lunch counter sit-ins, nonviolent demonstrations, and efforts to desegregate interstate busses and bus depots, Abernathy moved to Atlanta, Georgia, to become the pastor of West Hunter Baptist Church. In Atlanta he would be able to work more closely with the SCLC and King, who had returned to the city at an earlier date.

The SCLC attempted to coordinate a desegregation movement in Albany, Georgia, in December 1961, but were not as effective as they hoped to be with their work there. Abernathy was arrested along with King during the Albany demonstrations, but they were quickly released from jail because the city leaders did not want to attract national attention to conditions in the city. In the spring of 1963 the leaders of the SCLC began to coordinate their efforts to desegregate facilities in Birmingham, Alabama. Publicity about the rough treatment of African American demonstrators at the hand of Eugene "Bull" Conner, the city's director of public safety, directed the eyes of the world on that city's civil rights protest. Abernathy found himself in jail with King once again. More than 3,000 other African Americans in the city also endured periods of incarceration in order to dramatize their demands for equal rights. The Birmingham demonstrations were successful and the demands for desegregation of public facilities were agreed upon. In the wake of the demonstrations, desegregation programs commenced in over 250 southern cities. Thousands of schools, parks, pools, restaurants, and hotels were opened to all people regardless race.

March On Washington

The success of the Birmingham demonstration also encouraged President John F. Kennedy to send a civil rights bill to Congress. In order to emphasize the need for the bill, leaders of all the nation's major civil rights organizations, including the SCLC, agreed to participate in a massive demonstration in Washington, D.C. The "March on Washington" on August 28, 1963, attracted over 250,000 African American and white demonstrators from all over the United States. By the next summer the Civil Rights Act had been signed into law, and a year later, in 1965, the Voting Rights Act had passed.

On April 4, 1968, during a strike by city sanitation workers in Memphis, Tennessee, King was assassinated, and Abernathy succeeded him as the leader of the SCLC. Abernathy's first project was the completion of King's plan to hold a Poor People's Campaign in Washington during which white, African American, and Native American poor people would present their problems to President Lyndon B. Johnson and the Congress. Poor people moved into Washington in mule trains and on foot and erected "Resurrection City." Abernathy once again found himself in jail, this time for unlawful assembly. After the Poor People's Campaign, Abernathy continued to lead the SCLC, but the organization did not regain the popularity it held under King's leadership.

Abernathy resigned from the SCLC in 1977 and made an unsuccessful bid for the Georgia fifth district U.S. Congressional seat vacated by prominent African American statesman Andrew Young. Later, he formed an organization called Foundation for Economic Enterprises Development (FEED), designed to help train African Americans for better economic opportunities. He continued to carry out his ministerial duties at the West Hunter Street Baptist Church in Montgomery, and lectured throughout the United States. In 1989 Abernathy published his autobiography, *And The Walls Come Tumbling Down* (Harper, 1989), which garnered criticism from other civil rights leaders for its revelations about the alleged extramarital affairs of Martin Luther King.

Abernathy died of a heart attack on April 30, 1990 in Atlanta, Georgia.

Further Reading

Ralph Abernathy's biography is *And the Walls Came Tumbling Down: An Autobiography* (1991). The first published biography of Abernathy is Catherine M. Reef, *Ralph David Abernathy (People in Focus Book)* (1995). There is a substantial amount of biographical material about him in Stephen Oates' biography of Martin Luther King, Jr., *Let the Trumpet Sound*

(1982). Some information about Abernathy is also available in Flip Schulke, editor, *Martin Luther King, Jr.; A Documentary . . . Montgomery to Memphis* (1976) and in David J. Garrow, *The FBI and Martin Luther King, Jr.* (1981). There is information about Abernathy in a publication by the Southern Christian Leadership Conference entitled *The Poor People's Campaign, a Photographic Journal* (1968). □

Dean Gooderham Acheson

The American lawyer and statesman Dean Gooderham Acheson (1893-1971) served as secretary of state in President Harry Truman's Cabinet.

Dean Acheson was born in Middletown, Conn., on April 11, 1893, the son of Edward Campion and Eleanor Gooderham Acheson. His father, the Episcopal bishop of Connecticut, provided a genteel upbringing which led to Groton and afterward Yale, where Acheson received his bachelor's degree in 1915. During the succeeding 3 years he served briefly as an ensign in the U.S. Navy and earned his law degree at Harvard. In May 1917 he married Alice Stanley. Three children were born to the Achesons—Jane, David Campion, and Mary Eleanor.

From the beginning Acheson seemed destined for a successful career. Possessed of high intelligence, a deep sense of moral rectitude, and aggressive energy, he had in addition the grace of the patrician and the friendship of such distinguished and influential people as Felix Frankfurter of the Harvard Law School and, later, the Supreme Court of the United States.

Following his graduation from Harvard, Acheson became private secretary to Supreme Court Justice Louis D. Brandeis. In 1921 he entered the prominent Washington law firm of Covington, Burling, and Rublee, where he practiced for the next 12 years. President Franklin D. Roosevelt first brought Acheson into public service in May 1933 with an appointment as undersecretary of the Treasury. Acheson resigned 5 months later following a disagreement on the President's gold-purchasing program and returned to his Washington law practice.

In 1941 Acheson again entered the government, this time as assistant secretary of state for economic affairs. He remained in the State Department, except for one brief interlude, until 1953. His long and significant record there reflected a practical rather than a contemplative mentality, which attracted him especially to Harry Truman's forthright leadership. As undersecretary of state from 1945 to 1947, Acheson broke with Truman only on the Palestinian question, convinced that the nation was embarking on a unilateral commitment to Israel's defense against the Arab states which could ultimately prove embarrassing, if not costly.

Acheson's most memorable contributions, as undersecretary and, from 1949 to 1953, as secretary of state, came in his implementation of the containment policy from the Marshall Plan to NATO. Despite his achievements, these years in the State Department were trying ones. The alleged loss of China to Communist leadership in 1949 exposed the Truman administration to charges of treason. Acheson, always loyal to his friends and associates, refused to testify against Alger Hiss, then under trial for spying, or to condemn past American policy toward China. These actions rendered him totally vulnerable and roused a storm of accusations such as few commanding public figures in American history have faced.

Upon his retirement from the State Department in 1953, Acheson returned to Covington and Burling, remaining in public life only as a member of special governmental committees, as a presidential adviser, and as a critical observer of men and events. He served in the late fifties as foreign policy chief of the Democratic Advisory Council of the Democratic National Committee. He died in Sandy Spring, Md., on Oct. 12, 1971.

Further Reading

Acheson's own writings are voluminous. Three of his books which develop his views of external policy, politics, and government are *A Democrat Looks at His Party* (1955), *A Citizen Looks at Congress* (1957), and *Power and Diplomacy* (1958). His autobiography, *Morning and Noon* (1965), terminates with his appointment to the State Department in 1941. Acheson's personal record of his State Department experience is *Present at the Creation: My Years in the State Department* (1969).

Very little is written exclusively about Acheson. One of the most thorough biographies of Acheson is James Chace, *Acheson: the Secretary of State Who Created the American World* (1998). McGeorge Bundy, ed., *The Pattern of Responsibility* (1952), includes excerpts and paraphrases of Acheson's many speeches during his secretarial years and is a good source of information on his views toward world affairs. The volumes covering the years 1949 to 1952 of *The United States in*

World Affairs (1950-1953), prepared by Richard P. Stebbins for the Council on Foreign Relations, are replete with observations on Acheson's leadership. Also useful is the survey of postwar American foreign policy, William Reitzel and others, *United States Foreign Policy, 1945-1955* (1956). Acheson's role as an adviser to Kennedy is discussed in Seyom Brown, *The Faces of Power* (1968). □

Ansel Adams

Ansel Adams (1902-1984) was not only a masterful photographic technician but a lifelong conservationist who pleaded for understanding of, and respect for, the natural environment. Although he spent a large part of his career in commercial photography, he is best known for his majestic landscape photographs.

Ansel Easton Adams was born on February 20, 1902, in San Francisco, California, near the Golden Gate Bridge. His father, a successful businessman, sent his son to private, as well as public, schools; beyond such formal education, however, Adams was largely self-taught.

His earliest aspiration was to become a concert pianist, but he turned to photography in the late teens of the century; a trip to Yosemite National Park in 1916, where he made his first amateurish photos, is said to have determined his direction in life. Subsequently, he worked as photo technician for a commercial firm.

He joined the Sierra Club in 1919 and worked as a caretaker in their headquarters in Yosemite Valley. Later in

life, from 1936 to 1970, Adams was president of the Sierra Club, one of the many distinguished positions that he held.

Ansel Adams decided to become a full time professional photographer at about the time that some of his work was published in limited edition portfolios, one entitled *Parmelian Prints of the High Sierras* (1927) and the other, *Taos Pueblo* (1930), with a text written by Mary Austin.

His first important one-man show was held in San Francisco in 1932 at the M. H. de Young Memorial Museum. Subsequently, he opened the Ansel Adams Gallery for the Arts, taught, lectured, and worked on advertising assignments in the San Francisco area; during the 1930s he also began his extensive publications on the craft of photography, insisting throughout his life on the importance of meticulous craftsmanship. In 1936 Alfred Stieglitz gave Adams a one-man show in his New York gallery, only the second of the work of a young photographer (in 1917 Paul Strand was the first) to be exhibited by Stieglitz.

In 1937 Adams moved to Yosemite Valley close to his major subject and began publishing a stream of superbly produced volumes including *Sierra Nevada: The John Muir Trail* (1938); *Illustrated Guide to Yosemite Valley* (1940); *Yosemite and the High Sierra* (1948); and *My Camera in Yosemite Valley* (1949).

In 1930 Adams met the venerable Paul Strand while they were working in Taos, New Mexico, and the man and his work had a lasting effect on Adams' approach to photography by shifting his approach from a soft formulation of subjects to a much clearer, harder treatment, so-called "straight photography." This orientation was further reinforced by his association with the shortlived, but influential, group which included Edward Weston and Imogen Cunningham and called itself f/64, referring to the lens opening which virtually guarantees distinctness of image.

Throughout much of his early career Adams worked both on commercial assignments and in pursuit of his own vision. He saw no inherent conflict between the two approaches since, as he affirmed, "I don't have any idea that commercialism or professionalism is on one side of the fence and the creative side is on the other. They're both interlocked."

In one sense Ansel Adams' work is an extensive documentation of what is still left of the wilderness, the dwindling untouched segment of the natural environment. Yet to see his work only as documentary is to miss the main point that he tried to make: without a guiding vision, photography is a trivial activity. The finished product, as Adams saw it, must be visualized before it is executed; and he shared with 19th century artists and philosophers the belief that this vision must be embedded within the context of life on earth. Photographs, he believed, are not *taken* from the environment but are *made* into something greater than themselves.

During his life, Ansel Adams was criticized for photographing rocks while the world was falling apart; he responded to the criticism by suggesting that "the understanding of the inanimate and animate world of nature will aid in holding the world of man together."

Further Reading

A great deal has been written by and about Ansel Adams; of particular value are two books that are superbly illustrated with his work. Nancy Hewhall's *Ansel Adams: The Eloquent Light* (1963) provides a good analysis of his work and place in the history of photography; and Ansel Adams' book *Examples: The Making of 40 Photographs* (1983) is a firsthand account of his working methods. For a deeper understanding of his thinking see his essays "What is good photography?" (1940), "A personal credo" (1944), and "Introduction to Portfolio One" (1948) all in Nathan Lyons, *Photographers on Photography* (1966). In 1985 *Ansel Adams: An Autobiography,* written with Mary S. Alinder, was published with 277 illustrations. □

Hank Adams

Originally a staunch supporter of the Kennedys, Hank Adams (born 1944) moved into the arena of Native American activism in 1964. Eventually he became the director of the Survival of American Indians Association, a group dedicated to the Indian treaty-fishing rights battle.

Hank Adams was born in 1944 on the Fort Peck Indian Reservation in Montana at a place known as Wolf Point, but more commonly referred to as Poverty Flats. He graduated in 1961 from Moclips High School, where he was student-body president, editor of the school newspaper and annual, and a starting football and basketball player. Following graduation he developed an interest in politics and moved to California where he was a staunch

supporter of President John F. Kennedy and a campaign worker for the president's brother, Robert F. Kennedy, in the 1968 Democratic primary.

In 1964, Adams played a behind-the-scenes role when actor Marlon Brando and a thousand Indians marched on the Washington State capitol in Olympia to protest state policies toward Indian fishing rights. Indians reserved the right to take fish in "the usual and accustomed places" in numerous treaties negotiated in the 1850s. State officials and commercial and sports fisherman tried to restrict the amount, time, and places where Indian people could fish, thus prompting the treaty-fishing rights battles.

Adams began his activist career in April 1964 when he refused induction into the U.S. Army until Indian treaty rights were recognized. His attempt failed and he ultimately served in the U.S. Army. In 1968, Adams became the director of the Survival of American Indians Association, a group of 150 to 200 active members primarily dedicated to the Indian treaty-fishing rights battle. Late in 1968, he actively campaigned against state regulation of Indian net fishing on the Nisqually River near Franks Landing, Washington. For this and his role in the fishing-rights battles, Adams was regularly arrested and jailed from 1968 to 1971. In January 1971, on the banks of the Puyallup River near Tacoma, Washington, Adams was shot in the stomach by an unknown assailant. He and a companion, Michael Hunt, had set a fish trap about midnight and remained to watch it. That section of the Puyallup River had been the scene of recent altercations as Indian people claimed fishing rights guaranteed by treaties, despite state laws to the contrary. Adams recovered from the gunshot wound and continued to fight for Indian fishing rights in the state of Washington into the mid-1970s.

John Adams

The second president of the United States, John Adams (1735-1826) played a major role in the colonial movement toward independence. He wrote the Massachusetts Constitution of 1780 and served as a diplomatic representative of Congress in the 1780s.

John Adams was born in Braintree (now Quincy), Mass. His father was a modest but successful farmer and local officeholder. After some initial reluctance, Adams entered Harvard and received his bachelor's degree in 1755. For about a year he taught school in Worcester. Though he gave some thought to entering the ministry, Adams was repelled by the theological acrimony resulting from the period of the Great Awakening and turned to the law. After studying under James Putnam, Adams was admitted to the Boston bar in 1758. While developing his legal practice, he participated in town affairs and contributed his first essays to the Boston newspapers. In 1764 he married Abigail Smith of Weymouth, who brought him wide social connections and was to share with sensitivity and enthusiasm in the full life that lay ahead.

Early Political Career

By 1765 Adams had achieved considerable distinction at the Boston bar. With the Stamp Act crisis he moved into the center of Massachusetts political life. He contributed an important series of essays, *Dissertation on the Canon and Feudal Law,* to the *Boston Gazette* and prepared a series of anti-Stamp Act resolutions for the Braintree town meeting, which were widely copied throughout the province.

In April 1768 Adams moved to Boston. He defended John Hancock against smuggling charges brought by British customs officials and acted as counsel for Capt. Thomas Preston, the officer in charge of British troops at the Boston Massacre. Adams undertook the Preston defense somewhat reluctantly, fearing its consequences for his own local popularity, but the need to provide Preston with a fair trial persuaded him to act—with no damage, in the end, to his own reputation or practice. Indeed, a few weeks later Adams was elected representative from Boston to the Massachusetts Legislature.

In the spring of 1771, largely for reasons of health, Adams returned to Braintree, where he divided his attention between farming and the law. Within a year, however, professional and political considerations drew him back to Boston. In 1773 he celebrated the Boston Tea Party as a dramatic challenge to British notions of parliamentary supremacy. The next year he was one of the representatives from Massachusetts to the First Continental Congress, where he took a leading role in developing the colonists' constitutional defense against the Coercive Acts and other British measures. Although Adams favored the various petitions

Congress made to the King, Parliament, and the English people, as well as the scheme of nonimportation agreements, he nonetheless hoped for more vigorous measures. All the while, however, he had to guard against the suspicion held by many other delegates that the New Englanders were plotting independence. Upon his return to Massachusetts, Adams was chosen for the governor's council but was negatived. During the winter of 1774-1775 he carried on, under the pseudonym Novanglus, an extended debate with Daniel Leonard over the proper constitutional relations between the Colonies and Parliament. Adams's recommended solution at this point was a commonwealth system of empire, with a series of coequal parliaments joined by common allegiance to the Crown.

After the battles of Lexington and Concord, Adams returned to Congress, carrying the welcome instructions from the General Court for measures to establish American liberties on a permanent basis, secure from attack by Britain. He now believed that independence would probably be necessary. Congress, however, was not yet willing to agree, and Adams fumed while still more petitions were sent off to England. The best chance of promoting independence, he concluded, was through the device of instructing the various colonies to adopt new forms of government following the breakdown of their provincial regimes. Replying to petitions from several provinces seeking advice on their governments (petitions which Adams and others had solicited), he recommended that they adopt new governments modeled on their colonial regimes and framed by special conventions.

By February 1776 Adams was back in Congress. There he presented, first privately in response to the requests of several delegates and then publicly in a pamphlet entitled "Thoughts on Government," his specific proposals for the reconstruction of the provincial governments. Adams was at last fully committed to American independence. In May, Congress finally passed a resolution that, where no adequate governments existed, measures should be taken to provide for the "happiness and safety" of the people. For this resolution Adams wrote a preamble which in effect asserted the principle of independence. A month later he seconded Richard Henry Lee's resolution for the formal declaration of independence, the contracting of foreign treaties, and the construction of a continental confederation. A member of the committee appointed to bring in the formal statement, Adams contributed little to the content of the Declaration of Independence but served, as Thomas Jefferson later reported, as "the pillar of its support on the floor of the Congress." On another committee Adams drew up a model treaty that encouraged Congress to enter into commercial but not political alliances with European nations. Exhausted by his duties, he temporarily left Philadelphia in mid-October for Massachusetts. For the next year or so he continued to serve in Congress.

Diplomatic Career

On Nov. 28, 1777, Congress elected Adams commissioner to France, replacing Silas Deane, and in February Adams embarked from Boston for what was to prove an extended stay. Upon arrival, Adams found that France had already granted diplomatic recognition to the United States and contracted treaties of commerce and amity. With nothing specific to do, Adams spent the next year and a half trying to keep busy: attempting to secure badly needed loans for Congress, transmitting lengthy letters on European affairs, and learning with mixed fascination and repugnance about the ways of French court and national life.

When he learned that Benjamin Franklin, one of his fellow commissioners, had been appointed sole American plenipotentiary in France, Adams returned to Boston, where in the fall of 1779 he was elected from Braintree to the state constitutional convention. For the next few months he devoted his time to the convention, preparing what became the basic draft of the new Massachusetts constitution.

In the meantime Adams had been tapped by Congress for another diplomatic post, this time as commissioner to contract peace and then a commercial treaty with Great Britain. He embarked in mid-November and arrived in Paris on Feb. 9, 1780. Again he found his situation frustrating, largely because he had been instructed to make no significant moves without the prior approval of the Comte de Vergennes, the French foreign minister. Between Adams and Vergennes there quickly developed a mutual dislike— duplicated in Adams's relations with Franklin, a man more flexible and less demanding in his relations with the French foreign minister. In the face of all this, Adams spent considerable time writing his friends in Congress to complain of his difficult position. Having been further commissioned minister plenipotentiary to the United Provinces, Adams finally secured recognition by The Hague in the spring of 1782, and in October he signed the first of several desperately needed loans with a group of Dutch bankers.

He returned to Paris to negotiate the terms of peace with the British representatives. Adams and the other two American commissioners, Franklin and John Jay, ignored their instructions to make no agreement without first consulting Vergennes; they feared (correctly) that France wished to pressure the United States into peace arrangements inconsistent with national interest (for example, leaving certain coastal areas in British hands). The American commissioners concluded provisional articles of peace and sent the results home to Congress. These were duly signed as the definitive treaty of peace on Sept. 3, 1783.

The Dutch loans and the treaty of peace were the major products of the diplomatic phase of Adams's public career. Before returning permanently to the United States, however, he spent 3 frustrating years as American envoy to the Court of St. James in London, attempting without success to negotiate a commercial treaty and to clear up various diplomatic issues carried over from the Revolution. Rebuffed by British officials and unsupported by a weak Congress, Adams finally asked to resign. Formal letters of recall were sent in February 1788. During the last year and a half of his stay, he composed his three-volume *Defense of the Constitutions of Government of the United States of America,* an extended attempt to defend the American concept of balanced government against the criticisms of the French statesman A.R.J. Turgot.

The Presidency

With his return to Boston, Adams began the final stage of his public career. He was chosen vice president in 1789 under the new Federal constitution, a position he was to fill, again with considerable frustration because of its power-lessness, during both of Washington's administrations.

As the election of 1796 approached, the Jeffersonian Republicans began forming an opposition to the Federalists' financial program and seemingly pro-British foreign policy. The Republicans presented Jefferson as their presidential candidate. The Federalists split into two factions, with Adams as one candidate and Thomas Pinckney (backed by Alexander Hamilton) as the other. In spite of Hamilton's efforts, Adams ran well ahead of Pinckney and became the second president of the United States. Jefferson, a scant three electoral votes behind, became vice president.

Adams took office on March 4, 1797. From the first his presidency was a stormy one. His Cabinet, inherited from Washington and dominated by Hamilton's followers, proved increasingly difficult to control. Foreign policy problems, generated by the outbreak of war between revolutionary France and a counterrevolutionary coalition of European nations, created internal political crises of magnitude. The outbreak of revolution in France had tended to polarize political discussion in the United States as well as in Europe between "aristocratic" and "democratic" positions. More particularly, the war between England and France raised questions of whether the United States would maintain a strict neutrality—in fact impossible because of efforts by both England and France to control American trade—or align itself, at least sympathetically, with one of the countries. While most Americans professed the desire to remain neutral in the contest, the Jeffersonians were sympathetic with France and the Federalists with England. Adams found himself caught in the middle.

In 1797 French diplomats attempted to bribe the three-man commission sent by the United States to negotiate various points in dispute between the two nations. The immediate result was an outburst of anti-French sentiment, which the Hamiltonians worked hard to inflame. Adams became caught up in the furor as well, making numerous statements during the spring and summer of 1798 that fanned emotions even higher. Taking advantage of the situation, the Federalists in Congress, with Adams's tacit approval, developed a war program consisting of substantial increases in the American navy, a large provisional army, the Alien and Sedition Acts (aimed at controlling potential subversives within), and a system of tax measures to finance the entire program. The Federalist goals were two: to prepare for an expected war with France and to attack the Jeffersonian opposition.

For a while it seemed that the Federalist measures would carry the day. But during the late summer and fall of 1798 the prospect of peaceful accommodation with France increased, and public discontent with the Federalist war program (helped along by the cries of the Jeffersonians) broke through the surface. President Adams, at home in Massachusetts during much of this time, became convinced that war with France was not necessary and that the Fed-eralist policies, if continued, were likely to result in serious internal disorder. Early in 1799 he committed himself to a plan of peaceful accommodation with France—a decision that enraged most of the Hamiltonians and left them sitting far out on a political limb, with a military establishment and no foreign invader to fight.

By 1800 the split between Adams and the Hamiltonian wing of the Federalist party was complete. Adams dismissed the main Hamiltonians from his Cabinet, and Hamilton openly opposed Adams for reelection. But the President's peace initiatives were both enlightened statesmanship and good politics. The young nation was unprepared for any major external war, and the possibility of serious internal conflict if the war program was continued seems to have been real. Moreover, as various individuals reported, by late 1799 France was prepared for an honorable accommodation with the United States, so there was no longer reason for conflict. Politically, Adams's peace decision made comparable sense. The Federalist split no doubt weakened his chances in 1800, but the Jeffersonians were already scoring heavily in their attacks on Federalist policies. Continued defense of such policies would almost certainly have led to political disaster. In the end Adams lost the election to Jefferson by a narrow margin.

Adams later described his peace decision as "the most splendid diamond in my crown," more important than his leadership in the revolutionary crisis, his constitutional writings, or his diplomatic service. He left the capital, however, bitterly disappointed over his rejection by the American people, so distressed that he even refused to remain for Jefferson's inaugural in 1801.

Adams spent the remainder of his life in political seclusion, though he retained a lively interest in public affairs, particularly when they involved the rising career of his son, John Quincy Adams. John Adams divided his time between overseeing his farm and carrying on an extended correspondence concerning both his personal experiences and issues of more general political and philosophical significance. He died at the age of 91, just a few hours after Jefferson's death, on July 4, 1826.

Further Reading

The most complete modern biography is Page Smith, *John Adams* (2 vols., 1962), although Smith does not differentiate clearly enough the central themes of Adams's career. Still useful is Gilbert Chinard, *Honest John Adams* (1933). For the early career of John Adams see Catherin Drinker Bowen, *John Adams and the American Revolution* (1950). Adams's election to the presidency is fully detailed in Arthur M. Schlesinger, ed., *History of American Presidential Elections* (4 vols., 1971). Manning J. Dauer, *The Adams Federalists* (1953), and Stephen G. Kurtz, *The Presidency of John Adams: The Collapse of Federalism, 1795-1800* (1957), examine Adams's feud with Hamilton and the split within the Federalist party. For the political thought of Adams three studies are relevant: Correa M. Walsh, *The Political Science of John Adams* (1915); Edward Handler, *America and Europe in the Political Thought of John Adams* (1964); and John Howe, *The Changing Political Thought of John Adams* (1966). □

John Quincy Adams

John Quincy Adams (1767-1848) was the sixth president of the United States. A brilliant statesman and outstanding secretary of state, he played a major role in formulating the basic principles of American foreign policy.

B orn in Braintree (now Quincy), Mass. on July 11, 1767, John Quincy Adams was the eldest son of John and Abigail Smith Adams. In 1779, at the age of 12, he accompanied his father to Europe. Precocious and brilliant—at 14 he accompanied Francis Dana, the American minister, to Russia as a French translator—he served as his father's secretary during the peace negotiations in Paris. Except for brief periods of formal education, he studied under his father's direction. When he entered Harvard in 1785, he was proficient in Greek, Latin, French, Dutch, and German.

After his graduation Adams studied law and began to practice in Boston in 1790. More interested in politics than the law, he made a name for himself with political essays supporting the politics of President George Washington. Those signed "Publicola" (his answer to Thomas Paine's *Rights of Man*) were so competent that they were ascribed to his father, who was then vice president.

The Diplomat

In 1793 Washington appointed young Adams minister to the Netherlands. From this vantage point he supplied the government with a steady flow of information on European affairs. Sent to London in connection with Jay's Treaty, he met Louisa Catherine Johnson, the daughter of the American consul, and married her on July 26, 1797. Although it was not a love match, the marriage was a happy one marked by deep mutual affection. In 1797 Adams became minister to Prussia, concluding a commercial treaty incorporating the neutral-rights provisions of Jay's Treaty.

On his return to the United States in 1801, Adams was elected to the Massachusetts Senate. Two years later he became a U.S. senator. Nominally a Federalist, he pursued an independent course. He was the only Federalist senator from New England to vote for the Louisiana Purchase. The Massachusetts Federalists forced him to resign in 1808 because they were angered by his support of Jefferson's commercial warfare against Great Britain and his presence at a Republican presidential nominating caucus.

Adams severed his connections with the Federalists and in 1809 accepted an appointment from Republican president James Madison as minister to Russia. He did much to encourage Czar Alexander's friendly disposition toward the United States. It was partly due to Adams's encouragement that Russia made an offer to mediate between Great Britain and the United States, which led to direct peace negotiations to end the War of 1812. As a member of the peace commission at Ghent, Adams and his colleagues (Henry Clay, Albert Gallatin, James A. Bayard, and Jonathan Russell) found the British commissioners so intransigent that they were obliged to conclude a treaty short of American expectations. In 1815, as minister to great Britain, Adams worked to lessen the tension between the two nations by welcoming Lord Castlereagh's friendly overtures.

The Secretary of State

In March 1817 President James Monroe appointed Adams secretary of state. Adams, who was then 50, was not a prepossessing figure. He was short, plump, and bald; his best feature was his penetrating black eyes. Inclined to be irascible, and very much aware of his own intellectual powers, he disciplined himself to conceal his impatience. "I am," he wrote in his diary, "a man of reserved, cold, austere, and forbidding manners. . . ." He was ill at ease in large gatherings, but in intimate circles he could be an entertaining companion. Imposing rigid moral standards on himself, he was inclined to judge others harshly. He had an almost Puritan sense of duty and a passion for work, which kept him at his desk for long hours not only in connection with official duties but in the scholarly researches that gave him so much pleasure. Every day he found time to make lengthy entries in his diary, which constitutes one of the most revealing sources for the political events of his era. His wife, witty and gracious, somewhat compensated for her husband's social shortcomings; Louisa Adams's weekly evening parties were among the most popular in the capital.

Adams and Monroe worked together in the greatest harmony and understanding, for they were in complete agreement on the basic objectives of American foreign policy. They wished to expand the territorial limits of the nation, to give American diplomacy a direction distinct from that pursued by the European states, and to compel the other powers to treat the United States as an equal. Monroe closely controlled foreign affairs, but he relied heavily on Adams, who proved a shrewd adviser, an adroit negotiator, and a talented writer whose state papers formulated administration policy with logic and a tremendous command of the relevant facts.

The most difficult negotiations undertaken by Adams were those culminating in the acquisition of Florida and the definition of the western boundary of Louisiana. In 1819 Adams was able to exploit Andrew Jackson's invasion of Florida to force Spain to settle both issues in the Transcontinental Treaty, which Spain ratified in 1821. Adams's familiarity with the complexities of the history of Louisiana enabled him to obtain a boundary settlement favorable to the United States and to fix the northern boundary so that American interests in the Columbia River region were protected. During the crisis precipitated by Jackson's unauthorized seizure of Spanish posts in Florida, Adams was the only Cabinet member to recommend that the administration completely endorse the general's conduct.

Equally taxing and less successful were the prolonged negotiations with the French minister over indemnities for confiscation of American ships and cargoes during the Napoleonic Wars, France's commercial rights in Louisiana, and trade relations in general. In 1822 Adams concluded a treaty providing only for a gradual reduction of discriminatory duties. His efforts to persuade Great Britain to open West Indian trade to American ships were unsuccessful. In the midst of these demanding negotiations, Adams conducted an extensive correspondence with American diplomats, reorganized the State Department, and drafted a masterly report for Congress on a uniform system of weights and measures. In 1822 Monroe formally recognized the new independent states in Latin America. Adams's instructions to the first American emissaries reflected his misgivings about the future of these states, which were largely dominated by authoritarian regimes.

When France intervened in Spain in 1823 to suppress a revolution, Adams did not share the view that this presaged a move on the European powers, who had banded together in the Holy Alliance, to restore Spanish authority in South America. He was far more concerned about Russian attempts to expand along the Pacific coast. Consequently, he welcomed Monroe's decision in 1823 to make a policy declaration expressing American hostility to European intervention in the affairs of the Americas. To the President's declaration, later known as the Monroe Doctrine, Adams contributed the noncolonization principle, which affirmed that the United States considered the Americas closed to further European colonization. In 1824 the American minister in Russia, acting on instructions from Adams, obtained an agreement in which Russia withdrew north of latitude 54′40″, but Adams was not able to persuade the British to vacate the Columbia River region.

The President

In 1824 Adams was involved in a bitter four-cornered presidential contest in which none of the candidates received a majority of the electoral votes. Adams with 84 votes, largely from New England and New York, ran behind Andrew Jackson with 99 but ahead of William H. Crawford with 41 and Henry Clay with 37. The contest was resolved in Adams's favor in the House of Representatives when Clay decided to support him. Adams's subsequent choice of Clay as secretary of state raised a cry of "corrupt bargain"; there was no overt agreement between them, but the charge was most damaging.

Adams's presidency added little to his fame. In the face of the absolute hostility of the combined Jackson-Crawford forces, he was unable to carry out his nationalist program. His proposals for Federal internal improvements, a uniform bankruptcy law, federally supported educational and scientific institutions, and the creation of a department of the interior were rebuffed. His sole success in dealing with Congress was the appointment in 1826 of two delegates to attend the Panama Congress, arranged by Simón Bolívar. This Adams achieved only after acrimonious debates in which hostile congressmen made much of the fact that American delegates would be participating in a conference attended by black representatives from Haiti.

Committed to a protectionist policy, Adams signed the Tariff of Abominations (engineered by the Jacksonians in 1828), although it was certain to alienate the South and displease New Englanders, whose manufactures were not granted additional protection. He never permitted political expediency to override his rigid sense of justice. Consequently, he alienated much Southern and Western opinion by his efforts to protect the interests of the Cherokees in

Georgia. He also declined to use the power of patronage to build up a national following, although Postmaster General John McLean was appointing only Jackson men. Pilloried as an aristocrat hostile to the interests of the "common man," Adams was overwhelmingly defeated by Jackson in the election of 1828.

The Congressman

At the end of his presidency, Adams expected to concentrate on the scholarly interests which had always absorbed so much of his time, but his retirement was brief. In 1831 he was elected to the House of Representatives, where he served for eight successive terms until his death. Although generally associated with the Whigs, he pursued an independent course. For 10 years he was chairman of the Committee on Manufactures, which drafted tariff bills. He approved Jackson's stand on nullification, but he considered the compromise tariff of 1833, which was not the work of his committee, an excessive concession to the nullifiers. After 1835 he was identified with the antislavery cause, although he was not an abolitionist. From 1836 to 1844, when his efforts were finally successful, he worked to revoke the gag rule that required the tabling of all petitions relating to slavery. Session after session "old man eloquent," as he was dubbed, lifted his voice in defense of freedom of speech and the right to petition. True to his nationalist convictions, he continued to advocate internal improvements and battled to save the Bank of the United States.

Adams suffered a stroke on the floor of the House of Representatives on Feb. 21, 1848. He was carried to the Speaker's room, where he died 2 days later without regaining consciousness.

Further Reading

The most important printed sources are Adams's diary, *Memoirs of John Quincy Adams…*, edited by Charles Francis Adams (12 vols., 1874-1877), and Worthington Chauncey Ford's edition of *The Writings of John Quincy Adams* (7 vols., 1913-1917), which stops in 1823. The best biography is Samuel Flagg Bemis's two volumes, *John Quincy Adams and the Foundations of American Foreign Policy* (1949) and *John Quincy Adams and the Union* (1956). Another useful biography is Paul Nagel, *John Quincy Adams: A Public Life, a Private Life* (1997). Adams's election to the presidency is covered fully by Arthur M. Schlesinger, Jr., ed., *History of American Presidential Elections* (4 vols., 1971). Studies of Adams's diplomacy are Dexter Perkins, *The Monroe Doctrine, 1823-1826* (1927; new ed. 1966); Philip C. Brooks, *Diplomacy and the Borderlands: The Adams-Onis Treaty of 1819* (1939); Arthur Preston Whitaker, *The United States and the Independence of Latin America, 1800-1830* (1941); Bradford Perkins, *Castlereagh and Adams: England and the United States, 1812-1823* (1964). See also George A. Lipsky, *John Quincy Adams: His Theory and Ideas* (1950). □

Samuel Adams

The colonial leader Samuel Adams (1722-1803) helped prepare the ground for the American Revolution by inflammatory newspaper articles and shrewd organizational activities.

Afundamental change in British policy toward the American colonies occurred after 1763, ending a long period of imperial calm. As Great Britain attempted to tighten control over its colonies, Adams was quick to sense the change, and his invective writings at first irritated and finally outraged the Crown officials. As a prime mover in the nonmilitary phases of colonial resistance, Adams undoubtedly pushed more cautious men, such as John Hancock, into leading Whig roles. However, his service in the Continental Congress and as a state official lacked political finesse. Once the struggle shifted from a war of words to one of ideas and finally of military encounters, Adams's influence declined.

Samuel Adams was born on Sept. 27, 1722, in Boston, Mass., the son of a prosperous brewer and a pious, dogmatic mother. When he graduated from Harvard College in 1740, his ideas about a useful career were vague: he did not want to become a brewer, neither did work in the Church appeal to him. After a turn with the law, this field proved unrewarding too. A brief association in Thomas Cushing's firm led to an independent business venture which cost Adams's family £1,000. Thus fate (or ill luck) forced Adams into the brewery; he operated his father's malt house for a livelihood but not as a dedicated businessman. In 1749 he married Elizabeth Checkley.

When his father suffered financial reverses, Adams accepted the offices of assessor and tax collector offered by the Boston freeholders; he held these positions from 1753 to 1765. His tax accounts were mismanaged and an £8,000 shortage appeared. There seems to have been no charge that he was corrupt, only grossly negligent. Adams was honest and later paid off the debts.

Adams's wife died in 1757 and in 1764 he married Elizabeth Wells, who was a good manager. His luck had changed, for he was about to move into a political circle that would offer personal opportunity unlike any in his past.

Growth in Politics

Adams became active in politics, and politics offered the breakthrough that transformed him from an inefficient taxgatherer into a leading patriot. As a member of the Caucus Club in 1764, he helped control local elections. When British policy on colonial revenues tightened during a recession in New England, passage of the Sugar Act in 1764 furnished Adams with enough fuel to kindle the first flames of colonial resistance. Thenceforth, he devoted his energies to creating a bonfire that would burn all connections between the Colonies and Great Britain. He also sought to discredit his local enemies—particularly the governor, Thomas Hutchinson.

Enforcement of the Sugar Act was counter to the interests of those Boston merchants who had accepted molasses smuggling as a way of life. They had not paid the old sixpence tax per gallon, and they did not intend to pay the new threepence levy. Urged on by his radical Caucus Club associates, Adams drafted a set of instructions to the colonial assemblymen that attacked the Sugar Act as an unreasonable law, contrary to the natural rights of each and every colonist because it had been levied without assent from a legally elected representative. The alarm "no taxation without representation" had been sounded.

Mature Propagandist

During the next decade Samuel Adams seemed a man destined for the times. His essays gave homespun, expedient political theories a patina of legal respectability. Eager printers hurried them into print under a variety of pseudonyms. Meanwhile Parliament unwittingly obliged men of Adams's bent by proceeding to pass an even more restrictive measure in the Stamp Act of 1765. Unlike the Sugar Act, this was not a measure that would be felt only in New England; Adams's audience widened as moderate merchants in American seaports now found more radical elements eager to force the issue of whether Parliament was still supreme "in all cases whatsoever." In one of many results, Governor Hutchinson's home was nearly destroyed by a frenzied anti-Stamp Act mob.

Adams's hammering essays and unceasing activities helped crystallize American opinion into viewing the Stamp Act as an odious piece of legislation. Through his columns in the *Boston Gazette,* he sent a stream of abuse against the British ministry; effigies of eminent Cabinet members hanged from Boston lampposts testified to the power of his incendiary prose. Adams rode a crest of popularity into the provincial assembly. As calm returned, he knew that the instruments of protest were developed and ready for use when the next opportunity showed itself.

The Townshend Acts of 1767 furnished Adams with a larger and more militant forum, projected his name into the front ranks of the patriot group, and earned him the hatred of the British general Thomas Gage and of King George III. Working with the Caucus Club, the radicals overcame local mercantile interests and demanded an economic boycott of British goods. This nonimportation scheme became a rallying point throughout the 13 colonies. Though its actual success was limited, Adams had proved that an organized, skillful minority could keep a larger but diffused group at bay. Adams worked with John Hancock to make seizure of the colonial ship *Liberty* seem a national calamity, and he welcomed the tension created by the stationing of British troops in Boston. Almost singlehandedly Adams continued his alarms, even after repeal of the Townshend duties.

In the succession of events from the Boston Massacre of 1770 to the Boston Tea Party and the Bill, Adams deftly threw Crown officials off guard, courted the radical elements, wrote dozens of inflammatory newspaper articles, and kept counsel with outspoken leaders in other colonies. In a sense, Adams was burning himself out so that, when the time for sober reflection and constructive political activity came, he had outlived his usefulness. By the time of the battles of Lexington and Concord in 1775, when he and Hancock were singled out as Americans not covered in any future amnesty, Adam's career as a propagandist and agitator had peaked.

Declining Power

Adams served in the Continental Congress between 1774 and 1781, but after the first session he occupied himself with gossip, uncertain as to what America's next steps should be or where he would fit into the scheme. He failed to perceive the forces loosed by the Revolution, and he was mystified by its results. While serving in the 1779 Massachusetts constitutional convention, he allowed his cousin John Adams to do most of the work. Tired of Hancock's vanity, he let their relationship cool; Hancock's repeated reelection as governor from 1780 on was a major disappointment. Against Daniel Shays's insurgents in 1786-1787, Adams shouted "conspiracy," showing little sympathy for the hard-pressed farmers.

As a delegate to the Massachusetts ratifying convention in 1788, Adams made a brief show as an old-time liberal pitted against the conservatives. But the death of his son weakened his spirit, and in the end he was intimidated by powerful Federalists. He was the lieutenant governor of Massachusetts from 1789 to 1793, when he became governor. As the candidate of the rising Jeffersonian Republicans, he was able to exploit the voter magnetism of the Adams name and was reelected for three terms. He did not seek reelection in 1797 but resisted the tide of New England federalism and remained loyal to Jefferson in 1800. He died in Boston on Oct. 2, 1803.

Further Reading

Harry Alonzo Cushing edited *The Writings of Samuel Adams* (1904-1908). Ralph V. Harlow, *Samuel Adams, Promoter of the American Revolution: A Study in Psychology and Politics* (1923), is a brave attempt at interpretive analysis. John C. Miller, *Sam Adams, Pioneer in Propaganda* (1936), is readable and reliable. An older standard work is William V. Wells, *The Life and Public Services of Samuel Adams* (1865). Stewart Beach, *Samuel Adams: The Fateful Years, 1764-1776* (1965), is a useful study. Philip Davidson, *Propaganda and the American Revolution, 1763-1783* (1941), and Arthur M. Schlesinger, Sr., *Prelude to Independence: The Newspaper War on Britain, 1764-1776* (1958), provide background information. ☐

Spiro Theodore Agnew

Between the time of his nomination as Richard Nixon's running mate in August 1968 to his resignation in October 1973, Vice President Spiro T. Agnew (1918-1996) was a leading spokesman for those Nixon called "The Silent Majority" of Americans. The charge of bribe-taking, which forced Agnew's resignation from office, preceded by less than one year President Nixon's own resignation.

Spiro Theodore Agnew was born November 9, 1918, in Baltimore, Maryland, to Greek immigrant restaurant owner Theodore S. Anagnostopoulous and a Virginia-born widow named Margaret Akers. The family surname went through two changes after it left Gargaliani, Greece, metamorphosing from Anagnostopoulous to Aganost before arriving at Agnew. The elder Agnew lost his business during the Depression, but had restored his fortunes by the time his son was ready for high school. Agnew attended public schools in Baltimore before enrolling in Johns Hopkins University in 1937, where he studied chemistry. He was, in his own words, a "typical middle class youth" who spoke and wrote very well, gaining experience writing speeches for his father's many appearances before civic, ethnic, and community groups.

After three years of studying chemistry Ted Agnew transferred to law school at the University of Baltimore, where he attended night classes. He supported himself by working for an insurance company, where he met his future wife "Judy," Elinor Isabel Judefind.

Service in Two Wars

In September of 1941 Agnew became one of the early draftees in President Franklin D. Roosevelt's peace time Selective Service System. After the attack on Pearl Harbor, Agnew was sent to Fort Knox to train as a tank officer. He married Judy after graduation in May 1942. Sent to the European theater, Agnew commanded a tank company in the 10th Armored Division, won the Bronze Star, took part in the Battle of the Bulge, and was discharged a captain.

He returned to civilian life with the great wave of hundreds of thousands of veterans seeking to recover their old lives or build new ones. The first of four children was born to Agnew and his wife in 1946, spurring Agnew to complete his interrupted legal studies in 1947. He had a good job with an insurance company and had just purchased a new home in Baltimore County when the Korean War broke out in 1950. Abruptly recalled to active duty for a year, he lost both his income and his home.

Successful Legal Career

Mustered out a second time, Agnew joined the lower management levels of a Baltimore supermarket chain. He was not only a skillful personnel manager, but developed a friendship with Judge Herbert Moser, who served on the company's board of directors. Moser helped him make connections, and soon Agnew's legal career took off.

Agnew had all the attributes of the successful American attorney. He was articulate, persuasive, flexible, knowledgeable, confident, well-groomed, and energetic. As clients became more numerous, the growing Agnew family prospered.

Entrance into Politics

Despite his growing law practice, or perhaps because of a desire to expand it, Agnew became involved in Baltimore County local politics. His father was a well-connected Democrat, and Agnew registered as a Democrat early in his adult life. A friend and associate, Judge E. Lester Barrett, persuaded him to switch to the Republican party where he began working for local and national campaigns. In 1957 he served his first public office when he was appointed to the Zoning Board of Appeals of Baltimore County. In 1960 he ran his first campaign, for associate circuit judge. Although he lost that election, the next year saw him winning the seat of Baltimore county executive, the first Republican to do so in seventy years.

His run as county executive was generally considered to be very successful, and he gained a popular following which served him well when he ran for governor of Maryland in 1966 and won. He ran against Democratic civil rights hard-liner and millionaire contractor, George Mahoney. Notwithstanding the overwhelming Democratic edge in registration, Agnew captured half of the votes, defeating Mahoney 453,000 to 371,000.

Turn to the Right

Governor Agnew proved to be a progressive, urban-oriented executive with moderate civil rights leanings and liberal credentials. While in office he passed tax reform, increased funding for anti-poverty programs, passed legislation removing barriers to public housing, repealed a law banning interracial marriage, spoke out against the death penalty, passed a more liberal abortion law, and drafted the nation's toughest clean water legislation. However, around the time of the urban riots and the rise of the anti-war movement in 1968, the tone and tolerance of Agnew's administration began to undergo alteration. He began arresting civil rights demonstrators, speaking harshly against the rising waves of protest, encouraging a sharp increase in police powers and the use of the military in civil disturbances.

At the 1968 Republican Convention in Miami Beach, Agnew was persuaded to place Richard Nixon's name in nomination. When Nixon won the nomination he accepted Agnew as his running mate. A key sentence uttered by Agnew in his vice presidential acceptance speech was, "I fully recognize that I am an unknown quantity to many of you." In truth, as the governor of a small southern state he was relatively unknown within the party. Former Vice President Nixon wanted someone who was a Southerner, an ethnic American, an experienced executive, a civil rights moderate, a proven Republican vote-getter with appeal to Democrats, and a law and order advocate. Agnew fit all these qualifications.

Agnew's strengths generally helped the ticket, although several of his racially offensive gaffs created momentary fears about the wisdom of the choice. The Nixon-Agnew victory over Humphrey-Muskie was close yet clear cut, with a half million popular votes separating victors and losers.

Vice President—and Resignation

As vice president, Agnew was assigned a then-unprecedented office in the White House and was urged to help shape federal-state policies and other domestic matters. He learned his job quickly, making up for a lack of foreign and national experience by attacking administration opponents through attention-getting speeches. Relying on a crack team of writers led by William Safire, Patrick Buchanan, and Cynthia Rosenwald, the vice president became noted for coining phrases, lashing out against college radicals, dissident intellectuals, American permissiveness, and a "liberal" media elite. In New Orleans on October 19, 1969, he lamented that "a spirit of national masochism prevails, encouraged by an effete corps of impudent snobs who characterize themselves as intellectuals." At the Ohio State graduation ceremony of June 1969 he characterized the older generation's leadership as the "sniveling hand-wringing power structure." With these and similar speeches Agnew became widely known and much sought after as a speaker. The media became attracted to him and gave him considerable attention.

Resigning In Disgrace

Agnew won renomination to Nixon's team in 1972 and undoubtedly contributed to the overwhelming victory over McGovern-Shriver in that year. However, early into his second term he was advised that he was under investigation by federal prosecutors looking into allegations that he had regularly solicited and accepted bribes during his tenure as county executive and Maryland governor. As the cloud of Watergate began to envelope Richard Nixon and the presidency, the situation became increasingly untenable.

This intolerable political situation developed into an intricate plea bargaining process. As a result, federal authorities produced Agnew's "nolo contendere" plea of October 1, 1973. He pleaded no contest in Federal court to one misdemeanor charge of income tax evasion and was fined $10,000 and put on probation for three years. He was also forced to resign his office. His legal expenses, fines and other fees, totaling $160,000, were paid by his good friend Frank Sinatra. He was disbarred by the state of Maryland in 1974. The second of America's vice presidents to resign (John C. Calhoun had done so the previous century), Agnew was the only one to quit under a cloud of scandal.

After retreating from politics Agnew rearranged his life with considerable resiliency, becoming an international business consultant and the owner of several lucrative properties in Palm Springs, California, and in Maryland. He also wrote a best selling novel, *The Canfield Decision* (1986), and a book defending his record, *Go Quietly... Or Else* (1980), in which he suggests that Richard Nixon and Alexander Haig had planned his assassination if he refused to leave his post. In 1981 he was sued by three citizens of Maryland who sought to have the money he had reportedly received illegally from the state returned. After a few years of legal maneuvers the citizens won their case and Agnew had to reimburse $248,735 to the state coffers.

Agnew died of leukemia on September 17, 1996, at the age of 77.

Further Reading

The key to Spiro Agnew's importance to America lies in his speeches, which take up a good part of John R. Coyne, Jr.'s *The Impudent Snobs* (1972). Other collections are found in Spiro T. Agnew, *Frankly Speaking* (1970). Early biographies by Jim G. Lucas, *Agnew Profile in Conflict* (1970), and Robert Curran, *Spiro Agnew: Spokesman For America* (1970), shed light on Agnew's pre-vice-presidential career. His own book, *Go Quietly . . . Or Else* (1980), alleged his innocence of the charges that drove him from the office of vice-president. □

Conrad Aiken

Conrad (Potter) Aiken (1889-1973), poet, essayist, novelist, and critic, was one of America's foremost men of letters and a major figure in American literary modernism.

I n Conrad Aiken's "Silent Snow, Secret Snow," a young boy named Paul withdraws from his parents, teacher, and people with authority over his life. He enters a private, autistic world in which it seems as if he were cut off from everyone else by a wilderness of silence and snow. That private world seems mysterious in a delightful way, and by the end of the story, Paul has completely enveloped himself in it. There is no sign that anyone will ever be able to reach him again.

"Silent Snow, Secret Snow" is one of Aiken's most powerful stories. One of its principal achievements lies in making the reader sense the force and pleasure that a private world like Paul's can have.

A world like that might once have been attractive to Aiken himself. He was the son of wealthy, socially prominent New Englanders who had moved to Savannah, Georgia, where his father became a highly respected physician and surgeon. But then something happened for which, as Aiken later said, no one could ever find a reason. Without warning or apparent cause, his father became increasingly irascible, unpredictable, and violent. Then, early in the morning of February 27, 1901, he murdered his wife and shot himself. Aiken (who was eleven years old) heard the gunshots and discovered the bodies.

The violent deaths of his parents overshadowed Aiken's life and writings. Throughout his life, he was afraid that, like his father, he would go insane, and, like Paul in "Silent Snow, Secret Snow," he withdrew from threats in

the world around him. He disliked large gatherings and refused to give public readings from his works. He became deeply interested in psychoanalytic thought, and it became a central concern in his works.

After the tragedy, Aiken was taken to Massachusetts to live with relatives. He graduated from the Middlesex School and Harvard, where his classmates included T.S. Eliot, with whom he established a lifelong friendship. He lived in England for several years, but his main home for most of his life was Massachusetts. During his last 12 years, however, his home was the brickfront rowhouse in Savannah next to the one in which his parents died.

Aiken wrote or edited more than 50 books, the first of which was published in 1914, two years after his graduation from Harvard. His work includes novels, short stories (*The Collected Short Stories* appeared in 1961), criticism, autobiography, and, most important of all, poetry. He was awarded the National Medal for Literature, the Gold Medal for Poetry from the National Institute of Arts and Letters, the Pulitzer Prize, the Bollingen Prize, and the National Book Award. He was awarded a Guggenheim Fellowship, taught briefly at Harvard, and served as Consultant in Poetry for the Library of Congress from 1950 to 1952. He was also largely responsible for establishing Emily Dickinson's reputation as a major American poet.

The best source for information on Aiken's life is his autobiographical novel *Ushant* (1952), one of his major works. In this book he speaks candidly about his various affairs and marriages, his attempted suicide and fear of insanity, and his friendships with Eliot (who appears in the book as The Tsetse), Ezra Pound (Rabbi Ben Ezra), and other accomplished men.

In an interview for the *Paris Review* toward the end of his life, Aiken claimed that Freud's influence could be found throughout his work. In both his poetry and his fiction, Aiken tried to realize motivations buried in the subconscious. He believed that if they were left there, unspoken and unacknowledged, they could have as disastrous an effect as they had on his father's life. For Aiken, literature was a means to awareness, a route by which a man could become aware of the dark motivations hidden within himself.

Psychoanalytic thought is central in Aiken's writings. In his novel *Great Circle* (1933), for example, the central character has to learn to accept his past—with, of course, the help of a psychoanalyst. *Blue Voyage* (1927) is ostensibly about a voyage to England, but in fact the real voyage in this stream-of-consciousness novel is in the mind.

Aiken was principally successful as a poet, but his poetry has also been severely criticized. The central problem with much of the poetry is that it seems to lack great intensity. It conveys feelings of indefiniteness; emotion seems dispersed or passive. But those who criticize the poetry in this way have missed the nature of Aiken's poetic task. He cannot speak with the intensity and precision of other poets because he is, as it were, seeing and showing us things for the first time. He is dealing with aspects of man's psychology that are by their very nature indefinite and, in any precise way, undefinable. In this respect, his poetry reminds us strongly of the work of Mallarmé and other French symbolists.

Like the symbolists, Aiken is also a master of poetic music. Some poets are read less for the sound of their verse than for their ideas. Although Aiken presents grand intellectual schemes rooted in psychoanalytic thought, his greatest achievement is in the sound of his poetry—that is, in the creation of formal patterns of sound. There is great pleasure in simply reading and hearing the sound of his verse.

Aiken trained himself comprehensively in traditional English prosody, but his poetry shows little awareness of the revolutions in prosody that Pound and William Carlos Williams were effecting during his life. But the poetic effects he created are reminiscent of experiments in other arts in the late 19th and early 20th centuries. The sound of his poetry reminds one of the music of Debussy or, to name one of Aiken's American contemporaries, Charles Tomlinson Griffes. In painting, he reminds one of Whistler, particularly the Whistler of the Nocturnes.

Aiken sketches out moods, sensations, feelings, and attitudes with the music of his verse, but it is done as impressionistically as in, for example, Griffes' "The White Peacock" and "Nightfall." Aiken was at his best in poetic evocations of emotional and subconscious states which are better understood through suggestion than through direct statement.

Aiken's experiments with poetic music link him to some of the major poets of the New York School, particularly John Ashbery. The New York poets have generally been somewhat more experimental technically, but in the creation of "pure poetry"—poetry dependent on internal music for its unity and effect—they have clear affinities with him. Aiken should be seen in part as a transitional figure between the fin-de-siècle world of aestheticism and symbolism, on the one hand, and the poetic experiments of Ashbery and the New York School, on the other.

The magic of Aiken's poetry is in its ability to suggest through sound, image, and rhythm the things that would otherwise remain unknown to us. That accomplishment by itself places him among the most significant American poets of his generation.

Further Reading

The critical work on Aiken is vast. Reuel Denney's *Conrad Aiken* (1964), Frederick John Hoffman's *Conrad Aiken* (1962), and Jay Martin's *Conrad Aiken, a Life of His Art* (1962) are essential works. *Selected Letters of Conrad Aiken,* Joseph Killorin, ed., was published in 1978.

Additional Sources

Butscher, Edward, *Conrad Aiken, poet of White Horse Vale,* Athens: University of Georgia Press, 1988.

Conrad Aiken: a priest of consciousness, New York: AMS Press, 1989. □

Alvin Ailey

Alvin Ailey (1931-1989) founded the Alvin Ailey American Dance Theatre and won international fame as both a dancer and choreographer.

During the 1960s and 1970s, Alvin Ailey shaped modern dance into a popular art form. In 1969, he founded the American Dance Center, a dance school that teaches a variety of techniques. Five years later he founded the Alvin Ailey Repertory Ensemble, a junior dance company. But mainly through the auspices of the Alvin Ailey American Dance Theater established in 1959, Ailey greatly impacted the dance world. Known for its "vibrant artistry and repertory, and for Ailey's motivating humanist vision," his company drew enthusiastic responses from audiences, while touring the world.

The 30-member company has executed more than 150 pieces in some 67 countries. Ailey's modern dance company has presented classic pieces by early dance pioneers, including the dancer, choreographer, and anthropologist Katherine Dunham, whose Afro-Caribbean-based works had a lasting impact on Ailey. In addition, his company has performed many works by younger black choreographers such as Bill T. Jones, Ulysses Dove, Judith Jamison, and others.

Ailey also produced his own celebrated dance pieces, dealing with his memories of church services and forbidden dance halls in the all-black neighborhood of the Texas town where he spent his early years. His energetic, diverting dances also used blues, jazz, Latin, and classical music. About Ailey's works John Gruen wrote in *The Private World of Ballet,* "His work is marked by the free use of disparate

elements of the dance vocabulary. At its best, the Ailey group generates an uncommon exhilaration, achieved by a tumultuous and almost tactile rhythmic pulse. Ailey's own best works are charged with a dazzling and uninhibited movement and life. The exuberance and poignancy of the black experience are well served in Ailey's splendid [dance pieces] *Revelations, Blues Suite,* and *Cry.*"

In addition, Ailey staged dance productions, operas, ballets, and had works performed on television. He received honorary degrees in fine arts from colleges and universities and prizes for his choreography, including a *Dance* magazine award in 1975; the Springarn Medal, given to him by the National Association for the Advancement of Colored People (NAACP) in 1979; and the Capezio Award that same year. In 1988 he was awarded the Kennedy Center Honors prize.

Inauspicious Beginnings

Alvin Ailey, Jr. was born into a large extended family on January 5, 1931, in Rogers, Texas, a small town not far from Waco. Alvin Sr., a laborer, left his son's mother, Lula Elizabeth, when Alvin Jr. was less than one-year-old. While the United States was in the midst of the economic Great Depression, jobs were particularly scarce for black men and Alvin Sr. struggled to make ends meet. Six years later, Alvin Jr. was sent to his mother. At the age of six, Alvin Jr. moved with his mother to Navasota, Texas, where he recalled in an interview in the *New York Daily News Magazine,* "There was the white school up on the hill, and the black Baptist church, and the segregated theaters and neighborhoods.

Like most of my generation, I grew up feeling like an outsider, like someone who didn't matter."

In 1942, when Ailey was 12, he and his mother relocated to Los Angeles, where his mother worked in an aircraft factory. As a teenager Ailey showed an interest in athletics, joining his high school gymnastics team and playing football. An admirer of pioneering dancers Gene Kelly and Fred Astaire, Ailey took tap dancing lessons at the home of a neighbor. But his interest in dance was really stimulated when a high school friend took him to visit the Hollywood modern dance school run by Lester Horton, whose company was the first racially integrated one in America. Unsure of what opportunities would be available for him as a dancer, however, he left Horton's school after one month.

After graduating from high school in 1948, Ailey contemplated becoming a teacher. He entered the University of California in Los Angeles and began studying the romance languages. When Horton offered him a scholarship in 1949, Ailey went back to the dance school but left again after one year, this time to attend San Francisco State College.

Directed Horton's Troupe

For a time Ailey danced in a San Francisco nightclub, then he returned to the Horton school to finish his training. By 1953, when Horton took the company east for a New York City debut performance, Ailey was with him. When Horton died of a heart attack, the young Ailey took charge as the company's artistic director, choreographing two pieces in Horton's style to be presented at the Jacob's Pillow festival. After the works received poor reviews from the festival manager, the troupe broke up.

Despite the setback, Ailey's career stayed on track. A Broadway producer invited him to dance in *House of Flowers,* a musical adaptation of Truman Capote's book. While a member of the cast, Ailey spent the next five months broadening his dance knowledge by taking classes at the Martha Graham school with Doris Humphrey, and with Charles Weidman and Hanya Holm. He also studied ballet with Karel Shook, cofounder of the Dance Theatre of Harlem, and acting with legendary acting instructor Stella Adler. From the mid-1950s through the early 1960s, Ailey appeared in theatrical and musical productions on and off-Broadway, among them *The Carefree Tree; Sing, Man, Sing; Jamaica;* and *Call Me By My Rightful Name.* He also played a major theatrical part in the play, *Tiger, Tiger, Burning Bright.*

In the spring of 1958, Ailey and another dancer with an interest in choreographing recruited 35 dancers to perform several concerts at the 92nd Street Young Men's and Young Women's Hebrew Association (YM-YWHA) in New York City, a place where modern dances and new choreographers were seen. Ailey's first major piece was inspired by blues music. Viewers saw the debut performance of *Blues Suite,* set in a Southern "bawdyhouse." Observed Julinda Lewis-Ferguson in her book, *Alvin Ailey, Jr.: A Life in Dance,* "The characters interact with anger, tenderness, love, and a whole range of familiar and recognizable emotions." The performance drew praise, with Jack Anderson of the *New York Times* calling *Blues Suite* "one of Mr. Ailey's best pieces." Ailey scheduled a second concert at the Y, to present his own works, and then a third, which featured his most famous piece, *Revelations.* Accompanied by the elegant jazz music of Duke Ellington, *Revelation's* audience is deftly pulled into African-American religious life. Julinda Lewis-Ferguson described the piece in her book: "*Revelations* begins with the dancers clustered together in a group, in the center of the stage, arms stretched over their heads. . . . They appear to be bathed in a golden blessing from heaven. . . . The highly energetic final section of the work starts off with three men running, sometimes on their knees, trying to hide from their sins or from the punishment for their sins. . . . The finale, "Rocka My Soul in the Bosom of Abraham," is both a spiritually powerful conclusion to the suite and a purely physical release of emotion." In the *New York Post* Clive Barnes described *Revelations* as "powerful and eloquent" and a "timeless tribute to humanity, faith, and survival."

Established Own Dance Company

Ailey established the Alvin Ailey American Dance Theater, composed of a troupe of eight black dancers, in 1959. One year after formation, Alvin Ailey's dance theater became the resident dance company at the Clark Center for the Performing Arts at the 51st Street and Eighth Avenue Young Men's Christian Association (YMCA) in New York City. In 1969, they moved to Brooklyn, New York, as the resident dance company of the Brooklyn Academy of Music, an arts center with three theaters. But they were unable to create the Lincoln Center they had hoped for in that borough and moved back to midtown Manhattan in 1971.

By the mid-1960s Ailey, who struggled with his weight, gradually phased out his dancing and replaced it with choreographing. He also oversaw administrative details as the director of his ambitious dance company. By 1968, the company had received funding from private and public organizations but still had financial problems, even as its reputation spread and it brought modern dance to audiences around the world. Ailey also had the leading African-American soloist of modern dance, Judith Jamison, and having been using Asian and white dancers since the mid-1960s, Ailey had fully integrated the company. He had organized his dance school in 1969, and by 1974, he had a repertory ensemble too.

In the early 1960s the company performed in Southeast Asia and Australia as part of an international cultural program set up by President John F. Kennedy. Later they traveled to Brazil, Europe, and West Africa. Ailey was choreographing dances for other companies too. He created *Feast of Ashes* for the Joffrey Ballet, three pieces for the Harkness ballet, and *Anthony and Cleopatra* for the Metropolitan Opera at Lincoln Center in New York City.

Ailey also worked on projects with other artists, including one with the jazz musician Duke Ellington for the American Ballet Theater. His company also gave a benefit performance for the Southern Christian Leadership Conference (SCLC). For Ailey the decade culminated with the performance of *Masekela Language,* a dance about the need for racial equality in South Africa, based on the music of Hugh Masekela, a black South African trumpeter who lived in exile for speaking out against apartheid. In her book Julinda Lewis-Ferguson described the piece as "raw, rough, almost unfinished, just like the buildings of the South African townships."

Ailey's Solo *Cry* A Smash Hit

By the late 1970s Ailey's company was one of America's most popular dance troupes. They continued touring around the world, with U.S. State Department backing. They were the first modern dancers to visit the former Soviet Union since Isadora Duncan's dancers performed there during the 1920s. In 1971, Ailey's company was asked to return to the City Center Theater in New York City after a performance featuring Ailey's celebrated solo, *Cry;* danced by Judith Jamison, she made it one of the troupe's best known pieces.

Dedicated to "all black women everywhere—especially our mothers," the piece depicts the struggles of different generations of black American women. It begins with the unwrapping of a long white scarf that becomes many things during the course of the dance, including a wash rag, and ends with an expression of unquestioning belief and happiness danced to the late 1960s song, "Right On, Be Free." Of this and of all his works, Ailey told John Gruen in *The Private World of Ballet,* "I am trying to express something that I feel about people, life, the human spirit, the beauty of things. . . . My ballets are all very close to me—they're very personal. . . . I think that people come to the theater to look at themselves, to look at the state of things. I try to hold up the mirror. . . ."

In 1980, Ailey suffered a mental breakdown which put him in the hospital for several weeks. At the time he had lost a close friend, was going through midlife crisis, and was experiencing financial difficulties. Still, he choreographed a number of pieces for the company during the 1980s, and his reputation as a founding father of modern dance grew during the decade.

Ending a legendary career, Ailey died of a blood disorder called dyscrasia, on December 1, 1989. Thousands of people flocked to the memorial service for him held at the Cathedral of St. John the Divine. "Alvin Ailey was a giant among American artists, a towering figure on the international dance scene," Gerald Arpino, the artistic director of the Joffrey Ballet, told the *Washington Post.* "His works have elated and moved audiences throughout the world. His spirit soars in his creations and he has enriched and illuminated our lives." Indeed, African American modern dance has firmly been entrenched in popular culture thanks to the presence of Ailey, creator of 79 dance pieces.

Further Reading

Earl Blackwell's Celebrity Register, Times Publishing Group, 1986, pp. 3-4; Gale Research Inc., 1990, pp. 2-3.

Ferguson, Julinda Lewis, *Alvin Ailey, Jr.: A Life in Dance,* Walker and Company, 1994, pp. 1-74.

Gruen, John, *The Private World of Ballet,* Viking, 1975, pp. 417-23.

Jamison, Judith, with Howard Kaplan, *Dancing Spirit: An Auto-biography,* Doubleday, 1993, pp. 66-236.

Newsmakers, Gale Research Inc., 1989, 1990.

Rogosin, Flinor, *The Dance Makers: Conversations With American Choreographers,* Walker and Company, 1980, pp. 102-117.

Ballet News, November, 1983, pp. 13-16.

Chicago Tribune, December 3, 1989, Sec. 2, p. 16.

Dance Magazine, December, 1983, pp. 44, 46, 48; October, 1978, pp. 63-4, 66, 68, 72-4, 76.

Los Angeles Times, December 2, 1989, Sec. A-38.

Newsday, December 4, 1988, Part II, pp. 4-5, 27.

New York Times, December 2, 1989, pp. 1, 14.

Washington Post, December 2, 1989, Sec. A-1, A-12; Sec. C-1, C-9. □

Edward Franklin Albee, III

American playwright Edward Franklin Albee, III (born 1928), achieved great success in the early 1960s with his one-act plays and the immensely popular full-length work *Who's Afraid of Virginia Woolf?*

Edward Franklin Albee, III, was born on March 12, 1928, and as an infant was adopted by Reed A. and Frances Albee. His adoptive father was a part owner of the Keith-Albee theater circuit, which controlled many playhouses across the country presenting vaudeville acts, plays, and movies.

Albee attended private schools and spent the year 1946-1947 as an undergraduate at Trinity College in Hartford, Connecticut. Leaving college, he went to New York City, where he worked as a continuity writer for radio station WNYC, an office boy in an advertising agency, a record salesman for a music publisher, a counterman in a luncheonette, and a Western Union messenger. While working at these jobs, he had modest success as a poet.

In 1958 he began to write for the theater, and his first two one-act plays, *The Zoo Story* and *The Death of Bessie Smith,* debuted in Berlin in German translations in 1959 and the following year were taken to New York.

He also wrote *The Sandbox* in 1959 for the Festival of Two Worlds in Spoleto, Italy, where it was not performed, but it was produced in New York the following year. *The American Dream,* seen by some as an expanded version of *The Sandbox,* was presented in Manhattan in 1961. The brief one-act *Fam and Yam* premiered in Westport, Connecticut, in 1960. Critics called some of these plays "brilliant" and "excellent" and found them "packed with untamed imagination." A few hailed Albee as the first American playwright of the absurd and hence a seminal figure.

The most exciting development in European drama in the post-World War II period was the advent of the so-called Theater of the Absurd, which had it philosophical roots in the existentialist school led by Jean-Paul Sartre and Albert Camus. As old as Aristotle, this school's undergirding was the view that existence precedes essence, or, in overly-simplified terms, that the concrete precedes the abstract. But the French existentialists added these refinements: reason alone is not adequate to explain human existence; anguish is common to all those who try to confront life's problems; and morality demands participation.

As filtered through the Theater of the Absurd, these ideas were altered or expanded to include the notions that the human condition is senseless and devoid of purpose or ideals and that, as psychoanalyst Philip Weiss puts it, "conventional logical communication" must be de-emphasized or regarded as well-nigh impossible. In Europe, Eugene Ionesco was considered the most consistent practitioner of Absurdist drama. In the words of Jacques Guicharnaud and June Beckelman, Ionesco's plays can be summarized as "a return to nihilism," offering "the message . . . that there is no message."

In the words of Tom Driver in *History of the Modern Theater,* "it was necessary, to have a popular playwright of the absurd [in America]. It was in this context that Edward Albee became a culture hero . . . after . . . *The Zoo Story,*" because, as John MacNicholas puts it, this play was "an exploration of the farce and agony of human isolation," a common Absurdist theme.

Years of Success and Criticism

After co-authoring the libretto of the opera *Bartleby* with James Hinton, Jr., in 1961, Albee had his greatest hit with *Who's Afraid of Virginia Woolf?* in 1962. Robert Corrigan in *The Theater in Search of a Fix* observed, "Great drama has always shown man at the limits of possibility. . . . In *Virginia Woolf* Albee has stretched them some, and in doing so he has given not only the American theatre but the theatre of the whole world, a sense of new possibility." John Gassner in *Dramatic Soundings* called it "pulsating moment-by-moment drama . . . [which] reaches the same order of harrowing dramatic power as Elizabethan melodrama." Even those whose general reception of the play was cool found something to praise, like Richard Gilman, who commented that "the rhetoric . . . is straight-forward, cocky, brutal, knowing . . . tremendously *au courant* . . . and very funny." The play won the 1963 Antoinette Perry Award (Tony) as the best new drama of the season.

In the next five years Albee divided his talents between adapting the works of others and continuing to compose original plays. In selecting works to adapt, Albee showed an unfortunate predilection for the second-rate: in 1963 he dramatized Carson McCuller's novella *The Ballad of the Sad Café;* in 1966 he produced *Malcolm,* based on a James Purdy novel of no distinction; and in 1967 he rewrote the play *Everything in the Garden* by the then-deceased Giles Cooper.

In 1964 Albee's *Tiny Alice* was staged and, like most of those which followed, was greeted by either raves or boos. Thomas Adler thought it reminiscent of Pirandello in showing "the universal human need to concretize the abstract, to discover or . . . to create a manageable representation of the unknown." Richard Gillman considered it "far and away the most significant play on Broadway this year." At the other end of the spectrum, novelist Philip Roth blasted *Tiny*

Alice for "its tediousness, its pretentiousness, its galling sophistication, its gratuitous and easy symbolizing, its ghastly pansy rhetoric and repartee."

In 1966 came *A Delicate Balance,* which won its author his first Pulitzer Prize, although such influential critics as Robert Brustein and John Simon dismissed it, the former declaring that "its empty chatter is passed off as profound observation with the aid of irrelevant portentous subordinate clauses. . . ."

In 1968 came a double-bill of short plays, *Box* and *Quotations from Chairman Mao Tse-Tung,* which, the playwright explained, "both . . . deal with the unconscious primarily" and which represented his closest approach to Absurdist theater. *All Over,* a play about death, came to New York in 1971 and encountered the range of critical reactions that was becoming standard.

Awarded a Second Pulitzer Prize

Albee won his second Pulitzer Prize with *Seascape* in 1975, which Harold Clurman (long an Albee supporter) in the *Nation* found "rather charming" and Brendan Gill in the *New Yorker* judged to be "wryly written and sometimes touching," its plot "a charming toy." But the naysayers were out in force again, with Jack Kroll in *Newsweek* summing it up as "the ultimate in pure nagging."

The year 1977 brought *Counting the Ways: A Vaudeville,* first presented in London, and *Listening: A Chamber Play,* which debuted in Hartford. Martin Esslin in *Plays and Players* found the former "full of beauties," and Thomas Adler in the *Educational Theatre Journal* thought it had "considerable charm and wit."

The Lady from Dubuque in 1980 fared rather badly with the critics. Brustein wrote, "It really is quite an awful piece," and Simon added that it featured "the ultimate in witless nastiness, gratuitous offensiveness and, above all, . . . verbal infelicity." Albee did little better with his adaptation of Nabokov's novel *Lolita* in 1981, although more than one critic raised the question of whether the novel itself was not dated.

The Man Who Had Three Arms in 1982 drew from Dan Sullivan in the *Los Angeles Times* the grudging admission that "[t]here is some juice in this one, even if it is mostly bile," but Frank Rich in the *New York Times* blasted it because "it isn't a play—it's a temper tantrum in two acts."

Finding the Sun (1983) provoked the comment from Linda Ben-Zvi in *Theater Journal,* "There is much that is strong and theatrical about the piece . . . it plays well." *The Marriage Play* (1987) drew from Dana Rufolo-Hörhagen in *Plays and Players* the encomium that it "is a resonant, poetical, and cleanly hewn-work." In 1994 *Three Tall Women* debuted in Manhattan. Essentially a monologue in the first act, it had an ingeniously-wrought second act in which the monologue was continued by three actresses, representing the protagonist at different stages in her life. This play won the Pulitzer Prize in 1994.

In 1998, Albee's *The Play About the Baby* premiered in London at the Almeida and received critical praise. Albee told Steven Drukman of *American Theatre* that the play concerns "a baby who ceases to exist." *Time International* described the play as "a dark witty account of two couples—the combination of jaded Man and Woman vs. innocent Boy and Girl that provided a similar dramatic tension in 1962's *Virginia Woolf."* Through *The Play About the Baby,* Albee gave a newness to many of his familiar themes such as memory, illusion, self-deception, and repetition.

Besides writing for the theater, Albee directed some of his own plays and those of others at various off-Broadway houses and in Los Angeles and won an award from the *Village Voice* for directing Len Jenkins' *Five of Us.* Further, he joined with Richard Barr and Clinton Wilder to form the New Playwrights Unit Workshop, which assisted aspirant writers for the theater. Albee also served as chairman of the Theater Department of Fordham University in New York.

Albee wrote four screenplays, including an adaptation of *The Death of Bessie Smith;* composed an introduction to *Three Plays by Noel Coward;* contributed to the *National Playwrights Directory;* and authored a biography of Louise Nevelson.

Albee's position in the history of American drama is difficult to assess. He had ardent admirers such as Ruby Cohn, who called him "the most skillful composer of dialogue that American has produced" in *Dialogue in American Drama,* and John MacNicholas, who wrote in the *Dictionary of Literary Biography* that his "ideals about man and art and his formidable technical skills . . . place him in the first rank of the dramatists of his century." On the other hand, Driver thinks he "achieved a popular and critical success out of all proportion to his substance and skill." The best and probably the fairest summary of Albee's career thus far is that of C.W.E. Bigsby in *Edward Albee: A Collection of Critical Essays:* "Albee has remained at heart a product of off-Broadway, claiming the same freedom to experiment, and, indeed, fail, which is the special strength of that theater." Another assessment is Albee's receipt of three Pulitzer Prizes. Tennessee Williams and August Wilson won two Pulitzers each, the only other multiple winners among American playwrights. In 1997 Albee was the recipient of the Steinbeck Award for literary and humanitarian contributions by a writer.

Further Reading

There has been no definitive biography of Albee; until one appears, the essay by MacNicholas in the *Dictionary of Literary Biography* (1981) will have to suffice. Three collections of essays about Albee's work are worth attention: the aforementioned anthology edited by Bigsby (1975) with contributions by such critics as Esslin and Clurman; *Edward Albee,* edited by Harold Bloom (1987); and *Critical Essays on Edward Albee,* edited by Philip Kolin and J. Madison Davis (1986). Information regarding the Steinbeck award can be reviewed at http://www.southhampton.liunet.com. ☐

Sherman Alexie

Winner of Washington State Arts Commission poetry and National Endowment for the Arts poetry fellowships, Sherman Alexie (born 1966) has published poems, stories, translations, and several books.

Sherman Alexie was born in 1966 and grew up in Wellpinit, Washington, on the Spokane Indian Reservation. Winner of a 1991 Washington State Arts Commission poetry fellowship and a 1992 National Endowment for the Arts poetry fellowship, Alexie has published more than two hundred poems, stories, and translations in publications such as *Another Chicago Magazine, Beloit Poetry Journal, Black Bear Review, Caliban, Journal of Ethnic Studies, Hanging Loose Press, New York Quarterly, Red Dirt, Slipstream, ZYZZYVA,* and others. His first book of poetry and short stories, *The Business of Fancydancing* was published by Hanging Loose Press in January 1992 and quickly earned a favorable front-page review from *The New York Times Book Review*. This first poetry book was the result of poems and stories written in Alexie's first creative writing workshop at Washington State University in Pullman. Alexie soon published a second collection, *I Would Steal Horses,* which was the winner of *Slipstream's* fifth annual Chapbook Contest in March 1992. In January 1993, he published a third poetry book, *Old Shirts and New Skins* (UCLA American Indian Studies Center). By early 1993, Alexie had written three books. Atlantic Monthly Press contracted to publish a collection of Alexie's short stories, *The Lone Ranger and Tonto Fistfight in Heaven.*

The Lone Ranger and Tonto Fistfight in Heaven was published to much critical acclaim. The short stories in this collection, like many of Alexie's other works, reveal his awareness of the despair, poverty, and alcoholism that is an unescapable part of the daily life of many Native Americans. Alexie poignantly stated: "[Indians] have a way of surviving. But it's almost like Indians can easily survive the big stuff. Mass murder, loss of language and land rights. It's the small things that hurt the most. The white waitress who wouldn't take an order, Tonto, the Washington Redskins."

While growing up in Wellpinit, Alexie read everything he could get his hands on, including auto repair manuals in the public library. He had aspirations of becoming a doctor until fainting three times in a high school anatomy class and deciding that an early career change was in order. He attended college for a while, but before dropping out, over 200 of his poems had been published. Alexie often refers to his writing as "fancydancing," a name given the changes Native American veterans of World War II made to their traditional dances. Through the early 1990s many of Alexie's characters were wrought with hopelessness fueled by alcohol. By 1995 however the thrust of his writing was beginning to change and *People* called his then just-published *Reservation Blues* " . . . a high-flying, humor spiked tale of culture and assimilation." Alexie told *People* that although many regard Native Americans as overly stoic, humor in fact is an essential part of their culture. In 1996 Alexie's next novel, *Indian Killer,* was released to favorable reviews. A thriller stocked with a cast of Indian characters representing facets of Native American culture, the novel presents a gripping mystery as well as historical facts and Indian myths. Judith Bolton-Fasman in the Christian Science Monitor commented, "Alexie has profound things to say about the identity and the plight of the American Indian" through his characters.

Although Alexie's writing is often emotionally cathartic, he writes for his people as well as for himself. In a 1995 interview he told the *Milwaukee Journal Sentinel* that he cherishes the difference his stories and poems have made in the lives of reservation Indians and he continues to write for this audience. Alexie feels that many Native American writers focus on the angst of Native Americans living in urban settings and the reservation Indians, who play prominent roles in his stories and poetry, are unfortunately ignored. Alexie told an audience of writers at the Native American Journalists Association that only American Indian writers can write of their people as only they, regardless of the sincerity of non-Indian writers, have the empathy and the intrinsic awareness of their people's emotions, lives, and humor.

Muhammad Ali

Muhammad Ali (born Cassius Clay, 1942) was the only professional boxer to win the heavyweight championship three times. With his outspoken political and religious views he has provided leadership and an example for African American men and women around the world.

Born Cassius Marcellus Clay on January 17, 1942, at Louisville, Kentucky, Muhammad Ali began boxing at the age of 12. A white policeman named Joe Martin featured Ali on his early television show, "Tomorrow's Champions," and started him working out at Louisville's Columbia Gym. An African American trainer named Fred Stoner taught Ali the science of boxing, instructing him to move with the grace and subtlety of a dancer.

"Float Like a Butterfly, Sting Like a Bee"

Ali built an impressive amateur record which led him to both the national Amateur Athletic Union (AAU) and Golden Gloves championships. At the age of 18 he competed in the 1960 Olympic games held at Rome, Italy, and won the gold medal in the light-heavyweight division. This led to a contract with a twelve member group of millionaires called the Louisville Sponsors Group, the most lucrative contract negotiated by a professional in the history of boxing. He worked his way through a string of professional victories, employing a style that combined speed with devastating punching power, described by one of his handlers as the ability to "float like a butterfly, and sting like a bee."

Ali's flamboyant style of boasting and rhyming and outspoken self-promotion garnered considerable media attention as he moved toward a chance to contend for the world heavyweight boxing championship. When he began to write poems predicting the outcome of his many bouts he became known by the another name: "The Louisville Lip."

Both the attention and his skill as a fighter paid off, and on February 15, 1964, at Miami, Florida, when he was only 22 years old, he fought and defeated Sonny Liston for the heavyweight championship of the world.

"Beloved of Allah"

Meanwhile Ali, inspired by human rights activist Malcolm X, embraced the Black Muslim faith and announced that he had changed his name to Cassius X. This was at a time when the struggle for civil rights was at a peak and the Muslims had emerged as a controversial but major force in the African American community. Later he was given the name Muhammad Ali, meaning "beloved of Allah," by the Muslim patriarch Elijah Muhammad.

In his first title defense, held at Lewiston, Maine, on May 25, 1965, he defeated the now challenger Sonny Liston with a first round knockout that many called a phantom punch because it was so fast and powerful that few in attendance saw it. Ali successfully defended his title eight more times.

On April 28, 1967, Ali was drafted into military service during the Vietnam War. As a Muslim and a conscientious objector he refused to serve, claiming an exemption as a minister of the Black Muslim religion. The press turned against him, calling him "unpatriotic, loudmouthed, bombastic." Although he had not been charged or convicted for violating the Selective Service Act, the New York State Athletic Commission and World Boxing Association suspended his boxing license and stripped him of his heavyweight title in May of 1967. Ali's comment to *Sports Illus-*

trated at the time was, "I'm giving up my title, my wealth, maybe my future. Many great men have been tested for their religious beliefs. If I pass this test, I'll come out stronger than ever." Eventually Ali was sentenced to five years in prison, released on appeal, and his conviction overturned three years later by the U.S. Supreme Court.

Vindication and Victory

The vindicated Ali returned to the ring in a victorious bout with Jerry Quary in Atlanta in 1971. Four months later he was defeated by Joe Frazier in Manila, who had replaced him as heavyweight champion when the title had been vacated. He regained the championship for the first time when he defeated George Forman (who had beaten Frazier for the title) in a bout held in Zaire in 1974. Ali fought Frazier again in the same year, and in 1975 won both matches and secured his title as the world heavyweight champion. In that year, to welcome Ali back, *Sports Illustrated* magazine named him their "Sportsman of the Year."

Ali began to employ a new style of boxing, one that he called his "rope-a-dope." He would let his opponents wear themselves down while he rested, often against the ropes; then he would lash out in the later rounds. During his ensuing reign Ali successfully defended his title ten more times. Ali held the championship until he was defeated by Leon Spinks on February 16, 1978, in a bout held in Las Vegas, Nevada. Seven months later, on September 15, 1978, Ali regained the heavyweight title by defeating Spinks in a bout held at New Orleans. Ali thus became the first boxer in history to win the heavyweight championship three times. At the end of his boxing career he was slowed by a neurological condition related to Parkinson's disease. His last fight, the 61st, took place in 1981.

Role as Statesman

As his career wound to a close, Ali became increasingly involved in social causes, diplomacy and politics. He has campaigned for Jimmy Carter and other Democratic political candidates and taken part in the promotion of a variety of political causes addressing poverty and children. He even played the role of diplomat, attempting to secure the release of four kidnapped Americans in Lebanon in 1985. As a result, his image changed from gadfly to highly respected statesman.

At the 1996 Summer Games in Atlanta, the world and his country honored Ali by choosing him to light the Olympic torch during the opening ceremonies. In 1999, Ali became the first boxer to ever appear on the cover of a Wheaties box.

Further Reading

There are numerous books about Muhammad Ali. Some of the best include Thomas Conklin, *Muhammad Ali: The Fight for Respect* (1992), Thomas Hauser's three books, *Muhammad Ali: His Life and Times* (1992), *Muhammad Ali in Perspective* (1996), *Muhammad Ali: Memories,* with photographer Neil Leifer. An engaging and thorough look at Ali's life and cultural signifigance is David Remnick's *King of the World: Muhammad Ali and the Rise of an American Hero* (1998). Other supplementary texts include Barry Denenberg, *The Story of*

Muhammad Ali: Heavyweight Champion of the World (Famous Lives) (1996), *The People's Champ (Sport and Society)*, edited by Elliott J. Gorn (1995), Arlene Schulman, *Muhammad Ali: Champion (Newsmakers)* (1996), Jack Rummel, *Muhammad Ali (Black Americans of Achievement)* (1989), William R. Sanford, Carl R. Green, *Muhammad Ali (Sports Immortals)* (1993), John Stravinsky, *Muhammad Ali: Biography (Biographies from A&E)* (1997). Outstanding accounts of particular events in Ali's life and career are Norman Mailer's book about the return bout with Forman in Zaire, *The Fight* (1997), and Suzanne Freedman, *Clay v. United States: Muhammad Ali Objects to War* (1997). Recent articles on Ali have appeared in *The Boston Globe* (Oct. 1, 1984, Jan. 17, 1992), *Newsweek* (June 22, 1987), *New York Daily News* (Feb. 2, 1989), *New York Post* (July 14, 1987), *New York Times Magazine* (July 17, 1988), *Philadelphia Inquirer* (Aug. 12, 1990), *Spin* (Oct. 1991), *USA Today* (Feb. 25, 1994), and *Washington Post* (June 9, 1991). □

Woody Allen

Woody Allen (born 1935) has been one of America's most prominent filmmakers, with a series of very personal films about the subjects that have always obsessed him: sex, death, and the meaning of life.

"If I sat down to do something popular, I don't think I could," Woody Allen told interviewer Stephen Farber in 1985. "I'm not making films because I want to be in the movie business. I'm making them because I want to say something." When Allen was one of America's most popular stand-up comedians, his fans might have mocked those words, coming from a man whose first role models were Bob Hope and Groucho Marx.

Allen's own films have been made on modest budgets in New York City, where he lives, with no concessions to studio taste or control. Despite the growing seriousness of his work, audiences have never lost sight of Allen the performer and the character he created for himself in his days as a comedian: a nerdy neurotic whose only defense against a hostile universe is his sense of the absurd, which he fearlessly directs at any and all targets, beginning with himself. A very private man, Allen has reluctantly become a public figure, but through all the changes and controversies, "The Woodman" has remained a symbol of uncompromising integrity to his loyal fans. On that subject, he told Farber, "I never hold them cheaply . . . I never write down to them . . . I always assume that they're at least as smart as I am, if not smarter, and . . . I try to do films that they will respect."

The Early Years

Woody Allen was born Allen Konigsberg on December 1, 1935, in the Bronx and grew up in Brooklyn. He changed his name to Woody Allen when at age 17 he began submitting jokes to a newspaper column, eventually attracting the attention of a publicist who hired him to write gags for his clients. After graduation, Allen enrolled in New York University as a motion picture major and then in night school at City College, but dropped out of both to pursue his career as a comedy writer. Years later he told his biographer Eric Lax that when a dean recommended he "seek psychiatric help"

if he ever wanted to get a job, he replied that he was already working in show business. "Well, if you're around other crazy people," the dean conceded, "maybe you won't stand out."

Fortunately, Allen had a remarkable gift for his chosen profession. In a recent *New Yorker* article, Adam Gopnik recalled, "Woody was famous among his contemporaries for possessing a pure and almost abstract gift for one-liners . . . that could be applied to any situation, or passed on to any comic, almost impersonally." Before he turned 20 Allen had sold 20,000 gags to the New York tabloids, married his childhood sweetheart Harlene Rosen and landed a job in the writer's development program at NBC. By the time he turned 23 he was writing for the network's biggest comedy star, Sid Caesar, and had signed with talent managers Jack Rollins and Charles Joffe, who would later produce his films. He had also hired a tutor from Columbia University to teach him literature and philosophy at home.

At the urging of his new managers, Allen began performing his own material in a small New York nightclub in 1960. Honing his craft in painful encounters with the audience night after night, six nights a week, he struck a gold mine of comedy material when he and Rosen divorced in 1962. (His jokes about his ex-wife eventually led to a lawsuit from Rosen that was settled out of court.) By this time Allen was beginning to appear on network television and was a hit at Greenwich Village's legendary coffee house, The Bitter End.

Unlike other comics of the time, who favored political humor, Allen made jokes about his own comic persona, the little guy tormented by big philosophical issues and his unfailing hard luck with women. This fact was appreciated by a *New York Times* reviewer, who called him "the freshest comic to emerge in many months."

National recognition was not long in coming. Success in clubs and on television led to a Grammy-nominated comedy album, *Woody Allen,* in 1964, followed by *Woody Allen, Volume Two* in 1965 and *The Third Woody Allen Album* in 1968. Allen's humor found a more up-scale outlet when he began writing humorous essays in the style of S. J. Perelman for the *New Yorker* in 1966. Three collections of these essays have been published: *Getting Even, Without Feathers,* and *Side Effects.*

Begins Film Career

Allen had long been a lover of movies, American and foreign, but the first one he wrote and acted in, *What's New, Pussycat?* (1965), was a bad experience. Recruited to write a comedy for hip young audiences, he found the experience of sixties-style, big-budget improvisational filmmaking appalling. "I fought with everybody all the time," he told *Cinema* magazine. "I hated everyone, and everyone hated me. When that picture was over, I decided I would never do another film unless I had complete control of it." But the film made a fortune and established Woody Allen as a "bankable" movie talent.

True to his word, he made his directorial debut with a film so modest that no one ever thought to tamper with it. Released by AIP, a company specializing in low-budget action and horror films, *What's Up, Tiger Lily?* (1966) was a Japanese James Bond movie with new dialogue composed of dream-like one-liners put into the characters' mouths by Allen and some friends. "All we did was put five people in a room and keep them there improvising as the film ran," Allen told *Rolling Stone.* Truly for the young and hip, *Tiger Lily* didn't make as much money as *Pussycat,* but it acquired an enduring cult following.

Besides the release of *Tiger Lily,* 1966 was also the year of Allen's marriage to actress Louise Lasser, who supplied one of the voices for *Tiger Lily,* and the Broadway opening of his first play, *Don't Drink the Water,* a comedy about an Jewish American family on vacation who get in hot water behind the Iron Curtain. *Don't Drink the Water* ran for over a year and spawned a movie directed by Howard Morris; Allen directed a television remake of *Don't Drink the Water* in December 1994. The marriage to Lasser ended in divorce after three years, but they remained friends, and she acted in Allen's first three hit comedies: *Take the Money and Run* (1969), *Bananas* (1971), and *Everything You Always Wanted to Know About Sex but Were Afraid to Ask* (1972).

Allen's early comedies, made for United Artists—a company that gave him complete control of his work as writer-director—recall the messy, anything-goes style of classic American comedies built around such free-wheeling talents as the Marx Brothers and W. C. Fields. Like the Marx Brothers, a reviewer for *Time* magazine wrote, Allen was ready "to subordinate everything—plot, plausibility, people—to the imperative of a good joke."

Perhaps because it demanded a more controlled style, he entrusted the film version of his second Broadway hit, *Play It Again, Sam* (1972), to veteran director Herbert Ross. But he played the lead himself, as he had done in the stage version of this romantic comedy about a man who fulfills his dream: to play the last scene of his favorite movie, *Casablanca,* in real life, with himself in the Bogart role. His co-star on stage and in the film was his new off-screen friend and romantic partner, Diane Keaton.

Keaton and Allen also co-starred in the two films written and directed by Allen which mark the end of his "early, funny" period. In *Sleeper* (1973), Allen's character wakes up from a cryogenic sleep to find himself trapped in a future society that looks suspiciously like Los Angeles. And in *Love and Death* (1975), which Allen considers his best comedy, he takes on his favorite themes in an epic satire of all of Russian literature.

First Serious Film

It was Keaton's talents as an actress that inspired Allen to make his first serious film, a bittersweet comedy about a failed romance between two neurotics, and it was undoubtedly her personality that inspired him to create the title character, *Annie Hall* (1977). (She won an Oscar for her performance; the film won a total of four of the prized gold statuettes.) "What is Woody Allen doing starring in, writing and directing a ruefully romantic comedy that is at least as poignant [distressing] as it is funny and may be the most autobiographical film ever made by a major comic?" asked *Time* magazine. "What he is doing is growing, right before our eyes, and it is a fine sight to behold."

Keaton went on to star for Allen in *Interiors* (1978), and *Manhattan* (1979), a somber black-and-white film about cheating New Yorkers which ends with a salute to the last scene of Charlie Chaplin's *City Lights.* His career as a serious filmmaker had definitely begun.

Annie Hall also marked the beginning of a nine-picture collaboration with cinematographer Gordon Willis in which Allen's growing mastery of film-making techniques enabled him to create a new style for each new film. He imitated the style of Italian director Federico Fellini in his next, most controversial film, *Stardust Memories* (1980), in which he plays a filmmaker who seems to hate his fans. Despite the ensuing hue and cry, Allen told an *Esquire* interviewer in 1987, "The best film I ever did, really, was *Stardust Memories.*"

Finds New Leading Lady

When the executives who had given him artistic control of his work left United Artists and founded Orion Pictures, Allen worked off his contract with UA and joined them. Coincidentally, the move to Orion also marked the beginning of his collaboration with his new off-screen partner, actress Mia Farrow. Their first four films together all have a fairy-tale quality: *A Midsummer Night's Sex Comedy* (1982) mixes fairies and moonstruck lovers on a country estate; *Zelig* (1983) uses special-effects wizardry to tell the story of a human chameleon who achieved a peculiar kind of fame in the 1920s; *Broadway Danny Rose* (1984) transforms present-day New York into a never-neverland of show-business losers for a poignant romance between a brassy beauty and a hapless agent, and *The Purple Rose of Cairo* (1985) darkens the fairy-tale mood when a hero of the silver screen steps down into real life, with tragic consequences for a Depression-era housewife, touchingly played by Farrow.

Hollywood bestowed three Oscars on their next collaboration, *Hannah and Her Sisters,* in which Hannah (Farrow) is divorced from a hypochondriac, played by Allen, and married to a philanderer, played by Michael Caine. "Tracking the career of Woody Allen is exhausting but exhilarating," began the *New York Times* review of *Hannah.* "Just when we reach the top, another peak appears." But Allen, who told Eric Lax that "the whole concept of awards is silly," was worried by the film's success. "When I put out a film that enjoys any acceptance that isn't mild or grudging," he explained to Lax, "I immediately become suspicious of it."

After *Radio Days* (1987), a light-hearted look at Allen's childhood and the Golden Age of radio, the mood of his films darkened again. *September* (1987) replays the grim psychological dramas of *Interiors,* and *Another Woman* (1988) pairs Farrow with one of America's greatest actresses, Gena Rowlands, in a story of mid-life crisis. Allen briefly returned to comedy in the short *Oedipus Wrecks* (1989), about a man whose problems with his mother take a supernatural turn. He then made his most pessimistic film to date, *Crimes and Misdemeanors* (1989), in which a respectable married man (Martin Landau) murders his mistress (Anjelica Huston) and gets away with it, while Allen's character loses the woman he loves (Farrow) to a shallow fool (Alan Alda).

Personal Life Hits the Rocks

Before their off-screen relationship ended in a bitter child-custody suit, Allen and Farrow made three more films together: *Alice* (1990), a fairy tale recalling their early collaborations, in which a neglected housewife discovers love and life with the help of a Chinese herbalist who dispenses magic potions; *Shadows and Fog* (1992), a comic salute to the novels of Franz Kafka set in a Middle European country out of some German silent film, and *Husbands and Wives* (1992).

Released in a firestorm of publicity over the custody battle, Allen's last film with Farrow had the press looking for parallels to Allen's real-life romance with Farrow's adopted-daughter, Soon-Yi Farrow Previn, whom Allen wed in December 1997. It also marked another new beginning for Woody Allen the filmmaker. Orion's impending bankruptcy obliged him to make the film for Tri-Star, while a less controlled style of filming, with a hand-held camera scampering to keep up with the actors, brought a new sense of life to this savagely funny contemporary look at marriage and infidelity. "It's a good movie," observed the reviewer for *New York* magazine, "yet a decade or so may have to pass before anyone can see it in itself."

The hand-held camera still wobbles noticeably in *Manhattan Murder Mystery,* which reunites him with Diane Keaton, playing a married couple who suspect their next-door neighbor of murder. A pure comedy, Allen's first in many years, *Manhattan Murder Mystery* was a pit-stop for the filmmaker and his loyal fans before his 1994 film *Bullets Over Broadway,* the critically acclaimed melodrama set in the 1920s that focuses on a group of old Broadway stereotypes. He continued with comedy in 1995, releasing *Mighty Aphrodite,* a contemporary tale of a man obsessed with his adopted son's mother interspersed with scenes parodying Greek tragedy. The next release, *Everyone Says I Love You,* surprised his cast and fans alike, marking the director's first foray into musicals. Reports noted that he waited until two weeks after the film's stars signed their contracts to mention that he was making a musical, and that he chose actors who were not necessarily musically trained on purpose in order to evoke more honest emotion in the songs. Reviews were mixed.

Allen's interest in music extended to his off-screen life as well— starting in 1997, he regularly began playing clarinet for the Eddy Davis New Orleans Jazz Band every Monday at a club in New York City. Despite his diverse talents, however, Allen in real life can demonstrate his neurotic tendencies that are trademarks in his films. He told Jane Wollman Rusoff on the "Mr. Showbiz" web site, "I've never made a movie where scholars sat around and said, 'This ranks with the greatest.' . . . It's a goal, but the trick is to have a great vision. That's not so easy.'"

Further Reading

Lax, Eric, *On Being Funny: Woody Allen and Comedy,* New York, 1975.

Yacowar, Maurice, *Loser Take All: The Comic Art of Woody Allen,* New York, 1979; rev. ed., 1991.

Palmer, M., *Woody Allen,* New York, 1980.

Jacobs, Diane, *. . . But We Need the Eggs: The Magic of Woody Allen,* New York, 1982.

Brode, Douglas, *Woody Allen: His Films and Career,* New York, 1985.

Pogel, Nancy, *Woody Allen,* Boston, 1987.

Sinyard, Neil, *The Films of Woody Allen,* London, 1987.

McCann, Graham, *Woody Allen: New Yorker,* New York, 1990.

Lax, Eric, *Woody Allen,* New York, 1992.

Groteke, Kristi, *Mia & Woody,* New York, 1994.

Björkman, Stig, *Woody Allen on Woody Allen,* New York, 1995.

Blake, Richard Aloysius, *Woody Allen: Profane and Sacred,* Metuchen, New Jersey, 1995.

Perspectives on Woody Allen, edited by Renee R. Curry, New York, 1996.

Christian Science Monitor, January 24, 1997.

Life (New York), 21 March 1969.

Esquire (New York), 19 July 1975.

Rolling Stone (New York), 16 September 1993.

Esquire (New York), October 1994. □

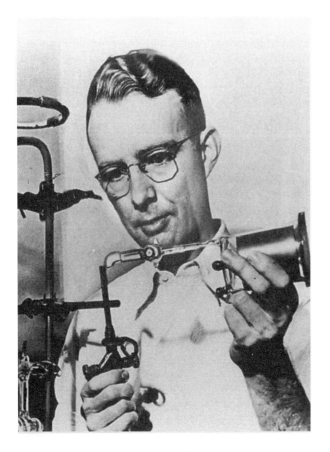

Luis W. Alvarez

The importance and variety of the discoveries and contributions of Luis W. Alvarez (1911-1988) are perhaps unmatched by any other 20th-century physicist. He received many awards for his work over the years, including the 1968 Nobel Prize in Physics for his work on a large liquid hydrogen bubble chamber.

Alvarez will probably be best remembered by the public for ingenious experiments that applied physics to other sciences. He x-rayed Chephren's pyramid in Egypt using cosmic radiation, only to find that there were no undiscovered chambers inside. His application of elementary physics to the evidence on the John F. Kennedy assassination verified the Warren Commission finding that only a single assassin was involved. But perhaps his most dramatic discovery was made after his "retirement" by jumping into a totally new field, paleontology and geology. With collaborators that included his son, Walter, he analyzed a 65 million year old clay layer and showed that the great ecological catastrophe that killed the dinosaurs was caused by the impact of an asteroid or comet.

Alvarez was born June 13, 1911, in San Francisco. He began his career at the University of Chicago. His first published paper (as an undergraduate) described a measurement of the wavelength of light using a phonograph record, a parlor lamp, and a yard stick. While reading the original physics literature, he found a paper by Hans Geiger that described a new type of detector for charged particles. He proceeded to construct one of the first Geiger counters in America. Alvarez was the first Chicago undergraduate to present results of his research at the weekly departmental colloquium, sharing the time with a professor who reported on James Chadwick's discovery of the neutron. After hearing the talk, Arthur Compton invited Alvarez to collaborate with him on a study to determine the electric charge of the primary cosmic radiation.

Alvarez's first summer as a graduate student was spent on the roof of the Geneva Hotel in Mexico City, his Geiger telescope resting in a wheelbarrow that allowed him to periodically reverse the east-west orientation of his apparatus. He and Compton determined that the cosmic rays were mostly positively charged, and therefore presumably protons. After receiving his Ph.D. in 1936 Alvarez began work with Ernest O. Lawrence at the University of California, in part through family connections. Alvarez's father, a physician on the staff of the Mayo Clinic, had helped Lawrence get money for one of his cyclotrons, and his sister was Lawrence's part-time secretary. Arriving at the Old Radiation Laboratory, Alvarez made the first of his dramatic career changes as he prepared himself to become a practicing nuclear physicist. First, he became thoroughly familiar with all instruments in the laboratory, their use, and the physics that was being done with them. He did this by helping everyone with their experiments while becoming a skilled machine operator and repairman.

Emerging from the laboratory at each day's end, Alvarez would pick up a couple of volumes of physics journals from the university library; he eventually read every published nuclear physics article held there. Years later he would astonish his colleagues by reproducing a curve or a little known fact gleaned in these early efforts. He could usually cite the authors, journal, year, and often the location of the volume in the library and whether the item was on a right-or a left-hand page. By 1937 Hans Bethe had published his three-part compendium of all that was known about nuclear physics. Alvarez chose first to make a measurement that Bethe said couldn't be done and then to disprove one of Bethe's assertions. In just four years Alvarez discovered the radioactivity of tritium and the stability of helium-3, the magnetic moment of the neutron, and that nuclei cannibalize their own atomic electrons. He also demonstrated the spin dependence of the nuclear force, established a new standard of length using mercury-198, and made the first experimental demonstrations in a field now called heavy-ion physics.

World War II ended Alvarez's nuclear physics career. He soon found himself in Boston, figuring how to apply high-frequency radio waves to achieve military goals. Using optics ideas learned in his thesis work, Luie invented the linear phased array, which formed the basis of EAGLE, the first radar bombing system. He also invented VIXEN, a system to outfox German submarines by diminishing an airborne acquisition radar's power as a surfaced sub was approached, so that the listening skipper would believe the attack plane was going away. Alvarez solved the problem of landing planes in bad weather by inventing the radar-based Ground Control Approach (GCA), for which he won the 1946 Collier Air Trophy.

Upon his return to the Berkeley laboratory after the war, Alvarez made another career change, to that of a particle accelerator physicist. He realized the importance of team research and looked to the methods of Lawrence and Ernest Rutherford. Like them, he displayed an ability to select good people to work with him.

His first postwar machine was the proton linear accelerator, which has become the standard injector for many subsequent higher energy circular machines and is still referred to as an "Alvarez accelerator." While preparing for his nuclear physics class one morning, he invented the Tandem van de Graaff, which was commercialized by High Voltage Engineering. Alvarez was a superb teacher. His course in physical optics was thorough. The students were introduced to the full spectrum of electromagnetic radiation from gamma rays to radio waves with spellbinding tales of how radar was used during the Battle of Britain.

In the mid 1950s Donald Glaser invented a new detector called a bubble chamber. Alvarez immediately saw the potential this had for the study of the newly available high-energy particles, if it could be made to work with liquified hydrogen. He established a group to develop the liquid-hydrogen bubble chamber from the first small steady-state chambers to large pulsed chambers. Characteristically, he grew impatient with the small chambers and proposed a large one 72 inches in length. This was nearly eight times the size of the one then in action at Berkeley, and some people thought this would be too big a step. Alvarez was confident that the chamber could be made to operate and he convinced the money sources to help. The 72-inch chamber aided in the identification of many new particles. It was for this work that he received the Nobel Prize in Physics in 1968.

In 1977 he was presented a piece of rock that had been cut from a hillside in Italy by his geologist son, Walter. The rock had a thin clay layer in it. He was shown how the microscopic fossils ("forams") in the rock became extinct right at the clay layer. These tiny forams had been destroyed at the clay layer. These tiny forams had been destroyed at the same time the dinosaurs had disappeared. Alvarez later described his experience in examining this rock as one of the most exciting moments in his life. The scientific consequences, which include the nuclear winter theory, are still being uncovered by geologists, paleontologists, physicists, chemists, and astronomers.

Alvarez was always solving practical problems that influenced his life. By his early fifties he needed bifocal lenses to correct his eyesight, and this convinced him that there must be a better way to solve this problem. The result was his invention of the variable focus lens and the formation of Humphrey Instruments.

While visiting Kenya, he was frustrated by how the image of the distant animals jumped around in the viewing port of his hand-held camera. He just couldn't hold the camera firmly enough to steady the image. He then invented a series of stabilized optical devices; and eventually he formed Schwem Technologies to develop and market them.

In addition to the 1946 Collier Air Trophy and the 1968 Nobel Prize in Physics, Alvarez also received the Einstein Medal in 1961, the 1964 National Medal of Science, a 1978 membership in the Inventors' Hall of Fame, and the 1981 Wright Prize.

Further Reading

Alvarez produced an extensive autobiography. A single volume version, *Alvarez: Adventures of a Physicist* was published in 1987, a paperback edition in 1989. He was honored by his colleagues with *Discovering Alvarez; Selected Works of Luis W. Alvarez with Commentary by His Students and Colleagues,* edited by W. Peter Trower (1987). □

Edwin Howard Armstrong

The American electrical engineer and radio inventor Edwin Howard Armstrong (1890-1954) was one of a small group who made fundamental contributions to the development of radio.

Edwin Armstrong was born in New York City, where his father was the American representative of the Oxford University Press. Armstrong rode his motorcycle to classes at Columbia University, and he took a degree in electrical engineering in 1913. He remained at Columbia for the rest of his life, serving as research assistant to Michael Pupin and, on the latter's death in 1934, as professor of electrical engineering.

Armstrong had one of those turbulent careers typical of so many inventors, especially those working in new and rapidly developing industries. Driven by a thirst for historical vindication and a love of legal combat, perhaps more

than by the desire for money, inventors have plagued each other's lives to a remarkable degree. Armstrong took out his first patent before he finished college in 1913, and patents and disputes over them always seem to have occupied an inordinate amount of his time and effort.

His early and long association with Prof. Pupin gave Armstrong direct access to one of the best and most fertile minds in the electrical field. Armstrong's academic base also kept him free of connection with any of the many companies then vying for dominance in the radio field; he was one of the few men to successfully maintain such independence.

The radio was not one invention but a combination of inventions, many of them of disputed origin. Armstrong's first important contribution was his realization of the value of Lee De Forest's audion vacuum tube as a means of amplifying current. To Armstrong this realization appeared to rank alongside the invention of the audion itself. Armstrong's second contribution was the feedback circuit, another means of amplifying current, which he (and others independently) worked out in 1912. The following year he discovered that the audion could be used to generate high-frequency oscillations; again, there were several contemporary claims to this discovery.

While serving as a signal officer in World War I, Armstrong developed in 1918 the superheterodyne circuit, in which incoming high-frequency signals were beaten against low-frequency signals from a local oscillator so that they could be detected. After the war he sold his feedback and superheterodyne patents to the Westinghouse Company for $350,000 and received even more from the Radio Corporation of America (RCA) for a superregenerative invention. His last great contribution was frequency modulation (FM), a method of overcoming static in broadcasting, on which he worked from 1924 to 1933 in the face of indifference and even hostility from large manufacturers and broadcasters.

During his last years perhaps 90 percent of Armstrong's time was taken up by court battles with the National Broadcasting Company, and others; this poisoned his life. He died, an apparent suicide, in 1954.

Further Reading

There is no biography of Armstrong. A brief discussion of his work is in John Jewkes, David Sawers, and Richard Stillerman, *The Sources of Invention* (1958). The standard history of the radio is William R. Maclaurin, *Invention and Innovation in the Radio Industry* (1949). Two other useful books are Donald M. McNicol, *Radio's Conquest of Space* (1946), and Carl F.J. Overhage, ed., *The Age of Electronics* (1962).

Additional Sources

Lewis, Thomas S. W., *The Legacies of Edwin Howard Armstrong: the regenerative circuit, the superheterodyne circuit, the superregenerative circuit, frequency modulatio,* Radio Club of America, 1990. □

Louis Daniel Armstrong

Louis Daniel Armstrong (1900-1971) was an early jazz trumpet virtuoso, and he remained an important influence for several decades.

Louis Armstrong was born into a poor African American family in New Orleans on July 4, 1900. As a youngster, he sang on the streets with friends. In 1913 he was arrested for a prank and committed to the Waif's Home, where he learned the cornet and played in the band. On his release he began performing with local groups. Joe "King" Oliver, leader of the first great African American band to make records, befriended him, and Armstrong joined Oliver in Chicago in 1922, remaining until 1924, when he went to New York to play with Fletcher Henderson's band.

When he returned to Chicago in the fall of 1925, Armstrong began to cut one of the greatest series in the history of recorded jazz. These Hot Five and Hot Seven recordings find him breaking free from the conventions of New Orleans ensemble playing, his trumpet work notable for its inventiveness, rhythmic daring, improvisatory freedom, and technical assurance. In 1928 he started recording with drummer Zutty Singleton and pianist Earl Hines, the latter a musician able to match Armstrong in virtuosity. Many of the resulting records are masterpieces, the performances highlighted by complex ensembles, unpredictable harmonic twists, and rhythmic adventurousness. During these years Armstrong was working with big bands in Chicago clubs and theaters. His vocals, featured on most post-1925 records, are an extension of his trumpet playing in their phrasing and rhythmic liveliness, and are delivered in a unique guttural style.

By 1929 Armstrong was in New York leading a nightclub band. Appearing in the theatrical revue *Hot Choco-lates,* he sang "Fats" Waller's "Ain't Misbehavin'," Armstrong's first popular song hit. From this period his repertoire switched mainly to popular song material, which presented a new challenge because of the relative harmonic sophistication. Some notable performances resulted. His virtuosity reached a peak around 1933; then his style underwent a process of simplification, replacing virtuoso display by a mature craftsmanship that used every note to maximum advantage. He re-recorded some of his earlier successes to considerable effect.

Armstrong continued to front big bands, often of inferior quality, until 1947, by which time the big-band era was over. He returned to leading a small group which, though it initially included first-class musicians, became over the years a mere background for his vaudevillian talents. During the 1930s Armstrong had achieved international fame, first touring Europe as a soloist and singer in 1932. After World War II and his 1948 trip to France, he became an inveterate world traveler, journeying through Europe, Africa, Japan, Australia, and South America. He appeared in numerous films, the best a documentary titled *Satchmo the Great* (1957).

In his later years the public thought of Armstrong as a vaudeville entertainer—a fact reflected in the bulk of his record output. But there were still occasions when he produced music of astonishing eloquence and brilliance. He died in New York City on July 6, 1971.

Further Reading

Armstrong's autobiographical *Satchmo: My Life in New Orleans* (1954) is informative and entertaining on his early years. *Swing That Music* (1936), though ostensibly by Armstrong, was almost certainly ghosted and is of limited interest. Max Jones and John Chilton, *Louis: The Louis Armstrong Story, 1900-1971* (1971), is a superb study and is particularly informative about his life during the 1930s. Laurence Bergreen, *Louis Armstrong: An Extravagant Life* (1997) provides a fascinating, moving, and honest depiction of Armstrong. An outstanding critical study of Armstrong's records of the 1924-1931 period is in Richard Hadlock, *Jazz Masters of the Twenties* (1965). See also Louis Terkel, *Giants of Jazz* (1957). □

Neil Alden Armstrong

The American astronaut Neil Alden Armstrong (born 1930) was the first person to walk on the moon.

Neil Armstrong was born on August 5, 1930, near Wapakoneta, Ohio, the eldest of three children of Stephen and Viola Engel Armstrong. Airplanes drew his interest from the age of six, when he took his first flight, and on his 16th birthday he was issued a pilot's license. A serious pilot even at this age, Armstrong built a small wind tunnel in the basement of his home and performed experiments on the model planes he had made.

Years of Training

Armstrong entered Purdue University in 1947 with a U.S. Navy scholarship. After two years of study he was called to active duty with the Navy and won his jet wings at Pensacola Naval Air Station in Florida. At 20 he was the youngest pilot in his squadron. He flew 78 combat missions during the Korean War and won three Air Medals.

Armstrong returned to Purdue and completed a degree in aeronautical engineering in 1955. He immediately accepted a job with the Lewis Flight Propulsion Laboratory of the National Advisory Committee for Aeronautics (NACA) in Cleveland, Ohio. A year later he married Janet Shearon.

An Aeronautical Career

Shortly afterward, Armstrong transferred to the NACA High Speed Flight Station at Edwards Air Force Base, California. Here he became a skilled test pilot and flew the early models of such jet aircraft as the F-100, F-101, F-102, F-104, F-5D, and B-47. He also flew a B-29 "drop plane," from which various types of rocket-propelled planes were launched. More important for his later role, he became a pilot of the X-1B rocket plane, an earlier version of which had been the first plane to break the sound barrier.

Armstrong was selected as one of the first three pilots of NACA for the X-15 rocket plane, and he made seven flights in this prototype spacecraft. Once he set a record altitude of 207,500 feet and a speed of 3,989 miles per hour. Armstrong received an invitation from the American space-flight program, but he demonstrated little enthusiasm for becoming an astronaut. His real love was piloting. Largely because of his experience with the X-15, he was selected as a pilot of the Dynasoar, an experimental craft that could leave the atmosphere, orbit earth, reenter the atmosphere, and land like a conventional airplane.

Astronautics: A Step into Space

In 1962, however, sensing that the days of the projected Dynasoar were numbered (it was canceled in 1963), Armstrong decided to become an astronaut and applied for selection and training. In September 1962 he became America's first civilian astronaut and moved to Houston, Texas, to begin training. Armstrong's attitude toward his job, at least prior to his first space mission, was summed up in a statement to a reporter in 1965: "I rule out the possibility of agreeing to go up if I thought I might not come back, unless it were technically indispensable. Dying in space or on the moon is not technically indispensable and consequently if I had to choose between death while testing a jet and death on the moon, I'd choose death while testing a jet."

Armstrong's first flight assignment as an astronaut was as backup, or alternate, command pilot for Gordon Cooper of the *Gemini 5* mission. Armstrong continued his specialized training on the Gemini spacecraft and was selected as the command pilot for the *Gemini 8* mission. With copilot David Scott he was launched from Cape Kennedy (now Cape Canaveral), Florida, on March 16, 1966. The *Gemini 8* achieved orbit and docked as planned with the Agena vehicle, but shortly afterward the vehicle went out of control. Armstrong detached his craft from the Agena, corrected the malfunction, and brought the Gemini down in the Pacific Ocean only 1.1 nautical miles from the planned landing point. His cool and professional conduct made a strong impression on the officials of the Manned Spacecraft Center in Houston. Armstrong continued his intensive training on the Gemini spacecraft and was selected as the backup command pilot for the *Gemini 11* mission, which was flown, however, by astronauts Charles Conrad, Jr., and Richard Gordon.

As the training for the Apollo program got under way, it was obvious that Armstrong rated high among those being considered for the important role of being the first American on the moon. He undertook his training program with the same cool, analytical, and almost detached approach that had always marked his attitude to flying.

During a routine training flight on the lunar landing research vehicle, a training device that permits astronauts to maneuver a craft in a flight environment similar to that in landing on the moon, Armstrong's craft went out of control. He ejected himself and landed by parachute only yards away from the training vehicle, which had crashed in flames. With his usual imperturbability he walked away and calmly made his report. Again, his behavior and attitude were noted by those who were evaluating candidates for the first crew to the moon.

Selection for the Moon Mission

In January 1969 Armstrong was selected as commander for *Apollo 11*, the first lunar landing mission. On July 16 at 9:32 A.M. Eastern Daylight Time (EDT), Arm-

strong, together with astronauts Michael Collins and Edwin Aldrin, lifted off from the Kennedy Space Center, Florida, aboard the Saturn 5 space booster.

Apollo 11 passed into the gravitational influence of the moon on July 18 and circled the moon twice. Armstrong and Aldrin entered the lunar module, named the *Eagle,* which then disconnected from the command and service module. As they descended toward the lunar surface, their computer became overloaded, but under continuous instructions from the mission control center at Houston, Armstrong continued the gradual touchdown. Suddenly a boulder field loomed in front of him. He quickly switched to manual control and guided the *Eagle* over it to a smooth landing with only 10 seconds of fuel left. At 4:17:40 P.M. EDT on July 20, a major portion of the earth population was listening to Armstrong's transmission, "Houston, Tranquility Base here. The *Eagle* has landed." At 10:56 P.M. he set foot on the moon, saying, "That's one small step for man, one giant leap for mankind." (Later, he stated that he had intended to say, "That's one small step for a man, one giant leap for mankind.")

Armstrong and Aldrin spent nearly two and a half hours walking on the moon. Armstrong reported: "The surface is fine and powdery. I can pick it up loosely with my toe. It does adhere in fine layers like powdered charcoal to the soles and sides of my boots. I only go in a fraction of an inch, maybe an eighth of an inch, but I can see the footprints of my boots." The astronauts deployed various scientific instruments on the moon's surface, including a seismograph and solar-wind particle collector, and collected rock and soil samples. They also left a mission patch and medals commemorating American and Russian space explorers who had died in the line of duty, along with a plaque reading, "Here men from the planet Earth first set foot upon the Moon. We came in peace for all mankind."

Armstrong and Aldrin returned to the *Eagle* and launched themselves to rendezvous with Collins, who had been orbiting in the *Columbia* spacecraft. On July 24 *Columbia* returned to earth. It splashed down at 12:50 P.M. EDT some 950 miles southwest of Hawaii and only 2.7 miles from its aiming point. After 18 days of quarantine to control any lunar microorganisms, Armstrong and the others traveled around the world for parades and speeches. The mission brought honors including the Presidential Medal of Freedom, the Harmon International Aviation Trophy, the Royal Geographic Society's Hubbard Gold Medal, and accolades from many nations. Armstrong became a Fellow of the Society of Experimental Test Pilots, the American Astronautical Society, and the American Institute of Aeronautics and Astronautics.

Career after NASA

Apollo 11 was Armstrong's final space mission. He joined Nasa's Office of Advanced Research and Technology, where he served as deputy associate administrator for aeronautics. One of his main priorities in this position was to further research into controlling high-performance aircraft by computer. In 1970 he earned a master's degree in aerospace engineering from the University of Southern California.

A private man, Armstrong rejected most opportunities to profit from his fame. He left NASA in 1971 and moved his family back to Ohio to accept a position at the University of Cincinnati. There he spent seven years engaged in teaching and research as a professor of aerospace engineering. He took special interest in the application of space technology to such challenges as improving medical devices and providing data on the environment. In 1978 Armstrong was one of the first six recipients of the congressional Space Medal of Honor, created to recognize astronauts whose "exceptionally meritorious efforts" had contributed to "the welfare of the Nation and mankind."

A member of the board of directors of Gates Learjet Corporation, in 1979 he piloted that company's new business jet to five world-altitude and time-to-climb records for that class of aircraft. Other boards Armstrong served on included those of USCX Corporation and United Airlines. In between his business ventures and such hobbies as fishing and sail-planing, he also chaired the board of trustees of the Cincinnati Museum of Natural History.

Armstrong did accept two further government appointments. In 1984 he was named to the National Commission on Space, which two years later completed a report outlining an ambitious future for American space programs. Also in 1986, Armstrong was named deputy chair of the Rogers Commission to investigate the explosion of the space shuttle *Challenger*. The commission's work resulted in major changes in NASA's management structure and safety practices.

From 1980 to 1982, Armstrong was chair of the board of Cardwell International. He accepted a similar post with Computing Technologies for Aviation (CTA) in 1982. CTA, which was based in Charlottesville, Virginia, provided software for flight scheduling and support activities, allowing corporate jet operators to maximize the efficient use of their aircraft. Armstrong stepped down as head of CTA in 1993. He later presided over the board of AIL Systems, Inc., an electronic systems company headquartered in Deer Park, New York.

In May 1997 Armstrong was named a director at Ohio National Financial Services Inc., a Cincinnati-based provider of diversified financial services. At that time, he also served on the boards of Cinergy Corp. and Cincinnati Milacron Inc. He maintained his residence at a farm near Lebanon, Ohio, and made occasional public appearances in nearby Wapakoneta, his boyhood home and the site of the Neil Armstrong Air & Space Museum.

Further Reading

Information on Armstrong's historic participation in the space program is contained in Chris Crocker, *Great American Astronauts* (1988), Buzz Aldrin and Malcolm McConnell, *Men from Earth* (1989), and Alan B. Shepard, *Moon Shot: The Inside Story of America's Race to the Moon* (1994). Armstrong, together with Michael Collins and Buzz Aldrin, wrote a memoir of the Apollo 11 moon voyage in *First on the Moon* (1970). □

Benedict Arnold

Although he fought with skill and courage in many campaigns during the American Revolution, Gen. Benedict Arnold (1741-1801) is best known as the man who betrayed his country.

B enedict Arnold was born on Jan. 14, 1741, in Norwich, Conn., of a prominent family. As a young man, he worked for a druggist, fought in the French and Indian War, and engaged in trade with the West Indies. In 1767 he married Margaret Mansfield.

Career as a Soldier

When news of the battles of Lexington and Concord reached Arnold in April 1775, he set out at the head of a company of Connecticut militia for Cambridge, Mass., where George Washington was gathering an army to fight the British forces. His first engagement was the attack the next month on Fort Ticonderoga, where the British had a concentration of artillery. The operation was successful but Arnold got little of the credit, which went mostly to Ethan Allen and his Green Mountain Boys. His second assignment was with an expedition against Canada. Leaving Cambridge on Sept. 19, 1775, Arnold led his troops the length of Maine, by land and water and in snow and storms, reaching Quebec in early November. There he was joined by another column under Gen. Richard Montgomery, which had come by way of Lake Champlain and Montreal. Together the two forces assaulted Quebec on December 31, but the attack failed, costing Montgomery his life and Arnold a severe leg wound. Arnold next went to Lake Champlain to prevent the British from using it as a highway from Canada to New York. He lost two naval battles on the lake in October 1776, but he had effectively delayed the British in their southward advance. In the same month Congress made Arnold brigadier general.

The winter of 1776-1777 was an unhappy one for Arnold. His hot temper, impulsiveness, and impatience had earned him many enemies, who now made all sorts of accusations against him—of misconduct on the march through Maine, of incompetence on Lake Champlain, and more. Worse yet, Congress in February 1777 promoted five brigadier generals, all Arnold's juniors, to major general. Only Washington's pleas kept Arnold from resigning from the army. Fortunately, the coming of spring gave him the chance for a successful operation. While visiting his home in New Haven, Arnold heard of a British attack on American supply depots in Danbury, Conn. He rounded up the local militia and raced to stop the enemy. Although he got there too late to prevent the destruction of the supplies, he did rout the British. A grateful Congress advanced him to major general on May 2, but he was still below the other five in seniority. Meanwhile, he faced a formal charge of stealing goods and property from Montreal merchants during the Canadian campaign. He was exonerated, but his anger at the charges moved him to resign his commission in July 1777.

Once again Washington pleaded with him, and Arnold reconsidered. Washington needed him for service in northern New York to block a bold British plan to split New England from the other colonies by sending Gen. John Burgoyne from Ticonderoga down the Hudson River to New York City. Burgoyne not only failed in his mission; he lost his whole army, which he surrendered at Saratoga, N.Y., in October 1777. Arnold played a major role in the two battles that culminated in the British defeat. Burgoyne himself said of Arnold that "it was his doing." Congress rewarded Arnold by restoring his seniority among the major generals.

Arnold's next assignment was command of the garrison at Philadelphia, which the British had evacuated in June 1778. He married Margaret Shippen, daughter of a wealthy Philadelphian, in April 1779. (His first wife had died some years earlier.) Moving in aristocratic circles, Arnold lived lavishly and beyond his means, and he soon found himself heavily in debt. At the same time he was being charged with a number of offenses connected with using his military office for private gain. He demanded a court-martial, which Congress convened in May. The verdict handed down in December found him not guilty of most charges but ordered Washington to reprimand him. The general did this, but mildly, in April 1780.

End as a Traitor

By this time, however, Arnold had already started on the road to treason. Personally hurt by Congress's treatment and sorely in need of money, he had begun to funnel information on troop movements and strength of units to the British in exchange for money as early as May or June 1779. Early in the summer of 1780, he conceived the idea of turning over the strategic post at West Point, N.Y., to the English for £10,000. He persuaded Washington to place him in command there, but Arnold's plan fell through when his contact, Maj. John André, was captured on September 21 with incriminating documents. André was executed and Arnold fled to the British lines.

Arnold spent the rest of the war in a British uniform fighting his own countrymen. In 1781 he went to London, where he died 20 years later on June 14, despised in America and forgotten in England.

Further Reading

The best biography of Arnold is Willard M. Wallace, *Traitorous Hero* (1954). Arnold's Canadian campaign is well presented by Justin H. Smith, *Our Struggle for the Fourteenth Colony: Canada, and the American Revolution* (2 vols., 1907). For his role in Burgoyne's defeat at Saratoga see Hoffman Nickerson, *The Turning Point of the Revolution* (1928; rev. ed. 1967). Carl Van Doren, *Secret History of the American Revolution* (1941), discusses Arnold's treason. ☐

Chester Alan Arthur

The twenty-first president of the United States, Chester Alan Arthur (1830-1886) was reputed to be one of the leading spoilsmen in American politics when he took office, but he proved to be a dignified and an able administrator.

Political enemies claimed that Chester A. Arthur was Canadian-born and therefore ineligible to be president of the United States. Arthur himself never replied to the charges and said that he was born on Oct. 5, 1830, in Fairfield, Vt., the eldest of seven children of a Scotch-Irish Baptist minister. He was educated at Union College in Schenectady, N.Y., taught school, and studied law. Moving to New York City, he built up a successful law practice and became interested in Republican party politics.

Arthur rose steadily, if undramatically, in the Republican party by virtue of his willingness to perform the less exciting labors necessary to building a new political movement. New York City was slipping into the clutches of the Democratic party machine of William Marcy Tweed during the Civil War, but Arthur moved up steadily as the protégé of the state's governor. He served as engineer in chief, inspector general, and quartermaster general of New York, raising, equipping, and dispatching state troops for the Federal government. In 1863, when the Republicans were turned out of office, he stepped aside for a Democratic successor. By unanimous agreement he had been an excellent administrator.

Arthur as a Spoilsman

As a reward for his work for the party, in November 1871 President U.S. Grant named Arthur to be collector of customs for the Port of New York. In an age when political

parties functioned almost primarily for patronage—the jobs and other "spoils" which accrued to the party in power—Arthur possessed one of the most powerful and lucrative positions in the patronage apparatus by the time he was 41. As collector, he supervised more than 1000 employees, and many of these were troops in the New York State Republican machine. Arthur helped oversee the distribution of the jobs and, at election time, supervised the collection of "assessments"—contributions to Republican campaign funds which were virtually a requirement for holding a Federal job. The Customs House was no stranger to graft but Arthur himself was honest. He once said that "if I had misappropriated five cents, and on walking down-town saw two men talking on the street together, I would imagine they were talking of my dishonesty and the very thought would drive me mad."

In a sense, corruption would have been superfluous. Arthur was paid by a fee of one-half of all monies he recovered for the government from importers misrepresenting what they owed. In one famous case Arthur and two other officials divided $135,000. His pay generally ran to $40,000 a year until 1874, when his salary was set at $12,000.

Not all of this money stayed in Arthur's bank account. Like all political appointees, he was expected to make large donations to the party. These expenditures earned Arthur a prominent place in New York State's patronage-oriented Republican party. With Alonzo Cornell and Levi Morton, he stood second only to Roscoe Conkling in the control of New York's powerful political organization. His reputation

among reformers was disgraceful but, until 1880, he could afford to ignore any pressures but Conkling's.

Arthur's nicknames—"the Gentleman Boss," "the Elegant Arthur," —indicate the figure he cut. Over 6 feet tall, stoutly built according to the specifications of the times, with a wavy moustache and bushy sidewhiskers, he dressed in fine, fashionable clothing. He was exquisitely urbane, dining well, drinking the best wines and brandies, and entertaining on a grand scale. None of this was extraordinary in middle-class New York City, but it made for a stunning contrast to the conservatively clothed and morally straitlaced Midwestern Republican politicians among whom he moved in Washington.

Accidental President

In 1880 Republicans divided sharply and bitterly over the nomination of a presidential candidate. The two principal hopefuls were former president U.S. Grant (Conkling and Arthur were among his chief advocates) and James G. Blaine. The deadlocked convention resolved the issue only by turning to a dark-horse candidate, James A. Garfield of Ohio. Conkling, the leader of the pro-Grant faction, was furious—for Garfield was friendlier to Blaine than himself—and he insisted that Levi Morton decline the offered vice-presidential nomination. Arthur was the Garfield group's second vice-presidential choice and, though Conkling remained adamant, Arthur accepted. Arthur continued to pay court to Conkling, however, even after the election had made him vice president of the United States. In fact, Arthur was in Albany, lobbying for Conkling's reelection, when news arrived that President Garfield had been shot in Washington by a deranged man who claimed he did it in order to make Arthur president. Garfield died on Sept. 19, 1881, and Arthur became president.

Historians tend to agree that Arthur was a much better president than anyone expected. He seemed sensitive to the dignity of his office, and, while he continued to send most patronage to his old allies, he generally extricated himself from their society. Though he offered Conkling a seat on the Supreme Court, he left one of Conkling's old enemies in the Customs House. Republicans on the side of reform were chagrined at this new president, but Arthur could be surprising. He even supported and signed a landmark civil service bill (providing, among other things, for examinations as a prerequisite to holding some government jobs), and he permitted an investigation of post office frauds, which implicated several cronies.

Arthur remained what he had always been, a good administrator. But, as H. Wayne Morgan (1969) points out, "Arthur liked the appearance of power more than its substance." He designed a flag for himself, relished military ceremonies, refurbished the shabby White House, and presented a perfect presidential appearance. He took little initiative in the significant events of his term, such as the Pendleton Civil Service Act and the construction of a modern navy.

Unfortunately for Arthur's political future (he would have liked to be reelected in 1884), he had alienated old supporters without winning over old enemies. In 1884 he had no real strength at the Republican Convention and was quietly shelved. He died in 1886. He had not inspired his contemporaries, and, though his biographers have been friendly, he has not inspired them either.

Further Reading

There are several biographies of Arthur, none of particular distinction. A standard account is George F. Howe, *Chester A. Arthur: A Quarter-century of Machine Politics* (1934). Matthew Josephson, *The Politicos: 1865-1896* (1938), is a highly readable, if sometimes inaccurate, history of 19th-century politics. H. Wayne Morgan, *From Hayes to McKinley: National Party Politics* (1969), updates Josephson's work and includes brief, incisive portraits of Arthur and other leading personalities of the era. □

Arthur Robert Ashe, Jr.

World champion athlete, social activist, teacher, and charity worker, Arthur Robert Ashe Jr. (1943-1993) was the first African American player to break the color barrier in the international sport of tennis at the highest level of the game. After early retirement from sports due to heart surgery in 1979, Ashe used his unique sportsman profile and legendary poise to promote human rights, education, and public health.

A rthur Robert Ashe Jr. was born on July 10, 1943, in Richmond, Virginia. He was a member of the eleventh identifiable generation of the Ashe family and a direct descendant of a West African slave. The family line reached back to ownership by Samuel Ashe, an early governor of North Carolina. When Ashe was six years old his mother, Mattie Cordell Cunningham Ashe, died of heart disease at the age of 27.

Ashe's father nurtured both Arthur and his younger brother, Johnnie, with love as a strict disciplinarian. He worked as a caretaker and special policeman for a park named Brook Field in suburban North Richmond. Young Arthur lived on the grounds with four tennis courts, a pool, and three baseball diamonds. This was the passkey to his development as a future star athlete. His early nickname was "Skinny" or "Bones," and he grew to six feet one inch with a lean physique. He was right-handed.

Ashe as Amateur Tennis Player

R. Walter ("Whirlwind") Johnson, an African American general physician and tennis patron from Lynchburg, Virginia, opened his home in the summers to tennis prospects, including the great Althea Gibson several years earlier. Johnson used military-style discipline to teach tennis skills and also stressed his special code of sportsmanship: deference, sharp appearance, and "no cheating at any time."

Ashe attended Richmond City Public Schools. He received an honorary diploma from Maggie L. Walker High School in 1961. After success as a junior player in the American Tennis Association (ATA, for African American players), he was the first African American junior to receive a United States Lawn Tennis Association (USLTA) national ranking. When he won the National Interscholastics in

1960, it was the first USLTA national title to be won by an African American in the South. The University of California at Los Angeles (UCLA) awarded him a full scholarship.

In 1963 Ashe became the first African American player to win the U.S. Men's Hardcourt championships. He also became the first African American to be named to a U.S. Junior Davis Cup team and played for ten years (1963-1970, 1975, 1976, 1978). (Earlier he could not make the U.S. Junior Davis Cup team because he was denied entry in two of five major events, in Kentucky and Virginia.) He became the National College Athletic Association (NCAA) singles and doubles champion, leading the UCLA Bruins to the NCAA title in 1965. He was All-American from 1963 to 1965.

A year later Ashe graduated from UCLA in the ROTC program with a bachelor's degree in business administration. After serving in the Army for two years, during which he was assigned time for tennis competitions, Ashe introduced a grassroots tennis program into U.S. innercities in 1968. This effort was the forerunner of today's national U.S. Tennis Association/National Junior Tennis League (USTA/NJTL) program, with 500 chapters running programs for 150,000 kids.

Ashe as Professional Tennis Player

Two events changed Ashe's life direction in the late 1960s. The first, in 1968, was a proposed boycott by African American athletes at the Olympic Games in Mexico City. The boycott issue partly involved a protest against racial segregation, or "apartheid," in the Republic of South Africa.

Ashe identified closely with such discrimination. The second event was in tennis. He was the first African American USLTA amateur champion and won the first U.S. Open Tennis Championships at Forest Hills, a new prize-money national event. The USLTA ranked him Co-Number One (with Rod Laver). His support changed from $28 per diem as a U.S. Davis Cup player to becoming a top money-winner when he turned professional in 1969. He took the Australian Open title in Melbourne in 1970. In 1971 he won the French Open doubles title with Marty Riessen. The next year he helped found the Association of Tennis Professionals (ATP).

In 1973 Ashe became the first African American to reach the South African Open finals held in Johannesburg and was the doubles winner with Tom Okker of The Netherlands. Black South Africa gave Ashe a name that day: They called him "Sipho," meaning "a gift from God" in Zulu.

The year 1975 was Ashe's best and most consistent season. He was the first and only African American male player to win the "Gentleman's Singles" title in an historic victory on center court at the All-England Lawn Tennis Club at Wimbledon. Ashe dethroned the defending champion, Jimmy Connors. President Lyndon Johnson's comment was "Brooke is the only Senator we got; and Marshall the only justice; and Ashe the only tennis player." In 1975 Ashe was ranked Number One in the world, won a singles title in Dallas, and was named ATP Player of the Year. He played as a member of the U.S. Aetna World Cup team, 1970 to 1976 and 1979.

Due to injuries, he sat out most of 1977. Wearing a footcast, Ashe (33) married Jeanne Moutoussamy (25), a professional photographer and television graphic artist. A decade later the couple had a daughter, Camera Elizabeth.

With Tony Roche, Ashe won the Australian Open doubles title in 1977. He almost defeated John McEnroe in the Masters final at Madison Square Garden in January 1979 and was a semi-finalist at Wimbledon in the summer, before a heart attack soon after the tournament ended his legendary career. After his quadruple bypass heart surgery, Ashe had to announce his retirement from competitive tennis.

Ashe as International Role Model

As his first post-retirement venture Ashe served as Davis Cup captain from 1981 to 1985. He was only the second captain in over 30 years to lead the U.S. team to consecutive victories, 1981 and 1982.

His new life was a rebirth with many directions. Ashe's Davis Cup campaigns, his protests against apartheid in South Africa, and his controversial support of higher academic standards for all athletes received much media attention. But he actually spent most of his time quietly dealing with the challenges of the "real world" through public speaking, teaching, writing, business, and voluntary public service.

In 1983 he had double bypass surgery. Ashe became national campaign chairman for the American Heart Association and the only nonmedical member of the National Heart, Lung and Blood Advisory Council. In the late 1970s

he had become a consultant to Aetna Life & Casualty Company. He was made a board member in 1982. He represented minority concerns and, later, the causes of the sick.

Ashe developed social programs such as the ABC Cities program, combining tennis and academics; Safe Passage Foundation for poor children, which includes tennis training; Athletes Career Connection; the Black Tennis & Sports Foundation to assist minority athletes; and 15-Love, a substance abuse program conducted through the Eastern Tennis Association.

Kappa Alpha Psi Fraternity gave him their Laurel Wreath Award in 1986. He was inducted into the UCLA Sports Hall of Fame, the Virginia Sports Hall of Fame, and the Eastern Tennis Association Hall of Fame. He became the first inductee into the U.S. Professional Tennis Association Hall of Fame. He was the first athlete without a link to the Olympic Games to be awarded the coveted Olympic Order.

Ashe spent six years and $300,000 of his own funds to write *A Hard Road to Glory: A History of the African-American Athlete,* a three-volume work published in 1988. Ashe won an Emmy Award for writing a television docudrama based upon his work. The research effort also earned him honorary doctorates from such universities as Virginia Union, Princeton, Dartmouth, Virginia Common-wealth, and South Carolina.

After brain surgery in 1988 came the shocking discovery that he had been infected with HIV, the virus which causes AIDS. Doctors traced this infection back to an unscreened blood transfusion after his second cardiac operation in 1983. To protect his family and his own privacy, he informed only a few friends and associates of his illness. But to avoid possible news reports he publicly disclosed that he was suffering from AIDS at a news conference in April 1992.

Ashe established the Arthur Ashe Foundation for the Defeat of AIDS as a new international organization, with half of the funds generated going to AIDS causes outside the United States. He rallied professional tennis to help raise funds and to increase public awareness of the AIDS epidemic. This foundation coordinated efforts with other groups to provide treatment to AIDS patients and to promote vital AIDS research. He addressed the General Assembly of the United Nations on World AIDS Day, December 1, 1992.

Arthur Ashe died of pneumonia related to AIDS on February 6, 1993, in New York City. Mourners paid their respects as Ashe's body lay in state at the Virginia governor's mansion, at a memorial service held in St. John's Cathedral in New York City, and at the funeral at the Ashe Athletic Center in Richmond. In 1996 Ashe's hometown of Richmond, Virginia announced plans to erect a statue in his honor on Richmond's Monument Avenue. The following year, a new tennis stadium at the National Tennis Center in Flushing Meadows, New York, was named for him. Up until his death, Ashe remained involved in tennis and sports. He served as a television commentator at tennis matches, sports consultant at tennis clinics and a columnist for the *Washington Post.*

Further Reading

Arthur Ashe: Portrait in Motion (written with Frank Deford, 1975, 1993) is a "tennis diary" written between Wimbledon 1973 and Wimbledon 1975. In 1981 he also wrote an autobiography (with Neil Amdur) dedicated to his slave ancestors, entitled *Off the Court.* The last autobiography, *Days of Grace: A Memoir,* co-authored with Arnold Rampersad, was completed by Ashe 48 hours before he died. Ashe's definitive work, *A Hard Road to Glory: A History of the African-American Athlete,* with Kip Branch, Ocania Chalk, and Francis Harris (1988) covered African-American athletic history from ancestral homelands to the present. For an intimate view of Ashe from a family perspective, see the touching book *Daddy and Me: A Photo Essay of Arthur Ashe and His Daughter Camera* (1993), with photographs and words by Jeanne Moutoussamy-Ashe. A balanced commentary by Kenny Moore, "He Did All He Could," appeared in *Sports Illustrated* (February 15, 1993). An article by Terry Pluto, "Statue Right of Way to Honor Ashe," appeared in the *Beacon Journal* (July 13, 1996). □

Isaac Asimov

The author of nearly five hundred books, Isaac Asimov (1920-1992) is esteemed as one of the finest writers of science fiction and scientific fact in the twentieth century.

Asimov was born on January 2, 1920, to middle-class Jewish parents in Petrovichi, Russia, then part of the Smolensk district in the Soviet Union. His family immigrated to the United States in 1923, settling in Brooklyn, New York, where they owned and operated a candy store. In 1934, while attending Boys High School of Brooklyn, Asimov published his first story, "Little Brothers," in the school newspaper. A year later he entered Seth Low Junior College, an undergraduate college of Columbia University. He transferred to the main campus in 1936, where he switched his major from biology to chemistry. During the next two years Asimov's interest in history grew and he read numerous books on the subject. He also read science fiction magazines and wrote stories. His first professionally published story, "Marooned off Vesta," appeared in *Amazing Stories* in 1939. Asimov graduated from Columbia University with a B.S. in chemistry in 1939. He later earned an M.A. and Ph.D. After serving in World War II, Asimov became an instructor at Boston University School of medicine. Asimov died in 1992.

Asimov received his greatest popular and critical acclaim for *The Foundation Trilogy: Three Classics of Science Fiction* and his robot series. Comprised of *Foundation, Foundation and Empire,* and *Second Foundation, The Foundation Trilogy* describes the "future history" of a vast galactic empire. His books about robots—most notably *I, Robot; The Caves of Steel;* and *The Naked Sun*—did much to legitimize science fiction by augmenting the genre's traditional material with the narrative structures of such established genres as mystery and detective stories, while displaying a thematic concern for technological progress and its implications for humanity. Many critics, scientists, and educators, however, believe Asimov's greatest talent was for popularizing or, as he called it, "translating" science for the lay reader. His many books on atomic theory, chemistry, astronomy, and physics have been recognized for their extraordinary clarity, and Asimov has been praised for his ability to synthesize complex data into readable, unthreatening prose. When asked about his prodigious output in such a wide range of fields, Asimov responded self-deprecatingly by saying he never had a thought that he didn't put down on paper. An editorial in *The Washington Post* concluded that he redefined the rule "as to how many things a person is allowed to be an expert on" and that his "extraordinary capabilities aside, [his] breadth of interest deserves more admiration than it gets."

Isaac Asimov is "the world's most prolific science writer," according to David N. Samuelson in *Twentieth Century Science-Fiction Writers,* who "has written some of the best-known science fiction ever published." Considered one of the three greatest writers of science fiction in the 1940s (along with Robert Heinlein and A. E. Van Vogt), Asimov has remained a potent force in the genre. Stories such as "Nightfall" and "The Bicentennial Man," and novels such as *The Gods Themselves* and *Foundation's Edge* have received numerous honors and are recognized as among the best science fiction ever written. As one of the world's leading writers on science, explaining everything from nuclear fusion to the theory of numbers, Asimov has illuminated for many the mysteries of science and technology. He is a skilled raconteur as well, who enlivens his writing with incidents from his own life. "In his autobiographical writings and comments," states James Gunn in *Isaac Asimov: The Foundations of Science Fiction,* "Asimov continually invites the reader to share his triumphs, to laugh at his blunders and lack of sophistication, and to wonder, with him, at the rise to prominence of a bright Jewish boy brought to this country from Russia at the age of three and raised in a collection of Brooklyn candy stores.''

Asimov's interest in science fiction began when he first noticed several of the early science fiction magazines for sale on the newsstand of his family's candy store. Although as a boy he read and enjoyed numerous volumes of nonfiction as well as many of the literary "classics," Asimov recalls in *In Memory Yet Green,* his first volume of autobiography, he still longed to explore the intriguing magazines with the glossy covers. But his father refused, maintaining that fiction magazines were "junk! . . . Not fit to read. The only people who read magazines like that are bums." And bums represented "the dregs of society, apprentice gangsters."

But in August of 1929, a new magazine appeared on the scene called *Science Wonder Stories.* Asimov knew that as long as science fiction magazines had titles like *Amazing Stories,* he would have little chance of convincing his father of their worth. However, the new periodical had the word "science" in its title, and he says, "I had read enough about science to know that it was a mentally nourishing and spiritually wholesome study. What's more, I knew that my father thought so from our occasional talks about my schoolwork." When confronted with this argument, the elder Asimov consented. Soon Isaac began collecting even those periodicals that didn't have "science" in the title. He notes: "I planned to maintain with all the strength at my disposal the legal position that permission for one such magazine implied permission for all the others, regardless of title. No fight was needed, however; my harassed father conceded everything." Asimov rapidly developed into an avid fan.

Asimov first tried writing stories when he was eleven years old. He had for some time been reading stories and then retelling them to his schoolmates, and started a book like some of the popular boys' series volumes of the 1920s: "The Rover Boys," "The Bobbsey Twins," and "Pee Wee Wilson." Asimov's story was called *The Greenville Chums at College,* patterned after *The Darewell Chums at College,* and it grew to eight chapters before he abandoned it. Asimov, in *In Memory Yet Green,* describes the flaw in his initial literary venture: "I was trying to imitate the series books without knowing anything but what I read there. Their characters were small-town boys, so mine were, for I imagined Greenville to be a town in upstate New York. Their characters went to college, so mine did. Unfortunately, a junior-high-school youngster living in a shabby neighborhood in Brooklyn knows very little about small-town life and even less about college. Even I, myself, was forced eventually to recognize the fact that I didn't know what I was talking about."

Despite initial discouragements, Asimov continued to write. His first published piece appeared in his high school's literary semiannual and was accepted, he says, because it was the only funny piece anyone wrote, and the editors needed something funny. In the summer of 1934, Asimov had a letter published in *Astounding Stories* in which he commented on several stories that had appeared in the

magazine. His continuing activities as a fan brought him to the decision to attempt a science fiction piece of his own; in 1937, at the age of seventeen, he began a story entitled "Cosmic Corkscrew." The procedure Asimov used to formulate the plot was, he says, "typical of my science fiction. I usually thought of some scientific gimmick and built a story about that."

By the time he finished the story on June 19, 1938, *Astounding Stories* had become *Astounding Science Fiction.* Its editor was John W. Campbell, who was to influence the work of some of the most prominent authors of modern science fiction, including Arthur C. Clarke, Robert Heinlein, Poul Anderson, L. Sprague de Camp, and Theodore Sturgeon. Since Campbell was also one of the best-known science fiction writers of the thirties and *Astounding* one of the most prestigious publications in its field at the time, Asimov was shocked by his father's suggestion that he submit "Cosmic Corkscrew" to the editor in person. But mailing the story would have cost twelve cents while subway fare, round trip, was only ten cents. In the interest of economy, therefore, he agreed to make the trip to the magazine's office, fully expecting to leave the manuscript with a secretary.

Campbell, however, had invited many young writers to discuss their work with him, and when Asimov arrived he was shown into the editor's office. Campbell talked for over an hour and agreed to read the story; two days later Asimov received the manuscript back in the mail. It had been rejected, but Campbell offered extensive suggestions for improvement and encouraged the young man to keep trying. This began a pattern that was to continue for several years with Campbell guiding Asimov through his formative beginnings as a science fiction writer.

Asimov's association with the field of science fiction has been a long and distinguished one. He is credited with the introduction of several innovative concepts into the genre, including the formulation of the "Three Laws of Robotics." Asimov maintains that the idea for the laws was given to him by Campbell; Campbell, on the other hand, said that he had merely picked them out of Asimov's early robot stories. In any case, it was Asimov who first formally stated the three laws: "1. A robot may not injure a human being or, through inaction, allow a human being to come to harm. 2. A robot must obey the orders given it by human beings except where such orders would conflict with the First Law. 3. A robot must protect its own existence as long as such protection does not conflict with the First or Second Laws." Asimov says that he used these precepts as the basis for "over two dozen short stories and three novels . . . about robots," and he feels that he is "probably more famous for them than for anything else I have written, and they are quoted even outside the science-fiction world. The very word 'robotics' was coined by me." The three laws gained general acceptance among readers and among other science fiction writers; Asimov, in his autobiography, writes that they "revolutionized" science fiction and that "no writer could write a *stupid* robot story if he used the Three Laws. The story might be bad on other counts, but it wouldn't be stupid." The laws became so popular, and seemed so logical, that many people believed real robots would eventually be designed according to Asimov's basic principles.

Also notable among Asimov's science fiction works is the "Foundation" series. This group of short stories, published in magazines in the forties and then collected into a trilogy in the early fifties, was inspired by Edward Gibbon's *Decline and Fall of the Roman Empire.* It was written as a "future history," a story being told in a society of the distant future which relates events of that society's history. The concept was not invented by Asimov, but there can be little doubt that he became a master of the technique. *Foundation, Foundation and Empire,* and *Second Foundation* have achieved special standing among science fiction enthusiasts. In 1966, the World Science Fiction Convention honored them with a special Hugo Award as the best all-time science fiction series. Even many years after the original publication, Asimov's future history series remains popular—in the 1980s, forty years after he began the series, Asimov added a new volume, *Foundation's Edge,* and eventually linked the Foundation stories with his robot novels in *The Robots of Dawn, Robots and Empire, Foundation and Earth,* and *Prelude to Foundation.*

Asimov's first fiction written specifically for a younger audience were his "Lucky Starr" novels. In 1951, at the suggestion of his Doubleday editor, he began working on a series of science-fiction stories that could easily be adapted for television. "Television was here; that was clear," he writes in *In Memory Yet Green.* "Why not take advantage of it, then? Radio had its successful long-running series, 'The Lone Ranger,' so why not a 'Space Ranger' modelled very closely upon that?" *David Starr: Space Ranger,* published under the pseudonym Paul French, introduced David 'Lucky' Starr, agent of the interplanetary law enforcement agency the Council of Science. Accompanying Lucky on his adventures is his sidekick, John Bigman Jones, a short, tough man born and raised on the great agricultural farms of Mars. Together the two of them confront and outwit space pirates, poisoners, mad scientists, and interstellar spies—humans from the Sirian star system, who have become the Earth's worst enemies.

Although the "Lucky Starr" series ran to six volumes, the television deal that Asimov and his editor envisioned never materialized. "None of us dreamed that for some reason . . . television series would very rarely last more than two or three years," Asimov writes. "We also didn't know that a juvenile television series to be called 'Rocky Jones: Space Ranger' was already in the works." Another problem the series faced was in the scientific background of the stories. "Unfortunately," state Jean Fiedler and Jim Mele in *Isaac Asimov,* "Asimov had the bad luck to be writing these stories on the threshold of an unprecedented exploration of our solar system's planets, an exploration which has immensely increased our astronomical knowledge. Many of his scientific premises, sound in 1952, were later found to be inaccurate." In recent editions of the books, Asimov has included forewords explaining the situation to new readers.

Asimov's first nonfiction book was a medical text entitled *Biochemistry and Human Metabolism,* begun in 1950

and written in collaboration with William Boyd and Burnham Walker, two of his colleagues at the Boston University School of Medicine. He had recognized his ability as an explainer early in life, and he enjoyed clarifying scientific principles for his family and friends. He also discovered that he was a most able and entertaining lecturer who delighted in his work as a teacher. He told *New York Times* interviewer Israel Shenker that his talent lies in the fact that he "can read a dozen dull books and make one interesting book out of them." The result was that Asimov was phenomenally successful as a writer of science books for the general public. Before his death in 1992, Asimov commented, "I'm on fire to explain, and happiest when it's something reasonably intricate which I can make clear step by step. It's the easiest way I can clarify things in my own mind."

Further Reading

Los Angeles Times, April 8, 1992.

New York Times, April 7, 1992.

Washington Post, April 7, 1992.

Asimov, Isaac, *The Bicentennial Man and Other Stories,* Doubleday, 1976.

Asimov, Isaac, *In Memory Yet Green: The Autobiography of Isaac Asimov, 1920-1954,* Doubleday, 1979.

Asimov, Isaac, *In Joy Still Felt: The Autobiography of Isaac Asimov, 1954-1979,* Doubleday, 1980.

Clareson, Thomas D., editor, *Voices for the Future: Essays on Major Science Fiction Writers,* Popular Press, 1976.

Contemporary Literary Criticism, Gale, Volume 1, 1973; Volume 3, 1975; Volume 9, 1978; Volume 19, 1981; Volume 26, 1983.

Dictionary of Literary Biography, Volume 8: *Twentieth-Century American Science Fiction Writers,* Gale, 1981. □

Fred Astaire

Fred Astaire (1899-1987) was a preeminent dancer and choreographer who worked in vaudeville, revue, musical comedy, television, radio, and Hollywood musicals. He achieved admiring recognition not only from his peers in the entertainment world, but also from major figures in ballet and modern dance.

Fred Astaire, born Frederick Austerlitz on May 10, 1899, in Omaha, Nebraska, began performing in vaudeville with his sister, Adele, in 1905. The Astaires eventually became featured performers, and in 1917 they moved to the musical stage where they appeared in ten productions, most of them hugely successful, particularly two musical comedies with songs by George and Ira Gershwin (*Lady, Be Good* in 1924 and *Funny Face* in 1927) and a revue with songs by Arthur Schwartz and Howard Dietz (*The Band Wagon* in 1931).

When his sister retired from show business in 1932 to marry, Astaire sought to reshape his career. He settled on the featured role in *Gay Divorce,* a "musical play" with songs by Cole Porter. This show proved Astaire could flour-

ish without his sister, and it also helped establish the pattern of most of his film musicals: it was a light, perky, unsentimental comedy, largely uncluttered by subplot, built around a love story for Astaire and his partner (Claire Luce) that was airy and amusing, but essentially serious—particularly when the pair danced together.

Astaire Goes to Hollywood

In 1933 Astaire married Phyllis Livingston Potter. Shortly after his marriage Astaire went to Hollywood. At RKO he had a featured part in the exuberant, fluttery *Flying Down to Rio* (1933). The film was a hit, and it was obvious Astaire's performance and screen appeal were a major factor in that success. *The Gay Divorcee* (1934), a film version of *Gay Divorce,* was the first of Astaire's major pictures with Ginger Rogers, and it scored even better at the box office than *Flying Down to Rio.* With this and seven more films in the 1930s (the most popular of which was *Top Hat* of 1935), they reached their full development as a team—one of the legendary partnerships in the history of dance, characterized by breathless high spirits, emotional richness, bubbling comedy, and beguiling romantic compatibility.

For these films Astaire created a rich series of romantic and playful duets for the team, as well as an array of dazzling and imaginative solos for himself. Astaire's musicality, together with the opportunity of working on such a classy, highly profitable project, made his films attractive to many of the top popular-song composers of the day: Irving Berlin, Jerome Kern, and the Gershwins.

By the end of the 1930s the revenues from the films with Rogers were beginning to decline and, after a disagreement over fees with the studio, Astaire left. The next years were nomadic but successful ones for Astaire. He made nine films at four different studios and continued to fashion splendid dances. He appeared with a variety of partners—tap virtuoso Eleanor Powell, Paulette Goddard, Rita Hayworth, Joan Leslie, and Lucille Bremer—and he also did a pair of films with Bing Crosby. Musically, Astaire continued to attract the best: Porter, Berlin, Kern, Harold Arlen, Harry Warren, and lyricist Johnny Mercer.

Retirement and Creation of Dancing Schools

In 1946 Astaire retired from motion pictures to create a chain of dancing schools, a venture that was eventually proved to be successful. In 1947 he returned to movies to make the highly profitable *Easter Parade* at MGM, opposite Judy Garland. Nine more musicals followed. His partners in these included Ginger Rogers for one picture, as well as Vera-Ellen, Cyd Charisse, Leslie Caron, Betty Hutton, Jane Powell, and Audrey Hepburn. This period was marked by a great personal tragedy for Astaire—the agonizing death of his beloved wife from cancer in 1954 at the age of 46.

By the mid-1950s the era of the classic Hollywood musical as Astaire had experienced it—indeed, defined it—was coming to an end, and Astaire moved into other fields. On television he produced four multiple award-winning musical specials with Barrie Chase as his partner. He also tried his hand at straight acting roles with considerable success in eight films between 1959 and 1982. Over the years he played a number of characters on television—usually suave ones—in dramatic specials and series. As he entered his 80s, Astaire, a life-long horse racing enthusiast, romanced, and in 1980 married, Robyn Smith, a successful jockey in her mid-30s. He died seven years later.

Ginger Rogers, Astaire's long time dance partner, passed away in April 1995. Rogers is often quoted as having said, "I did everything Fred did, only backwards and in high heels." Their partnership lasted sixteen years, from 1933 to 1949.

Astaire's Legacy

Over the course of his long film career, Fred Astaire appeared in 212 musical numbers, of which 133 contain fully developed dance routines, a high percentage of which are of great artistic value, a contribution unrivaled in films and with few parallels in the history of dance. And, because he worked mainly in film, Astaire is that great rarity: a master choreographer the vast majority of whose works are precisely preserved.

Although the creation of many of Astaire's dances involved a degree of collaboration with others, the guiding creative hand and the final authority was Astaire himself. His choreography is notable for its inventiveness, wit, musicality, and economy. Characteristically, each dance takes two or three central ideas and carefully presents and develops them—ideas that might derive from a step, the music, the lyrics, the qualities of his partner, or the plot situation.

Astaire's dances are stylistically eclectic, an unpredictable blend of tap and ballroom with bits from other dance forms thrown in. What holds everything together is Astaire's distinctive style and sensibility: the casual sophistication, the airy wit, the transparent rhythmic intricacy, and the apparent ease of execution. Astaire also focused his attention on the problems of filming dance and settled on an approach that was to dominate Hollywood musicals for a generation: both camerawork and editing are fashioned to enhance the flow and continuity of the dances, not to undercut or overshadow it.

A perfectionist, Astaire spent weeks working out his choreography. Although his perfectionism, his propensity to worry, his shyness, and his self-doubt could make him difficult, even exasperating, to work with, he was an efficient planner and worker. His courtesy, enormous professionalism, and tireless struggle for improvement earned him the admiration of his co-workers.

Astaire's legacy continues to be revisited, sometimes with controversy. In January 1997, Astaire's image returned to television through special effects editing when Dirt Devil grafted their vacuum cleaners into dance scenes from Astaire's films for three of their commercials. The advertisements were completed and run with Robyn Astaire's blessing. The commercials, which aired during the Super Bowl, were panned by the press, the general feeling being that replacing Ginger Rogers with a vacuum cleaner was in poor taste.

Further Reading

Fred Astaire's autobiography which, shattering Hollywood tradition, he wrote himself (in longhand) is *Steps in Time* (1959). His work is discussed and analyzed in Arlene Croce, *The Fred Astaire & Ginger Rogers Book* (1972) and John Mueller, *Astaire Dancing: The Musical Films* (1985). Useful interviews with Astaire are included in Morton Eustis, *Players at Work* (1937) and in *Inter/View* (June 1973). Astaire can also be found on the World Wide Web. A listing of his movies can be found at http://dolphin.upenn.edu/~amatth13/fred.html. Information on Astaire can also be found at http://www.mrshowbiz.com/scoop/news/archive. □

John Jacob Astor

An American fur trader, merchant, and capitalist, John Jacob Astor (1763-1848) used his profits from fur trading to invest in a wide range of business enterprises. By the time of his death he was the richest man in America.

John Jacob Astor was born in Waldorf, near Heidelberg, Germany, on July 17, 1763. He was named after his father, a poor but convivial butcher. In spite of the family's poverty, Astor was sent to the local schoolmaster, who provided him with an exceptional education, considering the times. When Astor reached the age of 14, his father decided that his son should work with him. The boy assisted for 2 years before, in 1779, he struck out on his own. He joined a brother in London, where he learned English and

worked to earn passage money to America. In 1783, after the peace treaty ending the American Revolution had been signed, he sailed for the United States to join another brother who had emigrated earlier. He landed at Baltimore in March 1784.

Astor soon joined his brother in New York and began to demonstrate his talent for business. He received a shipment of flutes from England, which he offered for sale. He also worked for several furriers and began buying furs on his own. In 1784 and 1785 Astor made furbuying trips to western New York for his employers, purchasing furs for himself at the same time. He acquired enough furs to make a trip to England profitable. In London he established connections with a reputable trading house, signed an agreement to act as the New York agent for a musical instrument firm, and used his profits from the furs to buy merchandise suitable for trade with the Native Americans. Not yet 22, he had already proved himself a shrewd and competent business man.

His initial success convinced Astor that a fortune could be made in the fur trade. He began to spend more time managing and expanding his business. Between 1790 and 1808 his agents collected furs from as far west as Mackinaw, Mich. The Jay Treaty and the British evacuation of forts in the Old Northwest worked to Astor's advantage, and he expanded his operations in the Great Lakes region. Through an arrangement with the British Northwest Company, he purchased furs directly from Montreal. By about 1809 he was recognized as one of the leading fur traders in the United States.

Following the Louisiana Purchase, Astor turned his attention to the fur trade in the Pacific Northwest. Through shrewd political maneuvers he obtained a charter for the American Fur Company. His plan was to establish a main fort at the mouth of the Columbia River, with sub-forts in the interior. His fleet of ships would collect the furs and sell them in China, where goods would be purchased for sale in Europe; in Europe merchandise could be bought to sell in the United States when the ships returned.

Although the town of Astoria was established on the Columbia, the company's operations were unsuccessful. After the War of 1812 Astor renewed his efforts to gain control of the fur trade in North America. Through influence in Congress he secured legislation that prohibited foreigners from engaging in the trade except as employees and that eliminated the government's trading post serving independent traders. By the late 1820's he monopolized the fur trade in the Great Lakes region and most of the Mississippi Valley. This monopoly put him into direct competition with the Rocky Mountain Fur Company and British fur interests in the Pacific Northwest. However, by 1830 Astor's interest in the company had begun to decline.

Through his dealings in the fur trade Astor became involved in general merchandising. During the 1790s he had begun to import and sell a large variety of European goods. During this early period he showed little interest in establishing trade relations with China. Between 1800 and 1812, however, his trade with China expanded and became an integral part of his business dealings in Europe. The War of 1812 temporarily disrupted his plans, but it gave him an opportunity to purchase ships at a bargain price since declining trade had made merchants anxious to dispose of their fleets. After the war Astor had a sizable fleet of sailing vessels and again became active in the China and Pacific trade. For a time he was involved in smuggling Turkish opium into China but found the profits were not worth the risk and abandoned this venture. Between 1815 and 1820 he enjoyed a commanding position in the China trade. Thereafter his interest declined, and he turned his attention to other business activities. One explanation for Astor's success as a merchant was that he had the capital to buy superior merchandise at a low cost and a fleet of ships that could transport the goods to markets more quickly than his rivals.

Astor retired from the American Fur Company and withdrew from both domestic and foreign trade in 1834. He turned to other investments, including real estate, moneylending, insurance companies, banking, railroads and canals, public securities, and the hotel business. The most important was real estate. He had invested some capital in land early in his career. After 1800 he concentrated on real estate in New York City. He profited not only from the sale of lands and rents but from the increasing value of lands within the city. During the last decade of his life his income from rents alone exceeded $1,250,000. A reliable estimate placed his total wealth at $20-30 million (the greatest source being his land holdings on Manhattan Island) at his death in 1848, at the age of 84.

Further Reading

The most complete biography of Astor is Kenneth Wiggins Porter, *John Jacob Astor, Business Man* (2 vols., 1931). A somewhat critical work which deals extensively with Astor's interest in the fur trade is John Upton Terrell, *Furs by Astor* (1963). See also Washington Irving, *Astoria* (1836; repr. 1961); Meade Minigerode, *Certain Rich Men* (1927); and Harvey O'Connor, *The Astors* (1941). A background discussion of the fur trade that includes Astor is provided by Bernard De Voto, *Across the Wide Missouri* (1947). Social histories of New York that discuss Astor are Arthur Pound, *The Golden Earth: The Story of Manhattan's Landed Wealth* (1935); Frederick L. Collins, *Money Town* (1946); and Edward Robb Ellis, *The Epic of New York City* (1966). □

John James Audubon

The work of American artist and ornithologist John James Audubon (1785-1851) was the culmination of the work of natural history artists who tried to portray specimens directly from nature. He is chiefly remembered for his "Birds of America."

When John James Audubon began his work in the first decade of the 19th century, there was no distinct profession of "naturalist" in America. The men who engaged in natural history investigations came from all walks of life and generally financed their work—collecting, writing, and publication—from their own resources. The American continent, still largely unexplored, offered a fertile field, giving the amateur an unrivaled opportunity to make a genuine contribution to science—for an afternoon walk in the woods might reveal a hitherto unknown species of bird, plant, or insect to the practiced eye. Especially fortunate was the man with artistic ability, for there was an intense popular interest in the marvels of nature during this, the romantic, era; and anyone who could capture the natural beauty of wild specimens was certain to take his place among the front ranks of those recognized as "men of science." This is the context in which Audubon worked and in which he became known as America's greatest naturalist—a title which modern scholars using other standards invariably deny him.

Audubon was born in San Domingo (now Haiti) on April 26, 1785, the illegitimate son of a French adventurer and a woman called Mademoiselle Rabin, about whom little is known except that she was a Creole of San Domingo and died soon after her son's birth. Audubon's father had made his fortune in San Domingo as a merchant, planter, and dealer in slaves. In 1789 Audubon went with his father and a half sister to France, where they joined his father's wife. The children were legalized by a regular act of adoption in 1794.

Life in France and Move to America

Audubon's education, arranged by his father, was that of a well-to-do young bourgeois; he went to a nearby school and was also tutored in mathematics, geography, drawing, music, and fencing. According to Audubon's own account, he had no interest in school, preferring instead to fish, hunt,

and collect curiosities in the field. Left to the supervision of his indulgent stepmother most of the time, while his father served as a naval officer for the republic, Audubon became a spoiled, willful youth who managed to resist all efforts either to educate or discipline him. When residence at a naval base under his father's direct supervision failed to have any effect, he was sent briefly to Paris to study art, but this disciplined study also repelled him.

With the collapse of a large part of his income following the rebellion in San Domingo, the elder Audubon decided to send his son to America, where he owned a farm near Philadelphia. At first the boy lived with friends of his father and they tried to teach him English and otherwise continue his education, but after a time he demanded to be allowed to live on his father's farm, which was being managed by a tenant. There Audubon continued his undisciplined ways, living the life of a country gentleman— fishing, shooting, and developing his skill at drawing birds, the only occupation to which he was ever willing to give persistent effort. He developed the new technique of inserting wires into the bodies of freshly killed birds in order to manipulate them into natural positions for his sketching. He also made the first banding experiments on the young of an American wild bird, in April 1804.

Business Career

In 1805, after a prolonged battle with his father's business agent in America, Audubon returned briefly to France, where he formed a business partnership with Ferdinand Rozier, the son of one of his father's associates. Together the

two returned to America and tried to operate a lead mine on the farm. Then in August 1807 the partners decided to move to the West. There followed a series of business failures, in Louisville, Henderson, and other parts of Kentucky, caused largely by Audubon's preference for roaming the woods rather than keeping the store.

During this period he married Lucy Bakewell. After the failures with Rozier, Audubon, in association with his brother-in-law, Thomas Bakewell, and others, attempted several different enterprises, the last being a steam grist and lumber mill at Henderson. In 1819 this enterprise failed and Audubon was plunged into bankruptcy, left with only the clothes he wore, his gun, and his drawings. This disaster ended his business career.

For a time Audubon did crayon portraits at $5 a head, then he moved to Cincinnati, where he became a taxidermist in the Western Museum recently founded by Dr. Daniel Drake. In 1820 the possibility of publishing his bird drawings occurred to him; and he set out down the Ohio and Mississippi rivers, exploring the country for new birds and paying his expenses by painting portraits. For a while he supported himself in New Orleans by tutoring and painting; then his wife obtained a position as a governess and later opened a school for girls. Thereafter she was the family's main support while Audubon tried to have his drawings published.

"Birds of America"

In 1824 Audubon went to Philadelphia to seek a publisher, but he encountered the opposition of friends of Alexander Wilson, the other pioneer American ornithologist, with whom he had had a bitter rivalry dating back to a chance encounter in his store in 1810. He finally decided to raise the money for a trip to Europe, where he was assured he would find a greater interest in his subject. He arrived at Liverpool in 1826, then moved on to Edinburgh and to London, being favorably received and obtaining subscribers for his volumes in each city. Audubon finally reached an agreement with a London engraver, and in 1827 *Birds of America* began to appear in "elephant folio" size. It took 11 years in all for its serial publication and subsequent reprintings. The success of Audubon's bird drawings brought him immediate fame, and by 1831 he was acclaimed the foremost naturalist of his country. This title was bestowed upon him despite the fact that he possessed no formal scientific training and no aptitude for taxonomy (the Latin nomenclature and the scientific indentification of most of the species in *Birds of America* is largely the work of a collaborator). He had, however, succeeded in giving the world the first great collection of American birds, drawn in their natural habitats with reasonable fidelity to nature.

With his great work finally finished in 1838, and the *Ornithological Biography* (a text commentary) in publication, Audubon returned to America to prepare a "miniature" edition. Simultaneously, he began to prepare, in collaboration with John Bachman, *Viviparous Quadrupeds of North America* (2 vols., 1842-1845). Audubon himself completed only about half the drawings in this last work; his powers failed during his last few years and his son contributed the remainder.

Final Years

With old age—and success—came a more kindly attitude toward his former rivals. In 1841 he bought an estate on the Hudson River and settled down to advise and encourage young scientists. It was during this period that the romantic picture of Audubon as the ''American Woodsman,'' the revered and adored sage and patron saint of the birds, began to emerge. (This image was kept alive by his daughter and granddaughter until 1917, when F. H. Herrick published the first critical biography of the artist-naturalist.) After several years of illness, Audubon suffered a slight stroke in January 1851, followed by partial paralysis and great pain, and died on the 27th.

Further Reading

Alice E. Ford, *John James Audubon* (1964), is a good biography by an art historian; Alexander B. Adams, *John James Audubon* (1966), gives a meticulous year-by-year chronicle of his activities. An earlier work, Francis H. Herrick, *Audubon the Naturalist* (2 vols., 1917), is still valuable for the scientific side. All of the earlier biographies, based on the account by Audubon's wife, are highly romanticized. Useful for background information on this period in American natural history is William M. and Mabel S. C. Smallwood, *Natural History and the American Mind* (1941). George H. Daniels, *American Science in the Age of Jackson* (1968), discusses the general scientific frame of reference. □

B

Amos Bad Heart Bull

Amos Bad Heart Bull (1869-1913) was an Oglala Lakota Sioux tribal historian and artist known for his pictographs.

Amos Bad Heart Bull was called "the Herodotus of his people" by Helen Blish, who rescued his 400 pictographs by having had them photographed before their interment. Through her intervention *A Pictographic History of the Oglala Sioux* was published to relate the transition of these proud Plains warriors into reservation Indians. The illustrations from this book have been featured in every television documentary about the Ghost Dance, the Battle of the Little Big Horn, and the deaths of Sitting Bull and Crazy Horse. The artist's pictures of Crazy Horse, his cousin, are the only surviving likenesses of him since Crazy Horse never allowed himself to be photographed. Fortunately, Blish was able to interview two of the artist's uncles, He Dog (Sunka Bloka) and Short Bull (Tatanka Ptecela), on the Pine Ridge Reservation in South Dakota, to learn a little about his life. Short Bull and He Dog told her that Amos Bad Heart Bull the Elder had been a band historian, a keeper of the winter count, and had created a hide chronicle on which the outstanding single event of each year was recorded. Since he died young, the task of bringing up his son fell to them, and to their brothers, Little Shield and Only Man. They told him stories of the battles they had fought in, and observed his interest in collecting treaties and documents about Indian-white encounters.

Self-Taught Artistry

Without any formal instruction, Bad Heart Bull began creating annotated drawings. Although he had been given no education, he taught himself to write using a system devised by the missionaries for the transcription of Lakota.

He also learned English from the soldiers at Fort Robinson, where he had enlisted as a scout for the United States Army in 1890. From a clothing dealer in Crawford, Nebraska, he bought a used ledger in which he began his 415 drawings using black pen, indelible pencil, and blue, yellow, green, and brown crayons, and red ink. In some instances he painted with a brush so fine that the strokes can be seen only under magnification. In addition, some of the pictures are touched with a gray or brown wash in places. He worked at this project for about two decades recording the civic, religious, social, economic, and military life of the Oglala.

His technical innovations permitted multiple perspectives of an event. He portrayed masses of people engaged in dramatic actions by assuming a panoramic view. Depicting hundreds of men and horses in battle, or in religious ceremonies, or in processionals to a buffalo hunt from above, he captured tribal activities in long-shots or topographic views. Then, he would render close-ups of some aspect on the same page, framed and set-off to one side, so that one could study the psychological impact of the sweeping event upon an individual participant by means of a near-view insert. He experimented with other than stylized profile renditions, using full-face depictions, rear-views, rendering wounded horses from below, or showing dancers in three-quarter view. Another innovation was his use of foreshortening. These techniques added drama and realism to his pictures.

Each set of drawings tells part of a heroic epic. The first group shows tribal events before 1856. The councilmen (wakicunza) and their marshals (akicita) are shown deliberating in the camp council, a buffalo hunt, a sun dance, and the eight warrior societies in their regalia are shown. The next set of pictures tells the story of the conflicts with the Crow, their hereditary enemies on the Plains in sporadic skirmishes from 1856 to 1875. The third set narrates the defeat of U.S. General George A. Custer on the Little Big Horn River in Montana. The next group of pictures shows the reorganization of Oglala society as it was forced to accept reservation existence. It opens with the ceremonies: the Sacred Bow, the Victory Dance, the Dance of the Black Tailed Deer, the Horse Dance, and the Vision Quest. These are followed by eight depictions of courting scenes, and ten of games. This section closes with the transition to agriculture. The next to last set depicts the Ghost Dance and the Battle of Wounded Knee. And the final set shows the fourth of July being celebrated in 1898 and in 1903 on the Pine Ridge Reservation. By grouping his pictures in these narrative sequences, the artist has conveyed the history of his band over 60 years. Because he preserved the most minute details of daily life, this constitutes an unparalleled historical record.

Rescued for Posterity

In 1926, Helen Blish was a graduate student at the University of Nebraska searching for examples of Plains art. From W. O. Roberts of the Pine Ridge Agency, she learned about Bad Heart Bull's drawings, which had been given, after the artist's death in 1913, to his sister, Dolly Pretty Cloud. Speaking through an interpreter, Blish spent her summer vacations from teaching in a Detroit high school, studying the art of Pretty Cloud's brother, kept in a trunk on the dirt floor of the one-room cabin on the reservation. It was only after much persuasion that she was permitted to rent it for a modest annual fee and to analyze the renderings for her master's thesis under the noted art historian Hartley Burr Alexander.

Following Lakota custom, the prized ledger book was buried with Pretty Cloud upon her death in 1947. Fortunately, though, Blish's work had been given to the American Museum of Natural History in New York City before her death in 1941. In 1959, the University of Nebraska Press decided to publish Bad Heart Bull's pictorial history and attempted to get permission to disinter the ledger, to no avail. However, it was found that Alexander had photographed the priceless document page-by-page in 1927; therefore, these illustrations were collated with Blish's manuscript and published in book form. Mari Sandoz, the biographer of Bad Heart Bull's cousin, Crazy Horse, encouraged the project from its inception, and wrote its introduction in the last year of her life. She said, "Without doubt, the Amos Bad Heart Bull picture history is the most comprehensive, the finest statement as art and as report of the North American Indian so far discovered anywhere."

Further Reading

Blish, Helen H., *A Pictographic History of the Oglala Sioux*, Lincoln, University of Nebraska Press, 1967.

Dockstader, Frederick J., *Great North American Indians*, New York, Van Nostrand Reinhold, 1977.

The Indians' Book, edited by Natalie Cirtis Burlin, New York, Harper, 1923.

Sandoz, Mari, *Crazy Horse: The Strange Man of the Oglalas*, Lincoln, University of Nebraska Press, 1942. □

Leo Hendrik Baekeland

An American chemist, inventor, and manufacturer, Leo Hendrik Baekeland (1863-1944) invented Bakelite, the first plastic to be used widely in industry.

Leo Hendrik Baekeland was born in 1863 in Ghent, Belgium. He took a bachelor of science degree from the University of Ghent in 1882 and began to teach there as an assistant professor; he received his doctorate in natural science in 1884 and continued to teach for another 5 years. In 1889 he went to the United States on a traveling scholarship, liked the country, received a job offer from a photographic firm, and decided to make America his home.

These were the years when science was first coming to the attention of American industry. In some European countries, notably Germany, industrial research was already helping to improve old products and processes and to develop new ones. This wedding of science and technology was just beginning in the United States, first in those industries that had been close to science from their beginnings, such as the chemical and electrical industries. The manufacture of photographic equipment and materials was one such industry. Baekeland began work to improve photographic film, and in 1893 he established the Nepera Chemical Company to manufacture Velox paper, a film of his invention which could be handled in the light. In 1899 he sold out to the leading firm in the field, Eastman Kodak, and used the money to set up his own private industrial research laboratory in a converted barn behind his home in Yonkers, N.Y.

At this laboratory Baekeland began a large number of experiments covering a range of subjects. One of these was an attempt to produce a synthetic shellac by mixing formaldehyde and phenolic bodies. Other experimenters had worked with these two substances, and it was known that the interaction was greatly influenced by the proportions used and the conditions under which they were brought together. Baekeland failed to synthesize shellac but instead discovered Bakelite, the first successful plastic.

Earlier plastics had only limited usefulness because of their tendency to soften when heated, harden when cooled, and interact readily with many chemical substances. Baekeland's new material did not suffer from any of these defects. Using temperatures much higher than previously thought possible, he developed a process for placing the material in a hot mold and adding both pressure and more heat so that a chemical change would take place, transforming the material in composition as well as shape.

He patented this process in 1909 and formed the Bakelite Corporation the following year to market the material. Bakelite soon became very successful and was widely used in industry as a substitute for hard rubber and amber, particularly in electrical devices. He retired from the company in 1939, honored for his success as a manufacturer and for his effectiveness as a spokesman for the whole concept of scientific research in the aid of industry.

Further Reading

There is no available biography of Baekeland. A sketch of his activities is in John Jewkes, David Sawers, and Richard Stillerman, *The Sources of Invention* (1958). An exhaustive study of the American Chemical industry is Williams Haynes, *American Chemical Industry* (6 vols., 1945-1954). The best study of plastics is Morris Kaufman, *The First Century of Plastics: Celluloid and its Sequel* (1963). □

George Balanchine

The Russian-born American choreographer George Balanchine (1904-1983) formed and established the classical style of contemporary ballet in America. His choreography emphasized form rather than content, technique rather than interpretation.

George Balanchine, born Georgi Melitonovitch Balanchivadze in St. Petersburg, Russia, on January 22, 1904, was the son of a famous Russian composer. At the age of 10, he entered the Imperial Ballet School, where he learned the technically precise and athletic Russian dancing style. After the Russian Revolution of 1917, Balanchine continued his training in a new government theater. In 1921 he entered the St. Petersburg Conservatory of Music to study piano while continuing work in ballet at the State Academy of Opera and Ballet. He used a group of dancers from the school to present his earliest choreographed works. One of the students was Tamara Gevergeyeva, later known as Tamara Geva, whom Balanchine married in 1922. She was the first of his four wives, who were all dancers. In 1924, when the group was invited to tour Europe as the Soviet State Dancers, Balanchine defected.

He was discovered in 1925 in Paris by the ballet impresario Sergei Diaghilev. When Diaghilev's most famous choreographer, Nijinska, left his ballet company, Balanchine took her place; at the age of 21 he was the ballet master and principal choreographer of the most famous ballet corps in the world. It was Diaghilev who changed the Russian's name to Balanchine. Balanchine did 10 ballets for him. When Diaghilev died and the company disbanded in 1929, Balanchine moved from one company to another until in 1933 he formed his own company, Les Ballets. That year he met Lincoln Kirstein, a young, rich American, who invited him to head the new School of American Ballet in New York City.

With the School of American Ballet and later with the New York City Ballet, Balanchine established himself as one of the world's leading contemporary classical choreographers. Almost single-handedly he brought academic excellence and quality performance to the American ballet, which had been merely a weak copy of the great European companies.

In 1934 the American Ballet Company became the resident company at the Metropolitan Opera in New York. Audiences were treated to three new Balanchine ballets: *Apollo, The Card Party,* and *The Fairy's Kiss*—works that revolutionized American classical ballet style. But Bal-

George Balanchine (right)

anchine's daring ballet style and the Metropolitan's conservative artistic policy caused a breach that ultimately terminated the alliance in 1938. His work in the next several years included choreography for Broadway shows and films and two ballets created in 1941 for the American Ballet Caravan, a touring group: *Ballet Imperial* and *Concerto Barocco.*

In 1946, following Kirstein's return from service in World War II, he and Balanchine established a new company, the Ballet Society. Initially financed by and limited to subscribers, in 1948 it was opened to the public. The performance of Balanchine's *Orpheus* was so successful that his company was invited to establish permanent residence at the New York City Center. It did so and was renamed the New York City Ballet. Finally, Balanchine had a school, a company, and a permanent theater. He developed the New York City Ballet into the foremost classical company in America, and to some critics, in the world. Here he created some of his most enduring works, including his *Nutcracker* and *Agon.* After the New York City Ballet moved to Lincoln Center's New York State Theatre in 1964, Balanchine added such wide-ranging works as *Don Quixote* and *Union Jack.*

Balanchine's choreography was not tied to the virtuosity of the ballerina, the plot, or the decor but to pure dance. The drama was in the dance, and movement was solely related to the music—a perfect dance equivalent to music. For Balanchine, the movement of the body alone created artistic excitement and evoked images of fantasy or reality. He emphasized balance, control, precision, and ease of movement. He rejected the traditional sweet style of romantic ballet, as well as the more acrobatic style of theatrical ballet, in favor of a neoclassic style stripped to its essentials—motion, movement, and music. His dancers became precision instruments of the choreographer, whose ideas and designs came from the music itself.

Balanchine died in New York City on April 30, 1983. Summing up his career in the *New York Times,* Anna Kisselgoff said, "More than anyone else, he elevated choreography in ballet to an independent art. . . . In an age when ballet had been dependent on a synthesis of spectacle, storytelling, décor, mime, acting and music, and only partly on dancing, George Balanchine insisted that the dance element come first."

Further Reading

Bernard Taper, *Balanchine* (1963), is a popular biography. Balanchine is given extensive coverage in George Amberg, *Ballet in America: The Emergence of an American Art* (1949); Olga Maynard, *The American Ballet* (1959); Joan Lawson, *A History of Ballet and Its Makers* (1964); and Ferdinando Reyna, *A Concise History of Ballet* (trans. 1965).

Additional Sources

Buckle, Richard, and John Taras, *George Balanchine: Ballet Master* (Random House, 1988).

Mason, Francis, *I Remember Balanchine: Recollections of the Ballet Master by Those Who Knew Him* (Doubleday, 1991).

New York Times (May 1, 1983). □

James Arthur Baldwin

The author James Arthur Baldwin (1924-1987) achieved international recognition for his bold expressions of African American life in the United States.

James Baldwin was born in Harlem, New York City, on August 2, 1924, the oldest of nine children. His father was a lay preacher in the Holiness-Pentecostal sect, and at the age of 14 Baldwin was also ordained a preacher. At 18 he graduated from DeWitt Clinton High School, and in 1944 he met Richard Wright, who helped secure a fellowship that allowed Baldwin the financial freedom to devote himself solely to literature. By 1948 Baldwin had concluded that the social tenor of the United States was stifling his creativity, and he went to Europe with the financial assistance of a Rosenwald fellowship. In Europe, Baldwin completed *Go Tell It on the Mountain* (1953), *Notes of a Native Son* (1955), and *Giovanni's Room* (1956).

Spokesperson for Civil Rights Movement

Returning to the United States after nine years abroad, Baldwin became known as the most eloquent literary spokesperson for the civil rights of African Americans. A popular speaker on the lecture circuit, Baldwin quickly discovered that social conditions for African Americans had become even more bleak while he was abroad. As the 1960s began—and violence in the South escalated—he became increasingly outraged. Baldwin responded with

three powerful books of essays: *Nobody Knows My Name* (1961), *The Fire Next Time* (1963), in which he all but predicts the outbursts of black anger to come, and *More Notes of a Native Son.* These highly inflammatory works were accompanied by *Another Country* (1962), his third novel. *Going to Meet the Man* (1965) is a group of cogent short stories of the same period. During this time Baldwin's commentary to Richard Avedon's photography was published under the title *Nothing Personal* (1964), and four years later came another novel, *Tell Me How Long the Train's Been Gone.*

In addition, the mid-1960s saw Baldwin's two published plays produced on Broadway. *The Amen Corner,* first staged in Washington, D.C., in 1955, was mounted at New York City's Ethel Barrymore Theatre in April 1965. Similar in tone to *Go Tell It on the Mountain,* it communicates the religious emotion of the Holiness-Pentecostal sect. *Blues for Mr. Charlie,* which premiered at Broadway's ANTA Theatre in April 1964, is based on the Emmett Till murder case.

The assassinations of three of Baldwin's friends—civil rights marcher Medgar Evers, the Reverend Martin Luther King, Jr., and the black Muslim leader Malcolm X—shattered any hopes Baldwin maintained for racial reconciliation in the United States, and he returned to France in the early 1970s. His subsequent works of fiction include *If Beale Street Could Talk* (1974) and *Just Above My Head* (1979). Nonfiction writings of this period include *No Name in the Street* (1972), *The Devil Finds Work* (1976), an examination of African Americans in the motion picture industry, and *The Evidence of Things Not Seen* (1985), a consideration of racial issues surrounding the Atlanta child murders of 1979 and 1980. A volume of poetry, *Jimmy's Blues* was issued in 1985.

Literary Achievement

Baldwin's greatest achievement as a writer was his ability to address American race relations from a psychological perspective. In his essays and fiction he explored the implications of racism for both the oppressed and the oppressor, suggesting repeatedly that all people suffer in a racist climate. Baldwin's fiction and plays also explore the burdens a callous society can impose on a sensitive individual. Two of his best-known works, the novel *Go Tell It on the Mountain* and the play *The Amen Corner* were inspired by his years with the Pentecostal church in Harlem. In *Go Tell It on the Mountain,* for instance, a teenaged boy struggles with a repressive stepfather and experiences a charismatic spiritual awakening. Later Baldwin novels deal frankly with homosexuality and interracial love affairs—love in both its sexual and spiritual forms became an essential component of the quest for self-realization for both Baldwin and his characters.

Themes and Techniques

Baldwin's prose is characterized by a style of beauty and telling power. His language seems deliberately chosen to shock and disturb, arouse, repel, and finally shake the reader out of complacency into a concerned state of action. His major themes are repeated: the terrible pull of love and hate between black and white Americans; the constant war in one possessed by inverted sexuality between guilt or shame and ecstatic abandon; and such moral, spiritual, and ethical values as purity of motive and inner wholeness, the gift of sharing and extending love, the charm of goodness versus evil. He tunes an inner ear to the disturbing social upheaval of contemporary life and to the rewarding ecstasy of artistic achievement. All such positive values are set in continual warfare against racism, industrialism, materialism, and a global power struggle. Everything demeaning to the human spirit is attacked with vigor and righteous indignation.

Final Works

Baldwin remained abroad much of the last 15 years of his life, but he never gave up his American citizenship. The citizens of France nevertheless embraced Baldwin as one of their own, and in 1986 he was accorded one of the country's highest accolades when he was named Commander of the Legion of Honor. He died of stomach cancer, November 30, 1987, in Saint-Paul-de-Vance, France, and was buried in Harlem. One of his last works to see publication during his lifetime was a well-regarded anthology of essays *The Price of the Ticket: Collected Nonfiction, 1948-1985*.

Further Reading

Biographical studies include David Adams Leeming, *James Baldwin: A Biography* (1994) and William J. Weatherby, *James Baldwin: Artist on Fire* (1989). Aspects of Baldwin's writings are examined in such studies as Bryan R. Washington, *The Politics of Exile: Ideology in Henry James, F. Scott Fitzgerald, and James Baldwin* (1995), R. Jothiprakash, *Commitment as a Theme in African American Literature: A Study of James Baldwin and Ralph Ellison* (1994), Jean-Francois Gounard, *The Racial Problem in the Works of Richard Wright and James Baldwin* (1992), and Horace A. Porter, *Stealing the Fire: The Art and Protest of James Baldwin* (1989). □

David Baltimore

The American virologist David Baltimore (born 1938) received the Nobel Prize in Physiology and Medicine for his work on retrovirus biochemistry and its significance for cancer research.

David Baltimore was born on March 7, 1938, in New York City, the son of Richard I. and Gertrude (Lipschitz) Baltimore. While still a high school student, he spent a summer at the Jackson Memorial Laboratory in Bar Harbor, Maine, experiencing biology under actual research conditions. This so affected him that upon entering Swarthmore College in 1956 he declared himself a biology major. Later he switched to chemistry to complete a research thesis and graduated in 1960 with a B.A. and high honors. Between his sophomore and junior years at Swarthmore, he spent a summer at the Cold Spring Harbor Laboratories, where the influence of George Streisinger led him to molecular biology.

Baltimore spent two years of graduate work at Massachusetts Institute of Technology (MIT) in biophysics, then

left for a summer with Philip Marcus at the Albert Einstein Medical College and to take the animal virus course at Cold Spring Harbor under Richard Franklin and Edward Simon. He then joined Franklin at the Rockefeller Institute, completing his thesis by 1964 and staying on as a postdoctoral fellow in animal virology with James Darnell.

In 1965 he became a research associate at the Salk Institute of Biological Studies, working in association with Renato Dulbecco. Here he first met Alice S. Huang, with whom he also conducted research. He and Huang were married on October 5, 1968, and that same year they returned to MIT, where he held the position of associate professor of microbiology until 1971. In 1972 he rose to full professorship, and in 1974 he joined the staff of the MIT Center for Cancer Research under Salvador Luria.

Received Recognition For Cancer and Immunology Research

Baltimore received many awards for his work. In 1971 he was the recipient of the Gustav Stern award in virology, the Warren Triennial Prize, and the Eli Lilly and Co. award in microbiology and immunology. A year after being promoted to full professorship at MIT, he was rewarded a lifetime research professorship by the American Cancer Society. In 1974 he was presented with the U.S. Steel Foundation award in molecular biology and the Gairdner Foundation Annual Award. His most prestigious award came in 1975 when he shared the Nobel Prize in Physiology and Medicine with Howard M. Temin and Renato Dulbecco for research on retro-viruses and cancer. Much of this work concentrated upon protein and nucleic acid synthesis of RNA (ribonucleic acid) animal viruses, especially poliovirus and the RNA tumor virus. His research demonstrated that the flow of genetic information in such viruses did not have to go from DNA (deoxyribonucleic acid) to RNA but could flow from RNA to DNA, a finding which undermined the central dogma of molecular biology—i.e., unilinear information flow from DNA to proteins. This process came to be called, facetiously, "reverse transcriptase."

Baltimore's interests later took him further into the study of how viruses reproduce themselves and into work on the immune systems of animals and humans, where he concentrated upon the process by which antibodies may develop. Central to much of this work was DNA technology, in which he maintained an active interest.

Baltimore proved himself an effective educator, conducting seminars with graduate students and younger colleagues. He also became successful at directing research rather than doing it himself, again working closely with students.

Research Debacle

In 1989 Thereza Imanishi-Kari, a collegue with whom he co-authored a 1986 paper on immunology for *Cell,* was charged with falsifying data. Imanishi-Kari, a Massachussets Institute of Technology Assistant Professor, was absolved when a top government ethics panel declared they found no wrongdoing in 1996. Although Baltimore was never implicated in any wrongdoing, the incident caused him to withdraw the paper. He was also pressured by colleagues to resign from his presidency at New York's Rockefeller University, which he did in 1991.

Baltimore Chairs AIDS Vaccine Research Panel

In December 1996, Baltimore became the head of a new AIDS vaccine research panel for the Office of AIDS Research at the National Institute of Health. The panel was formed to step up the search for an AIDS vaccine. He also became the President of the California Institute of Technology in 1997.

Further Reading

Short biographies of David Baltimore can be found in the 39th edition of *Who's Who in America* (1976-1977) and in the 14th edition of *American Men and Women of Science: Physical and Biological Sciences* (1979). He provided an autobiographical sketch in the *Nobel Lectures* (1977), and a *New York Times* interview (August 26, 1980) gives additional information.

For further reading, see: *Appeals Panel Reverses Fraud Finding* by K. Fackelmann in *Science News,* July 6, 1996; *Baltimore to Head New Vaccine Panel* by Jon Cohen in *Science,* December 20, 1996; and *A Shot In the Arm* by Mark Schoofs, *The Village Voice,* December 24, 1996. □

Benjamin Banneker

Benjamin Banneker (1731-1806), an African American mathematician and amateur astronomer, calculated ephemerides for almanacs for the years 1792 through 1797 that were widely distributed.

On Nov. 9, 1731, Benjamin Banneker was born in Baltimore County, Md. He was the son of an African slave named Robert, who had bought his own freedom, and of Mary Banneky, who was the daughter of an Englishwoman and a free African slave. Benjamin lived on his father's farm and attended a nearby Quaker country school for several seasons. He received no further formal education but enjoyed reading and taught himself literature, history, and mathematics. He worked as a tobacco planter for most of his life.

In 1761, at the age of 30, Banneker constructed a striking wooden clock without having seen a clock before that time, although he had examined a pocket watch. The clock operated successfully until the time of his death.

At the age of 58 Banneker became interested in astronomy through the influence of a neighbor, George Ellicott, who lent him several books on astronomy as well as a telescope and drafting instruments. Without further guidance or assistance, Banneker taught himself the science of astronomy; he made projections for solar and lunar eclipses and computed ephemerides (tables of the locations of celestial bodies) for an almanac.

In February 1791 Maj. Andrew Ellicott was appointed to survey the 10-mile square of the Federal Territory for a new national capital, and Banneker worked in the field as his scientific assistant for several months. After the base lines and boundaries had been established and Banneker had returned home, he prepared an ephemeris for the following year, which was published in Baltimore in *Benjamin Banneker's Pennsylvania, Delaware, Maryland and Virginia Almanack and Ephemeris, for the Year of Our Lord, 1792; Being Bissextile, or Leap-Year, and the Sixteenth Year of American Independence, which commenced July 4, 1776.*

Banneker forwarded a manuscript copy of his calculations to Thomas Jefferson, then secretary of state, with a letter rebuking Jefferson for his proslavery views and urging the abolishment of slavery of the African American, which he compared to the enslavement of the American colonies by the British crown. Jefferson acknowledged Banneker's letter and forwarded the manuscript to the Marquis de Condorcet, the secretary of the Académie des Sciences in Paris. The exchange of letters between Banneker and Jefferson was published as a separate pamphlet and given wide publicity at the time the first almanac was published. The two letters were reprinted in Banneker's almanac for 1793, which also included "A Plan for an Office of Peace," which was the work of Dr. Benjamin Rush. The abolition societies of Maryland and Pennsylvania were largely instrumental in the publication of Banneker's almanacs, which were widely distributed as an example of the work of an African American that demonstrated the equal mental abilities of the races.

The last known issue of Banneker's almanacs appeared for the year 1797, because of diminishing interest in the antislavery movement; nevertheless, he prepared ephemerides for each year until 1804. He also published a treatise on bees and computed the cycle of the 17-year locust.

Banneker never married. He died on Oct. 9, 1806, and was buried in the family burial ground near his house. Among the memorabilia preserved was his commonplace book and the manuscript journal in which he had entered astronomical calculations and personal notations.

Banneker's memory was kept alive by writers who described his achievements as the first African American scientist. Recent studies have verified Banneker's status as an extremely competent mathematician and amateur astronomer.

Further Reading

Two good biographical studies of Banneker are Martha E. Tyson, *A Sketch of the Life of Benjamin Banneker* (1854), and her *Banneker: The Afric-American Astronomer,* edited by Anne T. Kirk (1884). All the available source material has been brought together in Silvio A. Bedini, *The Life of Benjamin Banneker* (1972). Other treatments include a brief account in John Hope Franklin, *From Slavery to Freedom: A History of American Negroes* (1947; 3d ed. 1967); Shirley Graham's fictionalized biography, *Your Most Humble Servant* (1949); Wilhemena S. Robinson's sketch in *Historical Negro Biographies* (1968); and a chapter in William J. Simmons, *Men of Mark: Eminent, Progressive and Rising* (1968). Banneker's famous letter to Thomas Jefferson is in vol. 1 of Milton Meltzer, ed., *In Their Own Words: A History of the American Negro, 1619-1865* (3 vols., 1964-1967). For general background see E. Franklin Frazier, *The Negro in The United States* (1949; rev. ed. 1963), and Winthrop D. Jordan's monumental *White over Black: American Attitudes toward the Negro, 1550-1812* (1968). □

Imamu Amiri Baraka

The African American author Imamu Amiri Baraka (born 1934 as Everett LeRoi Jones) became influential during the 1960s as a spokesperson for radical black literature and theater.

Born as Everett LeRoi Jones in Newark, New Jersey, on October 30, 1934, Baraka studied at Rutgers, Columbia, and Howard universities and at the New School for Social Research. After taking a bachelor of arts degree at Howard in 1953, he spent two years in the U.S. Air Force in Puerto Rico.

Baraka's life may be divided into two major periods. As a resident of New York City's Greenwich Village, LeRoi Jones led the life of a typical white American. He married a caucasian woman, Hettie Cohen, and they had two children. He and his wife published *Yugen,* a poetry magazine, and he coedited a literary newsletter, *Floating Bear.* Jones's political commitment began when he visited Cuba in 1960.

In 1965 Jones moved to Harlem and began the second period of his life. Here he lived a totally African American and separatist life. As founder and director of the Black Arts Repertory Theatre School, he made every aspect of his life "black" and opposite to the "white" life he had previously known.

Religious Conversion and Political Activism

Converted to the Kewaida sect of the Muslim faith, he took the name Imamu Amiri Baraka and moved to Newark, New Jersey. "Imamu" is the Swahili word for spiritual leader; "Amiri Baraka" is the Arabic name Jones adopted. In Newark he directed Spirit House, a religious, cultural, and educational black community. He lived with his second wife, their son, and his wife's three daughters by a previous marriage.

During the 1967 racial rebellions in Newark, Baraka was severely beaten and then arrested and charged with carrying a concealed weapon. The judge fined him $25,000 and read one of Baraka's poems, which he regarded as obscene, as justification for the exorbitant fine. National indignation was aroused by this injustice, and the fine was paid by the contributions of Baraka's supporters. He later appealed the case and won. The 1970 election of the African American Kenneth Gibson as mayor of Newark was due partly to Baraka's leadership of a fervent voter registration campaign among African Americans of the city.

As a black nationalist political leader, Baraka was a key figure in the organization of the Congress of African Peoples in 1970 and the National Black Political Assembly in 1972. Political writings during this period cover such topics as the

development of a black value system and black political institutions and include the essay collection *Raise, Race, Rays, Raze: Essays since 1965* (1971). However, by 1974 Baraka had undergone yet another reassessment of his cultural and political orientation. In a dramatic turnabout he rejected black nationalism and proclaimed himself a Marxist-Leninist-Maoist. After 1974 Baraka produced a great deal of socialist poetry and essays espousing revolutionary politics.

Literary Achievement

The most startling feature of Baraka's literary work is his arresting vocabulary, which communicates shocking states of emotion as well as ideas that indicate new intellectual dimensions and frontiers of the mind. He was a brilliant myth-maker, breaking icons and clichés and destroying the stereotypes and shibboleths of the old racist myth—the myth of race and sex in America. As poet, essayist, and playwright, he pressed for new cultural understanding in the turbulent society of modern America.

Baraka's writing reveals the influence of black music on his sensibilities. Jazz especially influenced the rhythms of his poetry, although the imagery and style of his early poetry reflect wide reading in classical poetry of all countries and especially the influence of contemporary "beat" poetry. However, his subject matter was from the start almost entirely the plight of African Americans.

During the 1960s Baraka wrote three volumes of poetry: *Preface to a Twenty Volume Suicide Note* (1961), *The Dead Lecturer* (1964), and *Black Magic Poetry* (1969). His

many plays of the period include *Dutchman* (1964), which won the Obie Award and marked the beginning of black revolutionary theater, *The Slave, Slave Ship, Arm Yrself or Harm Yrself or Harm Yrself, Jello,* and *The Toilet. Experimental Death Unit #1, A Black Mass, Great Goodness of Life,* and *Madheart* were published as *Four Black Revolutionary Plays* (1969). He authored three collections of nonfiction, *Blues People* (1963), *Home,* a group of social essays (1966), and *Black Music* (1967); a novel, *The System of Dante's Hell* (1965); and a group of short stories entitled *Tales* (1967). During this period he also edited *The Moderns: An Anthology of New Writing in America* (1963) and coedited an anthology of new African American writing, *Black Fire* (1968).

Later Works

While Baraka produced numerous political writings during the 1970s—some of which were later collected in 1984's *Daggers and Javelins: Essays, 1974 1979*—his literary efforts of the decade include the drama collection *The Motion of History, and Other Plays* (1978), as well as *The Sidnee Poet Heroical, in Twenty-Nine Scenes* (1979). A first *Selected Poetry* was issued in 1979 in addition to such later verse collections as *Reggae or Not! Poems* (1981) and *Transbluesency: The Selected Poems of Amiri Baraka/LeRoi Jones (1961-1995)* (1995). *Funk Lore* (1996) features poems written from 1984 to 1995. Both 1995's *Wise, Why's, Y's* and 1996's *Eulogies* offer his insight into notable African American figures of the 20th century. Baraka's autobiography was published in 1984.

Further Reading

Examinations of Baraka's literary achievement may be found in William J. Harris *The Poetry and Poetics of Amiri Baraka: The Jazz Aesthetic* (1985), Henry C. Lacey, *To Raise, Destroy, and Create: The Poetry, Drama, and Fiction of Imamu Amiri Baraka* (1981), Lloyd Wellesley Brown, *Amiri Baraka* (1980), Werner Sollors, *Amiri Baraka/LeRoi Jones: The Quest for a "Populist Modernism"* (1978), Kimberly W. Bentson, *Baraka: The Renegade and the Mask* (1978), Theodore R. Hudson, *From LeRoi Jones to Amiri Baraka: The Literary Works* (1973), and Robert Elliot Fox, *Conscientious Sorcerers: The Black Postmodernist Fiction of LeRoi Jones/Amiri Baraka, Ishmael Reed, and Samuel R. Delany* (1987). □

Phineas Taylor Barnum

Phineas Taylor Barnum (1810-1891), America's greatest showman of the 19th century, instructed and amused a nation with his museum and later his circus.

Speaking of his youth, P. T. Barnum said, "I was always ready to concoct fun, or lay plans for moneymaking, but hard work was decidedly not in my line." Indeed, he succeeded in making a great deal of money by working hard at having fun. His love of a joke came to him naturally. When he was born in Bethel, Conn., in 1810, his grandfather deeded him a parcel of land known as Ivy Island. The

growing boy was constantly reminded of his property. When he was 10 years old, he went to visit his estate and discovered it to be "a worthless piece of barren land."

Early Occupations and Joice Heth

When Phineas was 15, his father died, leaving his widow and five children penniless. Phineas immediately became clerk in a country store, where he learned the fine art of Yankee trading. During the next 10 years he was a shop owner, director of lotteries, and newspaper publisher. When he was 19 he eloped with a local seamstress, Charity Hallett (who would remain his wife for 44 years and give him four daughters). At 22, as publisher of the *Herald of Freedom,* he was jailed for libelously accusing a deacon of usury; upon his release 60 days later, Barnum was met by a band and "a coach drawn by six horses" for a parade back to town.

The embryo showman was developing, but it was not until 1835, when he encountered Joice Heth, that the Prince of Humbugs was born. Joice Heth was a disabled African American woman who, her sponsors claimed, was 160 years old and had been the infant George Washington's nurse. Seeing her possibilities as a human curiosity, Barnum purchased the right to exhibit her, along with the documents validating her age, and set her upon her couch in Niblo's Garden in New York City. She was extremely popular, but when interest began to flag, a newspaper item appeared suggesting that Joice was not human at all but an "automaton" made of whalebone, indian rubber, and springs. The exhibition hall was full once more, for Barnum

always knew how to use the news as well as the advertising sections of newspapers. Finally, upon her death in 1836, when an autopsy proved that Joice had been no more than 80 years old, Barnum was as surprised and indignant as anyone else. He had learned, however, that "the public appears disposed to be amused even when they are conscious of being deceived."

American Museum

For the next four years Barnum was an itinerant showman in the West and South. By 1840 he was back in New York, poor, weary of travel, and without prospects. When he heard that the struggling Scudder's American Museum (with its collection of curiosity) was for sale, Barnum determined to buy it. "With what?" asked a friend. "Brass," Barnum replied, "for silver and gold I have none." He mortgaged himself to the building's owner, proposing for collateral good references, a determination to succeed, and a "valuable and sentimental" piece of property known as Ivy Island. By the end of 1842 the museum was his, and a year later he was out of debt.

Barnum's American Museum was to become the most famous showplace of the century. Here, in constantly changing and elaborately advertised parade, the public could see educated dogs and fleas, automatons, jugglers, ventriloquists, living statuary, albinos, obese men, bearded women, a great variety of singing and dancing acts, models of Paris and Jerusalem, dioramas of the Creation and the Deluge, glassblowing, knitting machines, African Americans performing a war dance, conjoined twins, flower and bird shows, whales, mermaids, virtuous melodramas such as *The Drunkard,* a menagerie of rare animals, and an aquarium—"all for twenty-five cents, children half price."

His showman's delight in seeking out the splendid and the curious knew no bounds. "The one end aimed at," he said, "was to make people think, and talk, and wonder, and . . . go to the Museum." His Great Model of Niagara Falls with Real Water was actually 18 inches high; the Feejee Mermaid was really a monkey's head and torso fused to a fish's tail; the Woolly Horse of the Frozen Rockies had in truth been foaled in Indiana. Only half in jest did Barnum seek to buy Shakespeare's birthplace, hire the Zulu leader who had recently ambushed a British force, and tow an iceberg into New York harbor. Altogether, the museum showed over 600,000 exhibits during its existence.

Tom Thumb and Jenny Lind

General Tom Thumb was Barnum's greatest attraction. Charles S. Stratton, a native of Bridgeport, Conn., was 25 inches tall and weighed 15 pounds when he entered Barnum's employ in 1842. When he died in 1883, at the age of 45, he had made millions of dollars and delighted international audiences. In the first of Barnum's many European junkets the General entertained Queen Victoria, King Louis Philippe, and other royalty with his songs, dances, and impersonations in miniature. Of the 82 million tickets Barnum sold during his lifetime for various attractions, Tom Thumb sold over 20 million.

In 1850 Barnum turned impresario, introducing the most renowned singer of her time, Jenny Lind, to the American public. The immensely profitable tour of this gracious "Swedish Nightingale" was prepared with ingenious public relations but conducted with dignity and generosity by Barnum. Its success initiated the vogue of European concert artists visiting the United States.

Fires and Bankruptcy

Barnum's irrepressibility helped him overcome numerous professional misfortunes. Five times he was almost ruined by fire, but each time he recouped. In 1857 his famous house, Iranistan, fashioned after George IV's Pavilion at Brighton, burned to the ground. The original museum burned in 1865, and new museums burned in 1868 and again in 1872. Finally, in 1887, the great circus in its winter quarters, with most of its menagerie, was lost. But the showman's greatest financial catastrophe had nothing to do with show business. For years he had cherished the dream of building a city out of the farmland of East Bridgeport—a benevolent endeavor, he thought. In order to attract business, he signed some notes guaranteeing the debts of the Jerome Clock Company. As a result, he lost all he owned. Thus, in 1855, at the age of 46, the great Barnum was bankrupt. But he worked his way back, in part from successful lectures on "The Art of Money Getting," and by 1860 he was free of debt once more.

Throughout his life Barnum was a political liberal, serving in the Connecticut Legislature in the late 1860s, where he diligently fought the railroad interests, and as mayor of Bridgeport in 1875-1876. A year after the death of his first wife, Charity, in 1873, Barnum married Nancy Fish, an English woman 40 years his junior.

"The Greatest Show on Earth"

In April 1874 Barnum opened his Roman Hippodrome in New York; this was to grow into the great circus. He did not invent the circus, an ancient form of entertainment, but along with his enterprising young partner, James A. Bailey, whose circus merged with Barnum's in 1881, he made it a three-ring extravaganza the likes of which had never been seen before. Barnum's last great coup was his 1881 purchase from the London Zoo of the largest elephant in captivity, Jumbo. Violent objections by the English only made Jumbo and the circus that much more appealing. The variety and splendor of the show delighted the American audiences that Barnum had trained, over the years, to be delighted. In 1882 the circus opened its season in Madison Square Garden, where it was to become an American institution; and everywhere the "big top" traveled, a "Barnum Day" was declared. Circling the arena in an open carriage as leader of the parade always brought roars of approval (and great satisfaction) to the aging genius.

By 1891 Barnum's body began to fail, though not his spirit. His child's delight in the joke, the curious, and the splendid had set an entire nation to wondering and laughing and buying. A few weeks before his death, Barnum gave permission to the *Evening Sun* to print his obituary, so that he might have a chance to read it. On April 7 he asked

about the box office receipts for the day; a few hours later, he was dead.

Further Reading

Barnum's autobiography, *Struggles and Triumphs of P.T. Barnum* (1871; rev. ed. 1967), was frequently revised by Barnum until 1888. It is detailed, though somewhat self-righteous and therefore less appealing than Waldo Brown, ed., *Barnum's Own Story: The Autobiography of P. T. Barnum . . .* (1927; rev. ed. 1961). This work combines Barnum's first autobiographical venture of 1855, which offended some readers for its frank confession of humbugs, and the more staid book of 1871. Irving Wallace, *The Fabulous Showman: The Life and Times of P. T. Barnum* (1959), is one of the most interesting treatments, providing not only a history of Barnum's career but sketches of his most famous associates and an analysis of Barnum's happy effect upon American society of the 19th century. For a history of the circus see Earl C. May, *The Circus from Rome to Ringling* (1932), and Fred Bradna, *Big Top: My Forty Years with the Greatest Show on Earth* (1952). □

Richmond Barthé

Richmond Barthé (1901–1989) was a pioneer in American sculpture in the 1930s and 1940s in that he was one of the first African American artists to focus thematically on the lives of blacks, both in the United States and in Africa.

Trailblazing artist Richmond Barthé's sculpted works were seminal in that they focused on the lives of his fellow African Americans. He depicted African Americans at work in the fields of the South (*Woman with Scythe*, 1944), African Americans of distinction, and, in *Mother and Son* (1939), African Americans as victims of racial violence. He also sculpted images of African warriors and ceremonial participants.

Barthé was born on January 28, 1901, in Bay St. Louis, Mississippi, to Richmond Barthé, Sr., and Marie Clementine Robateau. His father died before Barthé was a year old, and his mother's sewing supported the family. She later remarried, to William Franklin, an old friend and Barthé's godfather. Franklin worked in various odd jobs, including as an ice man, delivering ice throughout the rural community. According to Barthé, he was artistically inclined from a very young age. In *A History of African American Artists*, he is quoted as saying, "When I was crawling on the floor, my mother gave me paper and pencil to play with. It kept me quiet and she did her errands. At six years old I started painting. A lady my mother sewed for gave me a set of watercolors. By that time I could draw pretty well."

As a teenager, Barthé's artistic talent had attracted attention among several of his mother's clients, and among his stepfather's ice customers as well. Barthé used to help in the delivery during the summer. One of the customers, who knew of and admired Barthé's work, told the young boy that he would injure himself carrying such large chunks of ice all day long. She arranged for him to get a job with the Pond family in New Orleans, a very wealthy family with several homes and an interest in supporting the arts. Barthé stayed

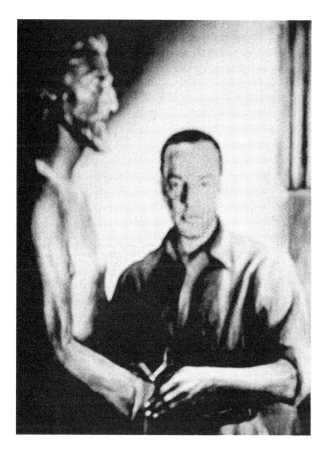

with the Ponds for several years, working as their houseboy while being encouraged to continue drawing and painting. Around this time, Barthé met Lyle Saxon, a writer working for the *New Orleans Times-Picayune,* and the two men became good friends. Saxon was very interested in Barthé's work and remained a champion of the artist after he became a well-known novelist.

Around 1923, a Catholic priest took an interest in Barthé's work and began looking for a local art school for him to attend. In the South, however, no school would admit a black, so the priest paid for Barthé to attend the prestigious Art Institute of Chicago. Here, Barthé rapidly developed as an artist, studying with several important teachers. Barthé's most influential teacher was Charles Schroeder. It was ultimately Schroeder who suggested that Barthé try sculpture. Schroeder did not intend to suggest that Barthé, who was mainly a painter then, shift his medium, but for him to incorporate three dimensions into his art. It turned out, however, that Barthé was a gifted sculptor, as was immediately apparent from the creation of his first busts in art school. An Art Institute show included three of his works. From that show, Barthé received his first commission as a sculptor. The Lake County Children's Home in Gary, Indiana, saw Barthé's work and hired him to do busts of Henry O. Tanner and Toussaint L'Ouverture for its home. Barthé, who had taken no classes in sculpting, thus began a career as a sculptor. His talents so impressed his teachers at the Institute that they advised him not to take any classes, fearing that formal training might ruin the creative spark in his work.

Having taken up sculpture, Barthé's began drawing the kind of critical attention artists dream about but rarely achieve at such a young age. In 1929, just out of art school, Barthé received an offer for a one-man show in New York, a tremendous honor. Barthé, however, was reluctant to accept, feeling he had not fully developed yet, not wanting to show in an important art center such as New York until he had refined his form more. Barthé declined the offer and spent a year studying at the Art Students League in New York. In 1930, after returning to Chicago, he had a large show at the Women's City Club. The show was a major success and it won him a Julius Rosenwald Fund fellowship.

In 1931, Barthé felt he was finally ready for a New York show and one was arranged at the Caz-Delbo Gallery, a prestigious showcase. Barthé's work at this show drew high praise and Barthé moved to the city when his Rosenwald fellowship was continued. In 1933, he exhibited at the Chicago World's Fair and, in 1934, Xavier University in New Orleans awarded him an honorary master of arts degree. In 1934, Barthé had a show at the Whitney Museum of American Art in New York, the preeminent contemporary art museum in the country. After the show, the museum purchased three of Barthé's sculptures for its permanent collection. By this time, Barthé was selling so much work that for the first time he could abandon side jobs and devote himself entirely to art.

Later in 1934, he went to Europe where the cultural heritage he observed fascinated him and where he also made several important sales to private collectors. In 1939, Barthé held his second one-man show in New York. It was his largest exhibition to date, including 18 bronze works, and was held at the Arden Galleries. Again, critical response was enthusiastic and on the strength of the work exhibited at these shows, Barthé was awarded a Guggenheim fellowship in 1940 and in 1941. In 1943, *The Boxer* was purchased by the Metropolitan Museum of Art in New York, America's largest and most important museum.

After the Second World War, the world of art began to change drastically, focusing on abstraction or distorted representations of reality. Barthé was not interested in these trends and was increasingly forgotten by the artistic establishment. As a result, Barthé began devoting much of his time to making portrait busts for wealthy New York clients, especially people involved in the theater. During and after the war, Barthé made busts of John Gielgud and Maurice Evans. Later works were of Lawrence Olivier, Katharine Cornell, and Judith Anderson. In 1946, he was inducted into the National Institute of Arts and Letters. By the end of the 1940s, Barthé had grown tired of the art scene in New York (and depressed over his exclusion from it) and he bought a house in Jamaica on the advice of his doctor who told him that living in the city was hurting his health.

Over the next several years, Barthé became a tourist attraction on the island, while continuing to work. In 1953, he completed a forty-foot statue for the city of Port au Prince, Haiti, depicting Jean Jacques Dessalines, leader of the 1804 revolution. He also designed several Haitian coins that are still in use. At first, Barthé enjoyed the prestige of being an expatriate black artist living in seclusion on a small

Caribbean island, but by 1969 he had grown restless and decided to move to Europe. He first went to Switzerland and then, in 1970, he moved to Florence. He stayed in Italy for the next seven years, then sold everything he owned and moved to California, where he rented an apartment from an admirer. Growing increasingly impoverished and old, and getting sick as well, Barthé became a charity case. The actor James Garner, who had only recently met him, was shocked that he should be living so poorly and began secretly paying his rent and medical expenses. Other artists and actors began to help Barthé too. The city of Pasadena renamed Barthé's street Barthé Drive. A fund-raising drive was also mounted to found the Barthé Historical Society and to fund thirty Barthé scholarships for artists.

Barthé's last known work was a bust of James Garner, made in appreciation for all of Garner's help late in Barthé's life. Barthé died on March 5, 1989.

Further Reading

Bearden, Romare, *A History of African American Artists, from 1792 to the present,* Pantheon Books, 1993.

Fine, Elsa Honig, "A Search for Identity," in *The Afro-American Artists,* Hacker Art Books, 1982.

New York Times, March 6, 1989. □

Count Basie

(William) Count Basie (1904-1984) was an extremely popular figure in the jazz world for half a century. He was a fine pianist and leader of one of the greatest jazz bands in history.

The story of Count Basie is very much the story of the great jazz band that he led for close to 50 years (1935-1984), an orchestra with a distinctive sound, anchored by a subtle but propulsive beat, buoyed by crisp ensemble work, and graced with superb soloists (indeed, a catalogue of featured players would read like a Who's Who of jazz). But perhaps the most startling aspect of the band's achievement was its 50-year survival in a culture that has experienced so many changes in musical fashion, and especially its survival after the mid-1960s when jazz lost much of its audience to rock music and disco.

William Basie was born in Red Bank, New Jersey, on August 21, 1904. His mother was a music teacher, and at a young age he became her pupil. But it was in Harlem, New York City, that he learned the rudiments of ragtime and stride piano, principally from his sometime organ teacher, the great Fats Waller. Basie made his professional debut as an accompanist for vaudeville acts. While on a tour of the Keith vaudeville circuit he was stranded in Kansas City. Here, in 1928, after a short stint as house organist in a silent movie theater, he joined Walter Page's Blue Devils, and when that band broke up in 1929, he was hired by Bennie Moten's Band and played piano with them, with one interruption, for the next five years.

Moten's death in 1935 altered Basie's career dramatically. He took over the remnants of the band (they called themselves The Barons of Rhythm) and, with some financial

and promotional support from impresario John Hammond, expanded the personnel and formed the first Count Basie Orchestra. Within a year or so the band had developed its own variation of the basic Kansas City swing style—a solidly pulsating rhythm underpinning the horn soloists, who were additionally supported by sectional riffing (i.e., the repetition of a musical figure by the non-soloing brass and reeds). This familiar pattern is evident in the band's theme song, "One O'Clock Jump," written by Basie himself in 1937, which has a subdued, expectant introduction by the rhythm section (piano, guitar, bass, and drums), then bursts into full orchestral support for a succession of stirring solos, and concludes with a full ensemble riffing out-chorus. Like any great swing band, Basie's was exciting in *any* tempo, and in fact one of the glories of his early period was a lugubrious, down-tempo blues called "Blue and Sentimental," which featured two magnificent solos (one by Herschel Evans on tenor saxophone and the other by Lester Young on clarinet) with full ensemble backing.

A Huge Success

By 1937 Basie's band was, with the possible exception of Duke Ellington's , the most highly acclaimed African American band in America. In the racially segregated context of the pre-World War II music business, African American bands never achieved the notoriety nor made the money that the famous white bands did. But some (Ellington's, Earl Hines's, Jimmy Lunceford's, Erskine Hawkins's, Chick Webb's, and Basie's, among them) did achieve a solid commercial success. Basie's band regularly worked some of the better big city hotel ballrooms and shared with many of the other 1,400 big bands of the Swing Era the less appetizing one-nighters (a series of single night engagements in a variety of small cities and towns that were toured by bus).

Some of the band's arrangements were written by trombonist Eddie Durham, but many were "heads"—arrangements spontaneously worked out in rehearsal and then transcribed. The band's "book" (repertory) was tailored not only to a distinctive orchestral style but also to showcase the band's brilliant soloists. Sometimes the arrangement was the reworking of a standard tune—"I got Rhythm," "Dinah," or "Lady, Be Good"—but more often a bandsman would come up with an original written expressly for the band and with a particular soloist or two in mind: two of Basie's earliest evergreens, "Jumpin' at the Woodside" and "Lester Leaps In" were conceived primarily as features for the remarkable tenor saxophonist Lester Young (nicknamed "Pres," short for "President") and were referred to as "flagwavers," up-tempo tunes designed to excite the audience.

Unquestionably the Swing Era band (1935-1945) was Basie's greatest: the superior arrangements (reflecting Basie's good taste) and the sterling performers (reflecting Basie's management astuteness) gave the band a permanent place in jazz history that even severe personnel setbacks couldn't diminish. Herschel Evans's death in 1939 was a blow, but he was replaced by another fine tenorist, Buddy Tate; a major defection was that of the nonpareil Lester Young ("Count, four weeks from tonight I will have been gone exactly fourteen days."), but his replacement was the superb Don Byas; the trumpet section had three giants—Buck Clayton, Harry "Sweets" Edison, and Bill Coleman—but only Edison survived the era as a Basie-ite.

Perhaps the band's resilience in the face of potentially damaging change can be explained by its model big band rhythm section, one that jelled to perfection—the spare, witty piano of Basie; the wonderful rhythm guitar of Freddie Green (who was with the band from 1937 to 1984); the rock-solid bass of Walter Page (Basie's former employer); and the exemplary drumming of Jo Jones. Nor was the band's excellence hurt by the presence of its two great blues and ballads singers, Jimmy Rushing and Helen Humes.

"April in Paris"

The loss of key personnel (some to the military service), the wartime ban on recordings, the 1943 musicians' strike, the economic infeasibility of one-nighters, and the bebop revolution of the mid-1940s all played a role in the death of the big band era. The number of 12 to 15 piece bands diminished drastically, and Basie was driven to some soul-searching: despite his international reputation and the band's still first-rate personnel, Basie decided in 1950 to disband and to form a medium-sized band (first an octet and later a septet), juggling combinations of all-star musicians, among them tenorists Georgie Auld, Gene Ammons, and Wardell Gray; trumpeters Harry Edison and Clark Terry; and clarinetist Buddy DeFranco. The groups' recordings (*Jam Sessions #2 & #3*) are, predictably, of the highest quality, but in 1951 Basie reverted to his first love—the big band—

and it thrived, thanks largely to the enlistment of two Basie-oriented composer-arrangers, Neil Hefti and Ernie Wilkins; to the solo work of tenorists Frank Wess and Frank Foster and trumpeters Joe Newman and Thad Jones; and to the singing of Joe Williams. Another boost was provided in the late 1950s by jazz organist Wild Bill Davis's arrangement of "April in Paris" which, with its series of "one more time" false endings, came to be a trademark of the band for the next quarter of a century.

A stocky, handsome, mustachioed man with heavy-lidded eyes and a sly, infectious smile, Basie in his later years took to wearing a yachting cap both off and on the bandstand. His sobriquet, "Count," was a 1935 promotional gimmick, paralleling "Duke" (Ellington) and "Earl" (Hines's actual first name). He was a shrewd judge of talent and character and, ever the realist, was extremely forbearing in dealing with the behavioral caprices of his musicians. His realistic vision extended as readily to himself: a rhythm-centered pianist, he had the ability to pick out apt chord combinations with which to punctuate and underscore the solos of horn players, but he knew his limitations and therefore gave himself less solo space than other, less gifted, leaders permitted themselves. He was, however, probably better than he thought; on a mid-1970s outing on which he was co-featured with tenor saxophone giant Zoot Sims he acquitted himself nobly.

Among Basie's many recordings perhaps the most essential are *The Best of Basie; The Greatest: Count Basie Plays . . . Joe Williams Sings Standards;* and *Joe Williams/ Count Basie: Memories Ad-Lib.* There are also excellent pairings of Basie and Ellington, with Frank Sinatra, with Tony Bennett, with Ella Fitzgerald, with Sarah Vaughan, and with Oscar Peterson.

In 1976 Basie suffered a heart attack, but returned to the bandstand half a year later. During his last years he had difficulty walking and so rode out on stage in a motorized wheelchair, his playing now largely reduced to his longtime musical signature, the three soft notes that punctuated his compositional endings. His home for many years was in Freeport, the Bahamas; he died of cancer at Doctors' Hospital in Hollywood, Florida, on April 26, 1984. His wife, Catherine, had died in 1983; they had one daughter. The band survived Basie's death, with ex-Basie-ite trumpeter Thad Jones directing until his death in 1986.

Further Reading

The best source for early Basie is Ross Russell's *Jazz Style in Kansas City & The Southwest* (1971). Two studies of the life of the band are Ray Horricks' *Count Basie & His Orchestra* and Stanley Dance's *The World of Count Basie* (1980), the latter a composite study of Basie and the band through bandsmen's memoirs. There is also a short biography, *Count Basie* (1985), by British jazz critic Alun Morgan. *Good Morning Blues: The Autobiography of Count Basie* as told to Albert Murray was published posthumously in 1985. □

George Wells Beadle

The American scientist, educator, and administrator George Wells Beadle (1903-1989) demonstrated the role of genes in the control of biochemical reactions in living organisms.

George Beadle was born on October 22, 1903, in Wahoo, Nebraska. He obtained an undergraduate degree in biology in 1926 and a master's degree in 1927 from the University of Nebraska, where he developed a specific interest in genetics, especially that of corn. Beadle continued graduate study at Cornell University under the joint guidance of geneticist R. A. Emerson and cytologist L. W. Sharp during a period when studies combining the methods of cytology and genetics were most profitable. After receiving a doctorate in 1931, he joined the California Institute of Technology, first as a fellow of the National Research Council and then, until 1936, as an instructor of biology. He later served Harvard University as an assistant professor of biology (1936-1937) and Stanford University as a professor of biology from 1937 to 1946.

Recombination and Gene Action

The two most puzzling problems in genetic research at that time involved the mechanisms by which recombination occurs between linked genes and the ways in which genes control the development of the hereditary traits for which they are responsible. Beadle's greatest successes came in studies of gene action, especially through the development of methods of experimentation permitting both extensive and selective observations of phenomena previously known only from sporadic spontaneous occurrences. Interactions between tissues of different genetic constitutions had been occasionally observed in spontaneously occurring mosaics. In 1935 Beadle and Boris Ephrussi at the Institut de Biologie Physico-Chimique in Paris succeeded in producing equivalent situations at will and involving any desired combination of genotypes by injecting organ buds from fruit fly (*Drosophila*) larvae into the body cavities of other larvae, where they continued to develop.

Enzyme-Gene Specificity

At about this time it was observed that, among species of microorganisms requiring a particular growth factor, some could use precursors not used by others. Presumably such differences were genetic, in which case it should be possible to induce mutations in genes responsible for nearly every step in the biosynthesis of every essential organic substance which could be fed to the organism. Selecting the mold *Neurospora* as an organism with suitable genetic and cultural characteristics, Beadle and E. L. Tatum in 1941 obtained definite support for that postulate. Afterwards the method became standard in biochemistry. Moreover, from the correlation between specific enzymes and specific genes, Beadle concluded that "each enzyme protein has its master pattern present in a gene." (It is now known that the master pattern is transferred to the enzyme through the agency of messenger ribonucleic acid.)

Later Career and Honors

In 1946 Beadle was recalled to the California Institute of Technology to direct the division of biology. He gave up his own research efforts at that time. In 1961 he became president of the University of Chicago, a position he maintained until his retirement in 1968. By then he had accumulated more than 30 honorary degrees from many universities around the country and had been awarded memberships into several prestigious academic societies. However, chief among his accolades remains the Nobel Prize for Physiology or Medicine, which he shared with Edward Lawrie Tatum and Joshua Lederberg in 1958 for his work on the "one gene-one enzyme" concept.

In the 1960s Beadle renewed his interest in the genetics of corn and became a prominent figure in the "corn wars," a debate among geneticists and archaeologists over the domestication of corn or maize in the Americas. Beadle contended that modern corn comes from a Mexican wild grass rather than a now-extinct species of maize. Beadle drew his conclusion from corn remains that show that domestication occurred at the time of the Mayans and Aztecs.

From 1968 to 1970 he directed the American Medical Association's Institute for Biomedical Research and from 1969 to 1972 served on the council of the National Academy of Science. He collaborated with his wife, Muriel Beadle, on the Edison Award-winning *The Language of Life: An Introduction to the Science of Genetics*. Beadle died June 9, 1989, in Pomona, California, at age 85 from complications of Alzheimer's disease.

Further Reading

Theodore L. Sourkes, *Nobel Prize Winners in Medicine and Physiology, 1901-1965* (rev. ed. 1967), contains a biographical sketch of Beadle and a description of his prize-winning work. Additional information is contained in Tyler Wasson, *Nobel Prize Winners* (1987) and in Maria Szekely, *From DNA to Protein* (1980). □

Romare Howard Bearden

The American painter-collagist Romare Howard Bearden (1914-1988) was a leading abstractionist until racial strife in the United States led him to focus more directly on African American subject matter, with related changes in his style and technique.

An only child, Romare Bearden was born on September 2, 1914, in Charlotte, North Carolina. When he was still a child, the family moved to Harlem, New York City, where his mother was a well-known journalist and political activist. He received a bachelor of science degree from New York University because, he said, "I thought I wanted to be a medical doctor." E. Simms Campbell, the renowned African American cartoonist, encouraged him to study painting with George Grosz, the German-born painter and satirical draftsman, at the Art Students' League in New York. "It was Grosz," Bearden remembered with gratitude, "who first introduced me to classical draftsmen like Hogarth and Ingres." Essential as formal institutions were to his development as a person and an artist, his association with African American artists and intellectuals of the Depression period cannot be minimized. Among these were the painters Norman Lewis and Jacob Lawrence and the writer Ralph Ellison, who maintained an atmosphere of social and political concern which heavily influenced Bearden's early work. Even though his concern for these problems in no way diminished later and all his works abound in ethnic subject matter, the mild-mannered, almost shy artist insisted that he was not a social propagandist. "My subject is people," he said. "They just happen to turn out to be Negro."

Early in his career he emulated the styles of Rufino Tamayo and José Clemente Orozco, painting simple forms and echoing the crude power he had come to admire in medieval art. His paintings of everyday black life were forceful in color; the figures followed simple patterns and their statements were literal, as in graphic art rather than painting. By 1945 he had begun to adopt a less literal, more personal style, which proved to be the most congenial for his unique artistic expressions. In the 1950s, while working as a New York City Welfare Department investigator, he expressed his feelings in lyrical abstractions.

First Solo Shows Bring Recognition

Caresse Crosby launched Bearden in her Washington, D.C., gallery in 1945, following his service in World War II. In his first one-person show in New York the same year, 18 works were sold during the first two weeks, and the critics were ecstatic in their praise, calling his work "vibrant," "propulsive," and "poetic." There were subsequent invitations to exhibit, including solo shows in Paris and New York.

By 1960 Bearden's personal style had firmly caught the imagination of the art world. Drawing on his boyhood memories of the Deep South and his experiences as a long-time resident of Harlem, he depicted the conditions in which African Americans lived with such stark reality that the collage or montage became a powerfully emotive art form. With the skill of a master, he made formidable use of disparate elements of photographs and documentary film, resulting in an uncommon immediacy in his work that extended its meaning.

Influenced by the Civil Rights Movement

The early 1960s brought a period of transition for Bearden. In 1963 a group of African American artists began meeting in his Harlem studio. Calling themselves the Spiral Group, they sought to define their roles as black artists within the context of the growing civil rights movement.

His "Projections" series, exhibited in 1964, caused a wave of controversy and excitement. The tormented faces of African American women hanging upside down on the cracked stoops of Harlem tenements, New York bridges soaring out of Carolina cotton fields, and African pyramids colliding with American folk singers strumming guitars prompted one critic to write that the show comprised "a collection of headhunters." These startling images, constructed from newspaper and magazine photographs, had been enlarged from their original color into huge black-and-white photographs that provided the artist's desired effect of urgency.

The shock turned into solid success that brought Bearden many honors, including cover commissions for *Time, Fortune,* and the *New York Times* magazines; the National Institute of Arts and Letters achievement award (1966); and a 1970 Guggenheim Memorial Fellowship to write a history of African American art. In 1969 his book *The Painter's Mind* (Carl Holty, coauthor) was published. He also wrote a biography of Henry O. Tanner, the towering but unheralded African American artist of the late 19th and early 20th centuries.

His first full-scale exhibition in a European museum was held in May 1971 at the Rath Museum in Geneva, Switzerland. In his widely acclaimed "Prevalence of Ritual" retrospective at New York's Museum of Modern Art, also held in 1971, many of the works displayed were collage paintings.

Focus on African American Life in the 1970s and 1980s

The primary subject of the last 25 years of Bearden's art was the life and culture of African Americans. His work covered rural themes based on his memories of the South as well as urban life and jazz. In the 1980s he produced a large body of work featuring compelling images of women. For many years he spent time annually on the Caribbean island of St. Martin, which brought tropical images to his work.

In 1986 Bearden was commissioned by the Detroit Institute of Arts to celebrate its centennial. He executed a mosaic mural, done in mosaic glass, titled "Quilting Time". The work is typical of Bearden in that it is rooted in his memories of his southern childhood and depicts an important aspect of African American culture. The brightly colored mosaic shows a group of women making a quilt. His use of mosaic tile late in his career developed from the technique of building his forms with very small pieces of paper, called *tesserae*. Since the paper was so fragile, Bearden preferred using mosaic tile for large public works.

Honors and Legacy

Bearden received the Medal of Arts from President Ronald Reagan in 1987. Less than a year later, on March 11, 1988, Bearden died of bone cancer in New York City. His estate made provisions for the establishment of the Romare Bearden Foundation to aid in the education and training of talented art students.

"Memory and Metaphor: The Art of Romare Bearden, 1940-1987" was a major retrospective show containing nearly 150 works from Bearden's half-century career in the visual arts. Beginning at the Studio Museum in Harlem in 1991, the show traveled through 1993 to major museums in Chicago, Los Angeles, Atlanta, Pittsburgh, and finally the National Museum of American Art in Washington, D.C. His massive survey *A History of African-American Artists from 1792 to the Present* was posthumously published in 1993.

Further Reading

A complete examination of Bearden and his work is available in Myron Schwartzman, *Romare Bearden: His Life and Art* (1990). Additional information on Bearden's career may be found in Elton C. Fax, *Black Artists of the New Generation* (1977), Sharon F. Patton, *Memory and Metaphor: The Art of Romare Bearden, 1940- 1987* (1991), and the Smithsonian Institution's, *African American Visual Aesthetics: A Postmodernist View* (1995). □

Harrison Begay

Harrison Begay (born 1917) is a Navajo artist who specializes in watercolors and silkscreen prints.

Harrison Begay is one of the most famous of all Navajo painters. His watercolors and silkscreen prints have been widely collected. His work, which has won 13 major awards, has a sinuous delicacy of line and is noted for its meticulous detail, restrained palette, and elegance of composition. His style has been so influential that disciples, like Baji Whitethorne, say that by studying his paintings one learns not only technique but also religion. The Navajo conception of the orderly balance of irreconcilable forces is exemplified in Begay's style, which is at once serenely still and vitally active.

Herds Family's Sheep

Harrison Begay was born on November 15, 1917, at White Cone, Arizona, to Black Rock and Zonnie Tachinie Begay. His mother belonged to the Red Forehead Clan, and his father adopted the Zuni Deer Clan. He was said to have been related to Manuelita, an esteemed medicine man. The boy herded his family's flock of sheep near Greasewood, where he still lives. In 1927, he was sent to school at Fort Wingate, from which he ran away to spend the next four years at home, studying alone as he tended the sheep. In 1934, he attended Fort Defiance Indian School in New Mexico, and later Tohatchi Indian School. He graduated from high school in 1939 as salutatorian.

The institution that conferred distinction upon him was Dorothy Dunn's studio at the Santa Fe Indian School. Among Begay's classmates were other Navajo painters: Gerald Nailor, Quincy Tahoma, and Andy Tsinajinnie. They were taught to depict pastoral landscapes and tribal traditions in smoothly-brushed forms placed flat on the picture plane. In *American Indian Painting,* Dunn summed up Begay's work as "at once decorative and lifelike, his color clear in hue and even in value, his figures placid yet inwardly animated. . . . [H]e seemed to be inexhaustibly resourceful in a quiet reticent way."

In 1940, Begay married Ramona Espinosa; the couple divorced in 1945. Also in 1940, he attended Black Mountain College in Blueridge, North Carolina, to study architecture for one year. In 1941, he enrolled in Phoenix Junior College in Arizona.

Serves in the United States Army

Begay was one of the 21,767 Native American veterans of the U.S. Army in World War II. From 1942 to 1945, Begay served in the signal corps. He participated in the Normandy campaign and was stationed in Iceland and in Europe. Upon his discharge, he stayed in Colorado until September of 1947. While there, he was briefly tutored by an artist in Denver. The army had trained him to be a radio technician, but his artistic talent enabled him to make a living as a full-time painter since his return to the reservation in 1947.

Works in Arts and Crafts Shops

He was given space to paint at Clay Lockett's Arts and Crafts Shop in Tucson, Arizona. He also painted in Parkhurst's Shop in Santa Fe, New Mexico, and in Woodard's Shop in Gallup, New Mexico. He prefers to work in watercolors, usually casein paints because oil painting takes too long. A prolific artist, he regularly exhibits at the Philbrook Art Center each May, and at the Gallery in New Mexico that sponsors exhibits for five days in August each year at the Intertribal Indian Ceremonials. He won two grand awards at the Intertribal festivities and has been a consistent winner at state and tribal fairs. The French government honored him with its Palmes d'Academiques in 1945.

Begay cofounded TEWA Enterprises, which made silkscreen prints of his work. His fine-lined, flat-colored designs were eminently suitable for serigraph reproduction. This method of duplication also made his work affordable to the general public. Begay has also specialized in sensitive renditions of animals such as fawns, antelope, deer, sheep, and horses. He is also fond of depicting looms as subjects, as in his often reproduced painting, "Two Weavers" of 1946.

In 1959, Begay had an Enemyway chant performed for him. He paid the singer who conducted the rite to protect warriors against the ghosts of slain enemies with a set of three paintings of the Navajo sacred mountains. A similar set of the four sacred mountains, each associated with a different color and a different direction, is now owned by the Museum of Northern Arizona at Flagstaff. In order to compose these paintings, Begay studied the Navajo origin myths recorded by Washington Matthews.

Begay also illustrated Ann Cromwell's *A Hogan for the Bluebird,* published in 1969. Cromwell's piece of Navajo fiction tells of a Navajo Indian girl who finds it difficult to readjust to the ways of her people after several years at the mission school.

In addition to Begay's considerable achievements in the art world, he is also the state champion long distance runner, having broken the record in the mile race.

Further Reading

Dockstader, Frederick J., *Indian Art in America,* Greenwich, Connecticut, New York Graphic Society, 1966.

Dunn, Dorothy, *American Indian Painting,* Albuquerque, University of New Mexico Press, 1968.

Fawcett, David M., and Lee A. Callander, *Native American Painting: Selections from the Museum of the American Indian,* Emerson, New Jersey, ALE Associates, 1982.

Wade, Edwin L., *The Arts of the North American Indian: Native Traditions in Evolution,* New York, Hudson Hills Press, 1986.

Wyman, Leland C., "Navajo Ceremonial System," in *Handbook of the North American Indians,* Volume 10, edited by Alfonso Ortiz, Washington, D.C., Smithsonian Institution, 1983. □

Alexander Graham Bell

Scottish-born American inventor and teacher of the deaf, Alexander Graham Bell (1847-1922) is best known for perfecting the telephone to transmit vocal messages by electricity. The telephone inaugurated a new age in communication technology.

Alexander Graham Bell was born on March 3, 1847, in Edinburgh. His father, Alexander Melville Bell, was an expert in vocal physiology and elocution; his grandfather, Alexander Bell, was an elocution professor.

After studying at the University of Edinburgh and University College, London, Bell became his father's assistant. He taught the deaf to talk by adopting his father's system of visible speech (illustrations of speaking positions of the lips and tongue). In London he studied Hermann Ludwig von Helmholtz's experiments with tuning forks and magnets to produce complex sounds. In 1865 Bell made scientific studies of the resonance of the mouth while speaking.

In 1870 the Bells moved to Brantford, Ontario, Canada, to preserve Alexander's health. He went to Boston in 1871 to teach at Sarah Fuller's School for the Deaf, the first such school in the world. He also tutored private students, in-

Alexander Graham Bell (on phone)

cluding Helen Keller. As professor of vocal physiology and speech at Boston University in 1873, he initiated conventions for teachers of the deaf. Throughout his life he continued to educate the deaf, and he founded the American Association to Promote the Teaching of Speech to the Deaf.

From 1873 to 1876 Bell experimented with a phonautograph, a multiple telegraph, and an electric speaking telegraph (the telephone). Funds came from the fathers of two of his pupils; one of these men, Gardiner Hubbard, had a deaf daughter, Mabel, who later became Bell's wife.

Inventing the Telephone

To help deaf children, Bell experimented in the summer of 1874 with a human ear and attached bones, a tympanum, magnets, and smoked glass. He conceived the theory of the telephone: an electric current can be made to change intensity precisely as air density varies during sound production. Unlike the telegraph's use of intermittent current, the telephone requires continuous current with varying intensity. That same year he invented a harmonic telegraph, to transmit several messages simultaneously over one wire, and a telephonic-telegraphic receiver. Trying to reproduce the human voice electrically, he became expert with electric wave transmission.

Bell supplied the ideas; Thomas Watson made and assembled the equipment. Working with tuned reeds and magnets to synchronize a receiving instrument with a sender, they transmitted a musical note on June 2, 1875.

Bell's telephone receiver and transmitter were identical: a thin disk in front of an electromagnet.

On Feb. 14, 1876, Bell's attorney filed for a patent. The exact hour was not recorded, but on that same day Elisha Gray filed his caveat (intention to invent) for a telephone. The U.S. Patent Office granted Bell the patent for the "electric speaking telephone" on March 7. It was the most valuable single patent ever issued, and it opened a new age in communication technology.

Bell continued his experiments to improve the telephone's quality. By accident, Bell sent the first sentence, "Watson, come here; I want you," on March 10, 1876. The first demonstration occurred at the American Academy of Arts and Sciences convention in Boston 2 months later. Bell's display at the Philadelphia Centennial Exposition a month later gained more publicity, and Emperor Dom Pedro of Brazil ordered 100 telephones for his country. The telephone, accorded only 18 words in the official catalog of the exposition, suddenly became the "star" attraction.

Establishing an Industry

Repeated demonstrations overcame public skepticism. The first reciprocal outdoor conversation was between Boston and Cambridge, Mass., by Bell and Watson on Oct. 9, 1876. In 1877 the first telephone was installed in a private home; a conversation was conducted between Boston and New York, using telegraph lines; in May, the first switchboard, devised by E. T. Holmes in Boston, was a burglar alarm connecting five banks; and in July the first organization to commercialize the invention, the Bell Telephone Company, was formed. That year, while on his honeymoon, Bell introduced the telephone to England and France.

The first commercial switchboard was set up in New Haven, Conn., in 1878, and Bell's first subsidiary, the New England Telephone Company, was organized that year. Switchboards were improved by Charles Scribner, with more than 500 inventions. Thomas Cornish, a Philadelphia electrician, had a switchboard for eight customers and published a one-page directory in 1878.

Contesting Bell's Patent

Other inventors had been at work. Between 1867 and 1873 Professor Elisha Gray (of Oberlin College) invented an "automatic self-adjusting telegraph relay," installed it in hotels, and made telegraph printers and repeaters. He tried to perfect a speaking telephone from his harmonic (multiple-current) telegraph. The Gray and Batton Manufacturing Company of Chicago developed into the Western Electric Company.

Another competitor was Professor Amos E. Dolbear, who insisted that Bell's telephone was only an improvement on an 1860 invention by Johann Reis, a German, who had experimented with pigs' ear membranes and may have made a telephone. Dolbear's own instrument, operating by "make and break" current, could transmit pitch but not voice quality.

In 1879 Western Union, with its American Speaking Telephone Company, ignored Bell's patents and hired Thomas Edison, along with Dolbear and Gray, as inventors and improvers. Later that year Bell and Western Union formed a joint company, with the latter getting 20 percent for providing wires, circuits, and equipment. Theodore Vail, organizer of Bell Telephone Company, consolidated six companies in 1881. The modern transmitter evolved mainly from the work of Emile Berliner and Edison in 1877 and Francis Blake in 1878. Blake's transmitter was later sold to Bell for stock.

The claims of other inventors were contested. Daniel Drawbaugh, from rural Pennsylvania, with little formal schooling, almost won a legal battle with Bell in 1884 but was defeated by a 4 to 3 vote in the Supreme Court. The claim by this "Edison of the Cumberland Valley" was the most exciting (and futile) litigation over telephone patents. Altogether, the Bell Company was involved in 587 lawsuits, of which 5 went to the Supreme Court; Bell won every case. A convincing argument was that no competitor claimed originality until 17 months after Bell's patent. Also, at the 1876 Philadelphia Exposition, eminent electrical scientists, especially Lord Kelvin, the world's foremost authority, had declared it to be "new." Professors, scientists, and researchers defended Bell, pointing to his lifelong study of the ear and his books and lectures on speech mechanics.

The Bell Company

The Bell Company built the first long-distance line in 1884, connecting Boston and New York. The American Telephone and Telegraph Company was organized by Bell and others in 1885 to operate other long-distance lines. By 1889, when insulation was perfected, there were 11,000 miles of underground wires in New York City.

The Volta Laboratory was started by Bell in Washington, D.C., with the Volta Prize money (50,000 francs, about $10,000) awarded by France for his invention. At the laboratory he and associates worked on various projects during the 1880s, including the photophone, induction balance, audiometer, and phonograph improvements. The photophone transmitted speech by light, using a primitive photoelectric cell. The induction balance (electric probe) located metal in the body. The audiometer indicated Bell's continued interest in deafness. The first successful phonograph record, a shellac cylinder, as well as wax disks and cylinders, was produced. The Columbia Gramophone Company exploited Bell's phonograph records. With the profits Bell established the Volta Bureau in Washington to study deafness.

Bell's Later Interests

Other activities took much time. The magazine *Science* (later the official organ of the American Association for the Advancement of Science) was founded in 1880 because of Bell's efforts. He made numerous addresses and published many monographs. As National Geographic Society president from 1896 to 1904, he fostered the success of the society and its publications. In 1898 he became a regent of the Smithsonian Institution. He was also involved in sheep breeding, hydrodynamics, and aviation projects.

Aviation was Bell's primary interest after 1895. He aided Samuel Langley, invented the tetrahedral kite (1903), and founded the Aerial Experiment Association (1907), bringing together Glenn Curtiss, Francis Baldwin, and others. They devised the aileron control principle (which replaced "wing warping"), developed the hydroplane, and solved balance problems in flying machines. Curtiss furnished the motor for Bell's man-carrying kite in 1907.

Bell died at Baddeck, Nova Scotia, on Aug. 2, 1922.

Further Reading

Catherine D. MacKenzie, *Alexander Graham Bell* (1928), is interesting and contains much personal information. Thomas Bertram Costain, *Chord of Steel* (1960), a recent history of the telephone, discusses Bell at length. Herbert Casson, *The History of the Telephone* (1910), is still useful for the early story. See also Arthur Pound, *The Telephone Idea. Fifty Years After* (1926), and Frederick Leland Rhodes, *Beginnings of Telephony* (1929). For the story of Bell's persistent rival see Warren J. Harder, *Daniel Drawbaugh* (1960). □

Saul Bellow

An American author of fiction, essays, and drama, Saul Bellow (born 1915) reached the first rank of contemporary fiction with his picaresque novel *The Adventures of Augie March*.

Saul Bellow, born of Russian immigrant parents in Lachine, Quebec, on July 10, 1915, grew up in Montreal, where he learned Hebrew, Yiddish, and French as well as English. When he was nine his family moved to Chicago, and to this city Bellow remained deeply devoted. After two years at the University of Chicago, Bellow transferred to Northwestern University and obtained a bachelor of science degree in 1937. Four months after enrolling as a graduate student at the University of Wisconsin, he fled formal education forever.

During the next decade Bellow held a variety of jobs—with the WPA Writers Project, the editorial department of the *Encyclopaedia Britannica,* the Pestalozzi-Froebel Teachers College, and the Merchant Marine. More importantly, he published two novels, both with autobiographical overtones. *Dangling Man* (1944), in the form of a journal, concerns a young Chicagoan waiting to be drafted into military service. *The Victim* (1947), a more ambitious work, describes the frustrations of a New Yorker seeking to discover and preserve his own identity against the background of domestic and religious (Gentile versus Jewish) conflicts. Neither novel was heralded as exceptional by contemporary critics.

After World War II Bellow joined the University of Minnesota English Department, spent a year in Paris and Rome as a Guggenheim fellow, and taught briefly at New York University, Princeton University, and Bard College. Above all, however, he concentrated on writing fiction. With the publication of *The Adventures of Augie March* (1953), Bellow won his first National Book Award. A lengthy, free-form liberating story of a young Chicago Jew

growing up absurd, *Augie March* combines comic zest and a narrative virtuosity rare in any decade. Bellow followed it in 1956 with *Seize the Day,* which is a collection of three short stories, a one-act play, and the novella that gives the title to the volume—a tautly written description of one day in the life of a middle-aged New Yorker facing a major domestic crisis. Some critics feel that Bellow never surpassed this novella.

Devotees of *Henderson the Rain King* (1959) enjoyed Bellow's return to a more free-flowing manner in describing an American millionaire's search to understand the human condition in his flight from a tangled marital arrangement and his adventures in Africa. His next novel, *Herzog* (1964), won him a second National Book Award and an international reputation. Doubtlessly based on personal sources, it portrays Moses Herzog, a middle-aged university professor, and his battles with his faithless wife Madeline, his friend Valentine Gersbach, and his own alienated self. Through a series of unposted letters, many of them highly comic, Herzog finally resolves his struggles, not in marital reconciliation but in rational acceptance and self-control.

In 1962 Bellow became a professor at the University of Chicago, a post which allowed him to continue writing fiction and plays. *The Last Analysis* had a brief run on Broadway in 1964. Six short stories, collected in *Mosby's Memoirs and Other Stories* (1968), and his sixth novel, *Mr. Sammler's Planet* (1969), elevated Bellow's reputation to the point where one critic wrote that if Bellow was not the most important American novelist, then whoever was had better announce himself quickly. Some critics called him the successor of Ernest Hemingway and William Faulkner.

Humboldt's Gift (1975) added the Pulitzer Prize and the Nobel Prize for Literature to Bellow's list of awards and led Frank McConnell to observe that his books "form a consistent, carefully nurtured *oeuvre* not often encountered in the works of American writers." In her glowing review of his short story collection, *Him with His Foot in His Mouth and Other Stories* (1984), Cynthia Ozick declared: "these five ravishing stories honor and augment his genius."

Bellow's later novels have not received the same unequivocal praise. *The Dean's December* (1982) and *More Die of Heartbreak* (1987) retained his distinctive style but some believed the cynicism of the characters signaled a lessening of Bellow's own trademark humanism.

Since 1987, Bellow has released a number of novellas: *A Theft* (1989), *The Bellarosa Connection* (1989), *Something to Remember Me By* (1991), and *The Actual* (1997). These works have met with similarly mixed reviews.

Despite the recent coolness towards his work, Bellow's place in American literature seems secure, most notably for his ability to combine social commentary with sharply drawn characters. His best fiction has been compared to the Russian masters, Tolstoy and Dostoevsky.

Robert Penn Warren's review of *Augie March* in *The New Republic* in 1953 seems to sum up subsequent reaction to his work: "It is, in a way, a tribute, though a back-handed one, to point out the faults of Saul Bellow's novel, for the faults merely make the virtues more impressive."

Further Reading

Full-length studies of Saul Bellow include Keith Michael Opdahl, *The Novels of Saul Bellow: An Introduction* (1967); John Jacob Clayton, *Saul Bellow: In Defense of Man* (1968); and Irving Malin, *Saul Bellow's Fiction* (1969). Useful introductory essays are Tony Tanner, *Saul Bellow* (1965); Earl Rovit, *Saul Bellow* (1967); and Robert Detweiler, *Saul Bellow: A Critical Essay* (1967). Irving Malin edited a collection of 12 essays, *Saul Bellow and the Critics* (1967). Another essay collection, edited by Harold Bloom, is *Saul Bellow* (1986). □

William John Bennett

The American teacher and scholar William John Bennett (born 1943) was chairman of the National Endowment for the Humanities (1981-1985), secretary of the Department of Education (1985-1988), and director of the Office of National Drug Control Policy (1989-1990) During the 1990s he was codirector of Empower America and an active spokesperson for conservatism.

William John Bennett was born in Flatbush (Brooklyn), New York, on July 3, 1943. His family was middle-class and Roman Catholic. He grew up on the streets of Flatbush and described himself as "streetwise." He first attended PS 92 but later transferred to Jesuit-run Holy Cross Boy's School. His family moved to Washington, D.C., where he graduated from Gonzaga High School, another Catholic institution.

Bennett was mostly raised by his mother, but he early found inspiration in such male American heroes as Abraham Lincoln, Roy Campenella, and Gary Cooper. From these life stories he derived an axiom that heroes are necessary for moral development of children and that this development requires adult guidance as well as inspiration. His high school football coach also provided a role model of mental and physical toughness and convinced Bennett of the value of competitive sports.

Bennett went to Williams College to play football. He was an interior lineman who earned the nickname "the ram" from an incident where he butted down a coed's door. He worked his way through Williams, and later through graduate school, with scholarships and part-time and summer jobs and with student loans that finally totaled $12,000.

Graduating in 1965, he studied philosophy at the University of Texas and wrote a dissertation on the theory of the social contract. (At that time John R. Silber was chairman of the Department of Philosophy and later dean of the College of Arts and Sciences.) He did not study all the time. In 1967 he had a blind date with Janis Joplin, and he also played guitar with a rock and roll band called Plato and the Guardians. While working on his Ph.D., which he earned in 1970, Bennett taught philosophy and religion at the University of Southern Mississippi for a year (1967-1968). He went on to study law at Harvard University, and worked as a social studies tutor and hall proctor (1970-1971) until he earned his J.D. degree.

He then moved across town to Boston University, where Silber had just become president. There he served as an associate dean of the College of Liberal Arts for a year (1971-1972) before becoming an assistant professor of philosophy and an assistant to Silber from 1972 to 1976. One of his duties was to escort military recruiters through crowds of antiwar protesters, a duty made easier by his football training.

Opening the Door to Government Service

Meanwhile, he was becoming better known nationally. He served on a review panel for the National Endowment for the Humanities (NEH) in 1973 and was chairman of the "Question of Authority in American High Schools" project of the National Humanities Faculty, a conservative group, the same year. He next was associate chairman of the group's bicentennial study, "The American Covenant: The Moral Uses of Power." He was also writing articles. Among these were "In Defense of Sports" in *Commentary* (February 1976); "The Constitution and the Moral Order" in *Hastings Constitutional Law Quarterly* (Fall 1976); and "Let's Bring Back Heroes" in *Newsweek* (April 15, 1977).

In May 1976 he became executive director of the National Humanities Center, which he had co-founded with Charles Frankel, a philosophy professor from Columbia University who took the office of president. When intruders murdered Frankel in 1979, Bennett assumed Frankel's position as well. The same year he co-authored *Counting by Race: Equality from the Founding Fathers to Bakke and Weber* with the journalist Terry Eastland. The book attacked affirmative action and the Supreme Court for legitimizing it.

A registered Democrat who described himself as sympathetic to "neoconservative" causes, Bennett drafted the arts and humanities section of the Heritage Fund"s *Mandate for Leadership* (1980), a series of recommendations for President-elect Ronald Reagan. He became a Republican and was rewarded by Reagan, who appointed him to replace Joseph Duffy as head of NEH in December 1981. One of his rivals for the job was Silber. As director, Bennett proved abrasive and controversial. He acceded to Reagan's budget cuts for the agency and criticized faddish projects, including three documentaries made with NEH funds: "From the Ashes . . . Nicaragua Today," "Women Under Siege," and "Four Corners, A National Sacrifice Area?" He argued for a return to a strict definition of the humanities and promoted summer seminars for high school teachers. His major goal, to teach students the core of Western values, appeared in *To Reclaim a Legacy: A Report on the Humanities in Higher Education* in November 1984. This report, along with Bennett's refusal to comply with Equal Employment Opportunity Commission affirmative action goals at NEH, earned him the enmity of women's and civil rights groups.

In November 1984 the office of secretary of the Department of Education became open when T. H. Bell resigned under right-wing pressure. Reagan had wanted to abolish the position, but decided instead to appoint Bennett after such conservatives as Jerry Falwell approved of him. In February 1985 he assumed the position.

Controversy in Two Jobs

Bennett proved even more controversial as the secretary of the Department of Education than he was at NEH. In his first press conference he supported Reagan's cuts in the student loan program, saying that some individuals should not go to college and that others should divest themselves of stereos, automobiles, and three weeks at the beach. Later the same year Americans United for the Separation of Church and State sued to force him to observe the Supreme Court ruling that public school teachers could not teach remedial education at private schools at federal expense. He attacked the educational establishment; said some colleges and universities were overpriced; deplored the high rate of student loan defaults, particularly in proprietary schools; and denounced Stanford University's revised curriculum, which de-emphasized Western civilization in favor of a broader study of world cultures.

He favored education vouchers, merit pay, and a constitutional amendment mandating the federal government to remain neutral in the matter of school prayer. He emphasized moral education based upon the Judeo-Christian ethic while denouncing values clarification and cognitive moral development. He remained in the limelight with appearances as a substitute teacher of social studies in a number of city schools and with many speeches and articles in the popular press. He was the author of *First Lessons: A Report on Elementary Education,* published by the U.S. Office of Education in 1987, which lists his personal convictions concerning elementary education. The same ideas appear in *Our Children and Our Country: Improving America's Schools and Affirming the Common Culture* (1988). Bennett also wrote *American Education: Making It Work* (1988) and *The De-valuing of America: The Fight for Our Culture and Our Children* (1992). Bennett's focus in education was on the three C's: content, character, and choice. It was his tireless advocacy of these that left his most lasting legacy on the education agenda of the 1980s.

Bennett resigned from the Department of Education in September 1988 to join the Washington law firm of Dunnels, Duvall, Bennett, and Porter. He had married Mary Elayne Glover late in life (1982) and needed the extra income to support his two sons.

However, the pull of public service proved too great. In January 1989 President George Bush appointed him head of the Office of National Drug Control Policy with the mission to rid the nation of drugs. Bennett was once again in the throes of controversy because of his outspoken views and his abrasive personality. He himself was an inveterate smoker and successfully kicked the habit in order to set an example. He pushed for more severe penalties for drug dealers, even saying that he had no moral qualms about beheading guilty parties as was done in Saudi Arabia. He used the metaphor of a war in urging the use of American military forces in Colombia and Peru to destroy supplies and set a goal of making Washington a drug-free city. Bennett announced his resignation November 8, 1990, claiming much progress. However his critics disagreed. Bennett considered becoming chairman of the Republican National Committee (RNC) but decided to devote his time to speaking, writing, and becoming a senior editor of the magazine *National Review.*

In 1993 Bennett published an anthology titled *The Book of Virtues,* which included stories, poems, essays, and fables intended to teach children values. The book sold very well, bringing in a profit of $5 million for Bennett and prompting him to publish similar books, including *The Moral Compass: Stories for a Life's Journey* (1995).

Spokesperson for Morality

Bennett was strongly favored as a presidential candidate by the conservative wing of the Republican Party in 1994, but he did not run. Instead, he continued to speak out on various topics. He joined the campaign protesting Time-Warner's investment in Interscope Records, which produced some of the most hardcore gangsta rap. He later took aim at some television talk shows. Bennett's issues found their way into the 1996 presidential campaign; even without running, he helped set the national agenda. He was also in demand on the public-speaking circuit, commanding $40,000 per speech. He served as codirector of Empower America, an organization dedicated to the promotion of conservative ideas and principles. Michael Kelly of the *New Yorker* called Bennett the pitchman of the new moral majority and "a leading voice of the force that is driving American politics right now—the national hunger for a moral society."

Further Reading

There is no full-length biography of Bennett, but his profile and critiques of his programs appeared frequently in popular magazines. Examples of these are portraits in the *Wilson Library Bulletin* (Spring 1982), *Time* (March 20, 1985; September 9, 1985), and the *New York Times* (January 11, 1985). Critiques of his programs at NEH can be found in *Nation* (April 14, 1984) and *National Review* (March 8, 1985). A critique of his tenure at the Office of Education can be found in the *Chronicle of Higher Education* (September 21, 1988), while an appraisal of his success in the drug war is in *Newsweek* (January 29, 1990). Also see *New Republic* (June 17, 1996). For articles by Bennett see *Harper's* (January 1996) and *Newsweek* (June 3, 1996; October 21, 1996). See the Empower America Web site at http://www.empower.org.

Bennett's ideas are best explained in his books, including *Counting by Race: Equality from the Founding Fathers to Bakke and Weber* (1979); *Our Children and Our Country: Improving America's Schools and Affirming the Common Culture* (1988); and *The De-valuing of America: The Fight for Our Children and Our Culture* (1992). □

Paul Berg

Paul Berg (born 1926) is best known for his development of a technique for splicing together DNA from different types of organisms. His achievement gave scientists a tool for studying the structure of viral chromosomes and the biochemical basis of human genetic diseases.

Paul Berg made one of the most fundamental technical contributions to the field of genetics in the twentieth century: he developed a technique for splicing together deoxyribonucleic acid (DNA)—the substance that carries the genetic information in living cells and viruses from generation to generation—from different types of orga-

nisms. His achievement gave scientists a priceless tool for studying the structure of viral chromosomes and the biochemical basis of human genetic diseases. It also let researchers turn simple organisms into chemical factories that churn out valuable medical drugs. In 1980 he was awarded the Nobel Prize in chemistry for pioneering this procedure, now referred to as recombinant DNA technology.

Today, the commercial application of Berg's work underlies a large and growing industry dedicated to manufacturing drugs and other chemicals. Moreover, the ability to recombine pieces of DNA and transfer them into cells is the basis of an important new medical approach to treating diseases by a technique called gene therapy.

Berg was born in Brooklyn, New York, on June 30, 1926, one of three sons of Harry Berg, a clothing manufacturer, and Sarah Brodsky, a homemaker. He attended public schools, including Abraham Lincoln High School, from which he graduated in 1943. In a 1980 interview reported in the *New York Times,* Berg credited a "Mrs. Wolf," the woman who ran a science club after school, with inspiring him to become a researcher. He graduated from high school with a keen interest in microbiology and entered Pennsylvania State University, where he received a degree in biochemistry in 1948.

Before entering graduate school, Berg served in the United States Navy from 1943 to 1946. On September 13, 1947, he married Mildred Levy and they had one son, John Alexander. After completing his duty in the navy, Berg continued his study of biochemistry at Western Reserve University (now Case Western Reserve University) in Cleveland,

Ohio, where he was a National Institutes of Health fellow from 1950 to 1952 and received his doctorate degree in 1952. He did postdoctoral training as an American Cancer Society research fellow, working with Herman Kalckar at the Institute of Cytophysiology in Copenhagen, Denmark, from 1952 to 1953. From 1953 to 1954 he worked with biochemist Arthur Kornberg at Washington University in St. Louis, Missouri, and held the position of scholar in cancer research from 1954 to 1957.

He became an assistant professor of microbiology at the University of Washington School of Medicine in 1956, where he taught and did research until 1959. Berg left St. Louis that year to accept the position of professor of biochemistry at Stanford University School of Medicine. Berg's background in biochemistry and microbiology shaped his research interests during graduate school and beyond, steering him first into studies of the molecular mechanisms underlying intracellular protein synthesis.

Experiments with Genetic Engineering

During the 1950s Berg tackled the problem of how amino acids, the building blocks of proteins, are linked together according to the template carried by a form of RNA (ribonucleic acid, the "decoded" form of DNA) called messenger RNA (mRNA). A current theory, unknown to Berg at the time, held that the amino acids did not directly interact with RNA but were linked together in a chain by special molecules called joiners, or adapters. In 1956 Berg demonstrated just such a molecule, which was specific to the amino acid methionine. Each amino acid has its own such joiners, which are now called transfer RNA (tRNA).

This discovery helped to stoke Berg's interest in the structure and function of genes, and fueled his ambition to combine genetic material from different species in order to study how these individual units of heredity worked. Berg reasoned that by recombining a gene from one species with the genes of another, he would be able to isolate and study the transferred gene in the absence of confounding interactions with its natural, neighboring genes in the original organism.

In the late 1960s, while at Stanford, he began studying genes of the monkey tumor virus SV40 as a model for understanding how mammalian genes work. By the 1970s, he had mapped out where on the DNA the various viral genes occurred, identified the specific sequences of nucleotides in the genes, and discovered how the SV40 genes affect the DNA of host organisms they infect. It was this work with SV40 genes that led directly to the development of recombinant DNA technology. While studying how genes controlled the production of specific proteins, Berg also was trying to understand how normal cells seemed spontaneously to become cancerous. He hypothesized that cells turned cancerous because of some unknown interaction between genes and cellular biochemistry.

In order to study these issues, he decided to combine the DNA of SV40, which was known to cause cancer in some animals, into the common intestinal bacterium *Escherichia coli* (*E. coli*). He thought it might be possible to smuggle the SV40 DNA into the bacterium by inserting it into the DNA of a type of virus, called a bacteriophage, that naturally infects *E. coli*.

A DNA molecule is composed of subunits called nucleotides, each containing a sugar, a phosphate group, and one of four nitrogenous bases. Structurally, DNA resembles a twisted ladder, or helix. Two long chains of alternating sugar and phosphate groups twist about each other, forming the sides of the ladder. A base attaches to each sugar, and hydrogen bonding between the bases—the rungs of the ladder—connects the two strands. The order or sequence of the bases determines the genetic code; and because bases match up in a complementary way, the sequence on one strand determines the sequence on the other.

Berg began his experiment by cutting the SV40 DNA into pieces using so-called restriction enzymes, which had been discovered several years before by other researchers. These enzymes let him choose the exact sites to cut each strand of the double helix. Then, using another type of enzyme called terminal transferase, he added one base at a time to one side of the double-stranded molecule. Thus, he formed a chain that extended out from the double-stranded portion. Berg performed the same biochemical operation on the phage DNA, except he changed the sequence of bases in the reconstructed phage DNA so it would be complementary to—and therefore readily bind to—the reconstructed SV40 section of DNA extending from the double-stranded portion. Such complementary extended portions of DNA that bind to each other to make recombinant DNA molecules are called "sticky ends."

This new and powerful technique offered the means to put genes into rapidly multiplying cells, such as bacteria, which would then use the genes to make the corresponding protein. In effect, scientists would be able to make enormous amounts of particular genes they wanted to study, or use simple organisms like bacteria to grow large amounts of valuable substances like human growth hormone, antibiotics, and insulin. Researchers also recognized that genetic engineering, as the technique was quickly dubbed, could be used to alter soil bacteria to give them the ability to "fix" nitrogen from the air, thus reducing the need for artificial fertilizers.

Questions the Ethics of Recombinant DNA Technology

Berg had planned to inject the monkey virus SV40-bacteriophage DNA hybrid molecule into *E. coli*. But he realized the potential danger of inserting a mammalian tumor gene into a bacterium that exists universally in the environment. Should the bacterium acquire and spread to other *E. coli* dangerous, pathogenic characteristics that threatened humans or other species, the results might be catastrophic. In his own case, he feared that adding the tumor-causing SV40 DNA into such a common bacterium would be equivalent to planting a ticking cancer time bomb in humans who might subsequently become infected by altered bacteria that escaped from the lab. Rather than continue his ground-breaking experiment, Berg voluntarily halted his work at this point, concerned that the tools of genetic engineering might be leading researchers to perform extremely dangerous experiments.

In addition to this unusual voluntary deferral of his own research, Berg led a group of ten of his colleagues from around the country in composing and signing a letter explaining their collective concerns. Published in the July 26, 1974, issue of the journal *Science,* the letter became known as the "Berg letter." It listed a series of recommendations supported by the Committee on Recombinant DNA Molecules Assembly of Life Sciences (of which Berg was chairman) of the National Academy of Sciences.

The Berg letter warned, "There is serious concern that some of these artificial recombinant DNA molecules could prove biologically hazardous." It cited as an example the fact that *E. coli* can exchange genetic material with other types of bacteria, some of which cause disease in humans. "Thus, new DNA elements introduced into *E. coli* might possibly become widely disseminated among human, bacterial, plant, or animal populations with unpredictable effects." The letter also noted certain recombinant DNA experiments that should not be conducted, such as recombining genes for antibiotic resistance or bacterial toxins into bacterial strains that did not at present carry them; linking all or segments of DNA from cancer-causing or other animal viruses into plasmids or other viral DNAs that could spread the DNA to other bacteria, animals or humans, "and thus possibly increase the incidence of cancer or other disease."

The letter also called for an international meeting of scientists from around the world "to further discuss appropriate ways to deal with the potential biohazards of recombinant DNA molecules." That meeting was held in Pacific Grove, California, on February 27, 1975, at Asilomar and brought together a hundred scientists from sixteen countries. For four days, Berg and his fellow scientists struggled to find a way to safely balance the potential hazards and inestimable benefits of the emerging field of genetic engineering. They agreed to collaborate on developing safeguards to prevent genetically engineered organisms designed only for laboratory study from being able to survive in humans. And they drew up professional standards to govern research in the new technology, which, though backed only by the force of moral persuasion, represented the convictions of many of the leading scientists in the field. These standards served as a blueprint for subsequent federal regulations, which were first published by the National Institutes of Health in June 1976. Today, many of the original regulations have been relaxed or eliminated, except in the cases of recombinant organisms that include extensive DNA regions from very pathogenic organisms. Berg continues to study genetic recombinants in mammalian cells and gene therapy. He is also doing research in molecular biology of HIV–1.

Nobel Prize Awarded for the Biochemistry of Nucleic Acids

The Nobel Award announcement by the Royal Swedish Academy of Sciences cited Berg "for his fundamental studies of the biochemistry of nucleic acids with particular regard to recombinant DNA." But Berg's legacy also includes his principled actions in the name of responsible scientific inquiry.

Berg was named the Sam, Lula and Jack Willson Professor of Biochemistry at Stanford in 1970, and was chairman of the Department of Biochemistry there from 1969 to 1974. He was also director of the Beckman Center for Molecular and Genetic Medicine (1985), senior postdoctoral fellow of the National Science Foundation (1961–68), and nonresident fellow of the Salk Institute (1973–83). He was elected to the advisory board of the Jane Coffin Childs Foundation of Medical Research, serving from 1970–80. Other appointments include the chair of the scientific advisory committee of the Whitehead Institute (1984–90) and of the national advisory committee of the Human Genome Project (1990). He was editor of *Biochemistry and Biophysical Research Communications* (1959–68), and a trustee of Rockefeller University (1990–92). He is a member of the international advisory board, Basel Institute of Immunology.

Berg received many awards in addition to the Nobel Prize, among them the American Chemical Society's Eli Lilly Prize in biochemistry (1959); the V. D. Mattia Award of the Roche Institute of Molecular Biology (1972); the Albert Lasker Basic Medical Research Award (1980); and the National Medal of Science (1983). He is a fellow of the American Academy of Arts and Sciences, and a foreign member of the Japanese Biochemistry Society and the Académie des Sciences, France. Berg worked as a Professor of Biochemistry at Stanford University.

Additional Sources

Antebi, Elizabeth, and David Fishlock, *Biotechnology: Strategies for Life,* MIT Press, 1986.

Magill, Frank N., editor, *The Nobel Prize Winners: Chemistry, Volume 3: 1969–1989,* Salem Press 1990, pp. 1027-1034.

Wade, Nick, *The Ultimate Experiment,* Walker, 1977.

Watson, James, *Recombinant DNA,* W. H. Freeman, 1983.

New York Times, February 2, 1975, p. A1; October 15, 1980, p. A1. □

Irving Berlin

The American composer Irving Berlin (1888-1989) produced about 800 songs, many of which attained worldwide popularity. His patriotic songs, especially "God Bless America," seemed to epitomize the mass American sentiments of the era.

I rving Berlin was born Israel Baline in Tyumen, Russia, on May 11, 1888. The family of nine fled the persecutions of Jews in Russia in 1893 and settled in New York City, where, like so many other immigrants of that time, they lived on the Lower East Side. The family's first years in America were very difficult—at one time they all sold newspapers on the streets. Israel, the youngest child, was first exposed to music in the synagogue in which his father occasionally sang as cantor; he also received singing lessons from his father.

When the boy left home at 14, he made money by singing in saloons on New York's Bowery. He attended school for two years but had no formal musical education; he never learned to read or notate music.

It was while working as a singing waiter that Israel Baline, collaborating with a coworker named Nicholson on a song entitled "Marie from Sunny Italy," became I. Berlin, lyricist. This was the name he chose to appear on the sheet music when the song was published shortly after, in 1907.

Subsequently, Berlin began to gain recognition as a clever lyricist. He provided words for "Queenie, My Own," "Dorando," and "Sadie Salome, Go Home." The last was something of a success, and he was hired by a Tin Pan Alley publisher to write words for new songs. Within a year, despite his continuing difficulty in writing English, Berlin was established as a rising talent in the popular-music business.

Somewhat belatedly music publishers became interested in exploiting ragtime, the highly original creation of African-American musicians in the South and Midwest during the 1880s and 1890s. Berlin contributed lyrics (and a few tunes) to several mild ragtime songs. In 1911 he wrote the words and music for "Alexander's Ragtime Band," which started toward worldwide popularity when sung by Emma Carus in Chicago that year. It is ironic that one of the most famous of all "ragtime" songs employs a few conventional syncopations but no real ragtime at all!.

Berlin's fame soared. He wrote his first complete musical score in 1914, *Watch Your Step,* followed by *Stop, Look, Listen.* In the Army during World War I he wrote a success-

ful soldier show entitled *Yip, Yip, Yaphank* (1919), which contained "Oh, How I Hate to Get Up in the Morning." In 1919 he founded his own music publishing company, Irving Berlin, Inc.

His most successful subsequent shows included *Ziegfeld Follies* (1919, 1920, 1927), *Music Box Revues* (1921-1924), *As Thousands Cheer* (1933), *This Is the Army* (1942), *Annie Get Your Gun* (1946), and *Call Me Madam* (1950). His best-known scores for films include *Top Hat* (1935), *Follow the Fleet* (1936), and *Holiday Inn* (1942).

Among Berlin's best known songs are "White Christmas" and "God Bless America" which are perennial holiday favorites to this day.

Commenting on the composer who produced more popular hits than any other of his generation, Harold Clurman wrote in 1949, "Irving Berlin's genius consists not so much in his adaptability to every historical and theatrical contingency, but rather in his capacity to discover the root need and sentiment of all our American lives."

Berlin's 100th birthday was celebrated in a televised special from Carnegie Hall. When he died in New York on September 22, 1989 he was remembered as a symbol of the nation. As fellow songwriter Jerome Kern was quoted in Alexander Woolcott's biography of Berlin: "Irving Berlin has no place in American Music. He *is* American Music."

Further Reading

Alexander Woollcott, *The Story of Irving Berlin* (1925), is an affectionate and stylishly written account of Berlin's early career. *The Songs of Irving Berlin* (1957?), a catalog of his works, was published by the Irving Berlin Music Corporation. For background on Berlin and American musical comedy see David Ewen, *Complete Book of the American Musical Theater* (1959; rev. ed. 1968) and *The Story of America's Musical Theater* (1961; rev. ed. 1968), Stanley Green, *World of Musical Comedy* (1960; rev. ed. 1968), and Laurence Bergreen, *As Thousands Cheer: The Life of Irving Berlin* (1990). More recent biography can be found in Philip Furia, *Irving Berlin: A life in Song* (1998). □

Joseph Cardinal Bernardin

Joseph Cardinal Bernardin (1928-1996) was a major leader in the U.S.-based Catholic Church during the modern progressive era.

Joseph Cardinal Bernardin became the symbol, even if unknowingly, of the U.S. Catholic Church's struggle with modernity. A quiet, devout man, he rose in the ranks of the church in the 1980s to lead American Catholicism into a more progressive era. He was an instrumental part of the creation of the National Conference of Catholic Bishops' pastoral letters on nuclear weapons, the economy, and AIDS. Bernardin's positions ranged between innovation and traditional Vatican teachings; yet, with his skills of negotiation he was almost always able to forge a compromise. It was his ability to listen clearly as well as speak strongly that separated his vision and actions from other officials in the

Joseph Cardinal Bernardin (right)

Catholic Church hierarchy. Bernardin's modesty did not allow him to view himself as a pure instrument of change, but only as a symbol doing the work that was required of him. As he once said in an interview with *Time* magazine, "There is a real spiritual hunger on the part of the people. They are not reaching out to me. They are reaching out to the Lord. Perhaps there is a personal dimension, but I am just a symbol."

Background

Born on 2 April 1928 in Columbia, South Carolina, to a family of Italian immigrants, Bernardin was the only Catholic boy on his block. These early experiences helped him acquire a great understanding and tolerance for other religions and opposite points of view. Initially intent on choosing a career in medicine, he attended the University of South Carolina for a year. Later, after deciding to enter the priesthood, he graduated with a degree in philosophy from St. Mary's Seminary in Baltimore in 1948. He received a master's in education from Catholic University in Washington, D.C., and was ordained a priest in 1952. Once ordained, Bernardin's skills shined, as he soon climbed the hierarchical ladder, moving to Atlanta and becoming the youngest bishop in the country by 1966. By 1968 Bernardin made Washington, D.C., his home as he became the general secretary of the National Conference of Catholic Bishops (NCCB) and its social action agency, the United States Catholic Conference. In 1972 he was named the archbishop of Cincinnati, Ohio, and was elected president of the NCCB

in 1974, serving in that role until 1977. Bernardin brought to every position a strong confidence and a progressive agenda toward church policies. In 1982 Bernardin was named archbishop of Chicago, the largest archdiocese in the nation. This new foothold of power placed Bernardin in a prominent location to express his social activism.

Pastoral Letters

In February 1983 Bernardin was elevated to the Sacred College of Cardinals by Pope John Paul II. Bernardin succeeded the late John Cardinal Cody, who in his last days had been plagued by financial scandals and dissent by priests and followers who believed him to be uncaring and rigid. With Bernardin now in power, Chicago's more than 2.4 million Catholic's felt they had a leader who would listen. Bernardin's outspoken position on social issues was evident in 1982 when the first draft of the NCCB's antinuclear weapons letter was issued—"The Challenge of Peace." The letter questioned the morality of possessing nuclear weapons, let alone the use of such destructive forces. After much debate, discussion, and modifications, the pastoral letter was issued 3 May 1983. Bernardin's determination did not stop there; he urged his fellow bishops, both liberal and conservative, to fight for reductions in the amounts of government money spent on the military in general, believing it wrong to waste resources on weapons while urban neighborhoods fell to ruin. In 1984 the NCCB examined the United States' economic structure. Once again Bernardin led the charge for the Catholic Church to take a moral stand, and the resulting pastoral letter, "Economic Justice for All," cited systematic flaws. Although seen as too much of an activist by some officials and church laity, Bernardin continued to work within the framework of the Catholic Church, always seeking biblical and Vatican confirmation for all maneuvers. In 1987 he witnessed the scourge of the AIDS virus sweeping the nation and felt it was time for the church to react officially. The issue of AIDS was complex for the Catholic Church, as it touched upon several issues—condoms, homosexuality, sexual activity—that the church preferred not to deal with publicly. Bernardin, acknowledging this, pushed for the Catholic Church to allow teaching the use of condoms as a prevention of future transmission of the disease. Opposition was severe as some bishops and cardinals felt any change in the official stance would appear as if the church were condoning sexual behavior outside of marriage. Bernardin saw silence and a lack of information as a sinful act on the church's part. In the end the document was adopted and discussion of the use of condoms was permitted on a limited basis.

Vision

Joseph Cardinal Bernardin was a visionary in the Catholic Church, always looking toward the future but never neglecting the Church's rich past. His strong relationships with the laity and to John Paul II in the early 1970s before his elevation to pope served Bernardin well during difficult periods in his career. His open style created a level of comfort not known to many elder Catholics, as he symbolized the pinnacle of post-Vatican II Catholicism. Unafraid to challenge the status quo, he became a star of the

American Catholic Church. In 1995 Bernardin was diagnosed with pancreatic cancer. After over a year of battling the illness, he died on November 14, 1996.

Further Reading

D. J. R. Bruckner, "Chicago's Activist Cardinal," *New York Times Magazine,* 132 (1 May 1983): pp. 42-45, 60, 63, 69, 82, 92.

Richard N. Ostling, "Bishops and the Bomb," *Time,* 120 (29 November 1982): pp. 68-77. ☐

Leonard Bernstein

Leonard Bernstein (1918-1990) was an American composer, conductor, and pianist. His special gifts in bridging the gap between the concert hall and the world of Broadway made him one of the most glamorous musical figures of his day.

Leonard Bernstein was born Louis Bernstein in Lawrence, Massachusetts, on August 25, 1918, to Russian-Jewish immigrants. He changed his name to Leonard at the age of sixteen. The family soon moved to Boston, where Leonard studied at Boston Latin School and Harvard University. Although he had taken piano lessons from the age of 10 and engaged in musical activities at college, his intensive musical training began only in 1939 at the Curtis Institute. The following summer, at the Berkshire Music Festival, he met Serge Koussevitsky, who was to be his chief mentor in the early years.

On Koussevitsky's recommendation two years later, Artur Rodzinski made Bernstein his assistant conductor at the New York Philharmonic. The suddenness of this appointment, coming after two somewhat directionless years, was superseded only by the dramatic events of November 14, 1943. With less than 24 hours' notice and no rehearsal, Bernstein substituted for the ailing Bruno Walter at Carnegie Hall and led the Philharmonic through a difficult program which he had studied hastily at best. By the concert's end the audience knew it had witnessed the debut of a born conductor. The *New York Times* ran a front-page story the following morning, and Bernstein's career as a public figure had begun. During the next few years he was guest conductor of every major orchestra in the United States until, in 1958, he became music director of the New York Philharmonic.

Bernstein's multi-faceted career might have filled several average lives. It is surprising that one who had never given a solo recital would be recognized as a pianist; nevertheless, he was so recognized from his appearances as conductor-pianist in performances of Mozart concertos and the Ravel Concerto in G.

As a composer, Bernstein was a controversial figure. His large works, including the symphonies *Jeremiah* (1943), *Age of Anxiety* (1949), and *Kaddish* (1963), are not acknowledged masterpieces. Yet they are skillfully wrought and show his sensitivity to subtle changes of musical dialect. He received more praise for his Broadway musicals. The vivid *On the Town* (1944) and *Wonderful Town* (1952) were followed by *Candide* (1956), which, though not a box-

office success, is considered by many to be Bernstein's most original score. *West Side Story* (1957) received international acclaim. Bernstein's music, with its strong contrasts of violence and tenderness, sustains—indeed determines—the feeling of the show and contributes to its special place in the history of American musical theater.

His role as an educator, in seminars at Brandeis University (1952-1957) and in teaching duties at Tanglewood, should not be overlooked. He found an even larger audience through television, where his animation and distinguished simplicity had an immediate appeal. Two books of essays, *Joy of Music* (1959) and *Infinite Variety of Music* (1966), were direct products of television presentations.

Bernstein had his greatest impact as a conductor. His appearances abroad—with or without the Philharmonic—elicited an excitement approaching frenzy. These responses were due in part to Bernstein's dynamism, particularly effective in music of strong expressionistic profile. It is generally agreed that his readings of 20th century American scores showed a fervor and authority rarely approached by those of his colleagues. His performances and recordings also engendered a revival of interest in Mahler's music.

There was some surprise when, in 1967, Bernstein resigned as music director of the Philharmonic. But it was in keeping with his peripatetic nature and the diversity of his activities that he should seek new channels of expression. After leaving the Philharmonic, Bernstein traveled extensively, serving as guest conductor for many of the major symphonies of the world including the Vienna Philharmonic and the Berlin Philharmonic. He became something of a fixture in those cities in the last few decades of his life.

More controversially, he also became caught up in the cultural upheaval of the late 1960s. He angered many when he claimed all music, other than pop, seemed old-fashioned and musty. Politically, too, he drew criticism. When his wife hosted a fund-raiser for the Black Panthers in 1970, charges of anti-Semitism were leveled against Bernstein himself. He had not organized the event, but the press reports caused severe damage to his reputation. This event, along with his participation in anti-Vietnam War activism led J. Edgar Hoover and the FBI to monitor his activities and associations.

In 1971 *Mass: A Theatre Piece for Singers, Players and Dancers* premiered at the Kennedy Center in Washington, DC. It was, according to biographer Humphrey Burton, "the closest [Bernstein] ever came to achieving a synthesis between Broadway and the concert hall." The huge cast performed songs in styles ranging from rock to blues to gospel. *Mass* debuted on Broadway later that year.

Later Bernstein compositions include the dance drama, *Dybbuk* (1974); *1600 Pennsylvania Avenue* (1976), a musical about the White House that was a financial and critical disaster; the song cycle *Songfest: A Cycle of American Poems for Six Singers and Orchestra* (1977); and the opera *A Quiet Place* (1983, revised 1984).

In the 1980s Bernstein continued his hectic schedule of international appearances and social concerns. He gave concerts to mark the fortieth anniversary of the bombing of Hiroshima and a benefit for AIDS research. On Christmas

Day, 1989, Bernstein led an international orchestra in Berlin, which was in the midst of celebrating the collapse of the Berlin Wall. In a typically grand gesture, Bernstein changed the words of "Ode to Joy" to "Ode to Freedom."

Despite health problems, Bernstein continued to tour the world in 1990 before returning to Tanglewood for an August 19th concert. He had first conducted a professional orchestra there in 1940, and this performance, 50 years later, was to be his last. He died in New York, on October 14, 1990, of a heart attack brought on by emphysema and other complications.

Further Reading

Humphrey Burton, *Leonard Bernstein* (1994) is a comprehensive biography with extensive comment from his friends and family. A more sensational biography is Joan Peyser, *Bernstein: A Biography* (1987). David Ewen, *Leonard Bernstein* (1960; rev. ed. 1967), is a solid biography and more comprehensive than John Briggs, *Leonard Bernstein: The Man, His Work, and His World* (1961). Evelyn Ames, *A Wind from the West* (1970), a sometimes-romanticized account of the New York Philharmonic's European tour of 1968, is valuable for its intimate detail. □

Chuck Berry

Chuck Berry (born 1926), creator of the "duck walk" and known as the "father of rock and roll," has been a major influence on popular music. Even though his career and life reached great peaks and declined to low valleys, he still prevails in music while his contemporaries have vanished.

"If there were a single fountainhead for rock guitar, Chuck Berry would be it," wrote Gene Santoro in *The Guitar.* Indeed, the list of artists influenced by the "father of rock and roll" is nearly endless. From the Beach Boys and the Beatles to Jimi Hendrix and on to Van Halen and Stevie Ray Vaughan, every popular musician knows the impact that Chuck Berry has had on popular music. As Eric Clapton stated, there's really no other way to play rock and roll.

Took up Guitar in Junior High

Born in 1926, Berry didn't take up the guitar until he was in junior high school thirteen years later. With the accompaniment of a friend on guitar, the two youths played a steamy version of *Confessin' The Blues* which surprised, and pleased, the student audience. The reaction from the crowd prompted Berry to learn some guitar chords from his partner and he was hooked from then on. He spent his teen years developing his chops while working with his father doing carpentry. But before he could graduate from high school, Berry was arrested and convicted of armed robbery and served three years in Algoa (Missouri). A year after his release on October 18, 1947, he was married and working on a family, swearing that he was forever cured of heading down the wrong path again.

In addition to carpentry, he began working as a hairstylist around this time, saving as much money as he could make (a trait that would cause him considerable grief later in his life). Near the end of 1952 he received a call from a piano player named Johnnie Johnson asking him to play a New Year's Eve gig at the Cosmopolitan Club. Berry accepted, and for the next three years the band literally ruled the Cosmo Club (located at the corner of 17th and Bond St. in East St. Louis, Illinois). At the beginning the band (which included Ebby Hardy on drums), was called Sir John's Trio and played mostly hillbilly, country, and honky tonk tunes. Berry's influence changed not only their name (to the Chuck Berry Combo) but also their style. He originally wanted to be a big band guitarist but that style had died down in popularity by then. Berry cited sources like T-Bone Walker, Carl Hogan of Louis Jordan's Tympani Five, Charlie Christian, and saxophonist Illinois Jacquet as his inspirations, borrowing from their sounds to make one of his own.

Met Idol Muddy Waters

While the swing guitarists had a major impact on his playing, it was the blues, especially that of Muddy Waters, that caught Berry's attention. He and a friend went to see the master perform at a Chicago club, and with some coaxing, Berry mustered the nerve to speak with his idol. "It was the feeling I suppose one would get from having a word with the president or the pope," Berry wrote in his autobiography. "I quickly told him of my admiration for his compositions and asked him who I could see about making a record. . . . Those very famous words were, 'Yeah, see Leonard Chess. Yeah, Chess Records over on Forty-seventh and Cottage.'" Berry flatly rejects the story of him hopping on stage and showing up Waters: "I was a stranger to Muddy and in no way was I about to ask my godfather if I could sit in and play." But he did take the advice and went to see the Chess brothers, Leonard and Phil. They were interested in the young artist but wanted to hear a demo tape before actually cutting any songs. So Berry hurried back home, recorded some tunes and headed back to Chicago.

"He was carrying a wire recorder," Leonard Chess told Peter Guralnick in Feel Like Going Home, "and he played us a country music take-off called 'Ida Red.' We called it 'Maybellene'. . . . The big beat, cars, and young love. . . . It was a trend and we jumped on it." Phil Chess elaborated, "You could tell right away. . . . He had that something special, that—I don't know what you'd call it. But he had it." After the May 21, 1955, recording session they headed back to the Cosmo Club, earning $21 per week and competing with local rivals like Albert King and Ike Turner. Unbeknownst to him, Berry shared writing credits for "Maybellene" with Russ Fralto and New York disc jockey Alan Freed as part of a deal Chess had made (also known as payola). The scam worked for the most part because by mid-September the song, which had taken 36 cuts to complete, was number 1 on the R&B charts. Berry was bilked out of two-thirds of his royalties from the song, but in later years he would reflect upon the lesson he learned: "Let me say that any man who can't take care of his own money deserves what he gets," he told Rolling Stone. "In fact, a man should be able to take care of most of his business himself." Ever since the incident that's just what Berry has done. He insists on running his career and managing his finances the way he sees fit.

Ten More Top Ten Hits

The next few years, until 1961, would see at least ten more top ten hits, including "Thirty Days," "Roll Over Beethoven," "Too Much Monkey Business," "Brown Eyed Handsome Man," "School Days," "Rock and Roll Music," "Sweet Little Sixteen," "Johnny B. Goode," "Carol," and "Almost Grown." Berry was a tremendous hit on the touring circuit, utilizing what is now known as his trademark. He explained its development in his autobiography: "A brighter seat of my memories is based on pursuing my rubber ball. Once it happened to bounce under the kitchen table, and I was trying to retrieve it while it was still bouncing. Usually I was reprimanded for disturbing activities when there was company in the house, as there was then. But this time my manner of retrieving the ball created a big laugh from Mother's choir members. Stooping with full-bended knees, but with my back and head vertical, I fit under the tabletop while scooting forward reaching for the ball. This squatting manner was requested by members of the family many times thereafter for the entertainment of visitors and soon, from their appreciation and encouragement, I looked forward to the ritual. An act was in the making. After it had been abandoned for years I happened to remember the maneuver while performing in New York for the first time and some journalist branded it the 'duck walk.'"

The money from touring and record royalties were filling his pockets enough for Berry to start spending on some of the dreams he had long held. Around 1957 he opened

Berry Park just outside of Wentzville, Missouri. With a guitar-shaped swimming pool, golf course, hotel suites, and nightclub, it was, next to his fleet of Cadillacs, his pride and joy. "Now that's what I call groovy," he told Rolling Stone. "To own a piece of land is like getting the closest to God, I'd say."

Remakes Weaker Than Originals

Things seemed to be going smoothly until 1961, when Berry was found guilty of violating the Mann Act. Berry was charged with transporting a teenage girl across a state line for immoral purposes. He spent from February 19, 1962 until October 18, 1963 behind bars at the Federal Medical Center in Springfield, Missouri. For years Berry denied this, claiming he was acquitted and never served time. He finally admitted the truth in his autobiography. He used his prison term constructively though, taking courses to complete his high school education and also by penning some of his most notable songs: "Tulane," "No Particular Place To Go," and "Nadine."

By the time Berry was released from jail the British Invasion was about to take over. Groups like the Beatles were churning out cover versions of Berry classics and turning whole new audiences on to him. While some artists might have cried rip-off (the Stones have done over ten of his tunes), Berry sees only the positive aspects. "Did I like it? That doesn't come under my scrutiny," he told Guitar Player. "It struck me that my material was becoming marketable, a recognizable product, and if these guys could do such a good job as to get a hit, well, fantastic. I'm just glad it was my song." Even so, remakes of Berry hits are more often than not considerably weaker than his originals. While his style is remarkably simple, it is also next to impossible to duplicate with the same feel and sense of humor.

A Shrewd Rock and Roller

"Chuck Berry dominated much of the early rock scene by his complete mastery of all its aspects: playing, performing, songwriting, singing and a shrewd sense of how to package himself as well," wrote Santoro. As shrewd as Berry was, by the mid-1960s his type of rock was losing ground to improvisors like Eric Clapton, Mike Bloomfield, and Jimi Hendrix (all three of whom acknowledged Berry's influence, but were trying to break new ground). A switch from Chess to Mercury Records from 1966 to 1969 did little to help. He would continue touring throughout the 1960s without the aid of a regular backup band.

Berry's method since the late 1950s has been to use pickup bands comprised of musicians from the city he's playing in. This has led to many complaints from fans and critics alike that his performances are sometimes shoddy and careless. In his book, Berry gives his own reasons, stating that "drinks and drugs were never my bag, nor were they an excuse for affecting the quality of playing so far as I was concerned. A few ridiculous performances, several amendments to our band regulations, and the band broke up, never to be reconstructed. Whenever I've assembled other groups and played road dates, similar conditions have prevailed." (Berry reportedly accepts no less than $10,000 per gig and plays for no more than 45 minutes; no encores.)

Another Hit and More Personal Strife

By 1972 Berry was back with Chess and produced his biggest seller to date, "My Ding-a-Ling," from *The London Chuck Berry Sessions*. Selling over two million copies, it was his first gold record and a number 1 hit on both sides of the Atlantic according to *The Illustrated Encyclopedia of Rock*. He had hit pay dirt, but his obsession to have a bank account with a $1 million figure led to another run-in with the law. In 1979 Berry was convicted of tax evasion and spent just over three months at Lompoc Prison Camp in California. Perhaps the one thing that has caused him more pleasure/pain than money is his fancy for women, stated simply in his book: "The only real bother about prison, to me, is the loss of love." He has said that he hopes to write a book one day devoted solely to his sex life.

Berry's legal troubles continued into his later years, when he was embroiled in accusations of drug possession and trafficking and various sexual improprieties in July of 1990. His estate was raided earlier that spring by the DEA, who had been informed that Berry was dealing in cocaine. The operation resulted in the confiscation of marijuana and hashish and pornographic videotapes and films, but charges against the entertainer were later dismissed. Berry was also involved in a class-action lawsuit regarding videotapes made of women without their consent. Meanwhile, more collections of Berry's hits continued to be released, including a well-received box set by Chess/MCA in 1989 and a live recording released in 1995.

While Berry's career has had the highest peaks and some pretty low valleys, he has survived while most of his contemporaries have vanished. In 1986 Rolling Stones guitarist Keith Richard, perhaps the ultimate student of the Chuck Berry School of Guitar, decided to put it all together with a 60th birthday party concert to be filmed and released as a movie, *Hail! Hail! Rock 'n' Roll*. It took place at St. Louis's Fox Theater, a venue which had at one time refused a youthful Berry entrance because of his skin color. The show featured Berry's classic songs with Richard, Johnnie Johnson, Robert Cray, Etta James, Eric Clapton, Linda Ronstadt, and Julian Lennon also performing. Berry has also been honored with a star in the Hollywood Walk of Fame, and induction into the Rock and Roll Hall of Fame. If that's not enough, "Johnny B. Goode" is riding around in outer space on the *Voyager I* just waiting to be heard by aliens.

Despite the accolades, in his own book Berry shrugs off his contributions, stating that "my view remains that I do not deserve all the reward directed on my account for the accomplishments credited to the rock 'n' roll bank of music." Nevertheless, *Rolling Stone*'s Dave Marsh's words seem to be more appropriate: "Chuck Berry is to rock what Louis Armstrong was to jazz."

Further Reading

Berry, Chuck, *The Autobiography*, Fireside, 1988.

Guralnick, Peter, *Feel Like Going Home*, Vintage, 1981.

Kozinn, Alan, and Pete Welding, Dan Forte, and Gene Santoro, *The Guitar*, Quill, 1984.

Logan, Nick, and Bob Woffinden, *The Illustrated Encyclopedia of Rock*, Harmony Books, 1977.

Rock Revolution, by the editors of *Creem* magazine, Popular Library, 1976.

The Rolling Stone Interviews, by the editors of *Rolling Stone*, St. Martin's Press/Rolling Stone Press, 1981.

The Rolling Stone Record Guide, edited by Dave Marsh and John Swenson, Random House/Rolling Stone Press, 1979.

Guitar Player, February, 1981; May, 1984; June, 1984; January, 1985; January, 1987; November, 1987; December, 1987; March, 1988.

Guitar World, March, 1987; November, 1987; December, 1987; March, 1988; April, 1988.

Rolling Stone, January 26, 1989; August 23, 1990. □

Owen Bieber

Owen Bieber (born 1929), president from 1983 to 1995 of the third-largest labor union in the United States—the United Automobile, Aerospace and Agricultural Implement Workers of America—is a central figure in the dramatic restructuring of the U.S. auto industry.

Elected UAW president in May 1983, Bieber led more than one million union members, most of whom work in the nation's auto plants. The plants and the U.S. companies that own them reeled in the 1980s from increased competition from lower-cost foreign carmakers and an early 1980s auto slump that saw sales fall to their lowest level since the Great Depression. More than 200,000 auto workers lost their jobs during that time because of the changes in the industry. Bieber struggled to find a balance between the companies' demands to be competitive and the needs of his members to keep their jobs.

Business Week reports one company negotiator as saying Bieber "is a deliberate, hard-working man of great integrity who tempers his comments and actions with an eye for the political consequences." Those attributes helped Bieber negotiate some novel labor agreements at the domestic Big Three automakers—General Motors Corporation, Ford Motor Company, and Chrysler Corporation. For example, Bieber negotiated historic job guarantee programs that prohibit the companies from laying off workers when new technology eliminates their jobs. Instead, the companies must find new work for the employees and retrain them if necessary. In return, the union agreed to more moderate wage increases than are traditional in auto contracts. Bieber also negotiated the first labor contracts for GM's innovative Saturn small-car project, which began producing a new generation of American cars in 1990. The pact, which drew attention from other industries because of its startling departure from past labor-management practices, lets auto workers share in some management decisions on how the plant is operated. In return, the UAW agreed that Saturn workers would receive starting base pay that is 85 percent of the going rate at traditional auto plants.

Bieber, a large man at six-foot-five and about 250 pounds, "is more purely a labor populist, not much given to trafficking with big thinkers outside the UAW or to serving on panels studying the problems of industry," writes Dale Buss of the *Wall Street Journal*. "One of his strengths, supporters maintain, is that he understands the wants of rank-and-file workers and is himself a true believer in the trade-union gospel," Buss states.

Bieber's baptism in that gospel goes back many years, to his first job out of high school. A native of the small, northwest Michigan farm community of North Dorr, Bieber went to work in 1948 at the same auto supply plant that employed his father—McInerney Spring and Wire Company in nearby Grand Rapids. The younger Bieber's first job was bending by hand the thick border wire on car seats. He told Kathy Sawyer of the *Washington Post:* "It was a hard job. After the first hour in there, I felt like just leaving. If my father hadn't worked there, too, I probably would have."

But a year later, at age 19, Bieber was elected to his first union position—shop steward—at UAW Local 687 at the plant. Immediately, he started bargaining. He told the *Detroit News* that the negotiating began "almost the second they gave me the steward button because there were grievances to take care of, and that's part of collective bargaining." Bieber was to become a highly skilled bargainer as he worked his way up the union ranks in Grand Rapids. In 1951 he became a member of the executive board of Local 687 and helped administer local union affairs. In 1955 he was elected to the local bargaining committee and helped run negotiations on local plant issues. In 1956, he was elected president of the

local. As Senator John Kennedy's campaign for the U.S. presidency got under way later in the decade, Bieber—a devout Democrat—joined the effort.

His hard work and dedication brought him to the attention of leaders at the UAW's regional office in Grand Rapids and by 1961, he was assigned part-time as a union organizer in the region, which encompasses 62 of Michigan's 83 counties, covering the western part of the state and the Upper Peninsula. A year later, Bieber became a full time regional organizer and international union representative. In 1964 he became a servicing representative, helping advise local union officials at plants in his area. "He was known as 'Big Dad' for the almost-paternal way he stood by union members in run-ins with management," writes Buss of the *Wall Street Journal*. In 1972, he was appointed director of the region, a position he held until 1980, when he was elected a vice-president of the UAW and moved to the union's Detroit headquarters. There, Bieber served as director of the UAW's GM department, the union's largest department with more than 400,000 members. It was Bieber's first public exposure beyond Michigan, as GM's plants stretch from shore to shore. But the spotlight was harsh. By early 1982, with all the domestic automakers in the red because of depressed car sales and foreign competition, Bieber found himself helping negotiate the first concessions contract in the history of GM. Accustomed to some of the most lucrative contracts in America, GM workers agreed, among other things, to put off annual wage increases and eliminate some paid time off the job. But the decision was by no means unanimous. The rank and file ratified the contract by only a slim margin. Recalling how difficult the negotiating had been at the small plants in outstate Michigan and how, until 1982, bargaining at GM had always been lucrative for the union, Bieber told the Associated Press: "I thought my life was going to get easier [in the GM department]. All of a sudden the bottom fell out and I got my baptism of fire."

Elected President

In 1983 the UAW was forced to find a successor for then-president Douglas Fraser, who had reached the mandatory retirement age of 65. Bieber, who has a reputation for being tight-lipped, was the last of three men to declare his candidacy in late 1982, and nonetheless, was selected by the union's 26-member executive board in a 15-11 vote. The nomination, supported by a vote of delegates to the UAW's three-year constitutional convention, surprised some who noted at the time Bieber's shy public demeanor and lack of lengthy experience on the national labor scene. But one member of the UAW executive board put it this way to Mark Lett of the *Detroit News:* "It's not that Owen bowled anybody over with his charisma. He isn't charismatic. But he also didn't offend anybody. I think we'd all agree that he's a good Christian gentleman who has integrity and can be trusted. . . . So what's wrong with a guy you can trust?"

Bieber's first three-year term was highlighted by the job security measures he won in the contracts with the Big Three automakers. Bieber, who sits on the Chrysler board of directors, also negotiated in 1985 a more than $2,100 payback for each Chrysler worker for concessions given to the automaker when it was struggling against bankruptcy from 1979 to 1983. That won Bieber overwhelming praise from UAW officials and workers and seemed to dispel past talk about his relative anonymity among union members nationwide. As John Coyne, president of UAW Local 212 in Detroit told John Saunders and Helen Fogel of the *Detroit Free Press:* "I don't think anybody will say, 'Owen who?' again. He's made his mark." Clyde Templin, a union official from a Chrysler plant in Sterling Heights, Michigan, told the *Free Press,* Bieber even compares favorably with late UAW President Walter Reuther who was largely responsible for making the union the social and political power that it is: "My own personal feeling is he [Bieber] is probably the best president we've had since Walter Reuther." Reuther, something of an idol in UAW circles, led the union from 1946 until his death in a plane crash in 1970. Bieber himself has often remarked that he plans to keep the UAW on the aggressive social and political course set by Reuther. "I never had the opportunity to work closely with Walter Reuther," Bieber told Lett of the *Detroit News.* "But all of us in the UAW leadership today identify with the Reuther era. You'll not see this ship of state veer from its established course."

Fights for Rights

But there were problems in Bieber's first term, most notably the pullout of the 120,000 Canadian UAW members in 1985. The action, which followed friction between Bieber and Canadian UAW leader Bob White during 1984's GM contract talks in Canada, deprived the UAW of its international image for the first time in its 50-year history. Bieber also saw the union's requests for protectionism in the auto industry fall on deaf ears in Washington. The UAW demanded a national industrial policy to help protect jobs. It also proposed a requirement that foreign carmakers build a certain percentage of car parts in the United States to help create jobs for American workers.

"It's tougher than I anticipated," Bieber told the *Detroit News.* "There are so many problems. I'm not feeling sorry for myself, but there are so many different problems today. Before, [union presidents worried about] how much money the companies made and if the workers would get their share. They never had the other problems that are out there now like world competition, the Japanese." The complex issues aside, however, Bieber said he was pleased to be the UAW president and looked for more years in that post. "The good Lord willing, [and] good health, I hope to be around for some time," he told Joe Espo of the *Flint Journal.* In 1984 Bieber was named to Chrysler Corporation's 21-member board of directors. Doug Fraser, formerly head of the UAW, was on the board from 1980 until his retirement in 1984. Chrysler claimed that Bieber was being named as an individual and that the UAW had no proprietary claim to the seat. Industry observer's remarked that the seat really belonged to the Chrysler workers who had granted major concessions during the company's earlier financial problems and were the single largest bloc of shareholders in the corporation. In 1985 Bieber was in the ironic position of calling a strike against Chrysler when labor negotiations broke down. The strike was settled a week later following a 42-hour bargaining session

amidst company accusations that the unnecessary $150 million strike was largely due to Bieber's confrontational and ineffectual bargaining style. Neither side was happy with the new contract. In 1989 Bieber told *WARD's Auto World* that future contract negotiations with the Big Three would center on non-economic issues such as job security, reduced work time, and in a precursor to the 1992 presidential election, national health care.

However, by 1992 Bieber and the UAW were mired in a bitter losing battle with Caterpillar Inc., a leading manufacturer of earth moving equipment. When contract negotiations failed, Caterpillar became entrenched and began hiring replacement workers. The strike lasted five months before the UAW, now crushed, ordered its members back to work without a contract. In a desperate attempt to re-assert the power of the UAW as 1993 Big Three contract negotiations approached, Bieber made a fiery and angry speech at a 1992 UAW convention in San Diego. He warned the auto companies against pushing the union too hard, saying that " . . . it takes two to make peace but only one to make a war." He warned the companies against "whipsawing" which is a union term for the policy of pitting one plant against another by threatening to close the one least cooperative and productive. Bieber also threatened the companies with future costly strikes:

> Do not forget that in the consumer-driven, retail, competitive markets in which you sell your products, you are especially vulnerable to lost production.

Bieber went on to defend the Union's policy with Caterpillar saying that the UAW hadn't capitulated and there is " . . . more than one way to skin a Cat!" Despite Bieber's speech, the UAW was still facing a bleak future and Bieber's stewardship of the union was doing little to improve the situation. The Caterpillar strike was a major defeat for the UAW and its ramifications were like shock waves to organized labor. In 1992 GM announced plans to close 21 plants and cut an estimated 50,000 UAW members from its workforce. By 1992 the UAW was successful in organizing only 8,000 of the estimated 100,000 workers employed by foreign car manufacturers with plants in the U.S. In 1978 the UAW represented 86 percent of the auto industry's workforce. It now represented only 68 percent, and since 1979 total UAW membership had fallen by 550,000 (1.5 million to 1.1 million). Consequently, Bieber was under tremendous pressure to cope with the falling fortunes of the UAW and pressure from within the Union for Bieber to retire before his scheduled departure in 1995.

However, Bieber did manage to hold onto his post and was succeeded in 1995 by Stephen Yokich, head of the UAW's GM department and long time rival.

Further Reading

Associated Press, November 13, 1982; May 12, 1983.

Automotive News, November 22, 1982.

Business Week, November 15, 1982; November 29, 1982; June 6, 1983; June 22, 1992.

Detroit Free Press, November 25, 1984; October 27, 1985; June 12, 1995.

Detroit News, July 29, 1980; November 14, 1982; May 20, 1984; June 15, 1992.

Flint Journal, November 18, 1982.

Industry Week, July 5, 1993.

New York Times, May 19, 1983.

Time, November 22, 1982; November 4, 1985.

U.S. News & World Report, May 30, 1983; September 24, 1984.

Wall Street Journal, February 14, 1984.

WARD'S Auto World, December 1989.

Washington Post, November 22, 1982. □

Billy the Kid

William H. Bonney, known as Billy the Kid (1859-1881), was the prototype of the American western gunslinger. He was the youngest and most convincing of the folk hero-villains.

On Nov. 23, 1859, William Bonney was born in New York City but moved as a young lad to Kansas. His father soon died, and his mother remarried and moved west to New Mexico. Having killed a man for insulting his mother, Bonney fled to the Pecos Valley, where he was drawn into the cattle wars then in progress. He became a savage murderer of many men, including Sheriff James Brady and a deputy, and scorned Governor Lew Wallace's demand that he surrender. "His equal for sheer inborn savagery," wrote journalist Emerson Hough, "has never lived." Such statements sent Bonney's reputation soaring and won him the nickname Billy the Kid.

Enjoying such notoriety, Billy the Kid gave no quarter to a hostile world. Condemned to hang, he heard a Las Vegas, Nev., judge say: "You are sentenced to be hanged by the neck until you are dead, dead, dead!" "And you can go to hell, hell, hell!" Billy spat back for an answer.

There are few facts about Billy the Kid's career that can be verified. It is known that women found him attractive. To Native American woman named Deluvina, who pulled off her shawl and wrapped it around him when he was a handcuffed prisoner, Billy gave the tintype of himself which remains the only authentic likeness. Sally Chisum, chatelaine of a large ranch, reported: "In all his personal relations he was the pink of politeness and as courteous a little gentleman as I ever met."

Sheriff Pat Garrett and a large posse vowed to track Billy down and destroy him. In the fall of 1881 they trapped him at Pete Maxwell's house in Fort Summer, N.Mex., ambushed him in a pitch-black room, and shot him to death. The next day he was buried in a borrowed white shirt too large for his slim body. Admirers scraped together $208 for a gravestone, which was later splintered and carried away by relic hunters. Billy had lived exactly 21 years 7 months 21 days.

From the first Billy's fame was part of a folkloric, oral tradition; it had more to do with western chauvinism than with literal history. If his crimes are dated, his appeal is not, as attested to by the many books and movies based on his life.

Further Reading

An important source for material on Billy is Jefferson C. Dykes, *Billy the Kid: The Bibliography of a Legend* (1952), which lists and evaluates all the earlier material. Writers and publicists most responsible for Bonney's fame include Charlie Siringo, *History of "Billy the Kid"* (1920), and Walter Noble Burns, *The Saga of Billy the Kid* (1926).

Additional Sources

The Capture of Billy the Kid, College Station, Tex.: Creative Pub. Co., 1988.

Cline, Donald, *Alias Billy the Kid: The Man Behind the Legend,* Santa Fe, N.M.: Sunstone Press, 1986.

Fable, Edmund, *The True Life of Billy the Kid, the Noted New Mexican Outlaw,* College Station, Tex.: Creative Pub. Co., 1980.

Garrett, Pat F. (Pat Floyd), *The Authentic Life of Billy the Kid: The Noted Desperado of the Southwest, Whose Deeds of Daring and Blood Made his Name a Terror in New Mexico, Arizona, and Northern Mexico,* Alexandria, Va.: Time-Life Books, 1980.

Priestley, Lee, *Billy the Kid: The Good Side of a Bad Man,* Las Cruces, N.M.: Arroyo Press, 1989; Las Cruces, N.M.: Yucca Tree Press, 1993.

Tuska, Jon, *Billy the Kid, a Bio-Bibliography,* Westport, Conn.: Greenwood Press, 1983.

Tuska, Jon, *Billy the Kid, a Handbook,* Lincoln: University of Nebraska Press, 1986, 1983.

Tuska, Jon, *Billy the Kid, His Life and Legend,* Westport, Conn.: Greenwood Press, 1994.

Utley, Robert Marshall, *Billy the Kid: A Short and Violent Life,* Lincoln: University of Nebraska Press, 1989. □

Larry Bird

No player has left a mark on 1980s professional basketball comparable to that of Larry Bird (born 1956), the renowned forward for the Boston Celtics.

Bird took the NBA by storm as a rookie in 1979 and dominated the league almost without a break throughout his career as a professional basket ball player. He transformed the lackluster Celtics into a basketball superpower, leading the team to three national championships in five attempts. Every sort of honor and superlative has been lavished on the blond Indiana native. *Sports Illustrated* contributor Frank Deford has called him "the greatest basketball player in the history of humankind," and few observers would argue the point. "Each Bird game is a rich tapestry of fundamentals," writes Mike Lupica in the New York *Daily News.* "He keeps the ball alive, he is the middleman on the fast break, he boxes out, he posts his man every chance he gets. He moves to the right place on defense, he blocks shots, he picks, he rolls. He dives after loose balls and makes perfect outlet passes. And four or five times down the court, he makes one of those plays that take your breath away."

Although he gained a noticeable measure of poise during his years with the Celtics, Bird is a product of his rural upbringing in French Lick, Indiana. He is a modest man who avoids media exposure (to the extent that it is possible to do so), and his name has never been linked to scandal or sensation. Deford notes: "Among those who know Bird well, the same catalog of qualities is cited again and again—honest, loyal, steadfast, dependable—his existence shaped by the contradictory, almost mystical ability to be the [center of attention], yet always to contribute to those around him." *New Yorker* correspondent Herbert Warren Wind concludes that Bird is the kind of man who derives one pleasure from life: "pride in playing good, sound, imaginative basketball. He hates to see his team lose if it can possibly win. He has almost unlimited determination. . . . A man has to love a game deeply to work so hard to play it well day after day and night after night."

Larry Bird was born on Pearl Harbor Day in 1956, the fourth of six children of Joe and Georgia Bird. His birthplace, West Baden, Indiana, is a small village just outside the slightly larger town of French Lick. Once a famous resort community with highly-prized mineral springs, French Lick had fallen upon hard times by the years of Bird's youth. His father managed to find factory work in the town, but the Bird family always struggled to make ends meet. According to Deford, Larry "knew damn well that he was poor. No, it was not oppressive. But, yes, it was there. The Birds had enough coal to stay warm, but too many nights the old furnace would break down, and the house would fill with black smoke, and they would all have to stand outside, freezing, while Joe Bird tried to fix things." Bird and his brothers were

all avid ball players, and as the next-to-youngest brother, he always competed valiantly to keep up with his older, bigger siblings. Wind writes: "Striving to be as good as Mark, who was three years older, made Larry a much better basketball player than he might otherwise have been, and a more competitive one, too."

Bird told the *New Yorker:* "Basketball wasn't really my only love. We played lots of baseball, softball, rubber ball—we played ball all the time. When we were growing up, before we got a real basketball hoop, we used a coffee can and tried to shoot one of those small sponge-rubber balls through it." In fact, Bird did not settle on basketball as his primary sport until he was well into high school, even though he played the sport on an organized level as young as ten. When it finally seemed apparent that he might excel in the sport, he began to practice—hard—day and night. "I played when I was cold and my body was aching and I was so tired," he told *Sports Illustrated.* "I don't know why, I just kept playing and playing. . . . I guess I always wanted to make the most out of it. I just never knew."

Bird honed his talents in one of the most rigorous basketball arenas, the celebrated Hoosier region where the sport reigns supreme. At Springs Valley High School in French Lick he played guard during his sophomore and junior years. He showed no spectacular ability at the time, and at six-foot-three he was not especially tall. Then fate—or rather, biology—intervened. By his senior year Bird had grown four inches. Almost overnight he had become an impressive physical specimen while retaining his agility and hustle. His senior year he averaged 30.6 points and 20 rebounds per game, and college scouts from all over the East flocked to see him play. He was actively pursued by a number of universities, but he decided to stay in state, entering Indiana University (of Bobby Knight fame) in the fall of 1974.

Bird lasted only twenty-four days at Indiana University. He was overwhelmed by the size and impersonality of the school, so he quickly returned to French Lick and entered junior college there. Within two months he had dropped out of that college as well and had entered into a brief and unhappy marriage. In order to support himself and his daughter, born after the marriage had dissolved, Bird took a job with the City Department of French Lick. He drove a garbage truck and helped to maintain parks and roads in the district. Such work may have seemed a low point to some people, but Bird told *Sports Illustrated* that he actually enjoyed it. "I loved that job," he said. "It was outdoors, you were around your friends. Picking up brush, cleaning it up. I felt like I was really accomplishing something. How many times are you riding around your town and you say to yourself, Why don't they fix that? Why don't they clean the streets up? And here I had the chance to do that. I had the chance to make my community look better."

Overcomes Tragedies

Bird faced further tragedy during the same period when his father committed suicide. Shortly after that unfortunate event, Bird decided to return to college, this time at Indiana State. He had little confidence in his scholastic abilities, but felt that he could help the struggling Sycamores win some respect. By that time he had added two more inches in height and was weighing in at 220 pounds; to quote Wind, he was "an altogether different commodity—a comparatively big man who could challenge the seven-footers at rebounding and in other phases of the game, because he was well built, had exceptional coordination for a man his size, and knew how to utilize the advantages his height gave him." Bird had to sit out his first season at Indiana State, and without him the Sycamores went 13-12. In 1976-77, his first year on the team, the same Sycamores earned a 25-3 record—their best in almost thirty years. The following summer Bird played for the United States team that won the basketball gold medal at the World University Games in Sophia, Bulgaria.

During his Indiana State years, Bird became "the most publicized college player in the country," to quote Wind. Even then Bird showed his penchant for team play and for sharing the glory both on and off the field. Still, he averaged thirty points per game through his junior year and led the Sycamores to the quarterfinals in the 1978 National Invitational Tournament. He was drafted by the Celtics in 1978. At that point he had the option of playing professional ball right away, but instead he chose to stay in school, finish his degree, and be a Sycamore one more season. In his senior year the Sycamores won thirty-three straight games—a collegiate record for a single season—and advanced to the NCAA championships against a formidable Michigan State team led by Earvin "Magic" Johnson. Michigan State won the game which marked the first of many encounters between Bird and Johnson, but Bird walked away with player of the year trophies from the Associated Press, United Press International, and the National Association of Coaches.

Negotiations began with the Celtics for Bird's professional services. Already known for his unwillingness to cooperate with the press, Bird offered no comment as his agent demanded a record salary. The contract signed on June 8, 1979 gave Bird $650,000 per year for five years, a total of $3,250,000. This sum was unheard of for an untested rookie in any sport, and the Boston fans made no secrets of their expectations for their new headliner. Bird did not disappoint. He made the NBA All-Star team his first year, played in every regular season Celtics game, and led the team to a first place finish in its league. Even though the Celtics lost the Eastern Conference finals to the Philadelphia 76ers, Bird was named Rookie of the Year and finished third in the Most Valuable Player balloting.

Bird Soars with Celtics

Those who had predicted that Bird could never turn the dismal Boston franchise around had to eat their words. After Bird's debut, the team became a regular championship contender with wins in 1981, 1984, and 1986. "There hasn't been a Celtics game at the Boston Garden in years that hasn't been sold out," writes Wind. "Most observers attribute this long run of sold-out games to Bird's astonishing virtuosity and the leading role he has played in making the Celtics once again a spirited, exciting team, which has been in contention for the championship just about every year."

The excitement of Bird's play has only been enhanced by his long-standing rivalry with Magic Johnson, the mainstay of the Los Angeles Lakers. In fact, Johnson's Lakers are the only team that have bumped the Celtics from the championship, beating them in 1985 and 1987. *Time* magazine contributor Tom Callahan concludes that even when the Celtics were bested by the Lakers, "somehow they [were] able to retrieve their preeminence in the next instant."

Few would list Larry Bird among the flashiest or most spectacular individual players in the NBA. He is not particularly fast on the court, nor is he a remarkable jumper. Bird has achieved greatness the old-fashioned way: by being consistent, by contributing not as a grand-standing superstar but as a team player, and by attacking every game with every ounce of effort. "The hours that Bird devotes to his job are astonishing," Deford notes. "From himself on the court he seeks only consistency and considers that the true mark of excellence." Years and years of practice and play have made Bird an expert on the shifting patterns of the game and even on the behavior of the ball when it hits the backboard. As Wind puts it, "he just knows where he should go, he beats other players to that spot, and his timing in going up for the ball is exceptional." Indeed, when "spectacular" is used to describe Bird's play, it is often in reference to passing and to diving for out-of-bounds balls. Wind concludes that Bird has showed "how imaginative and enthralling a well-played basketball game can be."

Perhaps not surprisingly, Bird has been dogged over the years by suggestions that he has been singled out for praise more because he is white than because he is good—that his superstardom is predicated on the general scarcity of great white players in the NBA. Deford is one of many who has sought to dispel this myth. "Larry Bird is not a Great White Hope," Deford claims. "Anybody who thinks that misses the point of Larry Bird. Little white boys today would much prefer to grow up to be Michael Jordan or Dominique Wilkins, for however clever and hardworking, they're also truly spectacular players. They can fly. But when kids imitate Larry Bird, mostly what they do, so humdrum, is reach down and rub their hands on the bottom of their sneakers. . . . He seems merely the sum of little bits—a bit more clever than you and me, a bit more dedicated, a bit better on his shooting touch. . . . In Bird's case, he probably has worked as hard as anyone in the ever has in sport, and he does possess an incredible sixth sense, but that has no more to do with his race than it does with his Social Security number." Wind too suggests that Bird's race has little to do with his stardom. "I do not believe that it is the underlying reason Bird and the Celtics have set attendance records at home and on the road," the critic writes. "As I see it, the explanation is that Bird's arresting over-all concept of basketball and his sturdy execution of it have made the Celtics game tremendously exciting to watch."

Always somewhat injury-prone, Bird missed much of the 1988-89 season after major surgery on both heels. He continued to battle back problems and other injuries throughout the next few seasons, but retired from the Celtics after an illustrious 13–year career. He played his last game of basketball as a member of the U.S. Olympic Dream Team at the 1992 games in Barcelona.

After retiring as a player, Bird worked for the Celtics Front Office as a Special Assistant. Many thought he would replace M.L. Carr as coach, but the position was awarded to Rick Pitino. As a result, Bird returned to his home state to succeed Larry Brown as coach of the Indiana Pacers for the 1997–1998 season. He was elected to the Basketball Hall of Fame in 1998.

Further Reading

Heinsohn, Tommy, *Give 'em the Hook,* Prentice Hall, 1989.

Levine, Lee Daniel, *Bird: The Making of an American Sports Legend,* McGraw-Hill, 1989.

Daily News, March 17, 1979; January 30, 1981.

Newsweek, February 26, 1979.

New Yorker, March 24, 1986.

New York Times, February 3, 1979.

Sports Illustrated, January 23, 1978; February 5, 1979; April 2, 1979; October 15, 1979; November 9, 1981; March 21, 1988; December 11, 1989.

Time, February 26, 1979; June 9, 1986.

Washington Post, February 9, 1979. □

Nicholas Black Elk

Nicholas Black Elk (1863-1950) was an Oglala Sioux medicine man in the transition period from nomadic to reservation life for his people and then, as an interviewee, a source for Native American tribal traditions and Plains Indian spirituality.

Born in December 1863 within a paternal lineage of shamans, or medicine men, Black Elk was nearly 70 years old when John Neihardt, Nebraska's poet laureate, interviewed him and several other Sioux elders in May 1931. This contact, the result of Neihardt's search to find survivors of the Wounded Knee Massacre of December 1890, produced the literary classic in American western and Native American writing, *Black Elk Speaks,* published in 1932. Black Elk became known to the world beyond Pine Ridge Reservation through Neihardt's literary interpretation, which covered the first 27 years of his life.

The actual interviews highlighted prominent features of Plains Indian nomadic life, including accounts of military conflict with the United States government, concluding with the 1890 tragic encounter at Wounded Knee Creek, South Dakota. As a teenager, Black Elk had also been at the Battle of the Little Big Horn, Montana, the last stand of General George Custer in 1876. Ten years later he joined William (Buffalo Bill) Cody's Wild West Show on tour in the United States, Great Britain, and the European continent between 1886 and 1889.

The central event in Black Elk's life, however, occurred when he was nine years old while suffering from a life-threatening illness. He had then "the great vision" that took him to the spiritual center of the Lakota world where he was presented to the Six Grandfathers that symbolized *Wakan*

Tanka or The Great Mysteriousness expressed in the powers of the four directions and of the earth and sky. In this transforming experience, Black Elk received instructions typical of shamanic initiation. For the rest of his life, the vision possessed determinative power. Especially in his young adult years, he sought to act out parts of it for the sake of preserving the unity and survival of his people. Aided by a wise elder and medicine man named Black Road, Black Elk launched his career as a shamanic healer at Fort Keogh, Montana, in the spring of 1881. Present as witnesses were his relatives, who had returned from Canada where they had been since 1877 following the death of the warrior Crazy Horse, a cousin of Black Elk's father.

The great vision, as told to Neihardt in 1931, became the center of the text of *Black Elk Speaks.* In remembering it so vividly, Black Elk resurrected its spiritual power, which had not waned despite his sincere conversion to Roman Catholicism in 1904. His depiction stands as a major source in visionary religious literature, attracting the interest in the last half century of symbologists, depth psychologists, and scholars in comparative mythology and prompting pan-Indian revitalization movements of traditional rituals.

Twice married, Black Elk's wife of 1892, Katie War Bonnett, died in 1903. Nicholas, added as a Christian name, lived with his second wife, Anna Brings White, from 1905 until her death in 1941. The father of four sons and a daughter, Black Elk was particularly dependent upon the third and last child by Katie, Benjamin, who provided him a home in his failing years and who also proved enormously helpful to Neihardt's projects. A victim of tuberculosis, Black Elk was treated first in 1912 and as late as the last years of his life. From the fifth decade of his life, he suffered from poor eyesight.

Traveling as a catechist for Roman Catholicism, Black Elk visited the Wind River, Winnebago, and Sisseton reservations between 1908 and 1910. But he kept some traditional practices alive in performing dances for pageants for summer tourists to the Black Hills, first probably in the late 1920s and certainly after 1935. When first hosting Neihardt, he ritualized the occasion of the telling of the great vision and of his deep involvement in the corporate life of his people. The event was so potent that Christian missionaries required Black Elk to disavow any intent to renew the traditional practices of the Sioux. Thirteen years later, he gave Neihardt another interview which became a novel entitled *When the Tree Flowered* when it was published the year after Black Elk died. After the interview of 1944, no disavowal was required of the octogenarian.

In 1947 Joseph Epes Brown, later a scholar of Native American religion and culture, met Black Elk in Nebraska. Brown spent the next winter with the elderly spiritual teacher in Manderson, South Dakota. Through that contact and their conversations Black Elk provided the details of seven traditional rituals of the Oglala people which Brown published as *The Sacred Pipe.* They included a purification ceremony (the sweat lodge), crying for a vision, female puberty, marriage, soul-keeping, throwing the ball, and the great medicine of all traditional Plains people, the Sun Dance.

Even though there is no public evidence that Black Elk practiced the healing rituals of a shaman after he converted to Catholicism, all of his adult life, beginning with his first major exposure to the world of "white" America and Europe, was spent creatively blending native and Christian perspectives. As catechist, he retained the role of spiritual leader, focused as always on the welfare and future of his people. Black Elk's bicultural religious orientation went far beyond the impression mediated by Neihardt's first book, which has no mention of his later Catholic roles and which presents an elegy to the last generation of Plains Indian survivors before the dominance of the reservation. With a spirituality infused by hopefulness and imaged as the sacred hoop and the flowering tree—symbols of the corporate reality of his people—Black Elk was continually devoted to trying to find a way for the tribe to live. His own long life, despite bad health and the economic difficulties of existence on the reservation, testified to a strong determination to endure while facing threatening cultural changes. Within a decade of his death the Sun Dance was renewed under his nephew, Frank Fools Crow. Such an action reflected the impact of Black Elk on the reservation where, coming full circle, what he described but no longer performed became a living practice again. Through the books with Neihardt and Brown, Black Elk made the world at large heirs of his spiritual wisdom, ensuring in them that the rituals of empowerment of the Sioux people would not depend on oral tradition. He died on August 19, 1950, at Manderson and was buried from St. Agnes Mission Chapel in a barren cemetery.

Further Reading

Raymond DeMallie has edited, with an introduction rich in detail and insight, the interview notes from both Neihardt visits with Black Elk in *The Sixth Grandfather* (1984). Joseph Epes Brown remembered Black Elk as a Heyoka or clown-trickster in an interview, "The Wisdom of the Contrary," in *Parabola* (1979). Several writers comment on Black Elk in Vine Deloria, Jr., editor, *A Sender of Words: Essays in Memory of John Neihardt* (1984). Clyde Holler has authored two articles that argue for Black Elk's bicultural religious perspective in *American Indian Quarterly* (Winter 1984) and *Journal of the American Academy of Religion* (March 1984). Will Gravely has reviewed the changing perspectives on Black Elk in *The Iliff Review* (Winter 1987). The place to begin, of course, is Neihardt, editor, *Black Elk Speaks* (reprinted in softcover 1991), and Brown, editor, *The Sacred Pipe*.

Additional Sources

Black Elk, *Black Elk speaks: being the life story of a holy man of the Ogalala Sioux,* Alexandria, Va.: Time-Life Books, 1991; Lincoln: University of Nebraska Press, 1932, 1979, 1988.

The Sixth Grandfather: Black Elk's teachings given to John G. Neihardt, Lincoln: University of Nebraska Press, 1984.

Petri, Hilda Neihardt, *Black Elk and Flaming Rainbow: personal memories of the Lakota holy man and John Neihardt,* Lincoln: University of Nebraska Press, 1995.

Rice, Julian, *Black Elk's story: distinguishing its Lakota purpose,* Albuquerque: University of New Mexico Press, 1991.

Rice, Julian, *Lakota storytelling: Black Elk, Ella Deloria, and Frank Fools Crow,* New York: P. Lang, 1989.

Steltenkamp, Michael F., *Black Elk: holy man of the Oglala,* Norman: University of Oklahoma Press, 1993. □

Mel Blanc

Known in Hollywood as "The Man of a Thousand Voices," Mel Blanc (1908-1989) was the versatile cartoon voice creator of such unforgettable characters as Bugs Bunny, Porky Pig, and Daffy Duck.

Blanc's voices have become standard-bearers for American popular culture throughout the world, heard, by some estimates, by more than 20 million people every day. Each of his characters is distinctive and many developed a trademark line that became famous, like "I tawt I taw a puddy tat!" (Tweety), "What's up, Doc?" (Bugs Bunny), "Thhhhufferin' Thhhhuccotash!" (Sylvester), and "Beep-beep!" (Road Runner). Blanc did the majority of his work for Warner Bros., performing in over 3,000 cartoons for that studio in a career that spanned more than 50 years, but he also worked for other animated film makers and as a memorable radio actor.

Porky Born

Born in 1908 and growing up in Portland, Oregon, Blanc studied music, becoming proficient on the bass, violin, and sousaphone. But he discovered a more amazing instrument in his own voice. "I used to look at animals and wonder, how would that kitten sound if it could talk," he said in the *New York Times.* "I'd tighten up my throat and make a very small voice, not realizing I was rehearsing." After marrying and working for a short time as a radio actor, Blanc moved to Los Angeles and joined Leon Schlesinger Productions, a cartoon workshop that eventually developed

the Looney Tunes and Merry Melodies characters for Warner Bros. While playing the part of a drunken bull in "Porky Picador," Blanc relates in his autobiography *That's Not All Folks,* the actor who was then portraying Porky actually did stutter. When Blanc was later asked to play Porky, he left the stutter in the act, and his first major character was born. Blanc next developed the character who was to become his favorite, Happy Hare, in another Warner Bros. short. He lent a brash, Bronx accent to the wiseguy rabbit that eventually became Bugs Bunny. "He's a little stinker," Blanc told the *New York Times.* "That's why people love him. He does what most people would like to do but don't have the guts to do." More famous characters followed, including Pepe LePew, Wile E. Coyote, Elmer Fudd, Speedy Gonzales, and Yosemite Sam.

Branches Out

Despite his proficiency, Blanc did not own the rights to any of his characters and never earned more than $20,000 in a single year from Warner Bros., so he, was forced to pursue other activities. In the 1960s he was co-producer and voice animator for ABC's "The Bugs Bunny Show," a Saturday morning series that featured Looney Tunes characters in new cartoons designed for television. He also provided the voices for Barney Rubble and Fred Flintstone's pet dinosaur, Dino, for the first prime-time cartoon series, "The Flintstones." Through the years, Blanc also kept up his work in radio, primarily as an actor and special effects creator for "The Jack Benny Show," on which he portrayed Benny's mexican gardener, Sy; his violin teacher, Mr. LeBlanc; his wise-cracking parrot; and his pet polar bear. Blanc also formed his own company to produce radio and television advertising. His last cartoon contribution came in the popular 1988 mixed-animation film "Who Framed Roger Rabbit," in which he performed the voices of Bugs Bunny, Daffy Duck, Tweety, and Porky Pig. In assessing why his characters have become so endearing to all age-groups, Blanc told the *New York Times:* "What we tried to do was amuse ourselves. We didn't make pictures for children. We didn't make pictures for adults. We made them for ourselves." Mel Blanc died in 1989.

Further Reading

Chicago Tribune, July 11, 1989.
New York Times, July 11, 1989. □

Guion Stewart Bluford, Jr.

As a fighter pilot in Vietnam, Guion Stewart Bluford, Jr. (born 1942) flew 144 combat missions and attained the rank of lieutenant colonel. On August 30, 1983, with the lift-off of the STS-8 Orbiter *Challenger,* he became the first African American in space.

D istinguished pilot and aeronautics engineer Guy Bluford was the first black American to experience space flight. Bluford has flown three missions on the Space Shuttle, performing various experiments and re-

turning to earth with exhilarating memories of his time in orbit. Although others have hailed the Philadelphia native as a hero and a role model for the black race, Bluford—who has earned a Ph.D. in aeronautical engineering—prefers to think of himself as a man whose accomplishments are not related to his skin color. He says that he would rather be seen simply as an astronaut, not a *black* astronaut, one of a hard-working corps and not a pioneer. "I felt an awesome responsibility, and I took the responsibility very seriously, of being a role model and opening another door to black Americans," he said of his Shuttle flights in the *Philadelphia Inquirer.* "But the important thing is not that I am black, but that I did a good job as a scientist and an astronaut. There will be black astronauts flying in later missions . . . and they, too, will be people who excel, not simply who are black . . . who can ably represent their people, their communities, their country."

Washington Post correspondent Bill Prochnau called Bluford's life "a study in contradictions: the story of a shy and reticent youth who will be known to history as a black pioneer, a youngster whose mother once thought him the least likely of her three sons to make a success of himself, a struggling student who persevered to earn a master's degree and a doctorate, a loner who says he has no best friends and no heroes but who is . . . seen as a hero himself, a self-described 'average guy' who became far more than average by pressing on when things got tough and by setting each new goal only after the last had been achieved."

Early Years in Philadelphia

Bluford, known in his youth by the nickname "Bunny," grew up in a middle-class, racially mixed neighborhood in Philadelphia. Both of his parents hailed from families of distinction. His mother, Lolita, was related to Carol Brice Carey, a well-known contralto and voice coach, and his father, Guion, Sr., was the brother of the editor of the *Kansas City Call.* Bluford's parents also had advanced educations. His father was a mechanical engineer until epilepsy forced him to retire early, and his mother worked as a special education teacher in the city's public schools.

Bluford was a quiet, private child who reportedly had few friends. He liked to spend his spare time building model airplanes and working crossword puzzles. He told the *Philadelphia Inquirer* that he was fascinated with his father's attitude toward work. "He would charge out of the house every morning, eager to get to work," Bluford said. "I thought if engineers enjoy work that much, it must be a good thing to get into."

Bluford was deeply moved and inspired by his father's courageous struggle with ill health. Determined to become an aeronautics engineer, the young man devoted himself to his studies. On one occasion, a guidance counselor at Overbrook, the mostly white high school he attended, suggested that Bluford might not be college material. Nevertheless, he was able to maintain a C-plus average in the school's most difficult math and science courses. Bluford's brother Kenneth told the *Washington Post:* "Bunny just had to work harder than the rest of us. He put in very long hours. He was always a little behind and trying to catch up. He was not like a kid who was unusually bright, with his mind darting all over the place, making discoveries here and there. In school, Bunny was always slugging it out."

Bluford's parents paid no attention to the suggestion that their son would not succeed in college. In 1960 they sent him to Pennsylvania State University, where he was the only black student in the engineering school. He attended college on the Reserve Officers' Training Corps plan and once again earned adequate, if not exceptional grades. Barnes McCormick, a professor of aerospace engineering at Penn State, told the *Washington Post* that Bluford was "a quiet fellow and an average student, not the sort you would expect to be interviewed about 20 years later."

Fighter Pilot in Vietnam

During his senior year at Penn State, Bluford married another Philadelphian, Linda Tull. After graduating in 1964, he joined the U.S. Air Force and took flight training. He was assigned to the 557th Tactical Fighter Squadron at Cam Ram Bay in Vietnam, where he flew 144 combat missions, 65 of them over North Vietnam. His family at home was split philosophically about the war, but Bluford saw his activities in Vietnam as a patriotic duty that he needed to perform to the best of his ability. He earned numerous medals and citations for his flying, including an Air Force Commendation medal. He returned home a lieutenant colonel and began to work as a test pilot for new air force equipment.

Referring to Bluford's transformation from average student to extraordinary military officer and engineer, *Philadelphia Inquirer* contributor Fawn Vrazo observed: "Between 1964, the year he graduated from Penn State, and 1978, the year he received a doctoral degree in engineering . . . something remarkable happened to Guy Bluford. School and military records suggest that he put himself through an incredible honing process—tightening up his determination and work habits until he became a perfectly disciplined and motivated specimen of an Air Force career pilot and engineer." Bluford was one of a handful of candidates chosen to attend the Air Force Institute of Technology near Dayton, Ohio. There he received his master's and doctoral degrees in aerospace engineering, with a minor in laser physics. He ranked consistently among the top ten percent of his class. He also continued to work as a test pilot and an instructor for would-be military aviators.

In 1978 Bluford submitted his application to the Space Shuttle program. He knew he had little chance of acceptance—some eight thousand other military personnel had also applied for only 35 openings. When he received the call telling him of his selection, he quietly celebrated the news with his wife and two sons. He told the *Philadelphia Inquirer* that he and several other black aviators who are now astronauts "had to be ready in 1977 and 1978, when the doors of opportunity were opened to us and the cloak of prejudice was raised. As black scientists and engineers and aviators, we had to prove that black people could excel."

Flew Space Shuttle Missions

Bluford was not the first black man in space—a Cuban astronaut had flown with the Soviet Union's space program. Bluford was, however, the first black American to be a member of a space flight. After years of training, he was named to the Shuttle's eighth mission, which commenced on August 30, 1983. The week-long mission marked the first nighttime Shuttle launch and landing, and multiple experiments were performed during the flight. Upon returning to earth, Bluford discovered somewhat to his dismay that he was a national celebrity. He was greeted ceremoniously in a number of America's biggest cities, especially Philadelphia, and was in great demand as a public speaker. Bluford accepted this role reluctantly, protesting that he was simply another member of the Space Shuttle team.

"It might be a bad thing [to be first], if you stop and think about it," Bluford told the *Washington Post.* "It might be better to be second or third because then you can enjoy it and disappear—return to the society you came out of without someone always poking you in the side and saying you were first." Tragically, the second black American in space, Ronald E. McNair, perished in the 1986 explosion of the Space Shuttle Challenger.

The Challenger disaster did little to dampen Bluford's enthusiasm for space travel, however. Of the two missions he has flown since 1983, one was a post-Challenger flight undertaken in 1991 to observe such phenomena as the Northern Lights, cirrus clouds, and the atmosphere. To date Bluford has clocked some 314 hours in space, and he is rarely at a loss for words when the subject turns to flying.

Asked by the *Philadelphia Inquirer* to describe how it feels to rocket into space on the Shuttle, he said: "Imagine driving down the street, and you look out the window, and all you see are flames. And your car is being driven by remote control, and you're saying to yourself, 'I hope this thing doesn't blow up.'" Bluford added that the Shuttle travels about three hundred miles *per minute.*

"The Right Stuff" Knows No Color

According to Prochnau, Bluford's career proves "that 'the right stuff' comes in hues other than white." Indeed, despite his disclaimers, Bluford has helped to open doors for minority scientists and aviators who want to be part of the nation's space program. He told the *Philadelphia Inquirer* that he is gratified that blacks and women have become part of the once all-white, all-male astronaut corps. "It's an indication that black Americans are starting to become a part of the mainstream in American society, particularly the professions," he asserted. "I'm sort of bringing black Americans into the astronaut program, breaking new ground. But I also anticipate that blacks in space will become more routine. All of this media attention will eventually fade away."

What won't fade for Bluford is the perspective he has gained from traveling into space and orbiting the earth at 180,000 miles per hour. "I've come to appreciate the planet we live on," he told the *Philadelphia Inquirer.* "It's a small ball in a large universe. It's a very fragile ball but also very beautiful. You don't recognize that until you see it from a little farther off." He told a reporter for the Los Angeles *Daily News* that after traveling well over two million miles in space, his work remains "a labor of love," and added, "You want to stay up forever."

In July 1993 Bluford resigned from NASA to become vice president and general manager of the Engineering Services Division of NYMA, Inc. The company, located in Greenbelt, Maryland, provides engineering and software expertise to several branches of the federal government—including NASA.

Additional Sources

Daily News (Los Angeles), February 12, 1988

Jet, April 30, 1990, pp. 8-9; July 5, 1993, p. 32.

Philadelphia Inquirer, July 21, 1983; August 9, 1983; August 29, 1983; August 31, 1983; November 5, 1983; November 22, 1983; May 19, 1986.

Washington Post, August 21, 1983. □

William Edward Boeing

Capitalizing on the need for new technology in fighting World War II, William Edward Boeing (1881-1956) became a key figure in American aviation.

William Edward Boeing went from being a general businessman to a giant in the aviation business during the 1940s. Most of this success came as a result of the need for new weapons. World War II was the first major war to be fought with the extensive use of air-

planes in a variety of capacities, and airplanes were what Boeing provided.

Background

Born in Detroit, Boeing studied at the Sheffield Scientific School at Yale University but left after two years without graduating. He then moved to Seattle, where he became a prominent timberman, landowner, and yachtsman. Inspired by the new field of aviation, he organized the Boeing Airplane Company in 1915 with a friend, Conrad Westervelt, hoping to build better airplanes than the wooden ones then being used. The Boeing Company began manufacturing airplanes in a seaplane hanger in Seattle, where he copied the designs of European planes used in World War I. Two of Boeing's seaplanes attracted the attention of the U.S. Navy, which encouraged Boeing to develop a new plane that would be used to train pilots. With America's entry into World War I the Boeing facilities expanded rapidly, but the company stagnated in the period between the wars. The company continued to have close ties to the military, and its reputation was based on building fighters during the 1920s and the 1930s. In 1934 his efforts were rewarded when he received the Daniel Guggenheim Medal for successful pioneering and achievement in aircraft design and manufacturing.

The Flying Fortress

During World War II the Boeing Company utilized technological innovations made during the 1930s. Boeing had begun expanding his factories in 1936 in anticipation of war, and the number of employees in the Seattle plants increased to 2,960 by the end of 1938, reaching 28,840 at the time of the Japanese attack on Pearl Harbor in December 1941. Boeing produced three basic types of planes for the military: the B-17 (designed in 1934), the B-29 (designed in 1938), and the Kaydet trainer. The B-17 Flying Fortress and the B-29 Superfortress were the foremost symbols of America's capacity to wage industrial warfare. Both bombers proved decisive in winning the war, particularly in the Pacific theater, where vast amounts of territory had to be covered. (A Boeing Superfortress carried the first atomic bomb dropped on Japan.) At the end of the war Boeing's contracts to produce the bombers ended as well. The company laid off temporary war workers, many of whom were women. He tried to diversify the company's products by experimenting with manufacturing other consumer goods, including furniture, but he quickly realized the difficulty of using airplane factories to manufacture other commodities.

A New Industry

During the 1950s the Boeing Company prospered, though Boeing's health failed and he no longer had any financial connection with it. In the years of prosperity that followed World War II the Boeing Company profited from the expansion of the commercial airline industry by building the Boeing 707 passenger plane. Furthermore, with the advent of the Cold War the government continued to place enough orders to keep weapons manufacturers in business. At the time of Boeing's death in 1956 the company that he had founded had made America's largest jet bomber, the B-52.

Further Reading

Peter M. Bowers, *Boeing Aircraft Since 1916* (Annapolis, Md.: Naval Institute Press, 1989). □

Humphrey Bogart

The American stage and screen actor, Humphrey Bogart (1899-1957), was one of Hollywood's most durable stars and a performer of considerable skill, subtlety, and individuality.

Humphrey Deforest Bogart was born on January 23, 1899, in New York City to Deforest Bogart, a surgeon, and Maud Humphrey Bogart, an illustrator. He attended several private schools, but performed poorly and was expelled at one point. Bogart spent several years with the U.S. Navy and worked briefly as a Wall Street clerk before entering the competitive world of Broadway theater. After a considerable struggle he achieved stature with his two most important stage appearances: in Maxwell Anderson's comedy *Saturday's Children* and Robert E. Sherwood's gangster morality play, *The Petrified Forest*. His characterization of the psychotic killer, Duke Mantee, in the latter, as well as in the popular film version with Bette Davis and Leslie Howard, led to typecasting him as a mobster in such movies as *Dead End* (1937), *Angels with Dirty Faces* (1938), and *The Roaring Twenties* (1940).

Achieved Star Status with Classic Films

Not until his performance as the cold, uncommitted private detective, Sam Spade, in John Huston's adaptation of Dashiell Hammett's *The Maltese Falcon* (1941), did Bogart reveal his potential as a screen personality. He projected, as one critic remarked, "that ambiguous mixture of avarice and honor, sexuality and fear." His co-starring role with Ingrid Bergman as Rick Blaine in Michael Curtiz's war drama *Casablanca* (1943) added to his legend and led to his first Academy Award nomination. He lost, but the film won Best Picture honors. *To Have and Have Not* (1944), Hemingway's novel of the Depression transformed into a comedy of social consciousness by William Faulkner and Howard Hawks, cast Bogart with Lauren Bacall. The following year Bogart divorced his third wife and the two stars married; they had two children.

Although Bogart appeared in several poor movies, most of his films were above the standard Hollywood level, and *The Treasure of Sierra Madre* (1948) may be one of the greatest films ever released. His best motion pictures of the 1940s include *Sahara* (1943), a realistic World War II drama; *The Big Sleep* (1946), Hawks's sophisticated detective thriller based on the Raymond Chandler novel; and *Key Largo* (1948), Huston's toughened filming of the Maxwell Anderson play. Of Bogart's portrayal of the pathetic psychopath in Huston's study of human greed, *The Treasure of Sierra Madre*, Pauline Kael wrote, "In a brilliant characterization, Humphrey Bogart takes the tough-guy role to its psychological limits—the man who stands alone goes from depravity through paranoia to total disintegration." What in

Duke Mantee was mere melodramatic villainy had been transformed into grim psychological reality. In a very different film, the Huston/James Agee adventure comedy, *The African Queen* (1951), Bogart won an Academy Award for his humorously expressive depiction of the earthy, gin-guzzling skipper who brings life to a straight-laced Katharine Hepburn.

In Joseph L. Mankiewicz's Hollywood exposé *The Barefoot Contessa* (1953), Bogart gave depth to his role as a shattered, alcoholic film director. In *Beat the Devil* (1954), he portrayed a disreputable adventurer. *The Caine Mutiny* (1954) provided Bogart with one of his finest roles, as the deranged Captain Queeg. In his last film Bogart gave a strong performance as an investigator of sports corruption in the sharp-edged boxing drama *The Harder They Fall* (1956). A year later, after a long struggle with throat cancer, he died in Hollywood. At his funeral, Bogart's long-time friend Huston paid him tribute: "He is quite unreplaceable. There will never be anybody like him."

Further Reading

Katz, Ephraim. *The Film Encyclopedia* (1979).

Sennet, Ted. *Warner Brothers Presents* (1971). ☐

Julian Bond

Julian Bond (born 1940) was a civil rights leader who was elected to the Georgia House of Representatives in 1965. Denied his seat because of his endorsement of an anti-Vietnam War statement, he was seated by the Supreme Court in the Georgia House one year after his election.

Horace Julian Bond, born on January 14, 1940, in Nashville, Tennessee, was the descendant of several generations of black educators and preachers. His father, Horace Mann Bond, was president of Fort Valley State College. When Bond's father was appointed to be the president of Lincoln University in Oxford, Pennsylvania, the family moved into an environment which was predominantly white. Bond's father caused quite a ferment at the university and in the surrounding community because of his protests against segregated facilities and white attitudes of racial superiority.

Young Julian, however, adjusted relatively easily to his new environment, attending elementary school with white children and winning the sixth grade award for being the brightest student in the class. He was sent to George School, a Quaker preparatory institution near Philadelphia, for his high school education. He encountered a few instances of racial prejudice during these years, but on the whole seemed to adjust well to the academic environment—although his grades were only average.

Civil Rights Movement

After deciding to attend Morehouse College in Atlanta, Georgia, for his higher education, Bond was somewhat fearful about moving there because of the stories of racial violence he had heard. He began college in 1957 when the

civil rights struggle was gaining momentum following the Supreme Court's 1954 school desegregation decision and the 1956 Montgomery, Alabama, bus boycott led by Martin Luther King, Jr. In February 1960 four freshmen from North Carolina Agriculture and Technical College staged a sit-in at Woolworth's white-only lunch counter in Greensboro, North Carolina, in order to force its desegregation. The daring action of these students captured the attention and imagination of black—and some white—students throughout the country.

Bond was swept into the incipient civil rights movement at Morehouse more as a coordinator and a spokesman than as a participant in the demonstrations and sit-ins. Bond was one of the founders of the organization directing the Atlanta student movement, which was called the Committee on Appeal for Human Rights. Because the students were so eager to be part of the civil rights movement, Ella Baker, secretary of the civil rights organization known as the Southern Christian Leadership Conference (SCLC) suggested that interested students meet in 1960 at Shaw University in Raleigh, North Carolina, to coordinate their efforts. King, who was president of the SCLC; and James Lawson, Jr., a clergyman and an exponent of nonviolent resistance, spoke to the students, inviting them to become part of an existing civil rights organization. Several hundred students, Bond among them, finally decided that they would form their own organization, which they named the Student Nonviolent Coordinating Committee (SNCC).

Because of the abilities he had demonstrated working on student newspapers such as the Atlanta *Inquirer*, Bond was appointed communications director for SNCC, a position he held from 1960 until 1966. He became so active in the movement during these years that he dropped out of college and dedicated his time to articulating SNCC's goals in press releases, feature stories, and fliers. He did not complete his degree at Morehouse until 1971.

Georgia State Legislator

Southern segregation meant that black faces were virtually nonexistent in public office, as policemen or firemen, on school boards, on juries, or in bar associations. Few blacks could pass the rigorous voting rights tests or pay poll taxes. As hundreds of Georgia blacks became eligible to vote because of the efforts of civil rights activists, SNCC workers felt that it was important that black candidates seek elective offices. When they sought a candidate for a seat in the Georgia House of Representatives in 1965, the SNCC workers encouraged Bond to run. The Bond name was well known; Bond was articulate and physically attractive; and the workers felt that he would be able to capture the votes needed for victory.

Bond, only after much coaxing, agreed to enter the race. He was 25 years old. He canvassed the 136th legislative district door to door, gained the confidence of the people, and easily won the seat. Bond stated that, proportionately, more people had voted in his district than in any other district in the state. Just before the legislative session opened in 1966, Bond was called by a newsman and asked if he endorsed an anti-Vietnam War statement released by SNCC. Bond said that he had not seen the release, so the newsman read it to him. Bond then said that he basically agreed with it. Unknown to Bond, the interviewing newsman had taped the conversation. When the other Georgia legislators learned about the interview indicating Bond's support of anti-war activists, they formally barred him from the House. That decision was appealed, and eventually reached the Supreme Court. The Court supported Bond and ordered the Georgia House to restore his seat. He was installed in January 1967, over one year after his election victory.

Bond was interested in securing effective civil rights laws, improved welfare legislation, a minimum wage provision, the abolition of the death penalty, increased funding for schools, and anti-poverty and urban renewal programs for the benefit of his constituents. Bond wrote that street protests were moving indoors. He said that it was the time to "translate the politics of marches, demonstrations, and protests" into effective electoral instruments.

The 1968 Democratic Convention

In 1968 Bond was one of the leaders of a delegation to the Democratic National Convention in Chicago whose purpose was to challenge the all-white Georgia delegation led by Governor Lester Maddox and to insure that black voters were represented by black delegates. The delegation won half of the seats from the traditional delegates, and Bond was subsequently nominated to be vice president of the United States. He declined because he was only 28

years old and the Constitution stated that a vice presidential candidate had to be 35.

Later Years

As the 1970s got underway, Bond started to fade from public attention. He limited his focus to helping the predominantly poor residents of his district, concentrating on such issues as street paving and garbage collection. He was criticized for involving himself in many other causes, especially those facing black Atlanta, and it sometimes seemed apparent that he was not entirely interested in politics. Bond continued to express his views, writing and giving speeches, but his popularity was on the wane. He served in the Georgia House until 1975 and then won election to the Georgia Senate. In 1977 Keith Thomas of the *Atlanta Constitution* wrote that a former colleague of Bond in the Georgia House had described him as the most ineffective legislator in the state. In 1976 he rejected an opportunity to join the administration of President Jimmy Carter and subsequently found himself somewhat isolated politically.

In the 1980s Bond narrowly survived a challenge to his Senate seat by an opponent who, according to Thomas, "charged him with inaccessibility, absenteeism, and inattention to local concerns." In 1986 Bond gave up his Senate seat to run for U.S. Congress, but lost the Democratic primary to longtime friend and SNCC colleague, John Lewis. In 1987 Bond's marital problems became headline news when his wife charged him with adultery and cocaine use. The couple divorced in 1989 and, in a paternity suit the following year, Bond admitted to fathering the child of his alleged mistress and was ordered to pay child support.

Bond survived this difficult period of his life by continuing to write and speak. He narrated the highly acclaimed Public Broadcasting Service (PBS) documentary on the civil rights movement, *Eyes on the Prize,* hosted the television program *America's Black Forum,* wrote a nationally syndicated newspaper column titled "Viewpoint," and contributed numerous newspaper and magazine articles. Since 1988 Bond has taught as a visiting professor at Drexel University, Harvard University, Williams College, the University of Virginia, and American University. In 1995 he was elected to his fourth term on the board of the National Association for the Advancement of Colored People (NAACP). Bond was elected as chairman of the NAACP in February 1998. He has made it clear that it is unlikely that he will reenter politics. "I gave it 20 years. That's enough," he told the *Atlanta Constitution.* Yet, the former legislator believes his career is far from over. "If people remember me, I hope it's not for what I've already done, but what I'm still going to do. And what that is, I have no idea. But I expect to be going a lot longer."

Further Reading

Bond wrote a book in which he discussed his political views from a historical perspective entitled *A Time to Act; The Movement in Politics* (1972). There is a full-length biography of Bond's accomplishments by age 31 written by John Neary called *Julian Bond: Black Rebel* (1971). Neary is somewhat critical of Bond and generally fails to recognize his leadership talents. Roger M. Williams wrote a far more analytical biography of several generations of the Bond family entitled *The Bonds: An American Family* (1971). However, Williams at times borrows heavily from Neary's account of Julian Bond's life. ☐

Daniel Boone

An American frontiersman and explorer, Daniel Boone (1734-1820) was the greatest woodsman in United States history. Hero of much farfetched fiction, Boone survived both legend making and debunking to emerge a genuine hero.

For all the myths about him, Daniel Boone was very much a real man born near Reading, Pa., on Nov. 2, 1734. At the age of 12 he became a hunter. He accompanied his family to North Carolina's Buffalo Lick on the Yadkin River in 1751 and, after working for his father, became a teamster and blacksmith. In 1755 he accompanied Brig. Gen. Edward Braddock as a wagoner on the ill-fated march to Ft. Duquesne. While on this march he met a teamster named John Finley, an old hunter, whose talk of the Kentucky wilderness eventually influenced Boone's career as a woodsman and explorer. When Braddock's command was destroyed at Turtle Creek (near modern Pittsburgh) by a French and Indian ambush, Boone fled for his life on horseback.

Early Expeditions

Daniel Boone married Rebecca Bryan on Aug. 14, 1756, and settled down in the Yadkin Valley, firmly believing that he had all the requisites of a good life—"a good gun, a good horse, and a good wife." But Finley's stories of fabled "Kentucke" never really vanished from his mind. In 1767 Boone led his first expedition as far westward as the area of Floyd County, Ky. On May 1, 1769, with Finley and four other companions, Boone opened the way to the Far West by blazing a trail through the Cumberland Gap. This trail soon became a highway to the frontier. As an agent for Richard Henderson and his Transylvania Company, Boone led the first detachment of colonists to Kentucky, reaching the site of Boonesborough on April Fool's Day 1775. There he began to build a fort to protect the settlement from the Indians, and that year he brought west another party, which included his own family.

Boone became the leader of the Kentucky settlement, as hunter, surveyor, and Indian fighter. He was a major of the Virginia militia when Kentucky was added to that state as an enormous county. The first of a series of misfortunes for Boone occurred in July 1776, when his daughter, Jemima, was captured by Shawnee and Cherokee tribespeople. He rescued her but 2 years later was himself captured by Shawnee tribespeople. Though he escaped and helped defend Boonesborough against Indian raiders, while on his way east with more than $20,000 in settlers' money (with which he was to buy land warrants) he was robbed of the entire sum. The settlers who angrily demanded satisfaction were repaid by Boone in land. But from this time on, Boone was dogged by debts, lawsuits, and land-record technicalities until, as one of his kin said—exaggerating

slightly—at the time of his death he did not own enough land to make a decent grave.

Moving Westward

Moving to Boone's Station, the scout held a succession of offices, including lieutenant colonel of Fayette County, legislative delegate, sheriff, county lieutenant, and deputy surveyor. In 1786 he moved to Maysville and was elected to the legislature. Misfortune continued to dog him, however: he lost his land because it had been improperly entered in the records. In 1788 he abandoned his beloved Kentucky and moved to Point Pleasant in what is now West Virginia. He was appointed lieutenant colonel of Kanawha County in 1789 and its legislative delegate in 1791.

When Boone lost the last of the Kentucky lands that he had discovered, protected, settled, and improved, he also lost faith. He moved all the way west to Spain's Alta Luisiana (or Upper Louisiana, now Missouri), where he obtained a land grant at the mouth of Femme Osage Creek. He had moved because the "Dark and Bloody Ground" of yore was filling up with settlers and he did not like to be crowded; when asked why he had left Kentucky, he answered, "Too many people! Too crowded, too crowded! I want some elbow room." Actually, however, he hoped to settle on some land that would not be taken away from him by legalistic trickery. The Spaniards were pleased to have the famous Kentuckian as a colonist and gave him a large land grant, making him magistrate of his district. He must have viewed the subsequent annexation of Louisiana Territory by the United States with mixed emotions, including apprehension. His fears were justified when, once again, U.S. land commissioners voided Boone's claim. However, in 1814 Congress confirmed a part of his Spanish grant.

Daniel Boone's greatest satisfaction was neither in opening up new territory to settlement nor in becoming the subject of laudatory books but simply in being able to journey back to Kentucky about 1810 to pay off his outstanding debts; he was left with only 50 cents. After his wife died 3 years later, the famous Kentuckian spent most of his remaining years in quiet obscurity in the Missouri home of his son, where he died on Sept. 26, 1820.

Boone was moderately well known for the wilderness exploits that had been described in several books when Lord Byron devoted seven stanzas of his poem *Don Juan* to him in 1823. The poet made the recently deceased woodsman world famous, with the result that Boone became a target for belittlers and debunkers as well as mythmakers. The latter sought to inflate his real-life adventures; the former tried to destroy his legend. All failed because the difference between legend and reality in Boone's case was so small. If he was not a dime-novel superman in buckskins, he was an unsurpassed woodsman; and he was strong, brave, loyal, and, above all, honest. Although he was hardly the "happiest of men" (as Byron described him) and had been forced to flee from American land sharks to Spanish territory, he shrugged off his shabby treatment and accepted his fate without rancor. In short, the rough woodsman was something of a stoic. He was also a true gentleman and a great figure of American history.

Further Reading

John Bakeless, *Daniel Boone* (1939), makes it unnecessary to consult such older works as Reuben G. Thwaites, *Daniel Boone* (1902), and Ella Hazel A. Spraker, *The Boone Family* (1922). More recent is Lyman C. Draper, *The Life of Daniel Boone* (1998). Good background studies of the American frontier include Ray Allen Billington, *Westward Expansion: A History of the American Frontier* (1949; 3d ed. 1967) and *America's Frontier Heritage* (1966), and Thomas D. Clark, *Frontier America: The Story of the Westward Movement* (1959; 2d ed. 1969). □

John Wilkes Booth

One of the most promising American actors of his time, John Wilkes Booth (1838-1865) was the assassin of President Abraham Lincoln in 1865.

John Wilkes Booth was born in Bel Air, Maryland, and attended school sporadically. A strikingly handsome youth, he attracted many people, and early decided to try the stage. Although unwilling to work at his parts, native talent enabled him to win acclaim as a Shakespearean actor, especially in the Richmond, Virginia stock company. In 1860—the year Lincoln was elected president—Booth achieved recognition across the country and played to approving audiences. Contemporary actors praised him as a "comer," and his reputation seemed assured.

A respiratory problem in 1863 forced Booth to leave the stage temporarily, and he began conceiving a romantic "conspiracy" to abduct President Lincoln and deliver him to Richmond for a ransom of peace or an exchange of Confederate prisoners.

Sympathized with the South

Unlike the rest of the Booth family, John had always been a Southern sympathizer. He believed the Civil War to be a simple confrontation between Northern tyranny and Southern freedom. He enrolled six other Confederate sympathizers in his kidnapping scheme. Their efforts in March 1865 to capture Lincoln on the outskirts of Washington, D.C. were foiled by the President's failure to appear. Booth's frustration undoubtedly contributed to his decision to assassinate Lincoln.

Booth learned at noon on April 14 that Lincoln would attend Laura Keene's performance of *Our American Cousin* at Ford's Theater in Washington that evening. Vice President Andrew Johnson and Secretary of State William Seward were also to be killed, but Booth's confederates failed to carry out these murders. Booth went to the theater in the afternoon and fixed the door of the President's box so that it could be barred behind him. At about ten o'clock Booth entered the theater, shot Lincoln, and jumped to the stage, shouting "Sic semper tyrannis! (Thus ever to tyrants!) The South is avenged!"

Pursued and Killed

Breaking a leg in his leap to the stage, Booth dragged himself from the theater to a waiting horse. The pain slowed him, and he and another conspirator were forced to seek a doctor. Dr. Samuel A. Mudd set the leg and fed the fugitives. For several days they tried to cross the Potomac, and when at last they succeeded, they journeyed to the farm of Richard H. Garrett, south of the Rappahannock River. Pursuers found them in Garrett's barn on April 26. When Booth refused to surrender, the barn was set afire. His figure was glimpsed briefly just as a shot was fired. Although one of the pursuers claimed to have shot Booth, it is unclear whether he was killed or committed suicide.

Booth's accomplices were rounded up and tried in one of the wildest travesties of justice ever perpetrated. Four of the conspirators were condemned to death. Dr. Mudd received a life sentence, as did two of Booth's accomplices. One accomplice died in 1867; the other and Mudd were pardoned by President Johnson in 1869.

Booth's tragedy lay in his twisted vision of patriotism. He never understood the horror caused by his act, and he died with these last words: "Tell Mother . . . I died for my country."

Further Reading

Lewis, Lloyd, and Mark Neely, Jr., *The Assassination of Lincoln: History and Myth* (1994). □

Ray Bradbury

Ray Bradbury (born 1920) was among the first authors to combine the concepts of science fiction with a sophisticated prose style. Often described as economical yet poetic, Bradbury's fiction conveys a vivid sense of place in which everyday events are transformed into unusual, sometimes sinister situations.

Bradbury began his career during the 1940s as a writer for such pulp magazines as *Black Mask, Amazing Stories,* and *Weird Tales.* The latter magazine served to showcase the works of such fantasy writers as H. P. Lovecraft, Clark Ashton Smith, and August Derleth. Derleth, who founded Arkham House, a publishing company specializing in fantasy literature, accepted one of Bradbury's stories for *Who Knocks?*, an anthology published by his firm. Derleth subsequently suggested that Bradbury compile a volume of his own stories; the resulting book, *Dark Carnival* (1947), collects Bradbury's early fantasy tales. Although Bradbury rarely published pure fantasy later in his career, such themes of his future work as the need to retain humanistic values and the importance of the imagination are displayed in the stories of this collection. Many of these pieces were republished with new material in *The October Country* (1955).

The publication of *The Martian Chronicles* (1950) established Bradbury's reputation as an author of sophisticated science fiction. This collection of stories is connected by the framing device of the settling of Mars by human beings and is dominated by tales of space travel and envi-

ronmental adaptation. Bradbury's themes, however, reflect many of the important issues of the post-World War II era—racism, censorship, technology, and nuclear war—and the stories delineate the implications of these themes through authorial commentary. Clifton Fadiman described *The Martian Chronicles* as being "as grave and troubling as one of Hawthorne's allegories." Another significant collection of short stories, *The Illustrated Man* (1951), also uses a framing device, basing the stories on the tattoos of the title character.

Bradbury's later short story collections are generally considered to be less significant than *The Martian Chronicles* and *The Illustrated Man.* Bradbury shifted his focus in these volumes from outer space to more familiar earthbound settings. *Dandelion Wine* (1957), for example, has as its main subject the midwestern youth of Bradbury's semiautobiographical protagonist, Douglas Spaulding. Although Bradbury used many of the same techniques in these stories as in his science fiction and fantasy publications, *Dandelion Wine* was not as well received as his earlier work. Other later collections, including *A Medicine for Melancholy* (1959), *The Machineries of Joy* (1964), *I Sing the Body Electric!* (1969), and *Long after Midnight* (1976), contain stories set in Bradbury's familiar outer space or midwestern settings and explore his typical themes. Many of Bradbury's stories have been anthologized or filmed for such television programs as *The Twilight Zone, Alfred Hitchcock Presents,* and *Ray Bradbury Theater.*

In addition to his short fiction, Bradbury has several adult novels. The first of these, *Fahrenheit 451* (1953), originally published as a short story and later expanded into novel form, concerns a future society in which books are burned because they are perceived as threats to societal conformity. In *Something Wicked This Way Comes* (1962) a father attempts to save his son and a friend from the sinister forces of a mysterious traveling carnival. Both of these novels have been adapted for film. *Death Is a Lonely Business* (1985) is a detective story featuring Douglas Spaulding, the protagonist of *Dandelion Wine,* as a struggling writer for pulp magazines *Dandelion Wine* and *The Martian Chronicles* are often included in the category of novel. Bradbury has also written poetry and drama; critics have faulted his efforts in these genres as lacking the impact of his fiction.

While Bradbury's popularity is acknowledged even by his detractors, many critics find the reasons for his success difficult to pinpoint. Some believe that the tension Bradbury creates between fantasy and reality is central to his ability to convey his visions and interests to his readers. Peter Stoler asserted that Bradbury's reputation rests on his "chillingly understated stories about a familiar world where it is always a few minutes before midnight on Halloween, and where the unspeakable and unthinkable become commonplace." Mary Ross proposed that "Perhaps the special quality of [Bradbury's] fantasy lies in the fact that people to whom amazing things happen are often so simply, often touchingly, like ourselves." In a genre in which futurism and the fantastic are usually synonymous, Bradbury stands out for his celebration of the future in realistic terms and his exploration of conventional values and ideas. As one of the first science fiction writers to convey his themes through a refined prose style replete with subtlety and humanistic analogies, Bradbury has helped make science fiction a more respected literary genre and is widely admired by the literary establishment.

Further Reading

Authors in the News, Gale, Volume 1, 1976, Volume 2, 1976.

Amis, Kingsley, *New Maps of Hell,* Ballantine, 1960, pp. 90-7.

Berton, Pierre, *Voices from the Sixties,* Doubleday, 1967, pp. 1-10.

Breit, Harvey, *The Writer Observed,* World Publishing, 1956.

Clareson, Thomas D., editor, *Voices for the Future: Essays on Major Science Fiction Writers,* Volume 1, Bowling Green State University Press, 1976.

Concise Dictionary of American Literary Biography: Broadening Views, 1968 1988, Gale, 1989.

Contemporary Literary Criticism, Gale, Volume 1, 1973, Volume 3, 1975, Volume 10, 1979, Volume 15, 1980, Volume 42, 1987. □

William Bradford

William Bradford (1590-1657), one of the Pilgrim Fathers, was the leader of the Plymouth Colony in America. His extraordinary history, "Of Plymouth Plantation," was not published until 1856.

On March 19, 1590, William Bradford was baptized at Austerfield, Yorkshire, England. His father, a yeoman farmer, died when William was only a year old. The boy was trained by relatives to be a farmer. He was still young when he joined a group of Separatists (Protestant radicals who separated from the established Church of England) in nearby Scrooby. For most of the rest of his life, the best source is his *Of Plymouth Plantation.*

Becoming a Pilgrim

In 1607 Bradford and about 120 others were attacked as nonconformists to the Church of England. They withdrew to Holland, under the religious leadership of John Robinson and William Brewster, living for a year at Amsterdam and then in Leiden, where they stayed nearly 12 years. They were very poor; Bradford worked in the textile industry. In these hard years he seems to have managed to get something of an education because he lived with the Brewsters near a university. Bradford was attracted to the ideal of a close-knit community such as the Scrooby group had established. At the age of 23 he married 16-year-old Dorothy May, who belonged to a group of Separatists that had come earlier from England.

The threat of religious wars, the difficulty of earning a decent living, the loss from the community of children who assimilated Dutch ways, the zeal for missionary activity—these forces led the Scrooby group to consider becoming "Pilgrims" by leaving Holland for America. After many delays they chose New England as their goal, and with financial support from London merchants and from Sir Ferdinando Gorges, who claimed rights to the American area they sought, the Pilgrims readied to leave for America.

Signing the Mayflower Compact

But the terms arranged for the colonists by their deacon were treacherous; the backers and the settlers were to share ownership in the land the colonists improved and the dwellings they constructed. Many of the Pilgrims' coreligionists backed out of the enterprise, and a group of "strangers" was recruited to replace them. When one of their two ships, the *Speedwell,* proved unseaworthy, the expedition was delayed further. Finally, in September 1620 the *Mayflower* departed alone, its 102 passengers almost equally divided between "saints" and "strangers." The men on board signed a compact that established government by consent of the governed, the "Mayflower Compact." John Carver (with Brewster, the oldest of the saints) was elected governor.

On landing at Cape Cod in November, a group led by Myles Standish went ashore to explore; they chose Plymouth harbor for their settlement. Meanwhile Dorothy Bradford had drowned. (In 1623 Bradford married a widow from Leiden, with whom he had three children.)

The settlers soon began to construct dwellings. The winter was harsh; one of many who died of the illness that swept the colony was Governor Carver. Bradford became governor, and under him the colonists learned to survive. Squanto, a Native American who had lived in England, taught the settlers to grow corn; and they came to know Massasoit, chief of the Wampanoag tribe. A vivid report on these early adventures written by Bradford and Edward Winslow was sent to England and published as *Mourt's Relation* (1622); with it went clapboard and other materials gathered by the settlers to begin paying off their debts. (Unfortunately the cargo was pirated by a French privateer—a typical piece of Pilgrim bad luck.)

Bradford was responsible for the financial burdens as well as the governing of the colony until his death, though for some five years he did not officially serve as governor. These years saw the debt continue to grow (with great effort it was paid off in 1648).

Developing Plymouth Colony

The population of the colony gradually increased, and by 1623 there were 32 houses and 180 residents. Yet during Bradford's lifetime the colony, which began for religious reasons mainly, never had a satisfactory minister. John Robinson, a great pastor in Holland who had been expected to guide the saints, never reached America. One clergyman who did come, John Lyford, was an especially sharp thorn in Bradford's side. Eventually he was exiled, with the result that the London backers regarded the colonists as contentious and incapable of self-rule.

Gradually as Plymouth Colony came to encompass a number of separate settlements, Bradford's particular idea of community was lost. After 1630 the colony was overshadowed by its neighbor, the Massachusetts Bay Colony. But in fact Plymouth never amounted to much as a political power. By 1644 the entire colony's population was still a mere 300. Plymouth did make other northern colonizing efforts attractive; it supplied important material aid to the Bay Colony, and it may have helped establish its Congregational church polity as the "New England way." Bradford was admired by Governor John Winthrop of Boston, with whom he frequently met to discuss common problems.

Bradford the Man

Bradford's private life was distinguished by self-culture. He taught himself Greek and came to know classical poetry and philosophy as well as contemporary religious writers. He worked on his great history, *Of Plymouth Plantation,* from 1630 until 1646, adding little afterward. Most of the events were described in retrospect. He wrote as a believer in God's providence, but the book usually has an objective tone. Though far from being an egotist, Bradford emerges as the attractive hero of his story. The last pages reflect his recognition that the colony was not a success, and the book has been called a tragic history. Though he stopped writing his history altogether in 1650, he remained vigorous and active until his death in 1657.

Further Reading

A convenient modern edition of Bradford's history was prepared by Samuel Eliot Morison, ed., *Of Plymouth Plantation, 1620-1647* (1952). Another edition was published in 1962, edited and with an introduction by Harvey Wish. The best biography is Bradford Smith, *Bradford of Plymouth* (1951). G. F. Willison, *Saints and Strangers* (1945), an account of the Pilgrims, contains much material on Bradford. Background works include Harvey Wish, *Society and Thought in Early America* (1950); Ruth A. McIntyre, *Debts Hopeful and Desperate: Financing the Plymouth Colony* (1963); and George D. Langdon, Jr., *Pilgrim Colony: A History of New Plymouth, 1620-1691* (1966). □

Ed Bradley

An award-winning broadcast journalist, Ed Bradley (born 1941) remains best known for his work on the weekly news program *60 Minutes.*

Born on June 22, 1941, in Philadelphia, Pennsylvania, Edward R. Bradley received a B.S. degree in education from Cheyney State College in Cheyney, Pennsylvania. From 1963 to 1967 Bradley worked as a disc jockey and news reporter for WDAS radio in Philadelphia. From there he moved on to WCBS radio in New York. He joined CBS as a stringer in the Paris bureau in 1971. Within a few months he was transferred to the Saigon bureau, where he remained until he was assigned to the Washington bureau in June 1974.

Until 1981, Bradley served as anchor for *CBS Sunday Night News* and as principal correspondent for *CBS Reports.* In 1981 he replaced Dan Rather as a correspondent for the weekly news program, *60 Minutes.* In 1992 Bradley was made host of the CBS news program, *Street Stories.*

Bradley has won seven Emmy Awards for broadcast journalism, two Alfred I. duPont-Columbia University Awards for broadcast journalism, a George Foster Peabody Broadcasting Award, a George Polk Award, and an NCAA Anniversary Award.

As a correspondent for CBS's *60 Minutes* since 1981, Bradley has become one of the most visible African-Americans on network television news. As Morgan Strong observed in *Playboy,* Bradley's "soft-spoken and often intensely personal reports made him the first black reporter to become a comfortable part of America's extended TV family."

Bradley's easygoing style belies his many achievements. Some have commented that he seems to have scaled the heights of the television news business more by a knack for being in the right place at the right time than by driving ambition. Michele Wallace of *Essence* called him "a maverick by happenstance, a trailblazer by accident, an inadvertent explorer on the frontier of racial barriers." But Bradley is driven not by ambition in the usual sense—"If I never anchor the national news, that's fine," he told Wallace—but by a less tangible standard. "I think I always need a new challenge," he commented to Kristin McMurran in *People.* "I do need some adventure in my life." And he pointed out to Wallace: "I've always been driven—but I'm not the kind of person who says 'This is going to take me here and that's going to take me there.' I don't have goals—I have standards of achievement."

Bradley grew up in Philadelphia, Pennsylvania, in a neighborhood where "if you didn't fight, you got beat up," he recalled to McMurran. "We were poor, but there was always food on the table. I was raised by people who worked 20-hour days at two jobs each. . . . I was told 'You can be anything you want, kid.' When you hear that often enough, you believe it."

Drifted Into Broadcast News

When Bradley graduated from college in 1964 he went to work as an elementary school teacher while moonlighting as an unpaid disc jockey at a local jazz radio station. He gradually moved into Philadelphia's WDAS news operation, reading hourly newscasts and still receiving no wages. He got the chance to cover his first hard news story when rioting broke out in north Philadelphia and WDAS found itself short-staffed.

"It must have been about two o'clock in the morning. . . . I was coming out of a club and turned on the radio," Bradley related to Tony Vellela in the *Christian Science Monitor.* "I heard Gary Shepard reporting on this rioting that was going on." Bradley proceeded to the station to get a tape recorder and an engineer. "For the next 48 hours, without sleep, I covered the riots. . . . I was getting these great scoops. . . . And that kind of hooked me on the idea of doing live stuff, going out and covering the news."

Bradley proved himself a capable newsman, and the station began paying him a small salary. In 1967 he moved to WCBS, an all-news CBS Radio affiliate in New York City. He worked there for three and a half years before restlessness prompted him to take a vacation in France. "I decided that I was born to live in Paris," he told Strong. After quitting his $45,000-a-year job and moving to the French capital, he planned to "write the great American novel," according to McMurran. "I didn't go to Paris for a career," Strong quoted him as saying, "I went to Paris for my life." Bradley wrote poetry and enjoyed the cultural life of the city until he ran out of money. He subsequently took the only opportunity that would allow him to stay in Paris, becoming a stringer for CBS's Paris bureau where peace talks between the United States and North Vietnam were in progress. Paid by the story, Bradley was able to earn a modest living covering the conference. "If they held the talks, I made the rent money," he told Strong. "I remember once when the talks were suspended for 13 weeks and I got a check for $12.50. But I managed to survive."

After a year, the journalist decided he wanted to get back into the news business full time. "My ego wouldn't let me be part time," he admitted in *People.* He noted in *Playboy,* "I decided I was either going all the way in or getting out," and became a war correspondent in Indochina for CBS-TV. He spent most of the next three years in Vietnam and Cambodia and was wounded in a mortar attack on Easter Sunday in 1973. Reassigned to Washington, D.C., in 1974, the journalist returned to Vietnam in 1975 to report on the end of the war.

Covered the Carter White House

After the fall of Saigon, South Vietnam, which marked the defeat of the anti-Communist government, Bradley returned to the United States to cover Jimmy Carter's campaign for the U.S. presidency. Following the election, CBS assigned him to its Washington, D.C., bureau, where he became the network's first African American White House correspondent. Though the White House beat is considered a prestigious position, Bradley hated it. For one thing, he was CBS's second-string reporter in the capital. Secondly, as

he told Strong, "it was an office job. You go to the same place every day and check in . . . down in the basement in this little nook in the back of the White House press room. And if Jimmy Carter jumps, I [had] to be there to say how high. But it [was] no great fun, and it wasn't the kind of work I wanted to do."

Chafing under the constraints of the assignment, Bradley acquired a reputation for being hard to get along with, one which has followed him ever since. He admits that his work in Washington did not bring out the best in him, but he feels the charge is unjustified. "I don't think I'm abrasive or egocentric. I think I have a healthy ego, but my problem in Washington was that there were too many bullshit assignments," he explained to Strong. "I had always worked overseas. . . . When I went out, I was the producer. So then to come back and have to report to a desk . . . it was all a big change for me. . . . I had not come up through the system."

As soon as he could, Bradley left the Washington bureau to join *CBS Reports* and produce documentaries. The new job took him back to Southeast Asia to make "What's Happening in Cambodia?," a program about refugees fleeing the country during the 1970s. While filming in the refugee camps in Thailand, Bradley and cameraman Norman Lloyd encountered some young Cambodians who were searching for missing relatives. "It's the kind of thing that Norman and I do best," Bradley recalled in *TV Guide.* "We breeze into this Cambodian joint, throw down some beers and say 'What are you guys doing here, man? No kidding! You're going to do *what?* Can we go with you? You can't get in, huh? *We'll* get you in.'" Bradley and Lloyd succeeded in getting the youths into the camp and after following them around for most of the day, captured a tearful mother-son reunion on camera.

Though Bradley resists being pigeonholed as a African American reporter and is said to hate covering "black" stories, some of his finest moments with *CBS Reports* came while focusing on racial issues. In "Murder—Teen-age Style," for example, the reporter examined the problem of violence among African American gangs in Los Angeles. Producer Howard Stringer, who had to talk Bradley into taking the assignment, was quoted by *TV Guide's* Rod Townley as saying "[Bradley]'s black . . . he's younger than most of our correspondents, hipper than most of our correspondents, and knows the world better than most of our correspondents." Stringer also noted that Bradley "doesn't like and doesn't do well at really abstract stories. . . . Ed is a reporter." But the journalist combined both reportage and analysis in his "Blacks in America: With All Deliberate Speed," a 1979 look at race relations in the United States that won him an Emmy and an Alfred I. duPont-Columbia University Award. The documentary contrasted the status of African Americans in Mississippi and Philadelphia in 1954 and 1979. "To the credit of Bradley and his producer, Philip Burton, Jr.," wrote Axel Madsen in *60 Minutes: The Power and the Politics of America's Most Popular News Show,* "the program reported both failures and occasional improvements and concluded that court actions, attempted enforcement, and massive media attention hadn't brought much change."

CBS Reports also sent Bradley to China and Saudi Arabia and to Malaysia to make a documentary on the Vietnamese refugees known as "boat people." "The Boat People" aired in 1979, earning Bradley an Emmy and several other awards. It was also excerpted on *60 Minutes* and may have been a deciding factor in the choice of Bradley to join the staff of America's most popular news program.

Bradley had been considered for *60 Minutes* when a fourth correspondent was added in the late 1970s, but Harry Reasoner was chosen instead. Then when Dan Rather left the news program to take over Walter Cronkite's position as anchor of the *CBS Evening News,* Bradley was asked to join Reasoner, Morley Safer, and Mike Wallace. In his book *Minute by Minute,* producer Don Hewitt wrote of Bradley, "He's so good and so savvy and so lights up the tube every time he's on it that I wonder what took us so long."

Bradley, as quoted by Hewitt, said, "It soon became apparent that I was the front runner, if I believed Hewitt, who went around saying to everybody but me, 'If there's a better reporter than Bradley, I wish someone would point him out,' but still he never said it to me. Finally I was in Los Angeles . . . for a [question] and [answer] session with the TV critics, when a reporter in the back of the room . . . asked Bob Chandler, the CBS News vice president who looked after 60 Minutes, about who was going to replace Rather. Either Chandler was writing Hewitt's lines or Hewitt was writing his: 'If there is a better reporter than Bradley, etc. . . . ' was the answer. . . . The next week I was named to replace Dan Rather."

The New Face on *60 Minutes*

Bradley's presence changed the chemistry of *60 Minutes,* with the substitution of his sensitive, compassionate approach to interviewing and reporting for Rather's more aggressive, sometimes pugnacious tactics. Aware that television audiences are notoriously fickle, Bradley felt that if ratings slipped, he would get the blame. But viewers seemed to accept him readily, though some critics have reacted less favorably. In 1983, for example, Mark Ribowsky wrote in *TV Guide* that Bradley had "not succeeded in establishing a familiar persona for viewers, or made a story sizzle." And four years later, David Shaw, in the same magazine, called Bradley one of the "least impressive of the correspondents [on *60 Minutes*]." Shaw faulted several of Bradley's stories for being "simple" and "superficial" and others for overlooking important questions, but nevertheless praised his "tough-minded report" on defects in the Audi 5000, a story which helped focus attention on a problem that led to the recall of 250,000 cars.

Coworkers and critics alike have pointed out Bradley's ability to establish a rapport with his subjects. Mike Wallace remarked that Bradley's approach is "instinctive—he has no idea how he does it." Bradley himself resists analyzing his style; he remarked to Townley, "I'd rather not think about it and just go out and do it, and it will come naturally." When Bradley profiled singer Lena Horne in December of 1981, for example, John Weisman of *TV Guide* described the journalist's work as "a textbook example of what a great television interview can be." Intercutting

Horne's performances with interview segments in which Horne discussed her personal and professional life, Bradley and producer Jeanne Solomon drew an intimate portrait of the singer that, as Bradley observed to Weisman, "told a lot of things about our society. It told a lot about the way women are treated, a lot of things about the way blacks are treated. It told a lot of things about interracial marriages, difficulties in the film and entertainment industries and how those things have changed and not changed." Bradley has said that he feels "Lena" is among his best work, and Wallace called it "as good a piece as I have seen on television in my life." "Lena" won Bradley his first Emmy as a member of the *60 Minutes* team.

Bradley's gift for winning his subjects' confidence was also crucial when he interviewed actor Laurence Olivier, who was ill at the time. There was some doubt about whether Olivier would have the stamina to complete the interview, but as Hewitt retold it, "gradually, prodded by Ed's questions, the frail old man who had tottered into the room became Laurence Olivier, the actor. The interview went on for another hour and a half as Laurence Olivier and Ed Bradley jousted with each other. When Jeanne finally said 'cut' neither had fallen off his horse, and we wrapped one of the more memorable *60 Minutes* interviews."

Not all of Bradley's interviews have been cordial ones. In one of his first pieces for *60 Minutes,* "The Other Face of the IRA," Bradley spoke with Northern Irish activist Bernadette Devlin McAliskey, prompting a heated discussion of politics and religion, which culminated with McAliskey declaring, "At the end of the day, God will be on the side of the winner, regardless of who wins, regardless of how he wins, because God always was and always will be." Other stories that required a more aggressive approach were Bradley's Emmy-winning study of convicted killer-turned-author Jack Henry Abbott and the story that Bradley described to *TV Guide* as the toughest he'd ever done: a report on the murder of CBS correspondent George Polk in post-World War II Greece.

The Polk investigation presented several difficulties. Many of the principals were dead, and as Bradley explained to Stephen Galloway in *TV Guide,* "for the people who are still alive, you're asking them to talk about something that happened 45 years ago. It's difficult to trust their memory." The piece presented a personal difficulty for Bradley as well: he discovered that one of his journalistic heroes, retired CBS correspondent Winston Burdett, might have been involved in a cover-up to protect Polk's killers. "I'd grown up listening to [Burdett] on the radio," reflected Bradley after what Galloway called "one of the most riveting interviews of one journalist by another."

After more than a decade of investigating and presenting thought-provoking subjects on *60 Minutes* and with six Emmy awards and numerous other honors to his credit, Bradley is no longer a new face but an "ominous and undeflectable presence . . . imperturbable and arguably beyond reproach," commented Johnathan Schwartz in *Gentlemen's Quarterly.* "He is adored without worship." In 1995 Bradley was the highest scorer in seven of eight categories among active CBS journalists in a viewers poll in *TV Guide.*

Occasional rumors of conflict with the *60 Minutes* production staff have subsided, as have speculations that Bradley is unhappy with his job. His need for adventure does not seem to have diminished, though, and he travels often, spending much of his life in hotels. The journalist summed up his attitude about his career in *People* in 1983: "The bottom line is this job is fun. And when it stops being fun, then I'll stop doing it."

Further Reading

Hewitt, Don, *Minute by Minute,* Random House, 1985.

Madsen, Axel, *60 Minutes: The Power and the Politics of America's Most Popular News Show,* Dodd, Mead and Company, 1984.

Christian Science Monitor, October 16, 1986.

Ebony, August 1983.

Essence, November 1983.

Gentlemen's Quarterly, May 1989.

Jet, February 20, 1995.

People, November 14, 1983.

TV Guide, October 18, 1980; February 20, 1982; January 22, 1983; February 25, 1984; March 28, 1987; January 19, 1991.

☐

Mathew B. Brady

The American photographer, publisher, and pictorial historian Mathew B. Brady (ca. 1823-1896) was famous for his portraits of eminent world leaders and his vast photographic documentation of the Civil War.

Mathew B. Brady (he never knew what the initial "B" stood for) was born in Warren County, N.Y. The exact place and year are not known; in later life Brady told a reporter, "I go back near 1823-24." He spent his youth in Saratoga Springs, N.Y., and became a friend of the painter William Page, who was a student of the painter and inventor Samuel F. B. Morse. About 1839/1840 Brady went to New York City with Page. Nothing certain is known of his activity there until 1843, when the city directory listed his occupation as jewel-case manufacturer.

The daguerreotype process had been introduced to America in 1839, and Morse became one of the first to practice the craft and to teach it. Possibly Brady met Morse through Page, and perhaps he learned to take daguerreotypes from him. In 1843 Brady added cases specially made for daguerreotypes to his line of goods, and a year later he opened a "Daguerreian Miniature Gallery." He was at once successful: the first daguerreotypes he put on public exhibition, at the Fair of the American Institute in 1844, won a medal, and he carried away top honors year after year.

Brady once said that "the camera is the eye of history." He began in 1845 to build a vast collection of portraits, which he named "The Gallery of Illustrious Americans," and two years later he opened a Washington branch, so that he could have portraits made of the presidents, cabinet ministers, congressmen, and other government leaders.

Brady sent 20 daguerreotypes to the Great Exhibition in London in 1851; they won him a medal and were greatly admired. In that year he traveled to England and the Continent. Shortly after his return he opened a second New York studio. His eyesight was now failing seriously, and he relied more and more upon assistants to do the actual photography. Chief among his many operators was Alexander Gardner, a Scotsman who was well versed in the newly invented collodion, or wet-plate, process, which was rapidly displacing the daguerreotype. Gardner specialized in making enlargements up to 17 by 20 inches, which Brady called "Imperials"; they cost $750 each. Gardner was put in charge of the gallery in Washington in 1858.

Perhaps the most famous of Brady's portraits was the standing figure of Abraham Lincoln taken at the time of his Cooper Union speech in 1861; Lincoln is reported to have said that the photograph and the speech put him in the White House.

When the Civil War broke out, Brady resolved to make a photographic record of it. The project was a bold one. At his own expense he organized teams of photographers— James D. Horan in his biography states that there were 22 of them—each equipped with a traveling darkroom, for the collodion plates had to be processed on the spot. Brady recollected that he spent over $100,000 and "had men in all parts of the Army, like a rich newspaper."

When the war ended, the collection comprised some 10,000 negatives. The project had cost Brady his fortune, and he became bankrupt. He could not afford to pay the storage bill for one set of negatives, which were sold at auction to the War Department. A second collection was seized by E. and H. T. Anthony, dealers in photographic materials, for nonpayment of debts. Today Brady's vast and brilliant historical record is divided between the National Archives and the Library of Congress in Washington, D.C.

Although he maintained his Washington gallery, Brady never fully recovered from his financial disasters. In 1895 he planned a series of slide lectures about the Civil War. While he was preparing them in New York, he became ill and entered the Presbyterian Hospital, where he died on Jan. 15, 1896.

Further Reading

James D. Horan, *Mathew Brady: Historian with a Camera* (1955), not only recounts the few known facts of Brady's career but gives a vivid account of life in America and the state of photography in the mid-19th century; Horan was the first biographer to have access to the records of Brady's heirs. Roy Meredith, *Mr. Lincoln's Camera Man: Mathew B. Brady* (1946), is somewhat conjectural and poorly documented; it is, however, useful for its illustrations. In 1911 the *Review of Reviews* published the 10-volume *The Photographic History of the Civil War,* edited by Francis Trevelyan Miller; a 5-volume reprint (1957) contains many Brady pictures. □

Louis Dembitz Brandeis

As an associate justice of the U.S. Supreme Court, Louis Dembitz Brandeis (1856-1941) tried to reconcile the developing powers of modern government and society with the maintenance of individual liberties and opportunities for personal development.

As the United States entered the 20th century, many men became concerned with trying to equip government so as to deal with the excesses and inequities fostered by the industrial development of the 19th century. States passed laws trying to regulate utility rates and insurance manipulations and established minimum-wage and maximum-hour laws. Louis Brandeis was one of the most important Americans involved in this effort, first as a publicly minded lawyer and, after 1916, as a member of the U.S. Supreme Court.

Brandeis was born on Nov. 13, 1856, in Louisville, Kentucky, to Adolph and Fredericka Dembitz Brandeis. His parents were Bohemian Jews who had come to America in the aftermath of those European revolutionary movements of 1848 that had sought to establish liberal political institutions and to strengthen the processes of democracy so as to safeguard the dignity and potential for self-development of the common man.

In 1875, at the age of 18, Brandeis entered the Harvard Law School without a formal college degree; he achieved one of the most outstanding records in its history. At the same time he tutored fellow students in order to earn money (necessary because of his father's loss of fortune in the Panic of 1873). Although Brandeis was not the required age of 21, the Harvard Corporation passed a special resolution granting him a bachelor of law degree in 1877. After a further year of legal study at Harvard, he was admitted to the bar.

Early Legal Career

In 1879 Brandeis began a partnership with his classmate Samuel D. Warren. Together they wrote one of the most famous law articles in history, "The Right to Privacy," published in the December 1890 *Harvard Law Review.* In it Brandeis enunciated the view he later echoed in the Supreme Court case of *Olmstead v. United States* (1928), in which he argued that the makers of the Constitution, as evidence of their effort "to protect Americans in their beliefs, their thoughts, their emotions and their sensations . . . conferred, as against the Government, the right to be let alone—the most comprehensive of rights and the right most valued by civilized men."

During this stage of his career, Brandeis spent much time helping the Harvard Law School. Though he declined an offer to become an assistant professor, in 1886 he helped found the Harvard Law School Association, an alumni group, and served for many years as its secretary.

Years of Public Service

By 1890 Brandeis had developed a lucrative practice and was able to serve, without pay, in various public causes. When a fight arose, for example, over preservation of the Boston subway system, he helped save it; similarly, he helped lead the opposition to the New Haven Railroad's monopoly of transportation in New England. The Massachusetts State Legislature's adoption of a savings-bank life insurance system was the result of his investigation of the inequities of existing insurance programs.

Brandeis also took part in the effort to bring legal protections to industrial laborers, and as part of this effort he contributed a major concept to Supreme Court litigation. In 1908, defending an Oregon law establishing wages and hours for women laborers, Brandeis introduced what came to be known as the "Brandeis brief," which went far beyond legal precedent to consider the various economic and social factors which led the legislature to pass the law. Many lawyers followed the Brandeis brief and presented relevant scientific evidence and expert opinion dealing with the great social problems of the day mirrored in judicial litigation.

Appointment to the Supreme Court

President Woodrow Wilson offered Brandeis a position in his Cabinet in 1913, but the Boston lawyer preferred to remain simply a counselor to the President. Brandeis continued his investigations of the implications for democracy of the growing concentration of wealth in large corporations. In 1914 he published *Other People's Money, and How the Bankers Use It,* in which he set down his antimonopoly views.

Wilson's nomination of Brandeis to the Supreme Court on Jan. 28, 1916, aroused a dirty political fight. Six former presidents of the American Bar Association and former president of the United States William Howard Taft denounced Brandeis for his allegedly radical political views. Some anti-Semitism was involved, for Brandeis was the first Jew ever nominated for America's highest court. Finally, however, the fight was won in the Senate, and Brandeis took his seat on June 5, 1916, where he served with distinction until Feb. 13, 1939.

Brandeis often joined his colleague Oliver Wendell Holmes, Jr. in dissenting against the Court's willingness to pose its judgments about economic and social policy against those of individual states. Also with Holmes, Brandeis bravely defended civil liberties throughout this era. If he did uphold wide use of state powers, it was only in the service of furthering individual self-fulfillment; he also rejected incursions of a state upon a citizen's liberty. Two examples are the Olmstead case (already noted), involving wiretapping, and *Whitney v. California,* in which Brandeis opposed a California law suppressing free speech.

Personal Interests

Brandeis married Alice Goldmark in 1891, and they had two daughters. Part of his personal life was his commitment to fellow Jews. He became a leading Zionist, supporting the attempt to develop a Jewish nation in Palestine.

Another of Brandeis's great interests was the building up of strong regional schools as a means of strengthening local areas against the threat of national centralization. To this end, beginning in 1924, he helped formulate and develop the law school and general library of the University of Louisville.

Brandeis died on Oct. 5, 1941. His commitments to justice, education, and Judaism were commemorated several years later in the founding of Brandeis University in Waltham, Mass.

Further Reading

The standard scholarly biography of Brandeis, unfortunately slim so far as his judicial career is concerned, is Alpheus Thomas Mason, *Brandeis: A Free Man's Life* (1946). A good introduction to his legal ideas is Samuel Joseph Konefsky, *The Legacy of Holmes and Brandeis* (1956). Alexander M. Bickel in *The Unpublished Opinions of Mr. Justice Brandeis* (1957) presents good examples of the justice's painstaking methods in preparing his judicial opinions. Paul A. Freund, Brandeis's former clerk, presents a moving portrait in Allison Dunham and Philip B. Kurland, eds., *Mr. Justice* (1964). For general historical background see Robert Green McCloskey, *The American Supreme Court* (1960), and Arthur M. Schlesinger, Jr.'s three volumes: *The Age of Roosevelt: The Crisis of the Old Order* (1957), *The Coming of the New Deal* (1959), and *The Politics of Upheaval* (1960). ☐

Marlon Brando

Beginning with his early career in the films of the 1950s, through his powerful roles in such classics as *On the Waterfront, A Streetcar Named Desire,* and *The Godfather,* Marlon Brando (born 1924) has captivated the American public with his intense onscreen presence, as well as with his personal life of controversy and excess.

Before James Dean, Marlon Brando popularized the jeans-and-T-shirt look, with and without leather jacket, as a movie idol during the early 1950s. The theatrically trained actor began to turn away from his youth-oriented persona with such movie roles as Mark Antony in *Julius Caesar* (1953). After winning an Academy Award for Best Actor for *On the Waterfront* (1954), he portrayed a wide variety of characters on-screen, garnering popular acclaim and critical consensus as one of the greatest cinema actors of the late twentieth century.

Early Career

Brando was born in Omaha, Nebraska, on April 3, 1924. He grew up in Illinois. After expulsion from a military academy, he dug ditches until his father offered to finance his education. Brando moved to New York to study with acting coach Stella Adler and at Lee Strasberg's Actors' Studio. While at the Actors' Studio, Brando adopted the "method approach," which emphasizes characters' motivations for actions. He made his Broadway debut in John Van Druten's sentimental *I Remember Mama* (1944). New York theater critics voted him Broadway's Most Promising Actor for his performance in *Truckline Cafe* (1946). In 1947 he played his greatest stage role, Stanley Kowalski—the brute who rapes his sister-in-law, the fragile Blanche du Bois—in Tennessee Williams's *A Streetcar Named Desire.* As *The New York Review* surmised, "The rest is stardom and gossip and a small handful of wonderful films."

Hollywood beckoned to Brando, and he made his motion picture debut as a paraplegic World War II veteran in *The Men* (1950). Although he did not cooperate with the Hollywood publicity machine, he went on to play Kowalski in the 1951 film version of A *Streetcar Named Desire,* a popular and critical success that earned four Academy

Awards. His next movie, *Viva Zapata!* (1952), with a script by John Steinbeck, traces Emiliano Zapata's rise from peasant to revolutionary to president of Mexico. Brando followed that with *Julius Caesar* and then *The Wild One* (1954), in which he played a motorcycle-gang leader in all his leather-jacketed glory. Next came his Academy Award winning role as a longshoreman fighting the system in *On the Waterfront,* a hard-hitting look at New York City labor unions.

Pinnacle

During the rest of the decade, Brando's screen roles ranged from Napoleon Bonaparte in *Désirée* (1954), to Sky Masterson in 1955's *Guys and Dolls,* in which he sang and danced, to a Nazi soldier in *The Young Lions* (1958). From 1955 to 1958 movie exhibitors voted him one of the top ten box-office draws in the nation. During the 1960s, however, his career had more downs than ups, especially after the MGM studio's disastrous 1962 remake of *Mutiny on the Bounty,* which failed to recoup even half of its enormous budget. Brando portrayed Fletcher Christian, Clark Gable's role in the 1935 original. Brando's excessive self-indulgence reached a pinnacle during the filming of this movie. He was criticized for his on-the-set tantrums and for trying to alter the script. Off the set, he had numerous affairs, ate too much, and distanced himself from the cast and crew. His contract for making the movie included $5,000 for every day the film went over its original schedule. He made $1.25 million when all was said and done.

Brando's career was reborn in 1972 with his depiction of Mafia chieftain Don Corleone in *The Godfather.* He refused his Academy Award for Best Actor as a protest of Hollywood's treatment of Native Americans. Brando did not appear at the awards show to personally deny the trophy. Instead, a Native American Apache named Sacheen Littlefeather read his protest. However, in September of 1994, Brando told the broker in possession of the award, Marty Ingels, that he now wishes to own it. Ingels would not return it.

Brando proceeded the following year to the highly controversial yet highly acclaimed *Last Tango in Paris,* which was rated X. Since then Brando has received huge salaries for playing small parts in such movies as *Superman* (1978) and *Apocalypse Now* (1979). Nominated for an Academy Award for Best Supporting Actor for A *Dry White Season* in 1989, Brando also appeared in *The Freshman* with Matthew Broderick. In 1995, he costarred in *Don Juan DeMarco* with Johnny Depp. Young people who have not seen Brando's amazing efforts in his early films will not find the same genius in his later movies. The small roles he has played do not demand the acting range for which he had once achieved so much praise. Janet Maslin of the *New York Times,* in her review of *Don Juan DeMarco,* wrote, "Mr. Brando doesn't so much play his role as play along." The critic added, "*Don Juan DeMarco* verges on the sad when its subject is vitality, since Mr. Depp's so clearly eclipses that of his co-star."

In early 1996 Brando costared in afilm called *The Island of Dr. Moreau. Entertainment Weekly* reported that

the actor was using an earpiece to remember his lines. His costar in the film, David Thewlis, told the magazine that he was nonetheless still impressed by Brando. "When he walks into a room," Thewlis noted, "you know he's around."

A Life of Turmoil and Self-Indulgence

There have been countless pages of print written about Brando's reclusive and self-indulgent lifestyle, including two books released in 1994: *Brando: The Biography,* by Peter Manso, and *Brando: Songs My Mother Taught Me,* by Marlon Brando with Robert Lindsey. The book by Marlon Brando is obviously the one he authorizes, but Manso's book is a result of seven years of research and interviews with more than a thousand people. *Time* magazine, though, questioned Manso's ethics in conducting such excessive research: "Driven to possess another man's life, Manso becomes the literary version of one of the late 20th century's scariest specimens, the celebrity stalker."

It has been observed that Brando has perhaps loved food and womanizing too much. His best acting performances are roles that required him to show a constrained and displayed rage and suffering. His own rage may have come from parents who did not care about him. *Time* magazine reported, "Brando had a stern, cold father and a dream-disheveled mother—both alcoholics, both sexually promiscuous—and he encompassed both their natures without resolving the conflict." Brando himself wrote in his autobiography, "If my father were alive today, I don't know what I would do. After he died, I used to think, 'God, just give him to me alive for eight seconds because I want to break his jaw.'"

Brando's acting teacher, Stella Adler, is often credited with helping him become a brilliant actor. Brando said in a reprint of Manso's book presented in *Premiere* magazine, "If it hadn't been for Stella, maybe I wouldn't have gotten where I am—she taught me how to read, she taught me to look at art, she taught me to listen to music."

Although Brando avoids speaking in details about his marriages, even in his autobiography, it is known that he has been married three times to three ex-actresses. He has at least 11 children ranging in age from two to thirty-eight. Five of the children are with his three wives, three are with his Guatemalan housekeeper, and the other three children are from other affairs. One of Brando's sons, Christian, told *People* magazine, "The family kept changing shape. I'd sit down at the breakfast table and say, 'Who are you?'" Christian is now at a state prison in California serving a 10-year sentence for voluntary manslaughter in the death of his sister's fiancee, Dag Drollet. He claimed Drollet was physically abusing his pregnant sister, Cheyenne. Christian said he struggled with Drollet and accidentally shot him in the face. Brando, in the house at the time, gave mouth-to-mouth resuscitation to Drollet and called 911. At Christian's trial, *People* reported one of Brando's comments on the witness stand, "I tried to be a good father. I did the best I could."

Brando's daughter, Cheyenne, was a troubled young woman. In and out of drug rehabilitation centers and mental hospitals for much of her life, she lived in Tahiti with her mother Tarita (one of Brando's wives whom he met on the set of *Mutiny on the Bounty*). *People* reported in 1990 that Cheyenne said of Brando, "I have come to despise my father for the way he ignored me as a child." After Drollet's death, Cheyenne became even more reclusive and depressed. A judge ruled that she was too depressed to raise her child and gave custody of the boy to her mother, Tarita. Cheyenne took a leave from a mental hospital on Easter Sunday in 1995 to visit her family. At her mother's home that day, Cheyenne, who had attempted suicide before, hanged herself.

Brando's years of self-indulgence are visible—he weighed well over 300 pounds in the mid-1990s. To judge Brando by his appearance and dismiss his work because of his later, less significant acting jobs, however, would be a mistake. His performance in *A Streetcar Named Desire* brought audiences to their knees, and his range of roles is a testament to his capability to explore many aspects of the human psyche. Brando seems perfectly content that his best work is behind him. As for his fans, they must accept that staying power is not what confirms the actor's brilliance.

Further Reading

Gary Cary, *Marlon Brando: The Only Contender* (London: Robson, 1985).

Christopher Nickens, *Brando: A Biography in Pictures* (Garden City, N.Y.: Doubleday, 1987).

Richard Schickel, *Brando: A Life in Our Times* (New York: Atheneum, 1991). □

Stephen Breyer

The general consensus on Stephen Breyer (born 1938), the 108th member of the United States Supreme Court, is that he has a brilliant legal mind. However, when those same observers try to label him as either a conservative or a liberal, or attempt to figure out how his decisions and opinions will shape the court, there is little agreement. Breyer is considered a centrist, a man who comes to the nation's highest court unlikely to radically transform the institution.

Like President Bill Clinton's other Supreme Court appointment, Ruth Bader Ginsburg, Breyer mirrors his president's political style: he has strong convictions, but he is known as much for his spirit of evenhandedness and compromise as for his passionate views on subjects.

Evidence of Breyer's centrist views became clear during his July, 1994 confirmation hearings before the United States Senate Judiciary Committee. Breyer sailed through the hearings with little rancor from either Republicans or Democrats, and won unanimous approval from the committee. Those hearings were vastly different from the contentious committee meetings that greeted other recent Supreme Court nominees. And, perhaps, Breyer's ability to appease political foes was one of the reasons President Clinton chose him as nominee.

Stephen Gerald Breyer was born on August 15, 1938, in San Francisco. His father was an attorney for the San Francisco School Board and his mother was active in

Democratic political circles. Upon his appointment to the court, Breyer was quoted as saying he was moved by the fact that he was able to rise so highly in America considering that his grandfather, a cobbler, came to the country just two generations ago. A brilliant student, Breyer attended Stanford University, choosing it over Harvard at the request of his parents, and graduated as a Phi Beta Kappa member with highest honors. He then studied at Oxford University in England as a prestigious Marshall Scholar. He received his law degree, *magna cum laude,* from Harvard.

Teaches at Harvard

Upon graduation, Breyer became a law clerk for Supreme Court Justice Arthur Goldberg. After a stint at the U.S. Department of Justice between 1965 and 1967, Breyer returned to Cambridge, where he taught law at Harvard. But "he is no stranger to Washington politics," the *Boston Globe* noted of him upon his appointment to the Supreme Court. That is because in 1973 he was involved in the biggest political story of the century: Watergate, the scandal that revealed then-President Richard M. Nixon's role in the break-in of Democratic Party headquarters at Washington's Watergate Hotel. Breyer became part of the special prosecutor's force led by his former law professor, Archibald Cox. That job led to the position of assistant special counsel to the Senate Judiciary Committee in 1975. Massachusetts Senator Edward Kennedy, who once chaired the committee, named Breyer as chief counsel in 1979. The Judiciary Committee is the same group that, 19 years later, held hearings and voted on Breyer's confirmation to the Supreme Court. The *Boston Globe* reported that one reason for Breyer's success before Judiciary was because "most of the lawmakers have long-standing ties to Breyer from his days as the committee's legal counsel."

Appointed to Court of Appeals

After the 1980 elections, President Jimmy Carter, who had lost the presidency to Ronald Reagan, made his final judicial appointment before leaving office; he chose Breyer to serve on the U.S. Court of Appeals. Republicans, who could have opposed the nomination and allowed Reagan to pick his own nominee, did not oppose Breyer. In supporting Breyer's nomination to the Supreme Court 14 years later, the *Wall Street Journal* noted of his 1980 nomination: "Mr. Breyer was the last Carter appointee confirmed by the Senate—confirmed even after the 1980 election because of his bipartisan support. For a president [Clinton] who needs a victory, this choice [of Breyer] is really easy." Breyer would become chief judge of the First Circuit Court of Appeals in Boston in 1990.

Once on the bench, Breyer began to develop the legal reputation that would lead to his Supreme Court nomination. Legal scholars describe his decisions in numerous cases before the appeals court as reasoned and moderate, and lacking passion. "Breyer has not used his writings to launch a perceptible constitutional manifesto," the *Boston Globe* opined in an article analyzing Breyer's "paper trail" of opinions. He has adhered to the theory that cases need not be decided within the strict formal structures of a particular law; that is, Breyer has been known to consider not just the laws Congress has made, but the "legislative intent" behind those laws. He looks at the legislative history of the struggle to pass a law, and what congressmen and senators meant the law to do when issuing his rulings. He has also been known to consider the effects of his rulings in the future, and not just consider past precedents.

"Law requires both a heart and a head," the *New York Times* quoted him as saying during his confirmation hearings. "If you don't have a heart, it becomes a sterile set of rules removed from human problems, and it won't help. If you don't have a head, there's a risk that in trying to decide a particular person's problem in a case that may look fine for that person, you cause trouble for a lot of other people, making their lives yet worse. . . . It's a question of balance."

Observers say that such opinions fly directly in the faces of other sitting justices, such as Antonin Scalia, who is regarded as forming decisions based on strict interpretations of the law. While Breyer may not be able to win over Scalia to his views, he is seen as a "coalition builder," someone who will occupy the political center of the court and woo other, centrist-leaning justices to his way of thinking. Or, as the *Boston Globe* reported, "Breyer's capacity for consensus-building causes some court analysts to believe he could lead a new moderate-liberal coalition."

On key controversial issues, Breyer has become known as a defender of First Amendment freedoms. On the First Circuit court he found that a federally-imposed " gag order" preventing family-planning clinics from providing abortion counseling was unconstitutional; it violated free speech provisions. He also wrote a majority decision that rejected the federal government's requirement that doctors working for the World Health Organization go through a "loyalty check." Allowing the government to examine someone's political leanings as a basis for judging loyalty violated that person's free speech rights, Breyer ruled. He also has a strong environmental record: in 1983 he ruled that oil companies and the federal government had no right to allow oil exploration in the environmentally sensitive George's Bank fishing area off the coast of Massachusetts.

Breyer is much more conservative when it comes to criminal cases. He has allowed improper police testimony to stand in a drug case, calling the police error "harmless" in light of the strong evidence against the drug dealers. Even friends, such as noted Harvard Law School professor and celebrity lawyer Alan Dershowitz, have expressed displeasure with some aspects of Breyer's opinions. Dershowitz was quoted in the *New York Times* as saying, "A lot of 'liberal' or 'moderate' judges establish their liberal credentials by supporting women's rights and press rights, which are very popular with their constituencies, and then establish their conservative credentials by an almost knee-jerk, pro-prosecutorial approach in criminal cases. . . . This certainly characterizes . . . Breyer."

Breyer's best known—and most controversial—work in the field of criminality occurred in 1987 when he served on the U.S. Sentencing Commission, a group dedicated to reviewing what sort of jail time criminals should receive across America. The commission's set of proposals drew

mixed reviews, with some crediting Breyer for finally getting something down on paper after extensive meetings. But others say the guidelines are too strict, that they do not allow judges enough flexibility, and that in some instances the proposed sentences are too harsh.

As regards the new Supreme Court justice's personal life, he has been married to the former Joanna Hare since 1967. She is the daughter of former British Conservative Party leader Lord John Blackenham. The pair met in Washington, D.C., and after 16 years of marriage Joanna Breyer went back to school and received a Ph.D. in psychology. She works at the Dana-Farber Cancer Institute with children stricken with cancer. The Breyers own 160 acres in Plainfield, New Hampshire, and often visit there to hike. The couple have three grown children. Breyer is known as an avid birdwatcher, a good cook, a fan of both old movies and football. "He has been known to wear the same suit for weeks while focusing on something he considers more important than wardrobe," the *Boston Globe* reported. He is Jewish, "speaks with a hint of a British accent," according to the *New York Times,* and "is more glib than smart and has an impish, often odd, sensibility that could come across as flakiness and could antagonize his potential colleagues on the Supreme Court."

Breyer's other major hobby—bicycle riding—probably cost him his first chance at being named to the Supreme Court. In May of 1993, Breyer was being considered to fill the seat of retiring Justice Byron White. But he was hit by a car while bicycling in the Boston area and was hospitalized. During his recuperation, President Clinton summoned the judge to Washington for an interview. The *Boston Globe* reported him as telling a friend "that he feared his prospects for the job were poor because he was ill at the meeting with the president . . . and nearly fainted afterward." But during the interview process it also became clear that Breyer had done what other recently rejected government nominees had done: he had failed to pay Social Security taxes on his part-time housekeeper. The same oversight forced Clinton to reject his first two choices for attorney general: Zoe Baird and Kimba Wood. Clinton eventually chose Ruth Bader Ginsburg over Breyer for the Supreme Court. But a year later, when Clinton chose Breyer to fill the seat of Justice Harry Blackmun, Breyer, quoted in the *Boston Globe,* was able to joke to the president, "I'm glad I didn't bring my bicycle down."

After being passed over in favor of Ginsburg in June of 1993, Breyer returned to Boston. Although many of his friends were critical of the way Clinton had dangled the job before Breyer and had made him travel while still feeling the ill effects of his bicycle accident, Breyer remained reserved and uncritical. After the rejection, according to the *Wall Street Journal,* Breyer called his friends, "cheering them up, rather than vice versa."

He returned to Boston to continue work on his biggest, non-legal project: helping design and construct a new $200 million federal courthouse in Boston. The courthouse is situated on the waterfront area known as Fan Pier. "This most beautiful site in Boston," Breyer was quoted as saying in the *New York Times,* "does not belong to the lawyers, it does not belong to the federal government, it does not belong to the litigants. It belongs to the people." According to all reports, Breyer threw himself into the project: interviewing and choosing architects, meeting with community groups, even visiting courts around the country that he and the architect either admired or wanted to avoid duplicating. In the end, the worldly and intelligent judge pressed for a courthouse that includes a community meeting hall, art exhibition space, and a restaurant.

Nomination Approved

In May of 1994, when Clinton was forced to fill another vacancy on the court, he returned to Breyer. White House officials were quoted as saying they liked the "classy" way Breyer handled his rejection a year before. Clinton called him "a jurist who I deeply believe will take his place as one of nation's outstanding justices," according to a report in the *Boston Globe.* His confirmation hearings before the Senate Judiciary Committee were not controversial. The biggest concern was Breyer's financial stake in Lloyd's of London, the giant insurance firm. Some senators questioned whether Breyer's financial interest in Lloyd's clouded his rulings on environmental cases. If Lloyd's had to pay for certain toxic waste cleanups, the senators wondered how Breyer could rule impartially in those cases. Breyer responded that Lloyd's was not a direct party to any clean-ups he was involved in, but added that he would sell off his investment in the insurance concern anyway. Breyer was also accused by consumer activists, such as Ralph Nader, of siding with big business in all of the antitrust cases on which he ruled. When asked about abortion, he said it was "settled law" that women have a right to an abortion under *Roe v. Wade,* the landmark 1973 ruling. The committee approved his nomination 18 to 0.

In ascending to the Supreme Court, Breyer "beat out" Clinton's other top choice, secretary of the interior Bruce Babbitt. For about a month during the summer of 1994, Washington engaged in a great guessing game about who would get the nomination: Babbitt or Breyer. Babbitt was opposed by many Western senators who did not like his tough stand on cattle-grazing fees. Clinton liked Babbitt, however, because he had said he wanted more than a legal mind on the court; the president wanted someone who would bring a politician's passion to the court. But Babbitt's political disadvantages proved too great. As the *Boston Globe* reported, "In the end, Breyer's greatest asset was the way he met a key element of Clinton's job description: someone with political skills who could sail through confirmation."

How Breyer would actually fit into the liberal-to-conservative spectrum on the court was unclear; and since his appointment he has been the focus of controversy. Supreme Court justices have a way of surprising the presidents who appointed them to the court; some are more liberal than expected, some more conservative. But most court observers agree that Breyer sits on the opposite spectrum of Antonin Scalia, arguing not so much on political lines, but for a broader interpretation of the law. As Breyer himself was quoted in the *New York Times* as telling senators during his confirmation hearing, "Consensus is important because law is not theoretical; law is a set of opinions and rules that lawyers have to understand, judges have to understand them, and eventually the labor union, the business, small business, everyone else in the country has to understand how they are supposed to act or not act according to the law."

Further Reading

Boston Globe, May 14, 1994; May 15, 1994; May 17, 1994; July 10, 1994; July 13, 1994; July 25, 1994.

Boston Magazine, October 1994, p. 60.

New Republic, July 11, 1994, p. 19.

New York Times, May 30, 1993; June 11, 1993; June 18, 1993; September 9, 1993; July 14, 1994.

Wall Street Journal, June 24, 1993. □

James Brown

"Godfather of Soul" James Brown (born 1933) is also known as "the hardest-working man in show business."

In the book about his life, *Living in America,* James Brown told the author, "I never try to express what I actually did," regarding his influence on the American soul scene. "I wouldn't try to do that, 'cause definition's such a funny thing. What's put together to make my music—it's something which has real power. It can stir people up and involve 'em. But it's just something I came to hear."

The music that James Brown heard in his head—and conveyed to his extraordinary musicians with an odd combination of near-telepathic signals and vicious browbeating—changed the face of soul. By stripping away much of the pop focus that had clouded pure rhythm and blues, Brown found a rhythmic core that was at once primally sexual and powerfully spiritual. Shouting like a preacher over bad-to-the-bone grooves and wicked horn lines, he unleashed a string of hits through the 1960s and early 1970s; he was also a formative influence on such rock and soul superstars as Parliament-Funkadelic leader George Clinton, Rolling Stones frontman Mick Jagger, Prince, and Michael Jackson, among countless others.

By the late 1970s, however, Brown's career was waning, and he was plagued by demands for back taxes, a nagging drug problem, and a combative relationship with his third wife. In 1988 he went to prison after leading police on a high-speed chase. And even as the advent of hip-hop has made him perhaps the most sampled artist in the genre, he has had frequent scrapes with the law since his release in 1991. Even so, his legacy—as bandleader, singer, dancer, and pop music visionary—is assured.

Brown was born in the South—sources vary, but generally have him hailing from Georgia or South Carolina—and grew up in Augusta, Georgia, struggling to survive. At the age of four, he was sent to live with his aunt, who oversaw a brothel. Under such circumstances, he grew up fast; by his teens he drifted into crime. In the words of Timothy White, who profiled the singer in his book *Rock Stars,* "Brown

became a shoeshine boy. Then a pool-hall attendant. Then a thief." At 16 he went to jail for multiple car thefts. Though initially sentenced to 8-16 years of hard labor, he got out in under four for good behavior. After unsuccessful forays into boxing and baseball, he formed a gospel group called the Swanees with his prison pal Johnny Terry.

"The Hardest-Working Man in Show Business"

The Swanees shifted toward the popular mid-1950s doo-wop style and away from gospel, changing their name to the Famous Flames. Brown sang lead and played drums; their song "Please, Please, Please"—a wrenchingly passionate number in which Brown wailed the titular word over and over—was released as a single in 1956 and became a million-seller. By 1960 the group had become the James Brown Revue and was generating proto-funk dance hits like "(Do the) Mashed Potato." Deemed the "King of Soul" at the Apollo Theater, New York's black music mecca, Brown proceeded over the ensuing years to burn up the charts with singles like "Papa's Got a Brand New Bag," "I Got You (I Feel Good)," "It's a Man's Man's Man's World," "Cold Sweat," "Funky Drummer," and many others. In the meantime, he signed with the Mercury subsidiary Smash Records and released a string of mostly instrumental albums, on which he often played organ.

Brown's declamatory style mixed a handful of seminal influences, but his intensity and repertoire of punctuating vocal sounds—groans, grunts, wails, and screams—came right out of the southern church. His exhortations to sax player Maceo Parker to "blow your horn," and trademark

cries of "Good God!" and "Take it to the bridge!" became among the most recognizable catchphrases in popular music. The fire of his delivery was fanned by his amazingly agile dancing, without which Michael Jackson's fancy footwork is unimaginable. And his band—though its personnel shifted constantly—maintained a reputation as one of the tightest in the business. Starting and stopping on a dime, laying down merciless grooves, it followed Brown's lead as he worked crowds the world over into a fine froth. "It was like being in the army," William "Bootsy" Collins—who served as Brown's bassist during the late 1960s—told *Musician,* adding that the soul legend "was just a perfectionist at what he was doing." Brown adopted a series of extravagant titles over the years, but during this period he was known primarily as "The Hardest-Working Man in Show Business."

"Guts"—and an Iron Hand

At the same time, Brown's harshness as a leader meant that bandmembers were constantly facing fines for lateness, flubbed notes, missed cues, violating his strict dress code, or even for talking back to him. His musicians also complained of overwork and insufficient pay, and some alleged that Brown took credit for ideas they had developed. The singer-bandleader's temper is legendary; as trombonist Fred Wesley told *Living in America* author Cynthia Rose, "James was bossy and paranoid. I didn't see why someone of his stature would be so defensive. I couldn't understand the way he treated his band, why he was so evil."

Charles Shaar Murray ventured in his book *Crosstown Traffic* that "playing with James Brown was a great way to learn the business and to participate in the greatest rhythm machine of the sixties. It was a very poor way to get rich, to get famous, or to try out one's own ideas." Even so, the group—which included, at various times, funk wizards like Maceo Parker, guitarist Jimmy Nolen, and drummer Clyde Stubblefield—reached unprecedented heights of inspiration under Brown. "He has no real musical skills," Wesley remarked to Rose, "yet he could hold his own onstage with any jazz virtuoso—because of his guts."

The increasingly militant stance of many black activists in the late 1960s led Brown—by now among an elite group of influential African Americans—to flirt with the "Black Power" movement. Even so, the singer generally counseled nonviolence and won a commendation from President Lyndon B. Johnson when a broadcast of his words helped head off a race riot. He was also saluted by Vice-President Hubert Humphrey for his pro-education song "Don't Be a Dropout." Brown's music did begin to incorporate more overtly political messages, many of which reiterated his belief that black people needed to take control of their economic destinies. He was a walking example of this principle, having gained control of his master tapes by the mid-1960s.

The year 1970 saw the release of Brown's powerful single "(Get Up, I Feel Like Being a) Sex Machine," a relentless funk groove featuring several hot young players, notably Bootsy Collins and his brother Phelps, aka "Catfish." Brown soon signed with Polydor Records and took on the moniker the "Godfather of Soul," after the highly successful mafia movie *The Godfather.* Further refining his hard funk sound, he released hits like "Get on the Good Foot," "Talking Loud and Saying Nothing," and "Soul Power." With the 1970s box-office success of black action films—known within the industry as "blaxploitation" pictures—Brown began writing movie soundtracks, scoring such features as Slaughter's Big Rip-Off and Black Caesar.

Taxes, Tragedy, and Trouble

James Brown may have been one of the biggest pop stars in the world—the marquees labeled him "Minister of New New Super Heavy Funk"—but he was not immune to trouble. In 1975 the Internal Revenue Service claimed that he owed $4.5 million in taxes from 1969-70, and many of his other investments collapsed. His band quit after a punishing tour of Africa, and most tragically, his son Teddy died in an automobile accident. Brown's wife later left him, taking their two daughters.

By the late 1970s, the advent of disco music created career problems for the Godfather of Soul. Though he dubbed himself "The Original Disco Man (a.k.a. The Sex Machine)," he saw fewer and fewer of his singles charting significantly. Things improved slightly after he appeared as a preacher in the smash 1980 comedy film *The Blues Brothers,* and he demonstrated his importance to the burgeoning hip-hop form with *Unity (The Third Coming),* his 1983 EP with rapper Afrika Bambaataa. But Brown's big comeback of the 1980s came with the release of "Living in America," the theme from the film *Rocky IV,* which he performed at the request of star Sylvester Stallone. The single was his first million-selling hit in 13 years. As a result, Brown inked a new deal with CBS Records; in 1986 he was inducted into the Rock 'n' Roll Hall of Fame. "Living in America" earned him a Grammy Award for best R&B performance by a male artist.

Jailed after 1988 Chase

Through it all, Brown had been struggling with substance abuse, despite his participation in the President's Council against Drugs. His and his third wife Adrienne's use of the drug known as PCP or "angel dust" led to frequent encounters with the law; in May of 1988 he faced charges of assault, weapons and drug possession, and resisting arrest. In December he was arrested again after leading police on a two-state car chase and was sentenced to six years in State Park Correctional Facility in Columbia, South Carolina. His confinement became a political issue for his fans, and Brown was ultimately released in early 1991. "We've got lots of plans," the soul legend declared to *Rolling Stone,* adding that the experience "has opened James Brown's eyes about things he has to do." He later announced plans to tape a cable special with pop-rap sensation M.C. Hammer.

That same year saw the release of Star Time, a four-CD boxed set that meticulously collected Brown's finest moments; much of which had never been released on compact disc before. The project's release date was set to coincide with the 35th anniversary of "Please, Please, Please."

Brown, meanwhile, set to work on a new album, *Universal James,* which included production by British soul star Jazzie B. "It'll be the biggest album I ever had," he declared to *Spin,* though this was not to be the case. The 1990s did, however, reveal just how influential James Brown's work had been in rap and hip-hop circles: hundreds of his records were sampled for beats, horn stabs, and screams; the group Public Enemy, which had taken its name from one of his singles, often elaborated on the political themes he had raised.

Meanwhile—thanks in part to his participation in *The Blues Brothers* and the use of his music in feature films like *Good Morning, Vietnam*—Brown emerged as a "classic" mainstream artist. Indeed, *Time* magazine listed 32 appearances of "I Got You (I Feel Good)" in films, movie trailers, and television commercials, and this list was probably not exhaustive. In 1993 the people of Steamboat Springs, Colorado, christened the James Brown Soul Center of the Universe Bridge. The following year a street running alongside New York's Apollo Theater was temporarily named James Brown Blvd., and he performed at Radio City Music Hall; superstar actress Sharon Stone sang "Happy Birthday" to him on the occasion of his 61st. "I'm wherever God wants me to be and wherever the people need for me to be," he told the *New York Times.*

Unfortunately, his troubles were not at an end. In December of 1994, he was charged with misdemeanor domestic violence after yet another conflagration with Adrienne. And on October 31, 1995, Brown was once again arrested for spousal abuse. He later blamed the incident on his wife's addiction to drugs, stating in a press release, "She'll do anything to get them." Just over two months later, Adrienne died at the age of 47 after undergoing cosmetic surgery. In 1998, a South Carolina judge ordered Brown to complete a 90-day drug treatment program after he pleaded no contest to the charge that he fired a rifle while under the influence at his home in Beech Island, South Carolina.

Brown's penchant for survival and the shining legacy of his work managed to overshadow such ugly incidents. "No one in the world makes me want to dance like James Brown," wrote producer and record executive Jerry Wexler—one of the architects of modern soul—in his book *Rhythm and the Blues.* "I came from nothing and I made something out of myself," Brown commented in a *New York Times* interview. "I dance and I sing and I make it happen. I've made people feel better. I want people to be happy." The Godfather of Soul released a new live album in 1995.

In 1997 Brown appeared in *When We Were Kings,* a documentary also starring Muhammad Ali and George Foreman. The film by Leon Gast is about Ali and Foreman's 1974 fight in Zaire (now Congo).

Further Reading

Brown, James, *The Godfather of Soul,* 1990.

Murray, Charles Shaar, *Crosstown Traffic: Jimi Hendrix and the Rock 'n' Roll Revolution,* St. Martin's, 1989.

Rees, Dafydd, and Luke Crampton, *Rock Movers & Shakers,* ABC/CLIO, 1991.

Rose, Cynthia, Living in America: *The Soul Saga of James Brown,* Serpent's Tail, 1990.

Wexler, Jerry, *Rhythm and the Blues,* Knopf, 1993.

White, Timothy, *Rock Stars,* Stewart, Tabori & Chang, 1984.

Augusta Chronicle (Augusta, GA), April 30, 1995.

Entertainment Weekly, December 23, 1994.

Los Angeles Times, September 10, 1994; December 10, 1994.

Musician, November 1994.

New York Times, April 13, 1994.

Oakland Press (Oakland County, MI), November 4, 1995; January 7, 1996.

Rolling Stone, April 18, 1991.

Spin, December 1992; December 1993.

Starwave, ''http://web.3starwave.com/starbios/jamesbrown/ b.html,'' July 18, 1997.

Time, April 25, 1994; May 16, 1994.

Additional information for this profile was taken from Scotti Bros. Records publicity materials, 1995. ☐

John Brown

John Brown (1800-1859) has been revered for generations as a martyr to the American antislavery cause. His attack on Harpers Ferry, Va., just before the Civil War freed no slaves and resulted in his own trial and death.

John Brown was born at Torrington, Conn., on May 4, 1800, to Owen Brown, a tanner, and Ruth Mills Brown, whose family had a history of mental instability. He spent his childhood there and on the family farm at Hudson, Ohio. A devoutly religious youth, Brown studied briefly for the ministry but quit to learn the tanner's trade. He married Dianthe Lusk in 1820, who bore him 7 children (two mentally deficient) before her death in 1832; a year later he married Mary Ann Day, who bore 13 children in the next 21 years. Of Brown's 20 children, 12 survived.

He said later that he had realized the sin of slavery, ''the sum of all villainies,'' at 12, and that seeing an African American boy mistreated had ''led him to declare, or *swear:* eternal war with slavery.'' He also developed a great interest in military history, especially in the guerrilla warfare of the Napoleonic Wars and in the Haitian slave rebellion. According to family testimony, he finally concluded that slavery could be destroyed only by atonement in blood, deciding in 1839 that the South, ''Africa itself,'' should be invaded and the slaves freed at gunpoint. If he actually made such a plan, he kept it to himself for another decade, meanwhile trying and failing at a number of business ventures, always in debt. He moved his family 10 times until in 1849 he settled on a farm at North Elba, N.Y., that was part of a project financed by philanthropist Gerrit Smith for the training of free African Americans.

Kansas Controversy

After the Kansas-Nebraska Act of 1854 the territory hung in the balance between slave- and free-state status while pro- and antislavery settlers contested for control. Five of Brown's sons went to Kansas, joined the free-staters, and appealed to their father for help. Brown traveled through the East, speaking on the Kansas question and gathering money for arms, for ''without the shedding of blood,'' he said, there could be ''no remission of sin'' in Kansas. In September he went to Kansas, settling near Osawatomie. ''I am here,'' he said grimly, ''to promote the killing of slavery.'' In spring of 1856 he led a retaliatory raid on a proslavery settlement at Pottawatomie, killing five men in cold blood. John Junior spent 3 months in jail as an accomplice, but Brown himself escaped. The Pottawatomie affair made him nationally known, and while some antislavery sympathizers disowned him, to others he seemed a hero.

Brown spent the summer of 1856 collecting money for Kansas in New England, where prominent public figures, some not wholly aware of the details of his Kansas activities, were impressed by his dedication to the abolitionist cause. The Massachusetts Kansas Committee, whose directors included such civic leaders as Theodore Parker, Samuel Gridley Howe, and Thomas W. Higginson, helped him to gather recruits, guns, and money. In August he led a skirmish at Osawatomie in which his son Frederick was killed. ''I will die fighting for this cause,'' Brown wrote. ''There will be no peace in this land until slavery is done for.''

He went East in early 1857 with plans for a Southern invasion apparently in hand, ordered a thousand 6-foot pikes from a Connecticut firm, and in late summer gathered a band of recruits at Tabor, Iowa, for training. He held frequent conferences with Eastern abolitionists and in early 1858 sent John Junior to survey the country around Harpers Ferry, Va., the site of a Federal arsenal. In April he held a curious 10-day meeting of sympathizers in Chatham, Ontario, Canada, during which he explained his plan to invade the South, arm the slaves, and set up a free state under a new constitution; the meeting adopted his plan and then voted him commander in chief. He returned to Kansas under the name of Shubel Morgan to lead a raid into Missouri, killing one man and taking some slaves back to Canada.

Brown was now considered a criminal in the eyes of Missouri and the U.S. government, and both offered rewards for his capture; still he was hailed in parts of the North as a liberator, and donations poured in. In early 1859 he again toured the East to raise money, and in July he rented a farm 5 miles north of Harpers Ferry, where he recruited 21 men (16 white and 5 black) for final training. He intended to seize the arsenal, distribute arms to the slaves he thought would rally to him, and set up a free state for african Americans within the South. Though Harpers Ferry was an isolated mountain town, with few slaves in the vicinity, the irrationality of his plan seemed to occur to no one.

Raid on Harpers Ferry

On the night of Oct. 16, 1859, Brown set out for Harpers Ferry with 18 men and a wagonload of supplies, leaving 3 men behind to guard the farm. After cutting the telegraph wires, Brown's party slipped into the town and easily captured the armory watchmen. Inexplicably, Brown allowed the midnight train to go through; the conductor telegraphed an alarm the next morning. Shooting broke out early on the 17th between Brown's men and local residents, while militia soon arrived from Charles Town. By nightfall Brown's band lay trapped in the armory enginehouse, all but 5 wounded, Brown's sons Oliver and Watson fatally. That night Col. Robert E. Lee and Lt. J. E. B. Stuart, commanding 90 marines, arrived from Washington. The next morning the marines stormed the enginehouse, bayoneting 2 men and slashing Brown severely with sabers. Of Brown's original party 10 died and 7 were captured; on the other side the toll was a marine and 4 civilians, one of them, ironically, a free African American killed by mistake.

Brown was jailed at Charles Town and tried a week later, lying wounded on a stretcher, in a fair trial which some, however, felt to be unduly hasty. He put up no defense. "I believe that to have interfered as I have done," he said, "in behalf of His despised poor, I did no wrong, but right. . . . I am ready for my fate." The jury indicted him on three counts—treason against Virginia, conspiracy with African Americans, and first-degree murder. The court imposed the death sentence on November 2, to be executed a month later.

Beginning of a Legend

News of Brown's deed—"so surprising, so mixed, so confounding," Bronson Alcott called it—shocked the nation. Was he martyr or murderer? Many praised him (Ralph Waldo Emerson called him "that new saint who will make the gallows like a cross"), and many condemned him. Seventeen of Brown's acquaintances sent affidavits to Governor Wise of Virginia raising, on good evidence, the issue of Brown's sanity, but Wise did not act on them. Brown was

hanged at Charles Town on Dec. 2, 1859, with four of his men, after handing a prophetic note to his jailer on his way to the gallows: "I John Brown am now quite certain that the crimes of *this guilty land: will* never be purged *away; but* with Blood." Mass meetings of mourning were held throughout the North, and church bells tolled at the hour of his execution. He was buried at North Elba, N.Y., and the cause of abolition had its martyr. When a penny ballad about him, set to the music of an old revival hymn and named "John Brown's Body," appeared on the streets of Boston in early 1861, he was already a legend.

Further Reading

The best book on Brown, well written and soundly researched, is Joseph C. Furnas, *The Road to Harper's Ferry* (1959). James C. Malin, *John Brown and the Legend of Fifty-Six* (1942), is a study of the Kansas years. David Karsner, *John Brown: Terrible Saint* (1934), and Oswald Garrison Villard, *John Brown* (1943), are good biographies. Allan Keller, *Thunder at Harper's Ferry* (1958), is an hour-by-hour account of the raid. One of the Massachusetts Kansas Committee leaders, Franklin B. Sanborn, published *The Life and Letters of John Brown* (1885; 4th ed. 1910), which is still interesting reading. □

Ronald H. Brown

After a very successful tenure as Chairman of the Democratic National Committee, Ronald Brown (1941-1996) was appointed Commerce Secretary by President Bill Clinton. His reign as Secretary was cut short when his plane crashed during a mission to Bosnia-Herzegovina, killing all on board.

Ron Brown made history in 1989 when he became the first African American chosen to lead a major U.S. political party. From 1989 through 1992, Brown served as the highly visible deputy chairman of the Democratic National Committee (DNC). Prior to that, he was Jesse Jackson's manager at the 1988 Democratic National Convention. But Brown's liberal roots go even deeper: he was earlier the National Urban League's chief Washington lobbyist, the deputy campaign manager for U.S. Senator Edward (Ted) Kennedy's 1980 presidential bid, and a chief counsel for the Senate Committee on the Judiciary. Brown's confirmation in 1993 as President Bill Clinton's secretary of commerce, however, focused the nation's attention on him even further.

As a boy growing up in the Theresa Hotel in Harlem managed by his father—boxer Joe Louis and actor Paul Robeson were guests there—Ronald Harmon Brown learned early to straddle two worlds. The Theresa, near the famed Apollo Theater, was an oasis for the black entertainment and professional classes of the day. Brown, whose parents were graduates of Howard University, was bused to exclusive preparatory schools and attended the virtually all-white Middlebury College in Vermont. Because of such a background, Brown, unlike many black political leaders of his generation, had for the most part no involvement in the civil rights movement of the 1960s. While Jesse Jackson led 278 students arrested at sit-ins over civil rights at all-black

North Carolina A and T State University, Brown was fulfilling ROTC responsibilities at his private rural college.

One instance of activism came far from the beaten paths of Southern civil rights battlefields but would characterize his later skill at nonconfrontational negotiations. The only black student in his freshman class at Middlebury, Brown was rushed by white classmates from the Sigma Phi Epsilon fraternity, the campus "jock house." But the national organization objected because of an exclusionary clause that barred blacks. As the debate dragged on, reported *Time* magazine, "Brown let it be known that he was unwilling to finesse the issue by accepting house privileges without full membership." Finally, fraternity members rallied to his side, provoking their expulsion by the national chapter leaders. Middlebury then barred all exclusionary charters from campus. Brown became a trustee at the mostly white school.

After college Brown served as the only black officer at his U.S. Army post in West Germany. Back home, he earned a law degree, worked as an inner-city social worker, and then joined the National Urban League—considered the most moderate of civil rights groups—as its Washington lobbyist. Later, he became the first African American attorney at the high-powered Washington law firm of Patton, Boggs and Blow.

Political Savvy Paid Off

Brown's election as head of the Democratic party came despite his carrying all the wrong credentials as far as many party regulars were concerned: he had served as Jesse Jackson's campaign manager in the 1988 bid for the party's presidential nomination. Brown's ties to the aggressive and somewhat controversial Jackson made some observers feel he was too volatile for the job, but his role as peacemaker between the Jackson and Michael Dukakis camps during the 1988 Democratic Convention helped cement his reputation as a suave negotiator. Jackson, who knew his '88 bid for the Democratic nomination was out of gas, at least wanted respect from Dukakis.

Such respect, however, was hard to elicit from the Dukakis camp, since it seemed to have the nomination—if not that 1988 general election against the Republicans—all wrapped up. Divisiveness within the party could have been a disaster for the Democrats, with even worse repercussions than Dukakis's eventual defeat against George Bush. But Brown helped to avoid an irreparable split in the party along color lines. "He is not bragging when he says that his conciliation efforts 'played a part in turning a potential disaster into a love-in,'" wrote David Broder in the *Washington Post.* And Donna Brazile, a Democratic activist aligned with Michael Dukakis in the 1988 election campaign, told the *Atlanta Journal and Constitution,* "If Ron was a pop singer, he would have crossover appeal."

Brown was the consummate Washington insider who learned how to work the levers of power by being a team player. Before becoming party chairman, he served on the DNC's Executive Committee as deputy chairman and chief counsel for the party and worked for Ted Kennedy and other Democrats in Congress. "His political formation is within

national political processes and not within ethnic political processes," Harvard professor Martin Kilson told the *Washington Post.* "Brown is the new black transethnic politician." Soon after his election to the DNC in 1989, Brown made a vow to the committee, stating, as reprinted in the *Washington Post,* "I promise you, my chairmanship will not be about race, it will be about the races we win."

Brown's political savvy was evident in his engineering of his own election as party chairman. He began the campaign as just one of five candidates for the post, but he deployed his lobbying skills early. One call Brown made looking for support went to his former boss, Senator Kennedy, chair of the crucial Labor Committee. Soon after the call, the AFL-CIO endorsed Brown. The *New York Times* wrote, "Mr. Brown's election, the product of a meticulously organized campaign, gave him such an overwhelming advantage that his four competitors dropped out of the contest weeks before the voting."

However, Brown faced scrutiny for trying to be too many different things to too many people. "If you asked people in the Fifties and Sixties what it was to be a Democrat, they could easily tell you," Brown told *Gentleman's Quarterly.* "Somehow in recent years, it has become harder and harder. If we continue to let our opponents . . . define us . . . there's no way we're going to win elections." But some critics feel that Brown's own self-analysis betrays just that weakness. When the magazine asked him to define his own beliefs, Brown replied, "Let's see, what did we come up with? I'm a mainstream progressive Democrat . . . meaning I embrace the traditional values of the Democratic party, but I'm progressive."

Chairman of Democratic National Committee

The role of Democratic National Committee chairman became increasingly important during the dozen years between 1980 and 1992 when Democrats were out of the White House. As party chairman, Brown was successful in raising funds against the odds and helping to elect approved candidates. The 1989 off-year elections were, in Brown's own words, "a slam dunk," according to the *New York Times.* Democrats registered two firsts: a black governor in Virginia and a black mayor in New York City. Just as significantly, the Democrats picked up four congressional seats in special elections, including winning former Vice-President Dan Quayle's seat in heavily Republican Indiana. Brown remarked to the *New York Times,* "What the party does over here and over there should be strategically connected. The voter registration, the redistricting, the state party building and the campaigns—everything should be connected to winning elections." That the party, and Brown, succeeded in that to a good degree is made even more impressive given President Bush's sky-high approval ratings during that period.

Still, potentially thorny racial questions—exactly the kind that could alienate jumpy white Southern Democrats—always threatened to grab headlines. There too, though, Brown found a way to defuse the many pressures facing him. In the Chicago mayoral election of 1989, for instance, Brown dodged a tricky, racially-charged issue—

whether to support white Democratic nominee Richard Daley, son of the late mayor, over black alderman Tim Evans, a Jackson ally running as an independent. He vowed to toe the party line and back the Democratic nominee, Daley.

But there was nowhere to escape to, no corner of America in which Brown could hide, when the political theater expanded from local elections to the presidential campaign of 1992. After the Persian Gulf War with Iraq, President Bush was enjoying high favorability ratings with the American electorate, and it appeared the Democratic party would again face an uphill battle to wrest White House control from the Republicans. Initially, because of Bush's popularity, Brown had difficulty raising money for the Democratic National Committee. Another problem was that, in the eyes of some Jewish contributors, Brown had not sufficiently distanced himself from Jesse Jackson, whose anti-Semitic remarks several years earlier were still a festering sore spot in Jewish/African American relations.

Worked for Democratic Unity

But Brown's greatest challenge, in terms of attracting dollars and, ultimately, the votes of Americans, was to remold the image of the party, shedding the "tax and spend" label that the Republicans had successfully applied to democratic candidates in the past. "We need to define ourselves as a party," Brown was quoted as telling *Black Enterprise*. "When you allow your adversaries to define you, you can be assured that the definition is going to be a very unpleasant one and that you find yourself on the defensive trying to dig yourself out of a hole. We can't let that happen again."

The answer, as many political observers had long known, lay in the middle. Brown understood that for the party to reclaim the so-called Reagan Democrats, it would need a candidate with fiscally conservative economic policies that would not adversely affect the struggling middle class. While he could not keep liberals such as Iowa senator Tom Harkin out of the primaries, Brown did muzzle the potential candidacy of Jesse Jackson, who, Brown feared, would unwittingly tarnish the new, moderate image that the party desperately needed.

Brown's plan was to minimize any acrimony among the primary candidates, hoping to focus their disparate voices on the need to unseat the Republican president. Bush, meanwhile, had suffered a precipitous fall in popularity, as his success in the Persian Gulf was overshadowed by a lingering recession in the United States. At a time when the citizenry had grown tired of politics as usual and were calling on the U.S. president to focus on domestic affairs, the Democratic party became the agent of "change."

In addition to nudging the party toward the center of the political spectrum, Brown's plan was to throw the party's support behind its candidate early in the political season. Indeed, one primary candidate, former California governor Jerry Brown, accused the party chairman of coddling to then-Arkansas governor Bill Clinton, who was emerging as the leading democratic figure, in spite of several personal and professional scandals in the Clinton camp that might have led to yet another Democratic loss in the general elections.

At the Democratic National Convention in July of 1992, Clinton won the nomination despite the various controversies surrounding him, and Brown, having calmed many of the voices of dissent, earned widespread praise for a smooth democratic crowning whose central messages were unity and enthusiasm for the party candidate. "Ron sensed what he had to do right from the start," former DNC chairman Kirk was quoted as saying in the *New York Times*. "He knew the party had to show it could govern itself before it could hope to govern the country." Brown's public trumpeting about a redefined Democratic party, and his behind-the-scenes maneuvering to generate support for Clinton, were seen as key to the first democratic presidential victory since 1976.

Named Secretary of Commerce

Brown's departure from the DNC was as controversial as his election as its chairman. In what some skeptics viewed as a political payback and an effort to create a racially diverse cabinet, Clinton nominated Brown as secretary of commerce. Immediately, Brown's past experience as a lobbyist took on the weight of a political liability. As secretary, he would make administrative and policy decisions that might affect his former clients, to whom, it was feared, he would feel some sort of allegiance. Moreover, several political commentators found it ironic that Clinton, who had campaigned against the status quo and the government-insider lobbyist crowd, had nominated Brown, the Washington power broker who played the political game with expert finesse. Illustrative of the ethical questions raised by Brown's nomination was a celebration in his honor that several of the largest American and Japanese corporations had planned. These companies, whose financial interests are impacted by decisions of the commerce secretary, were to have donated $10,000 each for the gala, which was abruptly canceled by Brown after Clinton expressed disapproval. Despite these setbacks, Brown was confirmed by the U.S. Senate in 1993 as the nation's first African American secretary of commerce. He pledged to make the department more responsive to the country's needs and concentrate on the promotion of American business interests both at home and in the international arena.

Brown's tenure as commerce secretary was a troubled one, however, as he was the target of numerous allegations that he acted improperly in his business dealings prior to his cabinet appointment. These allegations included charges that he failed to disclose his investment in a low-income apartment complex and that he did not report a $400,000 payment from a former business partner. By May of 1995, Brown was being investigated by the Justice Department, the Federal Deposit Insurance Corporation, and Congressional Republicans.

Brown's policy at the commerce department was one which emphasized trade over nuclear proliferation and human rights. His backslapping friendly manner resulted in American businessmen signing memoranda for new projects worth $4 billion in India on a January 1995 visit and over $6 billion in China during a September 1994 visit. On the China trip, Brown had 24 American CEOs accompany him to insure that the potential for some dealmaking would exist. He also led delegations bringing CEOs to South Africa, Northern Ireland, and Gaza. As a result of this policy Brown managed to acquire more foreign business for the United States than had any of his predecessors.

It was on a similar trip to Croatia, hoping to rebuild the war-torn region's infrastructure and economy, that Ron Brown died. Thirty-three people, including the secretary, business executives, and commerce staffers, were killed when their plane went down in the midst of a storm between Kalamota, near Dubrovnik, and the Cilipi airport on April 3, 1996. There were no survivors. As quoted in *USA Today,* President Clinton called Brown "one of the best advisers and ablest people I ever knew."

Further Reading

Atlanta Journal and Constitution, January 7, 1989; February 12, 1989; May 22, 1989.

Black Enterprise, March 1992, p. 48.

Boston Globe Magazine, October 22, 1989.

Business Week February 13, 1989, p. 54; June 18, 1990, p. 30; January 11, 1993, p. 31; September 12, 1994, p. 54.

The Economist January 21, 1995, p. 37.

Gentleman's Quarterly, July 1989.

Nation, February 20, 1989.

Newsweek, February 6, 1989, p. 20.

New York Times, February 11, 1989; March 28, 1992, p. A9; July 20, 1992, p. A11; January 14, 1993, p. A1.

New York Times Magazine, December 12, 1989.

Oakland Press (Oakland County, MI), December 13, 1992, p. A12.

Time, January 30, 1989, p. 56.

USA Today, April 4, 1996, pp. 1A, 2A, 13A.

Wall Street Journal, January 8, 1993, p. A14.

Washington Post, February 5, 1989; February 11, 1989. □

Blanche Kelso Bruce

Blanche Kelso Bruce (1841-1898), African American political leader in Mississippi, was the first member of his race to serve a full term in the U.S. Senate.

On March 1, 1841, Blanche Kelso Bruce was born a slave near Farmville, Prince Edward County, Va. His master had him educated, and before the Civil War he went to Missouri, where he organized the first school for African Americans in the state. In 1868, after 2 years at Oberlin College, he moved to Floreyville, Bolivar County, Miss., where he became a planter in the rich Mississippi Delta and acquired considerable property.

Soon after his arrival, Military Governor Adelbert Ames appointed him conductor of elections for a nearby county, and in 1870 he became sergeant at arms in the state senate. Bruce was highly regarded in Bolivar County, where he served as assessor, sheriff, county school superintendent, and member of the Board of Levee Commissioners. He was

also tax collector, with prominent Republicans and Democrats posting the bond required for the position. When Ku Klux Klan-inspired violence began to rise, he was able to use his influence to prevent race riots in his home county. As a leader of the Republican party in Mississippi, he was elected in 1874 to the U.S. Senate.

Bruce was a handsome man with erect bearing and polished manners, and he and his wife were active in Washington society. In the Senate he served on important committees, spoke on behalf of the Native Americans and Chinese, advocated improvements on the Mississippi River, and worked to obtain pensions for African American Union Army veterans. He tried to prevent the removal of Federal troops from Mississippi, where their presence acted as a deterrent to terrorism. After the Democrats took over control of the state through intimidation and violence at the polls in 1875, he was instrumental in providing for an investigation of the election.

At the end of his 6-year term in the Senate he was appointed register of the Treasury by President James A. Garfield and later served as recorder of deeds for the District of Columbia during the Harrison administration. Bruce continued to be a leader of the Republican party in Mississippi in the 1880s, often speaking from the same platform with white political friends and opponents, and he was a trustee of Howard University. President McKinley appointed him register of the Treasury again in 1895. He died in Washington, D.C., on March 17, 1898.

Further Reading

A sketch of Bruce's life is in Benjamin G. Brawley, *Negro Builders and Heroes* (1937). More detailed information on his career is in Vernon Lane Wharton, *The Negro in Mississippi: 1865-1890* (1947). See also Philip Sterling and Rayford Logan, *Four Took Freedom: The Lives of Harriet Tubman, Frederick Douglass, Robert Smalls, and Blanche K. Bruce* (1967), and William J. Simmons, *Men of Mark: Eminent, Progressive and Rising* (1887; repr. 1968). □

William Jennings Bryan

The American lawyer, editor, and politician William Jennings Bryan (1860-1925) was the Democratic party's presidential nominee three times and became secretary of state. Called the "Great Commoner," Bryan advocated an agrarian democracy.

For 30 years William Jennings Bryan was active in American politics, emerging first as a spokesman for those who felt disregarded or slighted by the urban, industrial forces revolutionizing the United States in the period after the Civil War. Giving voice to their values and protests, Bryan advocated measures which he believed would give the people more direct control of the government and would allow the common man more economic advantages. Seeking simple solutions to complex social and economic problems, Bryan talked in pietistic terms: the controversy over coinage was viewed as a struggle between good and evil, not merely between men of conflicting points of view.

Although the increasing industrialization and urbanization of American society and greater United States participation in world affairs made Bryan an anachronism and finally thrust him aside, his attacks helped to focus public attention on serious problems and indirectly led to measures of correction and reform in the early 20th century.

Bryan was born in Salem, Ill. In his middle-class family, great emphasis was placed on religion and morality, not only in one's personal life but in politics and in the conduct of national affairs. After graduating from Illinois College in 1881 and studying for 2 years at Union College of Law in Chicago, he opened a law office in Jacksonville. Shortly afterward he married Mary Baird.

Early Career

In 1887 Bryan moved to Lincoln, Nebr., practicing law and simultaneously turning toward politics. He won a seat in Congress in 1890 and was reelected in 1892. As a congressman, he was a foe of high tariffs and an exponent of free coinage of silver, both popular positions with Nebraska voters.

In the 1880s and 1890s debtors, farmers, and silver mine owners urged the expansion of the amount of money in circulation in the United States, arguing that more money in circulation would mean better times and that when money was scarce the wealthy benefited at the expense of the less well-to-do. Exponents of silver coinage argued that the Federal government should buy large quantities of silver, issue currency based on silver, and put 16 times as much silver in a

silver dollar as the amount of gold in a gold dollar. The movement had a magnetic appeal for those suffering from the agricultural depression of the 1880s and 1890s. Bryan took its rallying cries—"free silver" and "16 to 1"—as his own. A dynamic and dedicated speaker, he toured the country speaking on silver, as well as urging its merits in the *Omaha World Herald*. Defeated for the Senate in 1894, he had become editor of the paper. Known for his oratory rather than his brilliance or shrewdness, Bryan captured the imagination of small-town and rural people who were bewildered by the changes occurring around them, devastated by the depression of 1893, and angry with President Grover Cleveland's policies toward Coxey's Army and the Homestead strike.

Presidential Candidate and Political Leader

The silver forces, centered chiefly in western and southern states, had virtual control of the Democratic convention of 1896 before it opened in Chicago. Bryan's dramatic "Cross of Gold" speech helped him secure the presidential nomination, and he prosecuted the campaign against former Ohio governor William McKinley with unprecedented vigor. When the Populist party also nominated Bryan, the conservative "Gold Democrats" were alarmed and seceded from their traditional party and nominated another candidate. The campaign was extremely heated. To Bryan the "money men of the East" were agents of evil; to Republicans and conservative Democrats, Bryan was equally abhorrent. Bryan was the first presidential candidate to travel extensively and to use the railroads to take his case to the people.

Bryan lost the election but remained the Democratic party leader and immediately began campaigning for 1900. His activities were varied, designed to keep him before the public eye: he wrote magazine articles, made extensive speaking tours on the Chautauqua circuit, and, with his wife, compiled an account of the 1896 campaign called *The First Battle.*

When the Spanish-American War began, Bryan enlisted and served briefly, raising a regiment in Nebraska. The paramount issue arising from the war (which the United States won quickly) was whether the country should annex any of the overseas territories Spain had been forced to relinquish—whether the nation should embark on a policy of imperialism, as had most of the other major nations of the world. Bryan, a dedicated anti-imperialist, felt certain that by referendum the people would repudiate any administration that declared for annexation. But he argued for approving the Treaty of Paris ending the war, by which the Spanish would cede Puerto Rico and the Philippines to the United States, saying that the United States should first secure the freedom of the Philippines from Spain and then award them independence when the international situation was more favorable.

Bryan coupled anti-imperialism with free silver as the major issues of the 1900 campaign, in which he again opposed President McKinley and was again defeated. The gradual disappearance of hard times had lessened the appeal of free silver, and the American people were too pleased with the outcome of the Spanish-American War to support anti-imperialism.

Bryan launched a weekly newspaper, the *Commoner,* in 1901 and kept himself before the public, although many Democratic party leaders considered him a failure as a candidate. Bypassed in 1904 by the Democratic party, Bryan supported the presidential candidacy of conservative Judge Alton B. Parker. Parker and the conservatives did so poorly in the election that Bryan was able to secure the 1908 nomination for himself. Another defeat, this time at the hands of William Howard Taft, ensued, but Bryan remained active in the Democratic party. In 1912 he helped to secure the nomination of Woodrow Wilson for the presidency, and Wilson named the Great Commoner secretary of state in 1913.

Bryan's durability as a political leader stemmed from a number of sources: his control of a party faction, his appeal to the common man and his personification of traditional American values, his identification with a large number of reform issues, his constant and unremitting labor, and the paucity of successful Democratic leaders. In particular, his capacity for pointing out areas of reform turned the public's attention toward problems of trusts and monopolies, paving the way for corrective legislation. Many of the reforms he suggested were carried out, several by President Theodore Roosevelt. Federal income tax, popular election of senators, woman's suffrage, stricter railroad regulation, initiative and referendum provisions, and publicity of campaign contributions were all reforms for which Bryan had worked.

Secretary of State

Bryan helped to obtain passage of domestic legislation, most notably the Federal Reserve Act. He strove to master foreign policy, bringing more energy and dedication than insight. He had no experience in foreign policy and had been chosen secretary of state because that was the most important position in the Cabinet. For Latin America he advocated a policy of protection of American business interests, suggesting that more financial intervention by the U.S. government might prevent European influence. He was particularly interested in negotiating arbitration treaties with some 30 countries, for he believed that such treaties would prevent war. He advocated a policy of neutrality in World War I, hoping that the United States might play the role of arbitrator between the opposing sides. Wilson, however, did not follow his advice; in protest over the tone of the President's second note about the sinking of the *Lusitania,* Bryan resigned in June 1915.

Last Decade

Bryan remained active in politics and also promoted Florida real estate, wrote copiously, and lectured on prohibition. The old-fashioned Protestantism that had made him a hero to many people became more prominent in his thinking even as it became less prevalent in American society; he spoke out for the fundamentalists, even to the point of refusing to condemn the Ku Klux Klan because of their Christian guise. Shortly after he was howled down at the 1924 Democratic convention, he appeared for the prosecu-

tion in the Scopes trial in Tennessee, opposing the teaching of theories of evolution in public schools. The naiveté and narrowness of his thinking emerged clearly in this trial, which was Bryan's last appearance in public before his death in 1925.

Further Reading

Books about Bryan, like books by him, are abundant. The most detailed biography is Paolo E. Coletta, *William Jennings Bryan: Political Evangelist, 1860-1908* (1964). Louis W. Koenig, *Bryan: A Political Biography of William Jennings Bryan* (1971), is a useful study. Paul W. Glad, *The Trumpet Soundeth: William Jennings Bryan and His Democracy, 1896-1912* (1960), treats the rural context from which Bryan emerged. Glad's *McKinley, Bryan and the People* (1964) focuses on the election. The last years of Bryan's life are handled skillfully by Lawrence W. Levine, *Defender of the Faith: William Jennings Bryan; The Last Decade, 1915-1925* (1965). By far the best brief treatment of Bryan is Richard Hofstadter, "The Democrat as Revivalist," in Paul W. Glad, ed., *William Jennings Bryan: A Profile* (1968). □

William Cullen Bryant

The American poet and newspaper editor William Cullen Bryant (1794-1878) helped introduce European romanticism into American poetry. As an editor, he championed liberal causes. He was one of the most influential and popular figures of mid-19th-century America.

William Cullen Bryant was born on Nov. 3, 1794, in Cummington, Mass. His well-established New England family was staunchly Federalist in politics and Calvinist in religion. Encouraged to write poetry by his father, a physician of wide learning, the boy reflected in his earliest poems his family's political and religious attitudes. Bryant's Federalist satire on Thomas Jefferson, *The Embargo, or Sketches of the Times* (1808), by a "Youth of Thirteen" was published through his father's influence. In later years the liberal, democratic, Unitarian Bryant understandably wished to forget this youthful indiscretion, and he did not reprint it in any of his collections.

"Thanatopsis" and Other Poems

Bryant entered Williams College in 1810 and left after a year. In 1811 he wrote the first draft of his best-known poem, "Thanatopsis" (literally, view of death), reflecting the influence of English "graveyard" poets such as Thomas Gray.

Perhaps the most remarkable feature of "Thanotopsis" is its anti-Christian, stoical view of death. There is no heaven or hell beyond the grave; death ends life, and that is all: "Thine individual being, shalt thou go/To mix forever with the elements,/To be a brother to the insensible rock/And to the sluggish clod. . . ." Published in 1817, the poem was a marked success; it was reprinted in 1821 in the final, revised version familiar today.

A few years later Bryant modified his attitude to death in "To a Waterfowl," in which a "Power" (God) is omnipresent and beneficent. The later English poet Matthew

Arnold considered this to be the finest short poem in the English language. As the 1876 poem "The Flood of Years" makes clear, Bryant held this view of death to the end of his life.

Shortly after Bryant wrote the first draft of "Thanotopsis," he came under the influence of the romantic British poets William Wordsworth and Samuel Taylor Coleridge. In the opening lines of "Inscription for the Entrance to a Wood," Bryant conveyed a love of nature that he retained throughout his career: "Thou wilt find nothing here [in nature]/ Of all that pained thee in the haunts of men,/ And made thee loathe thy life." However, like Wordsworth and other romantics, Bryant saw the world of nature less as an escape from the evils of life in the city than as a positive, vital force in itself. He explored this idea in other poems of this period, such as "The Yellow Violet," "I Cannot Forget with What Fervid Devotion," "Green River," and "A Winter Piece," and later in "A Forest Hymn," "The Death of Flowers," and "The Prairies."

Following his year at Williams College, Bryant read for the law and in 1815 was admitted to the Massachusetts bar. From 1816 to 1825 he practiced law in Great Barrington, Mass. He also kept up his literary activities, writing poetry and essays. In 1821 he published his first volume, *Poems*, and read his Phi Beta Kappa poem "The Ages" at Harvard. That same year he married Frances Fairchild, his "Fairest of the Rural Maids."

In 1826 Bryant became assistant editor of the liberal *New York Evening Post* and in 1829 editor in chief. He served in this capacity for 50 years.

Poetic Theories

Bryant formulated his poetic theories in a series of four lectures on poetry, which he delivered in 1826 before the New York Athenaeum Society (they were published in 1884). He stressed, "The most beautiful poetry is that which takes the strongest hold of the feelings. . . . Important, therefore, as may be the office of the imagination [and of understanding, as well] in poetry, the great spring of poetry is emotion." (He expressed a similar view in the 1864 poem "The Poet.") Models from the past which the poet chooses to follow should be used only as guides to his own originality. While acknowledging that America's historical and cultural past was not as rich for the creation of poetry as England's, Bryant nevertheless felt that when America did produce a great poet he would draw on the best the young country had to offer.

The Editor

As an editor espousing liberal causes, Bryant had considerable impact on the life of New York and of the nation. Typical of his editorials was "The Right of Workmen to Strike" (1836), in which he upheld the workers' right to collective bargaining and ridiculed the prosecution of labor unions: "Can any thing be imagined more abhorrent to every sentiment of generosity or justice, than the law which arms the rich with the legal right to fix . . . the wages of the poor? If this is not *slavery*, we have forgotten its definition."

Similarly, Bryant was firmly committed to many other liberal causes of the day, including the antislavery movement, the "free-soil" concept, and free trade among nations. He also helped in the formation of the new Republican party in 1855.

Bryant published nine volumes of poetry from 1832 on. He also translated the *Iliad* (1870) and the *Odyssey* (1871-1872). He died in New York City on June 12, 1878.

Though Bryant was not a great poet, his poems were much admired in his own time, and a number of them are eminently readable today. As the guiding force of the *Evening Post,* he left his mark not only on the city his liberal paper served but on the nation as well.

Further Reading

Parke Godwin, Bryant's son-in-law, edited the standard editions of both *The Poetical Works of William Cullen Bryant* (2 vols., 1883) and Bryant's *Prose Writings* (2 vols., 1884). The best one-volume edition of the poems is Henry C. Sturges and Richard Henry Stoddard, eds., *The Poetical Works of William Cullen Bryant* (1903). The standard biography of Bryant is Parke Godwin, *A Biography of William Cullen Bryant, with Extracts from His Private Correspondence* (2 vols., 1883). A more balanced assessment is Harry H. Peckham, *Gotham Yankee: A Biography of William Cullen Bryant* (1950). Tremaine McDowell edited and wrote an excellent introduction to *William Cullen Bryant: Representative Selections* (1935). Allan Nevins, *The Evening Post: A Century of Journalism* (1922), discusses Bryant as an editor. Recommended for general background are Roy Harvey Pearce, *The Continuity of American Poetry* (1961), and Hyatt H. Waggoner, *American Poets, from the Puritans to the Present* (1968). □

James Buchanan

James Buchanan (1791-1868) was the fifteenth president of the United States. His administration was dominated by fighting between pro- and antislavery forces. In 1860, at the close of his term in office, South Carolina became the first state to secede from the Union.

James Buchanan was born on April 23, 1791, on a farm in Lancaster, Pa., the son of a Scotch-Irish immigrant. After graduating from Dickinson College in 1809, Buchanan became a lawyer. As a Federalist, he was elected to the Pennsylvania Assembly in 1814 and to the U.S. House of Representatives in 1820. He was an early supporter of Andrew Jackson's presidential aspirations and became a leading member of the new Democratic party in Pennsylvania. Buchanan was elected to the U.S. Senate in 1834, serving there until 1845. As a senator, he supported Southern demands that all abolitionist petitions to the Senate be immediately tabled without consideration.

Presidential Contender

At the 1844 Democratic convention, Buchanan was one of the leading contenders for the presidential nomination but lost out to James K. Polk. When Polk won the presidency and formed his Cabinet, Buchanan was named secretary of state. In this position he played a key role in Polk's expansionist policies. He successfully negotiated a treaty with England over the Oregon Territory, thus avoiding a possible war. At the beginning of the administration, he often acted as a moderating influence on the President, but later Buchanan became a leading imperialist. He urged rejection of the Treaty of Guadalupe Hidalgo (1848) in favor of annexation of large areas of Mexico. He also tried to secure the purchase of Cuba from Spain for $120 million.

At the 1848 and 1852 Democratic conventions, Buchanan was a leading contender for the presidential nomination but was again passed over. In 1853, he was appointed ambassador to England by President Franklin Pierce. While on this mission, in order to win Southern support for his nomination in 1856 he helped draft the Ostend Manifesto, which called for United States acquisition of Cuba, by force of arms if necessary. Returning to the United States in 1856, he received the Democratic nomination for president, and won the election.

A Crisis President

Buchanan sought to restore unity within his party and within the country by appointing Democrats from all geographical sections to the Cabinet. He was doomed to failure. A week after he was inaugurated, the Supreme Court handed down the Dred Scott decision, which upheld the Southern position that Congress had no right to legislate on the question of slavery in the territories. The decision alienated a great many Northerners.

Another stumbling block of Buchanan's administration was the constitution submitted by the territory of Kansas to Congress. A proslavery convention had drawn up the Lecompton Constitution. Governor Robert Walker warned

that unless the whole document was submitted for a vote, Congress would reject it. In defiance of the threat, only one section of the constitution was submitted. Buchanan put great pressure on Congress to accept it and to admit Kansas as a state but ran into opposition from Stephen A. Douglas, his party's most powerful senator. Douglas argued that the document was fraudulent and violated the provisions of the Kansas-Nebraska Act, which had provided for popular sovereignty. This dispute split the Northern and Southern wings of the Democratic party.

Buchanan's handling of the Kansas problem was complicated by several other difficulties. Shortly after he had taken office, the country went into a depression. Adhering to a strict states'-rights doctrine, Buchanan cut the budget and urged stricter regulation of banks but refused to commit the Federal government to relief measures. He also had difficulty with the Mormons, who had settled in the Utah Territory. As a consequence of Brigham Young's refusal to accept a governor appointed in Washington, the President sent 2,500 troops to bring Utah under Federal control. After the Mormons fled Salt Lake City and threatened a scorched-earth policy, Buchanan reached a compromise with Young that granted the Mormons a high degree of autonomy.

The administration also failed to achieve its diplomatic goals, which were to repudiate the Clayton-Bulwer Treaty and to establish American control over Central American and Cuba. In his last year and a half of the presidency, Buchanan faced a hostile Republican majority in Congress and had no hopes of securing ratification of a treaty on either subject, even had one been negotiated.

By the time of the Democratic convention in April 1860, the administration had been completely repudiated. The Democratic party broke into two factions—the North supporting Douglas for president and the South supporting Vice President John C. Breckinridge of Kentucky.

When Lincoln won in November 1860, Buchanan faced his final crisis—the secession of South Carolina. Unable to secure support in Congress and unable to overcome his own scruples against the use of force to restore the Union, Buchanan found his administration paralyzed. This paralysis was compounded by Lincoln's refusal to agree to any policy before actually becoming president. Buchanan did support efforts to conciliate the two sides, especially the Crittenden Compromise and the Peace Conference called by Virginia in 1861, but when these failed, so did the Union. Many Northerners blamed him for the dissolution of the Union and the ensuing Civil War. Thus, as the new president took office, Buchanan left Washington, a bitter and tired old man. He returned to Lancaster, where he died on June 1, 1868, at the age of 77.

Further Reading

The best biography of Buchanan is Philip Shriver Klein, *President James Buchanan* (1962), a well-researched work sympathetic to the subject. For the problems of the Buchanan administration see Allan Nevins, *The Emergence of Lincoln* (2 vols., 1950). For a summation of Buchanan's work as secretary of state see the chapter on Buchanan by St. George L. Sioussat in Samuel Flagg Bemis, ed., *The American Secretaries of State and Their Diplomacy,* vol. 5 (1928). □

Patrick Joseph Buchanan

Commentator, journalist, and presidential candidate Patrick Joseph Buchanan (born 1938) represented the hardline conservative wing of the Republican Party.

Patrick Buchanan was born in Washington, D.C., on November 2, 1938. His father, William Baldwin Buchanan, was a partner in a Washington, D.C., accounting firm. His mother, Catherine Elizabeth (Crum) Buchanan, was a nurse, an active mother, and a homemaker.

Buchanan traced his father's family as coming from Scotland and Ireland and settling in the southern region of America in the late 1700s. He related how some of his ancestors fought for the Confederacy, while another family branch lived in the North. His mother's side of the family were of German immigrant heritage and had settled in the Midwest.

Buchanan grew up in an energetic household. He was the third of nine children. He had six brothers and two sisters. He learned his combatative personality from his father. The elder Buchanan encouraged good manners, debates, sibling rivalries, and fisticuffs.

As did all his siblings, he attended a local Catholic elementary school. He went on to Jesuit-run Gonzaga High School, following in the steps of his father and brothers. Deciding to stay in Washington and to continue at a Catho-

lic school, he enrolled in Georgetown University in 1956 on a scholarship. While there, Buchanan majored in English, lived at home, and had an active social life. He joined intramural boxing and tore the cartilage in his knee during a fight. The damage was later to keep him out of military service.

In his senior year he received a traffic violation. Believing that his ticket was wrongfully given, he verbally and physically assaulted the police. He was arrested, fined, and had a minor police record. The incident had a marked effect on his life. The university suspended him for a year. During that period he learned accounting and took a serious look at his future. He decided on a career in journalism and returned to complete his undergraduate education with a more mature attitude. He graduated with a Bachelor of Arts degree, with honors, in 1961.

Buchanan entered the journalism school at Columbia University with a fellowship. He enjoyed writing, but disliked studying the technical side of newspaper publishing. He earned his Master of Science degree in 1962.

The future media personality began his career as a reporter with the *St. Louis Globe-Democrat.* He quickly became an editorial writer for this conservative Midwest newspaper. He was appointed the paper's assistant editorial editor in 1964. Thinking it would be years before he could become an editor, and wanting some challenges in his life, he thought about a new career direction.

In 1966 he arranged a meeting with Richard Nixon, whom he impressed with his conservative outlook and aggressive political style. Nixon hired him as an assistant. At that time the former vice-president (1953-1961) was a partner in a New York City law firm, was involved in Republican Party activities, and was anticipating a run for the 1968 presidential nomination. Buchanan assisted Nixon on his speeches, newspaper articles, study tours, and campaign.

Following Nixon's 1968 election, Buchanan joined the new presidential administration as a special assistant. He wrote speeches for Nixon and for Vice President Spiro Agnew. He helped plan strategies for the 1972 reelection campaign. During this time he met Shelly Ann Scarney, who was a receptionist at the White House. They married in 1971.

In 1973 Buchanan was appointed a special consultant to President Nixon. He devoted his attention to the Watergate crisis, which revolved around political sabotage in the 1972 presidential campaign. He testified before the Senate Watergate Committee later that year. Although he was not accused of any wrongdoing by the committee members, Buchanan denied suggesting or using any illegal or unethical tactics.

After Nixon's resignation from office in August 1974, Buchanan stayed on for several months as an adviser to President Gerald Ford. Buchanan then left the White House and became a syndicated columnist and lecturer. He later worked as a radio and television commentator on political and social issues. With his style and viewpoints, he became nationally known as a spokesman for a right-wing conservative philosophy.

He returned to the White House in 1985 as director of communications at the start of President Ronald Reagan's second term. His sister, Angela Marie Buchanan-Jackson, had served as treasurer of the United States in Reagan's first term. Buchanan took a major loss of income in his switch back to public service. He stayed only two years, then went back to broadcasting, writing, and lecturing.

In 1992 Buchanan declared his candidacy for the Republican Party presidential nomination. His campaign against President George Bush, who sought reelection, was designed to position himself as an "outsider" and to promote a strong conservative program. He ran with an "American First" theme, arguing that the country should limit its obligations abroad in the post-Cold War decade.

Buchanan attracted attention from a public facing an economic recession, lay-offs of workers, depressed real estate values, increased taxes, and general frustration with government. He spoke against abortion on demand, homosexual rights, women in combat, pornography, racial quotas, free trade, and an activist U.S. Supreme Court. He spoke for aid to religious schools, prayer in public schools, and curbs on illegal immigrants. Buchanan called his political beliefs "street corner" conservatism, which he learned at the dinner table, soaked up in parochial schools, and picked up on the street corners of his youth.

In the early 1992 New Hampshire primary he won 37 percent of the votes. That was his highest percentage of support. The figure dropped in each succeeding primary. In some primaries where Republican voters could vote uncommitted, "uncommitted" finished ahead of Buchanan.

He found it difficult to maintain a campaign organization and to raise funds, but he pressed on through the spring and summer.

Buchanan vied for the White House a second time in 1995, basing his campaign on conservatism. However, he lost once again. Buchanan also founded and directs The American Cause, an educational foundation that emphasizes his political beliefs.

Buchanan announced his candidacy for the 2000 presidential race in 1999.

Further Reading

Buchanan has written a lively autobiography, *Right from the Beginning* (1988), which describes the life and times of growing up in Washington, D.C., and attending Catholic schools in the mid-to-late 20th century. His conservative call to arms is colorfully written in his book *Conservative Votes, Liberal Victories: Why the Right Has Failed* (1975). The 1992 election campaign can be reviewed in the 1992 *Congressional Quarterly* weekly reports. Buchanan examines economic issues in 1998's *The Great Betrayal: How American Sovereignty and Social Justice are Being Sacrificed to the Gods of the Global Economy*. Many facts about Buchanan can be obtained from his Web site entitled "The Buchanan Brigade" available at http://www.buchanan.org. □

Warren Buffett

Warren Buffett (born 1930) is America's most brilliant investor, compiling a year-after-year record of phenomenal returns for the shareholders of his holding company, Berkshire Hathaway, Inc.

For example, if someone had given him $10,000 to invest in 1956 he or she would be worth over $60 million by 1994. Buffett is one of the richest men in America, and he is a success story in the classic mold. As of 1995 Buffett, with a personal fortune of some $12 billion in Berkshire stock, was the second-wealthiest individual in America, right after his friend, Microsoft chairman Bill Gates.

Throughout it all Buffett has retained a seeming simplicity that goes along with his down-home, Midwestern roots. His associates, however, say his hayseed manner disguises a brilliant sophisticate. He shuns New York and Los Angeles, preferring to run his far-flung empire from modest offices in Omaha, Nebraska. The periodic insights into his success that he dispenses are usually witty and simple. However, each time Buffett—known in the financial world as the "Oracle of Omaha"—speaks, just about everyone, from the most accomplished professional prognosticator to the stock-playing hobbyist, pays attention.

Born in 1930 in Omaha, Nebraska, Buffett always "wanted to be very, very rich," as a *Time* article put it. The boy received an early, close-up look at the stock market: his father Howard was a broker, and young Warren, just nine years old, often visited the shop and charted stock performances. He chalked in stock prices on the big blackboard at his father's office, and at age 13 ran paper routes and published his own horse-racing tip sheet.

In 1942 Buffett's father was elected to the U.S. House of Representatives and the family moved to Fredricksburg, Virginia. Young Warren Buffett expanded his business interests by placing pinball machines in Washington, D.C. barbershops. At age 16, a prodigy in statistics and mathematics, he enrolled at the University of Pennsylvania. He stayed two years, moved to the University of Nebraska to finish up his degree, and emerged from college at age 20 with $9,800 in cash from his childhood businesses. Harvard Business School rejected him, but Columbia University's Graduate School of Business accepted his application.

Finds Niche

Columbia was a key turning point in Buffett's life, for it was there that he met Benjamin Graham, co-author with David Dodd of the landmark textbook *Security Analysis.* "I don't want to sound like a religious fanatic or anything, but it really did get me," Buffett was quoted as saying in the *New York Times Magazine* about Graham's writings.

Graham's philosophy has permeated most of Buffett's decision in the 40-plus years since they first met. Essentially, Graham's theory, called value investing, urges stock pickers to buy shares that are much cheaper than a company's net worth would indicate. That is, look for stocks that sell below their "intrinsic value," a measurement Graham calculated by subtracting a company's liabilities from its assets. Eventually, Graham theorized, the stock market will catch on to the true value of a company and its share price will rise; by that time, a savvy investor following Graham's principles already will be locked into the stock at a low price. It's a

simple enough theory, but one that requires much research into companies to determine their net worth, their "book value," and other factors. It is research for which Buffett is eminently suited.

After graduate school, at his father's brokerage firm, Buffett would often travel to Lincoln, Nebraska and pore through company reports. As he told *Forbes* magazine, "I read from page to page. I didn't read brokers' reports or anything. I just looked at raw data. And I would get all excited about these things." Today, he conducts his business the same way. Buffett does not have a stock ticker in his office, nor a computer or calculator. According to numerous published reports, he spends about five to six hours each day reading annual reports and trade publications. *Fortune* magazine reported that in Omaha, Buffett "does what he pleases, leading an unhurried, unhassled, largely unscheduled life. . . . He spends hours at a stretch in his office, reading, talking on the phone, and, in the December to March period, agonizing over his annual report, whose fame is one of the profound satisfactions in his life."

Buffett left Omaha and joined Graham's investment firm on Wall Street in 1954. There he was able to view his mentor's work first-hand. Over the next two years, Buffett got married, fathered two children, and made $140,000 by the time he was 25. Graham shut down his investment firm in 1956 and Buffett gladly left New York. When he returned to Omaha family members asked him for advice, so Buffett set up an investment partnership. As he told the *New York Times Magazine,* he said to his investors, "I'll run it like I run my own money, and I'll take part of the losses and part of the profits. And I won't tell you what I'm doing."

While he might have kept investors in the dark about his methods, Buffet's bottom-line returns were crystal clear: over the next 13 years Buffett Partnership Ltd. generated a 29.5 percent compounded annual return. He raised $105,000 from investors to start the partnership, and when he closed it 13 years later, the partnership was worth $105 million, and Buffett worth $25 million.

One of the investments along the way was Berkshire Hathaway, a textile manufacturer in Massachusetts. Buffett would create his multibillion-dollar empire around that business, although the textile company itself remains—in Buffett's opinion—one of the biggest investment mistakes he made. Sure, Berkshire Hathaway's stock price was cheap, satisfying a requirement of the Graham strategy. But the textile industry as a whole, and the company itself, was weak. In one of his much-anticipated annual reports, quoted in *Fortune* magazine, Buffett summed up part of his philosophy in the wake of that mistaken textile purchase: "It's far better to buy a wonderful company at a fair price than a fair company at a wonderful price." (He would shut down the textile mill in the mid-1980s.)

Buffett ended the lucrative partnership in 1969. As the *New York Times Magazine* reported, "The partnership's capital had grown so large that small investments were no longer reasonable, and he could find no big investments to his liking. In addition, the market was too speculative for his taste." He then focused on Berkshire Hathaway, buying up companies under its umbrella, investing "where and when he pleased," according to the *Times.*

Buffett's holdings, and his strategies, from the late 1960s on are clear. He first bought a series of insurance companies, which are considered excellent sources of cash. (People regularly pay insurance premiums; insurance companies usually pay claims on those insurance policies—if they have to pay them at all—years down the line. Therefore, there is usually a great amount of cash on hand for the company owners.) Buffett used that cash to buy a series of businesses, which have remained at the core of his investments.

His so-called "Sainted Seven Plus One" are sizeable, profitable companies that, according to the *Wall Street Journal,* "provide a steady stream of profits and capital to fund the investments that bring him renown." Among the eight core businesses are: the *Buffalo News,* World Books, Kirby vacuum cleaners, Fechheimer Brothers uniform company, and See's Candies. According to *Money* magazine, those businesses alone generated $173 million in cash in 1990, and the *New York Times* estimated in 1991 that their combined worth was approximately $1.6 billion. The cash generated by the eight companies is, in turn, invested in other corporations, which comprise the other core chunk of Berkshire Hathaway's holdings.

All of the companies in which Buffett invested are businesses he understands, underlining one of Buffett's main rules: "Stick to what you know." *Forbes* once quoted him as explaining why he had not invested in the immensely profitable computer company, Microsoft: "Bill Gates is a good friend, and I think he may be the smartest guy I ever met. But I don't know what those little things do."

Instead Buffett bought into what the *New York Times Magazine* called his "permanent holdings": The *Washington Post,* Geico (an insurance company), Capital Cities/ABC, and Coca Cola. He bought $45 million of Geico stock, which by 1989, according to the *New York Times,* was worth $1.4 billion. His $10.6 million investment in the *Washington Post* group of publications ballooned to an investment worth $486 million 16 years later. When he purchased seven percent of Coca Cola for $1 billion in 1988, some said he had bought too high, too late. But Buffett predicted Coke's expansion into foreign markets and thought the company could grow. It did, more than doubling his investment.

Investments in the big, brand-name companies is an example of how Buffett's buying strategy has evolved from the teachings of his mentor, Graham. Buffett became interested in what he called "franchise" businesses, or companies that are well-managed, with an established product line, and which are not subject to low-cost competition. His strategy changed because the market changed. The companies that Graham liked—companies trading far below their actual value—are rarer.

White Knight

Also in the 1980s, Buffett engaged in a series of transactions that are available only to someone with enormous wealth. He stepped in as a so-called "white knight" to help

companies fend off hostile takeovers by other corporations. Buffett's strategy works like this: a company, such as Gillette, faces a takeover and needs an infusion of cash. Buffett invests in the company's "preferred stock." According to the *Wall Street Journal,* the preferred stock options are "not available to other investors. Typically [Buffett] gets preferred stock bearing a healthy dividend—assuring a modest return no matter what happens—and the ability to convert to common stock if the company's fortunes rise." In the case of Gillette, Buffett invested $600 million in 1989, and in converting the stock two years later, received 11 percent of the company, which was worth, at the time, $1.05 billion.

In 1991 Buffett stepped in as interim chairman of Solomon Brothers brokerage firm after that it was accused of making false bids at Treasury auctions. Buffett, who had invested $700 million of Berkshire Hathaway cash in Solomon Brothers, was its largest shareholder. He is credited with streamlining the company and, over his six-month tenure as interim chairman, helping to rebuild its reputation after the scandal.

But the shareholders are not complaining. Berkshire Hathaway stock was trading for $12 a share in 1965. As of December, 1994, a single share of the investment company was the most expensive traded on the New York Stock Exchange: it cost $19,900 a share. Buffett owns over 40 percent of Berkshire Hathaway, which accounts for his $8.3 billion net worth. (Incidentally, Buffett does his own taxes.) And in August 1995, Buffett brokered a spectacular deal when his Berkshire Hathaway arranged the $19 billion purchase of Cap Cities/ABC by the Walt Disney Company. While the brokerage already had a $345 million in investments, this one merger raised the value to $2.3 billion.

Those not fortunate enough to own Berkshire Hathaway often mimic Buffett's buys. *Fortune* reported that when the general public learns Buffett has bought a particular stock, the public also buys the stock, running up the price. That led the magazine to quip: "Now there are two ways to make a killing in the stock market. The first, goes the old saw, is to shoot your broker. The second, it seems, is to shadow Warren Buffett."

The strategy doesn't always work, as a 1995 *Money* article warned. "Awe-inspiring though Buffett's record is, he's had a few clunkers. The $322 million investment he made last spring in Salomon common stock is down roughly 26%, and an albeit tiny (for him) $38.7 million stake in [an aircraft leasing company] has plummeted 68% since 1990." Prior to that, Buffett had bought Disney low and sold it later for a small profit; but that company rose spectacularly after Buffett's sale. He bought a $358-million chunk of USAir only to see the investment sour. (He was later quoted in *Fortune* as telling a group of business students at Columbia, "Don't invest in airlines.") In his 1989 annual report, quoted in *Fortune,* Buffett candidly wrote, "It's no sin to miss a great opportunity outside one's area of competence. But I have passed on a couple of really big purchases that were served up to me on a platter and that I was fully capable of understanding. For Berkshire's shareholders, myself included, the cost of this thumb-sucking has been huge."

Aside from his business acumen and opinions, many people are interested in Buffett himself, asking: What's a billionaire like? He does not give frequent interviews, preferring to let his corporate report speak for him. He lives in the same Omaha home he bought in 1958 for $31,500. He lives in that home with his girlfriend and former housekeeper, Astrid Menks, 17 years his junior. His wife of 40-plus years lives in California and is friends with his girlfriend. (Mrs. Buffett is the second largest shareholder of Berkshire Hathaway and is slated to take over the company after Buffett's death.)

One of his few extravagances is his corporate jet, and playing bridge by computer with friends from around the country. According to the *Wall Street Journal,* he wears rumpled suits, although very expensive Italian ones, and drinks about five cherry Cokes a day. He says he is an agnostic. As Roger Lowenstein related in his unauthorized biography *Buffett: The Making of an American Capitalist,* the investor once promised his young daughter a $10,000 check if he didn't lose a certain number of pounds by a certain date. He lost the weight, and kept the cash.

"He is a standard bearer for long-term investing, the perfect antidote to the get-rich-quick schemers of *Wall Street,*" the *Wall Street Journal* said of Buffett. *Forbes* opined that "He has not the psychological need for the constant wheeling and dealing, buying and selling that afflicts so many successful business and financial people." His philosophy—as well as his enormous wealth—allows him to be pickier and choosier. As he stated in his 1989 annual report, "We do not wish to join with managers who lack admirable qualities, no matter how attractive the prospects of their business. We've never succeeded in making a good deal with a bad person."

Which leads to the obvious question he is often asked: How do you succeed in the stock market? Throughout the years Buffett has offered bits of advice, such as: 1) If you buy into a great business, stick with it no matter how high the stock price goes; 2) avoid staggering debt; 3) think long term and don't hop in and out of the market; 4) in a bidding war between companies, buy stock in the side you think will lose; 5) easy does it (meaning, avoid businesses with big problems), and 6) concentrate on a small number of stocks.

Buffett has already made preparations for his money when he dies. He intends to set up a philanthropic foundation which, given the 23 percent annual rate of return he has averaged throughout his career, could generate a multibillion-dollar legacy to put the Ford and Rockefeller foundations to shame. He wants the fund's trustees to focus on halting population growth and nuclear proliferation. His three children will not make out that well; Buffett has said he plans to leave them "only" about $5 million apiece. He was quoted in *Esquire* as saying, "I think kids should have enough money to be able to do what they want to do, to learn what they want to do, but not enough money to do nothing."

Further Reading

Lowenstein, Roger, *Buffett: The Making of an American Capitalist* (unauthorized biography), Random House, 1995.

Business Week, May 10, 1993, p. 30; July 18, 1994, p. 46.

Economist, May 23, 1992, p. 86.

Esquire, October 1988, p. 103.

Forbes, March 19, 1990, p. 92; October 18, 1993, p. 40, p. 112.

Fortune, April 11, 1988, p. 26; April 9, 1990, p. 95; January 11, 1993, p. 101; November 29, 1993, p. 10; April 18, 1994, p. 14; July 25, 1994, p. 17.

Money, November 1990, p. 72; August 1991, p. 70; April 1995, p. 106.

New York Times, March 26, 1992, p. D1.

New York Times Magazine, April 1, 1990, part 2, p. 16.

Time, August 21, 1995.

U.S. News & World Report, June 20, 1994, p. 58.

Wall Street Journal, November 8, 1991, p. A1. ☐

Ralph Johnson Bunche

Ralph Johnson Bunche (1904-1971) was the highest American official in the United Nations. For his conduct of negotiations leading to an armistice in the First Arab-Israeli War, he received the Nobel Peace Prize in 1950, the first African American to do so.

A barber's son, Ralph Bunche was born in Detroit, Mich., on Aug. 7, 1904. His parents died when he was 13, and his maternal grandmother took Ralph and his young sister to live in Los Angeles. While going to school Ralph helped support the family by working as a janitor, carpet-layer, and seaman. His grandmother's indomitable will and her wisdom had a lasting influence on him.

Bunche attended the University of California at Los Angeles on scholarships and graduated in 1927. He earned a master's degree at Harvard University in 1928 and a doctorate in government and international relations at Harvard in 1934. His doctoral dissertation won the Tappan Prize as the best one in the social sciences that year. Later he did advanced work in anthropology at Northwestern University, the London School of Economics, and the University of Cape Town.

From 1928 to 1942 Bunche was a member (and chairman from 1937) of the department of political science at Howard University. He married Ruth Harris, one of his students, in 1930; the couple had three children. In 1950 he was appointed to the faculty of Harvard University, but after two successive leaves of absence he resigned in 1952 without having taught there.

An expert on colonialism, Bunche worked during World War II in the Office of Strategic Services as an analyst of African and Far Eastern affairs, moving in 1944 to the State Department, where he became head of the Division of Dependent Area Affairs. At Dumbarton Oaks in 1944, San Francisco in 1945, and London in 1946, he was active as an authority on trusteeship in the planning and establishment of the United Nations (UN). In 1947, at the invitation of Secretary General Trygve Lie, Bunche joined the UN Secretariat as director of the Trusteeship Division.

Lie and his successors, Dag Hammarskjöld and U Thant, gave special troubleshooting assignments to Bunche. In 1947 he was a member of the UN Special Committee on Palestine that recommended partition of the country into Jewish and Arab states. Arab refusal to accept the UN plan resulted in the First Arab-Israeli War. When the UN's chief mediator in that conflict, Count Folke Bernadotte, was assassinated in 1948, Bunche took his place. From January to June 1949 he presided over the difficult negotiations between Arab and Israeli delegations on the island of Rhodes that led eventually to an armistice. Both sides praised his achievement, and in 1950 he was awarded the Nobel Peace Prize for his work.

In 1955 Bunche was named undersecretary without portfolio in the UN Secretariat and in 1957 undersecretary for special political affairs (in 1969 this title was changed to undersecretary general). He directed UN peace-keeping operations in the Suez area (1956), in the Congo (1960), and on the island of Cyprus (1964) and was also responsible for the UN's program in the peaceful uses of atomic energy. He became U Thant's most influential political adviser. In June 1971, fatally ill, Bunche retired from his post. He died in New York City on December 9.

The grandson of a slave, Bunche bore with great reserve the indignities of racial prejudice that he experienced. His lifelong concern about race relations was the source of his early desire to be a teacher and his later specialization in colonial problems. In 1936 he was codirector of the Institute of Race Relations at Swarthmore College. From 1938 to 1940, as a staff member of the Carnegie Corporation of New York, he served as chief aide to Swedish sociologist Gunnar Myrdal in his investigation of the race problem in the United States that led to Myrdal's influential book *An American Dilemma*. Bunche wrote or supervised 13 of the 81 volumes of manuscripts and memoranda submitted to Myrdal for the book. For 22 years Bunche was a member of the board of directors of the National Association for the Advancement of Colored People. In 1965 he participated in marches in Selma and Montgomery, Ala., led by Martin Luther King, Jr., to protest racial discrimination.

Bunche received many honorary degrees and awards, and President John F. Kennedy presented him with the Medal of Freedom in 1963. Bunche was president of the American Political Science Association and a member of the Harvard University board of overseers.

Further Reading

Bunche wrote *A World View of Race* (1936; repr. 1968). Howard P. Linton compiled *Ralph Johnson Bunche: Writings by and about Him from 1928 to 1966* (1967). A biography is J. Alvin Kugelmass, *Ralph J. Bunche: Fighter for Peace* (1962). There is a short biography of him in Wilhelmina S. Robinson, *Historical Negro Biographies* (1968). For examinations of the UN Secretariat and the UN's peace-keeping efforts see Sydney D. Bailey, *The Secretariat of the United Nations* (1962; rev. ed. 1964), and James M. Boyd, *United Nations Peace-keeping Operations: A Military and Political Appraisal* (1971). □

Luther Burbank

The American plant breeder Luther Burbank (1849-1926) originated many varieties of garden plants, grains, and fruits. He was popularly known as a "wizard" because of the stream of new and improved forms that came from his experimental farm.

In Luther Burbank's youth, botany was beginning to shed its taxonomic preoccupation and the interest of scientists was shifting to questions related to the theory of evolution—variation, species formation, modes of reproduction, and environmental effects. To a long-standing American interest in importation of foreign plant varieties was added an interest in the experimental production of improved forms. Agricultural experimental stations began to dot the country during the 1890s. Although Burbank was not a scientist and was essentially uninterested in scientific questions, he nevertheless drew his inspiration from this new scientific work, and his own success served to intensify public interest in such investigations.

Burbank was born on March 7, 1849, in Lancaster, Mass., the son of a farmer and maker of brick and pottery. He attended the district school until he was 15 and then spent four winters at the Lancaster Academy. Most of his scientific education, however, was obtained from reading at the public library in Lancaster. According to his own account, his reading of Charles Darwin's *Variation of Animals and Plants under Domestication* in 1868 proved the turning point in his career, causing him to take the production of new species and varieties of plants as his life's work.

Beginning the Work

In 1870, 2 years after the death of his father, Burbank used his inheritance to help purchase a tract of 17 acres near the small town of Lunenburg, where he took up the business of market gardening. Here he produced his first "creation," the Burbank potato, and began the work that was to make him famous.

Despite his success as a market gardener, in 1875 Burbank decided to sell his land and move to California, where his three older brothers had already moved. He settled in Santa Rosa, where he would carry on his work for the next 50 years. Later he added a small amount of acreage adjoining a nearby town.

Following the Empirical Method

Although Burbank had read the scientific literature, he never operated as a scientist and apparently never thought of himself as one. His methods were empirical; he imported plants from foreign countries, made crosses of every conceivable kind—often for no apparent reason except, as he said, to get "perturbation" in the plants so as to get as wide and as large a variation as possible—and grew hundreds of thousands of plants under differing environmental conditions. He kept records only for his own use; once a project was completed and a new plant on the market, the records were generally destroyed. An effort made by the Carnegie Institution of Washington to collate the scientific data that came out of Burbank's experiments collapsed after a few years.

Although Burbank's methods were empirical, he did develop a store of knowledge that proved invaluable. This special knowledge (as emphasized by two scholars who studied the scientific aspects of his work) concerned correlations. Thus a minute, almost undetectable, variation in a young leaf, for example, may imply (or correlate with) a sweeter or plumper fruit, or a larger and more perfect flower. In his years of experimentation, Burbank gained an unrivaled mastery of such correlations, which, combined with his unusually keen sensory abilities, largely accounted for his success.

Originating New Forms

Burbank's creative work ranged over a long list of plants, but his strongest interests were in plums, berries, and lilies. He originated more than 40 new varieties of plums and prunes, mostly from multiple crossings in which Japanese plums played a prominent part. His work with berries, extending over 35 years, resulted in the introduction of at least 10 new varieties, mostly obtained through hybridizations of dewberries, blackberries, and raspberries. His years of experimentation with lilies resulted in a brilliant array of new forms, many of which became the most popular varieties in American gardens.

Best known among Burbank's flowers are the Shasta daisy, the blue Shirley poppy and the Fire poppy, and the fragrant calla. His wide range of techniques is illustrated by these. The Shasta daisy, a favorite of Burbank, was the result of a multiple crossing between a European and an American species of field daisy and then between these hybrids and a Japanese variety. The Shirley poppy was obtained by long selection from a crimson European poppy. The Fire poppy was a hybrid from a butter-colored species and a pure-white species that had a dull red in its ancestry. The fragrant calla, which has a perfume resembling that of the violet, was discovered by accident in a flat of Little Gem calla seedlings. His new fruits, besides the many plums and prunes, included varieties of apples, peaches, quinces, and nectarines. One of his less profitable creations, the result of an effort to excite "perturbations," was a cross between the peach and the almond. At one time or another, he worked with virtually all the common garden vegetables. One of his most unusual experiments resulted in the production of a series of spineless cacti useful for feeding cattle in arid regions.

Applying Principles to Humans

Burbank's work with plants convinced him that the key to good breeding was selection and environment, and he, like so many others of his time, tried to apply his concepts to human society. The product of his thinking on this subject was first published in 1907 as *The Training of the Human Plant*. Yet despite his vast experience in plant breeding, this book revealed his firm belief in the then-discredited theory of the inheritance of acquired characteristics; accordingly, unlike most eugenists of the period, he stressed education and the provision of a good environment generally as the best way to remake human society.

Burbank was an honorary member of leading scientific societies all over the world. He was a fellow of the American Association for the Advancement of Science and of the Royal Horticultural Society. In 1905 he was awarded an honorary doctor of science degree by Tufts College. He died on April 11, 1926.

Further Reading

Luther Burbank: His Methods and Discoveries and Their Practical Application, edited by John Witson (12 vols., 1914-1915), was written under Burbank's direction. For an intimate account by Burbank's sister, Emma Burbank Beeson, see *The Early Life and Letters of Luther Burbank* (1927), which had been published in 1926 as *The Harvest of the Years*. Biographical material is also in Henry Smith Williams, *Luther Burbank: His Life and Work* (1915). For a favorable assessment of Burbank's scientific work see David Starr Jordan and Vernon L. Kellogg, *The Scientific Aspects of Luther Burbank's Work* (1909).

Additional Sources

Dreyer, Peter, *A gardener touched with genius: the life of Luther Burbank,* New York: Coward, McCann & Geoghegan, 1975, Santa Rosa, Calif.: L. Burbank Home & Gardens, 1993. □

Warren E. Burger

As Chief Justice of the U.S. Supreme Court (1969-1986), Warren E. Burger (born 1907) was tough on criminal defendants and generally negative toward civil rights and civil liberties claims, but did much to improve the administration of justice.

man, he earned his LL.B. *magna cum laude* from St. Paul College of Law in 1931.

After admission to the bar, Burger joined the St. Paul law firm of Boyesen, Otis & Faricy. In 1935 he became a partner in the successor firm of Faricy, Burger, Moore & Costello, with which he remained affiliated until 1953. In addition to handling a variety of civil and criminal cases, he taught contract law at his alma mater for a dozen years.

Political Career

Burger was active in Republican politics. He helped to organize the Minnesota Young Republicans in 1934 and played an important role in Harold Stassen's successful 1938 campaign for governor. Rejected for World War II military service because of a spinal injury, he served from 1942 to 1947 on his state's Emergency War Labor Board. At both the 1948 and 1952 Republican National Conventions, Burger acted as floor manager for Stassen's presidential campaign. At a crucial moment during the 1952 gathering he threw his support to Gen. Dwight Eisenhower, helping Ike to win the nomination on the first ballot.

After the election President Eisenhower made him head of the Justice Department's Civil Division. Assistant Attorney General Burger supervised a staff of about 180 lawyers who handled all civil cases except antitrust and land litigation. When Solicitor General Simon E. Sobeloff refused to defend the dismissal of Yale professor John Peters from a part-time position with the Public Health Service as a security risk, Burger volunteered to argue the case before the Supreme Court. He lost and, by involving himself in the matter, aroused the ire of liberals.

Law and Order Judge

Nevertheless, in 1955 Eisenhower named him to the U.S. Court of Appeals for the District of Columbia. While on that prestigious bench, Burger demonstrated a capacity for legal scholarship, writing several law review articles and lecturing on a variety of topics ranging from the insanity defense to judicial administration. His opinions in criminal procedure cases attracted more attention. They were consistently pro-prosecution. He urged that confessions be admitted into evidence even when the police who obtained them had violated legal rules requiring the prompt arraignment of suspects and that physical evidence not be excluded because it had been obtained through forcible entry. Pragmatic rather than legalistic, Judge Burger sought to ensure that the judiciary would not interfere with law enforcement.

He was just what Nixon wanted in a chief justice. Ironically, in Burger's most famous criminal case the loser was the president. In *United States* v. *Nixon* (1974) Burger ordered his patron to turn over to Watergate special prosecutor Leon Jaworski tape recordings, one of which contained unequivocal evidence that Nixon had committed the crime of obstruction of justice. This ruling led directly to the president's resignation.

In more routine criminal cases, Burger was everything Nixon had hoped for. He spent his first years on the Court dissenting as holdovers from the Warren era continued to expand the rights of defendants. When other Nixon appoin-

Duringthe 1968 presidential campaign, Richard Nixon told a public worried about the rising crime rate that the Supreme Court was "seriously hamstringing the peace forces in our society and strengthening the criminal forces." He promised, if elected, to ensure that the Court would no longer hamper law enforcement. The victorious Nixon's first step toward that goal was appointing Warren E. Burger to succeed Earl Warren as chief justice. Liberals worried that Burger would soon sweep away the many legal reforms initiated during the Warren era, but their fears proved unfounded. Although more conservative than his predecessor, he led no counterrevolution, but rather made his mark as an administrative reformer.

Indeed the contrast between the Burger and Warren courts was less striking than that between the humble origins of the new chief and the background of the typical appointee. Most members of the Court have come from prominent or well-to-do families and have attended prestigious colleges and law schools. Burger, though, was the son of a railroad cargo inspector and travelling salesman. He was born on September 17, 1907, in St. Paul, Minnesota, and grew up in modest circumstances. By age nine he was delivering newspapers to help his family financially. When Burger graduated from high school, where he was student council president and engaged in a wide range of extracurricular activities, Princeton offered him a partial scholarship. Because of his family's limited resources, he had to decline it. Burger took extension courses at the University of Minnesota for two years and then enrolled in a night law school. Combining study with work as a life insurance sales-

tees joined him on the bench, Burger launched a successful counterattack, which lasted from 1971 until 1976. It resulted in decisions partially undercutting Warren Court precedents, such as *Harris* v. *New York* (1971), in which he announced that a statement obtained without giving the warnings required by *Miranda* v. *Arizona* (1966) could be used to impeach a defendant's testimony. About 1977 the Burger Court's hostility toward the work of its predecessor seemed to subside, but the chief justice frequently dissented when it rendered decisions favorable to defendants. He also continued to criticize the "exclusionary rule," which made illegally obtained evidence inadmissible. Prodded by Burger, the Court returned to the attack in 1981. During the years that followed, it handed down decisions which, among other things, created significant exceptions to both the exclusionary rule and the requirement that police give suspects *Miranda* warnings before interrogating them.

During the same period, Burger also helped give new life to the death penalty, which for several years after the Court re-legalized it in 1976 had existed more in theory than in practice. With the chief justice lashing out at lawyers who resorted to endless legal maneuvering to keep their clients alive, the Supreme Court rejected almost all appeals in such cases. Executions began to occur again with relative frequency.

Civil Rights and Liberties

Besides being a law and order hard-liner, Burger also proved to be a conservative authoritarian. He believed "the community" (which he tended to equate with those having a bare majority in the legislature) had a right to impose its values on nonconforming individuals. Consequently, he was far less sympathetic toward civil liberties claims than Earl Warren had been.

That held for those claims based on the First Amendment's establishment of religion clause. In *Lemon* v. *Kurtzman* (1971) Burger announced a test for determining whether state attempts to subsidize parochial education violated that constitutional prohibition. This generated a collage of inconsistent decisions, striking down some and upholding others. The results of *March* v. *Chambers* (1983) and *Lynch* v. *Donnelly* (1984) were clearer but even more difficult to reconcile with the language of the establishment clause. In those cases Burger upheld respectively Nebraska's practice of opening legislative sessions with a prayer delivered by a state-paid Protestant chaplain and Pawtucket, Rhode Island's right to display a nativity scene in front of its city hall.

He was also, despite a background of service in Minnesota with groups seeking to improve race relations, an inconsistent supporter of claims based on the equal protection clause of the Fourteenth Amendment. Use of that provision against gender-based discrimination began with the Burger Court, and it was the chief justice who wrote the seminal opinion in *Reed* v. *Reed* (1971). On the other hand, he refused to support Justice William Brennan's effort to have the Court adopt for sex cases the same stringent constitutional test already employed in racial ones, and he accepted as valid policies which penalized pregnancy.

Also indicative of Burger's lack of sympathy for civil rights and civil liberties was his support of procedural innovations making it more difficult to litigate such claims in federal court. The Burger Court's decisions on such technical issues as standing, justiciability, abstention, and the requirements for bringing class action suits all tended toward closing the courthouse door. In addition, the Court lengthened the list of officials immune from suits for damages for violating citizens' constitutional rights and expanded the "good faith" defense available to those who can still be sued.

Reformer or Counterrevolutionary?

Yet, despite being less receptive to civil rights and civil liberties claims, the Burger Court was not as different from the Warren Court as casual observers supposed. It was, for example, equally "activist." That is, it proved equally willing to substitute its own value judgments for those of popularly elected lawmakers. In *Roe* v. *Wade* (1973), for example, the Burger Court on tenuous constitutional grounds invalidated the states' abortion laws and spelled out precisely how they might regulate abortion in the future.

Furthermore, although often critical of its predecessor's work, the Burger Court did not undo it. Not a single one of the Warren Court's landmark decisions was reversed. Neither segregation, nor malapportioned legislatures, nor prayer in public schools became constitutional again. Even in the area of criminal procedure, the Burger Court limited the effect of, rather than overturned, Warren Court precedents.

Ironically, after 17 years on the Court the "conservative" chief justice had better credentials as a reformer than as a counterrevolutionary. Early in his tenure he launched a crusade to reshape and improve the administration of justice, which had broken down under the burden of a vastly expanded volume of litigation. At his urging many courts began to employ professional administrators, and an institute was set up to train them. Burger got continuing education for judges whose numbers had increased substantially, and his attacks on the competency of trial lawyers inspired innovations in the training of litigators. He also improved the coordination between federal and state courts serving the same geographic areas. In 1986 Warren Burger resigned as chief justice to spend full time as head of the U.S. Constitution Bicentennial Commission.

Further Reading

Although the literature on the Burger Court is extensive, that on Warren Burger himself is not. Andrew Norman, "Warren E. Burger," in *The Burger Court 1969-1978,* ed. Leon Friedman (1978) is a disappointing article which does no more than analyze Burger's work on the Supreme Court. Although poorly focused, Dennis E. Everette's "Overcoming Occupational Heredity on the Supreme Court," *American Bar Association Journal* (January 1980), is a spirited defense of Burger's humble origins. Charles M. Lamb analyzes his work on the court of appeals in "The Making of a Chief Justice: Warren Burger on Criminal Procedure, 1956-1969," *Cornell Law Review* (June 1975). Robert Douglas Chesler, "Imagery of Community, Ideology of Authority: The Moral Reasoning of

Chief Justice Burger," *Harvard Civil Rights/Civil Liberties Law Review* (Summer 1983) is helpful in understanding Burger's negative attitude toward civil rights and civil liberties claims. Edward A. Tamm and Paul C. Reardon, "Warren E. Burger and the Administration of Justice," *Brigham Young University Law Review* (1981), is a good survey of Burger's efforts to promote judicial efficiency.

The book which provides the most insights into the inner workings of the Burger Court and the sometimes highhanded conduct of its chief justice is Bob Woodward and Scott Armstrong, *The Brethren* (1979), written by two investigative journalists. For scholarly evaluations of the Burger Court's decisions and direction, see Richard Y. Funston, *Constitutional Counterrevolution? The Warren Court and the Burger Court: Judicial Policy Making in Modern America* (1977); Vincent Blasi, editor, *The Burger Court: The Counter-Revolution That Wasn't* (1983); and Alpheus Thomas Mason, "Whence and Whither the Burger Court? Judicial Self Restraint: A Beguiling Myth," *Review of Politics* (January 1979). *The Nation* devoted its entire September 29, 1984, issue to an assessment of the Burger Court's first 15 years. The articles it contained examine numerous facets of the Court's work and are easy for readers with little legal background to understand. □

George Burns

Comedian and actor George Burns (1896–1996) is a show business legend. When he died at the age of 100 in 1996, he had spent 90 years as a comic entertainer, making numerous television and film appearances and earning an enduring popularity with his obligatory-cigar-in-hand comedy routines.

In his ninety years in show business, George Burns had time for three careers. His first two decades were spent as a small-time vaudeville performer. Later, as part of a comedy duo with his wife, Gracie Allen, he achieved wide popularity on the stage, radio, television, and in films. Finally, after Allen's death, Burns performed as a stand-up comedian and comic actor, winning an Academy Award at the age of 80.

George Burns was born Nathan Birnbaum on January 20, 1896, the ninth of twelve children of an Orthodox Jewish family. The Birnbaums, recent immigrants from Eastern Europe, lived on New York City's impoverished lower East Side. His father was a cantor (a painfully out-of-tune one, according to Burns's account), who worked as a last-minute substitute at various New York synagogues.

After his father's death, Burns began a career in show business at the age of seven. To help support the family, he formed the Pee Wee quartet, a group of child performers who sang and told jokes on street corners. He and his brothers also helped out by stealing coal from a nearby coal yard—earning the nickname the Burns Brothers. He would later settle on this as a stage name, changing his first name to George after an idolized older brother.

Burns's early performing years were spent doing whatever he could to earn money. In 1916, under the name Willy Delight, he performed as a trick roller-skater on the Keith Vaudeville Circuit. Later, as Pedro Lopez, he taught ballroom dancing. Over the years, he tried several other names—Billy Pierce, Captain Betts, Jed Jackson, Jimmy Malone, Buddy Lanks—appearing in a wide range of vaudeville acts with many different partners. "When I first started in vaudeville I was strictly small-time," he reminisced in his book, *How to Live to be 100—or More.* "I'd be lying if I said I was the worst act in the world; I wasn't that good."

Formed Partnership with Gracie Allen

By 1923, he was appearing at the Union Theatre as George Burns, comedian, when he met his future partner, Gracie Allen. Allen, ten years younger than Burns, came from a San Francisco show business family, and had also been performing since she was a child. However, by the early 1920s, she had given up her fledgling career in entertainment to train as a stenographer. Allen was accompanying a friend on a backstage visit at the theater when she was introduced to Burns. In tune with her scatterbrained image, she confused him with someone else, and called him by the wrong name for several days.

Burns and Allen made their performing debut in 1924. In his previous act, Burns was both the writer and the comedian, while his partner played the straight man. Burns initially stuck to this format in his act with Allen, but quickly learned that she was the funny one. "Even her straight lines got laughs," Burns was quoted as saying in *The Guardian.* "She had a very funny delivery .... they laughed at her straight lines and didn't laugh at my jokes."

Soon Burns and Allen developed the act that would make them famous: he played the bemused, cigar-smoking boyfriend and comic foil to her dizzy, muddled girlfriend. In a distracted, little-girl voice, Allen told rambling stories about her family, while Burns asked questions. "I just asked Gracie a question, and she kept talking for the next 37 years," he later recalled (quoted in *The Daily Telegraph*).

After performing together in vaudeville for three years, Burns and Allen were married in Cleveland on January 7, 1926. Theirs was a famously happy marriage. "I'm the brains and Gracie is everything else, especially to me," Burns once said (quoted in *The Daily Mail*). Later, they adopted two children, Sandra Jean and Ronald John.

Around the time of their marriage they were signed to a six-year contract with Keith theaters, which took them on tours of the United States and Europe. In 1930 Burns and Allen joined Eddie Cantor, George Jessel, and others in a headline bill marking the end of vaudeville at the Palace Theatre in New York. After this appearance, as well as appearances on the Rudy Vallee and Guy Lombardo shows, CBS signed the team for their own radio program.

Launched Successful Radio Show

The George Burns and Gracie Allen Show debuted on February 15, 1932. The team became famous for one exchange that ended that show, and every show. After a program filled with one non sequitur after another, Burns would say, long sufferingly, "Say goodnight, Gracie" and Allen would respond brightly, "Goodnight, Gracie."

During nineteen years in radio, Burns and Allen attracted an audience estimated at more than 45 million listeners. In 1940 their salary was reported to be $9,000 a week. Always modest about his role in the series, Burns claimed that Allen was solely responsible for their enduring success. "With Gracie, I had the easiest job of any straight man in history," he said (quoted in *The Guardian*). "I only had to know two lines—'How's your brother?' and 'Your brother did *what?*'"

Meanwhile, in 1931 they signed a contract with Paramount Studios to star in short films and, when not making pictures, to play on the stage of the Publix theaters. Their first full-length movie was *The Big Broadcast of 1932*. In addition to many short films, the team made an average of two films a year for Paramount. Their last film for Paramount was *Honolulu* (1939), which starred Eleanor Powell and Robert Young.

To attract attention for their radio show, Burns masterminded several publicity stunts. In 1933, Allen appeared on radio shows throughout the country, searching for her imaginary lost brother. The joke was so convincing that her real brother, an accountant in San Francisco, had to go into hiding until public interest in him had waned. During the 1940 election, Allen declared herself a nominee for the "Surprise Party," and campaigned on various radio shows, even holding a three-day convention in Omaha. She received several thousand write-in votes.

In October 1950, *The Burns and Allen Show* made the transition to television. The program used the same format as the successful radio program. The following exchange was typical of their humor: "Did the maid ever drop you on your head when you were a baby?" "Don't be silly, George. We couldn't afford a maid. My mother had to do it" (quoted in *The Independent*).

Began to Perform as Solo Act

In 1958, angina forced Allen to retire—an event that merited the cover of *Life* magazine. At the time, *The George Burns and Gracie Allen Show* was then television's longest-running sitcom. Burns continued to perform in *The George Burns Show,* but the series only lasted one season. "The show had everything it needed to be successful, except Gracie," Burns recalled (quoted in *The Independent*).

Six years later, Allen died of cancer at the age of 59. Burns was devastated, and made almost daily visits to her grave. "The good things for me started with Gracie and for the next 38 years they only got better," he was quoted as saying in *The Guardian*. "But everything has a price. It still doesn't seem right that she went so young, and that I've been given so many years to spend without her."

After Allen's death, Burns devoted his time to McCadden, his television production company, which made such popular programs as *The People's Choice* (1955-58) and *Mr. Ed* (1961-66). Burns also appeared as a guest in various television specials throughout the sixties. However, his attempts to develop a new double act failed; he was unacceptable to the public with new partners like Carol Channing or Connie Stevens.

Won Academy Award at Age 80

It was not until 1975 that Burns was given the opportunity to re-launch his performing career. After the death of Jack Benny, a contemporary and close friend from the vaudeville days, Burns took Benny's role opposite Walter Matthau in Neil Simon's film, *The Sunshine Boys*. The role of the ancient straight man, coming out of retirement for one last get-together with his shambling former partner, could not have been more perfect for Burns. At age 80, he won an Academy Award for best supporting actor—the oldest person to do so. "My last film was in 1939," he said at the time (quoted in *The Daily Telegraph*). "My agent didn't want me to suffer from over-exposure."

He followed his success with *Oh God!,* in which he played the deity wearing baggy pants, sneakers, and a golf cap. Two sequels followed, *Oh God! II* (1980) and *Oh God! You Devil* (1984), as well as several other comedies. None of these films was very successful, but Burns was undisturbed. "I just like to be working," he was quoted as saying in *The Daily Telegraph.*

Throughout the 1980s, Burns appeared often on television, hosting *100 Years of America's Popular Music* (1981), *George Burns and Other Sex Symbols* (1982) and *George Burns Celebrates 80 Years in Show Business* (1983). By this time, his comic material, mostly one-liners, centered almost exclusively on his age and longevity.

Burns also published various books, including *Dr. Burns' Prescription for Happiness* (1985) and a tribute to his wife, *Gracie, A Love Story* (1988), in which he revealed that Allen was actually his second wife. During his vaudeville days, Burns had formed a dancing act with Hannah Siegel, whom he had rechristened Hermosa Jose, after his favorite cigar. When their act was booked for a 26-week tour, her parents refused to let her travel the country with Burns unless he married her. The marriage lasted as long as the tour, and then was dissolved.

Although Burns never remarried, during his 80s and 90s he developed an enthusiasm for taking out young women—which became another endless source for comic material. At 97, Burns was still writing, making stage appearances, and numbering Sharon Stone among his escorts.

Burns had planned shows to celebrate his 100th birthday at the London Palladium for January 20, 1996. However, after a bad fall in 1994, his health declined, and the performances were canceled. A few days before his 100th birthday, he was suffering from the flu, and was unable to attend a party in his honor. Burns died at his home in Los Angeles on March 9, 1996.

Further Reading

Daily Mail, March 11, 1996, p. 23.
The Daily Telegraph, March 11, 1996, p. 23.
The Guardian, March 11, 1996, p. 12.
The Independent, March 11, 1996, p. 16.
The Times (London), March 11, 1996. □

Aaron Burr

American lawyer and politician Aaron Burr (1756-1836) was vice president under Thomas Jefferson. After his term of office he conspired to invade Spanish territory in the Southwest and to separate certain western areas from the United States.

Aaron Burr was born in Newark, N.J., on Feb. 6, 1756, the grandson of the Calvinist theologian Johathan Edwards, and the son of a Presbyterian minister. The family soon moved to Princeton, where the Reverend Burr became president of the College of New Jersey (later Princeton University). Burr was soon orphaned.

From an early age Burr prepared for an education at the College of New Jersey. Denied admission at the age of age 11, the precocious youth was accepted as a sophomore 2 years later. An eager and industrious student, he graduated with distinction in 3 years. He studied theology for a while but found himself disenchanted with the religious controversies generated by the Great Awakening. He turned instead to the study of law and for a period worked under the famous jurist Tapping Reeve.

Officer in the Revolution

Attracted by the drama and opportunity of the Revolutionary War, Burr secured a letter of recommendation from John Hancock, the president of the Continental Congress, and appeared before Gen. Washington to request a commission in the Continental Army. Washington refused, thus opening the first in a series of conflicts between the two men. Burr, however, persisted. He joined the Army and

behaved commendably in the illfated expedition against Quebec. In the spring of 1776 he secured appointment, with the rank of major, to Washington's official household in New York. Mutual distrust quickly deepened between the two men, partly because of Burr's disenchantment with the tedium of administrative duties and partly because of the glaring contrast between his own spontaneous behavior and Washington's stiff and humorless manner.

Again through the intercession of Hancock, Burr transferred to the staff of Gen. Israel Putnam. For the next several years he served effectively in a variety of posts, developing a reputation both for vigilance and the effective disciplining of his troops.

In March 1779, his health impaired by exhaustion and exposure, Burr resigned his commission. By 1780, however, he was ready to launch a heavy program of legal study. Burr was licensed as an attorney in January 1782 and 2 months later was admitted to the bar.

At least equal to Burr's pursuit of fame and fortune was his passion for women. Throughout his long life he carried on numerous affairs. Though he was only 5 feet 6 inches tall, his erect military bearing and graceful manner, his sparkling conversation and elegant appearance made him very attractive to women. In July 1777 he began regular visits to Mrs. Theodosia Prevost, 10 years his senior and wife of a British officer frequently away on duty. In July 1781 she was widowed; 9 months later she and Burr were married. The marriage lasted until her death in 1794, though Burr carried on a number of amours during the interval. In 1783 a daughter, Theodosia, was born, with whom Burr developed a deep and affectionate relationship. Indeed, much of Burr's life came to revolve around his ambitions and concerns for her.

Lawyer in New York

After establishing a successful legal practice in the booming town of Albany, Burr moved in 1783 to New York City. For 6 years he stuck to his practice, generating a substantial reputation and income. He never compiled a large fortune, however, for his generosity and his own lifestyle drained his money away.

Local and National Politics

Gradually during the 1790s Burr worked his way into New York politics. Nominally a member of the emerging Jeffersonian opposition, he took care not to break completely with the Federalists. The results of this were twofold. By carefully balancing group against group, he could present himself as a nonsectarian, coalition candidate. On the other hand, this generated suspicions among both Jeffersonians and Federalists about his "unsettled" political loyalties. In 1791 Burr won election to the U.S. Senate, defeating Philip Schuyler, Alexander Hamilton's father-in-law. Burr and Hamilton had been for some time political and professional antagonists; this election elicited Hamilton's unrelenting hatred. In the Senate, Burr occupied a somewhat ambiguous position, opposing Hamilton's financial program and the Jay Treaty, yet not becoming a full Jeffersonian partisan.

Burr failed to drum up support for the vice presidency in 1796 and also lost his seat in the Senate. From 1797 to 1799 he served in the New York Legislature but was defeated for reelection when he came under fire for promoting legislation to aid a land company and banking corporation in which he had financial interests.

Vice Presidency

Burr's opportunity to fashion a national political career came with the presidential election of 1800. With the support of the Tammany organization (which he never formally joined), he organized New York City and enabled Jefferson to carry the state's crucial electoral votes. Meanwhile Burr had secured a pledge from the Jeffersonians in Congress to support him equally with Jefferson in the election as a way of ensuring that neither of the Federalist candidates would have a chance. (In 1800 presidential electors simply cast two ballots, making no distinction between presidential and vice-presidential preferences.) The result was a tie. Jefferson and Burr each received 73 votes, and the election shifted to the House of Representatives. For 35 ballots neither man received a majority, while rumors circulated that Burr was scheming for Federalist support. A number of Federalists did state their strong preference for him, but Hamilton argued just as strongly that Jefferson was a more honorable man. Finally several Federalists withheld their votes and permitted Jefferson's election, thus ending a major constitutional crisis.

Burr was now vice president, but his political career was near its end. His relations with Jefferson's supporters were further strained during his 4 years in office. In 1804 Burr was passed over by the Jeffersonian congressional caucus and was not renominated for vice president.

Hamilton-Burr Duel

In July 1804 the famous duel with Hamilton took place. Burr had tried to avoid it, but it was forced upon him by Hamilton's mounting public attacks. As word of Hamilton's death spread, the public outcry forced Burr to flee for his safety. His political base, both within New York and in the Jeffersonian party, was now completely gone. To fulfill his obligation as vice president, Burr returned to Washington to preside over the impeachment proceedings against Justice Samuel Chase, a task he carried out with justice and impartiality. The day after the trial was over, Burr left the Senate chamber for the last time.

Burr's Conspiracy

For at least a year prior to this, Burr had been making plans to recoup in the West some of the power denied him in the East. The precise motive behind his western adventures has never been clarified. There seems to have been two options: to gather a force to invade Spanish–held territory across the Mississippi out of which an independent republic was to be fashioned, or to separate certain southwestern territories (east of the Mississippi) from the United States and incorporate them with the Spanish lands to form an independent nation. Burr's primary goal seems to have been the Spanish venture, though he was clearly interested

in including New Orleans and territory along the Mississippi. If his proposals to England to aid in dismembering the Union had met with support, Burr might well have placed separation at the center of his planning. Whatever the case, his western adventure had the gravest implications for the young republic.

Burr's involved intrigue took form in 1804-1805, when he divulged his plans to various persons, among them Gen. James Wilkinson, commander of American forces in the West, and Anthony Merry, British minister to the United States, whom Burr asked for half a million dollars and the promise of aid from the British fleet. After a scouting trip down the Ohio and Mississippi rivers, Burr returned east and made further attempts to organize support. Failing to secure funds from England, he turned to various private sources.

When Jefferson's purchase of Spanish Florida ended the prospect of the Spanish-American border war that Burr had hoped to use as the occasion for his own invasion of Spanish territory, he decided to launch his enterprise. In August 1806 he started west into the Ohio Valley to rally men and supplies. Increasingly alarmed by rumors of Burr's operations, President Jefferson sent warnings to western officials to keep Burr under careful surveillance. Receiving a communication from Wilkinson (who had now turned against Burr), the President issued a proclamation describing the intended expedition and warning American citizens not to participate. At the beginning of 1807, unaware of Wilkinson's betrayal, Burr started down the Ohio with about 100 men. Within a few weeks the whole thing was over. Behind Burr, units of the Ohio militia organized for pursuit, and ahead of him Wilkinson was frantically arranging New Orleans's defense while preparing a force to intercept Burr. Learning of Wilkinson's opposition, Burr fled toward Mobile, Ala., leaving his force to be placed under detention. Burr was arrested a few miles from Spanish Florida and returned east for trial.

On Trial

Charged with the high misdemeanor of launching a military expedition against Spanish territory and the treasonous act of attempting to separate areas from the United States, Burr stood trial before Chief Justice John Marshall in the U.S. Circuit Court at Richmond, Va. The outcome hung upon Marshall's instructions to the jury concerning the technicalities of American treason law. Burr was acquitted on the treason charge, and the misdemeanor indictment was eventually canceled. The acquittal was extremely unpopular; Marshall was burned in effigy as a result.

Burr's Decline

Although Burr was legally free, his political career was finished. For the next 4 years he wandered through Europe, vainly trying to find support for plans to revolutionize Mexico, free the Spanish colonies, and instigate war between England and the United States. Finally, in 1812, he returned to America, broken in health and financially destitute. After some discreet inquiries, he decided it was safe to return to New York. There he set about the task of reestablishing his legal practice. He was moderately successful, but his final years were not easy. In December 1812 his cherished daughter, Theodosia, was lost at sea. As the years passed, his fortunes again declined. By 1830 he had come to depend heavily upon contributions from a few friends for his survival. In 1833, at the age of 77, Burr married a wealthy widow 20 years his junior who quickly divorced him when it became apparent he would run through her fortune. Over the next several years a series of strokes left him paralyzed and utterly dependent for his care upon a cousin. Burr died on Staten Island, N.Y., on Sept. 14, 1836.

Further Reading

The best modern biography of Burr is Herbert S. Parmet and Marie B. Hecht, *Aaron Burr: Portrait of an Ambitious Man* (1967). The most detailed biographical study, however, is still James Parton, *The Life and Times of Aaron Burr* (1858; repr. 1967). Other biographies of Burr include Samuel H. Wandell and Meade Minnigerode, *Aaron Burr* (2 vols., 1925); Walter Flavius McCaleb, *The Aaron Burr Conspiracy* (1936); and Nathan Schachner, *Aaron Burr* (1937). For the fullest treatment of Burr's western adventures see Thomas P. Abernethy, *The Burr Conspiracy* (1954). Bradley Chapin explains many of the technicalities surrounding the famous trial of Aaron Burr in *The American Law of Treason* (1964).

Additional Sources

Lomask, Milton, *Aaron Burr,* New York: Farrar, Straus & Giroux, 1979-c1982.

Keunstler, Laurence S, *The unpredictable Mr. Aaron Burr,* New York: Vantage Press, 1974.

Chidsey, Donald Barr, *The great conspiracy; Aaron Burr and his strange doings in the West,* New York: Crown Publishers, 1967. □

William S. Burroughs

An innovative and controversial author of experimental fiction, William S. Burroughs (1914–1997) is best known for *Naked Lunch* (1959), a bizarre account of his fourteen-year drug addiction and a surrealistic indictment of middle-class American mores.

William S. Burroughs was the grandson of the industrialist who modernized the adding machine and the son of a woman who claimed descent from Civil War General Robert E. Lee. In 1936, he received his bachelor's degree in English from Harvard University. In 1944, after abortive attempts at, among other things, graduate study in anthropology, medical school in Vienna, Austria, and military service, he met Allen Ginsberg and Jack Kerouac and began using morphine. The meeting of these three writers is generally regarded as the beginning of the Beat movement; the writers who later became part of this group produced works that attacked moral and artistic conventions. The escalation of Burroughs's drug addiction, his unsuccessful search for cures, and his travels to Mexico to elude legal authorities are recounted in his first novel, *Junkie: The Confessions of an Unredeemed Drug Addict* (1953; republished as *Junky*). Written in the confessional style of pulp magazines under the pseudonym William Lee,

the novel received little critical notice. In 1957, Burroughs traveled to London to undergo a controversial drug treatment known as apomorphine. Following two relapses, he was successfully cured of his addiction.

Ostensibly the story of junkie William Lee, *Naked Lunch* features no consistent narrative or point of view. The novel has been variously interpreted as a condemnation of the addict's lifestyle, as an allegory satirizing the repressiveness of American society, and as an experiment in literary form, exemplified by its attacks upon language as a narrow, symbolic tool of normative control. Consisting of elements from diverse genres, including the detective novel and science fiction, *Naked Lunch* depicts a blackly humorous, sinister world dominated by addiction, madness, grotesque physical metamorphoses, sadomasochistic homosexuality, and cartoon-like characters, including Dr. Benway, who utilizes weird surgical and chemical alterations to cure his patients. Escape from the imprisoning concepts of time and space are dominant themes in this work and in Burroughs's later fiction, reflecting the addict's absolute need for drugs and his dependency on what Burroughs termed "junk time." Burroughs explained the book's title as "the frozen moment when everyone sees what is on the end of every fork."

Naked Lunch represents a selection from the wealth of material Burroughs had been writing for many years. The remaining work makes up the bulk of his immediately subsequent novels, *The Soft Machine* (1961), *The Ticket That Exploded* (1962), and *Nova Express* (1964). During the process of writing these works, Burroughs, influenced by artist

Brion Gysin, developed his "cut-up" and "fold-in" techniques, experiments similar in effect to collage painting. Collecting manuscript pages of his narrative episodes, or "routines," in random order, Burroughs folds some pages vertically, juxtaposing these with other passages to form new pages. This material, sometimes drawn from the works of other authors, is edited and rearranged to evoke new associations and break with traditional narrative patterns. In the surrealistic, quasi-science fiction sequels to *Naked Lunch,* Burroughs likens addiction to the infestation of a malignant alien virus, which preys upon the deep-seated fears of human beings and threatens to destroy the earth through parasitic possession of its inhabitants. The title of *The Soft Machine,* a novel emphasizing sexuality and drugs as a means of normative control throughout history, indicates the innate biological device which allows the virus entry into the human body. Mind control through word and image is the subject of *The Ticket That Exploded.* In this novel and in *Nova Express,* Burroughs suggests a number of remedies to the viral infestation. Although he expresses a cautious optimism, the crisis remains unresolved, and humanity's fate is uncertain at the saga's end.

In 1970, Burroughs announced his intention to write a second "mythology for the space age." Although his recent novels have generally received less acclaim than *Naked Lunch* and its sequels, critics have discerned a remarkably straightforward approach to these works, which rely less on cut-up strategies and horrific elements and more on complex, interrelated plots and positive solutions to escaping societal constraints. As Jennie Skerl noted: "In Burroughs's recent fiction, pleasure and freedom through fantasy balance the experience of repression, bondage, and death that the earlier works had emphasized." The universe of *The Wild Boys: A Book of the Dead* (1971) is similar to that of Burroughs's earlier books but is epic in proportion, encompassing galactic history and the whole of humanity in its scope. Time and space travel figure prominently in *Cities of the Red Night: A Boys' Book* (1981), in which detective Clem Snide traces the source of the alien virus to an ancient dystopian society. *The Place of Dead Roads* (1984) transfers the conflict to near-future South America, where descendants of the wild boys ally themselves with Venusian rebels in an escalating battle for galactic liberation.

Burroughs's novel *Queer* (1985) was written at the same time as *Junkie* and is considered its companion piece. According to Burroughs, the book was "motivated and formulated" by the accidental death of his wife in Mexico in 1951, for which Burroughs was held accountable. The novel centers once again on William Lee, chronicling a month of withdrawal in South America and his bitter, unrealized pursuit of a young American male expatriate. Harry Marten stated that the book functions as "neither a love story nor a tale of seduction but a revelation of rituals of communication which substitute for contact in a hostile or indifferent environment."

Burroughs is also well known for his nonfiction works. *The Yage Letters* (1963) contains his mid-1950s correspondence with Allen Ginsberg concerning his pursuit in Colombia of the legendary hallucinogen *yage.* Further correspondence is collected in *Letters to Allen Ginsberg, 1953-1957* (1982). During the mid-1960s, Burroughs became an outspoken proponent of the apomorphine treatment, claiming that its illegal status in the United States was the result of a conspiracy between the Food and Drug Administration, police, and legal authorities. His arguments are presented in *Health Bulletin, APO 33: A Report on the Synthesis of the Apomorphine Formula* (1965) and *APO 33, a Metabolic Regulator* (1966). Burroughs's observations on literary, political, and esoteric topics appear in a collaborative venture with Daniel Odier, *Entretiens avec William Burroughs* (1969; revised and translated as *The Job: Interviews with William Burroughs*), and in his collection *The Adding Machine: Collected Essays* (1985). *The Third Mind* (1979), written in collaboration with Brion Gysin, is a theoretical manifesto of their early "cut-up" experiments. Burroughs has also written a screenplay, *The Last Words of Dutch Schultz* (1970).

Burroughs's controversial novels have provoked extreme critical reactions, ranging from claims of genius to allegations that he was little more than a pornographer. While his work can be offensive, it has elicited much serious criticism, and Burroughs is regarded by many scholars as an innovative, even visionary writer. Critics credit Burroughs's hallucinatory prose and antiestablishment views with inspiring the Beat movement and such counterculture groups as hippies and punks. Among other accomplishments, Burroughs has, perhaps more effectively than any other author, rendered the nightmarish, paranoid mindset of the drug addict. Harry Marten observed that Burroughs "[mixed] the satirist's impulse toward invective with the cartoonist's relish for exaggerated gesture, the collage artist's penchant for radical juxtapositions with the slam-bang pace of the carnival barker. In the process, he has mapped a grotesque modern landscape of disintegration whose violence and vulgarity is laced with manic humor."

The former heroin addict lived in the quiet town of Lawrence, Kansas with several cats and a collection of guns until his death from a heart attack on August 2, 1997. Although his business affairs were handled by his staff at the high tech William Burroughs Communications, the writer himself still used a typewriter. One of his more recent publications, *The Letters of William S. Burroughs: 1945-1959* was used both as a journal and a sketchbook for his early work.

Additional Sources

Bartlett, Lee, editor, *The Beats: Essays in Criticism,* McFarland, 1981.

Bowles, Paul, *Without Stopping,* Putnam, 1972.

Bryant, Jerry H., *The Open Decision: The Contemporary American Novel and Its Intellectual Background,* Free Press, 1970.

Burgess, Anthony, *The Novel Now: A Guide to Contemporary Fiction,* Norton, 1967.

Burroughs, William, Jr., *Kentucky Ham,* Dutton, 1973.

Burroughs, William S., *Junky,* Penguin, 1977.

Burroughs, William S., *Cities of the Red Night,* Holt, 1981.

Caveney, Graham, *Gentleman Junkie: The Life and Times of William S. Burroughs,* Little, Brown, 1998.

Miles, Barry, *William Burroughs: El Hombre Invisible: A Portrait,* Hyperion, 1993.

Morgan, Ted, *Literary Outlaw: The Life and Times of William S. Burroughs,* Holt, 1988. □

George Bush

A successful businessman, George Bush (born 1924) emerged as a national political leader during the 1970s. After holding several important foreign policy and administrative assignments in Republican politics, he served two terms as vice president (1980, 1984) under Ronald Reagan. In 1988, he was elected the 41st president of the United States.

George Herbert Walker Bush was born on June 12, 1924, in Milton, Massachusetts. His father, Prescott Bush, was a managing partner in the Wall Street investment firm of Brown Brothers, Harriman and also served as U.S. senator from Connecticut from 1952 to 1962. His mother, Dorothy Walker Bush, was the daughter of another prominent Wall Street investment banker, George Herbert Walker (George Bush's namesake), and the founder of the Walker Cup for international golfing competition. George Bush grew up in the affluent New York City suburb of Greenwich, Connecticut, vacationing in the summers in Kennebunkport, Maine, where he later maintained a home.

Bush attended the Greenwich Country Day School and Phillips Academy, exclusive private schools, where he excelled both in the classroom and on the athletic field. After graduating from Phillips in 1942, he enrolled in the U.S. Navy Reserve and was commissioned a navy flight pilot in 1943, serving in the Pacific for the duration of World War II. Secretly engaged to Barbara Pierce, Bush married this daughter of the publisher of *Redbook* and *McCall's* in Rye, New York, on January 6, 1945. The Bushes became the parents of six children (one of whom died of leukemia when three years old).

Following severance from the navy, Bush enrolled at Yale University in September 1945. An ambitious, highly competitive student, he earned a B.A. in economics within three years. Although a married military veteran, Bush was nonetheless active in campus social and athletic activities (playing three years of varsity baseball and captaining the team). Following graduation in 1948, Bush became an oilfield supply salesman for Dresser Industries in Odessa, Texas. Rising quickly in an industry then in the midst of a postwar boom, in 1953 Bush started his own oil and gas drilling firm. After merging with another firm in 1955, Bush eventually (in September 1958) moved the corporate headquarters to Houston, Texas.

In addition to having become a millionaire in his own right, Bush was also active in local Republican politics and served as Houston County party chairman. In 1964 he took a leave of absence from his firm, Zapata Petroleum, to challenge incumbent Democratic Senator Ralph Yarborough. Bush campaigned as a Goldwater Republican, opposing civil rights legislation, calling for U.S. withdrawal from the United Nations should the Peoples Republic of China be admitted, and demanding a cutback in foreign aid spending. The strategy of Goldwater Republicans had been to promote a conservative realignment, specifically leading to Republican congressional victories in the South and Southwest. This strategy failed, and Bush also lost decisively in what was a nationwide Democratic landslide.

Bush did not withdraw from politics, however, and in 1966 he won election to the House of Representatives from a Houston suburban district. A two-term congressman, serving from 1966 through 1970, Bush compiled a conservative voting record (earning a 77 percent approval rating from the conservative Americans for Constitutional Action), specifically championing "right to work" anti-labor union legislation and a "freedom of choice" alternative to school desegregation. In an exception to an otherwise conservative record, in 1968, despite opposition from his constituents, Bush voted for the open housing bill recommended by President Lyndon Johnson.

A loyal adherent of the Nixon administration during 1969 and 1970, Bush supported the president's major legislative initiatives, including the family assistance plan. In 1970 he again sought election to the Senate, campaigning as an outspoken Nixon supporter on a "law and order" theme. His election chances, however, were submarined when the more moderate Lloyd Bentsen defeated Yarborough in the Democratic primary. Although Bush's electoral support had increased since 1966 (from 43 to 47 percent), he was once again defeated.

As a reward for his loyalty, in February 1971 President Nixon appointed Bush U.S. ambassador to the United

Nations. Given the nominee's lack of foreign policy experience, this appointment was initially viewed as a political favor. Bush, however, proved to be an able and popular diplomat, particularly in his handling of the difficult, if ultimately unsuccessful, task of ensuring the continued seating of the Taiwan delegation when the United Nations in a dramatic reversal voted to seat the Peoples Republic of China.

In December 1972 Bush resigned his United Nations appointment to accept, again at Nixon's request, the post of chairman of the Republican National Committee. This largely administrative appointment proved to be a demanding assignment when the Senate, in the spring of 1973, initiated a highly publicized investigation into the so-called Watergate Affair and then, in the winter/spring of 1973, when the House debated whether to impeach President Nixon. Throughout this period Bush publicly championed the president, affirming Nixon's innocence and questioning the motives of the president's detractors. As the scandal unfolded, Bush sought to minimize its adverse consequences for the political fortunes of the Republican party. Following Nixon's forced resignation in August 1974 his successor, Gerald Ford, appointed Bush in September 1974 to head the U.S. liaison office in Peking, China.

Serving until December 1975, Bush proved again to be a popular and accessible ''ambassador'' (formal diplomatic relations with the People's Republic had not at this time been established). He left this post to accept appointment in January 1976 as director of the Central Intelligence Agency. Bush served as a caretaker director, acting to restore morale within the agency and to deflect public and congressional criticisms of the agency's past role and authority. Resigning as CIA director in January 1977 following the election of Democratic presidential candidate Jimmy Carter, Bush returned to Houston to accept the chairmanship of the First National Bank of Houston.

Bush was an unannounced candidate for the Republican presidential nomination of 1980 starting in 1977. He sought to exploit the contacts he had made as Republican National Committee chairman and as a businessman in Texas with family and corporate interests in the East as well as his record of public service. Travelling to all 50 states and establishing his own fund-raising organization, the Fund for Limited Government, Bush formally announced his candidacy in May 1979. Modeling his campaign after Jimmy Carter's successful strategy of 1975-1976 of building a well-organized grass roots organization in the early primary/caucus states of Iowa and New Hampshire, Bush quickly emerged as the principal opponent of former governor of California Ronald Reagan, the Republican frontrunner.

While as conservative as Reagan in his economic and foreign policy views, Bush nonetheless successfully projected the image of a moderate candidate. He lacked substantive programmatic differences from Reagan except for his support for the Equal Rights Amendment, his qualified stand on abortion, and his questioning of Reagan's proposed intention to increase defense spending sharply while reducing taxes and balancing the budget. His failure to find a major issue and his lackluster campaign style eventually forestalled his candidacy. Although recognizing that he did not have the needed

delegate votes, Bush did not drop out of the race before the Republican National Convention. In a surprise decision, made on the eve of the balloting, Reagan announced his selection of Bush as his vice presidential running mate.

Becoming vice president with Reagan's decisive victory over incumbent Democratic President Jimmy Carter in 1980, Bush proved to be a loyal, hard working supporter of the president. Careful to demonstrate his loyalty and to accept the largely ceremonial public responsibilities of the vice presidency, Bush provided quiet counsel to the president and thereby gained his respect. Renominated in 1984, Bush retained the vice presidency with the resultant Reagan landslide. Bush's record of demonstrated loyalty and competence, and the series of important administrative offices he had held since 1971, nonetheless had not created for him a broad-based nationwide constituency. As such, he was not assured the Republican presidential nomination in 1988. Despite his nationwide campaign for the Republican presidential nomination in 1980, Bush remained an untested vote getter, his only electoral victory coming as a candidate from a safe Republican congressional district. Bush's other governmental positions were all attained through appointment. His career was thus marked by the ability to handle difficult administrative assignments, and yet a seeming failure to demonstrate the promise of leadership with the voters.

In 1988, Bush defeated Massachusetts governor Michael Dukakis to become the 41st president of the United States. With this victory, many felt he had overcome his weak image and allegations that he had known more than he admitted about the Iran-Contra (arms-for-hostages trade with Iran) scandal. As chief executive he was widely viewed as a foreign policy president. He was in office when the Communist governments of the Soviet Union and eastern Europe fell. The Persian Gulf War of 1990 also boosted Bush's popularity to a point where many thought he would be unbeatable in the next election.

However, Bush also had his share of problems. Many historians believe that Bush ran a negative campaign in 1988 which affected his ability to govern the country. Congress refused to confirm his nomination of former Texas senator John Tower for secretary of defense. He inherited problems with the Department of Housing and Urban Development (HUD). Other critics said he lacked vision and leadership. He also had a relatively inexperienced vice president in former Indiana Senator Dan Quayle. In 1992, in the midst of a recession, he lost his re-election bid in a three-way race to Democrat Bill Clinton.

In retirement, Bush kept a relatively low profile, preferring to travel and spend time with his grandchildren. He did make the news when, in March 1997, at the age of 72, he became (many believe) the first American President to jump out of an airplane. He also received a honorary doctorate from Hofstra University in April 1997. In 1998 he co-authored *A World Transformed,* a memoir of his dealings with foreign policy during his time as President.

Bush the politician will always be remembered. On November 30, 1994, the ground breaking ceremony for the George Bush Presidential Library and Museum was held.

This facility was constructed on the campus of Texas A & M University, in College Station, Texas, and opened in November 1997. It is the tenth presidential library administered by National Archives and documents Bush's long public career, from ambassador to world leader. Located within the complex will be The Bush School of Government & Public Service, which will provide graduate education to those who wish to lead and manage organizations serving the public interest.

Further Reading

Having been married for over 50 years, Barbara Bush's *Barbara Bush: A Memoir* (1994) will provide insight to the "real" George Bush. Michael Duffy's *Marching in Place: The Status Quo Presidency of George Bush* (1992) will also offer an interesting perspective. George Bush has also been profiled on the television show *A&E Biography*. Information on The George Bush Presidential Library and Museum can be accessed through the World Wide Web at http://www.csdl.tamu.edu/bushlib/ (July 29, 1997). Readers also might profitably consult Eleanora Schoenebaum (editor), *Political Profiles: The Nixon/Ford Years*, Vol. 5 (1979); Roy Reed, "George Bush on the Move," *New York Times Magazine* (February 10, 1980); and Elizabeth Drew, "A Reporter at Large: Bush 1980," *The New Yorker* (March 3, 1980); *New York Times* (March 26, 1997 and April 20, 1997). □

George W. Bush

When George W. Bush (born 1946) won a disputed election to become president of the United States, it capped a meteoric rise to power in a relatively short political career that combined good timing, a powerful family, and uncanny campaigning skills. A late bloomer in terms of achievement, Bush's victory represented the second time in American history that the son of a former president took on the world's most powerful political job.

George Walker Bush was born in New Haven, Connecticut on July 6, 1946. His parents moved the family from New Haven, where they had lived next door to the president of Yale University, to Texas when George W. was two years old. His father, George Herbert Walker Bush, had just graduated from Yale and wanted to try his hand at the oil business. At first they lived in a ramshackle duplex in the roughneck town of Odessa, with two prostitutes renting the other half of the house. Two years later, after a brief time following the elder Bush as a drill-bit salesman in California, they moved to Midland, a more refined city that was better suited to raising a family.

One of their neighbors, Charlie Younger, described Midland as "a real Ozzie-and-Harriet sort of town." It was also bursting with optimism during the boom times of the 1950s, when the elder Bush made his fortune in drilling. Young George W. was a strong-willed and wisecracking child who posed a challenge for his mother, Barbara. His father, who had played baseball at Yale, coached his Little League baseball team, and the young boy became a baseball fanatic, memorizing statistics and trivia from his collection of baseball cards. The Bushes had five more children: a son Jeb; a daughter Robin, (who died of leukemia in child-

hood); then sons Neil and Marvin and daughter Dorothy. As the eldest, George W. was expected to shine. He was an all-around athlete, fair student, and occasional troublemaker in school—he was once paddled for painting a mustache on his face during a music class. In seventh grade, he ran for class president and won. The next year, his father, who had become a millionaire, moved the family to Houston.

Two years later, George W. was sent back East to enroll at Phillips Academy, an elite private prep school in Andover, Massachusetts. At Andover, he was a whirlwind of physical activity, playing varsity baseball and basketball and junior varsity football. In basketball he often made self-deprecating jokes about riding the bench. Instead of trying out for varsity football, he became the squad's head cheerleader. He also organized a stickball league and was nicknamed Tweeds Bush, after the political organizer Boss Tweed. Against the school's intense competition Bush arrayed his sense of humor. "I was able to instill a sense of frivolity," Bush later said. "Andover was kind of a strange experience."

His high school academic record was far from topnotch. However, drawing on his family connections, Bush landed a spot at Yale, where both his father and grandfather had attended. Bush, extremely gregarious and a notoriously poor dresser, made many friends, somehow bridging the growing divide between the public school graduates who were entering Yale and the "preppies." Bush's interest in politics faded temporarily after his father lost a close election for a seat in the U.S. Senate, in which his grandfather had served. He remained uninterested in politics even after his father won the Senate seat on a second try in 1966. Instead, he became president of the Delta Kappa Epsilon fraternity and enjoyed parties, drinking, watching and playing football, and dating. Grades weren't a high priority. "He was a serious student of people," recalled classmate Robert McCallum. He was booked on a misdemeanor charge for being part of a prank that involved stealing a Christmas wreath for the frat house, but the charges were dropped. He was also questioned by police for helping to tear down the goalposts at Princeton University after a football game. For a brief time, he was engaged to a Rice University student, Cathryn Wolfman. In his senior year, he joined the notorious secret society, Skull and Bones. Despite his background of privilege, Bush became more at ease with all kinds of people in college. "I was never one to feel guilty," he said about his wealth and family connections. "I feel lucky." Moving back to Houston after graduating from Yale, Bush took up residence in a trendy apartment complex, the Chateaux Dijon—a hub for young single people. Cocky and loud, Bush played volleyball in the swimming pool, flirted with women, and drove a sports car. He worked, for a time, for an agribusiness company and for a mentoring program. "I was rootless," he later said. "I had no responsibilities whatsoever." Later, he would fend off reporters' questions about rumors of drug use in those days. "How I behaved as an irresponsible youth is irrelevant to this campaign," he said during his 1994 race for governor. "What matters is how I behave as an adult." Other questions later arose about how he had managed to avoid serving in Vietnam. He was a member of an elite Texas Air National Guard unit stationed at Ellington Air Force Base that included the sons of other prominent politicians and civic leaders. The National Guard had a long waiting list of young men eager to avoid military service during the war, but Bush managed to sail through easily. He has denied any impropriety, but political writer Molly Ivins claims that a family friend used Ben Barnes, then speaker of the House of Representatives in Texas, to recommend Bush for a spot in the Guard unit.

Texas Oil Business

Bush was rejected by the University of Texas Law School, but gained admittance to Harvard's Business School. After graduation, he retraced his father's footsteps and returned to Midland, Texas in 1975 to try his luck in the oil business. Bush started by searching deeds for other oilmen who wanted mineral rights. His first attempt at exploration, Arbusto Energy, failed to strike oil.

In 1977 Bush suddenly announced that would run for a seat in the U.S. Congress. Asked later about his renewed interest in politics, Bush said it was because President Jimmy Carter was trying to control natural gas prices and "I felt the United States was headed toward European-style socialism." A friend set up Bush for a date with Laura Welch, a librarian. She had grown up near him in Houston and even lived at the Chateaux Dijon, but they had never crossed paths. Three months later, he married her and they immediately hit the campaign trail. In 1982, they would have twin daughters, Jenna and Barbara. In a primary, Bush prevailed over the Republican Party's handpicked choice, Odessa mayor Jim Reese, who portrayed him as an elitist

and a liberal. Bush then faced off against Democrat Kent Hance, who painted him as elite East Coast carpetbagger whose $400,000 in campaign contributions came from well-connected outsiders such as baseball commissioner Bowie Kuhn. Bush played into Hance's hands by airing a campaign ad showing him jogging—an activity considered alien to many west Texans. Hance's campaign used a last-minute attack ad that accused Bush of having given free beer to college students in order to win their vote. Bush refrained from retaliating, and lost the election.

Bush raised money from prominent family friends to support an oil drilling fund. However, Arbusto was still unable to find oil. He merged it with another company, Spectrum 7, which soon was three million dollars in debt. Many independent oil companies were going broke. Midland, the financial center of the Texas oil country, was in decline. Bush needed a miracle to survive in the oil business and was finally bailed out by Harken Oil and Gas (later Harken Energy Corporation). Harken wanted the name of the vice-president's son on its board of directors so badly that it assumed Spectrum 7's debt, paid Bush $320,000 worth of stock options, and offered him a consulting position at $80,000 a year. Government regulators later investigated the deal after Harken, which had no previous experience in the Persian Gulf, landed a lucrative contract to drill for oil off the coast of Bahrain. Bush's decision to sell 212,140 shares of Harken for $848,560—just before the company announced poor quarterly earnings—was also scrutinized, but he was not charged with any wrongdoing.

In 1985, Bush was in the family's Kennebunkport, Maine, complex, when evangelist Billy Graham paid a visit. George W. Bush said he had a "personal conversion" and began taking Biblical teachings more seriously. A year later, on the morning after a raucous party celebrating his 40th birthday, Bush suddenly swore off drinking. He had not considered himself an alcoholic, and neither had friends or family, but all admitted he drank to excess on occasion. The announcement was a turning point.

In 1988, Bush worked on his father's presidential campaign as a "loyalty thermometer," taking the pulse of campaign workers and making sure that they were ready to deflect any criticism that was directed against his father. He also traveled far and wide soliciting donations and help from powerful people. Bush was instrumental in hiring decisions, but found Washington to be a pompous, petty place. He left shortly after the work for the transition team was finished. In the process, however, he had, he said, "earned his spurs" in his father's eyes. He would return to work on the 1992 campaign, playing an instrumental role in getting rid of Chief of Staff George Sununu, who had failed the loyalty test.

Bought Baseball Team

Late in 1988, Bush heard that the Texas Rangers, a struggling professional baseball club, was up for sale. He put together a group of 70 investors who contributed $14 million to buy the team at a bargain price. Bush's own investment of $606,000—part of his booty from the Harken stock sale—was the smallest of any investor. But Bush became the driving force and public face of the new owner-ship group. During the next five years, he was managing general partner of the franchise. He organized a successful campaign to get voters to approve a sales tax for a new publicly funded stadium paid with $135 million in bonds. The lucrative stadium deal turned the franchise around financially, since the owners got to keep the stadium when the bonds were paid off. In 1994, when Bush ran for gover-nor, he put his share of the Rangers, along with his other assets, in a blind trust and resigned as managing general partner just before a players strike wiped out the World Series. His opponent, Ann Richards, accused Bush of bene-fiting from corporate welfare, but the charges didn't stick and Bush won the election. In 1998, his group sold the team, and got a personal windfall of $14.9 million. That was money he used to bankroll his run for the presidency.

His old friend, Joseph O'Neill, said of Bush's 1988 moves: "He really hated Washington, but it charged him up. Then, with the Rangers, he really hit stride. It took some hard times and big jobs to bring out the bigness in him." When his father lost to Bill Clinton in the 1992 presidential race, Bush the younger felt free to resume acting on his long-shelved political ambitions. His celebrity as the most well known owner of the Rangers and as the son of a former president gave him an advantage as he ran for governor in 1994. But his opponent was the popular governor, Ann Richards. With the help of political strategist Karl Rove, nicknamed "Bush's brain," Bush stayed doggedly "on mes-sage" and remained affable and unresponsive to Richards's attacks.

Governor of Texas

Famous for delegating details and making connections, Bush used his newly honed management skills in the gover-nor's office. Texas is also a weak-governor state, and Bush was adept at making compromises and taking credit. Bush's governing style in Texas depended on bi-partisanship, a political tradition in that state. Longtime Texas Lieutenant Governor Bob Bullock, a Democrat, endorsed Bush in his 1998 bid for re-election. Bullock, a tough negotiator, had been a mentor for Bush in Texas politics. He did not earn a reputation as a hard-driving executive, often taking time out in the middle of the day to go jogging or play video games. He complained that he did not like to read long books and that he hated meetings and briefings. But Bush did work hard on education reform, championing public schools.

A key to Bush's popularity in Texas was his ability to appeal both to the old-guard "country club" Republicans, who tended to be more moderate, and the Christian Right, which had come to control the GOP in that state. Bush described himself as a born-again Christian, that helped him with the fundamentalist voters, but downplayed issues like his opposition to abortion, keeping his appeal to moderates. He would use that same formula to secure the GOP presi-dential nomination and keep the party together during the 2000 campaign.

Presidential Campaign

Many months before the first presidential primaries were held for the 2000 election, Bush had virtually sewed up the GOP nomination by demonstrating his ability to attract millions in contributions. Business interests and Re-publican stalwarts closed ranks behind the Bush candidacy, making his nomination appear to be inevitable. To some critics such as Ivins, Bush was characterized as "a wholly owned subsidiary of corporate America." *Washington Post* writer Lois Romano and George Lardner Jr. said that "all along George W. harbored qualities that his father could only envy: a visceral and energetic charm, sound political instincts, an easy and convincing sense of humor, a com-mon touch." But then a formidable challenger emerged out of a large pack of contenders.

Arizona Senator John McCain rode a wave of media and popular enthusiasm in early 2000 to provide a point of coalescence for those opposed to Bush's nomination. Sounding his key theme of campaign finance reform, Mc-Cain attacked Bush as being the creation of special interest and business contributors. Bush's campaigned was ambushed by McCain in New Hampshire, where the chal-lenger pulled off an upset. The defeat prompted Bush to change the tone and tactics of his campaign. To win the South Carolina primary, Bush visited controversial Bob Jones University, a hotbed of far-right activism. He also launched a series of attacks on McCain's credibility. Mc-Cain, complaining about campaign dirty tricks, was soundly defeated, and Bush eventually won in enough other states to fend off McCain's challenge.

In the general election campaign, Bush selected Dick Cheney, who had been Secretary of Defense under his father, as his running mate. It signaled that Bush would surround himself with people he considered authoritative. Bush took an early lead in the polls but his opponent, Vice-President Al Gore, bounced back after the Democratic con-vention, when he started sounding a populist theme. The media had a field day with Bush's tendencies to malapropisms and Gore hammered at his foreign policy weaknesses and lack of experience. There was also some criticism of an alleged subliminal messages in a Bush cam-paign ad in which the word "Democrats" morphed into "rats" for a split-second. Bush immediately pulled the ads, and continued to display his people skills. "What Bush does with people is establish a direct, personal connection," wrote reporter Nicholas Lemann in the *New Yorker*. Lemann claims that Bush has "a talent for establishing a jovial connection with an unusually large number of peo-ple." The polls drew close and a series of three debates in October was expected to be decisive. Gore, portrayed as a man with more command of policies and details, was ex-pected to win. However, Bush more than held his own, and his folksiness made Gore look stiff by comparison. In a second debate Gore was more agreeable, and the two can-didates declared much common ground. However, Gore's dramatic mood shift made him appear insincere to some voters. Bush remained adamantly "on message," repeatedly sounding his issues of education reform, social security privatization, and tax cuts, while downplaying controversial issues such as abortion.

Although the 2000 presidential election was extremely close, and was finally resolved by a five to four decision of the U.S. Supreme Court, Bush emerged as the winner. Ivins had often said of Bush: "He is so lucky that if they tried to hang him, the rope would break."

Further Reading

Ivins, Molly and Lou Dubose, *Shrub: The Short But Happy Political Life of George W. Bush,* Vintage, 2000.

Ivins, Molly and Lou Dubose, *Shrub: The Short But Happy Political Life of George W. Bush,* Vintage, 2000.

New Yorker, January 31, 2000.

Newsweek, November 22, 1999.

Texas Monthly, June 1999.

Time, June 21, 1999.

US News and World Report, January 22, 2001.

Washington Post, July 25, 1999; July 26, 1999; July 27, 1999; July 28, 1999; July 29, 1999; July 30, 1999; July 31, 1999. □

Vannevar Bush

Vannevar Bush (1890-1974) was a leader of American science and engineering during and after World War II. He was instrumental in the development of the atomic bomb and the analogue computer, as well as an administrator of government scientific activities.

By any standard, Vannevar Bush was one of the movers of the 20th century. A prominent engineer, he rose through the ranks to become the first vice president and dean of engineering at the Massachusetts Institute of Technology (MIT). In 1939 he moved to Washington, D.C. to assume the presidency of the Carnegie Institution, one of the country's most prestigious and important private foundations and sources of support for scientific research. Within a year, however, the gathering clouds of war turned his energies in other directions. With the advantage of location in Washington and drawing on acquaintanceships with the leaders of American science and engineering, Bush moved quickly into the lead mobilizing the scientific community for war.

The roots of this man who became the czar of wartime science reach deeply into the soil of New England. Bush was the descendant of a long line of sea captains who made their home in Provincetown and he always kept something of the salty independence of the sea about him. He returned frequently to Cape Cod throughout his life, and often found himself drawing upon images of the sea in talking of his work in engineering. His father had left Provincetown in the 1870s, probably to escape religious tensions and a declining economy, and taken up residence in the suburbs of Boston in the small community of Everett to be near the new Universalist Tufts College. There he studied for his degree in divinity and over the next decades became one of the area's well known and well loved pastors. And there Vannevar

was born to Richard Perry and Emma Linwood Bush March 11, 1890, one of three children.

For over two decades Bush was associated with two of the country's best engineering schools. One was MIT; the earlier and, in some ways, the more formative was Tufts. While small, this Universalist school had nevertheless towards the end of the century encouraged the development of a strong and innovative engineering program under the guidance of Gardner Anthony, a master of drawing and mechanical design. Here Bush developed a lifelong romance with invention which eventually culminated in a series of pioneering analogue computers during the 1920s and 1930s. Here also he acquired that graphic mathematical approach to things which became a characteristic of his work in engineering. Not least, the profoundly ethical context in which the profession of engineering gestated at Tufts combined with the pastoral commitments of his father to shape Bush's deep belief that engineering could, in fact, be a ministry devoted to social welfare and public good. Bush graduated from Tufts in 1913 with both bachelor's and master's degrees.

Between 1913 and 1919 he worked at General Electric, taught mathematics to the women at Tufts, worked as an electrical inspector in the New York Navy Yard, earned his doctorate in electrical engineering at MIT in one year in 1916, and returned again to Tufts as a young assistant professor. Here he taught for part of his time and consulted for the rest with a small company devoted to the development of radio equipment. From these modest beginnings came the Raytheon Corporation, one of New England's largest companies and a mainstay of its defense industry. Bush was one of the company's founders in the early 1920s and maintained his connections until World War II.

In 1919, just as the academic market for engineering was turning bullish after World War I, Bush joined the faculty of MIT. Starting as an associate professor of electric power transmission, he rose rapidly through the department, bypassing the chairmanship to become in 1932 MIT's first vice president and dean of engineering under the new president, Karl Compton. During these years Bush became involved in many of the issues percolating through the country's community of engineers. They ranged over the curricula and conceptual development of electrical engineering, the relationship of the engineer and the government, the characteristics of professionalism, and the large role of the engineer in American society. In his early years at the institute, Bush cooperated with the department's dynamic chairman, Dugald Jackson, in modernizing the curriculum; assumed direction of graduate training; and coordinated the research activities of the department. By the middle 1930s, as Compton's righthand man, Bush had become not only a major figure at MIT but a respected spokesman within the country's technical community.

His inventive activity during these years revolved around the notion of mechanical analysis and the development of machine methods for the solution of mathematical problems in engineering. Between 1927 and 1943 Bush developed a series of electromechanical analogue computers which greatly facilitated the solution of complex mathematical problems. In 1936 the Rockefeller Foundation awarded a major grant to MIT which resulted in the famous Rockefeller differential analyzer of World War II. The analyzer was quickly superseded by faster digital computers, but in its time it was a significant achievement and clearly revealed the possibilities for machine computation not only in engineering but in more basic fields of science. Moreover, it embodied in a concrete way the culture of engineering in which Bush had come of age.

During the war Bush headed the vital National Defense Research Committee and its successor, the Office of Scientific Research and Development. From these organizations and the laboratories they oversaw came radar, the proximity fuse, penicillin, and, of course, the atomic bomb. Such accomplishments brought fame to Bush and enormous public respect to the country's scientists. They also provided Bush great influence in the public debates and legislative battles which followed the war and which eventually gave birth to the Atomic Energy Commission in 1947 and the National Science Foundation in 1950.

In the calmer times after the war, Bush returned to his responsibilities at the Carnegie Institution. When he retired in 1955 he went home to Cambridge. He took up duties as a member of the boards of directors of Merck and Company, AT&T, the Metals and Controls Corporation, and the MIT Corporation, becoming honorary chairman of the last in 1959. He died in 1974.

After his career took its pronounced public turn with the events of World War II, Bush became a prolific and popular author of books dealing with the nature of science and the problems of science and public policy in the period of the Cold War. *Science—The Endless Frontier* (1945), a report written for President F. D. Roosevelt dealing with the organization of postwar science, quickly became an influential bestseller, as did his 1949 book, *Modern Arms and Free Men: A Discussion of the Role of Science in Preserving Democracy.*

In many ways, Bush is the outstanding example of the expert whose role at the hub of an increasingly complex society captured the imagination of American society in the early part of the 20th century. These were years in which the figure of the engineer became not only a necessary fact of life but a value-laden symbol which presaged the contributions of science and technology to human progress. If the consequences of this turning to science and engineering, especially in the light of the nuclear predicaments which followed the war, have proved ambiguous blessings, Bush himself never lost faith. The pioneering spirit helped us conquer plains and forest, Bush wrote at the end of his life in his autobiographical *Pieces of the Action.* Given the chance, it would do so again.

Further Reading

The best account of Bush's life, which contains as well an extensive bibliography of his writings, is Jerome Wiesner's short biography in volume 50 of the National Academy of Science's *Biographical Memoirs.* More anecdotal material can be found in Bush's own collection of autobiographical reminiscences, *Pieces of the Action* (1970), as well as in *My Several Lives* (1970), the autobiography of James Conant, his closest wartime collaborator. Bush's importance as a wartime administrator, as well as his general significance in the history of modern American science, have been treated in Daniel Kevles' interpretive survey, *The Physicists—The Development of a Scientific Community.* □

Richard Evelyn Byrd

Richard Evelyn Byrd (1888-1957), American aviator, explorer, and scientist, was the first man to fly over both poles and for his daring feats became one of America's genuine folk heroes.

Richard E. Byrd was born in Winchester, Va., on Oct. 25, 1888, into a distinguished Tidewater family. His early education included study at the Shenandoah Valley Military Academy and a trip around the world alone at the age of 13. He attended Virginia Military Institute, the University of Virginia, and the U.S. Naval Academy, graduating in 1912. At the academy Byrd established himself as a class leader and athlete, although leg injuries suffered in football threatened his military career.

After briefly retiring from active duty, Byrd returned to the service when the United States entered World War I. He requested assignment to the Navy's aviation division. In 1918 Byrd developed a plan to fly the Navy's trimotored NC-1 flying boat across the Atlantic. His wartime assignment, however, was as commander of U.S. Navy aviation forces in Canada, where a submarine patrol was maintained. Byrd worked on improving aerial navigation when

neither land nor horizon was visible, and developed a "bubble" sextant and a drift indicator. After the war he took charge of the navigational preparations for a one-stop transatlantic flight of three Navy planes but was not himself permitted to make the May 1919 flight.

Exploration from the Air

Eight years later Byrd would make one of the early nonstop transatlantic flights; in the meantime he influenced flight development in other important ways. He successfully lobbied for legislation to establish a Bureau of Aeronautics in the Navy; and he commanded the Navy flying unit that accompanied Donald MacMillan's Arctic expedition of 1925, during which over 30,000 square miles of northern Greenland and Ellesmere Island were explored.

Convinced of the practicability of the airplane for polar exploration, in 1926 Byrd undertook a privately sponsored expedition to the North Pole. Flying from Kings Bay, Spitsbergen, Byrd and his copilot circled the North Pole on May 9, 1926. Byrd returned to the United States to a tumultuous reception and promotion to the rank of commander.

Byrd's new goal was to demonstrate the scientific and commercial value of multiengine planes on sustained flight over long distances. He entered the "transatlantic derby" of 1927, but the crash of his new plane during tests delayed his departure until after Charles Lindbergh's flight. His aviation experiences are detailed in his first book, *Skyward* (1928).

Antarctic Expeditions

Byrd's subsequent career centered on his Antarctic adventures. Buoyed by scientific and technological developments, he planned a large-scale exploration of Antarctica. Reaching the Bay of Whales in December 1928, Byrd established his camp, Little America, on the Ross Ice Shelf. In constant radio communication with the outside world, he and his companions carried out their scientific studies and aerial surveys. On Nov. 28-29, 1929, Byrd and three companions successfully completed a hazardous flight to the South Pole and back, a distance of 1,560 miles, discovering several new mountain ranges and obtaining valuable geological, meteorological, and radiowave propagation data. When Byrd came home in 1930, he was showered with additional honors and awards, including promotion to the rank of rear admiral. His *Little America* (1930) is a full account of the expedition.

Byrd returned to Antarctica in 1933-1935. He spent 5 months in solitude at Advance Base, making careful meteorological and auroral observations. This expedition nearly cost him his life when he was stricken by carbon monoxide fumes. Rescued in August 1934, Byrd could not return to Little America II until 2 months later. He wrote about this expedition in *Discovery* (1935) and later in *Alone* (1938).

In 1939 the United States government sponsored its first Antarctic expedition in a century, with Adm. Byrd in charge. He made several flights over the continent, delineated hundreds of additional miles of coastline, and mapped mineral deposits. Further work in the Antarctic awaited the cessation of World War II, a conflict in which Byrd served with distinction.

In 1946-1947 Byrd led his fourth expedition to the Antarctic as part of the Navy's Operation High Jump. Thirteen ships and 4,000 men participated, photographing and mapping vast areas of the ice continent. Byrd again flew over the South Pole, dropping a packet containing flags of all the members of the United Nations. Byrd's final labors in Antarctica were made in Operation Deep Freeze (1955-1956) and in planning the United States Antarctic Program for the International Geophysical Year (1957-1958). He died in Boston on March 11, 1957, survived by his wife and four children. A scientist and inventor as well as a daring adventurer, Byrd had also lent his name and energy to many humanitarian and world peace organizations.

Further Reading

The best biography of Byrd is Edwin P. Hoyt, *The Last Explorer: The Adventures of Admiral Byrd* (1968), although it was compiled only from the public record and should be read in conjunction with other accounts. See particularly Fitzhugh Green, *Dick Byrd: Air Explorer* (1928); Charles J. V. Murphy, *Struggle: The Life and Exploits of Commander Richard E. Byrd* (1928); and the brief appreciation by Alfred Steinberg, *Admiral Richard E. Byrd* (1960). Walter B. Hayward, *The Last Continent of Adventure: A Narrative of Gallant Men and Bold Exploits in Antarctica* (1930), puts Byrd's early work in context. Raimund Goerler compiled *To the Pole: The Diary and Notebook of Richard E. Byrd, 1925–1927* (1998). ☐

C

Alexander Calder

American sculptor, painter, and illustrator Alexander Calder (1898-1976), through his construction of wire mobiles, pioneered kinetic sculpture.

Alexander Calder was born in Philadelphia, the son of a well-known sculptor and educator and his wife, a talented painter. Calder's grandfather, also a sculptor, executed the figure of William Penn that graces the dome of the city hall in Philadelphia. Though he was brought up in an artistic atmosphere, Calder's own inclinations were mechanical. He trained as a mechanical engineer at the Stevens Institute of Technology in New Jersey, studying such things as descriptive geometry, mechanical drawing, and applied kinetics—the branch of science that deals with the effects of force on free-moving bodies—in preparation for receiving his degree in 1919.

After working at a number of jobs that allowed him time for travel and reflection over the next few years, Calder decided to explore his growing interest in art. In 1923, two years after beginning his study of drawing in night school, he enrolled full-time at the Art Students League in New York City. There he attended classes given by George Luks, Guy Pène Du Bois, and John Sloan, all important American painters of that period. Calder also did freelance work as an illustrator for the *National Police Gazette* for about two years. In 1926 he had his first one-man exhibition of paintings at the Artist's Gallery in New York City. While concentrating on painting, Calder also worked on wood sculpture, and when he visited Paris in 1926 he continued to carve.

Circus Brought Lasting Fame

Calder's first significant recognition as an artist came when he exhibited his now-famous miniature circus with its animated wire performers at Paris's Salon des Humoristes in 1927. The idea for the toy figures can be traced back to sketches he made in 1925 while reporting on the circus for the *Police Gazette*. Made from wire, rubber, cork, buttons, bottle caps, wood, and other small "found" objects, Calder's circus includes lions, acrobats, trapeze artists, elephants, a ringmaster, and numerous other figures. Unlike many art works of the period, the unusual creation drew crowds from outside the artistic community as well as within, and the thirty-year-old artist found himself suddenly widely known.

Calder's first wire sculpture, *Josephine Baker* (1926), a witty linear representation of the famous American-born chanteuse, was exhibited to the Paris art community during the same period that his circus was drawing attention. He decided to return to New York City late in 1927, where he gave a one-man show that included *Josephine Baker,* as well as several of his other wire portraits. Those portraits would grow increasingly three dimensional as the artist refined his technique.

Influenced by Modernists

In November 1928 Calder was again in Paris, supporting himself with performances of his miniature circus, one of which was attended by Spanish surrealist Joan Miró. Calder had his first one-man shows in Paris at the Galérie Billiet and in Berlin in 1929. In Paris he met a number of important modernists, including Fernand Léger, Theo Van Doesburg, and Piet Mondrian, the latter whose work particularly impressed him. By 1930 Calder was making large-scale abstract wire sculptures using flat metal ovals painted black or bright colors, as well as small balls or other shapes suspended by long wires. Many of these work suggested the solar system in their design. From these beginnings he de-

The Rime of the Ancient Mariner with Robert Penn Warren's essay on Coleridge (1945), and *The Fables of LaFontaine* (1946). At this time Calder's international reputation was reinforced by exhibitions in New York, Amsterdam, Berne, Rio de Janeiro, São Paulo, Boston, and Richmond, Virginia. In 1952 he designed the acoustical ceiling for the Aula Magna at the university in Caracas and received the first prize for sculpture at the Venice Biennale. Commissions for his designs continued to pour in as he created everything from jewelry to costume and stage-set designs for dance and theatrical performances. In the 1970s, at the height of Calder's fame, Braniff Airlines commissioned him to paint some of their jet planes with his unique, boldly colorful designs.

Calder's works are featured in permanent installations around the world. In 1955 he travelled to India to execute 11 mobiles for public buildings in Ahmadabad. He designed many monumental pieces, including those for Lincoln Center in New York City, for the Massachusetts Institute of Technology in Cambridge, for the gardens of UNESCO in Paris, and for Expo '67 at Montreal. In 1964, when the artist was in his late seventies, he was honored with a comprehensive retrospective at the Guggenheim Museum in New York City; a smaller one was given at the Museum of Modern Art in 1970. At his death in 1976, Calder was eulogized by Minneapolis, Minnesota, curator Marvin Friedman as "one of the greatest form-givers America has ever produced."

Further Reading

Excellent for its plates and its interpretations of Calder's sculptures is H. H. Arnason, *Calder* (1966). Also recommended are Calder's own *Calder: An Autobiography with Pictures* (1966), and James Johnson Sweeney, *Alexander Calder* (1943; rev. ed. 1951). □

Alberto P. Calderón

Alberto Calderón's (1920–1998) revolutionary influence turned the 1950s trend toward abstract mathematics back to the study of mathematics for practical applications in physics, geometry, calculus, and many other branches of this field. His award-winning research in the area of integral operators is an example of his impact on contemporary mathematical analysis.

Widely considered as one of the twentieth century's foremost mathematicians, Alberto Calderón's career spanned more than 45 years, during which he left behind many seminal works and ideas.

Calderón was born on September 14, 1920, in Mendoza, Argentina, a town at the foot of the Andes. His father was a descendant of notable nineteenth-century politicians and military officers and was a renowned medical doctor who helped found and organize the General Central Hospital of Mendoza.

After completing his secondary education in his hometown and in Zug, Switzerland, under Dr. Save Bercovici, who encouraged Calderón's interest in mathematics, he enrolled in the School of Engineering of the National Univer-

---

veloped motor-driven sculptures, which featured objects hanging from large bases, although the artist had no fondness for the regular, predictable motion provided by motors. An exhibition of Calder's kinetic sculptures was seen by Marcel Duchamp, who referred to them as "mobiles"—a term which became associated with this work. He made a number of sculptures during the thirties which employed the same forms as the mobiles but were static, and known as "stabiles."

Meanwhile, in 1931 Calder was married to Louisa James, who he had met on a voyage to New York City; that same year he illustrated an edition of *Aesop's Fables*. Two years later Calder made his first draft-propelled mobiles. Rather than following a monotonous path of motion as did his motor-driven sculptures, these pieces create myriad patterns once they are set in action by a breeze or gentle push. Their shapes, largely ovoid and biomorphic, may have been inspired by the art of Miró. In 1933 Calder and his wife bought a farm in Roxbury, Connecticut, where he established his studio. In 1935 and again in 1936 he designed stage sets for the dancer Martha Graham.

Commissioned Works Prompted Travel

The Museum of Modern Art in New York City gave a comprehensive exhibition of Calder's work in 1943, during which the artist gave performances of his famous circus; the show's catalog was the first extensive study on the artist. The following year he made sculptures out of plaster to be cast in bronze. These pieces moved at a slow, measured pace. During this period he illustrated *Three Young Rats* (1944),

sity of Buenos Aires, from which he graduated in 1947. He soon became a student of Alberto González Domínguez and of the celebrated mathematician Antoni Zygmund, who was a visiting professor in Buenos Aires in 1948. He continued his mathematical studies at the University of Chicago with a Rockefeller Foundation fellowship, and received his Ph.D. there in 1950.

Calderón began his academic teaching career as an assistant to the Chair of electric circuit theory at the University of Buenos Aires in 1948, and after graduating in the United States, continued it as a visiting associate professor at Ohio State University from 1950 to 1953. Calderón was also a member of the Institute for Advanced Study in Princeton (1954-1955) and later served as an associate professor at the Massachusetts Institute of Technology (MIT) between 1955 and 1959. He then moved to the University of Chicago, where he served as professor of mathematics from 1959 to 1968, Louis Block professor of mathematics from 1968 to 1972, and chairman of the mathematics department from 1970 to 1972.

By that time, Calderón's prestige was well established in scientific circles, and his research in collaboration with his longtime mentor Zygmund had already been dubbed "the Chicago School of Analysis," also known today as "the Calderón-Zygmund School of Analysis." Their contribution, which profoundly affected modern mathematics, included reversing a predominant trend towards abstraction and turning back to basic questions of real and complex analysis. This work, completed in tandem with Zygmund, came to be known as "Calderón-Zygmund theory."

A landmark in Calderón's scientific career was his 1958 paper titled "Uniqueness of the Cauchy Problem for Partial Differential Equations," which the American Mathematical Society has called "a real watershed in the theory of singular integral operators, taking it beyond its traditional role in the study of elliptic equations." Two years later, he used the same method to build a complete theory of hyperbolic partial differential equations.

His theory of singular operators, which is used to estimate solutions to geometrical equations, contributed to link together several different branches of mathematics. It also had practical applications in many areas, including physics and aerodynamic engineering. This theory has dominated contemporary mathematics and has made important inroads in other scientific fields, including quantum physics. Although some authors have introduced and used the notion of pseudo-differential operator, which is a sum of compositions of powers of the Laplacian with singular integral operators with kernels which are infinitely differentiable off the diagonal, the original idea and basic applications remain credited to Calderón.

Calderón's extensive work has transformed contemporary mathematical analysis. In addition to his work with singular integral operators, he also did fundamental work in interpolation theory, and was responsible, together with R. Arens, for what is considered one of the best theorems in Banach Algebras. Calderón also put forth an approach to energy estimates that has been of fundamental importance in dozens of subsequent investigations, and has provided a general model for research in this area.

A Brief Return Home

In 1971-1972, Calderón briefly returned to his home country to serve as professor and direct mathematical doctoral dissertation studies at his alma mater, the National University of Buenos Aires. He continued to encourage mathematics students from Latin America and the United States to pursue their doctoral degrees, in many instances directly sponsoring them. Some of his pupils, in turn, have become reputed mathematicians, as, for example, Robert T. Seeley, whose extension of the Calderón-Zygmund results to singular operators on manifolds became the foundation of the now famous Atiyah-Singer index theorem.

After his stay in Argentina, Calderón returned to MIT as a professor of mathematics, and in 1975 he became University Professor, a special position, at the University of Chicago until his retirement in 1985. Between 1989 and 1992, he was a professor emeritus, with a post retirement appointment at that same institution. In 1979 he was awarded the Bôcher prize for a paper on the Cauchy integral on Lipschitz curves. In 1989 he shared the Mathematics Prize of the Wolf Foundation of Israel with his American colleague John W. Milnor. He received innumerable other honors around the world. The American Mathematical Society honored Calderón again with the prestigious Steele Prize (fundamental research paper category) in 1989, and former U.S. president George Bush, in granting him the 1991 National Medal of Science, cited "his ground-breaking work on singular integral operators leading to their application to important problems in partial differential equations."

Author and Lecturer

As an author, Calderón has published more than 75 scientific papers on various topics, from real variables to partial differential equations and singular integrals. A number of those papers were written in collaboration with his teacher Antoni Zygmund. Calderón has lectured in major cities the world over.

A member of the American Mathematical Society for over 40 years, Dr. Calderón served as member-at-large of its Council (1965-1967) and in several of its committees. He was also associate editor of various important scientific publications, such as the *Duke Mathematical Journal,* the *Journal of Functional Analysis,* and others.

Dr. Calderón married in 1950. With Mabel Molinelli, his first wife who died in 1985, he had two children: María Josefina, who holds a doctorate in French literature from the University of Chicago, and Pablo Alberto, also a mathematician who studied in Buenos Aires and New York. In 1989 Calderón married again. His second wife, Dr. Alexandra Bellow, is also a distinguished mathematician and a professor of mathematics at Northwestern University in Evanston, near Chicago. Calderón died on April 16, 1998, at Northwestern Memorial Hospital in Chicago at the age of 77.

Further Reading

Atiyah, M. F. and Singer, I. M., "The Index of Elliptic Operators on Compact Manifolds," *Bulletin of the American Mathematical Society,* 69, 1963, pp. 442-53.

González Domínguez, Alberto, "Dr. Alberto P. Calderón—Premio Bocher 1979," *Ciencia e Investigación,* 34, November-December 1978, Buenos Aires, pp. 221-23.

Beals, R. W., Coifman, R. R., and Jones, P. W., "Alberto Calderón Receives National Medal of Science," *Notices of the American Mathematical Society,* 39, No. 4, April 1992.

Chicago Tribune, September 17, 1991. □

John Caldwell Calhoun

The American statesman John Caldwell Calhoun (1782-1850) became the most effective protagonist of the antebellum South. It was his tragedy to become the spokesman for the dying institution of slavery.

John C. Calhoun was born on March 18, 1782, in the uplands of South Carolina, the son of Patrick and Martha Caldwell Calhoun. The family was Scotch-Irish and Calvinist and was relatively wealthy; his father owned twenty or more slaves, was a judge, and served in the state legislature. John graduated from Yale in 1804. He studied in the law school of Tapping Reeves in Litchfield, Conn., and in an office in Charleston, S.C., and was admitted to the bar in 1807. He quickly established a practice in Abbeville near his family home.

In 1811 Calhoun married a distant cousin, Floride Bouneau, by whom he had nine children. The marriage brought him a modest fortune. He enlarged his holdings and in 1825 established a plantation, called Fort Hill, in his native area.

Handsome in early life and with a commanding presence and piercing eyes all his life through, Calhoun had a striking personality. He had a gracious manner, and Daniel Webster and others not his partisans paid tribute to his character and integrity. In later years he struck observers as a "thinking machine," speaking very rapidly and always terribly in earnest. The picture is conveyed in Harriet Martineau's phrase that Calhoun was a "cast-iron man who looks as if he had never been born and could never be extinguished." He was concerned almost exclusively with ideas, politics, and business; he had little humor and no broad, cultural interests. One Senate colleague said there was no relaxation with the man, and another complained that to be with Calhoun was to be made to think all the time and to feel one's inferiority.

Political Career

Calhoun was elected to the South Carolina Legislature in 1808 and 2 years later won election to the U.S. House of Representatives. Henry Clay made him chairman of the Foreign Affairs Committee, and Calhoun and other "War Hawks" moved the country to the unsuccessful War of 1812 against Great Britain. Calhoun led the effort in the House to supply and strengthen the Army, and after the war he continued to work for a stronger military establishment.

He advocated measures which he would later denounce as unconstitutional: Federal encouragement of manufactures by means of a protective tariff, and internal improvements to "bind the republic together with a perfect system of roads and canals." To objections that the Constitution did not authorize such Federal expenditures, Calhoun replied that "the instrument was not intended as a thesis for the logician to exercise his ingenuity on. It ought to be construed with plain, good sense. . . ."

Calhoun was secretary of war in James Monroe's Cabinet (1817-1825). He became less and less militaristic through his life. In 1812 he had said that "a war, just and necessary in its origin, wisely and vigorously carried on, and honorably terminated," would establish "the integrity and prosperity of our country for centuries." But in 1846 he refused to vote for the declaration of war against Mexico; he asserted that the grounds for war given by the President were false and said simply, "I regard peace as a positive good, and war as a positive evil."

In Monroe's Cabinet, Calhoun was a nationalist. In 1821 John Quincy Adams appraised Calhoun as "a man of fair and candid mind . . . of enlarged philosophic views, and of ardent patriotism. He is above all sectional and factional prejudices more than any other statesman of this Union. . . ." Calhoun was Adams's vice president (1825-1829) and was elected to the office again in 1828 under Andrew Jackson. He had expectations of becoming president following Jackson's tenure, but there was a rupture between them during Jackson's first term. The social contretemps over Peggy Eaton was involved, but more important was Jackson's discovery that Calhoun had criticized his invasion of Florida in 1818. Even without these irritants the clash would have come. Calhoun had anonymously written the "South Carolina Exposition" in response to the so-called Tariff of Abominations of 1828. He argued the right of a state to "nullify" a Federal enactment injurious to its interests if the state believed the law to be unconstitutional. By 1830 Calhoun was known as the author of the doctrine, and at a Jefferson's birthday dinner that year Jackson glared at Calhoun and proposed the toast, "Our Federal Union—it must be preserved!" Calhoun replied, "The Union—next to our liberty, the most dear!"

Jackson threatened military force to collect the duties in South Carolina, and in 1832 Calhoun in an unprecedented action resigned from the vice presidency and was elected by South Carolina to the Senate to defend its cause. Henry Clay brought forth a compromise, which Calhoun supported, to lower the tariff gradually over a decade; the crisis subsided for a time.

In the Senate in the 1830s, Calhoun attacked the abolitionists, demanding that their publications be excluded from the mails, that their petitions not be received by Congress, and finally that a stop be put to agitation against slavery in the North as had been done in the South. By 1837 he was defending slavery as "a positive good" and had become an advocate for the suppression of open discussion and a free press.

Calhoun's shift from a national to a sectional position had virtually destroyed his chances for the presidency, but he continued to aspire to that office. He declared his candidacy in 1843 but withdrew to accept appointment as secretary of state for the last year of John Tyler's term. In his efforts for the annexation of Texas, Calhoun wrote a famous letter to the British minister in Washington, arguing that annexation was necessary to protect slavery in the United States and asserting (against the position of the British government, which was urging the emancipation of slaves throughout the world) that freed African Americans tended to be deaf, blind, and insane in far higher proportions than those in slavery. The letter did not help his cause in Congress. The treaty of annexation which he negotiated with the Republic of Texas was rejected by the Senate, where it was impossible to muster the required two-thirds vote in its favor. Calhoun then supported the device, of doubtful constitutionality, of admitting Texas by a joint resolution of Congress.

Calhoun returned to the Senate in 1845, where he first opposed the war against Mexico and then the Wilmot Proviso, which would have prohibited slavery in all the territories acquired from Mexico by that war. He denounced the Compromise of 1850, which did not guarantee the right of Southerners to take their slaves into all territories of the Union. He did not live to see that compromise adopted, dying on March 31, 1850. His last words were, "The South! The poor South!"

Political Philosophy

The political theory Calhoun had developed from the time of the Nullification Crisis of 1828 he began to organize in a formal treatise in the middle 1840s. His two works, *Disquisition on Government* and *Discourse on the Constitution and Government of the United States,* were published posthumously. Calhoun argued that government by mere numbers must inevitably result in despotism by the majority, a proposition supported by the men who drew up the Constitution. He also insisted that the Constitution should be based upon the "truth" of the inequality of man and on the principle that people are not equally entitled to liberty.

Calhoun said the U.S. Constitution lacked the necessary restraints to prevent the majority from abusing the minority. He proposed to give the minorities (the minority he had in mind was the Southern slaveholders) a veto power over Federal legislation and action by means of what he called the "concurrent majority." In the *Discourse* he proposed the device of dual executives for the Union, each to be chosen by one of the great sections of the country, with the agreement of both necessary for Federal action.

The 20th-century experience of the dangers of centralized governmental power has brought a renewed interest in Calhoun's proposals for the protection of minority rights. But although Calhoun's critical analysis was perceptive, his proposed solutions have not been regarded as serious contributions to the problem. Indeed, as critics have pointed out, although he spoke in general terms and categories, he was really interested only in defending the rights of a specific propertied minority—the slaveholding South.

Further Reading

Calhoun's own *A Disquisition on Government* and *A Discourse on the Constitution and Government of the United States,* originally published in 1851, are now available together in several editions. *The Works of John C. Calhoun,* edited by Richard K. Crallé (6 vols., 1851-1856), has been the basic published collection of his writings. However, a more recent, definitive collection of Calhoun's writings is *The Papers of John C. Calhoun,* edited by Robert L. Meriwether (4 vols., 1959-1969).

A representative collection of essays by Calhoun scholars is John L. Thomas, ed., *John C. Calhoun: A Profile* (1968). It provides an excellent introduction to the literature on Calhoun. The comprehensive biography is Charles M. Wiltse, *John C. Calhoun* (3 vols., 1944-1951); however, it denigrates his rivals and justifies Calhoun's actions throughout his career. The best one-volume biography, with a better interpretive balance, is Margaret L. Coit, *John C. Calhoun: American Portrait* (1950). For a more critical account see Gerald M. Capers, *John C. Calhoun, Opportunist: A Reappraisal* (1960). Richard N. Current, *John C. Calhoun* (1963), provides a good analysis of Calhoun's political theory.

To examine the changing interpretations of Calhoun over the last century see the biographies by John S. Jenkins, *The Life of John Caldwell Calhoun* (1852); H. von Holst, *John C. Calhoun* (1882); Gaillard Hunt, *John C. Calhoun* (1908); William M. Meigs, *The Life of John Caldwell Calhoun* (2 vols., 1917); and Arthur Styron, *The Cast Iron Man: John C. Calhoun and American Democracy* (1935). ☐

Cab Calloway

Cab Calloway (1907–1994), blues and scat legend, entertained generations of people with his jazzy big band sounds. Even in his golden years, Calloway still traveled on the road and performed for his fans.

Cab Calloway was a famous singer and bandleader beginning in the lively era of the 1920s, and he remained active in music throughout his golden years. At an age when most people retire and rest on old laurels, Calloway kept a full schedule of touring with a band and singing his signature song, "Minnie the Moocher." Long ago dubbed the "Dean of American Jive," Calloway brought the joys of the jazzy big band sound to many generations, helping to preserve the very style he helped to create.

Calloway was born Cabell Calloway III, in Rochester, New York. When he was six his family moved to Baltimore, Maryland, where his father practiced law and sold real estate. Although young Cab enjoyed singing solos at the Bethlehem Methodist Episcopal Church, it was assumed that he would follow in his father's footsteps and study law. Cab had other ideas, however. His older sister had found work singing with a show in Chicago, and he appealed to her for advice. Her guidance was substantial—she sent him a train ticket, and when he arrived in Chicago, she set him up as a singer with a quartet. He was still in his teens.

Calloway has noted that his career began in 1925. By that time he had become a talented drummer and secured a position with the Sunset Cafe orchestra in Chicago. He did not hide behind a drum set for long. Within two years—or by his twentieth birthday—he had organized his own orchestra and was singing lead vocals again. The group, Cab Calloway and his Alabamians, became quite popular in Chicago and eventually took a booking at the Savoy Ballroom in New York City. That engagement did not go well, and Calloway dissolved the band. He was about to return to Chicago when he landed a part in a Broadway comedy, *Connie's Hot Chocolates.* The show was an all-black revue, and Calloway brought the house down with his rendition of "Ain't Misbehavin'."

Invited to the Cotton Club

Broadway manager Irving Mills encouraged Calloway to form another band, so the young musician gathered another orchestra and immediately found work in the well-attended Harlem speakeasies and nightclubs. In 1929 he was invited to fill in for Duke Ellington at the Cotton Club, and thereafter the two band leaders alternated engagements at the prestigious venue. It was during his years at the Cotton Club that Calloway developed his crisp, jazzy song-and-dance style, and it was there that he composed and debuted "Minnie the Moocher."

Calloway was one of the first performers to make deliberate use of scat singing—random use of nonsense syllables—in his act. As with so many others, he began scat singing when he forgot a song's lyrics. Audiences loved the sound, however, so he began to write tunes with scat cho-

ruses. "Minnie the Moocher," his best-known song, is one such composition. Its refrain—"hi de hi de hi de ho"—invites the audience to sing along in the old call-and-response style. Recordings of "Minnie the Moocher" have sold in the millions worldwide.

Hepster's Dictionary

Calloway's fame soared in the 1930s and 1940s. He appeared in such films as *International House* and *Stormy Weather,* he helped to popularize the jitterbug with tunes like "Jumpin' Jive," "Reefer Man," "It Ain't Necessarily So," and "If This Isn't Love," and he even wrote a popular book, *Hepster's Dictionary,* which sold two million copies and ran into six editions. Although Calloway's is not always associated with the big band era, he actually fronted a fine ensemble during the period. His ability to pay top salaries attracted a group of brilliant musicians, including sax players Chu Berry, Ben Webster, and Hilton Jefferson; trumpeters Dizzy Gillespie and Jonah Jones; bassist Milt Hinton; and drummer Cozy Cole. In his book *The Big Bands,* George T. Simon noted: "the *esprit de corps* of the Calloway band was tremendous, and the great pride that the musicians possessed as individuals and as a group paid off handsomely in the music they created."

The years of World War II found Calloway entertaining troops in the United States and Canada. After the war he returned to club work and to the Broadway stage, most notably as Sportin' Life in the George Gershwinoperetta *Porgy and Bess.* In the late 1960s he took another important Broadway role, that of Horace Vandergelder in the all-black version of *Hello, Dolly!* His work with Pearl Bailey in that show was the culmination of a long friendship—he had helped Bailey get a start in show business in 1945 by hiring her to help him with vocals. Even though he was 60 when he appeared in *Hello, Dolly!,* Calloway never missed a step in the strenuous show. In fact, he was just hitting his stride.

Shone in *The Blues Brothers*

The energetic performer's career received an enormous boost when he was asked to star in the 1980 film *The Blues Brothers.* The movie, which also starred John Belushi and Dan Aykroyd, gave Calloway the opportunity to perform "Minnie the Moocher" for an audience young enough to be his grandchildren—and, clad in a snazzy white zoot suit with tails, he made the number the highlight of the film. Critics who otherwise panned *The Blues Brothers* singled Calloway out for praise, and his popularity soared.

Into his 80s, Calloway stayed on the road most of the time, sometimes performing with his daughter Chris. *Philadelphia Inquirer* correspondent John Rogers observed that Calloway strutted around the stage "like some nimble tightrope walker." Rogers added: "[His] moves have slowed a bit since the '30s, a time when Calloway could have danced Michael Jackson or Mick Jagger into the ground. The hair is white and thinner now, the midsection thicker, and that classically handsome face lined and puffy after eight decades of full-throttle living. But every bit of his voice is still there—and every bit of the style and grace that made the legend."

In June of 1994 Calloway suffered a stroke and died that November. He was survived by his wife, Nuffie, whom he married in 1953. When once asked if he has any heroes in the music business, Calloway scoffed at the very idea. It is easy to undersand why he might not idolize Webster or Gillespie—he helped give them their start, along with other notables such as Pearl Bailey and Lena Horne. "I'll tell you who my heroes are," he said. "My heroes are the notes, man. The music itself. You understand what I'm saying? I love the music. The music is my hero."

Further Reading

Calloway, Cab, *Of Minnie the Moocher and Me,* Crowell, 1976.

Simon, George T., *The Big Bands,* Macmillan, 1967.

Simon, George T., *Best of the Music Makers,* Doubleday, 1979

Los Angeles Times, November 20, 1994, p. A1.

New York Times, November 20, 1994, p. 59.

Philadelphia Inquirer, August 16, 1990.

Times (London), November 21, 1994, p. 21.

Washington Post, November 20, 1994, p. B5. □

Melvin Calvin

American chemist Melvin Calvin (1911–1997) did research that yielded important discoveries over broad areas of physical and biological chemistry, from metal-organic chemistry to the chemical origin of life.

Melvin Calvin was born in St. Paul, Minnesota, on April 8, 1911, to Russian immigrant parents. The family moved to Detroit, Michigan when Calvin was a child. He attended Michigan College of Mining and Technology, and, after a break of several years during the Great Depression that found him working in a Detroit brass factory, he graduated in 1931. He received his Ph.D. in chemical engineering from the University of Minnesota in 1935. His doctoral thesis concerned the electron affinity of iodine and bromide. A Rockefeller fellowship allowed Calvin the opportunity to do postdoctoral study at the University of Manchester, England, after which he joined the chemistry department of the University of California, Berkeley, in 1937, working as an instructor in chemistry before becoming a professor in 1947. He married Genevieve Jemtegaard in 1942; they had three children.

Organic Chemical Systems

At Berkeley, Calvin became interested in the structure and behavior of organic molecules, an interest that had been inspired by research on the catalytic reactions of the organic molecules involved in photosynthesis that he had undertaken while in England. He pursued his own studies in addition to his teaching duties, but was interrupted from both upon the United States entry into World War II. During the war, although he continued to teach, Calvin gave up his research to work for the National Defense Research Council and, later, as part of the Manhattan project charged with developing the atomic bomb, where he developed a process for procuring pure oxygen from the atmosphere that

has since had significant peace-time applications for medical patients with breathing problems.

Resuming his research at Berkeley after the end of the war, Calvin studied the physical and chemical properties of organic compounds, writing *The Theory of Organic Chemistry* (1940) and *The Chemistry of Metal Chelate Compounds* (1952). His clear understanding of the nature of organic molecules was to prove valuable in his subsequent work in biological chemistry. He formed the bio-organic chemistry group, which later expanded to the Laboratory of Chemical Biodynamics, in the Lawrence Radiation Laboratory of the University of California in 1945.

Maps Process of Photosynthesis

Working with his University of California associates, Calvin used the radioactive isotope carbon-14—which had become available to scientists in 1945—as a tracer for investigations of complex organic chemical systems. They described these tracer techniques in *Isotopic Carbon* (1949). In Calvin's research, chorella, a green algae, was suspended in water and then exposed to light. Then carbon dioxide consisting of carbon-14 was added. When the algae went through its life processes, producing carbohydrates from the carbon dioxide, water, and minerals, the presence of carbon-14 could be traced using a new research tool, paper chromatography. The series of compounds containing the radioactive carbon at different stages of photosynthesis were thus identified, and the biochemical mechanism of photosynthesis was mapped. These discoveries were described in *The Path of Carbon in Photosynthesis* (1957) and

The Photosynthesis of Carbon Compounds (1962). Calvin's proposal that plants change light energy to chemical energy by transferring an electron in an organized array of pigment molecules and other substances was substantiated by research in his laboratory and elsewhere.

Calvin tested his theories of the chemical evolution of life with studies of organic substances found in ancient rocks and of the formation of organic molecules by irradiation of gas mixtures, thus simulating the atmosphere thought to exist on earth billions of years ago. These findings were described in *Chemical Evolution* (1969). He was author of over 400 publications and held a number of patents.

Consulted widely in industry, Calvin became a member of the Board of Directors of the Dow Chemical Company in 1964. He served on many scientific boards for the United States government, including the President's Science Advisory Committee for presidents Kennedy and Johnson. He was president of the American Society of Plant Physiologists in 1963-1964, president of the American Chemical Society in 1971, and a member of the National Academy of Sciences and the Royal Society of London. In 1961 he received the Nobel Prize in chemistry for his work on the path of carbon in photosynthesis. The Royal Society awarded him the Davy Medal in 1964 for his pioneering work in chemistry and biology, particularly the photosynthesis studies.

Despite his important contribution to chemistry and biology, Calvin continued to involve himself in research. In the 1970s, as the shortage of the world's oil fuel supply was brought into sharp perspective by the Arab Oil Embargo, he began to contemplate the possibility of alternative nature-based fuels. From a farm in Northern California, he began testing the practicality of his theory: that a plantation growing certain species of rubber trees that secrete a sap with characteristics similar to petroleum, could produce enough of this sap to constitute a viable alternative fuel source. After retiring from the University of California, Calvin continued to be honored from his scientific peers, receiving the American Chemical Society's Priestly Medal in 1978 and that organization's Oesper Prize in 1981. He died at the age of 85 on January 1, 1997, in Berkeley, California.

Further Reading

There is no full-length biography of Calvin. Melvin Berger's, *Famous Men of Modern Biology* (1968), written in nontechnical language, contains a section on Calvin that emphasizes his work in photosynthesis. William Gilman, *Science: U.S.A.* (1965), devotes a section to Calvin and his work in chemical biosynthesis. A useful background source is John F. Hemahan, *Men and Molecules* (1966), which contains no biography of Calvin but discusses his work. Other information can be found in *McGraw-Hill Modern Men of Science* (1984), H.W. Wilson *Nobel Prize Winners* (1987), and David Swift *SETI Pioneers* (1990). □

Ben Nighthorse Campbell

As a result of his election on November 3, 1992, Ben Nighthorse Campbell (born 1933) of Colorado became the first Native American to serve in the U.S. Senate in more than 60 years. A member of the Northern Cheyenne Tribe, Campbell was also a renowned athlete and captained the U.S. judo team for the 1964 Olympics in Tokyo.

Ben Nighthorse Campbell was born in Auburn, California, on April 13, 1933, to Mary Vierra, a Portuguese immigrant, and Albert Campbell, a Northern Cheyenne Indian. He had a hard childhood, with a mother frequently hospitalized for tuberculosis and an alcoholic father. Indeed, by the time he turned ten years old Nighthorse had spent half of his life in St. Patrick's Catholic Orphanage in Sacramento, California. At home there was frequently no one to care for him or his younger sister, Alberta. As a result, the youngster spent much of his time in the streets getting into trouble.

While working as a fruit picker in the Sacramento Valley, Nighthorse befriended some Japanese youths who taught him judo. That sport, according to the senator, "kept me off the streets and out of jail." After graduating from high school, he served in the U.S. Air Force from 1951 to 1953. Stationed in Korea as an Airman 2nd class, he continued with his judo training. On completing his military service, Campbell entered San Jose State University and supported himself by picking fruit and driving a truck. He still was a member of the Teamsters and proudly displayed his union card while a senator. In 1957 he received a Bachelors degree in physical education and fine arts. Upon graduation, Nighthorse moved to Tokyo for four years to work on his judo and study at Meiji University.

Campbell's ability in judo not only won him All-American status in that sport and helped him become three-time U.S. judo champion but allowed him to win the gold medal in the Pan-American Games in 1963. The next year he captained the U.S. judo team at the Tokyo Olympics. Later, the Olympian coached the U.S. international judo team.

Although Campbell worked as a teacher, policeman, and prison counselor, as well as a farm laborer and a truck driver, his success came as a designer of Native American jewelry. He had been interested in this Indian art form since his childhood, but learned how to laminate different metals in Japan. Although traditionalists argued that this technique did not follow the style of Indian art, *Arizona Highways* recognized his creativity in a 1972 article that identified him as one of twenty Native Americans undertaking new forms of art. He won more than 200 design awards for his hand-crafted rings, bracelets, and pendants. Some of his work has sold for as much as $20,000. In 1977 Campbell moved to a 120-acre ranch on the Southern Ute Indian Reservation near Ignacio, Colorado. With his wife, Linda Price Nighthorse (Campbell's third marriage), and their two children, Colin and Shana, Campbell trained champion quarter horses on the ranch until a severe injury, incurred while breaking a colt, put an end to that career.

Nighthorse's involvement in politics came about because of bad weather. Unable to fly his single-engine airplane to the West Coast to deliver some jewelry due to heavy storms, he visited a meeting of Colorado Democrats seeking a candidate for the state's 59th House District. At that meeting Democratic leaders persuaded him to run for that office. To nearly everyone's surprise, he defeated his better known opponent and served in the state legislature for four years. In 1986 voters of Colorado's 3rd Congressional District, a normally Republican district, elected Democratic Campbell to the U.S. House of Representatives. He defeated incumbent Mike Strang in a closely fought election to become only the eighth Native American ever elected to Congress. He won reelection to that post three times by large margins.

In Congress he earned a reputation for having a "straight-shooting approach," and his charm, sincerity, charisma, and political blend helped him gain support from a wide variety of factions within and outside Congress. Although a strong fiscal conservative (he supported a balanced-budget amendment), he was a liberal on social issues (strongly pro-choice). As a congressman he served on the House Committees on Agriculture and on Interior and Insular Affairs. He played an important role in securing legislation to settle Native American water rights, and in 1991 he won a fight to change the name of Custer Battlefield Monument in Montana to the Little Bighorn Battlefield National Monument, in honor of the Native Americans who died in battle. He also initiated and guided through Congress legislation to establish the National Museum of the American Indian within the Smithsonian Institution.

After six years in the House of Representatives, Campbell decided to run for the Senate seat vacated by Tim Wirth, a liberal Democrat who declined to run for a second term. He defeated Josie Heath and former Governor Dick Lamm in the Democratic primary. And on November 3, 1992, after a nasty campaign, he bested Republican state senator Terry Considine, a conservative, for the Senate. That victory made him the first Native American to serve in the U.S. Senate in more than 60 years. In that office he almost always supported the programs of the Clinton administration.

On March 3, 1995 Campbell made a decision which shocked much of the political world. He decided to change from his political affiliation from the Democratic to the Republican party. It has been stated that the balanced budget amendment persuaded Campbell to change his political views. Campbell will serve the remainder of his six-year term as a Republican.

Campbell won his first election after switching parties in August of 1998 when he defeated conservative opponent Bill Eggert in the Senate primary in Colorado. He went on to retain his seat in the general election.

Further Reading

There are several good articles with excellent biographical data on Campbell. For instance, see "Big Ben," by Harland C. Clifford, in the *Boston Globe Magazine* (August 2, 1992). Also see a profile of him in the April 6, 1992, issue of *People* magazine. ☐

Al Capone

Al "Scarface" Capone (1899-1947) was a notorious American gangster of the prohibition era. His career illustrated the power and influence of organized crime in the United States.

Al Capone, whose real name was Alphonso Caponi, was born to Italian immigrant parents on Jan. 17, 1899, in Brooklyn, New York. Like other young Americans from minority backgrounds, Capone was taught that the main purpose of life was to acquire wealth and that the United States was a land of opportunity. But he also discovered that his family background made it impossible to succeed in school and his ethnicity and working-class status resulted in discrimination, both in the business world and socially. Embittered by the gap between the American dream and his own reality, Capone began to engage in illegal activities as a means of achieving success in what he saw as an unjust society.

Capone was a natural leader. He possessed a shrewd business sense, gained the loyalty of those working for him by showing his appreciation for a job well done, and inspired confidence through his sound judgments, diplomacy, and "the diamond-hard nerves of a gambler." He left school at 14, married at 15, and spent the next ten years with the street gangs of his Brooklyn neighborhood. During a barroom brawl, he received a razor cut on his cheek, which gained him the nickname "Scarface."

Finds Success in Chicago

In 1919, the same year the U.S. government ratified the Eighteenth Amendment prohibiting the manufacture, sale, and transport of alcoholic beverages, Capone fled Brooklyn for Chicago to avoid a murder charge. In Chicago he joined the notorious Five Points Gang and quickly moved up its ranks to become the right-hand man of boss Johnny Torrio. After Torrio fled the country, Capone found himself in control of part of the bootleg operation in the city that had sprung up after prohibition. Chicago had voted 6 to 1 against passage of the prohibition amendment, and its citizenry—rich and poor, officials included—felt that liquor deprivation had been unfairly imposed. Capone took advantage of the popular willingness to break the law, and openly plied his trade. As he would tell reporter Damon Runyan, "I make money by supplying a public demand. If I break the law, my customers . . . some of the best people in Chicago, are as guilty as me."

Capone protected his business interests by waging war on rival gangs. During the legendary St. Valentine's Day massacre in 1929, seven members of a rival gang led by George "Bugsy" Moran were gunned down in a Chicago garage. Other business strategies included bribing public officials, providing a ready market for the illegal home-brewed liquor produced by poor Italian ghetto residents, and becoming a supply source for the "respectable" customers of city speakeasies. Interacting in Chicago society in the manner of a well-to-do businessman rather than a shady racketeer, Capone gained a fabulously profitable bootleg monopoly, as well as the admiration of a large segment of the community, including members of the police and city government. Between 1927 and 1931 he was viewed by many as the de facto ruler of Chicago.

Seen as Common Thug outside Chicago

However, the rest of the country and certain elements in the Windy City regarded Capone as a menace. In the late 1920s President Herbert Hoover ordered his Secretary of the Treasury to find a way to jail Capone, who up until now had managed to evade being implicated in any illegal act. Perhaps more significantly than the efforts of the U.S. Treasury department, Capone's power had by now begun to wane due to both the coming of the Great Depression and the anticipated repeal of prohibition. Bootlegging was becoming less profitable.

After detailed investigations, U.S. Treasury agents were able to arrest Capone for failure to file an income tax return. Forced to defend himself while being tried for vagrancy in Chicago, Capone contradicted some previous testimony regarding his taxes, and he was successfully prosecuted for tax fraud by the federal government. In October 1931 Capone was sentenced to ten years' hard labor, which he served in a penitentiary in Atlanta, Georgia, and on Alcatraz. Because of syphilis Capone's mind and health deteriorated, and his power within the nation's organized crime syndicates ended. Released on parole in 1939, he led a reclusive life at his Florida estate, where he died in 1947.

Further Reading

John Kobler, *Capone* (1971), is the most thorough study of Capone's life. See also Fred D. Pasley, *Al Capone: The Biography of a Self-Made Man* (1930). For information on his life after imprisonment see James A. Johnston, *Alcatraz Island Prison, and the Men Who Live There* (1949). An excellent contemporary description of Capone's career and perhaps still the best analysis of the era is John Landesco, *Organized Crime in Chicago*, pt. 3 of the Illinois Crime Survey (1929). A reliable historical account is John H. Lyle, *The Dry and Lawless Years* (1960). Excellent for a sociological perspective is Kenneth Allsop, *The Bootleggers and Their Era* (1961). □

Truman Capote

Truman Capote (1924–1984) was one the most famous and controversial figures in contemporary American literature. The ornate style and dark psychological themes of his early fiction caused reviewers to categorize him as a Southern Gothic writer. However, other works display a humorous and sentimental tone. As Capote matured, he became a leading practitioner of "New Journalism," popularizing a genre that he called the nonfiction novel.

Because of his celebrity, virtually every aspect of Capote's life became public knowledge, including the details of his troubled childhood. Born in New Orleans, he seldom saw his father, Archulus Persons, and his memories of his mother, Lillie Mae Faulk, mainly involved emotional neglect. When he was four years old his parents divorced, and afterward Lillie Mae boarded her son with various relatives in the South while she began a new

life in New York with her second husband, Cuban business-man Joseph Capote. The young Capote lived with elderly relatives in Monroeville, Alabama, and he later recalled the loneliness and boredom he experienced during this time. His unhappiness was assuaged somewhat by his friendships with his great-aunt Sook Faulk, who appears as Cousin Sook in his novellas *A Christmas Memory* and *The Thanksgiving Visitor* (1967), and Harper Lee, a childhood friend who served as the model for Idabel Thompkins in *Other Voices, Other Rooms*. Lee, in turn, paid tribute to Capote by depicting him as the character Dill Harris in her novel, *To Kill a Mockingbird* (1960). When Capote was nine years old, his mother, having failed to conceive a child with her second husband, brought her son to live with them in Manhattan, although she still sent him to the South in the summer. Capote did poorly in school, causing his parents and teachers to suspect that he was of subnormal intelligence; a series of psychological tests, however, proved that he possessed an I.Q. well above the genius level. To combat his loneliness and sense of displacement, he developed a flamboyant personality that played a significant role in establishing his celebrity status as an adult.

Capote had begun secretly to write at an early age, and rather than attend college after completing high school, he pursued a literary apprenticeship that included various positions at *The New Yorker* and led to important social contacts in New York City. Renowned for his cunning wit and penchant for gossip, Capote later became a popular guest on television talk shows as well as the frequent focus of feature articles. He befriended many members of high society and

was as well known for his eccentric, sometimes scandalous behavior as he was for his writings.

Capote's first short stories, published in national magazines when he was seventeen, eventually led to a contract to write his first book, *Other Voices, Other Rooms*. Set in the South, the novel centers on a young man's search for his father and his loss of innocence as he passes into manhood. The work displays many elements of the grotesque: the boy is introduced to the violence of murder and rape, he witnesses a homosexual encounter, and at the novel's end, his failure to initiate a heterosexual relationship with Idabel Thompkins, his tomboy companion, leads him to accept a homosexual arrangement with his elder cousin Randolph, a lecherous transvestite. Each of these sinister scenes is distorted beyond reality, resulting in a surreal, nightmarish quality. Despite occasional critical complaints that the novel lacks reference to the real world, *Other Voices, Other Rooms* achieved immediate notoriety. This success was partly due to its strange, lyrical evocation of life in a small Southern town as well as to the author's frank treatment of his thirteen-year-old protagonist's awakening homosexuality. The book's dust jacket featured a photograph of Capote, who was then twenty-three, reclining on a couch. Many critics and readers found the picture erotically suggestive and inferred that the novel was autobiographical.

Many of Capote's early stories, written when he was in his teens and early twenties, are collected in *A Tree of Night and Other Stories*. These pieces show the influence of such writers as Edgar Allan Poe, Nathaniel Hawthorne, William Faulkner, and Eudora Welty, all of whom are associated to some degree with a Gothic tradition in American literature. Like these authors, as well as the Southern Gothic writers Carson McCullers and Flannery O'Connor, with whom critics most often compare him, Capote filled his stories with grotesque incidents and characters who suffer from mental and physical abnormalities. Yet Capote did not always use the South as a setting, and the Gothic elements in some of the tales are offset by Capote's humorous tone in others. Critics often place his early fiction into two categories: light and sinister stories. In the former category are "My Side of the Matter," "Jug of Silver," and "Children on Their Birthdays." Written in an engaging conversational style, these narratives report the amusing activities of eccentric characters. More common among Capote's early fiction, however, are the sinister stories, such as "Miriam," "A Tree of Night," "The Headless Hawk," and "Shut a Final Door." These are heavily symbolic fables that portray characters in nightmarish situations, threatened by evil forces. Frequently in these tales evil is personified as a sinister man, such as the Wizard Man feared by the heroine in "A Tree of Night" or the dream-buyer in "Master Misery." In other instances evil appears as a weird personage who represents the darker, hidden side of the protagonist. The ghostly little girl who haunts an older woman in "Miriam" is the best-known example of this doubling device in Capote's fiction. In later years Capote commented that the Gothic eeriness of these stories reflected the anxiety and feelings of insecurity he experienced as a child.

In *The Grass Harp* (1951), Capote drew on his childhood to create a lyrical, often humorous novel focusing on Collin Fenwick, an eleven-year-old boy who is sent to live in a small Southern town with his father's elderly cousins, Verena and Dolly Talbo. At sixteen years of age, Collin allies himself with the sensitive Dolly and other outcasts from the area by means of an idyllic withdrawal into a tree fort. There, the group achieves solidarity and affirms the value of individuality by comically repelling the onslaughts of the ruthless Verena and other figures of authority. The novel, which achieved moderate success, is generally considered to offer a broader, less subjective view of society and the outer world than Capote's earlier fiction, and was adapted as a Broadway drama in 1952. A light and humorous tone is also evident in such works as the novella *Breakfast at Tiffany's* and the three stories published in the same volume, "House of Flowers," "A Diamond Guitar," and *A Christmas Memory*. *Breakfast at Tiffany's* features Capote's most famous character, Holly Golightly, a beautiful, waif-like young woman living on the fringes of New York society. Golightly, like the prostitute heroine in "House of Flowers," is a childlike person who desires love and a permanent home. This sentimental yearning for security is also evident in the nostalgic novella *A Christmas Memory*, which, like the later *The Thanksgiving Visitor,* dramatizes the loving companionship the young Capote found with his great-aunt Sook.

In some of his works of the 1950s, Capote abandoned the lush style of his early writings for a more austere approach, turning his attention away from traditional fiction. *Local Color* (1950) is a collection of pieces recounting his impressions and experiences while in Europe, and *The Muses Are Heard: An Account* (1956) contains essays written while traveling in Russia with a touring company of *Porgy and Bess*. From these projects Capote developed the idea of creating a work that would combine fact and fiction. The result was *In Cold Blood*, which, according to Capote, signaled "a serious new art form: the 'nonfiction novel,' as I thought of it." Upon publication, *In Cold Blood* elicited among the most extensive critical interest in publishing history. Although several commentators accused Capote of opportunism and of concealing his inability to produce imaginative fiction by working with ready-made material, most responded with overwhelmingly positive reviews. Originally serialized in *The New Yorker* and published in book form in 1965 following nearly six years of research and advance publicity, this book chronicles the murder of Kansas farmer Herbert W. Clutter and his family, who were bound, gagged, robbed, and shot by two ex-convicts in November, 1959. In addition to garnering Capote an Edgar Award from the Mystery Writers of America, *In Cold Blood* became a bestseller and generated several million dollars in royalties and profits related to serialization, paperback, and film rights. Written in an objective and highly innovative prose style that combines the factual accuracy of journalism with the emotive impact of fiction, *In Cold Blood* is particularly noted for Capote's subtle insights into the ambiguities of the American legal system and of capital punishment.

In the late 1960s, Capote began to suffer from writer's block, a frustrating condition that severely curtailed his creative output. Throughout this period he claimed to be working on *Answered Prayers*, a gossip-filled chronicle of the Jet Set that he promised would be his masterpiece. He reported that part of his trouble in completing the project was dissatisfaction with his technique and that he spent most of his time revising or discarding work in progress. During the mid-1970s he attempted to stimulate his creative energies and to belie critics' accusations that he had lost his talent by publishing several chapters of *Answered Prayers* in the magazine *Esquire*. Most critics found the chapters disappointing. More devastating to Capote, however, were the reactions of his society friends, most of whom felt betrayed by his revelations of the intimate details of their lives and refused to have any more contact with him. In addition, Capote's final collection of short prose pieces, *Music for Chameleons* (1983), was less than warmly received by critics. Afterward, Capote succumbed to alcoholism, drug addiction, and poor health, and he died in 1984, shortly before his sixtieth birthday. According to his friends and editors, the only portions of *Answered Prayers* he had managed to complete were those that had appeared in *Esquire* several years previously.

Critical assessment of Capote's career is highly divided, both in terms of individual works and his overall contribution to literature. In an early review Paul Levine described Capote as a "definitely minor figure in contemporary literature whose reputation has been built less on a facility of style than on an excellent advertising campaign." Ihab Hassan, however, claimed that "whatever the faults of Capote may be, it is certain that his work possesses more range and energy than his detractors allow." Although sometimes faulted for precocious, fanciful plots and for overwriting, Capote is widely praised for his storytelling abilities and the quality of his prose.

Further Reading

Dictionary of Literary Biography Yearbook: 1984, Gale, 1985.

Chicago Tribune, August 27, 1984.

Los Angeles Times, August 26, 1984.

Newsweek, September 3, 1984.

New York Times, August 27, 1984.

Publishers Weekly, September 7, 1984.

Time, September 3, 1984, September 7, 1988.

Times (London), August 27, 1984.

Washington Post, August 17, 1984.

Brinnin, John Malcolm, *Truman Capote: Deat Heart, Old Buddy,* Delacourte Press, 1986.

Clarke, Gerald, *Capote: A Biography,* Simon & Schuster, 1986.

Contemporary Literary Criticism, Gale, Volume 1, 1973, Volume 3, 1975, Volume 8, 1978, Volume 13, 1980, Volume 14, 1981, Volume 34, 1986, Volume 38, 1986, Volume 58, 1990.

Dictionary of Literary Biography, Volume 2, *American Novelists Since World War II,* Gale, 1978.

Dictionary of Literary Biography Yearbook: 1980, Gale, 1981.

Grobel, Lawrence, *Conversations with Capote,* New American Library, 1985.

Hallowell, John, *Between Fact and Fiction: New Journalism and the Nonfiction Novel*, University of North Carolina Press, 1977. ☐

Chester F. Carlson

The American inventor Chester F. Carlson (1906-1968) invented the process of xerography which became the basis for the operation of the office copying machines first introduced by the Xerox Corporation in 1959.

Chester Floyd Carlson was born on February 8, 1906, in Seattle, Washington. Illness and poverty in his family forced him to become his parent's main financial support while he was in his teens. Despite these responsibilities and handicaps, Carlson worked his way through college, graduating with a Bachelor of Science degree in physics from California Institute of Technology in 1930.

After trying in vain to gain employment as a physicist in California he left for New York City, where the P. R. Mallory Company, an electrical manufacturing firm, offered him a position in its patent department. This job proved to be of crucial importance to Carlson's career as an inventor in two ways. First, he was introduced to patent law and procedures; second, the need to duplicate patent drawings and specifications made him aware of the inadequacies of the existing photostat process for copying documents.

Carlson stayed at Mallory until 1945, eventually becoming head of the patent department.

While working at Mallory, Carlson attended New York Law School at night, receiving his law degree in 1939. One year later he was admitted to the New York bar. At the same time he conducted research on a duplication process that would produce clean copies quickly without using the chemical solutions, film, and printing paper necessary for photographic reproduction.

Carlson began his search for an alternative process by reading the available literature on printing, photography, and various copying technologies. His study convinced him that in some yet unspecified manner it might be possible to duplicate documents by making use of photoconductivity. He decided that wet-process photography must be replaced by the dry techniques of what he called "electrophotography."

Using the little amount of money he possessed, Carlson bought chemicals and equipment and turned his New York apartment into a laboratory (1934). Unable to devote full time to this work, Carlson hired an unemployed German physicist and engineer named Otto Kornei to help him. Carlson and Kornei, limited to a research budget of $10.00 a month, were able in October 1938 to make the first electrophotographic copy. It read simply "10-22-38 Astoria."

This copy was produced by a primitive, but innovative, method that formed the foundation for Carlson's subsequent research and for the industry that grew out of it. First, a rabbit's fur or cotton cloth was rubbed vigorously over the surface of a metal plate coated with a layer of sulfur. The rubbing charged the plate with static electricity. The charged plate was then placed beneath a piece of glass upon which was inked the material to be copied. Metal plate and glass were next exposed to a bright light source for a few seconds. This exposure caused the sulfur coating to lose its charge in varying degrees depending upon how much light reached its surface. In effect, the intense illumination produced an invisible electrostatic image of the material being copied. This image could be made visible by dusting an electroscopic powder on the plate. The powder was attracted to the areas which had been less intensely illuminated. In order to make the fragile powder image permanent, Carlson carefully pressed a piece of wax-coated paper over the prepared plate. The powder adhered to, and fixed upon, the surface of the waxed paper.

Although there obviously remained much to be done in improving the new dry-copying technique—which came to be called "xerography"—Carlson applied for key patents on the process (1939, 1940). Carlson had neither the money, laboratory facilities, nor mechanical talent to transform his experiments into a working copy machine ready for public use. Therefore, in 1944 he reached an agreement with the Battelle Memorial Institute, a nonprofit industrial research laboratory, to develop his invention beyond its first stages. Three years later the Haloid Company of Rochester, New York, undertook the final conversion of xerography into a commercial product. Haloid, which became Haloid-Xerox and then Xerox, publicly demonstrated xerography in 1948 and offered the first Xerox copying machines for sale in 1959.

As xerography became a complex technical and business venture Carlson withdrew from active involvement with it, except for serving as a consultant to the Xerox Corporation. By 1945 his invention brought him sufficient financial security so that he could retire from Mallory. Royalties from his xerography patents made Carlson a multimillionaire, and in later life he engaged in many philanthropic endeavors.

Further Reading

For Carlson's life and work, and the commercial development of xerography, see John H. Dessauer, *My Years With Xerox: The Billions Nobody Wanted* (1971). The technical side of xerography is treated in John H. Dessauer and Harold E. Clark (editors), *Xerography and Related Processes* (London, 1965). ☐

Stokely Carmichael

Stokely Carmichael (1941–1998) was a "militant" civil rights activist and stood at the forefront of the "Black Power" movement. He soared to fame by popularizing the phrase "Black Power" and was one of the most powerful and influential leaders in the Student Non-Violent Coordinating Committee (SNCC).

Stokely Carmichael was born in Port of Spain, Trinidad, on June 29, 1941. His father, Adolphus, who died when he was in his late forties, moved with Stokely's mother, Mabel, to the United States when their son was only

two-years-old. Although his father had been swept up by the cause of Trinidad's independence, he left his homeland to better his family's economic fortunes and moonlighted as a New York City cab driver, while Mabel found work as a maid. Young Carmichael was left in the care of two aunts and his grandmother and attended Tranquillity Boy's School. Carmichael joined his parents in New York City's Harlem when he was eleven-years-old and became the only black member of a street gang called the Morris Park Dukes. His status as a foreigner and his self-described "hip" demeanor assured him of popularity among many of his liberal, affluent white schoolmates. He said in an interview with *Life* that he dated white girls and attended parties on swank Park Avenue during this period. But Carmichael, a bright student, settled down after his family moved to the Bronx and he discovered the lure of intellectual life. After his parents moved to the Bronx, he was admitted to the Bronx High School of Science, a school for gifted youths.

Carmichael was interested in politics even then, especially the work of African-American socialist Bayard Rustin, whom he heard speak many times. At one point, he volunteered to help Rustin organize African-American workers in a paint factory. But the friendliness, doctrinal and otherwise, of Rustin and other African-American intellectual leftists with the white liberal establishment would eventually alienate Carmichael.

Joined Civil Rights Movement

While he was in school the civil rights movement was gaining momentum. The Supreme Court had declared that

school segregation was illegal, and African-Americans in Montgomery, Alabama, successfully desegregated the city's busses through a yearlong boycott. During Carmichael's senior year in high school, four African-American freshmen from North Carolina Agricultural Camp; Technical College in Greensboro, North Carolina, staged a sit-in at the white-only lunch counter in Woolworth's.

The action of these young students captured the imagination of African-Americans and some sympathetic white students throughout the United States. Some young people in New York City, including Carmichael, joined a boycott of the city's Woolworth stores which was sponsored by the youth division of the Congress on Racial Equality (CORE). CORE hoped that the boycott would pressure Woolworth's owners to desegregate all of its stores' facilities throughout the country. Carmichael traveled to Virginia and South Carolina to join anti-discrimination sit-ins and because of his growing sensitivity to the plight of African-Americans in the United States, especially in the segregated South, he refused offers to attend white colleges and decided to study at the historically black Howard University in Washington, D.C.

At Howard from 1960 to 1964, Carmichael majored in philosophy while becoming increasingly involved in the civil rights movement. He joined a local organization called the Non-Violent Action Group which was affiliated with an Atlanta-based civil rights organization, the Student Non-Violent Coordinating Committee (SNCC, called "Snick"). During his summers or whenever there was free time, Carmichael traveled South to join with the Congress of Racial Equality sponsored "freedom riders," composed of integrated groups riding interstate busses in an attempt to make the federal government enforce statutes which provided that interstate busses and bus terminals be desegregated. In bus depots there were separate toilet facilities for blacks and whites with signs that read something like "white ladies here, colored women in the rear."

Many southern whites were violently hostile to the efforts of these young people to force desegregation on them, and some of the freedom rider busses were bombed or burned. The riders were often beaten and jailed. A CORE leader remarked that for the seasoned freedom riders, jail was not a new experience, but that the determined exuberance of the young freedom riders was a shock to the jailers in Mississippi and other southern states. In the spring of 1961, when Carmichael was 20, he spent 49 days in a Jackson, Mississippi jail. One observer said that Carmichael was so rebellious during this period that the sheriff and prison guards were relieved when he was released.

After graduating in 1964 with a bachelor's degree in philosophy, Carmichael stayed in the South as much as possible, sitting-in, picketing, helping with voter registration drives, and working alongside of other leaders of SNCC. He was especially active in Lowndes County, Alabama, where he helped found the Lowndes County Freedom Party, a political party that chose a black panther as its symbol in order to comply with a state requirement that all political parties must have a visual symbol to assist voters. The black panther was indigenous to Alabama and seemed both a dignified symbol for empowered African-Americans and an effective response to the white rooster that symbolized the Alabama Democratic party. Southern response to the civil rights workers was often so violent that demonstrators were bruised, wounded, or even killed by policemen, by members of the Ku Klux Klan, or other individuals. There were six civil rights workers murdered that year, but this only made Carmichael, and others, more determined than ever to work for desegregation.

Turning From Non-Violence

The turning point in Carmichael's experience came as he watched from his locked hotel room while outside, African-American demonstrators were beaten and shocked with cattle prods by police. The horrified Carmichael began to scream and could not stop. As his activism deepened and he saw the violence doled out to violent and non-violent protesters alike, he began to distance himself from non-violent tactics and its proponents, including Martin Luther King, Jr.

In 1965, after Carmichael replaced the moderate John Lewis as the president of the SNCC, he joined Martin Luther King, Jr., Floyd McKissick of the National Association for the Advancement of Colored People (NAACP), and James Meredith, who had been the first African-American student to attend the University of Mississippi, on a "freedom march" in Mississippi which Meredith had first attempted alone. After he was shot during his solitary march, Meredith welcomed the help of other civil rights leaders. Carmichael and McKissick had trouble agreeing with King that the march would be non-violent and interracial. Carmichael had become increasingly hostile to the aid offered by white civil rights workers. During this march, Carmichael began to articulate his views about "Black Power" before the assembled television cameras. Americans reacted strongly to a slogan that seemed to indicate that African-Americans wanted to replace white supremacy with African-American supremacy. Carmichael later defined "Black Power" to mean the right of African-Americans to define and organize themselves as they saw fit and to protect themselves from racial violence. After the march, white members of the SNCC were not encouraged to stay and Carmichael and other SNCC leaders began to talk about "revolution."

Carmichael's articulation of "Black Power" evidenced by his 1967 book *Black Power* (co-written with Charles V. Hamilton), and his article "What We Want" advanced the idea that mere integration was not the answer to American racism, and that America formed only a piece in the puzzle. Carmichael and Hamilton linked the struggle for African-American empowerment definitively to economic self-determination domestically and the end of imperialism and colonialism worldwide. "What We Want" described the need for African-American communal control of African-American resources.

The term "Black Power," however disconcerting to moderate African-American leaders, absolutely terrified mainstream whites; many interpreted this term to mean not empowerment, but rather African-American domination and possibly even race war. Journalists demanded repeatedly that Carmichael define the phrase, and he soon began

to believe that no matter what his explanation, they would interpret it as sinister. Pressed by *Life* magazine, Carmichael said "For the last time, 'Black Power' means black people coming together to form a political force and either electing representatives or forcing their representatives to speak their needs [rather than relying on established parties]. 'Black Power' doesn't mean anti-white, violence, separatism or any other racist things the press says it means. It's saying 'Look buddy, we're not laying a vote on you unless you lay so many schools, hospitals, playgrounds and good jobs on us.'" However, Carmichael sometimes gave the term a different spin when he spoke to African-American audiences. As James Haskins recorded in his book, *Profiles In Black Power* (1972), Carmichael explained to one crowd, "When you talk of 'Black Power,' you talk of building a movement that will smash everything Western civilization has created." Through statements like this, Carmichael and his movement continued to be seen by many in mainstream America as a movement not to build, but to destroy.

International Focus

As the revolutionary fervor of the 1960s deepened, the SNCC became a "Black Power" vehicle, more or less replacing the hymn-singing integration of earlier days. Yet Carmichael had gone as far as he could with the organization, deciding not to run for re-election as its leader in 1967, just before the organization fell apart. Carmichael's political emphasis had shifted as well; he began speaking out not only against the war in Vietnam, but against what he called U.S. imperialism worldwide. *Time* reported that Carmichael had traveled the world denouncing his adopted country, speaking to cheering crowds in Cuba, and declaring, "We do not want peace in Vietnam. We want the Vietnamese people to defeat the United States." *Time* called him a purveyor of "negritude and nihilism" and noted that many U.S. politicians wanted to jail him for sedition upon his return to the country he called "hell."

Upon his return in 1968, U.S. marshals confiscated his passport. Meanwhile, the radical Oakland, California-based Black Panther Party, a Black group which advocated African-American liberation by "any means necessary," had made him their honorary prime minister. He would resign from that post the following year, rejecting Panther coalitions with white activists. He based himself in Washington, D.C. and continued to speak around the country. In March of 1968, he announced his engagement to South African singer-activist Miriam Makeba. They were wed two months later and the Tanzanian ambassador to the United States hosted their reception. They were permitted to honeymoon abroad after they promised not to visit any "forbidden" countries; even so, many nations refused them entrance. In 1969, Carmichael left the United States for Conakry, Republic of Guinea, in West Africa. He moved there, in part, to assist in the restoration to power of the deposed Ghanaian ruler Kwame Nkrumah, who lived in Guinea and served as an exponent of the sort of anti-imperialist, pan-African empowerment Carmichael had espoused in the United States.

While in Guinea, Carmichael took the name Kwame Ture and, over the next decades, founded the All-African Revolutionary Party and continued to speak as an advocate of revolution to answer the problems of racism and injustice. In 1993, speaking at Michigan State University, he made it clear that he still considered capitalism the source of most of the problems he had been studying during his career as an activist. In a *Michigan Chronicle* interview he stated, "Those who labor do not enjoy the fruits of their labor, we know that to be slavery," but his 1992 afterward to a new edition of *Black Power* showed that he felt real progress had been made in certain respects in the U.S., "From 1965 to 1992, no one could deny that change has occurred."

In 1996 Carmichael was diagnosed with prostate cancer and was honored by his birth nation with a $1,000 a month grant, awarded to him by the government of Trinidad and Tobago. Benefits in Denver, New York, and Atlanta were also held to help pay his medical expenses.

Steeped in the civil rights struggle, Carmichael emerged as one of the firebrands of the African-American militant movement in the 1960s, and unlike many of his compatriots from that time, he has in the intervening years experienced neither burnout nor conversion; the years have only refined the flame of his convictions, even in the face of cancer.

He continued to advance revolution to answer the problems of racism and unfairness until his death from prostate cancer in late 1998. "Since we shed blood continually and sporadically and in a disorganized manner for reforms," he stated in his afterward to *Black Power*, "let us permanently organize ourselves and make Revolution."

Further Reading

Carmichael discussed his views in *Black Power; the Politics of Liberation in America* (1967), co-authored with Charles V. Hamilton, and in *Stokely Speaks: Black Power to Pan-Africanism* (1971). Several authors have written about the history of SNCC. Two examples are Howard Zinn *SNCC, The New Abolitionists* (1964) and Cleveland Sellers with Robert Terrell *The River of No Return, the Autobiography of a Black Militant in the Life and Death of SNCC* (1973).

Further information on Carmichael and his views can be found in James Haskins *Profiles in Black Power* (1972), Jacqueline Johnson *Stokely Carmichael: The Story of Black Power* (1990), Milton Viorst *Fire in the Streets* (1979), and Robert Weisbrot *Freedom Bound: A History of America's Civil Rights Movement* (1990). For information on Carmichael's views in his own words, see the May 19, 1967 issue of *Life*, the February 24, 1993 issue of the *Michigan Chronicle*, the August 5, 1966 issue of the *New York Times*, and the December 15, 1967 issue of *Time*. Additional biographical material on Carmichael can be found in the April 14, 1996 issue of the *New York Times*, the February 8, 1992 issue of the *Chicago Defender*, and the March 30, 1997 issue of the *Denver Post*. □

Andrew Carnegie

The Scottish-born American industrialist and philanthropist Andrew Carnegie (1835-1919) was one of the first "captains of industry." Leader of the American steel industry from 1873 to 1901, he disposed of his great fortune by endowing educational, cultural, scientific, and technological institutions.

Andrew Carnegie typified those characteristics of business enterprise and innovation that changed the United States from an agricultural and commercial nation to the greatest industrial nation in the world in a single generation—between 1865 and 1901. The era has sometimes been called the "Age of the Robber Barons" on the assumption that because no public regulation or direction existed large fortunes were built by unprincipled men who corrupted officialdom, despoiled the country's natural resources, and exploited its farmers and laborers. Surely, there were some men who manipulated the corporate securities of the companies they controlled in the stockmarket for their own gain, but the only victims were their fellow speculators.

The entrepreneurs of the period not only built and modernized industry, but because they were technologically minded, they increased the productivity of labor in agriculture, mining, manufacturing, and railroading. As a result, the real wages of workers and the real wealth of farmers went up sharply.

In all this, Carnegie was a pacesetter. He was a stiff competitor; plowing back company earnings into new plants, equipment, and methods, he could lower prices and expand markets for steel products. In years of recession and depression he kept running his plants, undercutting competitors, and assuring employment for his workers.

These 19th-century entrepreneurs were successful in a dog-eat-dog world for several reasons. Government followed a hands-off policy: it did not regulate; it also did not tax. Government had not yet made commitments to social justice, protection of the poor, or more equitable distribution of the national product. At the same time, the customs, attitudes, and sanctions of the period—and the law writers, courts, economists, Protestant clergy, and even the trade unionists affiliated with the American Federation of Labor—accepted the unequal distribution of wealth. In fact, success in the marketplace was equated with the virtues of hard work, thrift, sobriety, and even godliness.

It was in this kind of world that Carnegie, a man of boundless imagination and great organizational skills, built his companies and made steel efficiently and cheaply. He fought competitors and also efforts at market and price controls by the mergers and oligopolies that began to appear in the 1890s. Because he was successful, he had to be bought off: this was the origin of the U.S. Steel Corporation in 1901, the greatest merger of the era; and it was the end of Carnegie's career as a steel-master. But it was not his end as a citizen, for he closely followed national and international developments, particularly the search for world peace, and expressed himself forcefully in writings and before legislative committees on questions of the day; and he helped lay plans for the organizations he set up to use his very large endowments.

Youth and Early Manhood

Carnegie was born on Nov. 25, 1835, in Dunfermline, Scotland, the son of William Carnegie, a home linen weaver, and Margaret Morrison Carnegie, daughter of a tanner and shoemaker. It was a time of ferment in Scotland as machine looms displaced skilled cottage workers like Carnegie's father, and social and political inequalities radicalized such humble craftsmen. Because they lived in a caste-ridden society, agitations for reform were unsuccessful. When he came to contrast Britain with America in his *Triumphant Democracy* (1886), Carnegie said, "it is not to be wondered at that, nursed amid such surroundings, I developed into a violent young Republican whose motto was 'death to privilege.'"

In 1848 the family moved to the United States, settling in Allegheny City, across the river from Pittsburgh. The father obtained employment in a cotton factory, which he soon quit to return to his home handloom, peddling damask linens from door to door; Andrew, in the same mill, became a bobbin boy at $1.20 a week. The fierce desire to rise and to help take care of the family (he was soon its chief support for the father died in 1855) pushed Andrew to educate himself and to learn a craft. He became an indefatigable reader, a theatergoer who knew his Shakespeare so well he could recite whole scenes, and a lover of music with a cultivated taste.

At the age of 14 Carnegie became a messenger boy in the Pittsburgh telegraph office, and 2 years later a telegraph operator. So quickly did he improve himself that at 18 Thomas A. Scott, superintendent of the western division of the Pennsylvania Railroad, made Carnegie his secretary at $35 a month, soon raised to $50—a large enough salary to buy a house for his mother.

Carnegie stayed with the Pennsylvania Railroad until 1865, by which time he was a young man of real means. During the Civil War, when Scott was named assistant secretary of war in charge of transportation, Carnegie went to Washington to act as Scott's right-hand man and to organize the military telegraph system. But Carnegie soon was back in Pittsburgh, succeeding Scott as head of the Pennsylvania's western division. He was one of the backers of the Woodruff Sleeping Car Company, the original holder of the Pullman patents, and also bought into a successful petroleum company. He became a silent partner in a number of local small iron mills and factories; the most important was the Keystone Bridge Company, formed in 1863, of which he owned a one-fifth share.

Between 1865 and 1870 Carnegie became a self-designated capitalist. He traveled in and out of England, peddling the bonds of small United States railroads and publicly chartered bridge companies. He probably sold as much as $30 million in bonds and may have made in commissions from them, and from the iron products he also sold, $1 million.

During this time Carnegie watched the revolutionary changes taking place in the English iron industry as a result of the adoption of the Bessemer converter. Steel, he saw, was bound to replace iron for the manufacture of rails, structural shapes, pipe, wire, and the like.

In 1870 Carnegie decided that instead of being a "capitalist" with diversified interests he was going to be a steelman exclusively. Using his own capital, he erected his first blast furnace (to make pig iron) that year and the second in 1872. In 1873 he organized a Bessemer-steel rail company, a limited partnership. Depression had set in and would continue until 1879, but Carnegie persisted, using his own funds and getting local bank help. The first steel furnace at Braddock, Pa., began to roll rails in 1874. Carnegie continued building despite the depression—cutting prices, driving out competitors, shaking off faltering partners, plowing back earnings. In 1878 the company was capitalized at $1.25 million, of which Carnegie's share was 59 percent; from these policies he never deviated. He took in new partners from his own "young men" (by 1900, he had 40); he never went public, capital being obtained from undivided profits (and in periods of stress, from local banks); and he kept on growing, horizontally and vertically, making heavy steel alone. From 1880 onward, Carnegie dominated the steel industry.

Continued Growth

In the 1880s Carnegie's two most important acquisitions were his purchase of majority stock in the H. C. Frick Company with vast coal lands and over 1000 coking ovens in Connellsville, Pa., and the Homestead mills outside of Pittsburgh. Frick became his partner and, in 1889, chairman of the Carnegie Company. Carnegie had moved to New York City in 1867 to be close to the marketing centers for steel products; Frick stayed in Pittsburgh as the general manager. Frick and Carnegie made an extraordinary team. Carnegie, behind the scenes, planned the expansion moves, installation of cost and chemical controls, and modernization of plants. Frick was the working director who rationalized the mass-production programs necessary to keep prices down. It was Frick who saw that vertical integration was imperative and achieved the company's control (by purchase and lease) of iron ore mines in the Lake Superior area, linking Carnegie ore ships and railroads with the Pittsburgh complex of furnaces and mills.

Carnegie was wise enough to use his leisure for traveling, writing, and expanding his tastes. His first book, *Round the World* (1881), was a modest recital of widening horizons. His second, *An American Four-in-Hand in Britain* (1883), related a coaching trip through England and Scotland with his mother. The third, *Triumphant Democracy* (1886), surveyed the social and economic progress of the United States from 1830 to 1880, but woven in was a secondary theme: the contrast between American egalitarianism and the unequal, class societies of Britain and the other European countries. To Carnegie, easy access to education was the key to American democracy's political stability and industrial accomplishments. He said, "Of all its boasts, of all its triumphs, this is at once its proudest and its best."

In 1889 Carnegie published an important article, "Wealth" (republished in England as "The Gospel of Wealth"), in which he held that it was the duty of rich men to get rid of their fortunes, administering them personally for the welfare of the community. He did not gloss over the inequality of wealth, but he saw wealth as a stewardship to be employed productively, for modern industrialization and mass production had wide social benefits. As a result, he said: "The poor enjoy what the rich could not before afford. What were the luxuries have become the necessities of life."

Carnegie remained a bachelor until his mother died in 1886; a year later he married Louise Whitfield (their only child, Margaret, was born in 1897). The couple began to spend 6 months each year in Scotland, but Carnegie kept in close touch with developments and problems in the ramifying Carnegie Company, no minute detail of management escaping his attention.

Trials of the 1890s

The 1890s presented three serious challenges: two were surmounted, and one left a deep hurt and stained Carnegie's reputation. The bitter nationwide depression of 1893-1896 resulted in plant shutdowns, mass unemployment, and collapsing markets. But the Carnegie Company, by following Carnegie's famous injunction "Take orders and run full," pushed prices down, retained its workers, and made profits. Carnegie was hostile to pools, that is, collusive arrangements among steel companies to limit production and steady prices. He withdrew from them and undersold his competitors.

Carnegie's absence from the United States, together with his silence during the Homestead strike of 1892, was a tragic error. The Carnegie Company had acquired Homestead in 1883, invested $4 million in new plants and equipment, increased production 60 percent, and automated many of its operations, thus sharply stepping up productivity per man-hour but cutting down the number of skilled manual workers needed. These workers belonged to a craft union, the Amalgamated Association of Iron and Steel Workers, a member of the American Federation of Labor. From 1875 on the Carnegie Company had been negotiating wage and work agreements on a 3-year basis with this union. Thus, the Carnegie Company was not antiunion, and in two articles that Carnegie wrote in 1886 he declared that workers had a right to negotiate with management through their unions. He recognized the right to strike, as long as the action was peaceably conducted; management on its part was to shut down its plants and make no effort to use strikebreakers or protect them with private guards. Strikes, he said, should not degenerate into warfare but were to be regarded as trials of strength, with peaceful negotiation terminating the contest.

To show his good faith, Carnegie suggested a so-called sliding scale for wage determination in his own shops. There would be a guaranteed wage minimum, but rates would go up or down as market prices for steel products rose or fell. The union accepted such a contract for Homestead in 1889, but it was terminating on July, 1, 1892, and the union sought to renegotiate with the sliding scale. Frick had submitted a counterproposal calling for a lowering of the minimums from which wage rates were to be scaled, because modernization had resulted (in modern terminol-

ogy) in more capital inputs and less labor inputs. Labor's contribution to the increased productivity had declined, as had the number of skilled manual workers. The two sides met head on; neither would yield, and on June 30, 1892, the Homestead mill shut down as a result of both a lockout and a strike.

Carnegie had departed for Scotland in the spring, having instructed Frick that in the event of a strike there was to be a complete shutdown and no strikebreakers. Apparently when Frick refused to meet with union spokesmen a second time, he meant to smash the union. Carnegie's silence, despite his previous statements, meant approval. In any event, Frick decided to open the company properties by force, and he hired the notorious strikebreaking Pinkerton Agency. It is beside the point whether Frick's intention was simply to protect the Carnegie properties (as he contended) or to recapture the plants and use strikebreakers (as the workers believed).

On July 6 two barges carrying 300 Pinkertons moved up the Monongahela River and were fired on from the hills and the shore. The Pinkertons also fired, but they were unable to land and surrendered, asking for safe conduct back to Pittsburgh. Five strikers were killed, three Pinkertons fatally wounded, and scores on both sides injured. The strikers had won the battle of Homestead; the company property was still virtually in their possession. Five days later the governor of Pennsylvania sent in 8,000 militia to restore order and open the plant.

Carnegie, from abroad, said nothing, except, in a letter dated July 17: "We must keep quiet and do all we can to support Frick and those at Seat of War. . . . We shall win, of course, but have to shut down for months." On July 27 the Homestead works reopened under military protection; new workers were hired, and old ones were permitted to return on an individual basis. The militia was withdrawn in September, and 2 months later the union called off the strike; thenceforth the Carnegie Company (and U.S. Steel which succeeded it) remained nonunion until the middle 1930s.

Carnegie never got over the consequences of Frick's actions. Years later he wrote: "I was the controlling owner. That was sufficient to make my name a by-word for years." But, as controlling owner, he had neither intervened nor repudiated Frick.

In the 1890s Carnegie, for the first time, began to meet with stiff competition from giant corporations which had been put together, recapitalized, and made public by the investment houses of J. P. Morgan and Company in New York and the Moore Brothers in Chicago. Because they were overcapitalized, these companies were interested in stability in an industry with excess capacity and fluctuating market conditions. They wanted controlled prices, prorations of the market, and tying agreements rather than Carnegie's ruthless competition with all comers.

The new combines made heavy steel and light steel; and because the second group was tied into the first by "communities of interest," they threatened to cut down their purchases from Carnegie unless he was willing to play their game.

Carnegie had thought of selling out and retiring in 1889: his annual income was $2 million, and he wanted to cultivate his hobbies and develop the philanthropic program that was taking shape in his mind. But the threats that now came from the West as well as the East were too much for his fighting spirit and his sense of outrage, and he took the war into the enemy camp. He would not join their pools and cartels; moreover, he would invade their territories by making tubes, wire and nails, and hoop and cotton ties and by expanding his sales activities into the West. He ordered a new tube plant built on Lake Erie at Conneaut, which at the same time would be a great transportation center with harbors for boats to run to Chicago and a railroad to connect with Pittsburgh.

Thus orignated the U.S. Steel Corporation in 1901, through the work of J.P. Morgan. The point was to buy Carnegie off at his own price—as he was the only disturbing factor that held back "orderly markets and stable prices." The Carnegie Company properties were purchased for almost $500 million (out of the total capitalization of the merger of $1.4 billion); Carnegie's personal share was $225 million, which he insisted upon having in the corporation's first-mortgage gold bonds. At last Carnegie was free to pursue his outside interests.

Development of Taste

Carnegie had started cultivating his interests in books, music, the fine arts, learning, and technical education early in life. He began to set up trust funds "for the improvement of mankind." The first were for "free public libraries"; some 3,000 were scattered over the English-speaking world. In 1895 the magnificent Carnegie Institute of Pittsburgh was opened, housing an art gallery (at his request, one of the first to buy contemporary paintings), a natural history museum (which also financed archeological expeditions), and a music hall. Originally under the institute (but separated in 1912) was a group of technical schools which blossomed into the Carnegie Institute of Technology, today the basis of the Carnegie Mellon University. The Carnegie Institution of Washington was set up to encourage pure research in the natural and physical sciences. He built Carnegie Hall in New York City. The Foundation for the Advancement of Teaching was created to provide pensions for university professors. Carnegie established the Endowment for International Peace to seek the abolition of war.

In all, Carnegie's benefactions totaled $350 million, $288 million going to the United States and $62 million to Britain and the British Empire. The continuation of his broad interests was put under the general charge of the Carnegie Corporation, with an endowment of $125 million. Carnegie died on Aug. 11, 1919, at his summer home near Lenox, Mass.

Further Reading

The *Autobiography of Andrew Carnegie* (1920) is fascinating. Burton J. Hendrick, *The Life of Andrew Carnegie* (2 vols., 1932), is an objective and sound account of Carnegie as man and steelmaster. Joseph F. Wall, *Andrew Carnegie* (1970), is the most recent life and very full; it is also critical of Carnegie as a businessman. Louis M. Hacker, *The World of Andrew Carnegie, 1865-1901* (1968), describes the times in which

Carnegie flourished. The best discussion of the steel industry is Peter Temin, *Iron and Steel in Nineteenth-Century America: An Economic Inquiry* (1964). ☐

Christopher Carson

Christopher Carson (1809-1868), commonly called Kit Carson, was an American hunter, Indian agent, and soldier. He was one of the best-known and most competent guides available to explorers of the western United States.

Kit Carson's career in the West spanned the years from 1825 to 1868, a period of rapid national expansion, exploration, and settlement. His most important Western contributions came as a guide to the expeditions of John C. Frémont, as a messenger and soldier under Gen. Stephen W. Kearny in California, and as an Indian agent just prior to the Civil War. His name is inseparably connected with American expansion into the Far West.

The sixth child of Lindsay and Rebecca Robinson Carson, Kit was born on Dec. 24, 1809, in Madison County, Ky. He spent his childhood in frontier Missouri and apparently received little formal education, because he was illiterate most of his life. In 1824 he became apprentice to a saddlemaker in one of the largest of the early Missouri river towns. After less than 2 years he deserted the saddlemaker and joined traders headed for Santa Fe, N. Mex.

Descriptions of Carson vary, but most agree that he was small, probably about 5 feet 8 inches, had blue-gray eyes, and light brown or sandy-colored hair. To the wife of explorer Frémont, Kit looked "very short and unmistakably bandy-legged, long-bodied and short-limbed." A quiet man with a soft voice, Carson was considered modest, brave, and truthful by contemporaries—characteristics which helped him acquire a reputation as a heroic frontiersman.

Career as a Trapper

Young Carson worked for several years as a teamster, cook, and interpreter in the Southwest. In 1829 he joined Ewing Young's party of trappers and for the next year and a half trapped along the streams of Arizona and southern California. This jaunt into the mountains served Carson as a sort of training exercise, and for most of the next decade he continued in this occupation. Trapping most of the major streams in the West prepared Carson for his later work as a guide.

While living in the mountains, Carson married an Arapaho woman, who bore him a daughter, Alice. When his wife died a few years later, he took the child to Missouri. In 1841 or 1842 he married a second Native American woman but soon left her and acquired a mistress in Taos, N. Mex. A year later he wed again.

Career as a Guide

In the summer of 1842 Carson met Lt. Frémont on a river steamboat. Apparently Frémont had hoped to hire the well-known Andrew S. Drips to guide him on an expedition, but when he could not find Drips he hired Carson. From June until September, Kit guided Frémont's party west

through South Pass to the Wind River Mountains and then back to Missouri. When Frémont published his report of the expedition, Carson gained widespread fame.

The following year Carson rejoined Frémont traveling west on a second expedition. This time Carson shared the guide duties with Thomas Fitzpatrick, his former associate. The two mountain men led the Frémont party to Salt Lake, up the Oregon Trail to the Dallas River, south to Klamath Lake, then west across the Sierra Nevadas over Carson Pass to Sutter's Fort, Calif. From there the explorers moved south to the Mojave River and then northeast to Colorado, where Carson left them at Bent's Fort.

In 1845 Carson guided Frémont's third expedition across the Rockies to Salt Lake, across the Nevada desert to the Humboldt River, and to Sutter's Fort. This ended Carson's significant work as a guide, although on at least five other occasions he led army units or explorers through the Far West.

Career as a Soldier

Carson participated in skirmishes with Mexican forces in California in 1846. Returning to Washington, D.C., with messages from Frémont, Carson met Gen. Kearny, who was leading a small army to California. The general demanded that Carson guide his party west. This he did, participating in the battle and siege near San Pasqual. Later Carson was appointed a lieutenant in the Mounted Riflemen, but the Senate rejected this and he returned to Taos.

At the outbreak of the Civil War in 1861, Carson helped organize the First New Mexico Volunteer Infantry Regiment

and became its colonel. He fought in the battle at Val Verde, participated in campaigns against the Mescalero Apaches and the Navahos, and led the campaign against the tribes of the southern plains. In 1865 he was breveted brigadier general of volunteers. For the next 2 years Carson held routine assignments in the West, and in 1867 he resigned from the army.

Career as an Indian Agent

Interspersed with this military activity, Carson also served the Office of Indian Affairs, first as agent and later as superintendent of Indian affairs for Colorado Territory. In 1854 he became the agent for the Jicarilla Apache, Moache Ute, and Pueblos. He worked to keep peace and to obtain just treatment for the Native Americans, but he also used his authority to punish those guilty of depredations and cooperated with military leaders to show the tribesmen that the U.S. Government meant business.

Carson often disagreed with his superior superintendent of Indian affairs, Territorial Governor David Meriwether, about polices. Carson suggested that the governor send the agents to live among the Native Americans, or at least within their area, so that tribesmen would not have to travel several hundred miles to talk with them. In fact, he went so far as to state that the Native Americans should not even enter the towns because every time one did he was hurt in some manner. However, Meriwether apparently liked to summon Native American leaders to councils, thus forcing them to travel long distances. Such continuing differences and Carson's Criticism of his superior caused Meriwether to arrest him in 1856. Meriwether suspended him and charged him with disobedience, insubordination, and cowardice. Carson soon apologized and was reinstated as agent, a position he held until 1861, when he resigned to enter the army. He was appointed superintendent of Indian affairs for Colorado Territory in 1868, but he never had a chance to assume the duties of that office for on May 23 he died at Fort Lyon, Colo.

Further Reading

Of the numerous "biographies" of Carson, those written before 1960 include half-truths and legendary materials. Somewhat more accurate are Bernice Blackwelder, *Great Westerner* (1962), and M. Morgan Esterngreen, *Kit Carson: A Portrait in Courage* (1962). A most useful addition is Harvey L. Carter, *Dear Old Kit: The Historical Christopher Carson* (1968). This includes a discussion of errors in earlier material and a newly edited and annotated version of Carson's memoirs.

Discussion of the Carson legends is found in Henry Nash Smith, *Virgin Land: The American West as Symbol and Myth* (1950), and in Kent L. Steckmesser, *The Western Hero in History and Legend* (1965). Carson's part in Western exploration is best discussed in Allan Nevins, *Frémont: Pathmarker of the West* (1939; new ed. 1955), and William H. Goetzmann, *Army Exploration in the American West, 1803-1863* (1959). For an understanding of the fur trade see Robert G. Cleland, *This Reckless Breed of Men: The Trappers and Fur Traders of the Southwest* (1950); Dale L. Morgan, *Jedediah Smith and the Opening of the West* (1953); and David S. Lavender, *Bent's Fort* (1954). □

Johnny Carson

Johnny Carson (born 1925), dubbed the King of Late Night Television, became a pioneer in show business as host of *The Tonight Show* for 30 years. His interviewing and comic techniques won over a huge audience and spawned numerous imitators.

There was no way of knowing the young magician performing before the local Rotary Club would one day become America's most recognized face. The Great Carsoni, or young Johnny Carson, had already begun to master the techniques that would become so useful when entertaining people like Bob Hope, Steve Martin, politicians, musicians, and other performers on *The Tonight Show*. Carson became a pioneer in the television industry when he got his chance to host the *Tonight Show* after Jack Paar left the show in 1962. After many memorable late night evenings with Carson, the King of Late Night Television stepped down from his throne May 22, 1992, after 30 highly successful years.

Johnny Carson came into the world October 23, 1925, in Corning, Iowa. At the age of eight, Carson's father, Kit, packed up the family: matriarch Ruth, older sister Catherine, Johnny, and his little brother Richard, and moved to Norfolk, Nebraska. It was there that Carson came of age and began nurturing his talent for entertaining. His first paid gig was at the Norfolk Rotary Club when he was 14 years old. With the Great Carsoni emblazoned on a black velvet cloth draped over his magician stand, Carson performed for his mother's bridge club and the Methodist Church socials.

Carson's ability to entertain came as no surprise to him or his family, according to a quote in *Carson, the Unauthorized Biography,* by Paul Cockery.

"I can't say I ever wanted to become an entertainer. I already was one, sort of—around the house, at school, doing my magic tricks, throwing my voice and doing Popeye impersonations. People thought I was funny; so I kind of took entertaining for granted . . . It was inevitable that I'd start giving little performances."

Carson was in his senior year of high school when Japan bombed Pearl Harbor on December 7, 1941. After graduating, he enlisted with United States Navy. For two years, he served in non-combative positions before being assigned to the *USS Pennsylvania,* which the Japanese torpedoed in Okinawa two days before his arrival. Carson also spent time on the island of Guam in the South Pacific, where he entertained the troops with his ventriloquist dummy named Eddie.

One favorite Johnny Carson anecdote came from his military period. On board the *USS Pennsylvania,* one of his duties was decoding and delivering messages. Once he had the opportunity to deliver a message to James Forrestal, the Secretary of the Navy. Forrestal, as the story goes, asked Carson if he wanted to make the Navy his career. Carson replied no and told him his dream was to become a magician and entertainer. Forrestal asked if Carson knew any

card tricks and Carson was only too happy to oblige the Secretary of the Navy with some jokes and card tricks.

After the Navy, Carson returned to Norfolk and attended the University of Nebraska. He became a Phi Gamma Delta fraternity member and graduated in 1949 with a major in speech and a minor in radio. So enthralled with radio and comedy, Carson made a recording of all his favorite comedians like Bob Hope, Jack Allen, and Milton Belle, for his final thesis on "How to Write Comedy Jokes."

In the Beginning

Carson joined the forces of WOW Radio, Omaha, directly out of college, and on August 1, 1949, *The Johnny Carson Show* went on the air for in the morning for 45 minutes. Two months later, Carson married Jody Wolcott, his college sweetheart and the first of four wives. During his time at the radio station, Carson was becoming known for his cheerful banter while reading the news, but something bigger was about to begin in Omaha—television. Carson was about to embark on a new territory, a pioneer in television, just like everyone else at the time. But with his pleasant on-screen personality and satirical wit, he quickly became a recognizable figure in the small broadcast area of WOW-TV.

With the success of his television debut show *Squirrel's Nest,* Carson decided to take his talents on the road and see if he could make it in Hollywood, California. After months of rejection, Carson was offered a job at KNXT to read the station call letters, the time, and the weather. The job did not offer the notoriety or prestige he experienced in Omaha, but it was Hollywood and it was where he wanted to be. The *Carson's Cellar* was introduced a year later at 7:00 p.m. and many skits and characters seen by millions on the *Tonight Show* made their television debut.

Being a hard worker by midwestern nature, Carson diligently plugged away at his job, often putting in extra hours in and out of the studio. After *Carson's Cellar* went off the air, he became a game show host for *Earn Your Vacation,* and a comedy writer for Red Skelton. His tenacity payed off when he was asked to fill in for Skelton, who had become injured during rehearsals. He signed a contract for CBS shortly after, and a year later, Johnny Carson had his own half hour comedy show, aptly titled *The Johnny Carson Show.* Rumors were beginning to rumble about Carson becoming the next George Gobel, the very successful television comedian. But it did not last. The program was canceled four months later due to network lay offs and interference. CBS failed to renew his contract. Carson was left unemployed with a wife and three sons. His only option was to accept a job as game show host for *Do You Trust Your Wife?,* which eventually became *Who Do You Trust?,* on the ABC network and move to New York City.

New York was not as easy as Hollywood, but Carson kept plugging away. In 1957, Carson interviewed a man who would become synonymous with Johnny Carson and *The Tonight Show*—Ed McMahon. Carson substituted for Jack Paar on *The Tonight Show* for two weeks in 1958 and did a comedy routine for *The Perry Como Show.* Slowly, Carson was making a name for himself again, and when time came to restructure *The Tonight Show,* he wanted a chance to be involved.

The Tonight Show

The Tonight Show, which originated with Steve Allen on the radio in 1951 in Los Angeles, made the jump to television in 1954 in New York. Allen lasted two-and-a-half years and was replaced with Jack Paar. The show aired from 11:15 p.m. to 1:00 a.m. every night. Several millions of viewers watched every night—there was not a whole lot to choose from then. Johnny Carson took over October 1, 1962. The rest is television history.

Over thirty years, Carson had the perfect stage presence. An opening monologue and golf swing, his attention to comic details like timing, delivery, and gestures, plus his fair treatment of guests, made him a natural host of the most popular television show of the time. Carson believed that if the guest sparkled, so would the show. Over the years, many of the country's greatest entertainers, plus some local folks, came out from behind the stage curtain and sat between Carson and McMahon. The guest list was plentiful— Ethel Kennedy, Buddy Hackett, Ed Ames and his tomahawk, Pearl Bailey, Bob Hope, Dean Martin, and George Gobel all took time to talk with Carson about their newest projects. Carson and his show could make or break a struggling performer's career, and comedians like David Letterman, Jay Leno, George Carlin, and Joan Rivers all got their big break from appearing on *The Tonight Show.* Wild animals were special guests too, often creating hilarious disasters on Carson or his desk.

Carson's stage demure was quite different from his off-the-air personality. The pleasantries he bestowed to his guests were often not shared with anyone else. Carson preferred to remain aloof, almost shy, and small talk did not impress him. Carson preferred to save himself for his audience. He was divorced three times and often worked the proceedings and settlements into his monologues. Currently, he is married to Alex Mass, whom he met in 1984.

After hosting *The Tonight Show* 4,531 times for millions of people over 30 years, Carson was ready to retire from the show. On Friday, May 22, 1992, Johnny Carson did his famous golf swing for the last time. He resides in Malibu with his wife and manages to play a few games of tennis when he is not putting in time at his company, the Carson Production Group. He was reportedly entertaining thoughts of releasing *The Tonight Show* reruns for cable syndication. In early 1999, Carson suffered a heart attack; however, he was expected to fully recover.

Further Reading

Leamer, Laurence, *King of the Night: The Life of Johnny Carson,* 1989.

Corkery, Paul, *Carson: The Unauthorized Biography,* Randt & Co., 1987. □

James Earl Carter

The first U.S. president to be elected from the deep South in 132 years, James Earl (Jimmy) Carter (born 1924) served one term (1977-1981). In 1980 he lost his bid for re-election to Republican candidate Ronald Reagan but went on to be a much admired worker for peace and human rights at home and abroad.

James Earl Carter was born in the small southern town of Plains, Georgia, on October 1, 1924. He was the first child of farmer and small businessman James Earl Carter and former nurse, Lillian Gordy Carter. When Carter was four, the family moved to a farm in Archery, a rural community a few miles west of Plains. At five, Jimmy was already demonstrating his independence and his talents for business: he began to sell peanuts on the streets of Plains. At the age of nine, Carter invested his earnings in five bales of cotton which he stored for several years, then sold at a profit large enough to enable him to purchase five old houses in Plains.

Following his graduation from high school in 1941, Carter enrolled in Georgia Southwestern College, but in 1942 he received word that a much desired appointment to the United States Naval Academy at Annapolis had been approved. Carter entered the academy in 1943, and showed a special talent for electronics and naval tactics, eventually going on to work on the nation's first nuclear powered submarines. During his time in the Navy he also met Rosalynn Smith who he married on July 7, 1947 and had four children with: John, James Earl III, Jeffrey, and a daughter born much later, Amy.

Civic Activist to Politician

Carter had ambitions to become an admiral, but in 1953, following his father's death from cancer, he returned to Plains to manage the family businesses. He took over both the farm and the peanut warehouses his father had established, enlarged the business and, in order to keep up with modern farming techniques, studied at the Agricultural Experimental Station in Tifton, Georgia.

During these years in Plains, Carter began to play an active role in local civic affairs. From 1955 to 1962 he was active in a number of local functions and served on the boards of several civic organizations. In this civic life, Jimmy Carter distinguished himself by his liberal views on racial issues which could be traced back to his mother's disregard for many of the deep South's racist traditions.

As far as Carter's interest in politics goes, this may have come from his father, who had served for a year in the Georgia legislature. In 1962 Carter ran for a seat in the Georgia Senate and defeated his Republican opponent by about 1,000 votes. As a state senator, Carter promised to read every single bill that came up and when it looked as if he wouldn't be able to keep this promise due to the great volume of bills, he took a speed reading course to solve the problem. In government he earned a reputation as one of the most effective legislators and an outspoken moderate liberal. Carter was reelected to the state Senate in 1964.

In 1966, after first declaring himself as a candidate for the U.S. Congress, Carter decided to run for the office of governor of Georgia. He was beaten by Lester Maddox in the Democratic primary election though. Disappointed and

spiritually bankrupt, Carter then became "born again" and pushed forward. Between 1966 and 1970 he traveled widely through the state, making close to 1,800 speeches, studying the problems of Georgia, and campaigning hard. In the 1970 gubernatorial election, Carter's hard work paid off and he won Georgia's top position.

Governor of Georgia

In his inaugural address Carter announced his intentions to aid all poor and needy Georgians, regardless of race. This speech won Carter his first national attention, for in it he called for an end to racial discrimination and the extension of a right to an education, to a job, and to "simple justice" for the poor. As governor, Carter worked for, and signed into law, a bill which stipulated that the poor and wealthy areas of Georgia would have equal state aid for education. Carter also worked to cut waste in the government, merging 300 state agencies into only 30. The number of African-American appointees on major state boards and agencies increased from three to 53 and the number of African-American state employees rose by 40 percent. During his term, laws were passed to protect historical sites, conserve the environment, and to encourage openness in government.

While governor, Carter became increasingly involved in national Democratic Party politics. In 1972 he headed the Democratic Governors Campaign Committee, and in 1974 was chair of the Democratic National Campaign Committee. That same year Carter officially declared his intention to run for president in the 1976 race. When Carter announced his intentions to seek the presidency, he was still little known outside the state of Georgia. As late as October 1975 a public opinion poll on possible Democratic candidates did not even list his name. Then, in January 1976, Carter's whirlwind rise to national prominence began and by March 1976 he was the top choice among Democrats for the presidential nomination.

The 1976 Election

Carter's success against ten other candidates began with a victory in the New Hampshire primary in February. He was successful in making himself a symbol of a leader without ties to the entrenched interest groups of the nation's capital. Carter convinced voters that without these ties he would be able to act independently and effectively. In his campaign he also vowed to restore moral leadership to the presidency which had been badly shaken in the wake of Richard Nixon and the Watergate scandal. Carter easily won 17 of 30 primary contests and was elected on the first ballot at the 1976 Democratic National Convention.

With his running mate, Minnesota liberal Democrat Walter Mondale, Carter made unemployment a central issue of his campaign, urging the creation of jobs through increased federal spending and the expansion of business. Carter also campaigned on promises of pardon for the draft evaders of the Vietnam War period, the reorganization of the federal government bureaucracy, and the development of a national energy policy.

When Carter defeated the incumbent, Gerald Ford, by 1,678,069 popular votes, winning 297 electoral college votes to Ford's 240, he became the first president from the Deep South since Zachary Taylor in 1844. Carter's victory was definitely regional and was definitely based on social and economic class as his winning margin came from African-Americans, those with low incomes, and others who thought that they were being hurt by the policies of the Ford administration. Four out of five African-Americans voted for Carter and he also did well among white southerners, receiving the highest number of votes for a Democratic candidate since Roosevelt, but lost over one-half of Catholic voters and 55 percent of the Italian vote. One of the challenges to Carter was to ease the regional and ethnic splits evident in the election and to create a unified support for his presidency.

His Record as President

The year 1977 began well for the new president with a series of quick victories for Carter-backed programs. These included congressional approval of his plans to eliminate or consolidate federal agencies which duplicated services and of legislation aimed at lowering federal income taxes. In August of 1977 Congress adopted Carter's proposal to establish the Department of Energy as a new executive department. At the same time, Carter used his executive powers to make good on campaign pledges, including the pardoning of Vietnam War draft evaders and ending production of the B-1 bomber, which he felt was wasteful.

The Carter Administration was not without its problems though. In 1977 economic conditions had improved somewhat and unemployment had fallen, but by 1978 inflation had, despite a variety of approaches to stabilize it, continued to rise, reaching 15 percent by mid-1980. Due largely to these economic problems, Carter's approval rating in a July 1980 poll measured only 21 percent, the lowest recorded for any American president.

Carter's term was also marked by mixed success in foreign affairs. In 1977 Carter attracted worldwide attention and praise for his strong support of human rights wherein he limited or banned entirely any United States aid to nations believed to be human rights violators, but mixed reviews came for two 1977 treaties dealing with the Panama Canal. The first of these gave control of the canal to Panama on December 31, 1979 and the second gave the United States the right to defend the neutrality of the canal. Carter was influential in the Camp David Accords as well as in the creation of a peace treaty between Israel and Egypt in 1979 and in the negotiation of SALT (Strategic Arms Limitation Treaty) II with the Soviet Union, although these negotiations were ultimately delayed by the Soviet invasion of Afghanistan.

Carter's most dramatic moments in foreign policy affairs began in November 1979 when Iranian student militants seized the United States embassy in Teheran and took 52 U.S. citizens hostage. The hostages were to be held, their captors said, until the deposed Shah, who was in the United States for medical treatment, was handed over. Carter responded first by cutting diplomatic relations with Iran

and stopping all imports from that country. When these measures failed he, in April 1980, ordered an attempt at armed rescue, which failed and led to the death of eight marines and the resignation of Secretary of State Cyrus R. Vance. In the end the crisis lasted for a total of 444 days with the hostages finally being released on January 20, 1981, the last day that Carter held office.

The hostage crisis overseas and economic difficulties at home left Carter vulnerable but still vying for the top spot in the 1980 presidential elections. Running again with Vice President Walter Mondale, Carter was defeated by former California governor and actor Ronald Reagan by a wide margin. He received only 35 million votes to Reagan's 44 million and lost the electoral college vote 489 to 44.

The Right Things to Accomplish Post Presidency

While seen as a somewhat lame-duck immediately following his departure as president in 1981, recent historical revisionism has cast him in a more favorable light, especially in lieu of his successor's later improprieties during the Iran-Contra scandal. Viewed as a basically honest man, not a small commodity in this age of popular mistrust of government, Carter has devoted his post presidential career to an array of peacekeeping and humanitarian efforts.

In 1981 Carter established the Carter Center which, with its sizable budget, has sponsored programs from promoting human rights in third world countries to maintaining databases of immunization for local Atlanta children. The Carter Center has also monitored elections in newly democratized countries, fought such diseases as polio and river blindness, and helped eradicate the harmful African Guinea worm in Pakistan. In addition to these humanitarian efforts, Carter and his wife, Rosalynn, have volunteered their summers building low-income housing through the Habitat For Humanity organization.

The international relations front has also been no stranger to Carter since his defeat to Ronald Reagan. In 1990 he persuaded Nicaraguan Sandinista leader Daniel Ortega to step down and let an elected president, Violeta Chamorro, step in, something that without the relative neutrality of Carter's position probably would not have been possible. Carter has also served as somewhat of a mediator between President Bill Clinton and various leaders of non-democratic nations. In the early 1990s Carter brought messages from Somali warlord Mohamed Farrah Aidid to President Clinton which helped avoid a military confrontation and in June 1994 Carter negotiated with North Korean dictator Kim Il Sung to freeze his country's nuclear program and allow inspection of their nuclear facilities. Interestingly enough, sometimes Carter's efforts haven't been completely appreciated. President Clinton was reportedly incensed at Carter going over his head in foreign matters and making statements that he wasn't authorized to make.

One further mixed victory from Carter came when in September 1994, he, with the help of former chairman of the Joint Chiefs of Staff Colin Powell and Georgia Senator Sam Nunn, negotiated an agreement with Haitian revolutionary leader Lt. Gen. Raoul Cédras. Haiti, since the ouster of their first democratically elected president, Jean-Bertrand

Aristide, in 1991, had been a cesspool of violence and poverty since the revolution. Boatloads of Haitians seeking an escape from the myriad human rights abuses were arriving on U.S. shores daily and the situation was pointing towards a military invasion. President Clinton called on Carter to help, which he did with an agreement wherein military leaders relinquished power and handed it over to American forces until democracy could be restored. The downside of the agreement being Cédras and his cronies being given permission to stay in Haiti instead of being exiled which drew much criticism.

Whatever flak Carter has received for his methods of handling foreign affairs they fade from view when compared to the tireless work he has done for humanity since the end of his presidency. No other former president has worked so hard in the public arena while still maintaining personal pursuits which in Carter's case involve hunting, fishing, teaching adult Sunday school, and writing several books including one of his own poetry. As Carter's former speech writer, James Fallows, put it in 1990, "..what becomes. . .admirable is precisely the idealism of (Carter's) vision, the energy and intelligence and morality he has put into figuring out what is the right thing to accomplish."

Further Reading

There are several books that tell Jimmy Carter's story. Carter himself has written a number of books which include: *Keeping Faith: Memoirs of a President* (1982),*The Blood of Abraham: Insights into the Middle East* (1985), *An Outdoor Journal: Adventures and Reflections* (1988), *Turning Point: A Candidate, A State, and a Nation Come of Age* (1993), *The Virtues of Aging* (1998), and his volume of poetry *Always a Reckoning* (1995). Edna Langford and Linda Cox have done a biography of Carter's wife, Rosalynn, entitled *Rosalynn, Friend and First Lady* (1980) and Rosalynn tells her own story in *First Lady From Plains* (1985). Hamilton Jordan's book, *Crisis: The Last Year of the Carter Presidency* (1982) deals largely with the Iranian hostage crisis, while Jack Germond and Jules Witcover's *Blue Smoke and Mirrors: How Reagan Won and Why Carter Lost the Election of 1980* (1981) analyzes Carter's defeat in his bid for reelection. Carter's greatest diplomatic success—the 1978-1979 agreement between Israel and Egypt—is detailed in *Camp David* (1986) by William Quandt, a member of the Carter administration. Other accounts of Carter's life can be found in Peter G. Bourne's *Jimmy Carter: A Comprehensive Biography* (1997) and Rod Troester's *Jimmy Carter as Peacemaker: A Post Presidential Biography* (1996). For those inclined to go online, the Carter Center's Web site address is http://www.emory.edu/CARTER_CENTER. □

George Washington Carver

George Washington Carver (1864-1943) started his life as a slave and ended it as a respected and world-renowned agricultural chemist.

Born in Kansas Territory near Diamond Grove, Mo., during the bloody struggle between free-soilers and slaveholders, George Washington Carver became the kidnap victim of night riders. With his mother and

brother, James, he was held for ransom; but before they could be rescued the mother died. Merely a babe in arms, Carver was ransomed for a $300 racehorse by Moses Carver, a German farmer. Thus he was orphaned and left in the custody of a white guardian from early childhood.

Carver had responsibility for his own education. His first school was in Neosho, Iowa, some 9 miles from his home. Neosho had once been a Confederate capital; by now it had become the site of the Lincoln School for African American children. With James he walked there every day. His first teacher was an African American, Stephen S. Frost. He and his brother went faithfully to school for several years. Finally James tired of formal schooling and quit to become a house painter, but not George. He continued until he was 17. Then he went on to complete his high school work in Minneapolis, Kans.

Carver really wished to become an artist. His sketch of the rose *Yucca gloriosa* won him a first prize at the World's Columbian Exposition (1893).

Carver applied to study at the Iowa State College of Agricultural and Mechanical Arts but was turned down when it was learned that he was of African heritage. He then applied to Simpson College at Indianola, Iowa, where he was the second African American to be admitted. Tuition was $12 a year, but even this small amount was hard to come by. Carver raised the money by working as a cook at a hotel in Winterset, Iowa.

After 3 years' attendance at Simpson College, he once again applied for admission to Iowa State. He was admitted and was placed in charge of the greenhouse of the horticultural department while doing graduate work. He earned his master's degree in agriculture in 1896.

In April 1896 Carver received a unique offer from the African American educator Booker T. Washington to teach at Tuskegee Institute in Alabama. Said Dr. Washington: "I cannot offer you money, position or fame. The first two you have. The last from the position you now occupy you will no doubt achieve. These things I now ask you to give up. I offer you in their place: work—hard, hard work, the task of bringing a people from degradation, poverty, and waste to full manhood. Your department exists only on paper and your laboratory will have to be in your head."

Carver accepted the challenge. He arrived at the tiny railroad station at Chehaw, Ala., on Oct. 8, 1896. In a report to Dr. Washington he wrote: "8:00 to 9:00 A.M., Agricultural Chemistry; 9:20 to 10:00 A.M., the Foundation of Colors (for painters); 10:00 to 11:00 A.M., a class of farmers. Additional hours in the afternoon. In addition I must oversee and rather imperfectly supervise seven industrial classes, scattered here and there over the grounds. I must test all seeds, examine all fertilizers, based upon an examination of soils in different plots."

Through the years Carver was gaining national and international stature. Chinese and Japanese farmers raised many unique problems for him. Questions were referred to him from Russia, India, Europe, South America. He later had to turn down a request to journey to the Soviet Union. In 1916 he was elected a member of the Royal Society for the Encouragement of Arts in England; he went to Washington to the War Department to demonstrate his findings on the sweet potato in 1918. He was awarded the Spingarn Medal of the NAACP in 1923.

An early close friend of Carver was Henry A. Wallace; the pair knew each other for 47 years. Wallace said that Carver often took him on botanical expeditions, and it was he who first introduced Wallace to the mysteries of plant fertilizers. Carver was a shy and modest bachelor. An attack of whooping cough as a child had permanently caused him to have a high-pitched tenor voice. He considered it a high duty to attend classes and was seldom absent. In 1908 he returned to the West to visit his 96-year-old guardian, Moses Carver, and to visit the grave of his brother, James, in Missouri.

A careful and modest scientist, Carver was not without a sense of humor. When one of his students, hoping to play a trick on him, showed him a bug with wings of a fly and body of a mosquito, Carver was quick to label it "a humbug."

Carver utilized the materials at hand. He was interested in crop rotation and soil conservation. From the clay soil of Alabama he extracted a full range of dyestuffs, including a brilliant blue. He created 60 products from the pecan. From the common sweet potato he extracted a cereal coffee, a shoe polish, paste, oils—about 100 products. From the peanut he developed over 145 products. Carver suggested peanuts, pecans, and sweet potatoes replace cotton as money crops. He published all of his findings in a series of nearly 50 bulletins.

The testimony of Carver before the congressional House Ways and Means Committee in 1921 led to the passage of the Fordney-McCumber Tariff Bill of 1922. Scheduled to speak a scant 10 minutes, he was granted several time extensions because of the intense interest in his presentation. (He appeared in a greenish-blue suit many seasons old, having refused to invest in a new suit: "They want to hear what I have to say; they will not be interested in how I look.")

In 1935 Carver was chosen to collaborate with the Bureau of Plant Industry of the U.S. Department of Agriculture. He received the Theodore Roosevelt Medal in 1939 for distinguished achievement in science. During his lifetime Carver had made many friends. Henry Ford was his frequent host. Carver was a treasured friend of Thomas A. Edison. It was Edison who offered to make him independent with his own laboratories and an annual stipend of $50,000. Other intimates of his were Luther Burbank, Harvey Firestone, and John Burroughs. He was also a friend of three presidents: Theodore Roosevelt, Calvin Coolidge, and Franklin Delano Roosevelt.

Dr. Carver had earned the salary of $125 a month from the beginning until the end of his service at Tuskegee. He might have had much more. In 1940 he gave his life-savings, $33,000, to establish the George Washington Carver Foundation at Tuskegee Institute to perpetuate research in agriculture and chemistry. He later bequeathed his entire estate to the foundation, making a total of about $60,000. He died on Jan. 5, 1943.

At the dedication of a building in his honor at Simpson College, Dr. Ralph Bunche, Nobel Prize winner, pronounced Dr. Carver to be "the least imposing celebrity the world has ever known." Dr. Carver's birthplace was made a national monument on July 14, 1953.

Further Reading

Of the many studies of Carver the best is Rackham Holt, *George Washington Carver: An American Biography* (1943). Also useful is Shirley Graham and George D. Lipscomb, *Dr. George Washington Carver, Scientist* (1944). ☐

Johnny Cash

"The Man in Black"—as Johnny Cash (born 1932) has long been known—has been one of the most influential figures in country music since the 1950s. In the 1990s he broke through to a younger, more alternative audience, performing songs by Soundgarden, Beck, and others.

H e has also reached a substantial audience of rock fans, thanks to his outlaw persona, deep, authoritative voice, and dark songs like "Folsom Prison Blues." After enjoying a string of hits in the 1950s and even greater success in the late 1960s, when he was briefly the best-selling recording artist in the world, he saw his edgy, close-to-the-bone style go out of fashion. Even as his 1980s work was neglected, however, he appeared before adoring throngs worldwide. In 1994, well past his sixtieth birthday,

he came roaring back with a sparsely recorded album that ranked among his best work and earned him a Grammy Award. "Can you name anyone in this day and age who is as cool as Johnny Cash?" asked *Rolling Stone* rhetorically. "No, you can't."

J. R. Cash was born into an impoverished Arkansas family in 1932 and grew up working in the cotton fields. His Baptist upbringing meant that the music he heard was almost entirely religious, and the hymns sung by country greats like the Carter Family and Ernest Tubb reached him on the radio and made an indelible impression. "From the time I was a little boy," he recollected to Steve Pond in a 1992 *Rolling Stone* interview, "I never had any doubt that I was gonna be singing on the radio." His brother Roy formed a band when he was young, increasing John's determination to do the same one day.

Cash had no idea, though, what path would lead him to his destiny. He held a few odd jobs after graduating from Dyess High School in 1950, but eventually opted for a four-year stay in the Air Force. Stationed in Germany, he endured what he would later describe as a lonely, miserable period. Fortunately, he learned to play the guitar and began turning the poetry he'd been writing into song lyrics. After seeing a powerful film about Folsom Prison, he sat down to write what would become one of his signature songs—"Folsom Prison Blues." His empathy for prisoners and other marginalized people would consistently inform his work. With his powerful position in a generally conservative musical world, he also championed Native American rights and other social ills.

Cash left the military in 1954 and married Vivian Liberto, whom he met before joining the air force; they had corresponded throughout his tour of duty. The two lived in Memphis, Tennessee, and he earned a meager living selling appliances. "I was the worst salesman in the world," Cash confided to Pond. Nonetheless, he summoned the passion to sell himself as a singer, playing with a gospel group and canvassing radio stations for chances to perform on the air.

Plays with Presley

Eventually Cash was granted an audience with trail-blazing producer Sam Phillips, at whose Sun Studios the likes of Elvis Presley, Jerry Lee Lewis, Carl Perkins, and others made recordings that would help change the course of popular music. Phillips was a hard sell, but Cash won the opportunity to record his first single; "Cry, Cry, Cry" became a number 14 hit in 1955, and Cash's group played some local gigs with Presley. Pond describes Cash's early records as "stark, unsettling and totally original. The instrumentation was spare, almost rudimentary" featuring bass and lead guitar supplied by his Tennessee Two and Cash's rhythm guitar, which had "a piece of paper stuck underneath the top frets to give it a scratchy sound."

In 1956 Cash left his sales job and recorded the hits "Folsom Prison Blues"—containing the legendary and much-quoted lyric "I shot a man in Reno just to watch him die"—and "I Walk the Line." The next year saw the release of the one album released by Sun before his departure from the label, *Johnny Cash With His Hot & Blue Guitar.* He and the Tennessee Two left the label after a string of hits and signed with CBS/Columbia Records in 1958. Singles he recorded on Sun at Phillips's insistence just before his contract lapsed continued to chart for years afterward, much to Cash's chagrin. Yet he charted on CBS as well with a bevy of singles and such albums as *Blood, Sweat and Tears* and *Ring of Fire.*

In the midst of his success, however, Cash grew apart from Vivian and their children. He grew dependent on drink and drugs and became increasingly dissolute. Such misery no doubt contributed force to such work as 1963's "Ring of Fire," which was co-written by June Carter, who also performed on the track. Cash and Carter—of the famed Carter family—became increasingly close, both professionally and personally. His marriage collapsed in 1966 and he nearly died of an overdose. Cash has long attributed his subsequent rehabilitation to two factors: Carter and God. He and Carter wed in 1968 and later had a son, John.

Cash Sells

In any event, Cash expanded his repertoire as the 1960s unfolded, incorporating folk music and protest themes. He recorded songs by folk-rock avatar Bob Dylan and up-and-comers like Kris Kristofferson, but by the end of the decade, driven perhaps by his generally out-of-control life, his hits came largely from novelty songs like Shel Silverstein's "A Boy Named Sue." Even so, by 1969 Cash was the best-selling recording artist alive, outselling even rock legends The Beatles. That year saw him win two Grammy Awards for *Johnny Cash at Folsom Prison,* a live album for a worshipful audience of prisoners that led, perhaps inevitably, to *Johnny Cash at San Quentin.* From 1969 to 1971 he hosted a smash variety program for television, *The Johnny Cash Show.*

The 1970s saw more career triumphs, notably a Grammy-winning duet with Carter on Tim Hardin's "If I Were a Carpenter," a command performance for President Richard Nixon, acting roles in film and on television, a best-selling autobiography, and several more hit albums, including *Man in Black,* the title of which would become his permanent show business moniker. While this label has been associated with his "outlaw" image, he and his bandmates originally wore black because they had nothing else that matched; besides, as Cash informed *Entertainment Weekly,* "black is better for church."

In 1980 Cash was inducted into the Country Music Association Hall of Fame. He had become a music hero worldwide, appearing in eastern Europe before the fall of the Soviet empire and praising those who agitated for democracy. Yet during the 1980s, Cash became less and less of a priority for his record label; country music had come to be dominated by younger, pop-inclined artists who favored slick production. He continued to struggle with drugs, eventually checking into the Betty Ford clinic. There, he has said, he experienced a religious epiphany.

Cash wrote a novel, *Man in White,* about the life of the apostle Paul, and continued indulging his eclectic musical tastes, recording songs by mavericks like Elvis Costello. Alongside Kristofferson, Willie Nelson, and Waylon Jennings, he participated in a collaborative album, *The Highwayman;* he also joined Jerry Lee Lewis, Carl Perkins, and country-rock giant Roy Orbison for a reunion recording called *Class of '55 (Memphis Rock & Roll Homecoming),* which enjoyed solid sales. A daughter by his first marriage, Rosanne, became a country star in her own right; Johnny Cash, himself, even as his albums sold poorly, was firmly established as a living legend of country music and a profound influence on rock and roll. In 1992 he was inducted into the Rock and Roll Hall of Fame, and 1993 saw him contribute a vocal performance to *Zooropa,* by rock superstars U2.

Yet Cash tired of record-business priorities. "I kept hearing about demographics [market studies of consumers] until it was coming out my ears," the singer told Christopher John Farley of *Newsweek.* The first label representative who seemed to understand him after this bitter experience was, ironically enough, best known for his work with hardcore rap, metal, and alternative acts. Rick Rubin had founded his own label, first called Def American and later changed to American Recordings, to support acts he believed in. Though not intimately acquainted with Cash's work, he admired the singer's artistic persona. "I don't see him as a country act," Rubin told Farley. "I would say he embodies rock 'n' roll. He's an outlaw figure, and that is the essence of what rock 'n' roll is."

Rubin's appeal to Cash lay in his idea for a record. After seeing one of the country legend's performances, the producer "said he'd love to hear just me and my guitar," Cash told *Los Angeles Times* writer Robert Hilburn. These were the words the veteran artist had waited decades to hear; he had suggested such a minimal approach many times to country producers, only to have it vetoed immediately on commercial grounds. Rubin simply set up a tape machine in his Hollywood living room and allowed Cash to do what he does best.

Rubin "was a lot like Sam [Phillips], actually," Cash ventured to Hilburn. "We talked a lot about the approach we were going to take, and he said, 'You know, we are not going to think about time or money. I want you to come out as much as you can." Without such constraints—which had clipped Cash's wings in his Nashville years—he was free to experiment with a wide range of material. Recording over 70 songs, mostly at Rubin's house but also at his own cabin in Tennessee and at the trendy Los Angeles nightspot The Viper Room, Cash had a valedictory experience. He later told *Time*'s Farley that the work was his "dream album."

The material was culled to 13 tracks, including traditional songs, some Cash originals, and compositions by such diverse modern songwriters as Kristofferson, Leonard Cohen, Tom Waits, Nick Lowe, Glenn Danzig, and Loudon Wainright III. The leadoff track, "Delia's Gone," grimly describes the murder of a faithless woman; Rubin seemed to invite comparisons between Cash and the controversial metal and rap acts on his label. Titled *American Recordings,* the album was released in 1994; Johnny Cash was 62 years old. The liner notes contained testimonials from both Rubin and Cash. "I think we made a brutally honest record," the producer declared. "Working with Rick," Cash averred, "all the experimenting, kinda spread me out and expanded my range of material. This is the best I can do as an artist, as a solo artist, this is it."

Critics seemed to agree. Karen Schoemer of *Mirabella* praised it as "a daring, deceptively simple album" that "operates on a mythic scale, which suits someone who's always been larger than life. What is breathtaking is Cash's ability to analyze his aging self, and the failures, weaknesses, strengths and wisdoms that time bestows." *Village Voice* critic Doug Simmons praised it as "fiercely intimate," while *Rolling Stone*'s Anthony DeCurtis called it "unquestionably one of his best albums," one which "will earn him a time of well-deserved distinction in which his work will reach an eager new audience."

While *American Recordings* didn't take the charts by storm, it restored Johnny Cash's sense of mission. It also earned him a 1995 Grammy Award for best contemporary folk album. He played a sold-out engagement in Los Angeles just before his nomination, before an audience studded with such music stars as Tom Petty, Sheryl Crow, and Dwight Yoakam. And in September of 1996 he played a set at the CMJ Music Marathon in Manhattan, previewing songs from his album *Unchained* as well as performing cover versions from younger artists such as Beck and Soundgarden.

About the prospect of an "eager new audience" Cash himself—who seriously considered playing at the alternative-rock festival known as Lollapalooza before declining the offer—was philosophical. "I no longer have a grandiose attitude about my music being a powerful force for change," he told *Entertainment Weekly.* Even so, he allowed, "I think [today's youth] sees the hypocrisy in government, the rotten core of social ills and poverty and prejudice, and I'm not afraid to say that's where the trouble is. A lot of people my age are." One thing remained constant, as he told *Rolling Stone:* "I feel like if I can just go onstage with my guitar and sing my songs, I can't do no wrong no matter where I am."

Further Reading

Rees, Dafydd, and Luke Crampton, *Rock Movers & Shakers,* Billboard, 1991.

Entertainment Weekly, February 18, 1994, pp. 57-67.

Hits, May 2, 1994.

Los Angeles Times, April 25, 1994, pp. F1, F5.

Mirabella, July 1994.

People, May 16, 1994.

Rolling Stone, December 10, 1992, pp. 118-25, 201; May 5, 1994, p. 14; May 19, 1994, pp. 97-98; June 30, 1994, p. 35.

Time, May 9, 1994, pp. 72-74.

Village Voice, May 18, 1994. □

Wilt Chamberlain

Wilt Chamberlain (born 1936) is considered one of the world's all-time greatest professional basketball players.

Wilt Chamberlain was born in Philadelphia and was one of nine children. His father lived in a racially-mixed middle class neighborhood, and Chamberlain had a relatively pleasant childhood. At Shoemaker Junior High School, Wilt began to play on the basketball team, and he also played on the playgrounds against older players who taught him a lot about the game. He later said, "I still think you could pick up a team from the street corners of Philly that would give most colleges a real hard time." Wilt attended Overbrook High School in Philadelphia beginning in 1952. At that time he was already 6'11" tall, and had developed what he termed a "deep love for basketball."

Recruited By More Than 200 Universities

Chamberlain's high school basketball career was astounding. In three seasons he scored more than 2200 points. More than two hundred universities recruited Chamberlain, but he wanted to get away from big cities and preferred to play in the midwest. After seriously considering Dayton, Michigan, Indiana, and Kansas Universities he chose Kansas because of the recruiting by Hall of Fame coach Phog Allen.

At the University of Kansas, Chamberlain continued his brilliant play on the basketball court, scoring fifty-two points in his first varsity game. During his first varsity season he led the Jayhawks to the finals of the National Collegiate Athletic Association tournament, but they lost to North Carolina in double overtime. During his college career he averaged over thirty points per game and was twice selected to All-American teams. Following his junior year, he decided to

quit college and become a professional because, he said, "The game I was forced to play at [Kansas] wasn't basketball. It was hurting my chances of ever developing into a successful professional player."

Because he did not play his final season at Kansas, Chamberlain was not eligible to join an NBA team until one more year. So he joined the Harlem Globetrotters and spent the year traveling the world and entertaining adults and youngsters alike. He still claims that his year with the Globetrotters was his most enjoyable season of basketball.

Scoring Machine

In 1959, Chamberlain joined the Philadelphia Warriors of the NBA. The great centers of the day were Clyde Lovellette, Johnny Kerr, Johnny Green, and, of course, Bill Russell of the Boston Celtics. But Chamberlain made an immediate impact on the league. He could score almost at will, and opposing teams gave up trying to stop him and instead tried only to contain him. His scoring average during the 1959-60 season of 37.9 points per game was more than eight points per game higher than anyone else had ever scored in the history of the league. He was named both rookie of the year and most valuable player, the first person to receive both awards in the same season.

For the next six seasons, Chamberlain led the league in scoring. In 1961-62 he averaged 50.4 points and scored 100 in one game. In 1962-63 he averaged 44.8 points per game. Chamberlain was simply the greatest scoring machine in the history of basketball.

Despite his scoring achievements, Chamberlain and his teammates were not winning NBA championships. The late 1950s and 1960s were dominated by the Boston Celtics and their center Bill Russell. Russell had revolutionized basketball as much with his defense as Chamberlain had with his offense, and Russell always had a great group of supporting players, including Bob Cousy, Bill Sharman, John Havlicek, and Sam Jones. Chamberlain often had strong supporting players as well, but Russell always seemed to pull out the championship. Chamberlain always took a great deal of abuse from the media and fans because of his lack of success against Russell.

Wins Championship with the 76ers

Finally, in 1967, Chamberlain reversed his fortunes. The Warriors had moved to San Francisco, and Wilt had gone with them, but he was later traded to the new Philadelphia team, the 76ers. In 1967, the 76ers had a great supporting cast, including Chet Walker, Luke Johnson, Hal Greer, Wally Jones, and Billy Cunningham. They finished the regular season with the best record in the history of the league. In the championship series, the 76ers polished off the San Francisco Warriors to win the first world title for Chamberlain.

Several years later Chamberlain was traded again, this time to the Los Angeles Lakers. The Lakers had featured numerous great players through the years, including Elgin Baylor and Jerry West, but had not won a championship since moving to Los Angeles from Minneapolis in 1960 (they *lost* in the championship series seven times between 1962 and 1970). For the last two losses, in 1969 and 1970, Chamberlain was on the team. The 1969 loss was particularly devastating, since it was to Russell and the Celtics again. In the final game, Chamberlain was injured and played very little. Russell later criticized Chamberlain for not playing, thus infuriating Chamberlain and removing the last remnants of friendship between the two men.

In 1972, however, the Lakers seemed poised to finally win a championship. They finished the year with the best regular season record in history, breaking the record set by Chamberlain and the 76ers in 1967. In addition to Chamberlain, the team now featured Happy Hairston, Gail Goodrich, Jim McMillan, Jerry West, and a strong set of reserves. In the playoffs, the Lakers first defeated the Milwaukee Bucks, with Chamberlain completely outplaying the Buck center, Kareem Abdul Jabbar. In the championship series, the Lakers played the powerful New York Knickerbockers, led by Willis Reed, Dave DeBusschere, Bill Bradley, and Walt Frazier. In the fourth game of the series, Chamberlain suffered a fractured wrist. Although the Lakers led the series three games to one the series still seemed in doubt because of Chamberlain's injury. Despite understandable pain, Chamberlain played the next game with football linemen's pads on both hands. He scored twenty four points, grabbed twenty-nine rebounds, and blocked ten shots. The Lakers won the game and the series, four games to one and brought the first world championship to Los Angeles. After the final game Wilt said, "For a long time, fans of mine had to put up with people saying Wilt couldn't win the big ones. Now maybe they'll have a chance to walk in peace, like I do."

Following the 1973 season, Chamberlain left the Lakers to become the coach of the San Diego Conquistadors of the old American Basketball Association (ABA). Chamberlain left the NBA as the all-time leader in points scored (more than 30,000) and rebounds (over 22,000), and with four Most Valuable Player awards and more than forty league records. The ABA was a different sort of challenge, however; the athletes were not generally as good as in the NBA, and Chamberlain had never been a coach before. The Conquistadors were a poor team, even by ABA standards, and Chamberlain left the coaching ranks shortly thereafter for a well-deserved retirement.

Since retiring from basketball, Chamberlain has been involved in a wide variety of activities. He has sponsored several amateur athletic groups, including volleyball teams and track clubs. He has invested wisely through the years and remains a wealthy man. He has also kept in outstanding physical condition. When he walks into a room or onto a basketball court today, he is a legendary presence.

Controversial Books

Chamberlain gained further notoriety in 1991 with the release of his second and most talked about autobiography, *A View from Above*. The book contains observations on athletes of the 90's, gun control, and his 14 years in the NBA, among other topics. But it's the claim that he has slept with 20,000 women that landed him in the celebrity spotlight and in the public hotseat. Reflecting upon this claim, Chamberlain regretted the way he discussed sex in the book and became an advocate of safe sex. In 1997, Chamberlain published *Who's Running the Asylum?: The Insane World of Sports Today*. His latest book provides a critical discussion of the sports industry and the NBA, including his own ranking of basketball's greatest players.

Further Reading

Chamberlain, Wilt, and David Shaw, *Wilt: Just Like Any Other 7-Foot Black Millionaire Who Lives Next Door*, MacMillan, 1973.

Libby, Bill, *Goliath: The Wilt Chamberlain Story*, Dodd, 1977.

Sullivan, George, *Wilt Chamberlain* Grosset, 1971.

Ebony, April, 1972, pp. 114-121.

Esquire, May, 1988, pp. 53-56.

Life, March 13, 1970, pp. 46-50.

Look, June 10, 1958, pp. 91-94; March 1, 1960, pp. 51-57.

Sports Illustrated, October 29, 1973, p. 44-48; August 18, 1986, pp. 62-76; December 9, 1991, pp. 22-26.

Time, May 22, 1972, pp. 47-50. □

Ray Charles

The American jazz musician Ray Charles (born 1932) was widely admired as a singer, pianist, and composer. He combined elements of jazz, gospel and rhythm-and-blues to create a new kind of African-American music, known as soul.

Ray Charles Robinson was born in Albany, Georgia, on September 23, 1932. His father, Bailey Robinson, worked as a mechanic and handyman; his mother, Reather Robinson, worked in a sawmill. In order to avoid being confused with boxing champion Ray Robinson, he dropped his last name and was known as Ray Charles.

Suffered Blindness and Loss

The family moved from Albany, Georgia, to Greenville, Florida, when Charles was still a child. In Greenville, at the age of five, he began to go blind. At the age of seven, his right eye was removed, soon after which he became totally blind. At the Saint Augustine School for the Blind, in Florida, he learned to read Braille and began his musicianship as a pianist and clarinetist/saxophonist. His blindness required that he exercise his formidable memory for music aided by his gift of perfect pitch.

At 15 years of age, Charles lost his mother; two years later his father passed away. Suffering, somehow, always produces the greater artist. Charles, early orphaned and blind, suffered and grew in the capacity for emotion which infused his music.

Began Career With Country/Western Bands

Upon graduation from the Saint Augustine School, Charles traveled with country/western road bands—an experience he was to capitalize on later when he added country/western songs to his repertoire. Shortly afterwards, he began touring with rhythm-and-blues bands, working as a pianist, clarinetist, saxophonist, arranger, and composer.

As a singer, Charles was early influenced by blues singers Guitar Slim and Percy Mayfield. At the piano he was influenced by the jazz arrangements of Lloyd Glenn. Forever present in his style was the idiom of gospel music, sometimes subsumed by the other styles he sang; sometimes emerging in his pronunciation; sometimes predominating, as soul music. Charles' romantic ballad singing continued fundamentally in the suave Nat Cole school, but was embellished by deep-throated gospel growls and phenomenal falsetto which was frequently mistaken for a female soprano voice. The texture of his voice, his mixing of styles, his consummate musicianship, his versatile falsetto range, and his emotional appeal produced a unique vocal artistry which crossed even language barriers, but for an English-speaking audience his story-telling power added the dimension of meaning that provided a totally emotional experience not often equaled in any quarter of musical art.

Invented Soul

In 1954 an historic recording session with Atlantic records fused gospel with rhythm-and-blues and established Charles' "sweet new style" in American music. One number recorded at that session was destined to become his first great success. Secularizing the gospel hymn "My Jesus Is All the World to Me," Charles employed the 8- and 16-measure forms of gospel music, in conjunction with the 12-measure form of standard blues. Charles contended that his invention of soul music resulted from the heightening of the intensity of the emotion expressed by jazz through the charging of feeling in the unbridled way of gospel. When "It Don't Mean a Thing, If It Ain't Got That Swing" combines with "Swing Low, Sweet Chariot," the result is a beat hard to beat, and Charles never sang a note that was not perfectly on pitch or did not swing in his exceptional rhythmical contexts.

In 1959, on the ABC-Paramount label, Charles recorded his legendary "Georgia on my Mind." In 1961 he won the first of five consecutive polls conducted among international jazz critics by *Downbeat* magazine. Charles won several Grammy Awards from the National Academy of Recording Arts and Sciences. His virtuosity was internationally recognized. In 1976, he recorded songs from Gershwin's *Porgy and Bess* with Cleo Laine.

A Pepsi endorsement in the 1990s ensured that Charles would be known to a new generation of music lovers. He kept the albums coming, including *My World, The Best of Ray Charles: The Atlantic Years,* and *Love Affair,* and he even had a cameo in the 1996 movie *Spy Hard.*

Views on Elvis

In 1994, Charles appeared on the NBC news show "Now," admitting that "I'm probably going to lose at least a third of my fans," but telling interviewer Bob Costas that Elvis imitated what African-American artists were already doing. "To say that Elvis was. . .'the king,' I don't think of Elvis like that because I know too many artists that were far greater than Elvis." While this statement caused a stir, it was known that rock-and-roll, especially in the early years, was heavily rooted in blues, and many rock artists performed and popularized music that originally belonged to African-American blues singers.

Although described by Nat Hentoff as living within "concentric circles of isolation," Charles was married to the former Della Altwine, herself a gospel singer, with whom he had three children. He was also known to enjoy good friendship with Stevie Wonder and other musicians. Yet there was a loneliness in his music, a kind of self- intimacy which was, perhaps, best reflected in his 1961 recordings with Betty Carter and his recordings from *Porgy and Bess.*

Of course, loneliness is inherent in the blues, but so much in the art depends upon the feelings of the interpreter that it is clear that there was a kind of loneliness inherent in Charles, himself; a loneliness that we are reminded that we share whenever we hear him sing. There is no more existential art than the art of music, which exists as creative experience only in the time of its performance. As Charles best put it himself, in a 1989 *Downbeat* interview with Jeff Levinson:

> And then you have another kind of person like myself, for whom music is like the bloodstream. It is their total existence. When their music dies, *they* die. That's me. That's the difference.

> How can you get tired of breathing? Music is my breathing. That's my apparatus. I've been doing it for 40 years. And I'm going to do it until God himself says, "Brother Ray, you've been a nice horse, but now I'm going to put you out to pasture."

Further Reading

There is no full-length biography of Ray Charles at this time. Information can be found in *Downbeat* (January 1989); *Ebony* (April 1963); *New York Post* (January 4, 1962); *New York Times* (October 8, 1961); *Newsweek* (November 13, 1961); *Saturday Evening Post* (August 24, 1963); *Show Business Illustrated* (March 1962); *TIME* (May 10, 1963); Leonard Feather, *Encyclopedia of Jazz* (1960); *American Heritage* (August-September, 1986); *Esquire* (May, 1986); *Rolling Stone* (February 13, 1986); and *Jet* (July 25, 1994). □

Cesar Chavez

Cesar Chavez (1927-1993) was a Mexican American labor leader who organized the first effective union of farm workers in the history of California agriculture.

Cesar Chavez was born on March 31, 1927, near Yuma, Arizona. His grandfather had homesteaded some 112 acres there in 1904, but the family lost the ranch during the Depression in 1939, when they could not pay the taxes. The family then joined the migrant laborers streaming into California.

Early Organizing

Chavez quit school after the eighth grade to work full-time in the fields, but in 1944 he joined the U.S. Navy. He served for two years in the Pacific, but racism kept him in menial jobs, so upon discharge he rejoined his family and

continued as a farm worker in California. In 1948 he married Helen Fabela of Delano, California.

In 1952 Chavez met Fred Ross, who was organizing Mexican-Americans in the barrios (quarters) of California into the Community Service Organization (CSO). They concentrated on voter registration, citizenship classes, and helping Mexican-American communities obtain needed facilities in the barrios as well as aiding individuals with such typical problems as welfare, contracts signed with unscrupulous salesmen, and police harassment.

Chavez's work in the voter registration drive in Sal Si Puedes, the notorious San Jose barrio, was so effective that Ross hired him as an organizer. Over the next 10 years Chavez rose to national director of CSO. In 1962, when the CSO rejected his proposal to start a farmworkers union, he quit the organization. At 35 years of age, with $1,200 in savings, he took his wife and eight children to Delano to begin the slow, methodical organizing process which grew into the National Farm Workers Association (NFWA). When, three years later, members of Agricultural Workers Organizing Committee of the AFL-CIO (American Federation of Labor and Congress of Industrial Organizations) struck the vineyards in Delano, they asked for support from Chavez's NFWA.

Thus began the great California table-grape strike, which lasted five years. In 1966, the two unions merged to form the United Farm Workers Organizing Committee (UFWOC) of the AFL-CIO, headed by Chavez. During the struggle to organize the vineyards Chavez initiated an international boycott of California table grapes that brought such pressure to bear on local grape growers that most eventually signed with his union. The boycott ended in September 1970. Soon after this victory, Chavez again employed the boycott strategy, this time against lettuce growers who used non-union labor. Chavez became the first man ever to organize a viable farm workers' union in California that obtained signed contracts from the agricultural industry.

Believed in Non-Violence

Chavez was an outspoken advocate of social change through nonviolent means. In 1968, to avert violence in the grape strike, he undertook a 25-day fast; the fast was broken at an outdoor Mass attended by some 8,000 persons, including Senator Robert F. Kennedy. Chavez also led a 200-mile march from Delano to Sacramento to dramatize the demands of the farm workers.

In July 1970 Chavez's union faced one of its most serious challenges when the Teamsters' union signed contracts that applied to farm workers with some 200 growers in California. Chavez met the challenge head on: within 3 weeks the largest agricultural strike ever to hit California had spread over 180 miles along the coastal valleys. About 7,000 farm workers struck to win recognition of Chavez's UFWOC as their bargaining agent, with the national boycott again used as the weapon.

From 1972 to 1974, membership in the union dwindled from nearly 60,000 to just 5,000. But Chavez's efforts were rewarded. From 1964 to 1980, wages of California migrant workers had increased 70 percent, health care benefits became a reality and a formal grievance procedure was established. Chavez continued to fight for the rights of workers up to the day of his death on April 22, 1993.

Further Reading

Collins, David R., *Farmworker's Friend: The Story of Cesar Chavez* Carolrhoda Books, 1996.

Ferris, Susan, et al, *The Fight in the Fields: Cesar Chavez and the Farmworkers Movement,* Harcourt Brace, 1997.

Gonzales, Doreen *Cesar Chavez: Leader for Migrant Farm Workers,* Enslow Publications, 1996. □

Dennis Chávez

The first Hispanic American to be elected to the United States Senate, Democrat Dennis Chávez (1888–1962) led a long and distinguished career in government service, first as a member of the U.S. House of Representatives and then as a senator from the state of New Mexico. Noted primarily for his long and unrelenting fight to create a federal Fair Employment Practices Commission, Chávez was also a staunch supporter of education and civil rights.

The third of eight children, Dionisio Chávez was born to David and Paz (Sanchez) Chávez on April 8, 1888. His family lived in in what was then the United States Mexican Territory. The area did not become the state of New Mexico until 1912. When he was seven, the family moved to Albuquerque. At school his name was changed to

Dennis. Chávez quit school in the eighth grade and went to work. For the next five years he drove a grocery wagon to help support the family. He joined the Albuquerque Engineering Department in 1905, earning a substantial increase in income. Even after Chávez left school, he spent evenings at the local public library, reading about Thomas Jefferson and politics—his passions.

Chávez worked as an interpreter for senate candidate Andrieus A. Jones during the 1916 campaign. Jones rewarded him with a clerkship in the U.S. Senate in 1918-1919. While clerking, Chávez also entered Georgetown University through a special entrance examination to study law. He earned a Bachelor of Laws degree from Georgetown in 1920, and returned to Albuquerque, where he established a successful law practice.

Political Career Began with State Legislature

A Democrat in the tradition of his hero Thomas Jefferson, Chávez became active in local politics, winning election to the New Mexico House of Representatives. In 1930 he ran successfully for a seat in the U.S. House of Representatives, handily defeating the incumbent Republican, Albert Simms. He served as the thinly populated state's only representative. He was reelected once and then turned his sights toward the U.S. Senate. In 1934 he ran against the powerful Republican incumbent, Bronson Cutting. After a hard-fought, bitter campaign and a narrow defeat, Chávez challenged the validity of Cutting's victory, charging vote fraud. The issue reached to the Senate floor. The matter was still pending in May 1935, when Cutting was killed in an airplane crash. Chávez was appointed by New Mexico's Governor Tingley to serve in Cutting's place. Five senators expressed their disapproval by walking out of the Senate as Chávez was being sworn in. Chávez, however, was the people of New Mexico's clear choice when he was officially elected to the position in 1936, defeating a popular Republican candidate.

Served with Distinction

New Mexico voters showed their support for Chávez by reelecting him to the Senate five times. Although his often independent stands on various issues generated controversy, Chávez was a strong supporter of President Franklin Roosevelt's New Deal programs. His service on important Congressional committees allowed him to fight for causes he believed in. Chávez was a member of the Committees on Territories and Insular Affairs, the Education and Labor, Appropriations and Indian Affairs. In the last, he protested measures affecting Navajo grazing stock and also demanded an investigation of Indian Affairs Commissioner Collier.

In 1938 Chávez co-authored the Chávez-McAdoo bill, which established a federal radio station to counter Nazi and Fascist broadcasts into South America. In a curious move the following year, he advocated U.S. recognition of Spain's fascist leader, General Francisco Franco. He usually took a liberal stance on farm issues, voting for the draft deferment of farm laborers and against reductions in farm security appropriations. He was also active in measures regarding tariffs, employment programs, and unemployment benefits.

Chávez earned the nickname "Puerto Rico's Senator" in 1942 when he initiated an investigation into the causes of social and economic conditions in Puerto Rico. His support of a Senate bill to extend public works projects in that territory and the Virgin Islands was decisive in its passage.

Chávez attracted national attention during his long fight for enactment of a federal Fair Employment Practices Commission. The bill was designed to prevent employers or labor unions doing government work from discriminating on the basis of race, creed, color, ancestry, or national origin. The bill was eventually defeated in 1946—by only an eight-vote margin.

Dennis Chávez worked tirelessly to further the interests of the state of New Mexico. He is credited for garnering significant amounts of federal funding as well as key defense installations for the state. Chávez married Imelda Espinoza in 1911. They had three children: two daughters and a son. Chávez died of a heart attack on November 18, 1962, at the age of 74.

Further Reading

Hispanic-American Almanac, edited by Nicolás Kanellos, Detroit, Gale Research, 1993.

Mexican American Biographies, A Historical Dictionary: 1836-1987, edited by Matt S. Meier, Westport, Connecticut, Greenwood Press, 1988. □

Benjamin Chavis

Lifelong political activist Benjamin Chavis (born 1948) overcame racial injustice and wrongful imprisonment to become a vocal leader in the civil rights movement.

The first political act of Benjamin Chavis came when he was a wide-eyed 13 year old. On his way home from school each day, Chavis would pass a whites-only library in Oxford, North Carolina. One day, tired of tattered hand-me-downs and desirous of a book with two intact covers on it, he boldly walked into the library. The librarians told him to leave, but he questioned that demand. "He asked why," a childhood friend told the *New York Times.* "A lot of us when we were told to go away . . . would just do so, but Ben would always challenge, always ask why." The librarians called his parents, but the incident, like the spunkiness of the boy at its center, could not be calmed, and tempers flared. In a short time, the library was opened to all races. A child's simple act of disobedience and intellectual curiosity had shattered the overt racism of an institution whose sole mission, young Chavis knew, should have been the enrichment of minds—those of blacks and whites.

Descended from Activists

The Reverend Benjamin Franklin Chavis, Jr., was born in 1948 in Oxford, North Carolina, into a long and distinguished line of preachers. His great-great-grandfather, John Chavis, is considered to be the first black graduate of Princeton University because he graduated from a New Jersey seminary that later became the university. John Chavis, according to Benjamin, was killed in 1938 for teaching black children to read and write.

In the mid-twentieth century, even as the walls of segregation began to tumble, many racist elements thrived in the United States, particularly in the South. But even though the nation's military services were integrated in the year of Benjamin Chavis's birth, and a judicial decision six years later struck down the practice of "separate but equal" education, closed-minded whites in some areas vehemently defended their racist institutions and laws. The worldviews of civil rights leaders like Chavis and Martin Luther King, Jr., were shaped against this backdrop of hatred and bigotry.

In 1968—the year of King's assassination, which some observers feel brought an end to the modern civil rights era—Chavis became a field officer for the United Church of Christ's Commission for Racial Justice. The Commission, organized in 1963 in response to the assassination of civil rights activist Medgar Evers and the infamous Birmingham, Alabama, church bombing, coordinated racial justice strategies for national and regional organizations and spearheaded community organization and criminal justice campaigns.

In February of 1971, Chavis was in Wilmington, North Carolina, to drum up support for a school desegregation lawsuit that had been brought by the NAACP. On a night of racial violence, one of many in a season of escalating tension, Mike's Grocery, a white-owned store in a black part of

town, was firebombed. A year later, the Wilmington 10 (as the nine black men, including Chavis, and one white woman came to be known) were convicted of arson and conspiracy and sentenced to a combined total of 282 years in prison, with the lengthiest term, 34 years, slapped on Chavis.

World Focused on his Imprisonment

The case immediately garnered worldwide attention and became a celebrated focus of the civil rights movement in the United States. Defense attorneys cited 2,685 errors in the trial, but appeals were denied, and the convicted agitators went to prison in 1976. A year later, Amnesty International, the human rights watchdog agency, listed the ten as political prisoners. Ironically, the NAACP—the organization that Chavis had joined when he was only 12 years old and would one day head—was seen by some as offering one of the weakest responses to the obviously wrongful convictions.

While in prison, Chavis, who had been taught by King to see the positive in a negative experience, was frequently escorted in leg irons and handcuffs to Duke University, where he earned a master's degree from the divinity school under a study-release program. A disciplined student—he had taken his undergraduate degree in chemistry from the University of North Carolina at Charlotte in 1969—Chavis dodged the prison's strict, 10 P.M., lights-out rule by reading his school books in the bathroom, which was lighted all night.

The Wilmington 10 case took a dramatic turn when three principal prosecution witnesses from the trial admitted they had made up their stories after being pressured by local law enforcement authorities. North Carolina governor James Hunt reduced the sentences but left the convictions intact. Finally in 1980, after Chavis and the other activists had been paroled, a Justice Department investigation led to a federal appellate court's reversal of the convictions. "Our case was a victory for the whole movement," Chavis noted in *Newsweek.* "It showed people what is possible."

In 1983, two years after receiving his doctorate in divinity from Howard University, Chavis returned to the United Church of Christ's Commission for Racial Justice as deputy director. (The commission was one of several groups that had championed the release of the Wilmington 10.) By 1985, Chavis had been elected executive director of the commission and soon emerged as a national figure willing to exercise his preacher's oratory on a wide variety of racial and social justice issues in the United States. He organized gang summits to denounce the skyrocketing violence, high drop-out rate, and rampant drug involvement plaguing America's young people. He also participated in mainstream national politics, lobbying with other black leaders against U.S. aid to Angolan rebels fighting the Marxist regime of Jose Eduardo dos Santos, and serving as the clergy coordinator for the Reverend Jesse Jackson's 1984 presidential campaign.

Pioneered Concept of "Environmental Racism"

During his tenure at the Commission for Racial Justice, Chavis became most associated with the burgeoning environmental movement. In 1983 Chavis had joined in a protest against the depositing of tons of contaminated soil in rural Warren County, North Carolina, where the population was 75 percent black—the highest concentration of black citizens in the state—and mostly poor. Although the Warren County battle was lost, the protesters succeeded in shelving the state's plans to put another landfill and an incinerator in the area. Chavis, educated in school as a chemist and in the streets as an activist, saw the political issue clearly: industry's garbage was being foisted on the lower-class, politically unempowered members of society.

Coining the term "environmental racism," Chavis ordered a study that documented the extent of the crisis: three of the five largest toxic waste landfills in the country were in minority neighborhoods. Chavis spared few in his condemnation of this previously overlooked embodiment of racism. He chastised federal, state, and local governments; the mainstream environmental organizations, which were headed by whites and, in his view, cared more about the integrity of a wetland than the health of a black person; and big businesses that cavalierly promised jobs in impoverished communities in exchange for support of environmentally ruinous industries. "One of the responsibilities of the civil rights movement is to define the postmodern manifestations of racism," Chavis explained in *Ebony.* "We must not only point to overt forms of racism, but also to institutionalized racism."

Speaking at the 1987 First National People of Color Environmental Leadership Summit, which was attended by activists, professionals, and politicians, Chavis impressed upon conference participants the need to "rescue the environment from the clutches of persons and institutions gone mad with racism and greed," according to an account in *Audubon*. The summit cast much needed light on the environmental devastation plaguing minority communities—not only those of African Americans, but of Mexican American farmers, Native Americans, and the indigenous peoples of Alaska. Chavis thus became one of the most prominent spokespersons on environmental policy. After the election of President Bill Clinton in 1992, Chavis served as a senior advisor to the transition team studying the departments of Energy, the Interior, and Agriculture, as well as the Environmental Protection Agency.

Some observers noted that when Bill Clinton named of dozens of African Americans to top administration positions, he depleted the ranks of candidates qualified to fill the position of NAACP executive director, a post that Benjamin Hooks was vacating after 16 years in office. Still, the names under consideration were hardly minor league: Chavis; minister-activist Jesse Jackson; Jewell Jackson McCabe, founder and president of the Coalition of 100 Black Women; and Earl F. Shinhoster, a regional NAACP official. The appointment process began to look like a high-pressure political campaign. McCabe urged the predominantly male 64-member board to elect the first woman to the post, while Chavis sent each board member a 14-minute videotape detailing his personal history, his commitment to the NAACP, and his vision of the organization's future. Most of the attention, however, focused on the controversial Jackson, who withdrew from the race two days before the election, apparently over a change in the NAACP's constitution that he felt would decrease the power of the executive director.

Upon his election in 1993, Chavis proclaimed: "Now is the time for healing. Now is the time for unity." However, it was soon discovered that Chavis had begun earmarking the organization's funds as hush money for a legal settlement on a sexual harassment case against him and for other controversial initiatives. In a bizarre twist of events, Chavis was fired by the NAACP's board of directors in 1994.

Further Reading

Audubon, January-February 1992, p. 30.

Black Enterprise, July 1993, p. 17.

Boston Globe, April 10, 1993, p. 3; April 18, 1993, p. 85.

Detroit Free Press, April 14, 1993.

Ebony, July 1993, pp. 76-80.

Economist, April 17, 1993, p. 27.

Emerge, June 1993, pp. 27-28; September 1993, pp. 38-42.

Jet, April 26, 1993.

Newsweek, August 1, 1983, p. 9; June 14, 1993, pp. 68-69; August 29, 1994, p. 27.

New York Times, April 10, 1993, p. 10; April 11, 1993, p. 20; May 2, 1993.

People, July 19, 1993, pp. 65-66.

Time, July 19, 1993, p. 33.

Wall Street Journal, April 12, 1993, p. B5.

Washington Post, April 10, 1993, p. A1; April 26, 1993. □

Richard B. Cheney

Loyal service under four Republican presidents and a decade of leadership in Congress brought Richard B. Cheney (born 1941) to the inner circle in President George Bush's cabinet as secretary of defense. President Bush's son and governor of Texas, George W. Bush, selected Cheney as his vice presidential running mate on the Republican ticket in the 2000 election. After controversial vote recounts in Florida, Bush and Cheney won by a narrow margin and were sworn in as president and vice president respectively on January 20, 2001.

Born in Lincoln, Nebraska, on January 30, 1941, "Dick" Cheney was raised in Casper, Wyoming, by his parents, Richard H., a Department of Agriculture employee, and Marjorie L. Dickey. After a stellar secondary school career, he floundered at Yale, leaving in his sophomore year to return home, where he worked for the next two years before returning to college. Beginning again at the University of Wyoming in 1963, he quickly won his B.A. in political science in 1965 and one year later was granted the M.A. in the same discipline.

The Road to Washington Through Wyoming

While at Wyoming he undertook several internships, one with the state legislature and another in the governor's office. These whetted his appetite for government service and led him to apply for a coveted fellowship which brought him to the Washington office of one of the House's most highly respected members, William A. Steiger of Wisconsin.

The assignment drew him to the capital in 1968, a year of turmoil marking the end of eight years of Democratic control of both White House and Congress. While some careers were eclipsing, Cheney's was just beginning to rise. The Nixon administration, hungry for youthful blood, put him to work as special assistant to Donald Rumsfeld, director of the Office of Economic Opportunity. Cheney and Rumsfeld worked well together, the latter taking Cheney with him as deputy when he became White House counsel and as assistant director of operations when Rumsfeld became director of the Cost of Living Council. These positions, which Cheney held from May 1969 to March 1973, gave him an enviable education in government from the inside.

But Watergate Washington in 1973 was no place for a non-lawyer in his early thirties, particularly one with limited private employment experience. He took the vice presidency of an investment advisory group named Bradley, Woods and Company. Agnew's resignation in 1973 and Nixon's departure the following summer thus passed him harmlessly by and in fact opened new horizons.

Joining the Ford Administration

In August 1974 the call came to join Donald Rumsfeld on President Gerald Ford's transition staff. Cheney began life in the new administration at a considerably higher level than he had left the old. He was to serve as deputy assistant to the president, seconding yet again his close associate, Rumsfeld.

In the heady air of the White House, where absurdity is often called reality, Cheney remained himself: loyal, good-natured, pragmatically conservative, extremely civil, and extraordinarily hard-working. These traits brought him to the post of assistant to the president and chief of staff when Rumsfeld became Ford's choice to head the Department of Defense.

Cheney served the president from November 1975 until the end of his administration in January 1977. In the execution of his duties, he cultivated an old-fashioned "passion for anonymity" that would have done justice to many in the eras of Franklin Roosevelt and Eisenhower.

As chief of staff he was privy to the issues confronting Ford those days and had a direct role in advisement on political matters as well as responsibilities for scheduling the president and managing the White House staff. Once more, this was an education no graduate school could impart.

Return to Wyoming, Then a Return to Washington

Ford's defeat by Jimmy Carter sent Cheney back to Wyoming and private employment. But the lure of Washington was too great, and in 1978 he entered the Republican primary, winning it despite being stricken by a coronary attack in the midst of his campaign. Defeating his Democratic opponent in November, he entered the 96th Congress as his state's solitary member of the House of Representatives.

During the next decade of his life, from January 1979 until March 1989, Congressman Cheney consistently defined himself as a compassionate conservative. He made friends easily in both parties, assuming a leadership position early in his career. Re-election came easy to him, and he captured Wyoming's seat five times. Well-liked by his party, he was elected chairman of the Republican House Policy Committee in his second term, an unprecedented feat.

Cheney's political career as a congressman was benefitted greatly by the return of the Republicans to the White House in 1981. In domestic matters he joined right-of-center Republicans on issues such as abortion. In defense policy, he enthusiastically endorsed Carter, then Reagan, defense build up, including the Strategic Defense Initiative (SDI, or Star Wars). And in foreign policy he supported Reagan's stands on Nicaragua and Afghanistan. Nor did he neglect Wyoming, espousing popular positions on environmental issues while supporting reasonable use of the state's mineral and forestry resources. For example, Cheney once refused the requests of other congressmen who only wanted to "borrow" some of Wyoming's share of Colorado River water. They would give it back, they promised, and were even willing to put it in writing, after the water shortage eased. "No way," said Cheney. "Once they get it we'll never get it back. That's how things work."

His standing in Congress made him a natural choice for service on the House Select Committee to Investigate Covert Arms Deals with Iran. Elected as the ranking Republican, and therefore co-chair, he disagreed strongly with the majority report, defending the Reagan administration on the Iran-Contra episode without whitewashing it.

Secretary of Defense

His ten years of service in the House made him a widely respected national figure. The combination of executive-legislative experience gave him an uncommon perspective and compensated for some of the shortcomings which might have impeded his confirmation as defense secretary. Lack of personal military service and little experience in dealing with the Pentagon were built-in objections to his suitability. But these were not seriously entertained, partly because of the circumstances of the Tower rejection but most probably and principally because of the character and nature of Cheney himself. He was up to the job, even if his resume might not trumpet the fact.

He came to the position with a track record of enthusiasm for weapons systems but at a time of severe retrenchment made imperative by the deficit crisis at home and possible by the disintegration of the Soviet Union as a world-class antagonist. He early established control over the massive military-civilian bureaucracy, reprimanding one general and removing another for remarks he deemed beyond their authority. It was clear that civilian control of the military as a principle would not suffer under his tenure.

His capacity for crisis management was demonstrated in the invasion of Panama, a foreign policy-military operation that proceeded successfully to the seizure of Panama's free-wheeling chief of state, General Manual Noriega. But Secretary Cheney's most important test came in August 1990 with the Iraqi invasion and occupation of Kuwait. Responding to President Bush's call for American troop involvement in the defense of Saudi Arabia, Secretary Cheney undertook a massive movement of material and personnel to the Persian Gulf, where, in response to United Nations Security Council resolutions, they joined other nations from all quarters in pursuing the restoration of the Kuwait monarchy and the protection of America's interests. On January 16, 1991 these resources were employed in a violent air war against Iraq. This was followed by a ground attack launched February 23 that destroyed the bulk of Iraq's military forces in 100 hours. Cheney's key role, along with Chief of Staff Colin Powell, made both men popular heroes. With the formal surrender of Iraq, Cheney turned to the task of reducing the strength of the U.S. military, closing surplus military bases, and other cost-cutting devices. His solid reputation and stand-out professionalism helped him carry out these largely unpopular measures.

During his tenure, President Bush, Secretary of State James Baker, and Cheney shaped their party's national security policy. The Bush team reduced the military budget, shrank the size of U.S. military forces, and engaged in a flurry of negotiations that ultimately produced the START I and START II treaties, the Conventional Forces in Europe agreement, and the Chemical Weapons Convention. Bush and Baker led the way to a doubling of the number of U.N. peacekeeping operations across the globe. They all grappled with the issue of disarmament. Cheney's statement, reflecting the Bush administration's course, attested to no new or emerging policy on arms and security: "Arms for America's friends and arms control for its potential foes."

A Voice in Government

Cheney remained Secretary of Defense until 1994, through the political changing of the guard which resulted in the election of Democrat Bill Clinton as president. After leaving his official duties as Secretary of Defense, Cheney remained a voice in government affairs, and frequently commented on Clinton administration choices. In January 1994, Cheney said that the United States should avoid "getting consumed with the problems in Moscow" and instead concentrate on building strong relationships with all the republics of the former Soviet Union, especially Ukraine. In September 1994, he described the U.S. attempts to withdraw quickly from Haiti as "serious misjudgement" while pointing to the difficulties faced while attempting to leave Somalia. With tight budget times and downsizing at the Pentagon under way under the Clinton administration, Cheney was one of the eight civilian Secretaries of Defense invited to give "advice to the re-elected commander in chief" at a special event in Atlanta. In April 1997, he sent a letter to the Senate to protest the imminent ratification of the Chemical Weapons Convention.

Cheney was regarded as corporate America's choice for the 1996 Republican presidential nomination, although he removed his name from consideration almost two years before the election. His name was published as one of 15 possible vice presidential candidates as selected by Republican presidential candidate Bob Dole.

Cheney became part of corporate America when he was named chief executive at the Halliburton Co. in 1995. Under his leadership the company grew to become the largest oil-drilling, engineering and construction services provider in the world. When Halliburton acquired Dresser Industries in 1999, it expanded its product lines and increased opportunities for future growth.

In 2000, Texas governor and presidential candidate, George W. Bush, asked Cheney to be his running mate on the Republican ticket. The issue of Cheney's health was raised during the campaign. Suffering from chronic coronary artery disease, he experienced the first of several heart attacks at the age of 37. Despite these concerns Cheney felt that he had recovered sufficiently to take on the responsibilities of the vice presidency. Bush and Cheney won by a narrow margin and were sworn in as president and vice president respectively on January 20, 2001.

His wife, Lynne (Vincent) Cheney, whom he married in 1964, was a distinguished author and public figure and chairperson of the National Endowment for the Humanities. She has a doctorate in English, is a former editor of Washingtonian magazine and taught at several colleges and universities. They have two daughters, Elizabeth and Mary.

Further Reading

Some biographical data on Cheney's governmental career can be gleaned from accounts of his White House contemporaries and from those of journalists. Gerald Ford's account, *A Time To Heal* (1979), and John Osborne's *White House Watch: The Ford Years* (1977), fit those categories. For Cheney's part in the Iran-Contra investigation, see *Congressional Quarterly Almanac, 1987,* Vol. LXIII. His views on congressional responsibilities over national security, delivered at the end of his first year at the Department of Defense, can be found in "Legislative-Executive Relations in National Security," *Vital Speeches* (March 15, 1990). ☐

Chief Joseph

The American Indian Joseph (ca. 1840-1904), a Nez Percé chief, fought to preserve his homeland and did much to awaken the conscience of America to the plight of Native Americans.

Joseph was born in the Wallowa Valley of northeastern Oregon. In 1871, upon the death of his father, he assumed leadership of the nontreaty Nez Percé. White settlers coveted the traditional homeland of these Native Americans, and Joseph, seeking confirmation of Nez Percé territorial rights, met with Federal commissioners to discuss a spurious treaty in which the Indians had supposedly ceded their land to the U.S. government. The commissioners were disconcerted by Joseph, who stood 6 feet tall, was amicable but firm, and spoke with amazing eloquence.

Despite the obvious fraudulence of the old treaty, President Ulysses S. Grant opened the Nez Percé lands to settlement and ordered the Native Americans onto reservations. White settlers moved onto the land and committed atrocities against the Indians. Against his will, Joseph was forced by his tribesmen to fight. Pressed hard by Gen. Oliver Otis Howard's forces, Joseph was convinced that he could not win and began a lengthy withdrawal toward Canada. Pursued by Howard and harassed by many small detachments, Joseph fled toward Canada and thrilled the nation, whose sympathies were with the Native Americans.

During the fall of 1877 Joseph led his 500 followers into Montana. In the fighting he showed rare military genius and great humanity; he refused to make war on women and children, bought his supplies when possible, and allowed no mutilation of bodies. On October 1, as the Nez Percé paused to rest at the Bear Paw Mountains just 30 miles from Canada, they were surprised by Col. N. A. Miles with approximately 600 soldiers. With only 87 warriors, Joseph chose to fight. He would not abandon the children, the women, and the aged. After a 5-day siege, however, he said to Miles and his followers: "It is cold and we have no blankets. The little children are freezing to death. . . . Hear me, my chiefs. I am tired; my heart is sick and sad. From where the sun now stands, I will fight no more forever."

The 431 remaining Nez Percé were taken to Kansas and subsequently to the Indian Territory (Oklahoma). There so many of them sickened and died that an aroused American public demanded action. Chief Joseph was moved to Colville Reservation in Washington, along with 150 of his followers; the others were returned to Oregon. Joseph made many pleas to be returned to his tribal homeland, but he died on Sept. 21, 1904, and was buried on the Colville Reservation.

Further Reading

The best of the many biographies of Joseph is Merrill D. Beal, *I Will Fight No More Forever: Chief Joseph and the Nez Percé War* (1963). Other interesting works include Helen Howard and Dan McGrath, *War Chief Joseph* (1941; published in 1965 as *Saga of Chief Joseph*), and Lucullus McWhorter, *Hear Me, My Chiefs,* edited by Ruth Bordin (1952). □

Noam Avram Chomsky

Noam Chomsky (born 1928), American linguist and philosopher, was responsible for the theory of transformational grammar. As a political commentator he was critical of American foreign and domestic policy.

Noam Avram Chomsky was born in Philadelphia on December 7, 1928. He studied at the University of Pennsylvania, receiving his Ph.D. in linguistics in 1955. After that year, he taught at the Massachusetts Institute of Technology, where he was Institute Professor of Linguistics.

Chomsky received international acclaim for his work in linguistics, philosophy, and social/political theory. A prolific writer, he revolutionized linguistics with his theory of transformational-generative grammar. His work in epistemology and philosophy of mind was controversial; his social and political writings were consistently critical of American foreign and domestic policy.

Transformational Grammar

In two seminal books on linguistic theory—*Syntactic Structures* (1957) and *Aspects of the Theory of Syntax* (1965)—Chomsky argued that the grammar of human language is a formal system consisting of abstract logical structures which are systematically rearranged by operations to generate all possible sentences of a language. Chomsky's theory is applicable to all components of linguistic description (phonology, morphology, syntax, semantics, and so forth). In phonology, for example, Chomsky argues that the sound system of a language consists of a set of abstract binary features (phonemic level) which are combined and recombined by means of phonological processes to produce the sounds which people actually say (phonetic level) (see Chomsky and Halle's *The Sound Pattern of English*, 1968). In syntax, which has received the most attention by linguists, the theory specifies a set of abstract phrase-structure rules (deep structures) which undergo transformations to produce all possible sentences (surface structures).

Chomsky's assumption was that a grammar is finite, but that the sentences which people produce are theoretically infinite in length and number. Thus, a grammar must generate, from finite means, all and only the infinite set of grammatical sentences in a language. Chomsky has further argued that all languages have the same underlying, abstract structure—universal grammar.

Evidence for these claims is strong. The most commonly cited evidence is that children learn language rapidly, totally, and similarly by the age of five or six, irrespective of the culture into which they are born or the language which they learn. Chomsky thus claimed that children have innate linguistic competence, a reflection of universal grammar.

Chomsky broke from previous structuralist dominance of linguistics and revolutionized the field in several ways. First, he converted linguistics into a theoretical discipline. Second, he pluralized the word "grammar": he showed that there are many possible theories of language—grammars—and he argued that the purpose of scientific linguistics is to demonstrate which of all possible grammars is the most explanatory feasible. Third, he linked linguistics to mathematics, psychology, philosophy, and neuropsychology, thereby broadening the discipline immensely.

Chomsky's later work in linguistics focused on spelling out the details of universal grammar. He was particularly concerned with the sorts of constraints that limit the power of transformations (see, for example, *Lectures on Government and Binding,* 1981).

Critics of Chomsky generally argued that grammar is not a formal system, but a social tool. They raised as counter-evidence such things as language variation, social and cultural differences in language use, and what they claim to be the unprovability of the innateness hypothesis: that innateness is a theorist's intuition, not an empirical fact. In all fairness to Chomsky, he never ruled out variation or the functional aspect of language, but preferred instead to focus on the similarities across languages. His work, furthermore, generated considerable interest in both the neuropsychology and biology of language, which provided considerable evidence for innateness.

Rationalist Philosopher, Political Theorist

Chomsky demolished any connection between linguistics and behaviorist psychology with the scathing "Review of B. F. Skinner's *Verbal Behavior*" (1959), in which he argued that stimulus-response theory could in no way account for the creativity and speed of language learning. He then produced a series of books in favor of rationalism, the theory that a human is born with innate organizing principles and is not a tabula rasa (blank slate): *Cartesian Linguistics* (1966), *Language and Mind* (1972), *Reflections on Language* (1975), and *Rules and Representations* (1980).

Chomsky's rationalism engendered a resurgence of work in faculty psychology, the theory that the human mind consists of discrete modules which are specialized for particular cognitive processes: vision and language, for example. One of his statements in rationalist philosophy was *Modular Approaches to the Study of Mind* (1984).

Critic of American Policy Motives

Chomsky was also an ardent critic of American domestic and foreign policy. His libertarian socialist ideas can be found in such works as *American Power and the New Mandarins* (1969), *For Reasons of State* (1973), *The Political Economy of Human Rights* (1979), and *Towards a New Cold War* (1982). Chomsky's position was always that American international aggression is rooted in the American industrial system, where capitalism, by its aggressive, dehumanizing, and dominating nature, spawns a corresponding militaristic policy. Historian Michael Beschloss, writing for the *Washington Post Book World* found in Chomsky's *American Power and the New Mandarins* a strong denunciation of the "system of values and decision-making that drove the United States to the jungles of Southeast Asia." Chomsky's strongest vitriol, however, was directed toward the so-called "New Mandarins"—the technocrats, bureaucrats, and university-trained scholars who defended America's right to dominate the globe. *Times Literary Supplement* contributor, Charles Townshend noted that Chomsky "[sees] a totalitarian mentality" arising out of the mainstream American belief in the fundamental righteousness and benevolence of the United States, the sanctity and nobility of its aims. Yet "the publicly tolerated spectrum of discussion" of these aims is narrow. Chomsky transcended that narrow spectrum by offering examples to illuminate how American policies proved otherwise. Chomsky's political views, though, caused his historical/political scholarship to be taken less seriously than his work in linguistics. Steve Wasserman wrote in the *Los Angeles Times Book Review* that Chomsky had been "banished to the margins of political debate. His opinions have been deemed so kooky—and his personality so cranky—that his

writings no longer appear in the forums . . . in which he was once so welcome."

In later years Chomsky continued his criticism of American foreign policy in works such as *The ABC's of U.S. Policy Toward Haiti* (1994), *Free Trade and Democracy* (1993), *Rent-A-Cops of the World: Noam Chomsky on the Gulf Crisis* (1991), and *The New World Order Debate* (1991). Appreciation, if not acceptance, attended Chomsky's later works. According to Christopher Lehmann-Haupt in the *New York Times,* Chomsky "continues to challenge our assumptions long after other critics have gone to bed. He has become the foremost gadfly of our national conscience." *New Statesman* correspondent Francis Hope concluded of Chomsky's lingering suspicions of government motives: "Such men are dangerous; the lack of them is disasterous."

Further Reading

Noam Chomsky's positions, written in readable form, are presented in his own two books, *Language and Responsibility* (1979) and *The Generative Enterprise* (1982). Good accounts of, and commentaries on, his ideas and theories can be found in Lyons' *Noam Chomsky* (1970), Newmeyer's *Linguistic Theory in America* (1980), Smith and Wilson's *Modern Linguistics: The Results of Chomsky's Revolution* (1979), and Piattelli-Palmarini's *Language and Learning: The Debate between Jean Piaget and Noam Chomsky* (1980).

For more insight on Chomsky's political views see Robert F. Barsky, *Noam Chomsky: A Life of Dissent,* 1997. □

Warren Minor Christopher

Lawyer and government official Warren Minor Christopher (born 1925) became U.S. secretary of state in 1993 by appointment of President Bill Clinton.

W arren Minor Christopher was born on October 27, 1925, in Scranton, North Dakota. His parents were Ernest W. and Catherine Anne (Lemen) Christopher. His father, a banker, died when Christopher was young. His mother moved the family to California.

Christopher attended Hollywood High School. In 1942 he entered the University of Redlands, but transferred to the University of Southern California to complete his studies. He graduated in 1945 with a B.S. degree with honors and finished serving his three years, from 1943 to 1946, in the U.S. Naval Reserve.

Christopher's plan to become a lawyer began by enrolling in Stanford University's law school in 1946. He earned his LL.B. degree in 1949. After graduation he was selected for a very prestigious position: law clerk to Justice William O. Douglas of the U.S. Supreme Court.

After one year in Washington, D.C., Christopher returned to his hometown and joined a law firm. From 1950 on he split his career between practicing law and public service. He was a special counsel to California Governor Edmund Brown and vice-chairman of a commission the governor established in 1965 to investigate the causes of the urban riots in Watts, Los Angeles. Christopher also served as

a consultant to the U.S. State Department and helped negotiate several international trade agreements.

President Lyndon Johnson appointed Christopher as deputy attorney general in June 1967. Johnson selected him to assist federal efforts to combat the urban riots in Detroit during July 1967 and in Chicago during April 1968. He served in that office until Johnson's term expired in January 1969. Christopher returned to his law firm in California.

President Jimmy Carter called Christopher back to work in the nation's capital in 1977. Christopher was appointed as deputy secretary of state. A highlight of his term in office occurred after militants in Iran seized the United States embassy and held its occupants as hostages from November 1979 to January 1981. Carter put Christopher in charge of negotiating the release of the 52 captured Americans. For his skillful and successful negotiations, he was awarded the Medal of Freedom, the nation's highest civilian award. When Carter left office in 1981, Christopher returned to California and resumed his law practice. He headed a commission to investigate charges of brutality and racism in the Los Angeles Police Department in 1991.

In 1992 Christopher was again called back into national public service. His record of having worked in every Democratic presidential administration since he was an adult continued with the election of President Bill Clinton. When Clinton won enough votes in the 1992 campaign to be assured of the Democratic Party's nomination, he asked Christopher to head the team to select a vice presidential running mate (Albert Gore). After the November 1992 election, Clinton asked Christopher to help select members to

the new cabinet and to head the transition staff for the newly elected president. Clinton appointed Christopher as secretary of state in his first round of cabinet choices.

In 1993, Christopher was sworn in as the 63rd U.S. secretary of state. A series of international problems gave the new secretary of state little time to relax. After establishing some degree of order in Somalia, American troops were withdrawn by the end of March 1994. Meanwhile, in April the civil war among the states of the former Yugoslavia entered its second year and peace negotiations in the Middle East continued to be a sensitive issue. After Clinton was re-elected in 1996 to a second presidential term, Christopher resigned. During his four years with the cabinet, he played an important role in several foreign policy successes. Including a historic peace accord between Israel and the Palestinian Liberation Organization (PLO).

Christopher married Marie Josephine Wyllis on December 21, 1956. An earlier marriage had ended in divorce. He had four children: Lynn, Scott, Thomas, and Kristen.

Further Reading

Warren Christopher co-edited a book on the negotiations to free the Americans held in the embassy takeover, *American Hostages in Iran: The Conduct of a Crisis* (1985). *In the Stream of History: Shaping Foreign Policy for a New Era* (1998), collects 45 of Warren's speeches from his time as secretary of state. Christopher is listed in *Who's Who in America* .

Additional Sources

New Republic, February 1, 1993.

Time, June 7, 1993, pp. 32-33; June 26, 1995, pp. 31-33.

U.S. News & World Report, July 5, 1993, p. 24. □

Walter Percy Chrysler

The American manufacturer Walter Percy Chrysler (1875-1940) was a self-trained engineer who formed one of the three major automobile companies in the United States.

The son of a Union Pacific Railroad engineer, Walter Chrysler was fascinated by machinery at an early age. He turned down a chance to go to college to become an apprentice in the Union Pacific shops at Ellis, Kans. Hard-working, intelligent, and determined to master every aspect of his craft, Chrysler then worked as a machinist in a series of railroad shops throughout the Midwest. Moving into positions of greater responsibility, he emerged in 1910 as superintendent of motive power for the Chicago Great Western Railroad. As an official in the mechanical branch of railroading, Chrysler knew he had little chance of moving into the top echelons of the corporate structure, and so in 1910 he took a position as works manager of the American Locomotive Company in Pittsburgh, beginning at a salary of $8,000 per year.

At this time General Motors Corporation, formed by William C. Durant in 1908, was in financial difficulties. In order to avoid bankruptcy for the $60-million group of plants manufacturing both automobiles and components, a syndicate of bankers holding GM securities forced Durant out in 1910 and made Charles W. Nash, a self-trained engineer, president. Aware of Chrysler's efficient management of American Locomotive, Nash in 1912 persuaded Chrysler to become works manager of Buick at a cut in salary from $12,000 to $6,000.

Increased Production at Buick

Production methods at Buick were inefficient and expensive because cars were still being made by slow, handwork methods traditional in the manufacture of expensive carriages. Chrysler immediately reorganized the Buick shops into efficient units centered on construction by machinery and introduced the production-line method of automobile building inaugurated by Henry Ford. The results were impressive. The output of cars rose from 45 to 200 per day. At the same time Buick was chiefly responsible for a rise in GM's profits from $7 million to $28 million between 1913 and 1916.

Through skillful financial manipulations, Durant returned to the presidency of GM in 1916 and appointed Chrysler president of Buick at a salary of $500,000 per year, payable largely in stock. During the next 4 years production surged ahead, and Buick continued to provide most of the profits for GM. But Chrysler found Durant's interference in Buick's affairs increasingly irritating. He disapproved strongly of Durant's wholesale purchase of new plants for GM, some of them of marginal value to the combination, financially unstable, and difficult to integrate into GM's operations. Finally, in 1920 Chrysler resigned, intending to retire on his considerable savings. But in 1922, at the behest of a banking syndicate, he took on the job of salvaging the Willys-Overland Company from bankruptcy at a salary of $1 million per year.

An important part of the recovery program was the designing of a high-performance car in the $1,500 range which would compete with luxury cars selling for $5,000 and up. Shortly after the start of the Willys-Overland undertaking, Chrysler accepted responsibility for a similar reorganization of the Maxwell Motor Company. Through the efforts of three capable engineers the new Chrysler car was completed at the Maxwell plant in 1924 and exhibited in New York.

Birth of Chrysler Corporation

Public enthusiasm for his new car enabled Chrysler to raise the funds to get it into mass production, and in 1925 the Maxwell Company was rechartered as the Chrysler Corporation. Because of increasing demand for the car, Chrysler purchased the Dodge Brothers Manufacturing Company in 1928. Capitalized at approximately $432 million, Chrysler Corporation was the second-largest automobile producer in the nation.

During the Depression, Chrysler followed a policy of rigorous reduction of debt and improvements on the line of cars—Chrysler, DeSoto, and Plymouth. Thus by 1937, when demand surged back, the company was in a secure position.

A bluff, abrupt man, Chrysler nevertheless had a warm, outgoing personality which enabled him to make and keep friends even in times of disagreement. His success was due primarily to his ability to rationalize production, cut costs to the bone, and constantly improve his product. Moreover, he showed a remarkable ability to grow with his job. During his automotive years he became as adept at managing the financial and marketing ends of his business as in the actual production of automobiles. He retired in 1935 and died 5 years later.

Further Reading

The most detailed information on Chrysler is in his autobiography, written with Boyden Sparkes, *Life of an American Workman* (1938). Chrysler describes his managerial methods in B. C. Forbes and O. D. Foster, *Automotive Giants of America: Men Who Are Making Our Motor Industry* (1926). Thomas C. Cochran gives an excellent account of Chrysler's business career in John A. Garraty, ed., *The Unforgettable Americans* (1960). Chrysler's years at Buick and the history of the Chrysler Corporation receive good coverage in two volumes by John B. Rae, *American Automobile Manufacturers: The First Forty Years* (1959) and *The American Automobile: A Brief History* (1965). □

Henry G. Cisneros

Politician, college professor, cabinet member, and network executive, Henry G. Cisneros (born 1947) was elected mayor of San Antonio in 1981, the first Hispanic mayor in Texas, and became by the mid-1980s the nation's most prominent and publicly visible Hispanic leader.

Born in 1947, Henry Cisneros was the eldest of five children of Mexican-American George and Mexican-born Elvira Cisneros. Henry was raised in what was later described as a model home environment for an upwardly mobile ethnic family. His father, a civil servant at a nearby military base, and his mother were keenly ambitious for their children, prescribing piano lessons, Scout memberships, visits to the opera and symphony, and limited television viewing only after their homework and family responsibilities had been fulfilled.

The Cisneros family switched from Spanish to English use in the home when the children were born because the language of the schools was English and home use of the language of instruction would certainly help them to do better. It paid off. All five children became college graduates, including two Ph.Ds. Future mayor Henry Cisneros, who received a B.A. degree from Texas A&M University, an M.A. from Harvard University, and a Ph.D. in public administration from George Washington University in 1975, was selected as a White House Fellow and later worked for the Department of Health, Education, and Welfare when it was under Elliott Richardson.

Entry Into Politics

In 1974 doctoral candidate Cisneros returned to San Antonio, where he was employed as an assistant professor at the University of Texas branch campus. Always interested in public policy and politics, Cisneros won a seat on the city council in 1975 and was reelected in 1977 and 1979.

Although sensitive to the special needs of the Hispanic community, Cisneros studiously avoided an association with one of the city's most controversial advocacy groups, Communities Organized for Public Service (COPS), which specialized in Saul Alinsky style 1960s confrontation politics with the city fathers, planners, and future employers. It was not only a matter of style but a deep conviction on Cisneros's part that confrontation tactics could be counterproductive to the city's economic health. He also had a strong belief in the socially redeeming power of economic growth.

Elected mayor in 1981 at the age of 33 by a landslide 63 percent of the vote, which included solid Hispanic support and a sizable Anglo vote, Cisneros went on to enlarge his election majority in 1983 to an astonishing 94 percent of the vote and to 73 percent in 1985. Clearly his style and programs had won over the hearts and minds of residents of all colors and creeds. Downtown development, job expansion, and new factories and businesses were the hallmarks of the Cisneros administrations. The mayor boasted that he spent 85 percent of his time recruiting and luring high technology industry to his city. An unabashed booster, he was a firm believer in the benefits of economic expansion and business growth. No growth, he warned, translates into fewer opportunities and stunted mobility for the citizens.

He described himself as a "technocrat" and seemed to be in tune with the temper of the times in helping to re-start the economic engines and rekindle economic growth. He stressed the need for economic expansion and not the expansion of welfare as a solution to social problems. As one observer noted: "A Martin Luther King he is not." The mayor backed up his boosterism with substance. When once told by a potential industrial re-locator that the city's University of Texas branch lacked programs in key engineering fields, Cisneros got together a committee that persuaded the state educational authorities to remedy that need.

Scandal Tarnishes Reputation

Cisneros married his high school sweetheart, Mary Alice Perez, in 1969 and was the father of two daughters and a son. In 1988 his public announcement of an extramarital affair with Linda Medlar led to his resignation as mayor and the near destruction of his marriage. He reunited with his wife primarily because his infant son had been born the previous year with a defective heart. Although Cisneros supposedly ended the affair with Medlar, he continued making support payments to her after he left office and founded Cisneros Assets Management Company. In 1993 Cisneros was appointed Secretary of Housing and Urban Development (HUD) by President Bill Clinton. As HUD secretary Cisneros worked hard to reverse decades of Federal housing policy that promoted racism and to make the department's programs more efficient. Despite his efforts, though, the Medlar controversy would not go away. Upon accepting his position with HUD, Cisneros had ended his payments to Medlar. In 1994 the former mistress sued Cisneros, citing that she had been promised $4,000 a month until her daughter graduated from college. For his part, Cisneros claimed that his $148,000 annual salary as HUD secretary was much less than he received as a private sector consultant and speaker, and made continued payments a financial impossibility. The core of Cisneros's problems, however, centered around his claim to the FBI of having provided $60,000 to Medlar between 1990 and 1992 while Medlar's records showed payments of $213,000.

The scandal worsened in late 1994 as tapes of conversations between Cisneros and Medlar surfaced in the press. From 1992 to 1993, Medlar had secretly taped her conversations with Cisneros. She sold the tapes to the tabloid TV news show *Inside Edition*. The fall-out from this unwanted publicity led to a further FBI investigation of Cisneros's financial reports used during his cabinet background check. In 1995 Attorney General Janet Reno appointed a special counsel to ascertain whether or not Cisneros had lied to the FBI. National Public Radio (NPR) reported Cisneros response as "I regret any mistakes that I may have made but affirm once again that I have at no point violated the public's trust." That same year Cisneros settled the Medlar suit for $49,000.

Cisneros was indicted by a federal grand jury in 1997 on 18 felony counts that included his failure to tell FBI agents about payments he made to Medlar. A federal appeals court denied Cisneros' request to dismiss the charges on March 9, 1999.

Resignation From HUD

Throughout his ordeal, Cisneros continued to receive the support of the Clinton administration, but decided in 1996 not to remain in his post during the president's second term in office. The *Associated Press* reported Cisneros's reasoning as financial. "Really, I came to do this for four years. I prayed I could stretch the finances that far," he said. "This is about as far as I can stretch it." At the time of Cisneros's departure from HUD in 1997, the investigation into his financial records was still ongoing.

In January of 1997 Cisneros was named president and chief operating officer of Univision Communications, the parent company of the dominant Hispanic network in the United States.

Further Reading

For his early life, see Richard Erickson, "Cisneros: Media Creation or Right Man," *Advertising Age* (June 1981), and biographical file from the mayor's office. For his later life and public career, see Nicholas Leman, "First Hispanic," *Esquire* (December 1984); Irwin Ross, "Mayor Cisneros of San Antonio," *Readers Digest* (December 1984); and *U.S. News and World Report* (December 10, 1984; May 20, 1985). A full-length biography *Cisneros: Portrait of a New American* by Kemper Diehl and Jan Jarboe, was published in 1985.

For more information on Cisneros's resignation from HUD, see *Lubbock Online* (http://lubbockonline.com/news/112296/cisneros.htm). In-depth coverage of Cisneros's move to Univision Communications can be found in an article by Tony Cantu at http://www.hisp.com/apr97/cisneros.html. (July 1997). □

Tom Clancy

Tom Clancy (born 1947) writes novels of adventure and espionage in the international military-industrial complex that have earned him enormous popularity in the 1980s as a creator of the "techno-thriller" genre.

Tom Clancy was born in Baltimore, Maryland, in 1947, the son of a mail carrier and a credit employee. After graduating Loyola College in Baltimore in 1969, Clancy married Wanda Thomas, an insurance agency manager, and became an insurance agent in Baltimore, and later in Hartford, Connecticut. In 1973, he joined the O.F. Bowen Agency in Owings, Maryland, becoming an owner there in 1980. His poor eyesight made him ineligible for a military career, but Clancy maintained an interest in the military and researched various aspects of the armed forces and military technology. The ideas for several novels and main characters he wrote in the 1980s were formed in the late 1970s while he was conducting research. During this time, Clancy wrote in his spare time while working and raising a family, and in 1984, his first novel, *The Hunt for Red October,* was published by The Naval Institute Press, a noncommercial publisher in Annapolis. The story of the defection of a Soviet submarine commander to the United States, the novel captured the spirit of the Reagan-era Cold War politics that called attention to Soviet military capabil-

ity and the United States' capacity to meet and surpass the Soviet challenge. *The Hunt for Red October* was noticed by President and Mrs. Reagan, who praised the book publicly and helped boost the novel to bestseller lists. Casper Weinberger, Reagan's Secretary of Defense, reviewed the book for *The Times Literary Supplement,* calling it "a splendid and riveting story" and praising the technical descriptions as "vast and accurate." Clancy's subsequent novels continued to feature plots based upon critical world political issues from the perspective of military or CIA personnel, including the international drug trade and terrorism. All of Clancy's popular novels have resided on bestseller lists, and *Clear and Present Danger* (1989) sold more copies than any other novel published in the 1980s, according to Louis Menand of *The New Yorker.* Today Clancy continues to write successful novels. Several of his books have been adapted as popular films, including *The Hunt for Red October, Patriot Games* (1987), and *Clear and Present Danger.*

Although, according to an interview with *Contemporary Authors* in 1988, Clancy claimed he did not create the "techno-thriller," his use of highly involved technical detail incorporated into complex, suspenseful plots made him the most successful practitioner of the genre and added a new level of military realism and sophistication to the traditional adventure novel. His books take their plots from the most pressing international concerns of his times. When the arms race was escalating in the 1980s, Clancy's novels *The Hunt for Red October, Red Storm Rising* (1986), and *The Cardinal of the Kremlin* (1988) used different aspects of the Soviet-American conflict for story lines. In the post-Cold War era, Clancy turned to the South American drug trade in *Clear and*

Present Danger, IRA terrorism in *Patriot Games,* and Middle East peace and nuclear proliferation in *The Sum of All Fears* (1991). Clancy takes his characters from various levels of military establishment insiders, from elite soldiers and crewman to commanders, generals, espionage operatives, and government officials. Their goals and motives are often clearly good or evil, and while later novels feature some ambivalence or introspection in lead characters, most of the moral choices characters face are straightforward questions of right and wrong. In addition to using declassified documents and tours of vessels and bases, Clancy conducted interviews with personnel in order to draw his characters accurately. The hero in many Clancy novels is Jack Ryan, a sometime CIA agent who epitomizes integrity, bravery, and ingenuity in a changing, high stakes world. Whether he is assigned to resolve a crisis, as in *Clear and Present Danger,* or stumbles accidently into an international incident and becomes a target for revenge, as in *Patriot Games,* Ryan is adept at using available technology to achieve his mission; as Clancy stated in the CA interview, "the superior individual is the guy who makes use of [new technology]." The accuracy of Clancy's descriptions of military-industrial technology and personnel has been characterized as remarkable for one outside the establishment, and his favorable portrayal of the American armed forces has earned him respect in military circles.

Ronald Reagan called *The Hunt for Red October* "the perfect yarn." This comment could be a summation of critical reception to Clancy's novels. Although some critics found the plots of *The Sum of All Fears* and *Clear and Present Danger* too lengthy and bogged down by the detailed technical descriptions, most agree that Clancy is successful in creating suspenseful, thrilling action stories. Appreciation of Clancy's technological details varies among critics; some find the insider's glimpse of weaponry and tactics presented with clarity, accuracy, and interest, while others, perhaps more knowledgeable about the technology described, find Clancy's renderings inaccurate and implausible. Critics are almost unanimous in their negative reaction to Clancy's skill at characterization, finding them underdeveloped, and the hero Jack Ryan too flawless and unbelievably virtuous. Clancy responded to criticism about Ryan by giving him some vices in later novels, a change some critics found unbelievable. Clancy's novels usually are received by critics in the spirit they are written, to entertain and educate while highlighting the important international issues of the times and showing how the United States can meet difficult challenges with moral integrity, courage, and the wise use of modern technology.

Further Reading

Bestsellers 89, Issue 1, Gale, 1989.

Bestsellers 90, Issue 1, Gale, 1990.

Contemporary Literary Criticism, Volume 45, Gale, 1987.

American Legion, December, 1991, p. 16.

Chicago Tribune Book World, September 7, 1986.

Detroit News, January 20, 1985.

Fortune, July 18, 1988; August 26, 1991.

Newsmakers, Cumulation, Gale, 1998. ☐

William Clark

The American explorer and soldier William Clark (1770-1838) was second in command of what has been called the American national epic of exploration, the Lewis and Clark expedition of 1804-1806, which traveled from the Missouri River to the Pacific Ocean.

William Clark was born on Aug. 1, 1770, in Caroline County, Va. He joined militia companies fighting local tribes in the Ohio country in 1789 and 3 years later won a lieutenant's commission in the U.S. infantry. He was on the Native American and Spanish frontier of the United States and served in Mad Anthony Wayne's successful campaign, terminated by the victory of Fallen Timbers (1794) over the Native Americans.

Clark resigned his commission in 1796, became a civilian, and tried to straighten out the chaotic financial condition of his famous brother, a hero of the Revolution, George Rogers Clark. However, when Meriwether Lewis offered him a role in what would be known as the Lewis and Clark expedition, he leaped at the opportunity.

In 1801 President Thomas Jefferson had chosen his White House secretary, Capt. Meriwether Lewis, to lead a corps of discovery up the Big Muddy (or Missouri) River and across the Rockies to the Pacific via the Columbia River. He gave Lewis complete freedom to choose his second in command. Without hesitation the Virginian picked his old Army buddy William Clark. When the Army failed to give Clark the promotion he deserved, Lewis ignored the "brass" and addressed Clark as captain, treating him as a virtual co-commander of the expedition.

It was Clark who led the fleet of boats upriver on May 14, 1804, while Lewis was detained in St. Louis by diplomatic and administrative matters. The two officers led their men up the Missouri to the Mandan Indian country of North Dakota, where they wintered before continuing in the spring of 1805. With great difficulty they shifted from canoes to horses and back to canoes as they crossed the unknown Rockies and followed the Columbia River to the sea. Clark was sharing leadership with Lewis in one of the most successful partnerships in the history of the nation.

After wintering at Ft. Clatsop on the Oregon coast, Lewis decided to split the party on its return to Missouri. He sent Clark to explore the Yellowstone River while he reconnoitered the Marias River. Although Lewis never yielded his command to Clark (except when accidentally wounded and incapacitated during a hunting expedition), Clark's wilderness and leadership skills contributed to the success of the corps of discovery. While Lewis was more brilliant and intellectual, Clark got along better with the men and was a fine map maker. Both men kept diaries, although spelling was not one of Clark's strong points.

Safe in St. Louis in September 1806, Clark resigned his commission to become brigadier general of militia and superintendent of Indian affairs for Louisiana Territory (later Missouri Territory) under the new governor, Meriwether Lewis. Clark was governor himself from 1813 to 1821, then became an unwilling—and unsuccessful—candidate for governor of the new state of Missouri. He devoted much of his time during the War of 1812 to Native American affairs and kept Missouri Territory almost unharmed by British-inspired Native American raids. He continued in Indian diplomacy after the conflict and by his good sense was able to avert trouble with the Indians, who came to trust him more than any other white man.

Clark died in St. Louis on Sept. 1, 1838. Highly respected as an administrator, soldier, and explorer, for a half century he had served his country well, particularly in keeping the peace on the Native American frontier.

Further Reading

There is no biography of Clark, although one has long been in preparation. The best sources are those on Meriwether Lewis, including John Bakeless, *Lewis and Clark: Partners in Discovery* (1947), and Richard Dillon, *Meriwether Lewis* (1965). An interesting retracing of Lewis and Clark's exploration is Calvin Tomkins, *The Lewis and Clark Trail* (1965). A one-volume abridgment of *The Journals of Lewis and Clark* was edited by Bernard DeVoto (1953).

Additional Sources

Ambrose, Stephen E., *Undaunted courage: Meriwether Lewis, Thomas Jefferson, and the opening of the American West*, New York: Simon & Schuster, 1996.

Bakeless, John Edwin, *Lewis and Clark: partners in discovery*, Mineola, N.Y.: Dover Publications, 1996. □

Leroy Eldridge Cleaver

Leroy Eldridge Cleaver (1935–1998), an American writer and a leader of the Black Panther party, was noted for advocating violent revolution within the United States.

Leroy Eldridge Cleaver was born August 31, 1935 in Wabbaseka, Arkansas, the son of Leroy Cleaver, a waiter and piano player, and Thelma Cleaver, an elementary school teacher. When his father became a dining car waiter on the Super Chief, a train running from Chicago to Los Angeles, the family moved to Phoenix, Arizona, one of the train's stops. Young Cleaver earned money by shining shoes after school. Two years later, the family moved to the Watts section of Los Angeles. Cleaver dropped out of Abraham Lincoln Junior High School after his parents separated. His petty crime record began at the age of 12 with the theft of a bicycle. He was sent to the Fred C. Nelles School for Boys in Whittier, California, where he was inspired to commit more sophisticated crimes. In 1953, he was released from Nelles and was soon sent to the Preston School of Industry for selling marijuana. Soon after his release from Preston, he was again arrested for possession of marijuana and, now an adult, was sentenced to a two-and-one-half-year sentence at the California State Prison at Soledad in June of 1954.

At Soledad, Cleaver completed his high school education and read the works of Karl Marx, W.E.B. Du Bois, and Thomas Paine. After his release from Soledad, he went back to selling marijuana and became a rapist on the weekend. This led him to be arrested for "assault with intent to mur-

der" at the end of 1957 and was sentenced to two to fourteen years at San Quentin Prison. He later was transferred to Folsom Prison in Represa, California.

In the early 1960s, while in jail, Cleaver decided to give up crime. He was influenced by the teachings of the Black Muslims and became a follower of Malcolm X. When Malcolm broke with the Black Muslims, so did Cleaver. Then he became an advocate of "black power," as this position was enunciated by Stokely Carmichael.

Also while in jail, Cleaver wrote essays, some published in 1962 in the *Negro History Bulletin;* these dealing mainly with racial pride and black nationalism. Out of these autobiographical essays came his first book, *Soul on Ice* (1968).

Ramparts magazine, which had brought Cleaver to public attention by publishing some of his prison articles, and Cleaver's lawyer were instrumental in securing his parole in 1966. He immediately began a new life as a writer and political activist. He helped found Black House, a social center for San Francisco youth. In 1967, he met the men who had founded the Black Panther party the year before. He became the party's minister of information, responsible for editing its newspaper. Later that year, he married Kathleen Neal. She became the communications secretary of the Black Panther party. The couple had two children.

With *Soul on Ice* Cleaver gained national prominence. On April 15, 1968, along with the widow of Martin Luther King Jr., and others, he addressed a mass rally against the Vietnam War in San Francisco.

As he became increasingly outspoken against racial, economic, and political injustices in America, Cleaver's parole officer advised him to discontinue his political activities. But Cleaver was becoming convinced that conditions for African-American people could not be alleviated without a violent revolution. To effect this, he felt, massive education was required to politicize the people. One method was to utilize a political campaign. In 1968, he urged the Black Panther party to unite with the predominantly white Peace and Freedom party in California to nominate candidates for local and state offices. Cleaver's wife became a candidate on the Peace and Freedom party ticket for the California State Assembly, along with the Black Panther's Huey P. Newton and Bobby Seale.

In April 1968, following the assassination of Martin Luther King Jr., and after harassment by the police of the Black Panther party, Cleaver was involved in a shoot-out with the Oakland police. One man was killed, and Cleaver was wounded in the foot and arrested. He was accused of violating his parole by possessing a gun, associating with people of bad reputation, and failing to cooperate with his parole agent. He was released on $50,000 bail.

In the next few months, Cleaver became a prominent spokesman of the radical, revolutionary left. He had moved from cultural, African-American nationalism to a more Marxist interpretation of revolutionary change. Cleaver believed that African-Americans should ally themselves with radical whites, and he criticized those African-American nationalists who refused such coalitions. During this period, he toured America as the presidential candidate of the Peace and Freedom party. He lectured on racism at the University of California in the fall of 1968.

Cleaver was scheduled to surrender to prison authorities in November 1968 for hearings on the charge of parole violation. Instead, he disappeared. He went to Cuba, North Korea, and Algeria and in September 1970 announced the establishment of an international office for the Black Panther party in Algiers.

While in exile, Cleaver championed "the angels of destruction" and the "great educational value" of murder. Cleaver accused Newton of putting the Black Panthers in the past by advocating community service programs over armed revolution. Cleaver was accused by others of abusing his wife while in Algeria and of having other Black Panthers killed. In March of 1971, Cleaver and Newton expelled each others' faction from the party, thus ending its heyday as the major voice for African-American activism in America.

In 1976, Cleaver returned to America to vote for Jimmy Carter and to face his accusers in California. Cleaver had changed his beliefs again while in Africa and now "stopped being a communist or socialist and developed an understanding and respect for free enterprise and the democratic political system." He joined the Mormon church and began to lecture on conservative issues and sell ceramic pots. He eventually set up a recycling business and tried, unsuccessfully, to get the backing of the Republican party for a 1984 run for the US Senate.

Cleaver later divorced his wife and went to Harvard Law School. He then moved back to Berkeley, California, and became a preacher. A recovering drug addict, Cleaver spoke in schools, prisons, and churches about the importance of resolving conflicts. He died at the age of 62 on May 1, 1998, in Pomona, California.

Further Reading

Eldridge Cleaver: Post Prison Writings and Speeches was edited by Robert Scheer in 1968. Lee Lockwood's talks with Cleaver were published as *Conversations with Eldridge Cleaver: Algiers* (1970). Books about the Black Panthers that include Cleaver are Gene Marine *The Black Panthers* (1969), Ruth Marion Baruch and Pirkle Jones *The Vanguard: A Photographic Essay on the Black Panthers* (1970), Philip S. Foner, ed. *The Black Panthers Speak* (1970), and Bobby Seale *Seize the Time* (1970). Two books critical of the Black Panthers are Earl Anthony *Picking Up the Gun* (1970), and *I Was a Black Panther*, as told to C. J. Moore (1970). Cleaver's own autobiography is *Soul On Fire* (1978). Much biographical information on Cleaver can be found in David Leon *Leaders From the 1960s: A Biographical Sourcebook of American Activism* (1994), and a biography of Cleaver to that point can be found in the 1970 issue of *Current Biography*. Cleaver also appears in August 1996 issue of *Ebony* magazine. □

James Cleveland

The Reverend James Cleveland (1932-1991) combined his talents as minister, singer, composer, and philanthropist to become known as the Crown Prince of Gospel Music.

Variously hailed as the King of Gospel Music and the Crown Prince of Gospel, the Reverend James Cleveland combined his talents as preacher, composer, singer, producer, and philanthropist to become one of the most outstanding exponents of the modern gospel sound. Indeed, with a voice that has earned acclaim as one of gospel's greatest, and a religious fervor that has refused the lure of secular music, Cleveland, more than any artist of his generation, served as a champion of gospel in its purest form. As he explained to Ed Ochs in an interview for *Billboard*, gospel is not only "a music, but . . . a representation of a religious thinking. Gospel singing is the counterpart of gospel teaching. . . . It's an art form, true enough, but it represents an idea, a thought, a trend."

Grew up Where Gospel Flourished

Born in Depression-era Chicago, the son of hard-working, God-fearing parents, Cleveland grew up in an environment where gospel flourished. His grandmother introduced him to Chicago's Pilgrim Baptist Church, where the budding musician was influenced by choir director Thomas A. Dorsey—also known as the father of gospel music. Under Dorsey's tutelage, the youth made his solo debut with the choir at the age of eight. The vocalist subsequently taught himself to play piano, often recounting how he practiced on imaginary keys until his parents could afford to purchase an upright for him. As Tony Heilbut quoted the star in *The Gospel Sound*: "My folks being just plain, everyday people, we couldn't afford a piano. So I used to practice each night right there on the windowsill. I took those wedges and crevices and made me black and white keys. And, baby, I

played just like Roberta [Martin]. By the time I was in high school, I was some jazz pianist."

Roberta Martin, a Dorsey disciple and one of the Chicago gospel pioneers to gain international recognition, was among Cleveland's idols. It was her group, the Roberta Martin Singers, who first helped shape the youth's singing and piano style, with Roberta Martin herself inspiring the youngster to begin composing. By the time he was a teenager, Cleveland was singing with a neighborhood group, the Thorn Gospel Crusaders. And once the group began featuring Cleveland's compositions, the artist found himself piquing the interest of prominent gospel talents. In 1948 Cleveland's "Grace Is Sufficient," performed at a Baptist convention, prompted Martin to begin publishing the new composer's work.

Founded the Gospel Chimes

The next decade proved a productive one for Cleveland. He made his recording debut on the Apollo label in 1950, singing "Oh What a Time" with the Gospelaires. He composed songs for Roberta Martin, including "Stand By Me," "Saved," and "He's Using Me." He worked frequently with the Caravans, first establishing himself as a superlative gospel arranger, then emerging as a singer—the Caravans scored their earliest hits, in fact, with Cleveland as lead vocalist on such tunes as "Old Time Religion" and "Solid Rock." And he founded the first of his own groups, the Gospel Chimes, which helped showcase his talents as composer, arranger, and singer.

By 1960 Cleveland, who had incorporated blues riffs and what Heilbut described as "sheer funkiness" in his work, had become associated with a new tenor in gospel music. That year "The Love of God," a song he recorded with Detroit's Voices of Tabernacle choir, was a sensation, and its success helped Cleveland secure a recording contract with Savoy Records, for whom he recorded more than sixty albums. The artist passed another milestone with Savoy's 1963 release *Peace Be Still.* A recording pairing Cleveland with the Angelic Choir of Nutley, New Jersey, the album, which held a spot on the gospel charts for more than fifteen years, has sold more than one million copies, an almost unheard of achievement for a gospel recording.

During the 1960s Cleveland also formed the James Cleveland Singers, gradually built an international reputation, and became one of the best paid of the gospel music entertainers. And although two of Cleveland's former pupils—Aretha Franklin and Billy Preston—went on to achieve celebrity status, the master himself declined to expand his audience by moving into secular music, and instead chose to devote himself strictly to gospel.

Worked to Preserve Gospel Tradition

Indeed, in the early sixties Cleveland became a minister and served Los Angeles's New Greater Harvest Baptist Church as pastor until he was able to build his own Cornerstone Institutional Baptist Church in 1970. For him, gospel music and gospel teaching were inseparable—different mediums conveying the same message. As the minister-musician explained to Ochs: "If we can't preach to people in a dry, talking sermon and get their attention, we'll sing it to them, as long as we get the message across. We have been instrumental in drawing more people to the church in recent years through singing and getting them to find favor with something in the church they like to identify with. Then when we get them into church, putting the same message into words without music is not as hard, for we have set some type of precedent with the music to get them into the church and get them focused on where we're coming from."

For Cleveland, gospel music was so vital that in 1968 he organized the first Gospel Music Workshop of America. Designed both to help preserve the gospel tradition and to feature new talent, the workshop has grown to include more than five hundred thousand members representing almost every state. "My biggest ambition is to build a school somewhere in America, where we can teach and house our convention," Cleveland told *Village Voice* interviewer David Jackson. This was the best way, in the artist's opinion, to assure that gospel's legacy continues.

One Last Message

Cleveland perpetuated an understanding of gospel music and gospel teaching as part of the same religious experience, believing that the music devoid of the mission is not genuine gospel. As Jackson articulated: "Through classics like 'Peace Be Still,' 'Lord Remember Me,' 'Father, I Stretch My Hands to Thee,' and 'The Love of God,' Reverend Cleveland retells a biblical love story for the plain purpose of reconciling people to God and to one another." And as his scores of devoted followers attest, concluded Jackson, "his message is widely appreciated and applauded."

Cleveland died of heart failure on February 9, 1991, in Los Angeles, California. He had not been able to sing for a year before his death due to respiratory ailments. But the last Sunday of his life, he faced his congregation at the Cornerstone Institutional Baptist Church and told them, "If I don't see you again and if I don't sing again, I'm a witness to the fact that the Lord answers prayer. He let my voice come back to me this morning," the *Los Angeles Times* reported. The same source reverently opined that Cleveland had been "not just . . . a record maker, but a mentor, producer, primary source of new material and fountainhead of artistic recognition for the form."

Further Reading

Broughton, Viv, *Black Gospel: An Illustrated History of the Gospel Sound,* Blandford Press, 1985.

Heilbut, Tony, *The Gospel Sound: Good News and Bad Times,* Simon & Schuster, 1971.

Billboard, September 27, 1980.

Chicago Tribune, February 17, 1991.

Detroit Free Press, February 18, 1991.

Ebony, December, 1984.

Los Angeles Times, February 10, 1991; February 15, 1991.

Village Voice, April 16, 1979.

Washington Post, February 11, 1991.

Baker, Barbara, "Black Gospel Music Styles: 1942-1979," Ph.D. dissertation, University of Maryland, 1978.

Casey, M. E., "The Contributions of James Cleveland," thesis, Howard University, 1980. □

Stephen Grover Cleveland

Twice elected president of the United States, Stephen Grover Cleveland (1837-1908) owed his early political successes to reformism. His efforts to stem economic depression were unsuccessful, and the conservative means he used to settle internal industrial conflicts were unpopular.

Grover Cleveland's political career developed while the wounds of the Civil War and Reconstruction were healing and just as the serious social and economic problems attendant upon industrialization and urbanization were unclearly emerging. Although a lifelong Democrat, Cleveland was not skilled in party politics; he had emerged from a reform wing of his party and had only a few years of public experience before becoming president. Interested in public issues, he used the presidency to try to shape legislation and public opinion in domestic areas. Yet, by his second term of office, the old, familiar debates over tariffs and currency had been called into question and traditional political alignments began to tear apart. Cleveland, however, was not sensitive to the problems of party harmony; instead, he stood on principle at the price of party unity and personal repudiation. In the depression of the 1890s, his concern for the flow of gold from the Treasury led him to force Congress to repeal the Sherman Silver Purchase

Act, and this action caused division of the Democratic party. The depression worsened, and by his intervention in the Pullman strike of 1894 he alienated the laboring class, thus losing all effectiveness as president. In 1896 Cleveland was rejected by his party.

Cleveland was born in New Jersey but spent most of his life in New York. Despite the early death of his father, a Presbyterian minister, and his consequent family responsibilities, he studied law in a respected Buffalo firm and gained admission to the New York bar in 1859. He joined the Democratic party, acting as ward delegate and ward supervisor before being appointed assistant district attorney for Erie County in 1863. Diligent and devoted, Cleveland set a good, though not brilliant, record. Enactment of the Conscription Act of 1863 caught him in the dilemma of whether to serve in the Army or find a substitute. To continue supporting his mother and sisters, he took the latter option, remaining in Buffalo to practice law. This was a costly decision, for a military record was expected of almost any aspirant to public trust. Though without public office from 1865 to 1870, he steadily enlarged his law practice and gained stature in the community.

Cleveland became sheriff in 1870, a post which promised large fees as well as frustrating experiences with graft and corruption. Although he was respected for his handling of official responsibilities, he made many enemies and won few admirers, for most citizens looked with disfavor on the office of sheriff. After 3 years he returned to legal practice, concentrating now on corporate law. His legal aspirations (and fees) were modest. His qualities as a lawyer were a good index to the whole of his public service: he was thorough, careful, slow, diligent, serious, severe, and un-yielding. His sober approach to his career contrasted sharply with the boisterous humor of his private life, for he was a popular, if corpulent, bachelor.

Quickly Up the Political Ladder

In 1881 Buffalo Democrats, certain that a reform candidate could sweep the mayoralty election, turned to Cleveland. In his one-year term as mayor he stood for honesty and efficiency—exactly the qualities the New York Democrats sought in a candidate for governor in 1882. New York State was alive with calls for reform in politics; a trustworthy candidate was much in demand. Elected governor by a handsome margin, Cleveland favored reform legislation and countered the interests of the New York-based political machine called Tammany Hall and its "boss," John Kelly, to such an extent that it caused a rift between them. After one term as governor, Cleveland was seen as a leading contender for the presidential nomination of 1884. His advantages lay in his having become identified with honesty and uprightness; also, he came from a state with many votes to cast, wealthy contributors, and a strong political organization. Pitted against Republican nominee James G. Blaine, Cleveland even won the support of reform-minded Republican dissidents known as Mugwumps. Several forces favored him: Tammany's eventual decision to support him in New York State, blame for the depression of the 1880s falling on the Republicans, and temperance workers' ire with the Republican party.

Thus, in 4 years, riding a crest of reform movements on municipal, state, and national levels, Cleveland moved from a modest law practice in upstate New York to president-elect. The rapidity of this political success had several implications for the balance of his career—he had not had to make compromises in order to survive, he had not become identified with new programs or different systems, he owed fewer debts to special-interest groups than most new presidents, and he had come to the presidency on the strength of his belief in simple solutions of honesty and reform.

First Term as President

Cleveland's victory margin in 1884 was slim. His Cabinet appointees were men of substance, though not of prominence: Thomas Bayard as secretary of state, Daniel Manning as secretary of the Treasury, and William Endicott as head of the War Department. All shared the conviction that government should be neither paternalistic nor favorable to any special group and that contesting economic groups should settle their differences without government intervention. With little administrative experience and few reasons to think highly of party organization, Cleveland in his first term advocated improved civil service procedures, reform of executive departments, curtailment of largesse in pensions to Civil War veterans, tariff reform, and ending coinage based on silver. He failed to stop silver coinage but achieved at least modest success in the other areas. In one regard Cleveland was an innovative president: he used his office to focus attention on substantive issues, to pressure for

legislation, and to define and determine the lines of congressional debate. Previously (and again after Cleveland), U.S. presidents left issues of legislation to Congress, spending most of their efforts on party leadership. Thus, in 1887 Cleveland took a strong position on tariff reform and later supported passage of the Mills Bill of 1888. Although the Mills Bill provided for only moderate tariff reductions, it was viewed as a step in the right direction, a way of reducing the embarrassingly large annual government surpluses.

Private Citizen

The Republicans mobilized to meet tariff reduction head on, stopping the Mills Bill and substituting a protective tariff measure, going into the election of 1888 with the tariff as the key issue. Renominated for the presidency in 1888 without challenge, Democrat Cleveland was opposed by Republican Benjamin Harrison of Indiana, who had the support of businessmen and industrialists favoring protective tariffs. Superior Republican organization, Democratic party feuding, and election fraud lost the 1888 election for Cleveland, although he won a plurality of the popular vote. He moved back to New York to practice law and enjoy his family.

Out of office, Cleveland withdrew from politics for a year but then began again to behave like an interested candidate. Stirred into attacking the McKinley tariff of 1890 and taking a strong position against currency expansion through silver-based coinage, he gained the Democratic presidential nomination in 1892.

Cleveland's campaign against incumbent President Harrison was a quiet one, with the Democrats aided by the 1892 Homestead strike, in which prominent Republicans were involved in the effort to break labor power and to maintain special benefits for the powerful steel magnates. The Democrats scored smashing victories in 1892, not only electing Cleveland but winning control of both House and Senate.

Second Term As President

To his second Cabinet, Cleveland named Walter Gresham as secretary of state, John G. Carlisle as secretary of the Treasury, Daniel S. Lamont as head of the War Department, and Richard Olney as attorney general. Like Cleveland's earlier Cabinet, these men agreed on extreme conservatism in handling economic issues. It was to Carlisle, Lamont, and Olney that Cleveland listened most closely, although in the final analysis he made his own decisions.

Policies in Time of Depression

Cleveland had scarcely taken his oath of office when the worst financial panic in years broke across the country. A complex phenomenon, the Panic of 1892-1893 had its roots in overexpansion of United States industry, particularly railroad interests; in the long-term agricultural depression that reached back to the 1880s; and in the withdrawal of European capital from America as a result of hard times overseas. As the panic broadened into depression, the American public tended to focus debate about its cause and cure on one item: the money question. On one side the argument was that businessmen (alarmed by the Sherman Silver Purchase Act requiring a purchase of silver each month) had lost confidence in the monetary system and feared depletion of the gold reserves; to regain their confidence and a return to prosperity, the buying of silver by the Federal government had to be halted. On the opposite side of the argument, silver exponents maintained that what was needed was more money in circulation, which could be achieved only if more, not less, silver was purchased by the government and used as a basis for coinage.

Cleveland, long afraid of silver as a threat to economic stability, determined that repeal of the Sherman Silver Purchase Act would stem the drain of gold reserves and end the depression by restoring confidence to businessmen; he called a special session of Congress for its repeal. Protracted and bitter debate ensued. The Democratic party divided along sectional lines, with western and southern Democrats standing against repeal. The repeal, however, was voted, but it was ineffective, and gold reserves continued to dwindle. Meanwhile the depression became worse during 1893 and 1894.

Wounds that had opened during the silver-repeal debate were not healed when Cleveland's administration turned to the long-promised issue of tariff reform. Cleveland had been identified for many years with downward revision of tariffs and more equitable distributions. Pressured by sectional interests, the Democrats in Congress were more divided than united over tariff legislation. In addition, the silver battle had virtually torn the party in half, leaving many Democrats with nothing but hatred for the President. The Wilson bill, from the viewpoint of the President, a fairly satisfactory measure for tariff reduction, was amended almost beyond recognition as it passed through the Senate, emerging with tariff rates only slightly lower than previous ones and carrying a host of provisions for special-interest groups. Highly dissatisfied but unsuccessful in his attempts to improve it, Cleveland allowed the Wilson-Gorman Act to become law without his signature.

To avert what he viewed as financial disaster, Cleveland became involved with four bond issues to draw gold into the Treasury. Not only was this effort to maintain gold reserves unsuccessful, but Cleveland was charged with having catered to Wall Street millionaires when other governmental policies had failed.

Beset by currency and tariff failures and hated by a large segment of the general population and by many in his own party, Cleveland further suffered loss of prestige by his actions in the Pullman strike of 1894. Convinced that the strike of the American Railway Union under Eugene V. Debs against the Pullman Company constituted an intolerable threat to law and order and that local authorities were unwilling to take action, Cleveland and Olney sent Federal troops to Chicago and sought to have Debs and his associates imprisoned. Although Cleveland prevailed and order was enforced, laborers throughout the country were angered by this use of Federal force.

Foreign Policies

The congressional elections of 1894 marked a sharp decline in Democratic power. Bitter at Cleveland and disheartened by worsening depression, American voters turned against the Democrats. Although Cleveland felt betrayed by his party and misunderstood by his constituents, he remained confident that his money policy had been correctly conceived and reasonably executed. Perhaps his party had split, but for him the defense of principle was more important than political harmony. Confronted with possibilities for compromise, Cleveland spurned such options and withdrew into isolation.

More successful in foreign policy, Cleveland exhibited the same determination and toughness. He would not be drawn into the Cuban rebellion against Spain; he would not sanction the Hawaiian revolution engineered by American commercial interests. Yet he took an equally stern posture vis-á-vis the boundary dispute between Venezuela and Great Britain in 1895-1896. Concerned about European influence in the Western Hemisphere, Cleveland and Olney carried the United States to the brink of war by insisting that the dispute be arbitrated. Business interests, clamoring for guarantees of open markets for their products, had considerable influence in shaping Cleveland's policy, which succeeded when Great Britain accepted arbitration.

Again a Private Citizen

Distrusted now and detested, Cleveland was convincingly repudiated by the Democratic Convention of 1896, which nominated William Jennings Bryan on a platform demanding free and unlimited coinage of both silver and gold at the rate of 16 to 1. Cleveland took no role in the campaign. He retired to Princeton, N.J., as soon as his term ended. He occupied himself with writing, occasional legal consultation, the affairs of Princeton University, and very occasional public speaking, but after 1900 he became less reluctant to appear in public. Sympathetic crowds greeted his appearances as the conservative Democratic forces with which he had been identified took party leadership from William Jennings Bryan. Briefly stirred into activity in 1904 to support Alton B. Parker's candidacy for the presidency, Cleveland spent most of his retirement years outside political battles, increasingly honored as a statesman. After offering to assist President Theodore Roosevelt in an investigation of the anthracite coal strike of 1902, he was active in the reorganization of the affairs of the Equitable Life Assurance Society in 1905. His death in 1908 was the occasion for general national mourning.

Further Reading

There is an abundant literature on Cleveland. Allan Nevins, *Grover Cleveland: A Study in Courage* (1944), is the best overall treatment. A less sympathetic portrayal of Cleveland is Horace S. Merrill, *Bourbon Leader: Grover Cleveland and the Democratic Party* (1957). Robert Wiebe, *The Search for Order, 1877-1930* (1967), credits Cleveland's efforts to shape legislation, whereas J. Rogers Hollingsworth, *The Whirligig of Politics: The Democracy of Cleveland and Bryan* (1963), criticizes him as a party leader. Cleveland's diplomacy is discussed in Walter LaFeber, *The New Empire: An Interpreta-*

tion of American Expansion, 1860-1898 (1963). A detailed account of the 1892 campaign is George H. Knoles, *The Presidential Campaign and Election of 1892* (1942), and of the 1896 campaign, Stanley L. Jones, *The Presidential Election of 1896* (1964). Arthur M. Schlesinger, Jr., ed., *History of Presidential Elections* (4 vols., 1971), is valuable as a source on the four campaigns of 1884-1896. □

George Clinton

The American patriot and statesman George Clinton (1739-1812) was the governor of New York for 21 years and vice president of the United States for two terms.

George Clinton's father, Charles, was an Ulster County, N.Y., farmer who had emigrated from Ireland in 1729. Charles Clinton achieved modest prominence through military and political office, but it was the marriage of his sons, James to Mary DeWitt in 1765 and George to Cornelia Tappen in 1769, that gave the Clintons status in New York society and future political allies among influential Dutch families.

Revolutionary Radical

Born in Ulster County, on July 26, 1739, George Clinton was educated at home and under a tutor, with the advantage of his father's better-than-average library. After studying law in New York City under William Smith, Jr., one of the famous Whig "triumvirate," he began practice in 1764. His political career was launched in 1768 with his election to the Assembly from Ulster County. There he allied himself with the minority "popular party" of the Livingstons against the DeLancey "court party" which controlled the legislature. For the next 7 years Clinton consistently opposed grants for supporting the king's troops, and he was one of a mere five assemblymen who in 1770 voted against jailing Alexander McDougall, a Whig "firebrand" who had publicly criticized the House for betraying its trust by its military appropriations. In the broader quarrel with Britain, Clinton sided with the radicals, denouncing parliamentary taxation and the Coercive Acts and urging support for the resolves of the First Continental Congress. A delegate to the Second Continental Congress, he was absent when independence was approved, having military obligations in New York, where he had been appointed brigadier general of the Ulster and Orange County militia in December 1775. Despite military shortcomings, the Continental Congress placed him in command of the forts in the Hudson Highlands. However, his energetic efforts did not prevent capture of the forts by the British in late 1777.

War Governor

The new state constitution of 1777 provided for a popularly elected governor. New York's aristocrats, led by Philip Schuyler, John Jay, John Morin Scott, and the Livingstons, expected Schuyler to be chosen. To their consternation the elections brought victory to Clinton—a tribute to his appeal to middle-class and small farmers and his popularity with the soldiers. Schuyler's postelection judgment that neither Clinton's family nor connections entitled him

"to so distinguished a predominance" but that he was "virtuous and loves his country, has abilities and is brave" is an apt commentary on Clinton's entire political career. He attracted the majority of New Yorkers by his loyalty to the Revolutionary cause, his honesty, and his devotion to his state. His reputation was enhanced by his able service as war governor, a post which was more often military than political. He organized the defenses of the frontier, procured supplies, suppressed loyalists, quieted the Native Americans, and organized campaigns against Tory and British raiders. His universal popularity was attested to by his successive elections to the governorship, often without opposition, until his voluntary retirement in 1795.

Antifederalist and Republican

Conservative in his administration during the Confederation period, committed to the protection of property and a stable financial system, Clinton was equally sensitive to popular liberties and republican government. It was the latter that made him suspicious of the movement for the U.S. Constitution in 1787. Willing to strengthen congressional powers under the Articles of Confederation, he feared the substitution of a "consolidated" for a "federal" government. The acknowledged leader of New York's Antifederalists, he was not so virulent an opponent of the Constitution as Alexander Hamilton made him out to be. He presided over the state's ratifying convention at Poughkeepsie with impartiality and spoke seldom, and then with moderation. There is some doubt that he wrote the Antifederalist essays attributed to him which appeared in the *New York Journal* (September 1787 to January 1788) as "Cato's Letters.'' Preferring ratification conditional upon amendments, he nevertheless promised to support the new Constitution when New York ratified it 30 to 27, on July 26, 1788, without such conditions.

Vice President

While Clinton continued to be popular personally, his political followers hereafter faced stiff opposition from the Federalists, who in 1789 secured control of the legislature and in 1792 just missed placing John Jay in the governor's chair. Pleading ill health and perhaps sensing defeat, Clinton declined to stand in 1795, and his party was beaten. For the next 6 years his nephew DeWitt Clinton led the newly formed Democratic-Republican party in New York, an alliance of Clintonites, Livingstons, and the followers of Aaron Burr. George Clinton returned as governor for a term in 1801, but his political mantle remained with his nephew. Clinton played out the remainder of his political career on the national scene. In 1792 he was the unsuccessful candidate of Republicans in New York, Virginia, North Carolina, and Georgia for the vice presidency in place of John Adams. In 1804 he replaced Burr for the second place on the Republican ticket and served as vice president during Jefferson's second term. Four years later his followers promoted his candidacy for president on a ticket with James Monroe. When this failed, he settled for another term as vice president under James Madison. His 7 years in Washington (1805-1812) did not enhance his reputation. He had little influence with either administration, presided over the Senate without much skill, and disliked Washington society. Perhaps his most important action was his tiebreaking vote in 1811 to prevent the recharter of the Bank of the United States. He died in office on April 20, 1812.

A moderate reformer who during his governorship promoted road and canal building, lent support for manufactures and reform of the criminal code, and gave aid to libraries and public funds for common schools, Clinton appealed to the middle-class democracy of New York State. He lacked the felicity of language and the talented pen of a Jefferson to extend his influence much beyond his state.

Further Reading

The standard biography of Clinton is E. Wilder Spaulding, *His Excellency George Clinton: Critic of the Constitution* (1938; 2d ed. 1964). It has been revised in many details by more recent works on early New York political history, most notably Linda Grant De Pauw, *The Eleventh Pillar: New York State and the Federal Constitution* (1966), and Alfred F. Young, *The Democratic Republicans of New York: The Origins, 1763-1797* (1967). *Public Papers of George Clinton* (10 vols., 1899-1914) is an essential source, although the introductory sketch of Clinton's life by the editor, Hugh Hastings, is inaccurate. The Clinton era in New York politics may be traced in Jabez D. Hammond, *History of Political Parties in the State of New York* (2 vols., 1842; 4th ed., 3 vols., 1852), and in De Alva Stanwood Alexander, *A Political History of the State of New York* (4 vols., 1906-1923). Clinton's war governorship is ably analyzed and evaluated in Margaret Burnham Macmillan, *The War Governors in the American Revolution* (1943).

Additional Sources

Kaminski, John P., *George Clinton: yeoman politician of the new republic,* Madison: Madison House, 1993. □

William Jefferson Clinton

William Jefferson (Bill) Clinton (born 1946) won the Democratic nomination for the presidency in 1992 and then defeated incumbent George Bush to become the 42nd president of the United States. He was re-elected to a second term in 1996.

William Jefferson (Bill) Clinton was born in Hope, Arkansas, on August 19, 1946. He was a fifth-generation Arkansan. His mother, Virginia Kelly, named him William Jefferson Blyth, IV, after his father, who had been killed in a freak accident several months before Bill's birth. When Bill was four years old his mother left him with her parents, Hardey and Mattie Hawkins, while she trained as a nurse-anesthesiologist. His grandparents ran a small store in a predominantly African American neighborhood and, despite the racist practices of the South in the early 1950s, Bill's grandparents taught him that segregation was wrong.

After his mother's marriage to Roger Clinton when Bill was eight, the family moved to Hot Springs, Arkansas. They lived outside of the town in a house that had no indoor plumbing, which was not unusual for rural Arkansas in the late 1950s and early 1960s. Though Bill changed his last name to Clinton when he was 15 in an expression of family solidarity, the Clinton household was a troubled one. Roger Clinton was an alcoholic, and the family was frequently disrupted by incidents of domestic violence. At the age of 15 Bill made it clear to his stepfather that he would protect his mother and half brother, Roger, Jr., from any further assaults.

Clinton considered several careers as a child. At one point he wanted to be a musician (a saxophonist), and at another he wanted to be a doctor, but in 1963, as part of a delegation of the American Legion Boys' Nation, he met then-President John F. Kennedy. As a result of that meeting Clinton decided that he wanted a career in politics.

Education of a Future President

He entered college at Georgetown University in 1964. As a college student Clinton was committed to the movement against the Vietnam War, as well as to the civil rights struggle. In 1966 he worked as a summer intern for Arkansas Senator J. William Fulbright, who was at that time the leader of antiwar sentiment in the U.S. Senate. He was still a college student in Washington, D.C., when Martin Luther King, Jr., was killed, and he and a friend used Clinton's car to deliver food and medical supplies to besieged neighborhoods during the unrest that followed King's assassination.

Bill Clinton graduated from Georgetown University in 1968 with a B.S. in International Affairs. It was already clear to those who knew him that he was a natural politician. Clinton was awarded a Rhodes scholarship and spent the next two years as a postgraduate student at Oxford Univer-

sity. It was in 1969, while at Oxford, that Clinton wrote a letter to an army colonel in the University of Arkansas ROTC program concerning his draft eligibility and his opposition to the war in Vietnam. In his letter he expressed concern about his position both in terms of the draft and in terms of his later "political viability." At the age of 23 Clinton was already concerned with his electability.

In 1970 Clinton entered law school at Yale University. In his first year at Yale Clinton served as a campaign coordinator for Joe Duffy, an antiwar candidate for the U.S. Senate from Connecticut. While still a law student, Clinton worked with the writer Taylor Branch as campaign coordinator in Texas for presidential candidate George McGovern.

At Yale Clinton met Hillary Rodham, a fellow law student. After graduation Clinton and Rodham were offered jobs on the staff of the House of Representatives committee that was considering the impeachment of Richard Nixon. Clinton chose to return to Arkansas while Hillary Rodham went to work as a member of the House staff. Clinton went into private practice in Fayetteville, the center of Arkansas politics, and also began teaching at the University of Arkansas Law School.

A Political Career in Arkansas

In 1974 he ran for Congress against John Paul Hammerschmidt, who was a strong Nixon supporter. He lost the election, but it was a very close vote. In a heavily Republican district, running as the incumbent, Hammerschmidt got only 51.5 percent of the vote.

Hillary Rodham moved to Fayetteville in 1974 and also began teaching at the University of Arkansas Law School. On October 11, 1975, Bill Clinton and Hillary Rodham were married. In 1976 the Clintons moved to Little Rock when Bill was elected attorney general of the State of Arkansas, an office he held from 1977 to 1979.

In 1978 Bill Clinton ran for the office of governor of Arkansas. He was elected, and was the youngest-ever governor of Arkansas; in fact, he was the youngest person to be elected governor of any state since Harold E. Stassen was elected in 1938 at the age of 31. In his first term in office Clinton attempted to make numerous changes, many of which were extremely unpopular, including an attempt to raise automobile licensing fees.

On February 27, 1980, Bill and Hillary Clinton had a daughter they named Chelsea Victoria. In November of that same year Ronald Reagan won a landslide victory against Jimmy Carter, and Bill Clinton lost his bid for reelection as governor of Arkansas to Republican candidate Frank White. Clinton was a strong Carter supporter, which accounted for some of his difficulties, but Clinton recognized that many of his own policies had cost him reelection. When Clinton campaigned for election in 1982 against White, he explained he had learned the price for hubris and the importance of adaptability and compromise. He was elected with 55 percent of the vote.

Clinton served as governor of Arkansas until 1992. He was considered to be an activist, pushing for school reform and for health care and welfare reform with mixed results. He continued in these years to be active in Democratic national politics. Increasingly, Clinton attracted interest as a new voice in post-segregation southern politics. In 1988 Clinton came to national prominence at the Democratic convention when he gave a lengthy speech nominating Massachusetts Governor Michael Dukakis as the party's presidential candidate. Clinton's speech was considered to be excessively long and was not well received. The audience, in fact, began to shout, "Get off, get off."

In spite of this unsuccessful debut, Clinton continued to be active in national politics. In 1991 he was voted most effective governor by his peers. That same year he was chosen as chair of the Democratic Leadership Conference. Along with such other southerners as Albert Gore of Tennessee, he worked to shift control of the party away from the northeastern liberal wing and to reshape a new party constituency. In October of 1991 Clinton announced that he was entering the 1992 race for president.

1992 Campaign and Election

Clinton had a lot of competition for the Democratic nomination, and many of those candidates claimed to be the alternative who offered a change from the party's past and a chance to beat the incumbent president, George Bush. Even before the New Hampshire primary in early 1992 Clinton had suffered many embarrassments and difficulties. He came from a state that was small and was regarded by many as unsophisticated and economically underdeveloped. Critics felt he had no experience on the federal level and no understanding of foreign policy. Clinton in turn insisted that his strengths lay in the fact that he was not connected to a Washington power base and therefore had a fresh perspective to bring to government.

Clinton's campaign was also plagued by charges of personal scandal that included allegations of sexual liaisons with women other than his wife and questions about his draft status during the Vietnam War. Clinton remained in the race, however, slowly gaining momentum until the 1992 Democratic convention, where he became his party's nominee. He selected Senator Albert Gore as his running mate. Clinton focused his campaign on economic issues, especially stressing his understanding of the plight of the unemployed and the underemployed as well as general concern over access to health care. In November 1992 Clinton was elected president, defeating Republican incumbent George Bush and third-party candidate Ross Perot.

Once in office Clinton addressed economic issues as interest rates and unemployment began to drop. He also appointed Hillary Rodham Clinton as the head of a task force mandated to explore possibilities for large-scale health care reform.

Helped by a Democratic majority in both the Senate and the House of Representatives, Clinton was able to have enacted most of his proposals for the "change" issue that keyed his campaign. Probably the most enduring of the passed legislation was the 1993 North American Free Trade Agreement (NAFTA) making a single trading bloc of the United States, Canada, and Mexico. As the end of Clinton's term approached a new scandal threatened the President's credibility. The scandal was termed Whitewater for the suspicious Arkansas land deal in which Bill and Hillary Clinton were involved.

In 1996 Clinton was re-elected to a second term. He won the election by a landslide, defeating Bob Dole with 49 percent of the popular vote and 379 electoral votes.

Clinton's second term became increasingly overshadowed by independent council Kenneth Starr's investigations into the Whitewater land deal. Although the investigation had been underway during his first term, it became more serious when allegations of Clinton's affair with White House intern, Monica Lewinsky, were released to the public. When the news first broke, he fervently denied the affair, but later stated that he had engaged in inappropriate activities with Lewinsky. This led to an impeachment hearing in the House of Representatives. On December 19, 1998, the House ruled to impeach Clinton on charges of lying under oath to a federal grand jury and obstructing justice in the Lewinsky affair. This made Clinton only the second president in U.S. history to face a Senate impeachment hearing. The Senate conducted a 21–day impeachment trial with Chief Justice William Rehnquist presiding. Following three days of secret deliberations, on February 12, 1999, the Senate voted 55 to 45 to reject the first article of impeachment, which alleged that President Clinton had lied while under oath in his grand jury testimony for the Paula Jones case, and voted 50 to 50 on the second article, which charged that the president had obstructed justice in covering up his relationship with Lewinsky. Without the two-thirds majority on either charge, Clinton was acquitted. He again apologized to the American

people for what he did and the burden his words and actions put on the Congress.

Clinton was found in contempt of court in the Paula Jones lawsuit by judge Susan Webber Wright in April of 1999, for testifying falsely about his relationship with Lewinsky.

To handle the most significant foreign crisis of his presidency, Clinton spearheaded a NATO—led military campaign that began in March of 1999 against Yugoslav President Slobodan Milosevic to end the exodus of ethnic Albanians being forced from the Yugoslav province of Kosovo.

In a deal with independent counsel Robert Ray shortly before leaving office, Clinton conceded that he gave misleading testimony in the 1998 lawsuit. In exchange for this admission, all criminal charges were dropped. Clinton was fined $25,000 and his Arkansas law license was suspended for five years.

Further Reading

There are a number of biographies of Bill Clinton, including *The Comeback Kid: The Life and Career of Bill Clinton* (1992) by Charles F. Allen and Jonathan Portis, *Clinton, Young Man in a Hurry* (1992) by Jim Moore with Rich Ihde, *America: A Place Called Hope?* (1993) by Conor O'Clery, *The Clinton Revolution: An Inside Look at the New Administration* (1993) by Koichi Suzuki, and *Partners in Power: The Clintons and Their America* (1996) by Roger Morris. Additional information may be obtained from the White House web site at http://www.whitehouse.gov □

Tyrus Raymond Cobb

Tyrus Raymond Cobb, better known as Ty Cobb (1886-1961), was most probably the greatest all-around baseball player who ever lived and also universally acknowledged as the "most hated man in baseball."

Ty was born on December 18, 1886, in Narrows, Banks County, Georgia, to William Herschel Cobb, a school administrator and state senator, and Amanda Chitwood. Cobb grew up in Royston, Georgia, and began playing sandlot ball as soon as he could swing a bat. Over his family's objections he signed with the Augusta baseball team of the South Atlantic League in 1904 and soon attracted notice. Grantland Rice, the famous sportswriter, saw him play for Augusta and named him the "Georgia Peach," a title that Cobb wore proudly.

At a time when pitchers dominated the game and batting averages were low, Cobb was a brilliant exception, hitting .326 in his last season in the minors before joining the Detroit Tigers of the American League on August 27, 1905. In 1906 Cobb hit .320, the fifth best average in the league and 35 points ahead of the nearest Tiger. The next year he won the American League batting championship, hitting .350 and leading Detroit to the World Series. He quickly became the biggest gate attraction in baseball and would hit .300 or better for 23 straight years. During that time he hit over .400 in three different seasons, his all-time high being .420 in 1911. Cobb led the league in hitting 12 times, nine of them in a row. During his peak years, 1909-1919, he so dominated baseball that historians refer to it as the era of the "Cobbian game."

In 1909, for example, he had the best year of any baseball player to that date, leading both leagues in hitting with an average of .377 and leading the American League in hits, runs, stolen bases, runs batted in, total bases, and home runs. Once again he led the Tigers to a pennant, though as usual they lost the World Series. As most of his teammates were markedly less talented than Cobb, he would never be on a world championship team, about the only honor available to a ball player that he did not win. This remained so even during his years as a player-manager for Detroit from 1921 to 1926, when the team never finished better than second place.

In addition to his peerless batting skills, amazing fielding, and audacity as a base runner, Cobb was the fiercest competitor in baseball. Not satisfied with simply winning, he had to run up the highest possible score and therefore put unrelenting pressure on the opposition until the last man was out. The terror of pitchers as a hitter and base runner, he was also the terror of infielders and catchers as he stormed down the base paths. A perfectionist in an era of what was called "inside baseball," which emphasized hit-and-run plays, base stealing, and bunting, he mastered every aspect of his craft. Cobb was also a supremely intelligent player, a kind of baseball genius. "Know thy enemy" was his guiding rule, and his thorough knowledge of every competitor enabled him to "read" the opposition as no one else could.

Why his brains were so much admired in his playing days can be seen in his autobiography. The chapter on hitting is a brilliant essay on how to keep the opposition off balance by never doing the same thing twice. "I tried to be all things to all pitchers," Cobb wrote, summing up his teachings nicely. If this chapter is all about technique, the next one, "Waging War on the Base Paths," is all about psychology. To Cobb base stealing was largely a matter of deceiving and demoralizing the enemy. Once Cobb, annoyed by a catcher who was always telling journalists that Cobb's reputation was overblown, performed an astonishing feat. On stepping up to the plate he told the catcher that he was going to steal every base. After singling to first, Cobb then stole second, third, and home on four straight pitches. Cobb's explanation of how he accomplished this is itself a masterpiece.

Cobb remained a star after 1920 when the rise of Babe Ruth and the introduction of a livelier ball changed the game to one in which sheer batting power mattered more than finesse and guile. But the new "Ruthian game" was not to Cobb's taste, and, although he remained a skillful batter, his legs began to give out. In 1927 Cobb signed with the Philadelphia Athletics, but, though he averaged .357 at the plate, it was clear that his days as a player were numbered. He spent most of 1928 on the bench and retired at season's end. When he left baseball Cobb held 43 records. Although all but one have since been broken, his fantastic lifetime batting average of .367 appears safe. That he was the best all-around player who ever lived was recognized in 1936

when he led everyone in votes for the first group of Baseball Hall of Fame inductees, coming in ahead of Babe Ruth, Honus Wagner, Christy Mathewson, and Walter Johnson—the other four original selectees.

As a player Cobb was godlike, but as a man he had little to offer. Angry, abrasive, touchy, a loner, he was hated by his teammates at first for what one called his "rotten disposition" and was tolerated only after his phenomenal value became evident. A brawler and bully on the field, Cobb was the same off it. In a racist age he was notably abusive to African Americans. Cobb was a poor husband and father too. Both his marriages ended in divorce and, though he had five children by his first wife, his relations with them were not close. As sometimes happens, he did better as a grandfather.

Like many ex-athletes Cobb was restless in retirement, living simply despite his wealth—much of which he gave away. In 1953 he founded the Cobb Educational Foundation, which awarded college fellowships to needy Georgia students. Among his other charitable endeavors was the hospital Cobb built in Royston as a memorial to his parents. This was a defiant act in part, as his mother had shot his father to death in 1905 under suspicious circumstances—although a jury found her not guilty of manslaughter. Cobb died in Atlanta, Georgia, on July 17, 1961, widely admired but not loved, unlike his great counterpart Babe Ruth.

Further Reading

The best biography is *Ty Cobb* (1984) by Charles C. Alexander. Must reading is *My Life in Baseball* (1961, paperback 1993) by Ty Cobb with Al Stump, a unique mixture of score-settling, revisionist self-history, and outstanding baseball analysis. The movie *Cobb* (1994) starring Tommy Lee Jones was based on Stamp's biography. □

Nat King Cole

The American musician Nat Cole (Nathaniel Adams Coles; 1919-1965) was beloved by millions as a singer of popular songs, but his forte was piano, in the "cool" jazz idiom.

Nathaniel Adams Coles, the youngest son of the Reverend Edwards Coles and Perlina (Adams) Coles, was born on March 17, 1917 (St. Patrick's Day), in Montgomery, Alabama. Cole and his family were moved to Chicago, Illinois, in 1921 by his father, who served as pastor of the Truelight Spiritual Temple on the South Side of Chicago. By the time he reached the age of 12, Cole was playing the organ and singing in the choir of his father's church under his mother's choir direction.

He took piano lessons "mostly to learn to read, you know. I could play more piano than the teacher." Infatuated with show business, Cole formed his own big band, the Rogues of Rhythm, joined by his older brother Eddie, previously bassist with Noble Sissle's orchestra. First recordings of the Rogues, for Decca Records, are now collector's items.

Working with the band in Chicago nightclubs and dance halls enabled Cole to develop both as a pianist and a singer. He was early influenced by the piano styling of Earl Hines and Jimmy Noone's band. Of Noone's theme song,

"Sweet Lorraine," he said, "Man, that was the first song I ever sang." The tune, written by the New Orleans clarinetist Mitchell Parish, became a Cole classic.

Leaving the Chicago circuit, Cole and the band joined the Shuffle Along show scheduled to play the West Coast. Brother Eddie declined the engagement and Cole went along to California where, in 1937, he met and married Nadine Robinson, a chorus girl with the show. When the show folded, he and the band played a short-lived booking at the Ubangi Club in Maywood. "Old musicians never die; they just run out of gigs," said Louie Armstrong once, and when Cole's Ubangi gig was over the band broke up and he went on to do a solo act at the Century Club. From the Century, Cole was hired by Bob Lewis, owner of the Swanee Inn in Hollywood. Lewis insisted on a trio. The booking was for two weeks, but lasted six months.

The Genius of Cole, Moore, and Miller

Cole's first bass player, later to be replaced by the legendary Johnny "Thrifty" Miller, was Wesley Prince, who introduced him to Oscar Moore, a movie studio-guitarist. Although the phenomenal Moore was replaced years later by the excellent guitarist Irving Ashby, the trio reached its apex with the combination of the genius of Cole, Moore, and Miller.

The trio wove a fabric of blues licks, riffs, runs, arpeggios, and scalewise invented melodies, classically composed in an original and precise musical logic, as if nothing were left to chance, when, in fact, every note was a calculated risk controlled by the artists' innate rhythmic, harmonic, and melodic sensibilities—absolute freedoms contained by absolute rules of the musical art. Head arrangements were worked up from sheet music in rehearsals, but were not written down. Rehearsal time nods of the head by Cole signaled Moore and Miller and resulted in smooth transitions from piano to guitar solos and piano-guitar riffs, in the Benny Goodman mode. The three musicians each possessed exceptional improvisational melodic gifts which melded original inventions with jazz conventions.

Their harmonic genius added to a constantly swinging rhythm rooted in Miller's unswerving bass line and Moore's driving four to the measure chordal accompaniment—a beat which inspired the envy of contemporary big bands. Cole's accompaniment style, which backed up Moore's improvisational guitar lines and his own singing, was characterized by piano bass-note rockers and comped (chopped) chords executed by the left hand against exquisitely tasteful fill-ins executed by the right hand.

The trio was an original of the jazz combo which prepared future audiences for the small ensembles later to emerge as a consequence of economic retrenchment in the music industry, causing the demise of the big bands on the road circuit at a time when live radio and television broadcasting costs, too, became, for a while, prohibitive of orchestration on the grand scale.

Legend has it that upon an occasion of Cole's afterhours venture into vocalization with the previously predominantly instrumental trio, a young woman present in the club figuratively crowned him the "King," an affectionate nickname which stuck ever after. Among the "Counts" of Basie and the "Dukes" of Ellington, the title of "King" was reverential and emphasized Cole's high place in the enduring art and history of jazz.

After the Swanee Inn, the trio worked night spots in Hollywood and its environs; later, in Chicago, they played on the same bill with the Bob Crosby band and cut eight sides with Decca, including an early rendition of "Sweet Lorraine," one almost identical to their eventual hit on the Capital label. Moving on through Washington, D.C., they arrived in Manhattan in 1941 to play Nick's in Greenwich Village, Kelly's Stable (uptown), and one week at the Paramount, but the pay was "slim pickens," impelling the trio to return to the West Coast, where they played the 331 Club followed by a 10-week tour of Omaha and a return engagement at the 331 for almost a year, which got them through the winter of 1943-1944.

Lean times were followed by big hits. With the arrival of the spring of 1944 came a second Capital recording of "Straighten Up and Fly Right" and, on the flip side, "I Just Can't See for Lookin'," a novelty lyric derived from an old preacher's joke that Cole had composed and set to music about a buzzard who took a monkey for a ride. With personification came gratification and a series of hits: "Gee, Baby, Ain't I Good to You?" "Bring Another Drink," "If You Can't Smile and Say Yes," "Shy Guy," and then, two real winners, "Frim Fram Sauce" and "Route 66."

Constantly together on the road, Cole, Moore, and Miller lived and breathed their music at work and at play, until they played as one. Most often Cole sang solo, but some tunes were rendered in a unison band chant. His piano talent, synthesized from cross-fertilization of Earl "Fatha" Hines, Fats Waller, Frankie Carl, Count Basie, Fletcher Henderson, Mel Powell, and Teddy Wilson, was the bridge between the preceding style of Art Tatum and the styles to follow of George Shearing and Oscar Peterson. This lineage is, perhaps, best exemplified in Cole's solo rendition of "Body and Soul." Such is the family way in which jazz musicianship develops: first imitation and then innovation; first convention and then invention. Moore had picked up a few tricks along the way from Django Rinehardt, Eddie Lang (Salvatore Mussaro), Charley Christian, and Danny Perri; Miller had profited from listening to "Slam" Stewart and "Bobby" Haggert—but the trio's synthesis was original.

Huge Success as a Single

Cole and some of his Californian friends, including songwriter-singer Frankie Laine, prepared original compositions for what proved to be a successful concert tour, but as success mounted, so the jazz lessened and the popular vocalization increased, and so, too, the trio faded into the background, sometimes appearing with full orchestra in concerti sections; sometimes not appearing at all. With his recording of Mel Torme's "Christmas Song," a new career was launched for Cole which left little room for Moore and Miller; the trio broke up, to be restaffed later on by Cole for occasional gigs. Unfortunately, new success marked the end of old friendship.

There are three major lineages in modern American popular singing. The earliest is the Neapolitan School, which resulted from a fusion of Al Jolson's and Carlo Buti's styles by Russ Columbo, who was the leader in a family of crooners including Harry Lillis "Bing" Crosby, Buddy Clark, Perry Como, Dean Martin, and Elvis Presley. The second, the Big Band School, traded Rudy Valley's megaphone for the more sensitive microphone and includes Bob and Ray Eberly, Frank Sinatra, Vic Damone, Steve Lawrence, and Jack Jones. The youngest of the three pre-rock schools is the Cool School, deriving from the harsher toned ancestry of Louis Armstrong, Jimmy Rushing, and Louis Prima to culminate in the smooth, relaxed delivery of Cole, who established a style out of which others grew, including the styles of Mel Torme, Johnny Ray, Johnny Mathis, Oscar Peterson (whose similarity of style with Cole's caused a lifetime contract between them requiring Peterson to refrain from singing), Frankie Laine, Tony Bennett, early Ray Charles, and later, John Pizzarelli, Jr. (son of Bucky).

After seven film contracts with the trio, a long-term contract with the NBC Kraft Music Hall, recording contracts with Decca and Capital, top-ten hits, Metronome Poll awards, Gold Piano and Silver Singing Esquire awards, and a Gold Esquire Guitar award for Moore; after the constant friendship, the countless one-night stands, the concert engagements, and the fame and the fortune, the trio gig was up and Cole was on his own.

Cole never belted a song in his life, but depended on interesting subtleties of vocal timbre and texture and the art of nuance. Even Sinatra admired his intonation. Cole never sang a sour note in his life. He well knew how to hold the vowels and let go of the consonants. He was master of the art of understatement and knew how to capitalize on brief spaces of pregnant silence, as dramatically important to music as sound itself. He mastered the art of rubato, which resulted in an intricate ability to phrase a melodic line and tell a lyric story. The consummate jazz artist became the consummate balladeer, the singer of art and folk songs of the future, an American troubadour.

Cole bought a home in Los Angeles—"my own home," he said, but two lives spent in show business had led to divorce from Nadine. He married for a second and last time to singer Marie Ellington, who, although not related, sang with Duke Ellington's band. He and Marie had three daughters: Carol, Timlin, and Natalie. Natalie followed in her father's swinging footsteps.

After the successes of "Dance, Ballerina, Dance," "Nature Boy," and "Lush Life," there came the sudden and most sad end to the artist's life and the beginning of a landmark of native American music. The sound quality of Cole's voice derived not only from his broad Southern dialect (the vowel sounds almost Italian in pronunciation), his impeccable ear, the microphonic amplification of his tone color, his idiosyncratic pronunciation of "I", or from his velvet falsetto, but also from his cigarette smoking. On a WNEW New York interview shortly before his untimely death in 1965 by throat cancer, he was asked by host William B. Williams how he could smoke so much and still be a singer. Cole responded by saying he had learned two things, the first thing being that the choice of the right key for a song meant everything, and the second being that smoking helps a singer get a husky sound in his voice that the audience loves—"so, if you want to sing, keep on smoking."

When Cole died, a consummate jazz artist and a voice millions knew as the voice of a friend was irreplaceably lost to the world.

Further Reading

Additional information on Nat "King" Cole can be found in *Look* (April 19, 1955); *Newsweek* (August 12, 1946); *Time* (July 30, 1951); *Saturday Evening Post* (July 17, 1954); *ASCAP Biographical Dictionary of Composers, Authors, and Publishers* (1952); and *Who Is Who in Music* (1951). □

Samuel Colt

The American inventor and manufacturer Samuel Colt (1814-1862) first developed and popularized the multishot pistol, or revolver, which found wide use in the last half of the 19th century, especially in the American West.

Samuel Colt was born in Hartford, Conn., the son of a prosperous cotton and woolen manufacturer. In 1824 his father sent him to work in one of his dyeing and bleaching establishments; Colt attended school at the same time. His behavior in school, however, was such that his father sought to discipline him by sending him on a sea voyage as an ordinary seaman. It was a one-year trip to India and the Orient, and it was apparently on this voyage that

young Colt began to work on a revolving pistol. On his return he worked for a year in his father's bleachery and then left to travel on his own. Little is known of his activities for the next few years, but for at least a part of that time he billed himself as "Dr. Coult" and gave popular lectures on chemistry and demonstrated the effects of laughing gas.

Colt continued to work on his idea for a pistol and by 1831 had constructed at least two versions of it. By 1833 he had made both a pistol and a rifle on the principles which he later patented in the United States. Just about this time he wandered off to Europe, where he acquired patents in both France and England. He returned to America in 1836 and received an American patent that year. The primary feature of his pistol was a revolving cartridge cylinder which automatically advanced one chamber when the gun was cocked.

During 1836 Colt built a factory in Paterson, N.J., to make his revolvers, but failing to receive a contract from the government he was unable to produce and sell the gun in quantity. Forced to sell the patent for his revolver, he turned to the problem of submarine warfare, receiving some financial help from the government to build an experimental submarine battery.

In 1846, with the declaration of war against Mexico, the demand for guns rose, and Colt was given a government contract for 1000 of his revolving pistols. Quickly he bought back his patents and opened an armory in New Haven, Conn. This new government patronage, coupled with the growing popularity of the gun in the West (where it was ideally suited to the new kind of horseback warfare being

carried out against the Indians) brought Colt financial success at last. His exhibit at the 1851 Crystal Palace international exhibition in London caused widespread comment—for the excellence of his weapons, but most importantly for the example they gave of the mass production of interchangeable parts, which came to be known as the American system of manufactures. In 1855 Colt built his great armory at Hartford, Conn. (the largest private armory of its time), and he lived out his life as a prosperous and respected manufacturer.

Further Reading

A good introduction to Colt's life and works is William B. Edwards, *The Story of Colt's Revolver: The Biography of Col. Samuel Colt* (1953). There is a vast literature on guns, written for buffs and collectors, much of which contains references to Colt and his pistol.

Additional Sources

Barnard, Henry, *Armsmear: the home, the arm, and the armory of Samuel Colt: a memoria*, s.l.: s.n., 1976.

Grant, Ellsworth S., *The Colt legacy: the Colt Armory in Hartford, 1855-1980*, Providence, RI: Mowbray Co., 1982.

Keating, Bern, *The flamboyant Mr. Colt and his deadly six-shooter*, Garden City, N.Y.: Doubleday, 1978. □

John Coltrane

Saxophone player John Coltrane (1926-1967) created an innovative form of music that continues to influence modern jazz musicians, even more than two decades after his death.

Legendary saxophone virtuoso John Coltrane continues to influence modern jazz even from the grave. Coltrane's death more than two decades ago only enhanced his reputation as an artist who brought whole new dimensions to a constantly innovative musical form. The "sheets of sound" and other bizarre stylistic elements that characterize Coltrane's jazz sparked heated debate at the time of their composition. Today his work is still either hailed as the very pinnacle of genius or dismissed as flights of monotonous self-indulgence. In an *Atlantic* retrospective, Edward Strickland calls Coltrane "the lone voice crying not in the wilderness but from some primordial chaos" whose music "evokes not only the jungle but all that existed before the jungle." The critic adds: "Coltrane was attempting to raise jazz from the saloons to the heavens. No jazzman had attempted so overtly to offer his work as a form of religious expression. . . . In his use of jazz as prayer and meditation Coltrane was beyond all doubt the principal spiritual force in music."

"Last Great Leader"

Andrew White, himself a musician and transcriber of many of Coltrane's extended solos, told *Down Beat* magazine that the jazz industry "has been faltering artistically and financially ever since the death of John Coltrane. . . . Besides being one of our greatest saxophonists, improvisors, innovative and creative contributors, Coltrane *was* our last

great leader. As a matter of fact, he was the *only* leader we've had in jazz who successfully maintained an evolutionary creative output as well as building a 'jazz star' image. *He merged the art and the money."*

John William Coltrane, Jr., was born on the autumn equinox, September 23, 1926. He was raised in rural North Carolina, where he was exposed to the charismatic music of the Southern church—both of his grandfathers were ministers. Coltrane's father also played several instruments as a hobby, so the young boy grew up in a musical environment. Quite on his own, he discovered jazz through the recordings of Count Basie and Lester Young. He persuaded his mother to buy him a saxophone, settling for an alto instead of a tenor because the alto was supposedly easier to handle.

Showed Saxophone Talent Immediately

Coltrane showed a proficiency on the saxophone almost immediately. After briefly studying at the Granoff Studios and at the Ornstein School of Music in Philadelphia, he joined a typical cocktail lounge band. Then he played for a year with a Navy band in Hawaii before landing a spot in the Eddie Vinson ensemble in 1947. He was twenty-one at the time. For Vinson's band Coltrane performed on the tenor sax, but his ears were open to jazz greats on both alto and tenor, including Charlie Parker, Ben Webster, Coleman Hawkins, Lester Young, and Tab Smith. After a year with Vinson, Coltrane joined Dizzy Gillespie's group for one of his longest stints—four years. By that time he had "paid his dues" and was experimenting with composition and technical innovation.

The 1950s saw a great flowering of modern jazz with the advent of artists such as Miles Davis and Thelonious Monk. Coltrane played horn for both Davis and Monk; the latter showed him tricks of phrasing and harmony that deepened his control of his instrument. Coltrane can be heard playing tenor sax on Davis's famous Columbia album *Kind of Blue,* a work that hints of the direction Coltrane would ultimately follow. Strickland writes of the period: "Coltrane's attempt 'to explore all the avenues' made him the perfect stylistic complement to Davis, with his cooler style, which featured sustained blue notes and brief cascades of sixteenths almost willfully retreating into silence, and also Monk, with his spare and unpredictable chords and clusters. Davis, characteristically, paid the tersest homage, when, on being told that his music was so complex that it required five saxophonists, he replied that he'd once had Coltrane."

Exhausted Every Possibility for His Horn

What Coltrane called "exploring all the avenues" was essentially the quest to exhaust every possibility for his horn in the course of a song. He devoted himself to rapid runs in which individual notes were virtually indistinguishable, a style quickly labeled "sheets of sound." As Martin Williams puts it in *Saturday Review,* Coltrane "seemed prepared to gush out every conceivable note, run his way a step at a time through every complex chord, every extension, and every substitution, and go beyond that by reaching for sounds that no tenor saxophone had ever uttered before him." Needless to say, this music was not easily understood—critics were quick to find fault with its length and monotony—but it represented an evolution that was welcomed not only by jazz performers, but by composers and even rock musicians as well.

In 1960 Coltrane formed his own quartet in the saxophone-plus-rhythm mode. He was joined by McCoy Tyner on piano, Elvin Jones on drums, and Jimmy Garrison on bass, all of whom were as eager as Coltrane to explore an increasingly free idiom. Finally Coltrane was free to expand his music at will, and his solos took on unprecedented lengths as he experimented with modal foundations, pentatonic scales, and triple meter. His best-known work was recorded during this period, including "My Favorite Things," a surprising theme-and-variations piece based on the saccharine Richard Rogers tune from "The Sound of Music." In "My Favorite Things," writes Williams, Coltrane "encountered a popular song which had the same sort of structure he was interested in, a folk-like simplicity and incantiveness, and very little harmonic motion. . . . It became a best seller."

Extent of Jazz Legacy Realized

By 1965 Coltrane was one of the most famous jazz artists alive, acclaimed alike in Europe, Japan, and the United States. Critics who had once dismissed his work "all but waved banners to show their devotion to him," to quote Strickland. Not surprisingly, the musician continued to experiment, even at the risk of alienating his growing audience. His work grew ever more complex, ametric, and improvisatorial. Coltrane explained his personal vision in *Newsweek.* "I have to feel that I'm after something," he said. "If I make money, fine. But I'd rather be striving. It's the striving, man, it's that I want."

Coltrane continued to perform and record even as advancing liver cancer left him racked with pain. He died at forty, only months after he cut his album *Expression.* The subsequent years have revealed the extent of his legacy to jazz, a legacy based on the spiritual quest for meaning and involvement between man, his soul, and the universe. Strickland concludes: "Those who criticize Coltrane's virtuosic profusion are of the same party as those who found Van Gogh's canvases 'too full of paint.' . . . In Coltrane, sound—often discordant, chaotic, almost unbearable— became the spiritual form of the man, an identification perhaps possible only with a wind instrument, with which the player is of necessity fused more intimately than with strings or percussion. . . . The whole spectrum of Coltrane's music—the world-weary melancholy and transcendental yearning that ultimately recall Bach more than Parker, the jungle calls and glossolalic shrieks, the whirlwind runs and spare elegies for murdered children and a murderous planet—is at root merely a suffering man's breath. The quality of that music reminds us that the root of the word *inspiration* is 'breathing upon.' This country has not produced a greater musician."

Further Reading

Cole, Bill, *John Coltrane,* Schirmer, 1977.

Terkel, Studs, *Giants of Jazz,* Crowell, 1975.

Atlantic, December 1987.

Down Beat, July 12, 1979; September 1986.

New Republic, February 12, 1977.

Newsweek, July 31, 1967.

New York Times, July 18, 1967.

Saturday Review, September 16, 1987. □

Arthur Holly Compton

The American physicist Arthur Holly Compton (1892-1962) discovered the "Compton effect" and the proof of the latitude intensity variation. He also played a critical role in the development of the atomic bomb.

Arthur Compton was born in Wooster, Ohio, on Sept. 10, 1892, the youngest child of Elias and Otelia Compton. It was midway during Arthur's early formal education that he became interested in science and carried out his first amateur researches. Although he wrote an intelligent student essay on the mammoth, it was chiefly astronomy and aviation that stimulated him. He purchased a telescope and photographed constellations and (in 1910) Halley's comet. Later he constructed and flew a 27-foot-wingspan glider.

During his undergraduate years at the College of Wooster (1909-1913) Compton had to choose a profession. His father encouraged him to devote his life to science. On his graduation from Wooster, therefore, Arthur decided to

pursue graduate study, obtaining his master's degree in physics from Princeton University in 1914; in 1916 he obtained his doctoral degree. Immediately after receiving his degree, Compton married Betty Charity McCloskey, a former Wooster classmate; the Comptons had two sons.

Compton Effect

Compton's first position was as an instructor in physics at the University of Minnesota (1916-1917), where he continued his x-ray researches. Leaving Minnesota, he became a research engineer at the newly established Westinghouse laboratory in East Pittsburgh, where he remained from 1917 to 1919, doing original work on the sodium-vapor lamp and developing instrumentation for aircraft. He left Westinghouse because he came to recognize that fundamentally his interest was not in industrial research but in pure research. In particular, he had become intrigued by a recent observation of the English physicist C. G. Barkla, who had scattered hard x-rays from aluminum and found that the total amount of scattered radiation was less than that predicted by a wellknown formula of J. J. Thomson. Compton found that he could account for Barkla's observation by assuming that the electrons in the scatterer were very large and therefore diffracting the incident radiation.

Anxious to pursue these studies further, Compton applied for and received a National Research Council fellowship to work with perhaps the foremost experimentalist of the day, Ernest Rutherford, at the Cavendish Laboratory in England. Compton's year in the extremely stimulating intellectual atmosphere at the Cavendish, during which time he carried out gamma-ray scattering experiments and pondered his results, marked a turning point in his career, as he became convinced that he was on the track of a very fundamental physical phenomenon.

Desiring to pursue it further on his own, Compton returned to the United States in 1920 to accept the Wayman Crow professorship of physics at Washington University in St. Louis. There he scattered x-rays from various substances and, eventually, analyzed the scattered radiation by use of a Bragg spectrometer. By the fall of 1922 he had definite experimental proof that x-rays undergo a distinct change in wavelength when scattered, the exact amount depending only on the angle through which they are scattered. Compton published this conclusion in October 1922 and within 2 months correctly accounted for it theoretically. He assumed that an x-ray—a particle of radiation—collides with an electron in the scatterer, conserving both energy and momentum. This process has since become famous as the Compton effect, a discovery for which he was awarded the Nobel Prize of 1927. The historical significance of Compton's discovery was that it forced physicists for the first time to seriously cope with Einstein's long-neglected and revolutionary 1905 light-quantum hypothesis: in the Compton effect an x-ray behaves exactly like any other colliding particle.

Cosmic Ray Work

While the discovery of the Compton effect was undoubtedly Compton's single most important contribution to physics, he made many others, both earlier and later. He proved in 1922 that x-rays can be totally internally reflected from glass and silver mirrors, experiments which eventually led to precise values for the index of refraction and electronic populations of substances, as well as to a new and more precise value for the charge of the electron. After Compton left Washington University for the University of Chicago in 1923 (where he later became Charles H. Swift distinguished service professor in 1929 and chairman of the department of physics and dean of the physical sciences in 1940), he reactivated a very early interest and developed a diffraction method for determining electronic distributions in atoms. Still later he and J. C. Stearns proved that ferromagnetism cannot be due to the tilting of electronic orbital planes.

Perhaps the most important work Compton carried out after going to Chicago was his work on cosmic rays. Realizing the importance of these rays for cosmological theories, Compton developed a greatly improved detector and convinced the Carnegie Institution to fund a world survey between 1931 and 1934. The globe was divided into nine regions, and roughly 100 physicists divided into smaller groups sailed oceans, traversed continents, and scaled mountains, carrying identical detectors to measure cosmic-ray intensities.

The most significant conclusion drawn from Compton's world survey was that the intensity of cosmic rays at the surface of the earth steadily decreases as one goes from either pole to the Equator. This "latitude effect" had been noted earlier by the Dutch physicist J. Clay, but the evidence had not been conclusive. Compton's survey therefore proved that the earth's magnetic field deflects at least most of the incident cosmic rays, which is only possible if they are charged particles. Compton's world survey marked a turning point in knowledge of cosmic rays.

Atomic Bomb and Postwar Endeavors

When World War II broke out, Compton was called upon to assess the chances of producing an atomic bomb. If it were possible to develop an atomic bomb, Compton believed it should be the United States that had possession of it. Detailed calculations on nuclear fission processes proved that the possibility of developing this awesome weapon existed. Compton recommended production, and for 4 years thereafter, as director of the U.S. government's Plutonium Research Project, he devoted all of his administrative, scientific, and inspirational energies to make the bomb a reality.

Compton was under extraordinary pressure as he made arrangements for the purification of uranium and the production of plutonium and many other elements that went into the construction of the atomic bomb. Ultimately, Compton was asked for his personal opinion as to whether the bomb should be dropped on Hiroshima. He gave an affirmative response in the firm conviction that it was the only way to bring the war to a swift conclusion and thereby save many American and Japanese lives.

Between 1945 and 1953 Compton was chancellor of Washington University in St. Louis and strove unceasingly to make that institution a guiding light in higher education. Between 1954 and 1961, as distinguished service professor of natural philosophy, he taught, wrote, and delivered lectures to many groups and, as always, served on numerous boards and committees. In 1961 he became professor-at-large, intending to divide his time between Washington University, the University of California at Berkeley, and Wooster College. His plans were cut short by his sudden death on March 15, 1962, in Berkeley.

Compton was an extraordinarily gifted human being. At the age of 35 he won the Nobel Prize and was also elected to the National Academy of Sciences; later, he was elected to numerous other honorary societies, both foreign and domestic. He received a large number of honorary degrees, medals (including the U.S. government's Medal for Merit), and other honors. In spite of his many achievements and honors, however, he remained a modest and warm human being.

Further Reading

The Cosmos of Arthur Holly Compton, edited by Marjorie Johnston (1968), contains Compton's "Personal Reminiscences," a selection of his writings on scientific and nonscientific subjects, and a bibliography of his scientific writings. Compton discusses his role in the development of the atomic bomb in *Atomic Quest* (1956). The early life of the Compton family is the subject of James R. Blackwood, *The House on College Avenue: The Comptons at Wooster, 1891-1913* (1968). General works on modern physics which discuss Compton include Gerald Holton and Duane H.D. Roller, *Foundations of*

Modern Physical Science (1958); Henry A. Boorse and Lloyd Motz, eds., *The World of the Atom* (2 vols., 1966); and Ira M. Freeman, *Physics: Principles and Insights* (1968). □

John Calvin Coolidge

John Calvin Coolidge (1872-1933) was the thirtieth president of the United States. He has become symbolic of the smug and self-satisfied conservatism that helped bring on the Great Depression.

Calvin Coolidge (he dropped the John after college) was born July 14, 1872, at Plymouth Notch, a tiny, isolated village in southern Vermont; he was descended from colonial New England stock. His father was a thrifty, hard-working, self-reliant storekeeper and farmer, active in local politics. Calvin was a shy and frail boy, sober, frugal, industrious, and taciturn. But he acquired from his mother, whom he remembered as having "a touch of mysticism and poetry," a yearning for something better than Plymouth Notch.

Coolidge entered Amherst College in 1891 and graduated *cum laude*. While there he became an effective debater, and his professors imbued him with the ideal of public service. Unable to afford law school, he read law and clerked in a law office in Northampton, Mass. In 1897 he was admitted to the bar and the following year opened an office in Northampton. He built a modestly successful local practice. In 1905 he married Grace Goodhue, a charming and vivacious teacher. They had two sons: John, born 1906, and Calvin, born 1908.

Apprentice Politician

Coolidge became active in local Republican politics, serving as a member of the city council, city solicitor, clerk of the Hampshire County courts, and chairman of the Republican city committee. He spent two terms in the Massachusetts House of Representatives and two terms as mayor of Northampton. In 1911 he was elected to the state senate and 2 years later—thanks to luck, hard work, and cautious but skillful political maneuvering—he became president of the state senate. This was a traditional stepping-stone to the lieutenant governorship; he was elected to this post in 1915 and reelected in 1916 and 1917. Meanwhile, he gained a reputation as a loyal party man and follower of the powerful U.S. senator W. Murray Crane, a safe and sound man as regards business and a champion of governmental economy and efficiency. And Coolidge won the friendship of Boston department store owner Frank W. Stearns, who became his enthusiastic political booster.

But Coolidge was no narrow-minded standpatter. His credo was the promotion of stability and harmony through the balancing of all legitimate interests. Thus, he supported woman's suffrage, popular election of U.S. senators, establishment of a public service commission, legislation to prohibit the practice of undercutting competition by charging less than cost, protection of child and woman workers, maternity aid legislation, and the state's savings-bank insurance system.

Governor of Massachusetts

Elected governor in 1918, Coolidge pushed through a far-reaching reorganization of the state government, supported adoption of legislation against profiteering, and won a reputation for fairness as a mediator in labor disputes. But what brought him national fame was the Boston police strike of 1919. He avoided involvement in the dispute on the ground that he had no legal authority to interfere. Even when the police went out on strike, Coolidge failed to act until after Boston's mayor had brought the situation under control. Yet again Coolidge's luck held; and he, not the mayor, received the credit for maintaining law and order. His reply to the plea of the American Federation of Labor president Samuel Gompers for reinstatement of the dismissed strikers—"There is no right to strike against the public safety by anybody, anywhere, any time"—made him a popular hero and won him reelection that fall with the largest vote ever received by a Massachusetts gubernatorial candidate. At the Republican National Convention the following year the rank-and-file delegates rebelled against the party leaders' choice for the vice-presidential nominee and named Coolidge on the first ballot.

Sudden Thrust to the Presidency

Coolidge found the vice presidency frustrating and unrewarding. He presided over the Senate and unobtrusively sat in on Cabinet meetings at President Warren G. Harding's request but took no active role in administration decision making, gaining the nickname "Silent Cal."

Harding's death in 1923 catapulted Coolidge into the White House. The new president's major problem was the exposure of the corruption that had gone on under his predecessor. But his own reputation for honesty and integrity, his early appointment of special counsel to investigate the Teapot Dome oil-lease scandal and prosecute wrongdoers, and his removal of Attorney General Harry Daugherty when Daugherty refused to open Justice Department files to Senate investigators, effectively defused the corruption issue. Simultaneously, he smoothed the path for his nomination in 1924 through skillful manipulation of patronage. The Republican themes in the 1924 election were prosperity, governmental economy, and "Keep Cool with Coolidge." He won decisively.

Except for legislation regulating and stabilizing the chaotic radio industry, the subsidization and promotion of commercial aviation, and the Railroad Labor Act of 1926 establishing more effective machinery for resolving railway labor disputes, the new Coolidge administration's record in the domestic sphere was largely negative. Coolidge was handicapped by the split in Republican congressional ranks between the insurgents and regulars; furthermore, he was not a strong leader and remained temperamentally averse to making moves that might lead to trouble. He was also handcuffed by his conviction that the executive's duty was simply to administer the laws Congress passed. Most important, he was limited by his devotion to governmental economy, his belief in allowing the widest possible scope for private enterprise, his faith in business self-regulation, his narrow definition of the powers of the national government under the Constitution, and his acceptance of the "trickle-down" theory of prosperity through the encouragement of big business.

Domestic Program

Coolidge's domestic program was in line with this philosophy. He strongly backed Secretary of the Treasury Andrew Mellon's proposals for tax cuts to stimulate investment, and the Revenue Act of 1926 cut the maximum surtax from 40 to 20 percent, abolished the gift tax, and halved the estate tax. He vetoed the World War I veterans' bonus bill (1924), but Congress overrode his veto. He packed the regulatory commissions with appointees sympathetic to business. He twice vetoed the McNary-Haugen bills for the subsidized dumping of agricultural surpluses abroad in hopes of bolstering domestic prices. Coolidge unsuccessfully urged the sale or lease of Muscle Shoals to private enterprise and in 1928 pocket-vetoed a bill providing for government operation. He succeeded in limiting expenditures for flood control and Federal development of water resources. He resisted any reductions in the protective tariff. And he not only failed to restrain, but encouraged, the stock market speculation that was to have such disastrous consequences in 1929.

Foreign Affairs

Coolidge left foreign affairs largely in the hands of his secretaries of state, Charles Evans Hughes and then Frank B. Kellogg. The administration's major achievements in this area were its fostering of a professional civil service, its cautious sympathy toward Chinese demands for revision of the tariff and extraterritoriality treaties, and its efforts to restore friendship with Latin America.

Coolidge had a vague, idealistic desire to promote international stability and peace. But he rejected American membership in the League of Nations as then constituted and, whatever his personal feelings, regarded the League as a dead issue. He felt bound by Harding's prior commitment to support American membership on the World Court, but he never fought for its approval and dropped the issue when other members balked at accepting the reservations added by the Senate anti-internationalists. Although Coolidge did exert his influence to secure ratification of the Kellogg-Briand Pact (1928) outlawing war, his hand was forced by public opinion and he had no illusions about its significance. He supported Hughes's efforts to resolve the reparations tangle; but he was adamant against cancellation of the World War I Allied debts, reportedly saying, "They hired the money, didn't they?" His major effort in behalf of disarmament, the Geneva Conference of 1927, was a failure.

Leaving the White House

Yet Coolidge was popular and could have been reelected in 1928. But on Aug. 2, 1927, he publicly announced, "I do not choose to run for president in 1928." The death of his son Calvin in 1924 had dimmed his interest in politics; both he and his wife felt the physical strain of the presidency, and he had doubts about the continued soundness of the economy. He left the White House to retire to Northampton, where he died on Jan. 5, 1933, of a coronary thrombosis.

Coolidge was not a leader of foresight and vision. But whatever his shortcomings as seen in retrospect, he fitted the popular yearning of his day for stability and normalcy.

Further Reading

Two illuminating works are *The Autobiography of Calvin Coolidge* (1929) and a record of his press conferences, *The Talkative President: The Off-the-Record Press Conferences of Calvin Coolidge,* edited by Howard H. Quint and Robert H. Ferrell (1964). The most thorough and scholarly biography of Coolidge is Donald R. McCoy, *Calvin Coolidge: The Quiet President* (1967). Two earlier but still useful biographies are Claude M. Fuess's sympathetic *Calvin Coolidge: The Man from Vermont* (1940) and William Allen White's more hostile and less accurate *A Puritan in Babylon: The Story of Calvin Coolidge* (1938). Robert Sobel attempts a revisionist examination of Coolidge in *Coolidge: An American Enigma* (1998). □

James Fenimore Cooper

Novelist and social critic James Fenimore Cooper (1789-1851) was the first major American writer to deal imaginatively with American life, notably in his five "Leather-Stocking Tales." He was also a critic of the political, social, and religious problems of the day.

James Cooper (his mother's family name of Fenimore was legally added in 1826) was born in Burlington, N.J., on Sept. 15, 1789, the eleventh of 12 children of William Cooper, a pioneering landowner and developer in New Jersey and New York. When James was 14 months old, his father moved the family to a vast tract of wilderness at the headwaters of the Susquehanna River in New York State where, on a system of small land grants, he had established the village of Cooperstown at the foot of Otsego Lake.

Here, in the "Manor House," later known as Otsego Hall, Cooper grew up, the privileged son of the "squire" of a primitive community. He enjoyed the amenities of a transplanted civilization while reading, in the writings of the wilderness missionary John Gottlieb Heckewelder, about the Native Americans who had long since retreated westward, and about life in the Old World in the novels of Sir Walter Scott and Jane Austen. Meanwhile, he attended the local school and Episcopal church. The lore of the wilderness learned from excursions into the surrounding forests and from local trappers and hunters, the stories of life in the great estates of neighboring Dutch patroons and English patentees, and the gossip of revolution-torn Europe brought by refugees of all classes furnished him with materials for his later novels, histories, and commentaries.

For the present, however, Cooper was a vigorous and obstreperous young man who was sent away to be educated, first by a clergyman in Albany, and then at Yale, from which he was dismissed for a student prank. His father next arranged for him to go to sea, first in a merchant vessel to England and Spain, and then in the Navy; these experiences stimulated at least a third of his later imaginative writing.

When Cooper returned to civilian life in 1811, he married Susan Augusta DeLancey of a formerly wealthy New York Tory family and established himself in Westchester County overlooking Long Island Sound, a gentleman farmer involved in the local militia, Agricultural Society, and Episcopal church. It was here, at the age of 30, that he published his first novel, written on a challenge from his wife.

First Period of His Literary Career

Precaution was an attempt to outdo the English domestic novels Cooper had been reading, which he imitated in choice of theme, scene, and manner. But he soon realized his mistake, and the next year, in *The Spy*, he deliberately attempted to correct it by choosing the American Revolution for subject, the country around New York City he knew so well for scene, and the historical romance of Scott for model. Thereafter, although many of his novels combined the novel of manners with the historical romance, as well as with other currently popular fictional modes, he never again departed from his concern for American facts and opinions, even though for some of his tales he chose, in the spirit of comparative analysis, scenes in foreign lands and waters.

All of the novels of the first period of Cooper's literary career (1820-1828) were as experimental as the first two. Three dealt with the frontier and Native American life (*The Pioneers, The Last of the Mohicans,* and *The Prairie*), three with the sea (*The Pilot, The Red Rover,* and *The Water Witch*), and three with American history (*The Spy, Lionel Lincoln,* and *The Wept of Wish-ton-Wish*).

Discovering the "American Problem"

The success of his first America-oriented novel convinced Cooper that he was on the right track, and he decided to turn to his childhood memories for a truthful, if not wholly literal, tale of life on the frontier: *The Pioneers* (1823). Judge Temple in the novel is Judge Cooper, and Templeton is Cooperstown; and originals for most of the characters can be identified, as can the scenes and much of the action, although all of it is given what Cooper called "a poetical view of the subject." Though the traditional novel of manners deals realistically with a group of people in a closed and stable community using an agreed-upon code of social ethics, Cooper tried to adapt this form to a fluid and open society, thereby illuminating the core of the "American problem": how could the original trio of "unalienable rights"—life, liberty, and property (not, as Jefferson had it, the pursuit of happiness)—be applied to a society in which the rights of the Native American possessors of the land were denied by the civilized conqueror who took it from them for his own profit, thus defying the basic Christian ethic of individual integrity and brotherly love?

Natty Bumppo (or Leather-Stocking as he is called in the series as a whole) is neither the "natural man" nor the "civilized man" of European theorists such as John Locke and Jean Jacques Rousseau; he is the American individualist who is creating a new society by a code of personal fulfillment under sound moral self-guidance, improvising as he goes along. In *The Pioneers* Natty is a somewhat crotchety old man whose chief "gift" is his ability to argue his rights with both Indian John and Judge Temple. The central theme which knits this complex web of people and adventures into the cycle of a single year is the emergence of Leather-Stocking as the "American hero."

At this point Cooper was feeling his way toward a definition of his social concern, but in the novel itself the problem is almost submerged in the excitement, action, and vivid description and narrative. In the next of the Leather-Stocking series, *The Last of the Mohicans,* Natty is younger and the romantic story line takes over, making it the most popular of all Cooper's novels. In *The Prairie* Natty in his last days becomes a tragic figure driven west, into the setting sun, in a futile search for his ideal way of life. To most of Cooper's readers these stories are pure romances of adventure, and their social significance is easily overlooked.

In *The Pilot* (1824) Cooper was drawn to the sea by what he felt was Scott's mishandling of the subject, and he thus discovered a whole second world in which to explore his moral problem. The American hero, John Paul Jones, like other patriots of the time, is in revolt against the authority of the English king, and yet, in his own empire of the ship, he is forced by the dangers of the elements to exert an even more arbitrary authority over his crew. There is a similar problem in *The Red Rover,* the story of a pirate with a Robin Hood complex, and in *The Water-Witch,* a tale of a gentleman-rogue, which is less successful because Cooper turned from the technique of straight romantic narrative to that of symbolism.

Cooper's two historical novels of the period (other than *The Spy*), *Lionel Lincoln* and *The Wept of Wishton-Wish,* are set in New England, where Cooper was never at home. The former, although thoroughly researched, is trivial, but in the latter, in spite of lack of sympathy, Cooper made a profound study of the conflict between Puritan morality and integrity and the savage ethic of the frontier.

Second Period

His reputation as a popular novelist established, Cooper went abroad in 1826 to arrange for the translation and foreign publication of his works and to give his family the advantages of European residence and travel. He stayed 7 years, during which he completed two more romances, but thereafter, until 1840, he devoted most of his energy to political and social criticism—both in fiction and in nonfiction. Irritated by the criticisms of English travelers in America, in 1828 he wrote a defense of American life and institutions in a mock travel book, *Notions of the Americans Picked Up by a Travelling Bachelor.*

Settling his children in a convent school in Paris, he traveled from London to Sorrento, Italy, and also stayed in Switzerland, Germany, France, and England. Europe was astir with reform and revolutionary movements, and the outspoken Cooper was drawn into close friendships with the Marquis de Lafayette and other liberal leaders. One product of this interest was a trio of novels on European political themes (*The Bravo, The Heidenmauer,* and *The Headsman*), but the American press was so hostile to them

that Cooper finally declared, in his 1834 *A Letter to His Countrymen,* that he would write no more fiction.

This resolution, however, lasted only long enough to produce five volumes of epistolary travel essay and commentary on Europe (*Gleanings in Europe* and *Sketches of Switzerland*); *The Monikins,* a Swiftean political allegory; and various works on the American Navy, including a definitive two-volume history, a volume of biographies of naval officers, and miscellaneous tracts.

In 1833 Cooper returned to America, renovated Otsego Hall in Cooperstown, and settled his family there for the rest of his life. There is much autobiography in the pair of novels *Homeward Bound* and *Home as Found* (1838), in which he reversed himself to attack the people and institutions of his own land with the same keen critical insight that he had applied to Europe. One reason for this was that a series of libel suits against Whig editors helped personalize his quarrel with the equalitarian and leveling tendencies of the Jacksonian era. He won the suits but lost many friends and much of his reading public. His social and political position is succinctly summed up in *The American Democrat* (1838).

Third Period

The third period of Cooper's literary career began in 1840-1841 with his return to the Leather-Stocking series and two more chapters in the life of Natty Bumppo, *The Pathfinder,* in which Cooper used his own experiences on Lake Ontario during the War of 1812, and *The Deerslayer,* which fills in the young manhood of his hero. These romances were followed by equally vigorous tales of the sea, *The Two Admirals* and *Wing-and-Wing.*

But the most significant development of this period was Cooper's final success in blending the romantic novel of action and the open spaces with the novel of manners and social concern. Returning for subject to the scenes of his first interest, the estates and villages of early upstate New York (with their mixed population of Dutch patroons, English patentees, small farmers and woodsmen, and variegated adventurers carving out civilization in a wilderness peopled by Native Americans and rife with unexploited wildlife of all kinds), he wrote five novels in two series: *Afloat and Ashore* (1844) and its sequel, *Miles Wallingford,* and the "Littlepage Manuscripts" (1845-1846), depicting in a trilogy (*Satanstoe, The Chainbearer,* and *The Redskins*) the four-generation history of a landed family from their first days of settlement to the days of the disintegration of their privileged way of life in the face of rampant, classless democracy. Largely unread and unappreciated in their day, these five novels, especially *Satanstoe,* have since become recognized as Cooper's most successful fulfillment of his intention. He had always wished to write a chronicle of his times in fictional form in order to interpret for his countrymen and the world at large the deeper meanings of the "American experiment" in its formative years.

Meanwhile, Cooper's concerns for individual and social integrity and for change had hardened into moral and religious absolutes, and the novels of his last 4 years were less story and more allegory. The best of these, *The Crater* (1847), succeeds where *The Water-Witch* and *The Mon-*

ikins failed, in using symbolism to convey a narrative message.

Cooper's Achievement

The power and persistence of this first major American author in attempting a total imaginative redaction of American life, coupled with an equal skill in the description of place and the depiction of action, overcame the liabilities of both the heavy romantic style current in his day and his substitution of the character type for the individual character. Appreciated first in Europe, the most action-packed of his novels survived the eclipse of his reputation as a serious literary artist (brought about through attacks on his stormy personality and unpopular social ideas) and have led to a restudy of the whole of his work in recent years. In this process Cooper has been restored to his rightful place as the first major American man of letters.

Further Reading

Probably the most satisfactory short biography of Cooper is James Grossman, *James Fenimore Cooper* (1949), although Donald A. Ringe, *James Fenimore Cooper* (1962), gives fuller critical treatment of Cooper's works, and Robert E. Spiller, *Fenimore Cooper: Critic of His Times* (1931), provides more background analysis of Cooper's social ideas. None of these biographers had the advantage of James F. Beard, who edited *The Letters and Journals of James Fenimore Cooper* (6 vols., 1960-1968), and a new biography is needed. □

Aaron Copland

Aaron Copland (1900-1990) was one of the most important figures in American music during the second quarter of the 20th century, both as a composer and as a spokesman who was concerned about making Americans conscious of the importance of their indigenous music.

Aaron Copland was born on November 14, 1900, in Brooklyn, New York, the youngest of five children born to Harris Morris Copland and Sarah (Mittenthal) Copland. He attended Boys' High School and studied music privately (theory and composition with Rubin Goldmark, beginning in 1917). In 1921 he went to France to study at the American Conservatory in Fontainebleau, where his principal teacher was Nadia Boulanger. During his early studies, he had been much attracted by the music of Scriabin, Debussy, and Ravel; the years in Paris provided an opportunity to hear and absorb all the most recent trends in European music, notably the works of Stravinsky, Bartók, and Schoenberg.

Upon completion of his studies in 1924, Copland returned to America and composed the *Symphony for Organ and Orchestra,* his first major work, which Boulanger played in New York in 1925. *Music for the Theater* (1925) and a Piano Concerto (1926) explored the possibilities of jazz idioms in symphonic music; from this period dates the interest of Serge Koussevitzky, conductor of the Boston Symphony Orchestra, in Copland's music—a sponsorship that proved important in gaining a wider audience for his own and much of America's music.

In the late 1920s Copland turned to an increasingly abstract style, characterized by angular melodic lines, spare textures, irregular rhythms, and often abrasive sonorities. The already distinctive idiom of the early works became entirely personal and free of identifiable outside influence in the *Piano Variations* (1930), *Short Symphony* (1933), and *Statements,* and the basic features of these works remained in one way or another central to his musical style thereafter.

The 1920s and 1930s were a period of intense concern about the limited audience for new (and especially American) music, and Copland was active in many organizations devoted to performance and sponsorship, notably the League of Composers, the Copland-Sessions concerts, and the American Composers' Alliance. His organizational abilities earned him the sobriquet of *American music's natural president* from his colleague Virgil Thomson.

Beginning in the mid-1930s, Copland made a conscious effort to broaden the audience for American music and took steps to adapt his style when writing works commissioned for various functional occasions. The years between 1935 and 1950 saw his extensive involvement in music for theater, school, ballet, and cinema, as well as for more conventional concert situations. In the ballets, *Billy the Kid* (1938), *Rodeo* (1942), and *Appalachian Spring* (1944; Pulitzer Prize, 1945), he made use of folk or folklike melodies and relaxed his previous highly concentrated style, to arrive at an idiom broadly recognized as "American" without the sacrifice of craftsmanship or inventiveness. Other well-known works of this period are *El Salón México* (1935) and *A Lincoln Portrait* (1942), while the

Piano Sonata (1943) and the Third Symphony (1946) continue the line of development of his concert music. Among his widely acclaimed film scores are those for *Of Mice and Men* (1939), *Our Town* (1940), *The Red Pony* (1948), and *The Heiress* (1949).

Copland's concern for establishing a tradition of music in American life was manifested in his activities as teacher at The New School for Social Research and Harvard and as head of the composition department at the Berkshire Music Center in Tanglewood, Massachusetts, founded by Koussevitzky. His Norton Lectures at Harvard (1951-1952) were published as *Music and Imagination* (1952); earlier books, of similar gracefully didactic intent, are *What to Listen for in Music* (1939) and *Our New Music* (1941).

Beginning with the Quartet for Piano and Strings (1950), Copland made use of the serial methods developed by Arnold Schoenberg, amplifying concerns of linear texture long present in his music. The most important works of these years include the *Piano Fantasy* (1957), *Nonet for Strings* (1960), *Connotations* (1962), and *Inscape* (1967); the opera *The Tender Land* (1954) represents an extension of the style of the ballets to the lyric stage.

After his return from France, Copland resided in the New York City area. He engaged in many cultural missions, especially to South America. Although he had been out of the major spotlight for almost twenty years, he remained semi-active in the music world up until his death, conducting his last symphony in 1983.

Copland died on December 2,1990 in New York City and was remembered as a man who encouraged young composers to find their own voice, no matter the style, just as he had done for six decades.

Further Reading

An autobiographical sketch is included in Copland's *The New Music, 1900-1960* (titled *Our New Music*)(1968). Arthur V. Berger *Aaron Copland* (1953), contains more penetrating observations about Copland's music, but Julia F. Smith *Aaron Copland: His Work and Contribution to American Music* (1955), is also useful. An extensive biography with musical commentary can be found in Howard Pollack, *Aaron Copland: The Life and Work of an Uncommon Man* (1999). A detailed biography appears in the 1951 issue of *Current Biography.*

Copland's obituary appears in the December 17, 1990, issue of *Time* magazine. □

Francis Ford Coppola

Schooled in low-budget filmmaking, Francis Ford Coppola (born 1939) has gone on to direct some of the most financially successful and critically acclaimed movies in U.S. cinematic history.

Francis Ford Coppola, director of *The Godfather* and its two sequels, would be considered one of the masters of modern cinema based on those credits alone. But the writer/director/producer has been behind the scenes on numerous commercial and critical successes outside the

gangster genre. Coppola's uncommon craftsmanship has enabled him to make a dizzying variety of films, from low-budget labors of love to mainstream Hollywood crowd-pleasers. All his projects have the earmarks of a Coppola production: a respect for storytelling and a passionate commitment to the filmmaker's art. It was these qualities that led David Thomson, in his *Biographical Dictionary of Film,* to say of Coppola: "No one retains so many jubilant traits of the kid moviemaker."

Raised in Show-Business Family

Coppola was born in Detroit, Michigan, on April 7, 1939. His father, Carmine, was a concert flautist who played with Arturo Toscanini's NBC Symphony Orchestra. His mother, Italia, was an actress who at one time had appeared in films. Coppola's younger sister Talia would later follow in her mother's footsteps into the world of film acting, changing her name to Talia Shire and starring in the film *Rocky* alongside Silvester Stallone. A few years after his birth, Coppola and his family moved to the suburbs around New York City, where he would spend most of his childhood.

All the Coppola children were driven to succeed in show business and the arts. Leading by example was Coppola's father, who had achieved success as a musician for hire but longed to compose scores of his own. Francis seemed the least likely to redeem his father's promise, however. He was an awkward, myopic child who did poorly at school. At age nine, he was stricken with polio. The illness forced him into bed for a year, a period during which he played with puppets, watched television, and became lost in an inner fantasy world. After his recovery, he began to make movies with an eight millimeter camera and a tape recorder.

Interest in Film Sparked in High School and College

While a student at Great Neck High School on Long Island, Coppola began to study filmmaking more formally. He soon became enamored with the work of Soviet director Sergei Eisenstein. Coppola also trained in music and theater to round out his education. In 1956 he enrolled at Hofstra College in Hempstead, New York on a drama scholarship. Here he acted in and directed student productions, and founded his own cinema workshop. So determined was Coppola to direct his own pictures that he once sold his car to pay for a 16-millimeter camera.

After graduating from Hofstra, Coppola moved to the West Coast to attend film school at the University of California—Los Angeles (UCLA). But he was impatient to escape the classroom and start making his own films. He signed on to direct an adult movie, which caught the attention of low-budget impresario Roger Corman. Corman hired Coppola to work on his movies as a jack-of-all-trades. Coppola's strong work ethic prompted Corman to allow him to direct his own picture. The result was *Dementia 13* (1963), a gory horror movie Coppola had written in three days and shot for $40,000. That year, Coppola married Eleanor Neil, his set decorator on the picture.

Establishes His Reputation

Coppola submitted his next film, *You're a Big Boy Now* (1966), as his master's thesis at UCLA. The sweet coming-of-age drama anticipated the style and themes of *The Graduate* and received many positive reviews. Warner Brothers selected the promising young filmmaker to direct their big-budget musical *Finian's Rainbow*. But the subject matter took Coppola away from his strengths and the film was savaged by critics. *The Rain People* (1969) represented Coppola's attempt to return to "personal" (not to mention low-budget) moviemaking. A somber travelogue about a housewife on the run, the movie was made up as the crew went along, evidence of Coppola's flair for the experimental.

Coppola might have remained in an avant-garde rut were it not for his next project. As co-writer of the mega-hit biopic *Patton,* Coppola earned an Academy Award and added considerable luster to a tarnished reputation. Paramount Pictures next asked him to take the reins on its screen adaptation of Mario Puzo's bestselling novel *The Godfather.* It would prove to be Coppola's greatest triumph.

Glory Gained from *Godfather*

Filming *The Godfather* posed many challenges. Coppola fought hard to retain control of casting decisions. He also resisted studio attempts to cut his budget and make the setting more contemporary. Italian-American groups protested the depiction of organized crime in the original screenplay. Even Coppola's own crew at times lost faith in

his ability to control the mammoth project. Nevertheless, he steered the movie to completion.

The Godfather tells the sweeping story of the Corleone crime family, focusing on the ascension of young Michael Corleone to control of the family's empire. It is a violent epic on the scale of classic American films like *Gone with the Wind.* Propelling the drama forward are powerful performances by Marlon Brando and newcomer Al Pacino. At its release in 1972, critics were floored by the film's depiction of America's criminal underworld. The film became a sensational hit with moviegoers as well, and the *The Godfather* swept the Academy Awards that year. Coppola was a winner in the Best Director and Best Screenplay categories; suddenly he was the toast of Hollywood.

Now a wealthy man thanks to the success of *The Godfather,* Coppola could at last pick and choose his own projects. In 1974 he made *The Conversation,* an edgy drama about secret surveillance. He returned to the world of organized crime with 1974's *The Godfather Part II,* which continued the Corleone family saga through the 1950s and, via flashback, to the early 1900s. The intricate storyline resonated once again with critics and moviegoers alike. Coppola accepted a second Academy Award statuette as Best Director of 1974. The haunting score, by Nino Rota and family patriarch Carmine Coppola, also took home an "Oscar."

Apocalypse and Aftermath

Coppola's next project was *Apocalypse Now,* an ambitious film about the Vietnam War. But the expensive production was bedeviled by bad weather, budget overruns, and the bizarre behavior of its star, Marlon Brando. The release date was pushed back repeatedly as Coppola struggled to come up with an ending for the film. When it finally reached the screen in 1979, the film was hailed by many critics as a visionary masterpiece. It was nominated for several Academy Awards and did well at the box office. But many in Hollywood never forgave Coppola for letting the project get so out of control. For many years, Coppola could not get funding from a major studio to make his movies.

Unable to make mainstream movies, Coppola instead crafted independent films which he released through his own Zoetrope Studio. These pictures, including *Rumble Fish* (1983) and *The Cotton Club* (1984), received mixed reviews and had many wondering if Coppola was a spent force in the industry. He did manage to create a hit with the offbeat *Peggy Sue Got Married* (1985), about a woman who travels back in time to her own high school days, but the project seemed like a work-for hire. Closer to Coppola's heart was *Tucker: The Man and His Dream,* a 1988 biopic about a maverick automaker who could have been a stand-in for the director himself.

Return to Prominence via *Godfather III*

In 1990 Coppola completed *The Godfather Part III.* While not as lavishly praised as the previous two installments, it nevertheless was a box office success and won back the confidence of the major studios. While receiving mixed critical response, his *Bram Stoker's Dracula* (1992) helped solidify Coppola's comeback. This lush, gory version of the horror classic was undermined by some poor performances but widely praised for its visual style. Audiences flocked to see stars Winona Ryder and Keanu Reeves, made the film a major hit, and returned Coppola to the ranks of "bankable" directors.

As the 1990s rolled on, Coppola continued to turn out Hollywood productions. The comedy *Jack* (1994) utilized the talents of Robin Williams, while *The Rainmaker* (1996) adapted the work of best-selling novelist John Grisham. Finally out of debt and at ease working for the major studios, Coppola in his late 50s seemed content with his cinematic legacy. He expanded his interests into publishing in 1997 with *Zoetrope Short Stories,* a magazine dedicated to literary, not Hollywood, material. "Coppola is hoping to revive the literary tradition of Ernest Hemingway, F. Scott Fitzgerald, . . . and maybe make a good movie in the process," noted Leslie Alan Horvitz in *Insight on the News.* In 1998 Coppola helped launch the first Classically Independent Film Festival in San Francisco, California; films shown included *One Flew Over the Cuckoo's Nest* and *Diner.* Also in 1998, Coppola won an $80 million lawsuit from Warner Bros. for blocking his plans to film a live-action Pinocchio. Outside the film industry, Coppola is the owner of a California winery that produces wine under the Niebaum-Coppola label.

Further Reading

Contemporary Literary Criticism, Volume 16, Gale, 1981.

Contemporary Theatre, Film, and Television, Volume 13, Gale, 1995.

Cowie, Peter, *Coppola: A Biography,* Scribner, 1990.

Dictionary of Literary Biography, Volume 44: *American Screenwriters, Second Series,* Gale, 1986.

Lewis, Jon, *Whom God Wishes to Destroy: Francis Coppola and the New Hollywood,* Duke University Press, 1995.

Thomson, David, *The Biographical Dictionary of Film,* Knopf, 1994.

American Film, April 1983.

Chicago Tribune, January 18, 1982; February 11, 1982; October 5, 1986; March 3, 1989; December 15, 1990.

Entertainment Weekly, February 7, 1997.

Film Quarterly, spring 1986.

Insight on the News, May 12, 1997.

Los Angeles Times, December 19, 1988; January 26, 1990; December 30, 1990.

New York Times, August 12, 1979; August 15, 1979; March 18, 1980; March 21, 1980; November 23, 1980; February 11, 1982; April 16, 1982; May 3, 1987; March 1, 1989; March 12, 1989; December 23, 1990; December 25, 1990.

Premiere, September 1996.

Time, April 17, 1995.

Times (London), January 21, 1988; November 14, 1988; February 11, 1989.

Vanity Fair, June 1990; December 1995; July 1996; April 1998.

Variety, November 17, 1997; January 26, 1998. □

William Henry Cosby, Jr.

An entertainer for three decades, William Henry Cosby, Jr. (born 1937) starred in live performances, record albums, books, film, and television. His long-running, hugely popular "The Cosby Show" was in the top of the Nielson television ratings from its debut in 1984.

William Henry Cosby, Junior, was born in Germantown, Pennsylvania, July 12, 1937, to Anna and William Cosby. There were four boys in the family, but one died from rheumatic fever at six years old. Soon after the young boy's death, William Cosby, Sr., left his family and joined the Navy. Bill, the oldest son, became the man of the family and helped his mother pay the bills by doing odd jobs such as delivering groceries and shining shoes. He tried to keep up with his school work, but he dropped out of high school to join the Navy in the early 1950s. Cosby's mother had always stressed the importance of education to her children, and so eventually Bill earned his diploma through correspondence school and was accepted at Temple University in Philadelphia on an athletic scholarship.

The athlete at Temple still needed spending money, so he took a job as a bartender in a neighborhood café called The Underground. The bar had a resident comedian who often didn't show up for his act, so Cosby began to fill in, entertaining the crowd with jokes and humorous stories. His reputation as a funny bartender spread throughout the city, and Cosby soon got offers to do stand-up comedy in other clubs. His act was influenced by Mel Brooks, Jonathan

Winters, Bob Newhart, and Lenny Bruce. Cosby's biggest chance came when he was asked to perform at the Gaslight Café, a Greenwich Village coffeehouse that regularly featured young performers such as Bob Dylan.

Cosby was soon making people laugh in large, well-known night spots all over the country, and he reached a point where his career showed him more promise than his education. He left Temple in 1962.

Cosby's first electronic medium for his comedy was the long-playing album. "Bill Cosby Is a Very Funny Fellow . . . Right!" (1963), produced by Roy Silver and Allan Sherman, was the comedian's first recording, as well as his first to win a Grammy Award. His second album, "I Started Out As a Child," released in 1964, received another Grammy honor as Best Comedy Album of the Year. All of Cosby's albums earned more than $1 million in sales. His popularity continued and he won consecutive Best Comedy Album awards every year from 1964 to 1969.

Allan Sherman was one of Cosby's biggest fans as well as his producer, and when Sherman filled in for Johnny Carson as guest host of "The Tonight Show" in 1963, he asked Cosby to be his guest. "The Tonight Show" producers were skeptical about having an African American comic on the show, but Sherman was adamant and Cosby was a big hit.

Sheldon Leonard, producer of mid-1960s hits including "The Danny Thomas Show," "The Dick Van Dyke Show," and "The Andy Griffith Show," was watching "The Tonight Show" the night Cosby was on. At the time, he was looking for a male actor to play opposite Robert Culp on a new dramatic series—and when he saw Cosby, he had his man. "I Spy" was an immediate success, and the fact that it was the first prime-time television program to star a black person added to its appeal. In 1967 Cosby won the Emmy Award for Best Actor in a Dramatic Series, and he did likewise in 1968 and 1969. His second prime-time series, "The Bill Cosby Show," began in 1969, just one year after "I Spy" went off the air. Starring Cosby as a high school sports instructor, it was number one in its first season. However, ratings steadily dropped over the next two years, and the show was canceled in the spring of 1971.

The following year marked the beginning of "Fat Albert and the Cosby Kids" as a regular series on CBS (it aired first in 1971 as a special). The Saturday afternoon cartoon featured a group of kids living and learning together in an urban area much like the impoverished section of Philadelphia where Cosby was reared. Cosby provided the voice for every character and bracketed the animated portion of the show in person to discuss the episode's message. So that his audience would learn good behavior and solid values, Cosby employed a panel of educators to act as advisers. The program won a variety of awards, and audience estimates numbered about six million.

Cosby made two more attempts at prime time with "The New Bill Cosby Show" and "Cos" in 1972 and 1976, respectively; both were unsuccessful variety shows which included dancing, skits, and monologue sessions.

Although Cosby dropped out of prime-time television for some time during the mid-1970s, he was still quite active in comedy, mostly through live performances and comedy albums such as "Why Is There Air?," "Wonderfulness," and "Revenge." The majority of the material for these albums came from Cosby's childhood experiences, such as plotting an escape from a bed he'd been told was surrounded by thousands of poisonous snakes, living through a tonsillectomy at age five, and having everything he ever made in shop class turn into an ashtray.

Cosby earned his undergraduate degree from Temple University in 1971 and in 1977 completed his Ph.D. in education at the University of Massachusetts. Cosby's commitment to education included regular appearances during the 1970s on "The Electric Company," produced by the Children's Television Workshop, which also produced "Sesame Street." He also appeared as the host of the Picturepages segment on "Captain Kangaroo" in the early 1980s.

Hollywood also employed the talent of Cosby, but with indifferent results. His first movie was "Man and Boy," a 1972 western film with Cosby in the lead; panned by critics, it quickly died at the box office. A much later movie (1978) with Richard Pryor, "California Suite," was written by Neil Simon. The film fared relatively well. In between, he made "Hickey and Boggs," "Uptown Saturday Night," "Let's Do It Again," "Mother, Jugs and Speed," "A Piece of the Action," "The Devil and Max Devlin," "Bill Cosby Himself," and "Leonard the Sixth."

By 1984 Cosby had become disillusioned with what he saw on television and came up with his own idea of a sitcom. The networks were skeptical, as his last two attempts at prime time were failures. Only NBC was interested; they ordered six provisional episodes only after seeing a pilot. Cosby gave them a segment featuring himself as Dr. Heathcliff Huxtable discussing sex with his two teenaged daughters. NBC liked it enough to agree to Cosby's major concessions, including complete creative control and a studio in New York. He would cast himself as an obstetrician-gynecologist married to an attorney. They would be parents to five children, and their names would be Huxtable (executives wanted him to change it to Brown). They would represent middle-class values and they would just happen to be black. They would not take on traditional television characteristics of blacks, neither Fred Sanford's dialect nor George Jefferson's anger. They would be a happy family dealing with everyday problems and incidents, and it would be called "The Cosby Show."

The first show aired in September 1984, and it was an immediate success. That season "The Cosby Show" finished as the third most watched prime-time television show, according to Nielsen ratings, and it was number one for the next four seasons. The show went into syndication in October 1988, and it sold to the Fox network for $550 million the rights to 182 programs to last for three and a half years.

On January 16, 1997, Cosby's life took a dramatic turn, as headlines nationwide broke the shocking news that his only son had been murdered. Ennis, 27, had stopped to change a flat tire along a Los Angeles freeway when he was allegedly shot to death by an 18-year-old Ukrainian immigrant. Details of the fated night were sketchy at first, and it was not certain that the killer would be found. National tabloid the *National Enquirer* offered $100,000 for information leading to the arrest of the shooter, which prompted one witness, a friend of defendant Mihkhail Markhasev, to come forward to testify. The District Attorney's office announced in June, 1997, that it would not seek the death penalty for Markhasev. In the summer of 1998, Markhasev was convicted of the crime and sentenced to life in prison with no possibility of parole.

Two days after the shooting, Cosby gained additional attention when a young woman alleged she was his illegitimate child. Prosecutors later claimed Autumn Jackson, 22, was one of three defendants who schemed to extort $40 million from the comedian. Cosby's lawyers alleged Jackson, along with failed children's television producer Jose Medina and Boris Sabas, tried to trash Cosby's reputation by threatening to sell the story to a supermarket tabloid. Cosby admitted to having had an affair with Jackson's mother, Shawn Upshaw, but has denied being Jackson's father. In July of 1997, Jackson was convicted of extortion.

Cosby and his wife, Camille, have been married since 1964 and have four daughters. Cosby has been his own manager and producer and wrote several books, including the best-selling "Fatherhood," published in 1986. He also became one of the most visible spokespeople in the nation, pitching products for Jell-O, Kodak, Del Monte, the Ford Motor Company and the Coca-Cola Company on television commercials.

"Cosby," which debuted in the fall of 1996 is the latest addition to the Cosby television archive. The CBS show, which also starred Madeline Kahn and Phylicia Rashad, was co-produced by Cosby for Carsey-Werner Productions.

Further Reading

In addition to numerous articles in the popular media, Bill Cosby has been the subject of books by Bill Adler, *The Cosby Wit* (1986); Ronald L. Smith, *Bill Cosby in Words and Pictures* (1986) and *Cosby* (1986); James T. Olsen, *Look Back in Laughter* (1974); and Caroline Latham, *Bill Cosby—For Real* (1987). Cosby himself has written *Fatherhood* (1986), *Time Flies* (1988), and *Love and Marriage* (1989). All are anecdotal, humorous, and matter-of-factly make fun of everyday activities. ☐

Charles Edward Coughlin

Charles Edward Coughlin (1891-1979) was a Canadian-born Roman Catholic priest who became a political organizer in the United States and, during the 1930s, a radical right-wing radio personality.

Charles Edward Coughlin was born on October 25, 1891, in Hamilton, Ontario, Canada, and received his education in Catholic schools and at St. Michael's College of the University of Toronto. At the age of 20, he began studies for the priesthood, receiving his ordination in 1916. After assisting in several parishes in the

Detroit area, Coughlin was formally incardinated into the Detroit diocese in 1923. Three years later, Coughlin's bishop assigned him to the new Shrine of the Little Flower Church in the suburban community of Royal Oak, Michigan.

In 1926, Coughlin started a weekly broadcast over the local radio station which proved so popular that, within four years, the Columbia Broadcasting System began carrying it nationally. A series of florid denunciations of communism in 1930 gave him a national reputation and occasioned his appearance before the Committee to Investigate Communist Activities, of the United States House of Representatives. By the end of the year, however, with the country in the throes of the Great Depression, Coughlin had shifted his broadcasts to emphasize the necessity for drastically altering American capitalism under a program keyed to monetary inflation called "social justice," which Coughlin based on the late-19th-century papal encyclical *Rerum novarum*.

In 1931, the network, worried by Coughlin's attacks on the Hoover administration and by other contentious material in his addresses, discontinued his weekly broadcasts. With contributions from his listeners, Coughlin organized his own radio network, which grew to 26 stations.

During the 1932 presidential campaign, Coughlin vigorously championed Franklin D. Roosevelt, proclaiming that America's choice was "Roosevelt or ruin." Roosevelt carefully cultivated Coughlin and benefited substantially from his support in the first year of the New Deal, but he always kept the priest at arm's length. Coughlin, however, saw himself as an unofficial member of the Roosevelt administration and assumed that the president would follow his advice for combating the Depression, particularly his advocacy of massive currency inflation through silver coinage. When Roosevelt refused to fully accept Coughlin's schemes, the priest became a loud critic of the administration.

In 1934, Coughlin formed the National Union for Social Justice to combat communism and to fight for currency inflation and government control of big business. In 1936 Coughlin, determined to stop Roosevelt's re-election, made the National Union the nucleus for the Union party, which also amalgamated much of the followings of the late Huey Long and of Francis E. Townsend, a crusader for old-age pensions. Roosevelt was overwhelmingly re-elected, while the Union party's candidate polled less than 900,000 votes.

After 1936, Coughlin's influence declined rapidly. He organized the Christian Front to succeed the National Union and trained his oratorical guns on Roosevelt's foreign policy, which he believed would inevitably involve the country in another war. He also concentrated on the fancied internal menaces of Communists and Jews (who seemed interchangeable in Coughlin's thinking). Fascist Italy and Nazi Germany, he announced, were bulwarks against "Jewish-Communist" power in Europe. Coughlin enunciated a program for an anti-Semitic, fascist-style corporate state, under which established political institutions in the United States would virtually disappear.

Coughlin's anti-Roosevelt oratory became more shrill when World War II broke out in Europe in 1939 and the administration provided more and more assistance to the Allied governments. In 1940, the larger stations in Coughlin's radio network, acting on the basis of a recent National Association of Broadcasters ruling barring "controversial" speakers, refused to renew his broadcasting contract. When he continued his attacks on the government after Pearl Harbor, his bishop officially silenced him and the Post Office Department banned his weekly newspaper from the mail.

With his newsletter banned, his radio network gone, and his bishop silencing him, Coughlin confined his activities to those of an ordinary parish priest, in 1942. He retired from his pastorate at the Shrine of the Little Flower in 1966. He concerned himself with his newly-built home in Birmingham, Michigan, and still wrote pamphlets denouncing Communism.

Coughlin died on October 27, 1979 at his home in suburban Detroit. He was remembered as the fiery, vibrant, and opinionated priest who followed the directive of his church over his own feelings towards the government. Near his death, Coughlin said he "couldn't take back much of what [he] had said and did in the old days when people still listened to [him]."

Further Reading

A biography officially authorized by Father Coughlin and written by a close friend and aide is Louis B. Ward *Father Charles E. Coughlin* (1933), it must be read with great caution. Charles J. Tull *Father Coughlin and the New Deal* (1965), is a detached, scholarly study of the radio priest's career during the 1930s. A

fuller account of the Union party movement of 1936, in which Coughlin was the central figure, is given in David H. Bennett *Demagogues in the Depression: American Radicals and the Union Party, 1932-1936* (1969). For information on the upsurge of Catholic social activism in the 1930s, which furnished much of the rationale for Coughlin's activities, see Aaron I. Abell *American Catholicism and Social Action: A Search for Social Justice, 1865-1950* (1960). There is also information about Coughlin in Arthur M. Schlesinger, Jr. *The Age of Roosevelt* (3 vols., 1957-1960), Rexford G. Tugwell *The Democratic Roosevelt* (1957), and George Wolfskill and John A. Hudson *All but the People: Franklin D. Roosevelt and His Critics, 1933-1939* (1969). Coughlin's obituary appears in the October 28, 1979 issue of the *New York Times*. □

Stephen Crane

Stephen Crane (1871-1900), an American fiction writer and poet, was also a newspaper reporter. His novel "The Red Badge of Courage" stands high among the world's books depicting warfare.

After the Civil War, William Dean Howells, Henry James, and others established realism as the standard mode of American fiction. In the 1890s younger writers tried to enlarge the territory of realism with impressionist, symbolist, and even new romantic approaches. Of these pioneers, Stephen Crane was the most influential.

Crane was born on Nov. 1, 1871, the fourteenth and last child of Mary Helen Crane and the Reverend Doctor Jonathan Townley Crane, presiding elder of the Newark, N.J., district of the Methodist Church. A frail child, Stephen moved with his family from one parsonage to another during his first 8 years. In 1880, with the death of his father, his mother moved her family to Asbury Park, N.J. Stephen was exposed early to writing as a career: his mother wrote on religious topics and lectured for the Women's Christian Temperance Union, and his brother Townley worked as a newspaper reporter.

In 1888 Crane entered military school, where he made an impressive record on the drill field and the baseball diamond but not in the classroom. Without graduating he went to Lafayette College, then to Syracuse University. He flunked out, but whatever his academic record, his time had not been wasted: in his fraternity house Crane, aged 20, had written the first draft of *Maggie: A Girl of the Streets*. Returning to Asbury Park as a reporter under his brother for the *New York Tribune*, Crane attended Hamlin Garland's lectures on the realistic writers. Garland was interested in the young writer, read his manuscripts, and guided his reading.

In 1891 Crane's mother died. Crane spent much of the next year in Sullivan County, N.Y., where another brother practiced law. Five "Sullivan County Sketches" were published in the *Tribune* and *Cosmopolitan* (his first magazine appearance). He went frequently to New York City, haunting the Bowery in search of experience and literary material. When he returned to Asbury Park, he lost his job on the *Tribune* (and his brother's too) by writing an accurate description of a labor parade that undermined his Republican

publisher's standing in an election campaign. This year also brought unhappy endings to two romances.

Career as Novelist

In autumn 1892 Crane moved to New York City. By spring he submitted a second version of *Maggie* to a family friend, Richard Gilder, editor of the *Century*. Gilder tried to explain his rejection of the manuscript, but Crane interrupted bluntly, "You mean that the story's too honest?" Honest the story is, and blunt and brutal. It shows Maggie as a simple, ignorant girl bullied by her drunken mother, delivered to a seducer by her brother, driven by the seducer into prostitution and, finally, to suicide. In approach the novel is akin to the "veritism" of Garland and the realism of Howells, but it differs stylistically in its ironic tone, striking imagery (especially color imagery), and its compression. "Impressionism" is the term often applied to the very personal style Crane was developing. Convinced that no publisher would dare touch his "shocking" novel, Crane printed it at his own expense, using the pseudonym Johnston Smith. The book went unnoticed and unpurchased, except for two copies. Garland, however, admired it and called it to the attention of Howells, then America's most influential man of letters, who recognized Crane's achievement and tried unsuccessfully to get the novel reissued.

By summer 1893 Crane was well into what was to be a Civil War novel. As research he read *Century* magazine's series "Battles and Leaders of the Civil War" and, it is believed, traveled in Virginia to interview Confederate veterans. What he found missing from the history books was

the actual sensation any single individual experiences in battle; this is what *The Red Badge of Courage* conveys. Just as Maggie represents every girl victimized by a slum environment, so Henry Fleming represents every recruit who reels through the noise and glare of war. Neither character had a name in Crane's first drafts: they are "every woman," "every man," buffeted by forces they neither control nor understand. Though there were delays—painful ones for the penniless author—this book was destined for early success. A shortened version was serialized in the *Philadelphia Press* and hundreds of other newspapers in 1894. The instant critical and popular enthusiasm spread to England when the complete book was published the following year. A revised version of *Maggie* was issued along with an earlier novel about slum life, *George's Mother,* in 1896. The syndicate that had arranged newspaper publication of *Red Badge of Courage* sent Crane to the West and Mexico to sketch whatever struck his fancy.

Poet and Journalist

Crane's first book of poems, *The Black Riders,* was on the press before his departure. "A condensed Whitman," the *Nation* aptly called him. His "lines," as he called his poems, are terse, natural, and forceful; ironic and unsentimental. Their language is in the best sense journalistic, just as Crane's reportage had been from the beginning poetic.

The excursion west and to Mexico produced sensitive sketches and materials for a number of Crane's finest stories. Back in New York, he published newspaper articles critical of the city's corrupt police. The police made New York uncomfortable for Crane, so he departed for Cuba to report the anti-Spanish insurrection there. Enroute he stopped in Jacksonville, Fla., where he met Cora Stewart, a handsome New England woman in her late 20s, separated from her husband, the son of a British baronet. She was the owner of the Hotel de Dream, an elegant boardinghouse-cum nightclub-cum brothel and gave it all up to become (quite without clerical or legal formalities) "Mrs. Stephen Crane."

In spite of this "marriage," Crane left for Cuba aboard a small steamer. It sank on its first day out. Crane's heroic role in the disaster—he barely escaped with the captain and two other men—evoked his best short story, "The Open Boat."

War Correspondent

For the Hearst newspapers Crane covered the war between Greece and Turkey. Crane, it appears, wanted to see if war was really as he had depicted it in *Red Badge of Courage:* it was. But the trip yielded mediocre war reportage and a bad novel, *Active Service* (1899). Cora had followed Crane to Greece; they next went to England, where Crane finished his powerful novella *The Monster* and three of his finest short stories, "The Bride Comes to Yellow Sky," "Death and the Child," and "The Blue Hotel."

The Spanish-American War in 1898 provided new employment. Crane sent distinguished reports to the *New York World.* He was with Cora in England when his second volume of poems, *War Is Kind,* appeared in 1899. Sick and aware of nearing death, he wrote furiously. That spring Cora took him to the Continent, where he died on June 5, 1900, in Badenweiler, Germany, of tuberculosis. His haunting tales of childhood, *Whilomville Stories,* and Cuban tales, *Wounds in the Rain* appeared later that year.

Further Reading

Robert W. Stallman, *Stephen Crane: A Biography* (1968), is the authoritative source on Crane's life. The two most interesting studies—one biographical, the other critical—are by poets: John Berryman, *Stephen Crane* (1950), and Daniel G. Hoffman, *The Poetry of Stephen Crane* (1956). Also recommended are Maurice Bassan, ed., *Stephen Crane: A Collection of Critical Essays* (1967) and Linda H. Davis, *Badge of Courage: The Life of Staphen Crane* (1998). For views of Crane in the context of his period, see Warner Berthoff, *The Ferment of Realism* (1965), and Larzer Ziff, *The American 1890s* (1966). □

Seymour Cray

Seymour Cray (1925-1996) is one of the founding fathers of the computer industry. Seeking to process vast amounts of mathematical data needed to simulate physical phenomena, Cray built what many consider the first supercomputer, which represented a technological revolution to such fields as engineering, meteorology, and eventually biology and medicine.

Seymour Cray is an electronics engineer and one of the founding fathers of the computer industry. His seminal work in computer design features the semiconductor as a component to store and process information. Cray's dense packing of hundreds of thousands of semiconductor chips, which reduced the distance between signals, enabled him to pioneer very large and powerful "supercomputers." Among his accomplishments was the first computer to employ a freon cooling system to prevent chips from overheating. However, Cray's most significant contribution was the supercomputer itself. Seeking to process vast amounts of mathematical data needed to simulate physical phenomena, Cray built what many consider the first supercomputer, the CDC 6600 (with 350,000 transistors). To such fields as engineering, meteorology, and eventually biology and medicine, the supercomputer represented a technological revolution, akin to replacing a wagon with a sports car in terms of accelerating research.

A maverick in both his scientific and business pursuits, Cray eventually started his own company devoted entirely to the development of supercomputers. For many years Cray computers dominated the supercomputer industry. A devoted fan of "Star Trek," a 1960s television show about space travel, Cray included aesthetically pleasing touches in his computers, such as transparent blue glass that revealed their inner workings.

Early Computer Innovations

Cray was born on September 28, 1925, in Chippewa Falls, Wisconsin, a small town situated in the heart of Wisconsin's dairy farm country. The eldest of two children, Cray revealed his talent for engineering while still a young boy, tinkering with radios in the basement and building an automatic telegraph machine by the time he was ten years old. Cray's father, a city engineer, and his mother fully supported his scientific interests, providing him with a basement laboratory equipped with chemistry sets and radio gear. Cray's early aptitude for electronics was evident when he wired his laboratory to his bedroom, and included an electric alarm that sounded whenever anyone tried to enter his inner sanctum. While attending Chippewa Falls High School, Cray sometimes taught the physics class in his teacher's absence. During his senior year, he received the Bausch & Lomb Science Award for meritorious achievement in science.

While serving in the U.S. Army during the final years of World War II, Cray utilized his natural gifts in electronics as a radio operator and decipherer of enemy codes. After the war, he enrolled in the University of Wisconsin, but later transferred to the University of Minnesota in Minneapolis, where he received his bachelor's degree in electrical engineering in 1950 and a master's degree in applied mathematics the next year. Cray began his corporate electronics career when he was hired to work for Engineering Research Associates (ERA). When Cray joined the company, it was among a small group of firms on the cutting edge of the commercial computer industry. One of his first assignments with ERA was to build computer pulse transformers for Navy use. Cray credited his success on the project to a top-of-the-line circular slide rule that enabled him to make a multitude of calculations needed to build the transformers. In a speech before his colleagues at a 1988 supercomputer conference, Cray recalled feeling "quite smug" about his accomplishment until he encountered a more experienced engineer working at the firm who told Cray that he did not use complicated slide rules or many of the other standard engineering approaches in his work, preferring to rely on intuition. Intrigued, Cray put away his slide rule and decided that he would do likewise.

For his next computer project, Cray and his colleagues developed a binary programming system. With the addition of magnetic core memory, which allowed Cray and his coworkers to program 4,096 words, the age of the supercomputer dawned. Although devoted to his laboratory work, Cray was also interested in the business side of the industry; his efforts to market ERA's new technology resulted in the Remington Rand typewriter company buying out ERA. With a formidable knowledge of circuits, logic, and computer software design, Cray designed the UNIVAC 1103, the first electronically digital computer to become commercially available.

Despite his growing success, Cray became dissatisfied with the large corporate atmosphere of ERA, which had been renamed the Sperry Rand Corporation. A friend and colleague, William Norris, who also worked at Sperry Rand, decided to start his own company, Control Data Corporation (CDC), and recruited Cray to work for him. Lacking the financial resources of larger companies, Cray and Control Data set out to make affordable computers. Towards this end, Cray built computers out of transistors, which he purchased at an electronics outlet store for 37 cents each. Although the chips were of diverse circuitry, Cray successfully replaced the cumbersome and expensive tubes and radio "valves" which were then standard in the industry.

Control Data began developing a line of computers like the CDC 1604, which was immensely successful as a tool for scientific research. Cray went on to develop the CDC 6600, the most powerful computer of its day and the first to employ freon to cool its 350,000 transistors. In 1969, the corporation introduced the CDC 7600, which many considered to be the world's first supercomputer. Capable of 15 million computations per second, the 7600 placed CDC as the leader in the supercomputer industry to the chagrin of the IBM corporation, CDC's primary competitor. Even with a legion of researchers, IBM was unable to match CDC's productivity, and eventually resorted to questionable tactics to overtake CDC, which eventually filed and won an antitrust suit against IBM. But as Control Data grew, so did its bureaucracy. As Russell Mitchell recounted in *Business Week,* Norris once asked Cray to develop a five-year plan. What Norris received in return was a short note that said Cray's five-year plan was "to build the biggest computer in the world," and his one-year plan was "to achieve one-fifth of the above." After developing the CDC 8600, which the company refused to market, Cray, in 1972, decided to leave CDC and set up his own company, Cray Research Corporation. Norris and CDC graciously invested $500,000 to assist Cray in his fledgling business effort.

The Supercomputer Emerges

Cray Research immediately set out to build the fastest supercomputer. In 1976 the CRAY–1 was introduced. Incorporating a revolutionary vector processing approach, which allowed the computer to solve various parts of a problem at once, the CRAY–1 was capable of performing 32 calculations simultaneously, outpacing even the best CDC computer. When the National Center for Atmospheric Research met the computer's $8.8 million price tag, Cray Research finally had solid financial footing to continue building faster and more affordable computers. For Cray, this meant manufacturing one product at a time, a radical approach in the computer industry. The first CRAY–2 was marketed in 1985 and featured a phenomenal 2-billion byte memory that could perform 1.2 billion computer operations per second, a tenfold performance increase over the Cray–1. Capable of providing computerized models of physical phenomena described mathematically, the CRAY computers were essential catalysts in accelerating research. For example, in such areas as pharmaceutical development, supercomputer modeling of a drug's molecules and its biological components eliminated much trial and error, reducing the time necessary to solve complicated mathematical equations.

In 1983, Cray turned his attention to developing gallium arsenide (GaA) circuits. Although the CRAY–2 was based on silicon chips, Cray continued to develop GaA chips in the spinoff Cray Computers Corporation. Although extremely difficult to work with because of their fragility, gallium arsenide computer chips marked a major advance in computer circuitry with their ability to conduct electrical impulses with less resistance than silicon. Adding even more speed to the computer, the GaA chip also effectively reduced both heat and energy loss.

While Cray's advances in computer technology enabled him to corner the market on the supercomputer industry for many years, the advent of parallel processing allowed others in the industry to make inroads into the same market. Utilizing hundreds of mini-computers to work on individual aspects of a problem, parallel processing is a less expensive approach to solving huge mathematical problems. Although Cray for many years denounced parallel processing as impractical, he eventually accepted this approach and made plans with other companies to incorporate it into his computer research and business.

Cray's first wife, Verene, was a minister's daughter. Married shortly after World War II, they had two daughters and two sons, who have characterized their father as a man intensely dedicated to his work; in fact, Cray demanded their absolute silence while traveling in the car so that he could think about the next advance in supercomputers. In 1975, Cray and Verene divorced, and he wed Geri M. Harrand five years later. Although he engaged in outdoor pursuits with his new wife, such as windsurfing and skiing, Cray remained devoted to his research. In 1972, he was awarded the Harry Goode Memorial Award for "outstanding achievement in the field of information processing." As Cray looked forward to the future of supercomputers, especially to the use of GaA computer chips, many experts in the field characterized his vision as impractical. Nonetheless, Cray's numerous conceptual breakthroughs in computer and information science have firmly established him as an innovator in computer technology. Cray died on

October 5, 1996, from injuries sustained in a car accident three weeks earlier.

Further Reading

Slater, R, *Portraits in Silicon,* MIT Press, 1989, pp. 195–204.

Spenser, Donald, *Macmillan Encyclopedia of Computers,* Macmillan Publishing Company, 1992.

Anthes, Gary H, ''Seymour Cray: Reclusive Genius,'' in *Computerworld,* June 22, 1992, p. 38.

Elmer-Dewitt, Philip, ''Computer Chip Off the Old Block: Genius Seymour Cray and the Company He Founded Split Up,'' in *Time,* May 29, 1989, p. 70.

Krepchin, Ira, ''Datamation 100 North American Profiles,'' in *Datamation,* June 15, 1993, p. 81.

Mitchell, Russell, ''The Genius,'' in *Business Week,* April 30, 1990, pp. 80–88. □

Crazy Horse

The Native American Crazy Horse (ca. 1842-1877), Oglala Sioux war chief, is best known as the leader of the Sioux and Cheyenne renegades who won the Battle of the Little Bighorn, where Gen. Custer died.

Born on Rapid Creek, S. Dak., near the present Rapid City, Crazy Horse (Tashunca-Uitco) was a strange, quiet Sioux youth, serious and thoughtful. His skin and hair were so light that he was mistaken for a captive white child and was called ''Light-Haired Boy'' and ''Curly.''

Crazy Horse grew to manhood wild and adventurous, implacably hating the reservations and the encroaching whites. He married a Cheyenne girl and thus had close ties with that tribe. After he came to prominence as a warrior, many Cheyenne followed him.

Crazy Horse probably participated in the Sioux wars of 1865-1868 but as a warrior, not a leader. By the last of these wars, in 1876, however, he had risen to prominence. He and his followers refused to return to the reservation by Jan. 1, 1876, as had been ordered by the U.S. Army following the outbreak occasioned by the Black Hills gold rush. Crazy Horse and his followers bore the first burden of this campaign. Their village of 105 lodges was destroyed by Col. J. J. Reynolds on March 17. The Native Americans' horses were captured, but Crazy Horse rallied his braves, trailed the soldiers 20 miles, and recaptured most of the horses. On June 17 he and 1,200 warriors defeated Gen. George Crook and 1,300 soldiers, turning them away from a rendezvous with the forces of Gen. Alfred Terry.

Crazy Horse next moved north, where he joined with Sitting Bull's followers on the Little Bighorn River. On June 25 he was in command of the warriors who massacred Gen. George Custer and 264 soldiers. Then, with 800 warriors he went into winter quarters in the Wolf Mountains near the headwaters of the Rosebud River. On Jan. 8, 1877, the village was destroyed in an attack led by Col. N. A. Miles. Crazy Horse continued to fight for 4 months before surrendering on May 6 with 1,100 men, women, and children at Red Cloud Agency near Camp Robinson, Nebr. An army officer there described Crazy Horse as 5 feet 8 inches tall, lithe and sinewy, with a weathered visage; wrote Capt. John G. Bourke: ''The expression of his countenance was one of great dignity, but morose, dogged, tenacious and melancholy. . . . He was one of the great soldiers of his day and generation.''

On Sept. 5, 1877, the officers at the post, convinced that Crazy Horse was plotting an outbreak, ordered him locked up. Crazy Horse drew his knife and began fighting. In the struggle he was mortally wounded in the abdomen, either by a soldier's bayonet or his own knife. His death deprived the Oglala Sioux of one of their most able leaders.

Further Reading

Details on Crazy Horse's life are in Mari Sandoz, *Crazy Horse: The Strange Man of the Oglalas* (1942), and Earl A. Brininstool, *Crazy Horse* (1949). A good, condensed version of his life is in Alvin M. Josephy, *The Patriot Chiefs* (1961). John G. Bourke, *On the Border with Crook* (1891), gives a contemporary assessment. □

John Michael Crichton

Michael Crichton (born 1942) is best known as a novelist of popular fiction whose stories explore the confrontation between traditional social and moral values and the demands of the new technological age. His most successful novel, *Jurassic Park* (1990), involves the re-creation of living di-

nosaurs from ancient DNA and examines what can go wrong when greedy people misconstrue the power of new and untested technologies.

Crichton was born in Chicago and raised on Long Island. At fourteen years of age, he wrote and sold articles to the *New York Times* travel section, and, in 1964, earned a B. A. in anthropology from Harvard University. The following year, while on a European travel fellowship in anthropology and ethnology, he met and married Joan Radam; they eventually divorced in 1970. Returning to Harvard University in 1965, Crichton entered medical school, where he began to write novels under the pseudonym John Lange in order to support his medical studies. While doing postdoctoral work at the Salk Institute for Biological Studies in La Jolla, California, Crichton published *The Andromeda Strain* (1969), a technological thriller, which garnered literary acclaim and national prominence for the author. Upon leaving medical studies, Crichton began a full-time writing career. Eventually, he also directed his screenplay of his novel *Westworld* (1973), starring Yul Brynner, and wrote the screenplay for his book, *The Great Train Robbery* (1978).

Crichton's stories generally take place in contemporary settings and focus on technological themes, although his earliest works were traditional mystery novels. Writing under the pseudonym John Lange, Crichton published a mystery novel entitled *Odds On* (1966), followed by *A Case of Need* (1968), written under the pseudonym Jeffrey Hudson. *A Case of Need* received favorable reviews and the 1968 Edgar Allan Poe Award of Mystery Writers of America. In

1969, Crichton published *The Andromeda Strain,* a novel that, Crichton acknowledges, was influenced by Len Deighton's *The Ipcress File* (1962) and H. G. Wells *The War of The Worlds. The Andromeda Strain* is a technological thriller about a seemingly unstoppable plague brought to earth from outer space; it became a Book-of-the-Month Club selection and a 1971 motion picture, directed by Robert Wise and starring Arthur Hill. In *Westworld* (1973), Crichton depicts the ability of technology to blur the line between reality and fantasy, and how that can affect people's lives. As the android creations of the Delos theme park begin to operate on their own recognizance, they attack and threaten the lives of the guests who have come there merely to play and live out their childhood fantasies in the make-believe Old West.

While *The Great Train Robbery* (1975) recalls the history of an actual train robbery in Victorian England, and *Eaters of the Dead* (1976) is set among tenth-century Vikings, and is supposedly the retelling of the *Beowulf* myth, *Congo* (1980) returns to the dangers of technology, greed, and power. *Congo* recalls the narrative tradition of Rider Haggard's novel *King Solomon's Mines,* as it relates the story of a behavioral specialist and Amy, a gorilla that is capable of communicating in human language. In the process of returning Amy to her African jungle home, the specialist and the gorilla encounter a series of dangers and catastrophes. These include the ruthless activities of a group of corporate-sponsored explorers who are searching for the lost City of Zinj, where a race of hostile apes guards rare diamonds capable of nullifying humanity's need for nuclear weapons and energy. An encounter with alein life forms and alien technology is the central focus of Crichton's next novel, *Sphere* (1987). Scientists undertake an underwater excavation of an alien spacecraft, believed to have landed in the ocean three centuries earlier. While a raging storm maroons the scientists on board the spacecraft, which is one thousand feet below the surface of the sea, the aliens wreak havoc on the contact team.

In 1990, Crichton published his nationally acclaimed best-seller, *Jurassic Park,* which recounts the classic tale of greed and a technological experiment gone awry. A wealthy entrepreneur and his scientists lose control of their experiment to re-create living dinosaurs for a wild animal park on a deserted island off the coast of Costa Rica. Steven Spielberg's 1994 Academy award-winning film of *Jurassic Park* also helped to ensure the world-wide popularity and success of the novel. Turning to Japanese-American relations in today's competitive business world, *Rising Sun* (1992) begins with the bizarre murder of a young woman, which is pivotal to a plot that explores the exploitative and unprincipled actions of Japanese technocrats. *Rising Sun* is often criticized for its stereotypical presentation of Japanese villains and Japan-bashing—criticisms that Crichton rejects. *Disclosure* (1994) continues to focus on the technological business community and its handling of sexual harassment. In a role-reversal, the new female executive of DigiCom seduces a former lover and present employee, and then accuses him of sexual harassment when he spurns her advances. The story focuses on the fight to save his job and the truth of what actually happened. In 1995, Crichton returned to the theme of genetic engineering in *The Lost World*. Scientist Ian Malcolm and entrepreneur Lewis Dodgson of *Jurassic Park* join rival expeditions sent to investigate an island thought to be inhabited by dinosaurs. Once again, twentieth-century human technology is challenged by the raw force of prehistoric nature.

Crichton's works have received mixed reviews. While most critics applaud his ability to make technological information understandable and engaging, some fault his traditional and predictable plotlines, such as *Disclosure*'s battle-of-the-sexes plot and *Jurassic Park*'s the-dangers-of-new-science theme. And too, while many critics favorably comment on Crichton's well organized plots and use of clear and simple prose, they fault his ability to develop realistic characters. For instance, John Hammond and Nedry of *Jurassic Park* are the traditional unprincipled entrepreneur and scientific genius whose greed precipitates a technological disaster, while Meredith Johnson of *Disclosure* is the predictable evil enemy of Tom Sanders, the harassed and innocent victim-hero of the story. As Robert L. Sims points out, most of "Crichton's characters are one-dimensional figures whose psychological makeups are determined by the particular drama in which they are involved." A few commentators also remark at Crichton's ability to identify and successfully capitalize on current public issues and concerns. For example, *Disclosure* examines the issue of sexual harassment in the business world, while *Rising Sun* focuses on Japan's growing power in the world of American business. Nevertheless, in spite of traditional plotlines and simplistic characterizations, Crichton's concise prose style, tightly organized plots, contemporary themes, and engaging action continue to make his works popular and successful.

Further Reading

Authors and Artists for Young Adults, Volume 10, Gale, 1993.

Contemporary Literary Criticism, Gale, Volume 2, 1974, Volume 6, 1976, Volume 54, 1989.

Dictionary of Literary Biography Yearbook: 1981, Gale, 1982.

American Spectator, May, 1992, p. 71.

American Way, September, 1975, pp. 66-69.

Atlantic Monthly, May, 1972, pp. 108-110.

Best Sellers, August 15, 1968, pp. 207-208; February, 1981, p. 388. □

David Crockett

David Crockett (1786-1836), American frontiersman and politician, became during his own lifetime a celebrity and folk hero, particularly to Americans living in the newly settled midwestern regions of the country.

Davy Crockett grew to manhood in a backwoods area. He experienced the crudeness and poverty of the frontier squatter and later used this knowledge in his political campaigns. A master storyteller, the semiliterate Crockett proved a formidable political campaigner, as well as the personification of the characters in the frontiersmen's "tall tales" of that day. Although he is known chiefly for his exploits as a hunter and soldier,

Crockett's major contributions included political efforts to get free land for frontier settlers, relief for debtors, and an expanded state banking system for Tennessee.

Davy Crockett, the son of John and Rebecca Crockett, was born on Aug. 17, 1786, in Hawkings County, East Tennessee. John Crockett failed as a farmer, mill operator, and storekeeper. In fact, he remained in debt, as did Davy, all his life. Because of continuing poverty, Davy's father put him to work driving cattle to Virginia when he was 12 years old. Returning to Tennessee in the winter of 1798, Davy spent 5 days in school. After a fight there, he played hookey until his father found out and then, to escape punishment, ran away.

Crockett worked and traveled throughout Virginia and did not return home for nearly 3 years. Several years later he decided that his lack of education limited his marriage possibilities, and he arranged to work 6 months for a nearby Quaker teacher. In return Crockett received 4 days a week of instruction. He learned to read, to write a little, and to "cypher some in the first three rules of figures."

In 1806 Crockett married Mary Finely; the young couple began their life together on a rented farm with two cows, two calves, and a loan of $15. Frontier farming proved difficult and unrewarding to Crockett, who enjoyed hunting more than work. After five years he decided to move farther west. By 1813 he had located his family in Franklin Country, Tenn.

Life on the Frontier

Shortly afterward the so-called Creek War began. During the summer of 1813 a party of frontiersmen ambushed a band of Creek Indian warriors in southern Alabama. Settlers in the area gathered at a stockade called Ft. Mims. The Native Americans attacked on Aug. 30, 1813, found the garrison undefended, and killed over 500 people. Within 2 weeks frontier militia units gathered for revenge, and Crockett volunteered for 3 months' duty that year. In September and October he served as a scout. During the famous mutiny against Andrew Jackson in December, Crockett was on leave, and reports that he deserted the militia during the Creek War are unfounded. He served again from September 1814 to February 1815. During this campaign Crockett was a mounted scout and hunter; apparently his unit encountered little fighting.

In 1815 Mary Crockett died. Within a year Crockett remarried. While traveling with neighbors in Alabama to examine the newly opened Creek lands during 1816, he contracted malaria and was left along the road to die. But he recovered and returned to Tennessee, pale and sickly, much to the surprise of his family and neighbors who thought he was dead. He has been quoted as remarking about his reported death, "I know'd this was a whopper of a lie, as soon as I heard it."

Local and State Politics

In 1817 Crockett was a justice of the peace and the next year was serving also as a county court referee. In 1818 his neighbors elected him lieutenant colonel of the local militia regiment, and that same year he became one of the Lawrenceburg town commissioners. He held this position until 1821, when he resigned to campaign for a seat in the state legislature. During the campaign Crockett first displayed his shrewd ability to judge the needs of the frontiersmen. He realized that their isolation and need for recreation outweighed other desires. Therefore, he gave short speeches laced with stories, followed by a trip to the ever present liquor stand—a tactic well received by his audience, who elected him. Crockett appears to have been a quiet legislator, but his first-term actions demonstrate the areas of his future legislative interest. Having grown to manhood among the debt-ridden and often propertyless squatters, Crockett served as their spokesman. He proposed bills to reduce taxes, to settle land claim disputes, and in general to protect the economic interests of the western settlers.

When the legislative session ended in 1821, Davy went west again, this time to Gibson County, Tenn., where he built a cabin near the Obion River. Two years later he was elected to the Tennessee Legislature. This victory demonstrates his improved campaign techniques and his realization that antiaristocratic rhetoric was popular. Again he worked for debtor relief and equitable land laws.

Congressional Career

During 1825 Crockett ran for Congress; he campaigned as an antitariff man, however, and the incumbent easily defeated him. Two years later Crockett won the election. Throughout his congressional terms he worked for the Tennessee Vacant Land Bill, which he introduced during his first term. This proposal would have offered free land to frontier settlers in return for the increase in value which they would bring about because of their improvements.

In 1829, although he opposed several of President Andrew Jackson's measures, Crockett's campaign for re-election as a Jacksonian was successful. But during his second term in Congress, Crockett grew increasingly hostile to Jackson. He opposed the President on the issues of Native American removal, land policy, and the Second National Bank. In the election of 1831 Crockett was defeated. Two years later he regained his congressional seat by a narrow margin. By 1834 he had become such an outspoken critic of Jackson that Whig party leaders used Crockett as a popular symbol in their anti-Jackson campaigns. It was during these activities that several purported biographies and autobiographies of Crockett appeared. Their purpose was to popularize him and to show that not all frontiersmen supported the Jackson administration. These literary efforts failed to sway most of the voters, and Crockett was defeated in 1835, ending his congressional career.

During his three terms in Washington, Crockett tried to represent the interests of his frontier district. In doing so, he became enmeshed in a dispute with the Tennessee Jackson forces. The continuing fight with this group not only prevented him from making any lasting legislative contributions but also ended his political career.

Death at the Alamo

In 1835 Crockett and four neighbors headed into Texas looking for new land. By January 1836 he had joined the Texas Volunteers, and within a month he reached San Antonio. In the first week of March he and the other defenders of the Alamo died during the siege and capture of that fort. Popular tradition places Crockett as one of the last defenders who died protecting the bedridden Col. William Travis during the final assault. The fact is, however, that Crockett was one of the first defenders to die, alone and unarmed.

Crockett's death at the Alamo engendered a notoriety and a lasting fame which his political activities would never have earned him. Through the newspaper accounts and other writings—fact and fiction—Crockett came to represent the typical westerner of that day. With the passage of time, tales and legends concerning his exploits grew. As a result, the popular image bears less relationship to the actual person than may be said about almost any other prominent figure.

Descriptions of Crockett are varied, but it is generally conceded that he was about 5 feet 8 inches tall, of medium weight, and with brown hair, blue eyes, and rosy cheeks. He was noted for a fine sense of humor, honesty, and ability as an entertaining public speaker. Those who knew him realized that he was a man of ability and character.

Further Reading

A lack of source material has limited the scholarly studies of Crockett but has not prevented numerous popular accounts. Beginning with Matthew St. Clair Clarke's anonymously published *Life and Adventures of Col. David Crockett of West Tennessee* (1833), such accounts have continued to appear. Of the 19th-century books only *A Narrative of the Life of David Crockett, of the State of Tennessee* (1834), written by Crockett himself, is at all reliable.

The best work on Crockett is James A. Shackford, *David Crockett: The Man and the Legend* (1956), which separates the myths surrounding him from the historical person. Crockett's position in folklore is examined in Franklin J. Meine, ed., *Tall Tales of the Southwest: An Anthology of Southern and Southwestern Humor, 1830-1860* (1930), and Richard M. Dorson, ed., *Davy Crockett: American Comic Legend* (1939). For an understanding of politics in the Old Southwest see Thomas P. Abernethy, *From Frontier to Plantation in Tennessee: A Study in Frontier Democracy* (1932); Arthur M. Schlesinger, Jr., *The Age of Jackson* (1945); and Charles G. Sellers, *James K. Polk, Jacksonian: 1795-1843* (1957). ☐

Walter Leland Cronkite, Jr.

Walter Leland Cronkite, Jr., (born 1916) was an American journalist and radio and television news broadcaster who became preeminent among the outstanding group of correspondents and commentators developed by CBS News after World War II.

Walter Cronkite was born in St. Joseph, Missouri, the only son of his dentist father and the former Helena Lena Fritsch. While he was still a youngster the family moved to Texas. His reading about the exploits of foreign correspondents inspired his interest in journalism. Preparation for that vocation began with his work on his high school yearbook and newspaper.

In 1933 he entered the University of Texas at Austin and took a part-time job with the *Houston Post.* This set him on a professional career which led him to abandon college after two years to serve as a general reporter for the *Post,* a radio announcer in Kansas City, and a sportscaster in Oklahoma City. After that his principal employer for several years was United Press International (UPI), for whom he covered World War II in Europe (1941-1945) and served as chief correspondent at the Nuremburg War Crimes Trials (1945-1946) and in Moscow (1946-1948).

Years at CBS

To this point Cronkite was largely unknown to the general public. In 1950 he joined CBS News where two years later he was narrator for "You Are There," a television program in which major historical events were re-created. In 1954 he became narrator of "The Twentieth Century," a monumental television documentary which established Cronkite's recognition with the viewing public. That was reinforced by his quadrennial service as anchor of the CBS coverage of the national political party conventions, which he first covered in 1952. With the exception of the 1964 Democratic convention, he continued this role until his retirement in 1981.

When Cronkite assumed the duties of anchor and editor for the "CBS Evening News" in 1962, NBC's "Huntley-Brinkley Report" dominated viewer ratings. Gradually the CBS broadcasts gained ground on the renowned team at NBC, which broke up in 1970. From then until his retire-

ment, Cronkite's program was consistently the most popular television news broadcast.

Although the evening news was his main platform, Cronkite maintained his prominence as narrator and correspondent on network specials, including space shots, major documentaries, and extensive interviews with world figures such as Presidents Truman, Eisenhower, and Johnson. After his retirement he continued this role in addition to the intermittent series, "Walter Cronkite's Universe."

For a society that emphasized youthfulness, it was a paradox that as Cronkite grew older his prestige increased. His white hair and moustache gave him a rather distinguished look, although Cronkite's reputation did not rest on appearance. He earned recognition and praise through hard work, a passion for accuracy, and an insistence on impartiality. Underlying that was a life-long competitive spirit that was sublimated before the microphone and camera but manifest in his leisure activities of sailing, tennis, and race car driving.

Among Cronkite's strengths were his believability, accuracy, and impartiality. He was also quite diligent about not becoming part of the story he was reporting. Yet there were memorable instances when he failed to remain completely detached from a story: his obvious emotional reaction when announcing the death of President John Kennedy in 1963; his characterization, on the eve of the 1968 Democratic convention, of the site as a concentration camp; his broadcast pronouncement in 1968, upon returning from Vietnam, that he doubted that U.S. policy for that region could prevail; and his undeniable enthusiasm when Neil Armstrong became the first person on the moon in 1969. Despite his philosophic disclaimer, Cronkite sometimes influenced the news, as in his televised interview with Anwar Sadat that led that Egyptian leader to visit Israel and the Israeli Prime Minister Menachem Begin to reciprocate. Inadvertently, Cronkite was a news topic in 1976 when John Anderson, running as an independent presidential candidate, mentioned Cronkite as his likely running mate.

The exceptions notwithstanding, Cronkite raised television news broadcasting to a level of professionalism that was lauded around the world. His credentials as a newspaperman and war correspondent, along with his unwillingness to deviate from a hard news format, demonstrated that acceptance and popularity in television news need not rest on superficiality.

The depth of respect for his work was reflected in the numerous awards he received: the Peabody for Radio and Television and the William Allen White Award for Journalistic Merit, as well as the Emmy. In 1981, during his final three months on the "CBS Evening News," Cronkite received 11 major awards, including the Presidential Medal of Freedom. In 1985 he became the second newsman, after Edward R. Murrow, to be selected for the Television Hall of Fame. At his retirement, Cronkite was the most commonly mentioned person on the "dream list" for lecturers at conventions, clubs, and college campuses.

Post CBS Retirement

After retiring as anchor of the "CBS Evening News," Cronkite served as CBS News special correpondent and on the network's board of directors from 1981 to 1991. He also anchored the CBS News science magazine series "Walter Cronkite's Universe," (1980-82), and from the late 1980s until 1992, hosted "Walter Cronkite's 20th Century", a daily 90-second account of same-day historical events. In 1993 he formed his own production company and produced several award-winning documentaries for The Discovery Channel, PBS, and other networks. One of those, "Cronkite Remembers", was sheduled to air in early 1997 in conjunction with the late 1996 publication of his autobiography, *A Reporter's Life.* During the 1996 presidential campaign, Cronkite headed efforts to convince networks to offer free television time for presidential candidates. When not making documentaries, Cronkite enjoyed sailing his 48-foot yacht, the "Wynje".

Further Reading

Cronkite tells the story of his years growing up in Kansas City and Houston; his early career working for newspapers, wire services, and radio stations; his time as a war correspondent for UPI; and his years at CBS in his autobiography *A Reporter's Life* (1997). An excellent overview of Cronkite's work habits, strengths and weaknesses, and rapport with his colleagues is "Uncle Walter," a chapter in *Air Time* (1978) by Gary Paul Gates. Briefer episodes of a similar vein about Cronkite are in *The Powers That Be* (1979) by David Halberstam. In *Challenge of Change* (1971), Cronkite set out his journalistic philosophy. The book is a collection of nine speeches he gave during 1967-1970. *Eye on the World* (1971) is useful mainly as an example of his editing skills. The volume is largely excerpts from interviews by other CBS newsmen on major topics of that period. Both philosophic and descriptive is his "What It's Like To Broadcast News," *Saturday Review* (December 12, 1970). *South by Southeast* (1983) with Ray Ellis and *South by Southwest* (1971) provide insight into Cronkite's leisure activities, especially sailing. One of Cronkite's daughters, Kathy, recorded her experiences as a child of a celebrity in *On the Edge of the Spotlight* (1981). □

Countee Cullen

The American Countee Cullen (1903-1946) was one of the most widely heralded African American poets of the Harlem renaissance, though he was less concerned with social and political problems than were his African American contemporaries. He is noted for his lyricism and his artful use of imagery.

Countee Cullen, whose real surname was Porter, was born May 30, 1903. Nothing is known about where he was born, and little is known of his parents. An orphan in New York City, he was adopted by the Reverend Frederick A. and Mrs. Carolyn Cullen, whose name he took. Following graduation from DeWitt Clinton High School, where he won a high school poetry contest, he attended New York University. In 1925 he took a baccalaureate degree, and his first book of poems, *Color,* was published. His metrical skill reminded many readers of the English poet Algernon Swinburne. He earned a master's degree at Harvard and then became assistant editor of *Opportunity: Journal of Negro Life,* which printed the fugitive pieces of African American writers and gave publicity to the African American artists who contributed so much to the cultural awakening of the 1920s.

Cullen knew what was going on in African American life, but he was not deeply involved. *Ballad of the Brown Girl* and *Copper Sun,* both published in 1927, contain mostly personal Keatsian lyrics, which, generally speaking, show no advance and no development from the poems in his first volume. The piece entitled "Heritage" is a noteworthy exception. In a critical preface to the collection of African American poetry, *Caroling Dusk* (1927), which he edited, Cullen argues that "Negro poetry . . . must emanate from some country other than this in some language other than our own." Though he later claimed that his poetry "treated of the heights and depths of emotion which I feel as a Negro," he did not want to be known as an African American poet.

Even after his marriage in 1928 to Yolande, the only daughter of the African American radical and activist W. E. B. Du Bois, Cullen stayed aloof from action and affirmative argument about race. His marriage lasted only through the first year of a 2-year visit to France, where he completed the long, narrative, parabolic poem "The Black Christ," which became the title poem of his fourth volume. *The Medea and Some Poems* (1935) was his last book of verse. From 1934 to 1945 he taught French in a New York public school.

Cullen's poetry is traditional in structure. His output in prose suffers from an absence of genuine commitment and is undistinguished. His novel, *One Way to Heaven,* satirizes upper-class African American life. *The Lost Zoo* and *My Nine Lives and How I Lost Them* are children's books. Cullen collaborated on a musical play, *St. Louis Woman* (1946), but whatever emotional power and integrity it had was supplied by Arna Bontemps. The play opened on March 31, 1949. Cullen had died earlier, on Jan. 9, 1946. *On These I Stand,* his own selection of his best poems, was published in 1947.

Further Reading

The only full-length work on Cullen is Blanche E. Ferguson, *Countee Cullen and the Negro Renaissance* (1966). Stephen H. Bronz, *Roots of Negro Racial Consciousness, the 1920's: Three Harlem Renaissance Authors* (1964), discusses Countee Cullen, James Weldon Johnson, and Claude McKay. Cullen is appraised in such anthologies and critical works as James Weldon Johnson, ed., *The Book of American Negro Poetry* (1922; rev. ed. 1931); Alain L. Locke, ed., *The New Negro: An Interpretation* (1925); J. Saunders Redding, *To Make a Poet Black* (1939); Margaret Just Butcher, *The Negro in American Culture: Based on Materials Left by Alain Locke* (1956); and Herbert Hill, ed., *Soon, One Morning: New Writings by American Negroes, 1940-62* (1963). □

Edward Estlin Cummings

The American poet Edward Estlin Cummings (1894-1962) presented romantic attitudes in technically experimental verse. His poems are not only ideas but crafted physical objects which, in their nonlogical structure, grant fresh perspectives into reality.

In his publications E. E. Cummings always gave his name in lowercase letters without punctuation (e e cummings); this was part of his concern for the typography, syntax, and visual form of his poetry. He worked in the Emersonian tradition of romantic transcendentalism, which encouraged experimentation, and may have been influenced also by Walt Whitman, the poet that Ralph Waldo Emerson had personally encouraged.

Born in Cambridge, Mass., on Oct. 14, 1894, of a prominent academic and ministerial family, E. E. Cummings grew up in the company of such family friends as the philosophers William James and Josiah Royce. Had he lived in Emerson's time, he too might have been described as a "Boston Brahmin." His father, Edward Cummings, after teaching at Harvard, became the nationally known Congregational minister of the Old South Church in Boston, preaching a Christian-transcendentalist theology. Eventually Cummings came to espouse a positive position similar to that of his father, but not before an early period of rebellion against the stuffiness of Cambridge ladies, the repressiveness of conventional moralism, and the hypocrisy of the churches.

After receiving his bachelor of arts degree (1915) and master's degree (1916) from Harvard, Cummings became an ambulance driver in France just before America entered World War I. He was imprisoned for 3 months on suspicion of holding views critical of the French war effort, and this experience provided the material for his first book, *The Enormous Room* (1922), an experiment in blending autobiographical prose reporting with poetic techniques of symbolism.

Early Career

Cummings's transcendentalism, which stressed individual feeling over "objective" truth in a period when critical canons of impersonal, rationalistic, and formalistic poetry were being articulated, resulted in early rejection of his work. For several decades he had to pay for the publication of his books, and reviewers revealed very little understanding of his intentions. His first volume of verse, *Tulips and Chimneys* (1923), was followed by a second book of poems 2 years later. Though Cummings received the Dial Award for poetry in 1925, he continued to have difficulty in finding a publisher.

In the 10 years following 1925 only two volumes of Cummings's poems were published, both at his own expense: *is 5* (1926) and *W* (*ViVa;* 1931). In that decade Cummings also arranged for the publication of one experimental play, *Him* (1927), and a diary like account of a trip to the U.S.S.R., *Eimi* (1933). With characteristic sarcasm Cummings named the 14 publishers who had rejected the manuscript of *No Thanks* (1935) in the volume itself and said "Thanks" to his mother, who had financed its publication.

Poetic Techniques

Despite his dedication to growth and movement, and in contrast to his reputation as an experimenter in verse forms, Cummings actually tended to lack fresh invention. Especially in the 1930s, when he felt most alienated from his culture and his fellow poets, he repeated himself endlessly, writing many versions of essentially the same poem. He tended to rely too much on simple tricks to force the reader to participate in the poems, and his private typography, although originally expressive and amusing, became somewhat tiresome. Cummings's other stylistic devices—the use of low dialect to create satire and the visual "shaping" of poems—often seem selfindulgent substitutes for original inspiration.

However, Cummings's most characteristic device, the dislocation of syntax and the breaking up and reconstituting of words, was more than just another trick when it operated organically within the context of a poem's meaning. When he wrote, in one of his own favorite poems, "i thank You God for most this amazing," he emphasized the nonlogical quality of the statement by its syntactical ambiguity. "Most" intensifies the entire line in its displaced position and indicates why he thanks God; it moves "this amazing" toward "most amazing" in an authentic recreation of the miraculous process of the natural world. In general, Cummings's best dislocations expressed his belief in that miraculousness of the ordinary which logical syntax could not convey, bringing the reader to a freshness of perception that was Cummings's way toward illumination.

Poetic Achievement

The love poems and religious poems represent Cummings's greatest achievements; usually the two subjects are interrelated in his work. For example, "somewhere i have never travelled, gladly beyond" is one of the finest love lyrics in the English language, and Cummings's elegy on the death of his beloved father, "my father moved through dooms of love," is a profoundly moving tribute. Often he used a dislocated sonnet form in these poems, but what makes them memorable is not their formal experimentalism but their unique combination of sensuality with a sense of transcendent spirit. Cummings wrote some of the finest celebrations of sexual love and the religious experience of awe and natural piety produced in the 20th century, precisely at a time when it was highly unfashionable to write such poems.

Early in his career Cummings had divided his time between New York and Paris (where he studied painting); later, between New York and the family home in North Conway, N.H. He was always interested in the visual arts, and his paintings and drawings, late impressionist in style, were exhibited in several one-man shows in the 1940s and 1950s.

Ripening into Honor

After World War II a new generation of poets in rebellion against their immediate predecessors began to find in Cummings an echo of their own distinctly Emersonian ideas about poetry, and Cummings began to receive the recognition that had eluded him so long. In 1950 the Academy of American Poets awarded this self-described "failure" a fellowship for "great achievement," and his collected *Poems, 1923-1954* (1954) won praise in critical quarters which earlier had tended to downgrade Cummings for his unfashionable lyric romanticism.

Harvard University honored its distinguished alumnus by asking Cummings to deliver the Charles Eliot Norton Lectures in 1952-1953, his only attempt at formal artistic autobiography, later published as *i: six nonlectures* (1953). In the lectures Cummings said that perhaps 15 poems were faithful expressions of his stance as artist and man. The total number of truly memorable short poems is certainly higher than this modest figure but still only a fraction of the nearly 1,000 poems published in his lifetime.

Although Cummings did not "develop" as a poet either in terms of ideas or of characteristic style between the publication of *Tulips and Chimneys* and his final volume, *73 Poems* (1963), his work does show a deepening awareness and mastery of his special lyrical gift as poet of the mysteries of "death and forever with each breathing," with a corresponding abandonment of earlier defensive-offensive sallies into ideology and criticism. His finest single volume, *95 Poems* (1958), illustrates Cummings's increasing ability toward the end of his life to give content to his abstractions through the artifact of the poem-object itself, rather than depending entirely on pure rhetoric. If only a tenth of his

poems should be thought worthwhile, Cummings will have been established as one of the lasting poets America has produced.

Late Works and Influence

Cummings's *Collected Poems* was published in 1960. In addition to the works mentioned, Cummings published several other experimental plays, a ballet, and some 15 volumes of verse. Shortly before his death at North Conway on Sept. 3, 1962, Cummings wrote the texts to accompany photographs taken by his third wife, Marion Morehouse. Titled *Adventures in Value* (1962), this work exemplifies his lifelong effort to *see* intensely and deeply enough to confront the miraculousness of the natural. Poets of neoromantic inclinations consider him, along with William Carlos Williams, one of their artistic ancestors, although Cummings produced no significant stylistic followers.

Further Reading

Good discussions of Cummings and his work include Charles Norman, *The Magic-Maker: E. E. Cummings* (1958); Norman Friedman, *E. E. Cummings: The Growth of a Writer* (1964); Barry A. Marks, *E. E. Cummings* (1964); and Robert E. Wegner, *The Poetry and Prose of E. E. Cummings* (1965). There is a section on Cummings in Hyatt H. Waggoner, *American Poets: From the Puritans to the Present* (1968). □

Mario Matthew Cuomo

Mario Matthew Cuomo (born 1932) was a progressive Democrat governor of New York state from 1982 to 1994. He emphasized lower taxes, balanced budgets, public education, and affirmative action, as well as a government-private sector partnership for economic progress. He was often mentioned as a possible Democratic candidate for president.

Mario Matthew Cuomo was born on June 15, 1932, in New York City. His parents, Andrea and Immaculata (Giordano) Cuomo, had immigrated from Salerno, Italy, in the late 1920s. His father dug and cleaned sewers and by 1931 had saved enough to open an Italian-American grocery store in the South Jamaica section of Queens, a borough of New York City. Cuomo was born in the family's apartment above the store. He was the youngest of three children; he had a brother and a sister. He spent much of his early life watching his parents work incredibly hard and absorbing their values of respect for family, personal obligations, education, and the law.

Cuomo spoke only Italian until he started local public schools. Seeking a more rigorous academic education, he transferred to a Roman Catholic high school, St. John's Preparatory. A boy who always liked to play ball games, at 19 Cuomo was recruited by the Pittsburgh Pirates to become a professional baseball player. He was sent to play with its minor league team, the Brunswick (Georgia) Pirates, as a center fielder. His doubts about making sports a career won out after a head injury received from a fastball. He returned to school on a scholarship given by St. John's

University. Cuomo earned his B.A. degree with high honors in 1953, then entered St. John's School of Law. In June 1954 he married Matilda Raffa, a student at St. John's, who became a school teacher. He earned his law degree in 1956, tied for first in his class.

After graduation, Cuomo became a law clerk with a New York state Court of Appeals judge. In 1958 he went into private practice, joining a Brooklyn law firm. In 1963 he started teaching law part-time at St. John's.

Cuomo soon was drawn into representing community groups in their legal problems. He earned a reputation as a skilled debater and arbitrator. Once, he represented a group of junkyard owners and scrap dealers who sought to save their businesses when their land was condemned by New York City as a proposed site for the 1964-1965 World's Fair. Another time he helped families save their homes from being bulldozed to build a school and athletic field in Corona, Queens. Mayor John Lindsey asked him to settle bitterly hostile neighborhood disputes arising from a plan to build a large-scale low-income housing project in middle-income Forest Hills, Queens. His victories were heavily publicized and the recognition led to suggestions that he seek public office.

Cuomo, with a deep sense of civic obligation, decided to enter public service. In 1974 he ran for lieutenant governor of New York, but lost in a three-way Democratic primary that year. Governor Hugh Carey, an acquaintance from law school, appointed Cuomo secretary of state, beginning January 1975. Cuomo left his law partnership and teaching post to devote his full attention to the office, although he was not required to do so. He worked to expand the duties of secretary of state, intervening in a series of state-wide crises, including a Mohawk Indian lands claim dispute, nursing home practices problems, and rent strikes. The position offered him an extraordinary education in state government.

In 1977 he ran for mayor of New York City. He lost the Democratic primary, facing six rivals. However, he stayed in the race as the nominee of the Liberal Party. Cuomo was defeated by Edward Koch.

Carey, seeking re-election in 1978, asked Cuomo to run on his ticket as lieutenant governor. Cuomo received his party's support. The ticket won in the election. As lieutenant governor, Cuomo traveled the state in the role of ombudsman for citizen problems. He led President Jimmy Carter's 1980 re-election campaign in New York state and was a delegate that year to the Democratic National Convention.

When Carey announced that he would not seek a third term in office in 1982, Cuomo decided to enter the race. He faced his old opponent, Edward Koch, in the struggle for the nomination. Koch, more widely known and far better financed, lost this round. Relying on volunteers and upstate voters, Cuomo won the Democratic primary and, also, a place on the Liberal Party ticket. He narrowly defeated his millionaire Republican opponent in the general election to become New York's 52nd governor.

In 1984 Cuomo delivered the keynote address at the Democratic Party's national nominating convention in San Francisco. He electrified the crowd with his oratorical skills. In 1992 at the Democratic National Convention he gave the speech which nominated Bill Clinton as the Democratic candidate for President. Cuomo himself was sought after to run for the presidential nomination in 1984, 1988, and 1992, but each time he refused.

Cuomo won re-election in 1986 and again, for a third term, in 1990. His vote-gathering abilities broke state records for the percentage of votes received for governor. As governor, Cuomo pushed for lower taxes and balanced budgets. He made public education a top priority. He emphasized a partnership between business and government for economic development. His affirmative action efforts won praise.

In 1994, even after a campaign that was supported by New York City's Republican mayor, Rudolph Guiliani, Cuomo was defeated for re-election by his Republican challenger, George Pataki. Critics have said that Cuomo's brand of social liberalism had been discredited in the public mind, in favor of less government. In 1995, shortly after taking office, Pataki passed a death penalty law, after two decades of vetoes by his two Democratic predecessors.

Cuomo spoke of his political orientation as "progressive pragmatism." He was influenced by his ethnic, religious, and lower-class upbringing. He reminded people of America's immigrant heritage and the upward mobility of its people. His political philosophy was a "family kind of politics" that conceived of people sharing their burdens and blessings and understanding that their individual well-being depends on the well-being of the community. Thus, he believed that government has a responsibility to help those who through no fault of their own are either permanently or temporarily unable to help themselves.

Cuomo is an introspective person, keeping diaries to explore his own motivations and sort his thinking. He has been described as being a workaholic, competitive, having a quick temper, and refusing to delegate authority. Cuomo considers himself devoted to his family and friends. He doted on his three daughters and two sons. His elder son, Andrew, managed his father's campaigns and served as a chief adviser to the governor. Andrew Cuomo became Secretary of Housing & Urban Development in the second term of President Bill Clinton.

Cuomo has authored books about public policy, social and cultural issues, New York, and his life, both personal and political. He also hosts a radio call-in show in New York City.

Further Reading

Mario Cuomo has written two books recording major episodes in his life, based on his diaries. Both have biographical portions and personal meditations that give insight into the many forces that shape his character: *Forest Hills Diary: The Crisis of Low-Income Housing* (1974); and *Diaries of Mario M. Cuomo: The Campaign for Governor* (1984). He described New York State, its challenges and accomplishments in *The New York Idea: An Experiment in Democracy* (1994). He also released *More Than Words* and *Lincoln On Democracy* (which he co-edited). A fascinating biography is Robert S. McElvaine, *Mario Cuomo: A Biography* (1988). A study of Cuomo's political support and issues is Lee M. Miringoff and Barbara L. Carvalho, *The Cuomo Factor: Assessing the Political Appeal of New York's Governor* (1986). Information about Cuomo's political career can be followed in a biennial series, *The Almanac of American Politics,* by Michael Barone and Grant Ujifusa. ☐

Harvey Williams Cushing

The American neurosurgeon Harvey Williams Cushing (1869-1939) developed operative techniques that made brain surgery feasible.

Harvey Cushing was born on April 8, 1869, in Cleveland, Ohio. He graduated from Yale University in 1891 and received a medical degree in 1895 from Harvard Medical School. After a year's internship at Massachusetts General Hospital he went to Johns Hopkins, where he was William Halsted's resident in surgery. From Halsted he learned meticulous surgical technique.

During a trip to Europe in 1900 Cushing worked with some of Europe's leading surgeons and physiologists, including Charles Scott Sherrington, Theodore Kocher, and Hugo Kronecker. They directed his attention to neurosurgery, to which he devoted the rest of his life. Shortly after his return to Johns Hopkins he was made associate professor of surgery. In 1902 he married Katharine Crowell.

In 1907 Cushing began studies of the pituitary gland. He unraveled many of the disorders affecting the gland and showed that a surgical approach to the pituitary was possible. In 1912 *The Pituitary Body and Its Disorders* was pub-

lished. In that same year he accepted the Moseley professorship of surgery at Harvard and an appointment as surgeon in chief at Peter Bent Brigham Hospital in Boston. During World War I he served in France as director of Base Hospital No. 5. His wartime experiences formed the basis of a book, *From a Surgeon's Journal* (1936). Cushing's active affiliation with Harvard continued until 1932, when he was named professor emeritus. The following year he accepted the Sterling professorship of neurology at Yale.

Throughout his career Cushing studied brain tumors and published many important books on the subject, including: *Tumours of the Nervus Acusticus and the Syndrome of the Cerebellopontile* (1917); *A Classification of the Tumours of the Glioma* (1926), with P. Bailey; *Tumours Arising from the Blood Vessels of the Brain: Angiomatous Malformations and Hemangioblastomas* (1928), with Bailey; *Intracranial Tumours* (1932); and *Meningiomas: Their Classification, Regional Behavior, Life History, and Surgical End Results* (1938). He published numerous historical essays, and his biography of Sir William Osler (1925) received the Pulitzer Prize in 1926.

Cushing's use of local anesthesia in brain surgery was an outstanding achievement, as were his many special surgical techniques. In 1911 he introduced special sutures to control the severe bleeding that accompanies brain surgery and often made it impossible.

In 1937 Cushing accepted a position as director of studies in the history of medicine at Yale. He guided the development of a historical library to which he left his own excellent collection of historical books. He was especially interested in Andreas Vesalius, the 16th-century anatomist, and was at work on the *Bio-Bibliography of Vesalius* at the time of his death, on Oct. 7, 1939. The work was completed by his friends and published in 1943.

Further Reading

The definitive biography of Cushing is John F. Fulton, *Harvey Cushing* (1946). A shorter biography for the general reader is Elizabeth Harriet Thomson, *Harvey Cushing: Surgeon, Author, Artist* (1950). On the occasion of Cushing's seventieth birthday, in 1939, *A Bibliography of the Writings of Harvey Cushing* was published by the Harvey Cushing Society.

Additional Sources

Fulton, John F. (John Farquhar), *Harvey Cushing, a biography*, New York: Arno Press, 1900, 1946. □

George Armstrong Custer

No figure of the Indian wars in America so typifies that era as George Armstrong Custer (1839-1876). He is known universally for the massacre that bears his name and for the blundering that brought it about.

George Custer was born in New Rumley, Harrison County, Ohio, on Dec. 5, 1839. His ambition from youth was to be a soldier, and he secured an appointment to West Point in 1857. A poor, mischievous student, he graduated at the bottom of his class in 1861, but was commissioned a second lieutenant in the 2d Cavalry.

The Civil War was in progress, and Custer fought on the Union side. For gallant conduct at the engagement at Aldie on June 16, 1863, he was breveted a brigadier general and given command of a brigade from Michigan. By the end of the war, at the age of only 25, he had been promoted to brevet major general. During the war he had married his childhood sweetheart, Elizabeth Bacon.

The conflict over, Custer reverted to his permanent rank of captain in the 5th Cavalry but soon was promoted to lieutenant colonel of the 7th Cavalry; he would actively hold this command until his death. In 1867 he was charged with absence from duty and suspended for a year but was reinstated by Gen. Philip H. Sheridan in 1868. On November 27 of that year he achieved a startling victory over Chief Black Kettle and the Cheyenne Indians at the battle of the Washita. His regiment was then fragmented, and he spent 2 years in Kentucky. In 1873 the regiment was reunited in the Dakota Territory. He was described at this time as tall, slender, energetic, and dashing, with blue eyes and long golden hair and mustache. At the post he wore velveteen uniforms decorated with gold braid, but in the field he affected buckskins. He rarely drank or used tobacco and spent his spare hours reading military history and studying tactics.

Rumors of gold in the Black Hills led to a government expedition in 1874, which Custer commanded. Scientists from the Smithsonian Institution confirmed the rumors, and the swarm of gold seekers to the area caused the Sioux Indians to go on the attack. Custer was to lead the campaign against the Sioux and Cheyenne in early 1876, but instead he was summoned to Washington to testify before a congressional committee investigating fraud in the Indian Bureau. Custer's testimony, unfavorable to Secretary of War W. W. Belknap, so angered President Grant that he removed Custer from command of the expedition to punish the Native Americans. Public outcry at the President's act, along with the request of Gen. Alfred Terry that Custer accompany the campaign, caused Grant to restore Custer to command of the 7th Cavalry, which then took the field.

On the Yellowstone River, Terry's scouts reported Indians in the vicinity, and Custer was sent to investigate, with orders to exercise caution. On the morning of June 25, 1876, he came upon a village later estimated to have contained from 2,500 to 4,000 Sioux and Cheyenne warriors under Chief Crazy Horse. Splitting his command into three parts, Custer personally led 264 men into battle. His force was surrounded on the hill that now bears his name, overlooking the valley of the Little Bighorn River. He and all the men under his personal command were massacred there, while Maj. Marcus Reno and Capt. Frederick Benteen took refuge on the bluffs overlooking the river and escaped.

The Custer massacre electrified the nation, although it had little effect on the outcome of the Sioux wars. Reno and Benteen were accused of cowardice by admirers of Custer, while Custer's detractors bemoaned the death of the troops under his command due to his rash order to charge so superior a Native American force. This controversy continues, for Custer was a man so paradoxical that he could fight corruption in the Indian Bureau to the disservice of his own carrier, yet also order a charge to kill Native Americans.

Further Reading

So many books have been written about Custer that no one book can be singled out as best. Custer's autobiography, *My Life on the Plains: or, Personal Experiences with Indians* (1874), gives insights into his character, as do the books by his wife, Elizabeth Bacon Custer, *Boots and Saddle: or, Life in Dakota with General Custer* (1885) and *Tenting on the Plains: or, General Custer in Kansas and Texas* (1887). See also Marguerite Merington, ed., *The Custer Story: The Life and Intimate Letters of George A. Custer and His Wife Elizabeth* (1950). ☐

D

Clarence Seward Darrow

As an American labor lawyer and as a criminal lawyer, Clarence Seward Darrow (1857-1938) helped sharpen debate about the path of American industrialism and about the treatment of individuals in conflict with the law.

Clarence Darrow was born on April 18, 1857, in Farmdale, Ohio, to Amirus and Emily Darrow. He was introduced early to the life of the dissenter, for his father, after completing studies at a Unitarian seminary, had lost his faith and had become an agnostic living within a community of religious believers. Furthermore, the Darrows were Democrats in a Republican locale.

After completing his secondary schooling near Farmdale, Darrow spent a year at Allegheny College in Meadville, Pa., and another year at the University of Michigan Law School. Like almost all lawyers of the time, he delayed his admission to the bar until after he had read law with a local lawyer; he became a member of the Ohio bar in 1878. For the next 9 years he was a typical small-town lawyer, practicing in Kinsman, Andover, and Ashtabula, Ohio.

Seeking more interesting paths, however, Darrow moved to Chicago in 1887. In Ohio he had been impressed with the book *Our Penal Machinery and Its Victims* by Judge John Peter Altgeld. Darrow became a close friend of Altgeld, who was elected governor of Illinois in 1892. Altgeld not only raised questions about the process of criminal justice but, when he pardoned several men who had been convicted in the aftermath of the Haymarket riot of 1886, also questioned the treatment of those who were trying to organize workers into unions. Both of these themes played great roles in Darrow's life.

Labor Lawyer

Darrow had begun as a conventional civil lawyer. Even in Chicago his first jobs included appointment as the city's corporation counsel in 1890 and then as general attorney to the Chicago and North Western Railway. In 1894, however, he began what would be his primary career for the next 20 years—labor law. During that year he defended the Socialist Eugene V. Debs against an injunction trying to break the workers' strike Debs was leading against the Pullman Sleeping Car Company. Darrow was unsuccessful, though; the injunction against Debs was finally upheld by the Supreme Court.

In 1906-1907 Darrow successfully defended William D. "Big Bill" Haywood, the leader of the newly formed Industrial Workers of the World, against a charge of conspiring to murder former governor Steunenberg of Idaho. But in 1911 disaster struck as Darrow, defending the McNamara brothers against a charge of blowing up the Los Angeles Times Building, was suddenly faced with his clients' reversing their previous plea of innocence to one of guilt. In turn, Darrow was indicted for misconduct but was not convicted. With this his career as a labor lawyer came to an end.

Criminal Lawyer

Darrow had always been interested in criminal law, in part because of his acceptance of new, psychological theories stressing the role of determinism in human behavior. He viewed criminals as people led by circumstance into committing antisocial acts rather than as free-willing monsters. For this reason he was a bitter opponent of capital punishment, viewing it as a barbaric practice. Now he embarked on a new major career as a criminal lawyer.

Without a doubt Darrow's most famous criminal trial was the 1924 Leopold-Loeb case, in which two Chicago

225

boys had wantonly murdered a youngster. For the only time in his career Darrow insisted that his clients plead guilty, then turned his attention to saving them from the death penalty. He was successful in this, partly because he was able to introduce a great deal of psychiatric testimony supporting his theories of the determining influences upon individual acts.

Scopes Trial

During this period Darrow also participated in another great American case, the Scopes trial of 1925 in Dayton, Tenn. The issue was the right of a state legislature to prohibit the teaching of Darwinian theories of evolution in the public schools. Darrow, as an agnostic and as an evolutionist, was doubly contemptuous of the motives behind the fundamentalist law that had been passed, and he sought to defend the young schoolteacher who had raised the issue of evolution in his class. Technically, he was unsuccessful, for Scopes was convicted and fined $100 for his crime. But Darrow's defense, and particularly his cross-examination of William Jennings Bryan (the three-time Democratic candidate for president who spoke for the biblical, antiscientific, fundamentalist side) served to discredit religious fundamentalism and won national attention.

Two books among Darrow's many writings typify his concerns toward the end of his life. In 1922 he wrote *Crime: Its Cause and Treatment;* in 1929 appeared *Infidels and Heretics,* coedited with Wallace Rice, in which he presented the case for freethinking. To these two issue-oriented books he added in 1932 his autobiography, *The Story of My Life.*

Darrow's last important public service was as chairman of a commission appointed by President Franklin D. Roosevelt to analyze the operation of the National Recovery Administration. He died on March 13, 1938.

Further Reading

The standard popular biography of Darrow is Irving Stone, *Clarence Darrow for the Defense* (1941). A more recent work is Miriam Gurko, *Clarence Darrow* (1965). A specialized, scholarly study is Abe C. Ravitz, *Clarence Darrow and the American Literary Tradition* (1962), which takes note of Darrow's participation in some of the literary controversies of his time. □

Jefferson Davis

Jefferson Davis (1808-1889) was president of the Confederate States of America during the Civil War. His honesty, character, and devotion elevated his cause above a quest for the perpetuation of slavery to a crusade for independence.

History has served Jefferson Davis badly by placing him opposite Abraham Lincoln. Davis is grudged even the loser's mite, for Fate chose Robert E. Lee to embody the "Lost Cause." Yet Davis led the Confederacy and suffered its defeat with great dignity, and he deserves a better recollection.

Davis was born on June 3, 1808, in what is now Todd County, Ky. The family soon moved to Mississippi. After attending Transylvania University for 3 years, he entered the U.S. Military Academy at West Point, from which he graduated in 1828. He served in the infantry for 7 years. At Ft. Crawford, Wis., he fell in love with Sarah Knox Taylor, daughter of post commandant Zachary Taylor. Col. Taylor disapproved of the proposed match. Davis resigned his commission in 1835, married Sarah, and took her to Mississippi; within 3 months she died of malaria. Davis contracted a light case of it, which, combined with grief, permanently weakened his health. From 1835 to 1845 he lived in seclusion at Brierfield, a plantation given him by his brother, Joseph. He and Joseph were close, shared reading habits, argued, and sharpened each other's wits and prejudices.

During these quiet years Davis developed a Southerner's fascination for politics and love for the land. In December 1845 Davis and Varina Howell, his new bride, went to Washington, where Davis took a Democratic seat in the House of Representatives. The Davises made a swift impression. Varina entertained well; Jefferson earned notice for his eloquence and the "charm of his voice."

War with Mexico interrupted Davis's congressional service. He resigned in 1846 to command a volunteer regiment attached to Zachary Taylor's army. Col. Davis and his men won quick approval from the crotchety old general, and the earlier hostilities between the two men were forgotten. Distinguished service by Davis's outfit at Monterey, Mexico, was followed by real heroism at Buena Vista (Feb. 22, 1847). Wounded, Davis returned to Mississippi and received a hero's laurels. In 1847, elected to the U.S. Sen-

ate, Davis became chairman of the Military Affairs Committee. But in 1851 Mississippi Democrats called him back to replace their gubernatorial candidate, thinking that Davis's reputation might cover the party's shift from an extreme secessionist position to one of "cooperationist" moderation. This almost succeeded; Davis lost to Henry S. Foote by less than 1,000 votes.

U.S. Secretary of War

When President Franklin Pierce appointed Davis secretary of war in 1853, Davis found his happiest niche. He enlarged the Army, modernized military procedures, boosted soldiers' pay (and morale), directed important Western land surveys for future railroad construction, and masterminded the Gadsden Purchase.

At the close of Pierce's term Davis reentered the Senate and became a major Southern spokesman. Ever mindful of the Union's purposes, he worked to preserve the Compromise of 1850. Yet throughout the 1850s Davis was moving toward a Southern nationalist point of view. He opposed Stephen A. Douglas's "squatter sovereignty" doctrine in the Kansas question. Congress, Davis argued, had no power to limit slavery's extension.

At the 1860 Democratic convention Davis cautioned against secession. However, he accepted Mississippi's decision, and on Jan. 21, 1861, in perhaps his most eloquent senatorial address, announced his state's secession from the Union and his own resignation from the Senate and called for understanding.

Confederate President

Davis only reluctantly accepted the presidency of the Confederate States of America. He began his superhuman task with very human doubts. But once in office he became the foremost Confederate. His special virtues were revealed by challenge—honesty, devotion, dedication, the zeal of a passionate patriot.

As president, Davis quickly grasped his problems: 9 million citizens (including at least 3 million slaves) of sovereign Southern states pitted against 22 million Yankees; 9,000 miles of usable railroad track against 22,000; no large factories, warships, or shipyards; little money; no credit, save in the guise of cotton; scant arms and no manufacturing arsenals to replenish losses; miniscule powder works; undeveloped lead, saltpeter, copper, and iron resources; and almost no knowledge of steelmaking. Assets could be counted only as optimism, confidence, cotton, and courage. Davis would have to conjure a cause, anneal a new nation, and make a war.

With sure grasp Davis built an army out of state volunteers sworn into Confederate service—and thus won his first round against state rights. Officers came from the "Old Army" and from Southern military schools. Supplies, arms, munitions, clothes, and transportation came from often reluctant governors, from citizens, and, finally, by means of crafty legerdemain worked by staff officials.

When supplies dwindled drastically, Davis resorted to impressing private property. When military manpower shrank, Davis had to ask the Confederate Congress for the greatest military innovation a democracy could dare—conscription. In April 1862 Congress authorized the draft.

Confederate Strategy

Nor was Davis timid in using his armies. Relying usually on leaders he knew, he put such men as Albert Sidney Johnston, Joseph E. Johnston, P. G. T. Beauregard, Braxton Bragg, James Longstreet, Thomas J. Jackson, Nathan Bedford Forrest, and Robert E. Lee in various commands. He developed a strategy to fit Confederate circumstances. Realizing that the weaker side must husband and hoard yet dare desperately when the chance came, Davis divided the Confederate military map into departments, each under a general with wide powers. He sought only to repel invaders. This strategy had political as well as military implications: the Confederacy was not aggressive, sought nothing save independence, and would fight in the North only when pressed. Davis's plan brought impressive results—First Manassas, the Seven Days, Second Manassas, and the clearing of Virginia by September 1862. Western results seemed equally promising. Shiloh, while not a victory, stabilized the middle border; Bragg's following campaign maneuvered a Union army out of Tennessee and almost out of Kentucky.

These successes led Davis to a general offensive in the summer and fall of 1862 designed to terrify Northerners, themselves yet untouched by war; to separate other, uncertain states from the Union; and to convince the outside world of Southern strength. Though it failed, the strategy had merit and remained in effect. Checks at Fredericksburg, Holly Springs, and Chancellorsville stung the North. When Union general U. S. Grant moved against Vicksburg in spring 1863, it looked as though he might be lost in Mississippi, with Gen. Joseph Hooker snared in Virginia's wilderness.

But Grant's relentless pressure on Vicksburg forced Davis to a desperate gamble that resulted in the Battle of Gettysburg, the loss of Vicksburg, and a cost to the South of over 50,000 men and 60,000 stands of arms. Men and arms were irreplaceable, and Davis huddled deeper in the defensive.

Davis had tried perhaps the most notable innovation in the history of American command when he adopted the "theater" idea as an expansion of departmental control. Joseph E. Johnston became commander of the Department of the West, taking absolute power over all forces from the Chattahoochee River to the Mississippi River, and from the Gulf of Mexico to Tennessee. It was a great scheme for running a remote war and might have worked, save for Johnston's hesitancy in exercising his authority. Davis lost faith in his general but not in his plan.

In 1864, after Atlanta's fall, Davis approved Gen. John Bell Hood's plan of striking along William T. Sherman's communications into Tennessee, with the hope of capturing Nashville. Logistical support for this bold venture was coordinated by P. G. T. Beauregard, the new commander of the Department of the West. But Beauregard also distrusted his own authority. Hood failed before Nashville; but by then things had so deteriorated that the blame could hardly be fixed on any one in particular.

Wartime Innovations

Innovation was essential: the armies had to be supported—and in this quest Davis himself changed. Ever an advocate of state rights, he became an uncompromising Confederate nationalist, warring with state governors for federal rights and urging centralist policies on his reluctant Congress. Conscription and impressment were two pillars of his program; others included harsh tax laws, government regulation of railroads and blockade running, and diplomacy aimed at winning recognition of Confederate independence and establishing commercial relations with England and France. Davis came to advocate wide application of martial law. Finally he suggested drafting slaves, with freedom as the reward for valor. These measures were essential to avoid defeat; many were beyond the daring of the Confederate Congress.

Congress's inability to face necessity finally infuriated Davis. Though warm and winning in personal relations, he saw no need for politicking in relations with Congress. He believed that reasonable men did what crisis demanded and anything less was treason. Intolerant of laxity in himself or in others, he sometimes alienated supporters.

Southern Defeat

As Confederate chances dwindled, Davis became increasingly demanding. He eventually won congressional support for most of his measures but at high personal cost. By the summer of 1864 most Southern newspapers were sniping at his administration, state governors were quarreling with him, and he had become the focus of Southern discontent. The South was losing; Davis's plan must be wrong, the rebels reasoned. Peace sentiments arose in disaffected areas of several states, as did demands to negotiate with the enemy. Davis knew the enemy's price: union. But he tried negotiation. Yet when the Hampton Roads Conference in February 1865 proved fruitless and Davis called for renewed Confederate dedication, the Confederacy was falling apart, and there was almost nothing to rededicate. Confederate money had so declined in value that Southerners were avoiding it; soldiers deserted; invaders stalked the land with almost no opposition. Lee surrendered on April 9, 1865; Johnston surrendered on April 26. Davis and a small party were captured at Irwinville, Ga., on May 10.

Years of Decline

Accused of complicity in Lincoln's assassination, and the object of intense hatred in both North and South, Davis spent 2 years as a state prisoner. He was harshly treated, and his already feeble health broke dangerously. When Federal authorities decided not to try him for treason, he traveled abroad to recuperate, then returned to Mississippi and vainly sought to rebuild his fortune.

Through a friend's generosity Davis and his family received a stately home on Mississippi's Gulf Coast. Here from 1878 to 1881 Davis wrote *Rise and Fall of the Confederate Government*. And here, at last, he basked in a kind of fame that eased his final years. He died in New Orleans on Dec. 6, 1889, survived by Varina and two of their six children.

Further Reading

A primary source is Dunbar Rowland, ed., *Jefferson Davis, Constitutionalist: His Letters, Papers and Speeches* (10 vols., 1923), which includes an autobiography in volume 1. Biographies include Varina H. Davis, *Jefferson Davis: A Memoir* (1890); William E. Dodd, *Jefferson Davis* (1907); Allen Tate, *Jefferson Davis, His Rise and Fall* (1929); Robert W. Winston, *High Stakes and Hair Trigger: The Life of Jefferson Davis* (1930); Robert McElroy, *Jefferson Davis: The Unreal and the Real* (2 vols., 1937); and Hudson Strode, *Jefferson Davis* (3 vols., 1955-1964). See also Burton J. Hendrick, *Statesmen of the Lost Cause* (1939); Robert W. Patrick, *Jefferson Davis and His Cabinet* (1944); Frank E. Vandiver, *Jefferson Davis and the Confederate State* (1964) and *Their Tattered Flags* (1970). □

Miles Davis

A jazz trumpeter, composer, and small-band leader, Miles Davis (1926-1991) was in the jazz vanguard for more than two decades. His legend continued to grow even after poor health and diminished creativity removed him from jazz prominence.

Miles Dewey Davis, 3rd, was born into a well-to-do Alton, Illinois, family on May 25, 1926. His father was a dentist, his mother a woman of leisure: there were two other children, an older sister and a younger brother. In 1928 the family moved to East St. Louis. At the age of 10 Miles began playing trumpet; while still in high

school he met and was coached by his earliest idol, the great St. Louis trumpeter Clark Terry.

After fathering two children by a woman friend, Miles moved to New York City in 1944. He worked for just two weeks in the talent-packed Billy Eckstine Band, then enrolled in the Juilliard School of Music, by day studying classical music and by night interning in jazz's newest idiom, bebop, with the leaders of the movement, notably Charlie Parker, Dizzy Gillespie, Fats Navarro, and Max Roach.

Miles's 1947-1948 stint in a quintet led by bebop genius Charlie Parker gained him a modicum of early fame; a fine trumpeter in the bebop idiom, he nevertheless began to move conceptually away from its orthodoxy. He felt a need to divest his music of bebop's excesses and eccentricities and to restore jazz's more melodic and orchestrated elements. The result was the seminal LP recording *Birth of the Cool* (1949), played by a medium-sized group, a nonet, featuring, in addition to Miles, baritone saxophonist Gerry Mulligan, alto saxophonist Lee Konitz, and pianist Al Haig. A highly celebrated record date, it gave "birth" to the so-called "cool," or West Coast, jazz school, which was more cerebral, more heavily orchestrated, and generally more disciplined (especially in its shorter solos) than traditional bebop, and it gave Miles a musical identity distinct from Parker and the other beboppers.

In the early 1950s Miles became a heroin addict, and his career came to a near halt for three years, but his ultimately successful fight against the drug habit in 1954 led to his greatest period, the mid-to-late 1950s. During that six-year span he made a series of small group recordings regarded as jazz classics. In 1954, with tenor saxophone titan Sonny Rollins, he made memorable recordings of three Rollins originals—"Airegin," "Doxy," and "Oleo"—as well as two brilliant versions of the Tin Pan Alley standard "But Not for Me." Additionally, in the 1954-1955 period Miles recorded with a number of other jazz giants—tenorist Lucky Thompson, vibist Milt Jackson, and pianist Thelonious Monk.

In 1955 Miles formed his most celebrated group, a remarkably talented quintet (later, a sextet, with the addition of alto saxophonist Julian "Cannonball" Adderley) that featured tenor saxophonist John Coltrane, pianist Red Garland, bassist Paul Chambers, and drummer Philly Joe Jones. Until Coltrane's defection in the 1960s, Miles's band was the single most visible and dominant group in all of jazz. The early 1960s saw a succession of personnel shifts until the band stabilized in 1964 around an excellent new rhythm section of pianist Herbie Hancock, bassist Ron Carter, and drummer Tony Williams, as well as a new tenor saxophonist, Wayne Shorter. Miles continued to be the greatest attraction (and biggest moneymaker) in all of jazz, but his new band couldn't match the impossibly high standards of its predecessor. Late in the decade his music took a radically new direction. In two 1968 albums, *Miles in the Sky* and *Filles de Kilimanjaro*, Miles experimented with rock rhythms and non-traditional instrumentation. For the last two decades of Miles' career his music was increasingly rhythm-and-drone and Miles himself became more of a jazz curiosity than a musician to be taken seriously.

A good part of Davis's fame owed less to his considerable musicianship than to his strange persona. He was notorious in performance for turning his back on audiences, for addressing them inaudibly or not at all, for expressing racial hostility toward whites, for dressing nattily early in his career and outlandishly later, and for projecting (especially in a series of motorcycle ads on television) a voice hoarse to a point of strangulation—all of which contributed to his charismatic mystique. Davis also had many health problems and more than his share of brushes with officialdom (widespread racism and his own racial militancy made the latter inevitable).

Miles was, in reality, a paradox. Himself the victim of a policeman's clubbing (reportedly, racially-inspired), he had the fairness and courage in the late 1950s to defy Black jazzmen's expectations by filling a piano vacancy with a white player, Bill Evans, but then, by all accounts, often racially taunted him. A physical fitness enthusiast (with his own private gym), he nevertheless ingested vast quantities of drugs (sometimes, but not always, for arthritic pain). Forbiddingly gruff and solitary, he was also capable of acts of generosity toward down-at-heels musicians, both African American *and* white.

Davis was married three times—to dancer Frances Taylor, singer Betty Mabry, and actress Cicely Tyson; all ended in divorce. He had, in all, three sons, a daughter, and seven grandchildren. He died on September 28, 1991, of pneumonia, respiratory failure, and a stroke.

Davis, in addition to the classic small group recordings of the 1954-1960 period, recorded memorable orchestral works with arranger and long-time friend Gil Evans, most notably *Miles Ahead* (1957), *Porgy and Bess* (1958), and *Sketches of Spain* (1960). Davis' extended works include scores for Louis Malle's film *Elevator to the Gallows* (1957) and for the full-length documentary *Jack Johnson* (1970). Among Davis' best-known shorter compositions are the early "Tune Up," "Milestones," "Miles Ahead," "Blue Haze," and "Four"; from 1958 on his best tunes, such as "So What" and "All Blues," are based on modal scales rather than chords. Early and late, both the compositions and the trumpet playing are trademarked by Davis' hauntingly "blue" sound.

Further Reading

Miles: An Autobiography (1989), written with Quincy Troupe, is inadvertently self-revealing—opinionated, irreverent, egotistical, obscene, abusive, and wrong-headed (e.g., he is almost totally dismissive of his finest work and aggressively defensive of his worst). More balanced is Ian Carr's *Miles Davis* (1982). The two most rewarding articles are both negative assessments—Whitney Balliett's "Miles" in the *New Yorker* (December 4, 1989) and Stanley Crouch's "Play the Right Thing" in *The New Republic* (February 12, 1990), which labels Miles as "the most brilliant sellout in the history of jazz" (for having abandoned his early artistry in favor of jazz-rock fusion). A 1993 biography, *Miles Davis: The Man in the Green Shirt*, by Richard Williams is little more than a coffeetable book. □

Richard Harding Davis

The American journalist Richard Harding Davis (1864-1916) was also a fiction writer and dramatist whose swashbuckling adventures were popular with the American public.

Richard Harding Davis was born into a well-to-do and rather pious Episcopalian family in Philadelphia. His father, an editorial writer, and his mother, a well-known fiction writer, often entertained Philadelphia artists and visiting actors and actresses, and the boy from the start was completely at ease with celebrities. After graduating from Episcopal Academy and Lehigh University, he studied political economy during a postgraduate year at Johns Hopkins University. In 1886 Davis became a reporter for the *Philadelphia Press*. The editor and other reporters confidently expected the cocky young dandy to fall on his face, but he shortly proved to be a superb reporter and a talented writer. From 1888 to 1890 he was in New York writing special stories for the *Sun*. He also published two volumes of short stories, *Gallegher and Other Stories* (1891) and *Van Bibber and Others* (1892). At the age of 26 he became the managing editor of *Harper's Weekly* and soon was writing accounts of his worldwide travels, which were collected in books such as *Rulers of the Mediterranean* (1894), *About Paris* (1895), and *Three Gringos in Venezuela and Central America* (1896).

As a picturesque and alert correspondent for New York and London newspapers, always appropriately attired for each adventure, Davis covered the Spanish War and the Spanish-American War in Cuba, the Greco-Turkish War, the Boer War, and—toward the end of his life (he died in 1916)—World War I. He based a number of books upon his experiences. More short stories filled 10 volumes, including *The Lion and the Unicorn* (1899), *Ranson's Folly* (1902), and *The Scarlet Car* (1907). A number of Davis's novels covered the international scene; notable were *Soldiers of Fortune* (1897), *The King's Jackal* (1898), *Captain Macklin* (1902), and *The White Mice* (1909). In addition, Davis wrote about two dozen plays, of which dramatizations of *Ranson's Folly* (1904), *The Dictator* (1904), and *Miss Civilization* (1906) were the most successful.

The critic Larzer Ziff in *The American 1890's* admirably summarized Davis's significance: "He demonstrated to those . . . who would listen that their capacity for excitement was matched by the doings in the wide world. But he also demonstrated to an uneasy plutocracy . . . that their gospel of wealth coming to the virtuous and their public dedication to genteel manners and gentlemanly Christian behavior were indeed justified."

Further Reading

For a complete list of Davis's writings consult Henry Cole Quinby, *Richard Harding Davis: A Bibliography* (1924). Two studies relate the author to his background admirably: Fairfax D. Downey, *Richard Harding Davis: His Day* (1933), and Gerald Langford, *The Richard Harding Davis Years: A Biography of a Mother and Son* (1961).

Additional Sources

Lubow, Arthur, *The reporter who would be king: a biography of Richard Harding Davis,* New York: Scribner; Toronto: Maxwell Macmillan Canada; New York: Maxwell Macmillan International, 1992. □

Sammy Davis, Jr.

American entertainer Sammy Davis, Jr. (1925-1990) had a career that spanned more than five decades. He started in vaudeville and progressed to Broadway, film, and performing on the Las Vegas strip.

Sammy Davis, Jr.'s death in 1990 robbed American audiences of a favorite entertainer, a star showman in the oldest vaudeville tradition. Davis was a well-rounded performer of the sort found only rarely these days: he could sing, he could act, he could dance, and he could make people laugh with clowning and impersonations. Davis's long career in show business was even more remarkable because he managed to break color barriers in an era of segregation and racism. His many honors and awards—including a prestigious Kennedy Center medal for career achievement—serve as reflections of the affection his fans felt for him.

Davis was a complete variety performer. With a microphone and a backup ensemble he could entertain solo for two hours at a time. He was one of the first blacks to be accepted as a headliner in the larger Las Vegas casinos and one of the very few stars, black or white, to receive Emmy, Tony, *and* Grammy Award nominations. *People* magazine contributor Marjorie Rosen notes that Davis "made beautiful music . . . and blacks and whites alike heard him and were touched by him. He was loved. And that, of course, is what he wanted most of all."

Learned to Tap Dance Like a Master

Sammy Davis, Jr. began performing almost as soon as he could walk. Both of his parents were vaudevillians who danced with the Will Mastin Troupe. In 1928, when he was only three, Davis joined the Mastin Troupe as its youngest member. He became a regular in 1930 and travelled with his father on the dwindling vaudeville circuit. The demanding schedule of train rides, practice, and performances left little time for formal education, and Davis was always just one step ahead of the truant officer. His unconventional childhood did provide him with important lessons, however. Young Sammy learned how to please an audience, how to tap dance like a master, and how to move people with a smile and a song.

The motion picture industry all but forced most vaudeville entertainers out of business. Few acts survived the competition from the silver screen. The Mastin Troupe felt the strain, dwindling gradually until it became a trio—Sammy Davis, Sr., Will Mastin, and Sammy Davis, Jr. By 1940 Sammy, Jr. had become the star attraction of the trio, with his father and friend providing soft shoe in the background. The act was popular enough to receive billings in larger clubs, and in that environment Davis met other per-

formers such as Bill "Bojangles" Robinson, Frank Sinatra, and various big band leaders.

Davis was drafted into the United States Army when he turned eighteen and was sent to basic training in Cheyenne, Wyoming. The boot camp experience was devastating for Davis. Although he was befriended by a black sergeant who gave him reading lessons, he was mistreated relentlessly by the white troops with whom he had to share a barracks. Transferred to an entertainment regiment, Davis eventually found himself performing in front of some of the same soldiers who had painted "coon" on his forehead. He discovered that his energetic dancing and singing could "neutralize" the bigots and make them acknowledge his humanity. This era may have marked the beginning of Davis's dogged pursuit of his audience's love, a pursuit that would sometimes earn him scorn in years to come.

Headliner in Vegas and New York

After the war the Mastin Trio re-formed, playing on bills with Davis's friends like Sinatra, Mel Torme, and Mickey Rooney. Davis went solo after signing a recording contract with Decca Records. His first album, *Starring Sammy Davis, Jr.,* contained songs and comedy, but another work, *Just for Lovers,* was composed entirely of music. Both sold well, and soon Davis was a headliner in Las Vegas and New York, as well as a guest star on numerous television shows.

On November 19, 1954, Davis nearly lost his life in an automobile accident in the California desert. The accident shattered his face and cost him his left eye. While recuperating, he spent hours discussing philosophy with a rabbi on staff at the hospital, and shortly thereafter he converted to Judaism. Rather than end his career, the accident provided a burst of publicity for Davis. Upon his return to the stage he sold out every performance and received thunderous ovations. Even his well-publicized conversion failed to dampen his popularity. While some critics suggested that he might have had ulterior motives, others—especially blacks— applauded his thoughtful observations about Jews, blacks, and oppression.

Davis began the 1960s as a certified superstar of stage and screen. He had turned an average musical comedy, "Mr. Wonderful," into a successful Broadway show, and he earned critical raves for his performance in the film *Porgy and Bess*. As a member of the high-profile "Rat Pack," he hobnobbed with Frank Sinatra, Dean Martin, Tony Curtis, and Joey Bishop at fashionable bistros in Las Vegas and Los Angeles. In 1965 he starred in another Broadway play, "Golden Boy," in which he played a struggling boxer, and then he turned in creditable film performances in *A Man Called Adam* and *Sweet Charity*. Somehow he was also able to star in two television shows during the same years, "The Sammy Davis, Jr. Show" and "The Swinging World of Sammy Davis, Jr."

Pitfalls of the "Swinging World"

Davis's "swinging world" had its pitfalls, however. His marriage to Swedish actress May Britt earned him the vitriol of the Ku Klux Klan. His "Rat Pack" habits of drinking and drug-taking threatened his health, and his ostentatious displays of wealth nearly bankrupted him even as he earned more than a million dollars a year. Throughout the 1960s Davis was a vocal supporter of the Black Power movement and other left-wing causes, but in the early 1970s he alienated blacks and liberals by embracing Richard Nixon and performing in Vietnam. By that time Davis was in the throes of drug and alcohol addiction. He developed liver and kidney trouble and spent some months in the hospital early in 1974.

The last fifteen years of Davis's life were conducted at the performer's usual hectic pace. In 1978 he appeared in another Broadway musical, "Stop the World—I Want To Get Off." He occasionally served as a stand-in host for the popular "Tonight Show," and he returned in earnest to the casino and show-hall stages. Even hip surgery failed to stop Davis from performing. His best-known act in the 1980s was a musical review with his friends Sinatra and Liza Minnelli, which played to capacity crowds in the United States and Europe just a year before Davis's death.

Doctors discovered a tumor in Davis's throat in August of 1989. The performer underwent painful radiation therapy that at first seemed successful. Then, early in 1990, an even larger cancerous growth was discovered. Davis died on May 16, 1990, as a result of this cancer—only some eight weeks after his friends of a lifetime feted him with a television special in his honor.

A Mentor and Pioneer

During his lifetime, Sammy Davis, Jr. was not universally adored. Some observers—including some blacks— accused him of grovelling to his audiences, of shamelessly toadying for admiration. Those sentiments were forgotten, however, when Davis died at the relatively young age of sixty-four. In eulogies across the country, other black entertainers cited Davis as a mentor and as a pioneer who reached mainstream audiences even though he hailed from minority groups in both race and religion. Record producer Quincy Jones told *People:* "Sammy Davis, Jr. was a true pioneer who traveled a dirt road so others, later, could follow on the freeway. He helped remove the limitations on black entertainers. He made it possible for the Bill Cosbys, the Michael Jacksons and the Eddie Murphys to achieve their dreams."

Davis, the quintessential song-and-dance man, recorded albums throughout his career and performed a number of signature songs. Chief among these were his tribute to Bill Robinson, "Mr. Bojangles," the ballads "What Kind of Fool Am I" and "I've Gotta Be Me," and his biggest hit, the spritely "Candy Man." Davis's singing was like everything else in his performance—energetic, spirited, and played to maximum effect. Rosen sees Davis as "a personal link to a vibrant mainstream of American entertainment" who "poured his jittery energy into virtuoso performances with all the intimacy of a saloon singer."

In an interview for *Contemporary Authors,* Davis analyzed his position in show business. "Nobody likes me but the people," he said. "Though I have been treated extremely well overall by the critics, I have never been a critic's favorite. But the people always had faith in me, and they were supportive of me. . . . They laugh. They have good times, and they come backstage. It's a joy."

Further Reading

Contemporary Authors, Volume 108, Gale, 1984.

Davis, Sammy, Burt Broyar and Jane Broyar, *Yes I Can: The Story of Sammy Davis, Jr.,* Farrar, Straus, 1965.

Davis, Sammy, Burt Broyar and Jane Broyar, *Why Me? The Sammy Davis, Jr. Story,* Farrar, Straus, 1989.

Dobrin, Arnold, *Voices of Joy, Voices of Freedom,* Coward, 1972.

Stambler, Irwin, *Encyclopedia of Pop, Rock & Soul,* St. Martin's, 1974.

New York Times, May 17, 1990.

People, May 28, 1990. □

Lee De Forest

The American inventor Lee De Forest (1873-1961) pioneered in radio, both in developing broadcasting and in inventing the audion. He is considered one of the fathers of radio.

Lee De Forest was born in Council Bluffs, Iowa, in 1873, where his father was a minister. While Lee was still a boy, his father became the president of the College for the Colored in Talladega, Ala. Because of his father's association with African Americans, young Lee was shunned by playmates and sought relief from his loneliness in invention and mechanics. He took bachelor of science

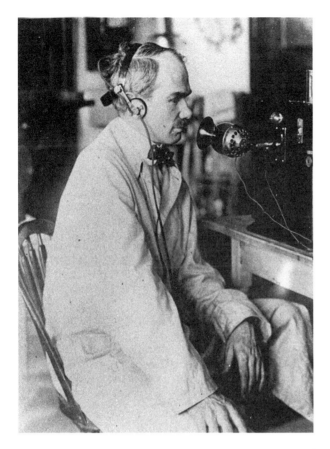

and doctor of philosophy degrees from Yale in 1896 and 1899. He then went to work for the Western Electric Company in Chicago.

During the 1890s Guglielmo Marconi transmitted radio waves over increasing distances; his work culminated in 1901 with a transatlantic message. The new field of radio attracted many inventors, among them De Forest. In 1910 he literally electrified the musical world by broadcasting the voice of Enrico Caruso by radio. In 1916 De Forest made what he believed to be the first news broadcast by radio.

The greatest single contribution De Forest made to the field, however, was his invention of the triode, or audion, as he called it, for which he received a patent in 1908. One of the major goals of inventors was to come up with a more powerful and sensitive detector, or receiver. In 1904 John Ambrose Fleming, a consultant to the Edison Electric Light Company, patented a two-electrode vacuum tube which he called a thermionic valve. Acting between the two electrodes, one of which was heated, the oscillating radio waves were made unidirectional. De Forest's contribution, which he claimed was made in ignorance of Fleming's earlier work, was to add a third element, thus converting the diode to a triode. This new element was a grid (or zigzag piece of wire) placed between the other two. Although no one, including the inventor himself, realized the importance or the exact action of the audion, it proved to be the basis of all subsequent radio development because it could be used to send, receive, or amplify radio signals better than any other device.

In 1902 De Forest became vice president of the De Forest Wireless Telegraph Company and in 1913 vice president of the Radio Telephone Company and the De Forest Radio Company. He worked on other electrical problems, including talking motion pictures and television, and eventually received over 300 domestic and foreign patents. He made and lost four fortunes during his lifetime and was extensively engaged in court litigation with such formidable foes as Irving Langmuir of the General Electric Company and Edwin Armstrong, with whom he disputed invention of the feedback circuit. This last dispute was decided in favor of De Forest in 1934. He retired to a private research laboratory in Hollywood, Calif.

Further Reading

De Forest's autobiography is *Father of Radio* (1950). A more balanced account of his contributions is the standard history of radio, William R. Maclaurin, *Invention and Innovation in the Radio Industry* (1949). The business side of radio is covered in Erik Barnouw, *A History of Broadcasting in the United States* (1966). ☐

James Dean

Actor James Dean (1931-1955) had a short-lived but intense acting career that began in 1952 and ended tragically in his death in September 1955. After his death he became a cult figure, and fans have marveled for decades at his ability to duplicate their adolescent agony on screen.

Born on February 8, 1931, in Marion, Indiana, James Byron Dean was the only child of Winton and Mildred (Wilson) Dean. Winton, a farmer-turned-dental-technician, moved his family to Santa Monica, California. when Dean was six years old. Receiving a lot of attention from both parents, he was particularly close to his mother. James Byron, as she called him, entered first grade in 1937 at the Brentwood Public School. He took violin lessons, playing well for a young child although his school friends taunted him about this activity.

In July 1940 his mother died of cancer. His father sent him, then nine, back to Indiana to live with Marcus and Ortense Winslow, his sister and brother-in-law. In Fairmount Dean grew up in the rural Quaker home, helping with farm chores and enjoying a reasonably carefree existence. Underneath, however, he harbored great pain. "My mother died on me when I was nine years old. What does she expect me to do? Do it all alone?" Dean was later to say.

Still, he got along well, riding his motorcycle with friends and playing guard on the high school basketball team. He excelled at debate and drama, coached and trained by teacher Adeline Nall. He won several state titles for his abilities, and on April 14, 1949, the Fairmount *News* read, "James Dean First Place Winner in Dramatic Speaking."

After graduating in 1949 he left for Los Angeles, where he lived briefly with his father and stepmother and entered Santa Monica City College, majoring in pre-law. But it was drama in which he shone: he received Cs and Ds in law

classes, As and Bs in acting. He transferred the following year to the University of California, Los Angeles, pledging Sigma Nu fraternity. Befriended by actor James Whitmore, Dean obtained a small part in a television drama, *Hill Number One.*

Soon Dean quit school, living precariously as a parking lot attendant and chasing auditions wherever they were available. In 1951, after landing only bit parts and a small role in *Fixed Bayonets,* a war picture, he left Hollywood for New York. There, in 1953, he landed a spot in the Actors Studio run by Lee Strasberg.

He obtained a small part in *See the Jaguar* which opened at the Cort Theatre on Broadway on December 3, 1952. After this his career took off. He did television plays and several more Broadway productions and developed a reputation as "difficult." Despite this he won the Daniel Blum Theatre World Award for "best newcomer" of the year for his role in *The Immoralist.*

In March 1954 Elia Kazan, who knew Dean from Actors Studio days, offered him a Warner Brothers contract. The film was *East of Eden.* The film's New York preview was March 10, 1955, but Dean declined to attend. "I can't handle it," he said, and flew back to Los Angeles.

Dean finished filming *Rebel Without a Cause* (with Sal Mineo and Natalie Wood) in June 1955 and began work on *Giant.* He co-starred in this with Elizabeth Taylor and Rock Hudson. Completing *Giant* in September of that year, Dean was to start rehearsing for *The Corn Is Green,* a play for the National Broadcasting Company. But Dean had a few days free time in which he decided to do some car racing.

Intrigued with fast automobiles, Dean had bought a $6,900 Porsche Spyder which he planned to race at Salinas, California, in September. On September 30th, he and his mechanic, Rolf Wuetherich, were involved in a head-on collision at Paso Robles, California. The Porsche was crumpled, Rolf suffered a smashed jaw and leg fracture. James Dean, dead at the age of 24, was buried in Fairmount, Indiana, on October 8, 1955. Three thousand people attended his funeral.

Less than a month later, *Rebel Without a Cause* opened in New York City, and the Dean legend began. Warner Brothers received landslides of mail—fans were obsessed with the curt, swaggering Dean. In February 1956 he was nominated for a Best Performance Oscar for his role in *East of Eden.* He also received numerous foreign awards, including the French Crystal Star award and the Japanese Million Pearl award. By June 1956 there were dozens of fan clubs, and rumors flourished that Dean was not dead, only severely injured.

Dean, interviewed in March 1955, commented on his craft, offering this curiously fatalistic view of life: "To me, acting is the most logical way for people's neuroses to manifest themselves. To my way of thinking, an actor's course is set even before he's out of the cradle."

Further Reading

Although countless articles appeared about James Dean during his short career and following his death, there are only a few substantial biographies. They include: William Bast's *James Dean* (1956), written by a former roommate and close personal friend; *James Dean: The Mutant King* (1974) by David Dalton; *James Dean, A Short Life* (1974) by Venable Herndon; and Dennis Stock's *James Dean Revisited* (1978). □

Eugene Victor Debs

Eugene Victor Debs (1855-1926), a leading American union organizer and, after 1896, a prominent Socialist, ran five times as the Socialist party nominee for president.

Eugene V. Debs was born on Nov. 5, 1855, in Terre Haute, Ind., where his French immigrant parents, after considerable hardship, had settled. Debs began work in the town's railroad shops at the age of 15, soon becoming a locomotive fireman. Thrown out of work by the depression of the 1870s, he left Terre Haute briefly to find a railroad job but soon returned to work as a clerk in a wholesale grocery company. Even though he was no longer a fireman, he joined the Brotherhood of Locomotive Firemen in 1874 and rose rapidly in the union. In 1878 he became an associate editor of the *Firemen's Magazine.* Two years later he was appointed editor of the magazine and secretary-treasurer of the brotherhood.

Debs also pursued a political career in the early 1880s. A popular and earnest young man, he was elected city clerk of Terre Haute as a Democrat in 1879 and reelected in 1881. Soon after his second term ended in January 1884, he was elected to the Indiana Legislature, serving one term.

Changing Concept of Unionism

During the 1880s Debs remained a craft unionist, devoted to "orthodox" ideals of work, thrift, and respectable unionism. With the Firemen's Brotherhood as his base, he sought to develop cooperation among the various railroad brotherhoods. A weak federation was achieved in 1889, but it soon collapsed due to internal rivalries. Tired and discouraged, Debs resigned his positions in the Firemen's Brotherhood in 1892, only to be reelected over his protest.

Debs's new project was an industrial union, one which would unite *all* railroad men, whatever their specific craft, in one union. By mid-1893, the American Railway Union (ARU) was established, with Debs as its first president. Labor discontent and the severe national depression beginning in 1893 swelled the union's ranks. The ARU won a major strike against the Great Northern Railroad early in the spring of 1894. Nevertheless, when the Pullman Company works near Chicago were struck in May, Debs was reluctant to endorse a sympathetic strike of all railroad men. His union took a militant stance, however, refusing to move Pullman railroad cars nationally. By July, Debs felt the boycott was succeeding, but a sweeping legal injunction against the union leadership and the use of Federal troops broke the strike. Debs was sentenced to 6 months in jail for contempt of court, and his lawyer, Clarence Darrow, appealed unsuccessfully to the U.S. Supreme Court.

Conversion to Socialism

Having moved from craft to industrial unionism, Debs now converted to socialism. Convinced that capitalism and competition inevitably led to class strife, Debs argued that the profit system should be replaced by a cooperative commonwealth. Although he advocated radical change, he rejected revolutionary violence and chose to bring his case to the public through political means. He participated in the establishment of the Social Democratic party in 1898 and its successor, the Socialist Party of America, in 1901.

Debs was the Socialist candidate for president five times. His role was that of a spokesman for radical reform rather than that of a party theorist. A unifying agent, he tried to remain aloof from the persistent factional struggle between the evolutionary Socialists and the party's more revolutionary western wing. As the party's presidential candidate in 1900 and 1904, he led the Socialists to a fourfold increase in national voting strength, from about 97,000 to more than 400,000 votes. While the party's vote did not increase significantly in 1908, Debs drew attention to the Socialist case by a dramatic national tour in the "Red Special," a campaign train. The year 1912 proved to be the high point for Debs and his party. He won 897,011 votes, 6 percent of the total.

Imprisonment for Sedition

When World War I began in 1914, the party met with hard times. The Socialists were the only party to oppose economic assistance to the Allies and the preparedness movement. Debs, while refusing the Socialist nomination for president in 1916, endorsed the party view that President Woodrow Wilson's neutrality policies would lead to war. In 1917 America's entrance into war resulted in widespread antagonism toward the Socialists. When Debs spoke out in 1918 against the war and Federal harassment of Socialists, he was arrested and convicted of sedition under the wartime Espionage Act. He ran for the last time as the Socialist presidential candidate while in prison, receiving nearly a million votes, more actual votes (but a smaller percentage of the total) than in 1912.

On Christmas Day 1921, President Warren G. Harding pardoned Debs, but Debs could do little to restore life to the Socialist party, battered by the war years and split over the Russian Revolution. Debs had welcomed the Revolution; yet he became very critical of the dictatorial aspects of the Soviet regime, refusing to ally himself with the American Communist party. Debs died on Oct. 20, 1926, having won wide respect as a resourceful evangelist for a more humane, cooperative society.

Further Reading

The most recent edition of Debs's writings is *Writings and Speeches of Eugene V. Debs,* with an introduction by Arthur M. Schlesinger, Jr. (1948). There are two excellent studies of Debs's career: Ray Ginger, *The Bending Cross: A Biography of Eugene Victor Debs* (1949), and H. Wayne Morgan, *Eugene V. Debs: Socialist for President* (1962). McAlister Coleman, *Eugene V. Debs: A Man Unafraid* (1930), is the best of the older biographies. Ira Kipnis, *The American Socialist Movement, 1897-1912* (1952), and David A. Shannon, *The Socialist Party of America* (1955), are invaluable sources on the Socialist party. □

John Deere

The American inventor and manufacturer John Deere (1804-1886) was one of the first to design agricultural tools and machines to meet the specific needs of midwestern farmers.

John Deere was born in 1804 in modest circumstances in Rutland, Vt., the third son of William Rinold and Sarah Yates Deere. After receiving the limited education available to a country boy, Deere was apprenticed at 17 to a blacksmith in Middleburn, Vt. He completed his apprenticeship in 4 years and became a master craftsman.

In 1836 Deere left Vermont for Grand Detour, Ill., where he found ready employment in his trade. He prospered, for the farmers kept him fully occupied supplying their customary needs. They also presented him with an unusual problem posed by the local soil. The soil of Illinois and other prairie areas was not only difficult to plow because of its thick sod covering but also tended to clog the moldboards of plows. Deere tried covering the moldboard and cutting a plowshare from salvaged steel. Steel surfaces tended to shed the thick soil and were burnished by the abrasive action of the soil. Deere's new plows, introduced in 1839, sold readily, and within a decade the production of plows by Deere and his new associate, Leonard Andrus, exceeded 1,000 per year. Deere parted company with his partners to move to Moline, Ill., which was better situated for a market, transportation, and raw materials.

Repeated experiments produced an excellent moldboard and demonstrated that further improvements in the plow were dependent on using better-quality steel. Deere imported such steel from an English firm until a Pittsburgh firm cast the first plow steel in the United States for him. Deere's production of plows soared to 10,000 by 1857 as agriculture in the Midwest grew to meet the unprecedented demands of the growing home and export market.

The business was incorporated in 1868 with Deere and his son, Charles, in the executive positions. During the Civil War the company prospered as it diversified its output to include wagons, carriages, and a full line of agricultural equipment. It also adopted modern administrative practices and built an efficient sales, distribution, and service organization which reached into all parts of America. Deere remained active in the management of the company until his fatal illness in 1886. He was succeeded by his son.

John Deere married twice. His first wife, Demarius Lamb, died in 1865. Two years later he married her younger sister, Lucinda Lamb.

Further Reading

Full-length studies of Deere are Neil M. Clark, *John Deere: He Gave to the World the Steel Plow* (1937), and Darragh Aldrich, *The Story of John Deere: A Saga of American Industry* (1942). See also Stewart H. Holbrook, *Machines of Plenty: Pioneering in American Agriculture* (1955), and Wayne D. Rasmussen, *Readings in the History of American Agriculture* (1960).

Additional Sources

Broehl, Wayne G., *John Deere's company: a history of Deere & Company and its times,* New York, N.Y.: Doubleday, 1984.

Collins, David R., *Pioneer plowmaker: a story about John Deere,* Minneapolis: Carolrhoda Books, 1990. □

Morris S. Dees, Jr.

Civil rights attorney Morris S. Dees, Jr. (born 1936) used the rule of law to fight against hate groups in the United States.

In the quarter of a century following the death of civil rights leader Dr. Martin Luther King, Jr. in 1968, there was an alarming rise in the number of hate groups and hate crimes in America. By 1994 it was estimated that there were over 250 hate groups across the United States, including the Ku Klux Klan, neo-Nazis, racist skinheads, and Christian Identity Movement, to name only a few of the most violent. Combatting these groups effectively was extremely difficult, since the very freedoms cherished in U.S. democracy, including and especially freedom of speech, allow bigots to spread their hateful ideas with little fear of prosecution by authorities.

One man made a stand against all of that. Morris S. Dees, Jr., a native of the deep South, led an innovative and effective campaign against America's most dangerous purveyors of hate by using the rule of law to put them out of business.

There is little in Dees' early biography that would hint of his later emergence as a crusader for the rights of minorities. He was born in 1936 in Shorter, Alabama, the son of a farmer and cotton gin operator. The South of his early youth provided equality for African Americans in theory only. Public schools and private institutions were segregated and most African Americans were eking out a living below the poverty line. In rural areas many lived on the land as sharecroppers, in effect little more than indentured servants to white landlords. There were few white citizens who ever questioned a system that rarely protected the rights of African Americans or provided them with opportunities to improve their economic status. Some, like Dees' uncle Lucien, were avowed racists. Others, while not fighting the status quo, still maintained a basic respect for their African American neighbors. Dees' father was such a man. He once took a belt to the young Dees when the teen used a racial epithet to describe a worker.

Originally, Morris Dees saw his future on the land; indeed, he was named the "star farmer" of Alabama in 1955. But his innovative business acumen would lead him on a different course. While an undergraduate at the University of Alabama, he founded a nationwide direct mail sales company that specialized in book publishing. He did not know it then, but Dees had not only discovered a way to secure his financial future, but a new way to communicate ideas directly to millions of Americans. In 1960 he graduated from the University of Alabama Law School, opened a law office in Montgomery, and continued to develop his direct mail business. Sales would reach

$15 million, and eventually he sold his business to the Times-Mirror Corporation.

As Dees grew professionally, he and many other Southerners began to be deeply affected by the emerging civil rights movement of the 1960s. He decided to apply his legal knowledge to aid minorities in the courts. His most notable achievement was a 1968 lawsuit he filed that successfully led to the integration of the all-white Montgomery Young Men's Christian Association (YMCA).

In 1971 Dees co-founded the Southern Poverty Law Center, which engaged in civil lawsuits ranging from defending an African American female inmate in a North Carolina jail to the integration of the Alabama state troopers. Utilizing direct mail, Dees eventually won the financial support of some 300,000 Americans, which enabled the center to pursue critically important but highly unpopular civil rights cases. Throughout, Dees and his colleagues exhibited great courage in standing up for unpopular and powerless clients. But armed with the truth and a belief in the ultimate fairness of the American justice system, they prevailed against the odds.

In 1980 Dees founded Klanwatch as a direct response to resurgence of the virulently anti-African American, anti-Semitic, and anti-Catholic Ku Klux Klan (KKK) and related groups. In more than one instance, violent leaders of the Klan and the White Patriot Party planned to assassinate Dees. Combining great personal heroism and an aggressive use of the law, the Klanwatch struck telling blows against some of America's most dangerous hate groups.

In 1981 a Klan leader, Louis Beam, led a group of renegade American fishermen who sought to block immigrant Vietnamese fishermen from operating in the waters near Galveston, Texas. The new Americans were scared by the terror tactics of boat burnings and threats of physical violence and were on the verge of giving up their livelihoods when the law center entered the picture and successfully sued the Texas Knights of the KKK.

In his native Alabama, Dees successfully used the courts to sue the Klan. Not only were Klan leaders convicted of breaking the law, they were stripped of their assets and left virtually penniless. In one case, a unique aspect of the court-imposed settlement mandated that the leader of the racist assaults was required to attend a Brotherhood seminar convened by the husband of an African American woman who was the target of their attack. In Georgia, Klansmen had to pay $100,000 to their intended victims and their office equipment was transferred to the Raleigh branch of the National Association for the Advancement of Colored People (NAACP). In 1984 Dees won a $7 million lawsuit against the United Klan following the lynching of an African American man by Klansmen. The suit forced the United Klan of America out of business.

The White Patriot Party, a paramilitary off-shoot of the KKK, had by the early 1980s some two thousand members who terrorized minorities in the Carolinas and Virginia. Some of the followers were actually active members in the United States Armed Forces. In 1985 legal action by Klanwatch against the group's leader, Glen Miller, led to the uncovering of thousands of dollars worth of explosives, including rockets stolen from the military, which were destined to be used in a "race war." Later, a Federal Bureau of Investigation (FBI) raid thwarted an assassination plot by Miller and his followers to kill Dees. As a result of the legal steps brought against them, the White Patriot Party no longer exists.

The legal and social basis of Dees' crusade can be shown in his summation before a Mobile, Alabama, court in 1987: "I do not want you to come back with a verdict against the Klan because they have unpopular beliefs. In this country you have the right to have unpopular beliefs just as long as you don't turn those beliefs into violent actions that interfere with someone else's rights. . . . But they put a rope around Michael MacDonald's neck and treated him to an actual death . . . so they could get out their message. . . . You have an opportunity to send a different message that will ring out all over Alabama and all over the United States: That an all white jury from the heart of the South will not tolerate racial violence in any way, shape or form. . . ." The jury found for the African American plaintiff and fixed damages at $7 million.

In the Southern Poverty Law Center's first quarter century the largest amount awarded by a court to the heirs and victims of a racist murder was the 1988 decision in Oregon to assess damages of $12 million against White Aryan Resistance leader Tom Metzger. His skinhead followers had murdered an Ethiopian immigrant. Obviously, money cannot compensate for murder and mayhem, but Dees had a remarkable track record in using the American justice system to financially bankrupt the groups and hate mongers who strove to promote racism in the United States.

Dees was honored by many groups and institutions. He received the Martin Luther King Jr. Memorial Award from the National Education Association. The American Civil Liberties Union presented him with the Roger Bladwin Award, and he was named the Trial Lawyer of the Year by the Trial Lawyers for Public Justice. He earned a reputation as a respected speaker and was asked to deliver the Ralph Fuchs lecture at Indiana University School of Law in 1996. He collaborated with James Corcoran to publish a chilling account of the militia groups in 1996. The book, *Gathering Storm: America's Militia Threat,* makes a strong case for the common thread which appeared to unravel from Ruby Ridge, Idaho in 1992, to Waco, Texas in 1993, to Oklahoma City in 1995.

Further Reading

Two of the most important sources of information on Morris S. Dees, Jr., are books he co-authored with Steve Fiffer: *A Season for Justice: The Life and Times of Civil Rights Lawyer Morris Dees* (1991) and *Hate On Trial: The Case Against America's Most Dangerous Neo-Nazi* (1993). Dees also co-authored with James Corcoran a book about militia groups, *Gathering Storm: America's Militia Threat* (Harper Collins, 1996). Information on hate groups, chiefly the KKK, can be found in Robert P. Ingalls, *Hoods: The Story of the Ku Klux Klan* (1979); Andy Oakley, *"88": An Undercover News Reporter's Expose of American Nazis and the Ku Klux Klan* (1987); Craig Wyn Wade, *The Fiery Cross: The Ku Klux Klan in America* (1987); Susan S. Lang, *Extremist Groups in America* (1990); James Ridgeway, *Blood in the Face: The Ku Klux Klan, Aryan Nations, Nazi Skinheads, and the Rise of a New White Culture* (1990); and Bill Stanton, *Klanwatch: Bringing the Ku Klux Klan to Justice* (1991). See also *Klanwatch Intelligence Report: A Project of the Southern Poverty Law Center,* Southern Poverty Law Center, 1981 to present, a bimonthly. □

Deganawida

Deganawida (1550–1600) was instrumental in founding the League of the Iroquois.

Deganawida is best known as the great leader who, with Hiawatha, founded the League of the Iroquois. Although the story of Deganawida's life is based primarily on legend, all accounts of the league's formation credit Deganawida for his efforts. In addition to his persuasive vision of unified Iroquois tribes, Deganawida was instrumental in defining and establishing the structure and code of the Iroquois league.

It is believed that Deganawida was born around the 1550s in the Kingston, Ontario, area and was one of seven brothers born to Huron parents. According to legend, Deganawida's birth was marked by a vision his mother had that her newborn son would be indirectly responsible for the destruction of the Hurons. She, along with Deganawida's grandmother, tried to protect the Hurons by attempting three times to drown him in a river. Each morning after the attempts, Deganawida was found unharmed in his mother's arms. After the third unsuccessful attempt,

Deganawida's mother resigned herself to her son's existence.

Creates the League of the Iroquois

When Deganawida was grown, he journeyed south to carry out his mission of peace among the Iroquois. He met Hiawatha (not the Hiawatha of Longfellow's poem), a Mohawk, who joined him in his efforts to create an alliance of the Oneidas, Cayugas, Onondagas, Senacas, and Mohawks. Deganawida acted as the visionary and, because Deganawida had a speech impediment, Hiawatha served as his spokesman. Deganawida's message to the Iroquois was that all men are brothers; therefore, they should cease their practices of killing, scalping, and cannibalism. Together, Deganawida and Hiawatha convinced the five tribes to make peace and join together in an alliance of friendship, rather than persist with their attempts to destroy each other. The powerful Onondaga chief, Thadodaho (also known as Atotarho, Adario), who initially had been strongly opposed to the union of the five tribes, marked the beginning of the alliance when he made the decision to join. Deganawida also tried, without success, to encourage the Erie and neutral tribes to join the alliance. Their refusal resulted in their eventual dispersal by the Iroquois in the 1650s. Deganawida's effort to persuade them to join may have been prompted by their friendly disposition toward the Hurons, unlike the other Iroquois. Sometime after Deganawida's death, his mother's earlier vision was realized when the Huron nation was destroyed by the Iroquois.

The alliance of the five tribes was referred to as the League of the Iroquois (also known as The Iroquois Five Nation Confederacy; after the Tuscaroras joined in the early eighteenth century, it was known as the Six Nations). The exact date of the founding of the league is unknown. The purposes of the league were to bring peace, to build strength, and to create goodwill among the five nations in order for them to become invulnerable to attack from external enemies and to division from within. The code of the league summarized the intent of Deganawida and the confederate chiefs to establish "The Great Peace." Out of this code was created the Pine Tree Chiefs. Deganawida served as one of those chiefs, who were chosen by merit rather than by heredity.

A grand council of all the chiefs of the five tribes gathered at Onondaga, the most centrally located of the five tribes, to establish the laws and customs of the league. Each tribe had an equal voice in the council despite the fact that the number of chiefs representing each tribe varied. As the council developed over the years, it became immersed in matters of diplomacy, including war and peace, associations with other tribes, and treaties with the European settlers on their borders. Deganawida is credited with the development of the advanced political system of the league, which was primarily democratic and also allowed women a major role. Many of the principles, laws, and regulations of the league are attributed to Deganawida.

By 1677, the league had developed into the most powerful of all the North American Indian confederations and consisted of approximately 16,000 people. The successful union begun by Deganawida flourished into the nineteenth century. After its peak of influence, the league began its collapse as a result of many contributing factors, including the influence of outsiders, the supply of trade goods, the control of military posts, the old covenants with the whites, the rivalry between warriors and chiefs, and structural weaknesses. However, the league owed the several centuries of influence it enjoyed to the prominent leadership of Deganawida, as evidenced by his astuteness in negotiations and by his wisdom in framing the laws and principles that served as the basis for the entire structure of the league.

Further Reading

Dockstader, Frederick J., *Great North American Indians,* New York, Van Nostrand Reinhold, 1977; 71-72.

Graymont, Barbara, *The Iroquois in the American Revolution,* New York, Syracuse University Press, 1972; 14, 47, 128, 296.

Handbook of American Indians, edited by Frederick Webb Hodge, New York, Rowman and Littlefield, 1971; 383-384.

Leitch, Barbara A., *Chronology of the American Indian,* St. Clair Shores, Michigan, Scholarly Press, Inc., 1975; 82.

Tooker, Elisabeth, ''The League of the Iroquois: Its History, Politics, and Rituals,'' in *Handbook of North American Indians,* edited by William C. Sturtevant, Smithsonian Institution, 1978; 422-424.

Waldman, Carl, *Who Was Who in Native American History,* New York, Facts on File, 1990; 96-97.

Wallace, Anthony F. C., *The Death and Rebirth of the Seneca,* New York, Knopf, 1969; 42, 44, 97-98. □

Martin Robinson Delany

African American intellectual Martin Robinson Delany (1812-1885), a journalist, physician, army officer, politician, and judge, is best known for his promotion before the Civil War of a national home in Africa for African Americans.

Martin Delany was born free in Charlestown, Virginia, on May 6, 1812. His parents traced their ancestry to West African royalty. In 1822 the family moved to Chambersburg, Pennsylvania, to find a better racial climate, and at the age of 19 Martin attended an African American school in Pittsburgh. He married Kate Richards there in 1843; they had 11 children.

In 1843 Delany founded one of the earliest African American newspapers, the *Mystery,* devoted particularly to the abolition of slavery. Proud of his African ancestry, Delany advocated unrestricted equality for African Americans, and he participated in conventions to protest slavery. Frederick Douglass, the leading African American abolitionist, made him coeditor of his newspaper, the *North Star,* in 1847. But Delany left in 1849 to study medicine at Harvard.

At the age of 40 Delany began the practice of medicine, which he would continue on and off for the rest of his life. But with the publication of his book *The Condition, Elevation, Emigration, and Destiny of the Colored People of the United States, Politically Considered* (1852; reprinted, 1968), he began to agitate for a separate nation, trying to get African Americans to settle outside the United States, possibly in Africa, but more probably in Canada or Latin America. In 1854 he led a National Emigration Convention. For a time he lived in Ontario. Despite his bitter opposition to the American Colonization Society and its colony, Liberia, Delany kept open the possibility of settling elsewhere in Africa. His 1859-1860 visit to the country of the Yorubas (now part of Nigeria) to negotiate with local kings for settling African Americans there is summarized in *The Official Report of the Niger Valley Exploring Party* (1861; reprinted, 1969).

When Delany returned to the United States, however, the Civil War was in progress and prospects of freedom for African Americans were brighter. He got President Abraham Lincoln to appoint him as a major in the infantry in charge of recruiting all-African American Union units.

After the war Delany went to South Carolina to participate in the Reconstruction. In the Freedmen's Bureau and as a Republican politican, he was influential among the state's population, regardless of race. In 1874 he narrowly missed election as lieutenant governor. In 1876, as the Republicans began losing control of the state, Delany switched to the conservative Democrats. Newly elected governor Wade Hampton rewarded him with an important judgeship in Charleston. As a judge, Delany won the respect of people of all races. In 1878 he helped sponsor the Liberian Exodus Joint Stock Steamship Company, which sent one ill-fated emigration ship to Africa. The next year his *The Principia of Ethnology* argued for pride and purity of the races and for Africa's self-regeneration.

When his political base collapsed in 1879, Delany returned to practicing medicine and later became a businessman in Boston. He died on January 24, 1885.

Further Reading

A recent biography of Delany is Victor Ullman, *Martin R. Delany: The Beginnings of Black Nationalism* (1971). A contemporary account is Frank A. Rollin, *Life and Public Services of Martin R. Delany* (1868; repr. 1969). William J. Simmons, *Men of Mark* (1968), includes a biographical sketch. For the significance of Delany's black nationalist thought before the Civil War see Howard H. Bell, *A Survey of the Negro Convention Movement 1830-1861* (1970). □

Max Delbrück

Max Delbrück (1906-1981) has often been called the founder of molecular biology. In 1969 he shared the Nobel Prize for physiology or medicine for work in the area of molecular genetics.

Max Delbrück has often been called the founder of molecular biology. Although educated as a physicist, Delbrück quickly became interested in bacteriophages, a type of virus that infects bacterial cells. He perfected a method of culturing bacteriophages and found that they could infect a bacterial cell and, within twenty minutes, erupt out of the cell in a hundredfold their original number. Each of these offspring bacteriophages was then ready to infect another bacterial cell. Among his many contributions to the field, Delbrück and another researcher together discovered that bacterial cells could spontaneously mutate to become immune to the bacteriophages. He also found that two different types of bacteriophages could combine to create a new type of bacteriophage. Perhaps as much or more than his discoveries, he forged the field of molecular biology through his involvement in the work of so many other scientists. While he was highly critical and not easily convinced of a new discovery, Delbrück also inspired many scientists to new heights. His work paved the way for an explosion of new findings in the field of molecular biology, including the discoveries that viruses contain the genetic material deoxyribonucleic acid (DNA), along with the eventual unveiling of the structure of DNA itself. In 1969, Delbrück won the Nobel Prize for physiology or medicine, which he shared with Alfred Day Hershey and Salvador Edward Luria, for their work in molecular genetics.

Delbrück was born on September 4, 1906, in Berlin as the youngest of seven children to Hans and Lina Thiersch Delbrück. Many of his relatives were prominent academicians, including his father, who was a professor of history at the University of Berlin and editor of the journal *Prussian Yearbook;* his maternal great-grandfather, Justus von Liebig, is considered the originator of organic chemistry. Throughout his youth in the middle-class suburb of Grünewald, Delbrück developed his interests in mathematics and astronomy, and carried those interests into college.

In 1924 he enrolled in the University of Tübingen, but switched colleges several times before enrolling at the University of Göttingen, where he obtained his Ph.D. in physics

in 1930. Delbrück began writing a dissertation about the origin of a type of star, but abandoned it because of his lack of understanding of both the necessary math and English, the language in which most of the pertinent literature was written. He took up a new topic, and completed his dissertation by explaining the chemical bonding of two lithium atoms, and why this bonding is much weaker than the bond between two hydrogen atoms.

Switches from Quantum Mechanics to Biology

For the next year and a half, through a research grant, he did postgraduate studies in quantum mechanics at the University of Bristol in England. There, he became friends with other researchers, several of whom went on to make major contributions in the fields of physics and chemistry. In the early 1930s, he continued his research as a Rockefeller Foundation postdoctoral fellow under Neils Bohr at the University of Copenhagen, one of the major intellectual centers in the world. Bohr's beliefs had a strong impact on Delbrück. Bohr had developed a theory of complementarity, stating that electromagnetic radiation could be described by either waves or particles, but not both at the same time. He followed that by a now-famous lecture in 1932 called "Light and Life." In it, Bohr suggested that a similar paradox existed in living things: they could be either described as whole organisms or as groups of molecules. Delbrück was hooked. He began to study biology. In 1932, Delbrück returned to Berlin and the Kaiser Wilhelm Institute. He remained at the institute for five years, and continued his shift from physics to biology. From 1932 to 1937, while an assistant to Professor Lise Meitner in Berlin,

Delbrück was part of a small group of theoretical physicists which held informal private meetings; he was devoted at first to theoretical physics, but soon turned to biology. In his acceptance speech for the Nobel Prize, Delbrück recalled that "Discussions of (new findings) within our little group strengthened the notion that genes had a kind of stability similar to that of the molecules of chemistry. From the hindsight of our present knowledge," he said, "one might consider this a trivial statement: what else could genes be but molecules? However, in the mid-'30s, this was not a trivial statement."

In 1937, by virtue of his second Rockefeller Foundation fellowship, Delbrück immigrated to the United States, where he began to study biology and genetics and the reproduction of bacteriophages, in particular, at the California Institute of Technology in Pasadena. A year later, he met Emory Ellis, a biologist also working on these viruses, and together they designed experiments to study bacteriophages and the mathematical system to analyze the results.

Publishes Milestone Paper on Bacterial Mutation

By 1940, Delbrück had joined the faculty of Vanderbilt University in Tennessee and during the following summers continued his phage research intensively at the Cold Spring Harbor Laboratory on Long Island in New York. Also in 1940 he met Italian physician Salvador Luria, with whom he would eventually share the Nobel Prize. Luria was conducting bacteriophage research at the College of Physicians and Surgeons of Columbia University in New York City. Their collaborative work began, and in 1943 Delbrück and Luria became famous in the scientific community with the publication of their landmark paper, "Mutations of Bacteria from Virus Sensitivity to Virus Resistance." The paper confirmed that phage-resistant bacterial strains developed through natural selection: once infected with a bacteriophage, the bacterium spontaneously changes so that it becomes immune to the invading virus. Their work also outlined the experimental technique, which became a standard analytical tool for measuring mutation rates. The publication of this paper is now regarded as the beginning of bacterial genetics.

Also in 1943, the so-called Phage Group held its first informal meeting, with Delbrück, Luria and microbiologist Alfred Hershey in attendance. At group meetings, members discussed research and ideas involving bacteriophages. The number of members grew along with the excitement over the possibilities presented by this area of research. The meetings were much like those Delbrück had so enjoyed while he was working in Meitner's lab in Berlin. In the following year, the Phage Group drafted guidelines—called the Phage Treaty of 1944—to ensure that results gained from different laboratories could be compared easily and accurately. The treaty urged all bacteriophage investigators to conduct their studies on a specific set of seven bacteriophages that infect *Escherichia coli* strain B and its mutants. It also spelled out the standard experimental conditions to be used.

While on the faculty at Vanderbilt University, Delbrück organized the first of his summer phage courses at Cold Spring Harbor in 1945, the year he also became a U.S. citizen. The course became an annual event and drew biologists, geneticists and physicists who traveled from laboratories all over the world to learn not only about the experimental and analytical methods of phage research but also about its potential.

In 1946, Delbrück's and Hershey's labs separately discovered that different bacteriophage strains that both invade the same bacterial cell could randomly exchange genetic material to form new and unique viral strains. They called the phenomenon genetic recombination. According to *Biographical Memoirs of Fellows of the Royal Society*, this finding "led, about 10 years later, to the ultimate genetic analysis of gene structure by Seymour Benzer."

Describes Cell as "Magic Puzzle Box"

The following year, Delbrück returned to the California Institute of Technology as a professor in the biology department. In 1949, he delivered an address, "A Physicist Looks at Biology," that recalled his scientific journey. "A mature physicist, acquainting himself for the first time with the problems of biology, is puzzled by the circumstance that there are no 'absolute phenomena' in biology. Everything is time bound and space bound. The animal or plant or microorganism he is working with is but a link in an evolutionary chain of changing forms, none of which has any permanent validity. . . . If it be true that the essence of life is the accumulation of experience through the generations, then one may perhaps suspect that the key problem of biology, from the physicist's point of view, is how living matter manages to record and perpetuate its experiences." He described the cell as a "magic puzzle box full of elaborate and changing molecules (that) carries with it the experiences of a billion years of experimentation by its ancestors."

In the late 1940s and early 1950s, Delbrück expanded his interests to include sensory perception, eventually studying how the fungus *Phycomyces* uses light and how light affects its growth. As he did with the phage research, Delbrück formed a *Phycomyces* Group to gather and discuss ideas. Despite his shift, he and his work continued to have an influence in bacteriophage research. In 1952 Hershey, one of the original three members of the Phage Group, and Martha Chase confirmed that genes consist of DNA and demonstrated how phages infect bacteria. The following year molecular biologist Francis Crick and physicist James Watson, once a graduate student of Luria's, determined the three-dimensional, double-helix structure of DNA. While their work was in progress, Watson would frequently write Delbrück to discuss ideas and to tell him about their results, including the first details of the double-helix structure.

Delbrück remained busy throughout the 1950s and 1960s as investigators and students sought his knowledge and advice, despite his reputation for being a tough critic with a brusque manner. Following an investigator's explanation of his research and results, Delbrück would often respond, "I don't believe a word of it," or if it was a more formal presentation, "That was the worst seminar I have ever heard." Once, according to Seymour Benzer in *Phage and the Origins of Molecular Biology*, Delbrück wrote to

Benzer's wife, "Dear Dotty, please tell Seymour to stop writing so many papers. If I gave them the attention his papers *used* to deserve, they would take all my time. If he *must* continue, tell him to do what Ernst Mayr asked his mother to do in her long daily letters, namely, *underline what is important.*" Yet, many scientists persisted in bringing their research to Delbrück. In his essay in *Phage and the Origins of Molecular Biology,* molecular biologist Thomas Anderson recalled Delbrück: "At each phase in our groping toward discovery, Max Delbrück seemed to be present not so much as a guide, perhaps, but as a critic. To the lecturer he was an enquiring, and sometimes merciless, logician. If one persevered, he would be fortunate to have Max as conscience, goad and sage."

Delbrück also had a lighter side. As reported in *Thinking About Science,* Delbrück remembered pitting his wits against those of his college professors. He would not take notes during the lectures, but would try to follow and understand the professor's mathematical argument. "When the professor made a little mistake, with a plus or minus sign or a factor of 2, I did not point that out directly but waited 10 minutes until he got entangled and then pointed out, to his great relief, how he could disentangle himself—a great game." When Delbrück joined the faculty ranks, he developed a rather unusual tradition with his students and peers. He often invited them along on camping trips with his family, including his wife and eventually their four children. Delbrück married Mary Adeline Bruce in 1941. They had two sons, Jonathan and Tobias, and two daughters, Nicola and Ludina.

Wins Nobel Prize and Peers' Accolades

In 1961, while still a professor at the California Institute of Technology, Delbrück took a two-year leave of absence to help the University of Cologne in Germany establish its Institute of Genetics. In 1966 back in California, the former Phage Group members celebrated Delbrück's sixtieth birthday with a book in his honor, *Phage and the Origins of Molecular Biology.* The book is a collection of essays by the group members, many of whom had gone on to make important discoveries in bacterial genetics. The larger scientific community also recognized Delbrück's contributions with a variety of awards. In December of 1969, Delbrück, Luria and Hershey accepted the Nobel Prize in physiology or medicine for their work in molecular biology, particularly the mechanism of replication in viruses and their genetic structure.

Delbrück continued his sensory perception research into the next decade. He retired from the California Institute of Technology in 1977, and died of cancer four years later in Pasadena on March 10, 1981. In *Phage and the Origin of Molecular Biology,* phage course alumnus N. Visconti recalled a conversation he had with Delbrück. "I remember he once said to me, 'You don't have the inspiration or the talent to be an artist; then what else do you want to do in life besides be a scientist?' For Max Delbrück it was as simple as that."

Further Reading

Biographical Memoirs of Fellows of the Royal Society, Volume 28, Royal Society (London), 1982.

Fischer, Ernst P., and Carol Lipson, editors, *Thinking about Science: Max Delbrück and the Origins of Molecular Biology,* W. W. Norton, 1988.

Hayes, William, "Max Delbrück and the Birth of Molecular Biology," in *Social Research,* autumn, 1984, pp. 641–673.

Kay, Lily, "Conceptual Models and Analytical Tools: The Biology of Physicist Max Delbrück," in *Journal of the History of Biology,* summer, 1985, pp. 207–246.

Physics Today, June, 1981, pp. 71–74. □

Vine Deloria, Jr.

Vine Deloria, Jr. (born 1933) is known as a revolutionary thinker who speaks out against the decadence of U.S. culture and insists that young Native Americans receive traditional teachings before exposing themselves to the philosophies of the dominant Euro-American culture. Through his widely published books, he has brought greater understanding of Native American history and philosophy to a vast global audience.

Vine Deloria, Jr., of the Hunkpapa Lakota, became well-known as a political activist whose publications explained to the American people what the Native American rights movement was seeking. His family heritage combined with academic training gave him credibility in his writings. Deloria was born on March 26, 1933, in Martin, South Dakota, the son of Vine and Barbara (Eastburn) Deloria. He joined a distinguished family: his great-grandfather Francois Des Laurias ("Saswe") was a medicine man and leader of the White Swan Band of the Yankton Sioux tribe; his grandfather Philip Deloria was a missionary priest of the Episcopal Church; his aunt Ella C. Deloria was a noted anthropologist who published works on Indian ethnology and linguistics; and his father, Vine Deloria, Sr., was the first American Indian to be named to a national executive post in the Episcopal Church. Deloria's own comment about his family gave context to his first major book. In its afterword he wrote: "As long as any member of my family can remember, we have been involved in the affairs of the Sioux tribe. My great grandfather was a medicine man named Saswe, of the Yankton tribe of the Sioux Nation. My grandfather was a Yankton chief who was converted to Christianity in the 1860's. He spent the rest of his life as an Episcopal missionary on the Standing Rock Sioux reservation in South Dakota." From 1923 to 1982 the Indian Council Fire, an organization in Chicago, presented fifty-four achievement awards to recognize quality of Indian initiative and leadership. Of these awards, three were to members of the Deloria family: Vine, Sr., Ella, and Vine, Jr.

After attending grade school in Martin, South Dakota, the younger Deloria graduated from high school at St. James Academy in Faribault, Minnesota. He served in the Marine Corps from 1954 to 1956, then attended Iowa State University where he received his B.A. degree in 1958. In his youth,

he had considered following his father in the ministry, but exposure to his father's frustrations convinced him that church life did not have the bearing on Indian life that he wanted his career to have. Before he gave up the idea entirely, however, he earned a B.D. in theology at Augustana Lutheran Seminary, Rock Island, Illinois, in 1963. The following year he was hired by the United Scholarship Service in Denver to develop a program to get scholarships for American Indian students in eastern preparatory schools. He successfully placed a number of Indian students in eastern schools through the program.

He served as the executive director of the National Congress of American Indians (NCAI) in Washington, D.C., from 1964 to 1967, an experience he claimed was more educational than anything he had experienced in his previous thirty years. He was expected to solve problems presented by Indian tribes from all over the country, but found that unscrupulous individuals made the task impossible. He was frustrated by the feeling that the interests of tribes were often played against one other. In addition the NCAI had financial difficulties, and was often close to bankruptcy, so that a majority of time had to be spent resolving funding issues. Increased memberships and a research grant gave the organization enough strength to successfully win a few policy changes in the Department of Interior. Although Deloria felt the organization had been successful, especially because of the support and hard work of organization members, he realized that other tactics would have to be used to further the cause for Indian rights.

Earns Law Degree

Two circumstances influenced his decision to return to college and earn a law degree from the University of Colorado in 1970. One was learning of the success of the National Association for the Advancement of Color People's Legal Defense Fund which had been established to help the black community. The second was the realization that local Indian tribes were without legal counsel and had no idea what their rights were. His goal when receiving his law degree was to start a program which would assist smaller tribes and Indian communities to outline their basic rights. Throughout his career his goal in life has been twofold: to support tribes through affiliation with various advocacy organizations and to educate Native Americans on aspects of the law through teachings and writings which stress the historical and political aspects of the relationships of Indians to other people. His role as an activist in the efforts of Native Americans to achieve self-government has focused on change through education rather than through violence.

From 1970 to 1972 Deloria was a lecturer at Western Washington State College in the division of ethnic studies. While there, he worked with Northwest Coast tribes in their effort to gain improved fishing rights. From 1972 to 1974 he taught at the University of California at Los Angeles. During the same period, from 1970 to 1978, he was the chairperson of the Institute for the Development of Indian Law, headquartered in Golden, Colorado. From 1978 to 1991 he was a professor of American Indian studies, political science, and history of law at the University of Arizona. In 1991 he moved to the University of Colorado in Boulder to join the faculty of the Center for Studies of Ethnicity and Race in America. In addition to his teaching positions, Deloria served in leadership positions in several organizations including the Citizens Crusade against Poverty, the Council on Indian Affairs, the National Office for the Rights of the Indigent, the Institute for the Development of Indian Law, and the Indian Rights Association.

Publishes Indian Activist Views

Deloria has been an activist writer, dramatically presenting his case for Indian self-determination. *Custer Died for Your Sins: An Indian Manifesto,* written while he was attending law school, captured the attention of reviewers and critics and bolstered Native American efforts for recognition. Written at the time the American Indian Movement (AIM) was drawing public attention to Native American rights, Deloria's book was an articulation of the activist goal: to become self-ruled, culturally separate from white society and politically separate from the U.S. government. While blasting America's treatment of Indian people, Deloria explained the concepts of termination and tribalism. Although contemporaneous with the civil rights movement of other American groups, he distinguished between black nationalism and Indian nationalism, explaining that because Indian civil rights issues were based upon treaties they needed to be addressed in a different way. Deloria explained his reasons for writing the book in its afterword: "One reason I wanted to write it was to raise some issues for younger Indians which they have not been raising for themselves. Another reason was to give some idea to white people of the unspoken but often felt antagonisms I have detected in Indian people toward them, and the reasons for such antagonism."

Deloria's second book, *We Talk, You Listen: New Tribes, New Turf,* also addressed the issue of tribalism and advocated a return to tribal social organization in order to save society. His third book, *God Is Red: A Native View of Religion,* again captured a national audience. In this book Deloria offered an alternative to Christianity which he explained had failed both in its theology and its application to social issues. He proposed that religion in North America should follow along the lines of traditional Native American values and seek spiritual values in terms of "space" by feeling the richness of the land. Most critics applauded his presentation of Indian religious practice, but were offended by his attack on the Judeo-Christian tradition. His later book *The Metaphysics of Modern Existence* followed up on this theme by questioning non-Indian world views of modern life and recommending a reassessment of reality about moral and religious property.

In all of Deloria's writings, he has emphasized the failure of U.S. treaties to adequately provide for the needs of Indian people. Using his legal training, he has analyzed past relationships between the U.S. government and Native American groups and has continually pressed for renewed treaty negotiation in order to allow more Indian self-control over their culture and government. His book *Behind the Trail of Broken Treaties* provided an account of events which led to the occupation of Wounded Knee, South Dakota, by supporters of the American Indian Movement. In this work he argued for reopening the treaty-making procedure between Indian tribes and the U.S. government. As an expert in U.S. Indian treaties, Deloria was called as first witness for the defense in the trial of Wounded Knee participants Russell Means and Dennis Banks in 1974. Later, in his writing about Indian activism of the early 1970s, Deloria blamed the failure of the Indian civil rights movement on the unwillingness of the American public to forget their perception of what an Indian should be. In the second edition of *God Is Red* he stated: "When a comparison is made between events of the Civil Rights movement and the activities of the Indian movement one thing stands out in clear relief: Americans simply refuse to give up their longstanding conceptions of what an Indian is. It was this fact more than any other that inhibited any solution of the Indian problems and projected the impossibility of their solution anytime in the future. People simply could not connect what they believed Indians to be with what they were seeing on their television sets." He castigated the American public for its avoidance of the real Indian world in a series of ironic contrasts between current events of the Indian movement of the 1970s and what the American public was reading. "While Dee Brown's *Bury My Heart at Wounded Knee* was selling nearly twenty thousand copies a week, the three hundred state game wardens and Tacoma city police were vandalizing the Indian fishing camp and threatening the lives of Indian women and children at Frank's Landing on the Nisqually River. . . . As Raymond Yellow Thunder was being beaten to death, Americans were busy ordering *Touch the Earth* from their book clubs as an indication of their sympathy for American Indians. As the grave robbers were breaking into Chief Joseph's grave, the literary public was reading his famous surrender speech in a dozen or more anthologies of Indian speeches and bemoaning the fact that oratory such as Joseph's is not used any more."

Deloria's writing style has been consistent. In his books he often attempts to peel away platitudes that his white readers have developed so that they begin to comprehend the issues and the Indian viewpoint. Not without humor, he cynically derides white culture, and then offers his replacement. He commented in an interview that Americans can be told the obvious fifty times a day and revel in hearing it, but not learn anything from it. Some critics have been disappointed that Deloria's books do not describe Indian culture. As Deloria stated in an interview in *The Progressive,* "I particularly disappoint Europeans. They come over and want me to share all the tribal secrets. Then I lecture and harangue about the white man." In the same interview he derided his own success as an Indian writer in the early 1970s. "I happened to come along when they [the media] needed an Indian. The writing is not very good at all. But Indians were new, so everybody gave *Custer* great reviews. I never fooled myself that it was a great book."

His second edition of *God Is Red,* published in 1992, built upon the arguments against Christianity he wrote in the first edition. Encouraged by trends in American society to be more concerned about religion and ecology, he raised additional issues in the revised edition. "I suggest in this revised edition that we have on this planet two kinds of people—natural peoples and the hybrid peoples. The natural peoples represent an ancient tradition that has always sought harmony with the environment." Hybrid peoples referred to the inheritors of Hebrew, Islamic, and Christian traditions who adopted a course of civilization which exploits the environment. When *The Progressive*'s interviewer asked Deloria his views on renewed interest in Native American spirituality, Deloria commented: "I think New Age shamanism is very interesting. Whites want to take our images, they want to have their Indian jewelry; at the same time, they need our valley to flood for a dam. People are desperately trying to get some relationship to Earth, but it's all in their heads. . . . New Age shamanism may be one of the few solutions." At the same time, he admitted his own dependence upon technology. "I wouldn't delude myself for a minute that I could go back to the reservation and live any kind of traditional life. I've been in the cities too long. . . . I would love to go back to the old shamanism. My great-grandfather was a very powerful man. But here I am in Tucson, Arizona, dependent upon Tucson Electric Power to stay comfortable."

Another of his major themes has been concern for the natural environment. He blames contemporary technological society for destroying the earth, and presents an apocalyptic view. He envisions the end of the earth if changes are not made soon to allow the natural environment to recover. He predicts in *The Progressive* interview that in 500 years "there will be fewer than 100,000 people on whatever this continent comes up as, there will probably be some Indians and all kinds of new strange animals—the Earth a completely different place, people talking about legends of the old times when iron birds flew in the air."

Other works by Vine Deloria include *Indians of the Pacific Northwest* (1977), *Of Utmost Good Faith* (1971), *A Better Day for Indians* (1976), *The nations within: the past and future of American Indian sovereignty* (1984), and *Behind the trail of broken treaties: an Indian declaration of independence* (1985).

Further Reading

Bruguier, Leonard Rufus, "A Legacy in Sioux Leadership: The Deloria Family," in *South Dakota Leaders,* edited by Herbert T. Hoover and Larry J. Zimmerman, Vermillion, University of South Dakota Press, 1989; 367-378, 471.

Contemporary Authors, edited by Linda Metzger and Deborah A. Straub, Detroit, Gale, 20NR, 1987; 130-132.

Contemporary Literary Criticism, edited by Sharon R. Gunton, Gale, 21, 1982; 108-114.

Deloria, Vine, Jr., "An Afterword," in *Custer Died for Your Sins: An Indian Manifesto,* New York, Avon Books, 1970; 262-272.

Deloria, Vine, Jr., "Introduction" and "The Indians of the American Imagination," in *God Is Red: A Native View of Religion,* 2nd Edition, Golden, CO, North American Press, 1992; 1-3, 25-45.

Gridley, Marion E., *Indians of Today,* Chicago, I.C.F.P., 1971; 347.

Native North American Almanac, edited by Duane Champagne, Detroit, Gale, 1994; 1043-1044.

Paulson, T. Emogene, and Lloyd R. Moses, *Who's Who among the Sioux,* Institute of Indian Studies, University of South Dakota, 1988; 58-59.

Reader's Encyclopedia of the American West, edited by Howard R. Lamar, New York, Thomas Y. Crowell, 1977; 295.

Something about the Author, edited by Anne Commire, Gale Research, 21, 1980; 27.

Warrior, Robert Allen, "Vine Deloria Jr.: 'It's About Time to be Interested in Indians Again,'" *The Progressive,* 54:4, April 1990; 24-27. □

Cecil Blount DeMille

Considered one of the founders of Hollywood, film producer and director Cecil B. DeMille (1881-1959) earned a place in moviemaking history with such religious epic films as *The Ten Commandments* and *King of Kings.*

Although he is one of the most commercially successful film directors of all time, Cecil B. DeMille has for a long time been considered at best a director of mediocre quality. Still his place in the history of Hollywood movie making is central; in fact, more than anyone else, he deserves to be called the man who founded Hollywood. As Lewis Jacobs has said—as quoted in *World Film Directors:* "If in the artistic perspective of American Film History, Cecil B. DeMille is valueless; in the social history of films, it is impossible to ignore him."

Religious and Theatrical Background

DeMille's father was split between wanting to be an actor and wanting to be an Episcopalian priest. It was an internal conflict strangely appropriate for the father of a man who would become identified with making sexually lurid motion pictures from Bible stories. The elder DeMille ended up teaching school until his friendship with David Belasco, the most successful American playwright of the late 19th century, led him to satisfy his theatrical urge by writing plays instead of acting in them. Both his sons followed him into the theater. Cecil's older brother broke in as a playwright, and Cecil tried to make it as an actor; but after ten years on the boards, he was still struggling to feed his family.

As he neared 30, DeMille gave up acting to join his mother in launching a theatrical agency. Working as the general manager, he met Jesse L. Lasky who along with a Samuel Goldfish—later to change his name to Goldwyn—was trying to break into motion picture production. At this time, feeling frustrated, DeMille was thinking of leaving show business altogether; but Lasky, after working on several musical plays with the younger man, convinced him to try his hand at directing a motion picture. After spending a day at Thomas Edison's studios in New York, DeMille took off for Arizona to shoot *The Squaw Man,* a melodrama based on a Broadway play and set in Wyoming. When the Arizona locations did not work out, DeMille got back on the train and headed off to the end of the line, Los Angeles.

The Man Who Founded Hollywood

DeMille was not the first person to ever shoot a film in Hollywood, but when he arrived in late 1913, he decided to stay. The southern California climate was perfect for motion picture making, because even the indoor scenes could be shot outside on sets with three walls and no ceilings, since plenty of sun and not much rain let the crews shoot without having to set up lights, a huge savings in time and money. The barn on the corner of Vine Street in which DeMille set up shop would soon be the world headquarters for Paramount Studios; but at the moment they were sharing facilities with a stable of horses, and things did not always smell nice around the studio. DeMille was the consummate showman from the start and not only in the movies. Writing in *World Film Directors,* Philip Kemp speaks about DeMille's making of the image of the Hollywood Filmmaker: "To direct his first movie, DeMille adopted a distinctive costume which he retained largely unaltered throughout his working career and which came to represent the publicly accepted image of an old-style movie director: open-necked shirt, riding breeches, boots and puttees along with a riding-crop, a large megaphone, and a whistle on a neck-chord. Charges of theatricality were met with pained denial from DeMille who always insisted that his garb was strictly functional . . . but his costume also undoubtedly reflected his favorite self-image—the movie director as bold and masterful adventurer, intrepid pioneer and empire-builder."

With the commercial success of *The Squaw Man,* DeMille's founding of Hollywood was complete. He had found the perfect location to make movies, he had developed the fashion style that would come to be associated with moviemaking, and, now with the money he was making for Paramount, he proved the viability of his creation. The reviews of DeMille's early directorial efforts were very favorable. He worked with Alvin Wyckoff, one of the most important of the first generation of cameramen in Hollywood. Besides shooting motion pictures, Wyckoff invented new camera lenses that had the ability to work under difficult conditions. By the end of 1914, after only three DeMille films, Lasky moved his whole enterprise to California. He bought the barn next door and established a vast studio in the desert.

In 1915, DeMille made what many still consider his most impressive film. Writing in the *International Dictionary of Films and Filmmakers,* Eric Smoodin writes, "Although he made films until 1956, DeMille's masterpiece may well have come in 1915 with *The Cheat.* . . . For the cinema's first 20 years, editing was based primarily on following action . . . [but] in *The Cheat,* through his editing, DeMille created a sense of psychological space." DeMille was the first to use film editing in such an intrusive way to show off what a character is thinking.

Produced First Epics

In the silent era, DeMille was fast becoming the middle-brow alternative to the high-brow films of D. W. Griffith, still the greatest innovator in film history, and the low-brow silent comedies pouring out of Mack Sennet's and Hal Roach's studios. In 1917, DeMille left his social comedies behind to make his first epic, *Joan the Woman,* the story of Joan of Arc. One of the longest and most extravagant pictures made to that time, it was a box office disaster. DeMille had made the first feature released in this country several years before, but audiences were not ready for the extra time he added to *Joan.*

The next years were difficult ones of DeMille. Two pictures he made with Mary Pickford flopped, and after several more mediocre films, he made *The Whispering Chorus.* The film meant a lot to him. In the film historian Kevin Brownlow's memorable phrase, he sunk not only his money, "but also his heart" into the film. The story of a man who tries to avoid a debt by faking his death, the film featured a chorus of whisperers who followed him through the movie, speaking his thoughts out loud. Whatever its artistic merit, it was a big failure. Some think it was the disappointment attendant on the reception of *The Whispering Chorus* which led DeMille to forsake artistic aspirations and concentrate on giving audiences what they wanted.

Still whatever his artistic disappointments, DeMille was able to regain his golden touch at the box office, primarily by making social comedies filled with both a bit of titillating sex and moralistic messages. Titles such as *We Can't Have Everything* and *Don't Change Your Husband* give a good sense of the message of these movies. By 1921, the critics held DeMille's work pretty much in contempt for the mix of sex and morality which he peddled so easily, satisfying his audience's erotic urges while at the same time satisfying their puritan tendencies. At the same time, DeMille was helping to set up the Hays Office, the self-policing branch of the Hollywood industry, which censored films for sexual or immoral content. DeMille's worry, shared by many in Hollywood at the time, was that if Hollywood did not censor itself, Congress would.

In 1923, he was powerful enough to return to the epic despite the failure of *Joan the Woman* at the box office. Costing $1,475,000, the first version of *The Ten Commandments* was probably the most expensive movie made to that time. Adolph Zukor, the studio head, threatened to pull the plug on the movie several times; but in the end, it was a blockbuster, making its huge budget back several times over. Some of the critics even liked it. He continued making expensive epics, but he did not return to the Bible until 1927 when he filmed a life of Christ entitled *King of Kings.* His first sound movie was *Dynamite,* which fared respectably, but his attempt to take advantage of the new medium to make a musical was another failure, *Madame Satan.*

The Crusades, another one of his epics, lost $700,000, perhaps the largest failure in Hollywood history up to that time. Five years later, after a couple of moderately successful westerns, DeMille made his first color film, *North West Mounted Police,* starring Gary Cooper. His next film, *Reap the Wild Wind,* distinguished itself by being the first motion picture edited by a woman, Anne Bauchens, to win the Oscar for Best Editing. Neither DeMille, nor any of his films had to that time an Oscar.

End of His Career

After World War II, DeMille set a new tone for himself when he made *Samson and Delilah* with Victor Mature and Hedy Lamarr. It was widely viewed as one of the most tasteless American films ever made with its tacky special effects and heavy-breathing sexuality. In 1950, he returned to acting, playing himself in Billy Wilder's acid portrait of Hollywood, *Sunset Boulevard.* In 1952 he made *The Greatest Show on Earth,* a film often considered to be the closest movie to a self-portrait that DeMille ever made. It was the first film he made to win an Oscar. The best directing Oscar that year went to John Ford.

Unfortunately for DeMille, he was involved in another dispute with John Ford, one which would forever damage DeMille's reputation. DeMille, a politically conservative man, got wrapped up in the McCarthy anti-communist campaign in Hollywood and decided that he wanted to oust Joseph Mankiewicz as president of the Director's Guild. Mankiewicz was a successful director himself and politically liberal. DeMille thought he was soft on communism. A special meeting of the Director's Guild was called to air DeMille's charges. It was a very rancorous meeting attended by nearly every director in the guild. After four hours of debate, John Ford, who had not said a word as of yet, rose to speak. In an *Esquire* Magazine article, Peter Bogdanovich recounts the scene with Ford rising and introducing himself, "My name is Jack Ford—I make westerns." He then went on to praise DeMille's ability to produce pictures that appealed to the public—more so, Ford said, than anyone else in the room; he turned to look across the hall now directly at DeMille: "But I don't like you, C. B.," he said, "and I don't like what you've been saying here tonight. I move that we give Joe a vote of confidence—and let's all go home and get some sleep."

It is worth noting that DeMille did not mention the episode in his memoirs. He also made his final film with one of the most conservative actors in Hollywood, Charlton Heston. Although the second version of *The Ten Commandments* is his most widely seen film, thanks to Easter-time television programming, it is not one of his most respected. Still it was a colossal success at the box office, capping a directing-producing career that was by far the most commercially successful of all time, at least until that of the much later director, Steven Spielberg. DeMille suffered a heart attack while shooting *The Ten Commandments,* but he refused to slow down; and soon after, in 1959, on a publicity tour for another picture, one which he produced but did not direct, he had another heart attack which led to his death.

Further Reading

Eric Smoodin, *International Dictionary of Films and Filmmakers,* Nicholas Thomas, ed., St. James Press, 1991, pp. 204-207.

Bogdanovich, Peter, "The Cowboy Hero and The American West . . . as Directed by John Ford," in *Fifty Who Made a Difference,* ed. Lee Eisenberg, Esquire Press Book, 1984, pp. 347-348. ☐

Jack Dempsey

One of the world's greatest heavyweight boxers, William Harrison "Jack" Dempsey (1895-1983) was so popular that he drew more million-dollar gates than any prizefighter in history.

William Harrison Dempsey, more commonly known as "Jack" after age 20, was born in Manassa, Colorado, on June 24, 1895, the ninth child of Hyrum and Cecilia Dempsey, both sharecroppers. The family was so poor that Jack began farming at the age of 8. From age 16 to 19 he lived in hobo jungles.

Dempsey's early boxing often took place in back rooms of frontier saloons under the name "Kid Blackie." His first fight of record was in 1915 against "One-Punch" Hancock. Dempsey's one-punch win earned him $2.50; his highest purse. Eleven years later his purse was $711,000 for his first match with Gene Tunney. Eventually called the "Manassa Mauler," Dempsey earned more than $3,500,000 in all in the ring.

Dempsey's appeal lay in his punching ability: he was a ruthless tiger stalking his prey, fast as any big cat and deadly with either paw. He won the world's heavyweight title on July 4, 1919, against Jess Willard in Toledo, Ohio. With his first real punch Dempsey shattered Willard's cheekbone and knocked him down seven times in the first round. Willard was unable to answer the bell for the start of the fourth.

Two years later Dempsey drew the world's first million-dollar gate against Georges Carpentier of France, in Jersey City, New Jersey, scoring a fourth-round knockout. Another million-dollar bout was in 1923 against Luis Angel Firpo of Argentina; few bouts have packed such unbridled fury and

spectacular savagery. Dempsey was knocked down twice, once through the ropes and out of the ring; 10 times Firpo went down, the tenth time for keeps—all within the span of 3 minutes 57 seconds. The Mauler was dethroned in Philadelphia in 1926, when Gene Tunney outpointed him before the largest crowd ever, 120,757 spectators, to witness the championship game.

Dempsey knocked out Jack Sharkey before the second Dempsey-Tunney fight a year later in Chicago. This last bout became the focus of an enduring controversy. Dempsey floored Tunney in the seventh round but refused to go to a neutral corner according to the rules. The countdown was delayed, and Tunney, given this extra respite, recovered sufficiently to outbox Dempsey the rest of the way.

For several years after his defeat, Dempsey refereed, announced boxing matches, and mentored young fighters. He attempted a comeback in 1931-32 but failed.

During the years of the Great Depression, Dempsey concentrated on various business interests including retailing, real estate, and two restaurants in New York City. After the outbreak of World War II, Dempsey joined the Coast Guard, serving as director of the physical fitness program. As the war drew to a close in the Pacific, he was sent on a three month's tour of combat areas to assess needs for athletic and physical training.

During his time as a highly respected restaurateur on Broadway, Dempsey enjoyed a fantastic popularity, revered as one of the true titans of American sports. He died on May 31, 1983.

Further Reading

The most authoritative book on Dempsey is his autobiography, *Dempsey,* written with Bob Considine and Bill Slocum (1960). The best statistical background is in *Nat Fleischer's Ring Record Book* (1970). Dempsey's manager, Jack "Doc" Kearns, appraises him in *The Million Dollar Gate,* written with Oscar Fraley (1966). The second Dempsey-Tunney fight is in Mel Heimer, *The Long Count* (1969). ☐

John Dewey

During the first half of the 20th century, John Dewey (1859-1952) was America's most famous exponent of a pragmatic philosophy that celebrated the traditional values of democracy and the efficacy of reason and universal education.

Born on Oct. 20, 1859, in Burlington, Vt., John Dewey came of old New England stock. His father was a local merchant who loved literature. His mother, swayed by revivals to convert to Congregationalism, possessed a stern moral sense. The community, situated at the economic crossroads of the state, was the home of the state university and possessed a cosmopolitan atmosphere unusual for northern New England. Nearby Irish and French-Canadian settlements acquainted John with other cultures. Boyhood jobs delivering newspapers and working at a lum-

beryard further extended his knowledge. In 1864, on a visit to see his father in the Union Army in Virginia, he viewed firsthand the devastating effects of the Civil War.

Educational Career

Dewey's career in Vermont public schools was unremarkable. At the age of 15 he entered the University of Vermont. He found little of interest in academic work; his best grades were in science, and later he would regard science as the highest manifestation of human intellect. Dewey himself attributed his "intellectual awakening" to T. H. Huxley's college textbook on physiology, which shaped his vision of man as entirely the product of natural evolutionary processes.

Dewey later remembered coming in touch with the world of ideas during his senior year. Courses on psychology, religion, ethics, logic, and economics supplanted his earlier training in languages and science. His teacher, H. A. P. Torrey, introduced him to Immanuel Kant, but Dewey found it difficult to accept the Kantian idea that there was a realm of knowledge transcending empirical demonstration. Dewey also absorbed Auguste Comte's emphasis on the disintegrative effects of extreme individualism. The quality of his academic work improved and, at the age of 19, he graduated Phi Beta Kappa and second in his class of 18.

Dewey hoped to teach high school. After a frustrating summer of job hunting, his cousin, principal of a seminary in Pennsylvania, came to his rescue. For 2 years Dewey taught the classics, algebra, and science, meanwhile read-

ing philosophy. When his cousin resigned, however, Dewey's employment ended. He returned to Vermont to become the sole teacher in a private school in Charlotte, near his alma mater. He renewed acquaintance with Torrey, and the two discussed the fruits of Dewey's reading in ancient and modern philosophy.

Intellectual Development

At this time most American teachers of philosophy were ordained clergymen who tended to subordinate philosophical speculation to theological orthodoxy. Philosophy was in the hands of laymen in only a few schools. One such school was in St. Louis, where William T. Harris established the *Journal of Speculative Philosophy*. Here Dewey published his first scholarly effort. Finally, Dewey decided to pursue a career in philosophy and applied for admission to the newly founded Johns Hopkins University, another haven for lay philosophers.

At Johns Hopkins in 1882 Dewey studied with George S. Morris, who was on leave as chairman of the philosophy department at the University of Michigan. Under Morris's direction Dewey studied Hegel, whose all-encompassing philosophical system temporarily satisfied Dewey's longing to escape from the dualisms of traditional philosophy. In 1884 Dewey completed his doctorate and, at Morris's invitation, went to teach at Michigan.

In Ann Arbor, Dewey met and married Alice Chipman. His interests turned toward problems of education as he traveled about the state to evaluate college preparatory courses. His concern for social problems deepened, and he adopted a vague brand of socialism, although he was unacquainted with Marxism. He still taught Sunday school, but he was drifting away from religious orthodoxy. In 1888 he accepted an appointment at the University of Minnesota, only to return to Michigan a year later to the post left vacant by Morris's death.

The next stage in Dewey's intellectual development came with his reading of William James's *Principles of Psychology*. Dewey rapidly shed Hegelianism in favor of "instrumentalism," a position that holds that thinking is an activity which, at its best, is directed toward resolving problems rather than creating abstract metaphysical systems.

In 1894 Dewey moved to the University of Chicago as head of a new department of philosophy, psychology, and pedagogy. Outside the academic world he became friends with the social reformers at Hull House. He also admired Henry George's analysis of the problems of poverty. To test his educational theories, he started an experimental school, with his wife as principal. The "Dewey school," however, caused a struggle between its founder and the university's president, William R. Harper. In 1904, when Harper tried to remove his wife, he resigned in protest. An old friend of Dewey's engineered an offer from Columbia University, where Dewey spent the rest of his teaching years. His colleagues, some of the most fertile minds in modern America, included Charles A. Beard and James Harvey Robinson.

Peak of His Influence

Living in New York City placed the Deweys at the center of America's cultural and political life. Dewey pursued his scholarship, actively supported the Progressive party, and, in 1929, helped organize the League for Independent Political Action to further the cause of a new party. He also served as a contributing editor of the *New Republic* magazine and helped found both the American Civil Liberties Union and the American Association of University Professors. After World War I, reaching the peak of his influence, he became a worldwide traveler, lecturing in Japan at the Imperial Institute and spending 2 years teaching at the Chinese universities of Peking and Nanking. In 1924 he went to study the schools in Turkey and 2 years later visited the University of Mexico. His praise for the Russian educational system he inspected on a 1928 trip to the Soviet Union earned him much criticism.

As a teacher, Dewey exhibited the distracted air of a man who had learned to concentrate in a home inhabited by five young children. Careless about his appearance, shy and quiet in manner, he sometimes put his students to sleep, but those who managed to focus their attention could watch a man fascinated with ideas actually creating a philosophy in his classroom.

In 1930 Dewey retired from teaching. A year earlier, national luminaries had used the occasion of his seventieth birthday to hail his accomplishments; such celebrations would be repeated on his eightieth and ninetieth birthdays. He continued to publish works clarifying his philosophy. In public affairs he was one of the first to warn of the dangers from Hitler's Germany and of the Japanese threat in the Far East. In 1937 he traveled to Mexico as chairman of the commission to determine the validity of Soviet charges against Trotsky. His first wife having died in 1927, Dewey, at the age of 87, married a widow, Roberta Grant. In the early years of the cold war Dewey's support of American intervention in Korea earned him criticism from the U.S.S.R. newspaper *Pravda*. He died on June 1, 1952.

Dewey's Philosophy

In his philosophy Dewey sought to transcend what he considered the misleading distinctions made by other philosophers. By focusing on experience, he bridged the gulf between the organism and its environment to emphasize their interaction. He rejected the dualism of spirit versus matter, insisting that the mind was a product of evolution, not some infusion from a superior being. Yet he avoided the materialist conclusion which made thought seem accidental and irrelevant. While he saw most of man's behavior as shaped by habit, he believed that the unceasing processes of change often produced conditions which customary mental activity could not explain. The resulting tension led to creative thinking in which man tried to reestablish control of the unstable environment. Thought was never, for Dewey, merely introspection; rather, it was part of a process whereby man related to his surroundings. Dewey believed that universal education could train men to break through habit into creative thought.

Dewey was convinced that democracy was the best form of government. He saw contemporary American democracy challenged by the effects of the industrial revolution, which had produced an overconcentration of wealth in the hands of a few men. This threat, he believed, could be met by the right kind of education.

The "progressive education" movement of the 1920s was an effort to implement Dewey's pedagogical ideas. Because his educational theory emphasized the classroom as a place for students to encounter the "present," his interpreters tended to play down traditional curricular concerns with the "irrelevant" past or occupational future. His influence on American schools was so pervasive that many critics (then and later) assailed his ideas as the cause of all that they found wrong with American education.

Philosophical Works

To the year of his death Dewey remained a prolific writer. Couched in a difficult prose style, his published works number over 300. Some of the most important works include *Outlines of a Critical Theory of Ethics* (1891), *The Study of Ethics* (1894), *The School and Society* (1899), *Studies in Logical Theory* (1903), *How We Think* (1910), *The Influence of Darwin on Philosophy and Other Essays in Contemporary Thought* (1910), *German Philosophy and Politics* (1915), *Democracy and Education* (1916), *Reconstruction in Philosophy* (1920), *Human Nature and Conduct* (1922), *Experience and Nature* (1925), *The Public and Its Problems* (1927), *The Quest for Certainty* (1929), *Individualism Old and New* (1930), *Philosophy and Civilization* (1931), *Art as Experience* (1934), *Liberalism and Social Action* (1935), *Logic: The Theory of Inquiry* (1938), *Freedom and Culture* (1939), *Problems of Men* (1946), and *Knowing and the Known* (1949).

Further Reading

For more information see Dewey's autobiographical fragment, "From Absolutism to Experimentalism," in George P. Adams and William Pepperell Montague, eds., *Contemporary American Philosophy: Personal Statements* (1930). His daughters compiled an authoritative sketch of his life in Paul Arthur Schilpp, ed., *The Philosophy of John Dewey* (1939), which also contains valuable summaries of aspects of his philosophy.

Indispensable for any examination of Dewey's thought is Sidney Hook, *John Dewey: An Intellectual Portrait* (1939). John E. Smith presents an excellent chapter on Dewey in *The Spirit of American Philosophy* (1963). Paul K. Conkin in *Puritans and Pragmatists: Eight Eminent American Thinkers* (1968) attempts an evaluation of Dewey's place in the context of American ideas. Morton G. White, *Social Thought in America* (1949), considers assumptions common to Dewey and his colleagues in other disciplines. Longer, more challenging treatments of Dewey's ideas are in George R. Geiger, *John Dewey in Perspective* (1958); Robert J. Roth, *John Dewey and Self Realization* (1962); and Richard J. Bernstein, *John Dewey* (1966). See also Jerome Nathanson, *John Dewey: The Reconstruction of the Democratic Life* (1951).

Additional Sources

Campbell, James, *Understanding John Dewey: nature and cooperative intelligence*, Chicago, Ill.: Open Court, 1995.

Ryan, Alan, *John Dewey and the high tide of American liberalism,* New York: W.W. Norton, 1995. □

Joe DiMaggio

Named the "Greatest Living Player" in a 1969 centennial poll of sportswriters, baseball star Joe DiMaggio (1914–1999) took the great American pastime to new heights during his enormously successful career and epitomizes the sports heroes of the 1940s and 1950s.

One of the most popular and fabled players to compete in Yankee Stadium, Joe DiMaggio was winner of three Most Valuable Player awards. His 1941 hitting streak of 56 games was one of the most closely watched achievements in baseball history, and he was so beloved by his fans that Japanese attempting to insult American soldiers on World War II battlefields called out insults to DiMaggio. His career batting average was .325, and he hammered 361 home runs. In 1949 he became the American League's first $100,000 player.

Before the Yankees

Son of Italian immigrant parents, Giuseppe Paolo DiMaggio Jr. grew up in the San Francisco area with his four brothers and four sisters. At seventeen DiMaggio elected to play minor league baseball with the San Francisco Seals, the team on which his brother was making his professional debut near the end of the 1932 season. With a salary of $250 a month, 6-foot-2-inch DiMaggio became a Bay Area celebrity in 1933, hitting safely in 61 consecutive games, an all-time record for professional baseball, while hitting .340 and driving in 169 runs. A year later DiMaggio hit .341 and was purchased by the New York Yankees for $25,000 and five minor league players. An impressive .398 batting average earned him a Yankee tryout in 1936, where he was billed as the next Babe Ruth. DiMaggio's debut was delayed because of an injury, yet when he appeared on the field for the first time, on 3 May 1936, 25,000 cheering, flag-waving Italian residents of New York showed up to welcome him to the team.

"Joltin Joe, the Yankee Clipper"

By 1936 "Joltin' Joe," as he was called, led the league with a career-high 46 home runs. Even with the depth of the left field fence in Yankee Stadium, DiMaggio hit 361 career home runs, placing him fifth on the major league all-time home run list when he retired in 1951. In 1937 he batted an impressive .346, driving in 167 runs. The next season DiMaggio hit .324, followed in 1939 with a .381 and his first batting championship and the league Most Valuable Player award. Late in the 1939 season DiMaggio was hitting at a .412 pace, but eye trouble, and possibly the pressure, kept him from staying above the .400 mark.

The Streak

During the 1940 season DiMaggio captured his second consecutive batting title with a .352, but for the first time since he had joined the Yankees his team failed to win the pennant—setting the stage for the 1941 season that would make baseball history. DiMaggio's 56-game hitting streak during the 1941 season began on 15 May, when he singled home a run, and ended on 17 July. In between he hit .406, and fans all over the country anxiously checked each game day to see if the Yankee Clipper had kept the streak going. People jammed the ballpark; radio programs were interrupted for "DiMag" bulletins, the U.S. Congress designated a page boy to rush DiMaggio bulletins to the floor, and newspaper switchboards lit up every afternoon with the question of the day, "Did DiMaggio get his hit?" Immediately after Cleveland pitchers Al Smith and Jim Bagby held DiMaggio hitless on 17 July, with the help of two great plays at third base by Ken Keltner, he started another hitting streak that ran 17 games. At the same time, twenty-two-year-old Red Sox slugger Ted Williams was setting a modern-age batting average of .406. During that same year, young pitcher Bob Feller won 25 games for the Cleveland Indians, and veteran pitcher Lefty Grove won his 300th game. In 1941 DiMaggio won his second Most Valuable Player award and like the rest of the nation began to feel the pressure of a nation readying itself for war. During the 1942 season DiMaggio batted .305 and was drafted into the army along with thousands of other young men. During his three years in the army DiMaggio played baseball in the Pacific and across the United States. The 1946 season was a disappointment (he batted .290), but by 1947 he was back in form, hitting .315 to win his third Most Valuable Player award and lead his team to the pennant.

Hall of Famer

Aided by the media machine of New York City and his own powerful statistics, DiMaggio became a national hero after the war—even though he played for the often-hated Yankees. He was even immortalized in a song called "Joltin' Joe DiMaggio," recorded by the Les Brown Orchestra. In 1948 DiMaggio had returned to the height of this form, winning the home run title with 39, the RBI crown with 155, and the batting title with a .320 average. DiMaggio sat out the first two months of the 1949 season with a bone spur in his heel, but as always his return was memorable. Although playing in pain, during his first games for new manager Casey Stengel, DiMaggio belted four homers in three games that broke the back of the league-leading Red Sox and helped the Yankees bring home another pennant. In 1951, with another soon-to-be Yankee superstar, young Mickey Mantle, on the scene, DiMaggio's average slipped to .263 with only 12 homers. Announcing his retirement at age thirty-seven in 1952, he turned down a fourth consecutive $100,000 contract because "when baseball is no longer fun, it's no longer a game." The Yankees, whose history is replete with heroes, retired his uniform, the world-famous pinstripe number five. In later years DiMaggio hosted pregame television shows, made television commercials, and was briefly married to the voluptuous Hollywood actress Marilyn Monroe. He was elected to the Baseball Hall of Fame in 1955, and in 1969 he was named the "Greatest Living Player" in a centennial poll of sportswriters. DiMaggio died at his home in Hollywood, Florida, on March 8, 1999.

Further Reading

Maury Allen, *Where Have You Gone, Joe DiMaggio? The Story of America's Last Hero* (New York: Dutton, 1975);

Jack B. Moore, *Joe DiMaggio: A Bio-Bibliography* (Westport, Conn.: Greenwood Press, 1986);

Michael Seidel, *Streak: DiMaggio and the Summer of '41* (New York: McGraw-Hill, 1988).

Durso, Joseph, *DiMaggio: the last American knight* (Boston: Little, Brown, 1995). □

David Dinkins

After defeating incumbent Mayor Edward I. Koch in New York's 1989 Democratic mayoral primary, David Dinkins (born 1927) went on in November to defeat Rudolph Giuliani and become the first African American mayor of New York City.

Calm, elegant, deliberate, and dignified, David N. Dinkins overcame the suspicions of many white New Yorkers that he lacked leadership qualifications and in November of 1989 was elected the first black mayor of the United States' largest city. After announcing his candidacy in February, Dinkins became the beneficiary of a changing public attitude, one exhausted with racial strife and adjustments caused by a constricting economy. Drawing heavily on his political stronghold in Harlem, the career politician and lifelong Democrat defeated incumbent Mayor Edward I. Koch in September. In the general election he was victorious over a political neophyte, the popular district attorney Rudolph W. Giuliani. Once in office, Dinkins faced the intimidating task of healing a city suffering from fiscal and racial hemorrhaging. The results have received mixed reviews, with supporters praising Dinkins for calming a populace that threatened to explode more than once, and detractors arguing that he has acted timidly at a time when the city was crying out for forceful leadership.

Celestine Bohlen expressed in the *New York Times:* "David Dinkins comes to the office of mayor after three decades of loyal, quiet service to the Democratic party—making him a man who is a groundbreaker and very much bound by tradition. In a race against two high-profile opponents, Mr. Dinkins was the candidate of moderation, a middle-of-the-road choice for a city that seemed eager to lower its own decibel level. His strategy was to soothe, not excite—and it worked."

Perceiving that the city he likes to call "our town" was ready for a candidate that would "take the high road," Dinkins led a campaign that was notable less for what he said than the way he said it. His English was formal and almost stilted, delivered in a calm baritone laden with "one oughts" and "pray tells." He did not raise his voice and unlike many politicians, spoke the same language at a breakfast meeting on Wall Street as he did at a street rally in Bensonhurst, a volatile area of the city. He fared well in comparison to Koch, known for his divisive politicking, and Giuliani, who transferred his prosecutorial style to the campaign trail.

Dinkins has been called a man of deep convictions by his admirers, although few concrete programs can be linked to those convictions. Others have called him a political Bill Cosby: "Dinkins projects the kind of personality that's not threatening to whites and is acceptable to blacks," Representative Floyd H. Flake, a black Democrat from Queens, told the *New York Times.* Yet throughout his career he has received only marginal support from black political groups or voters outside his Harlem base, losing as many elections as he has won. The "rap" against him cites his inadequate support for minority issues.

Emerged as a Peacemaker

By most accounts his finest moments in the campaign involved calming the city when it seemed on the brink of racial schism. A young white woman had been raped and brutalized by black youths in Central Park, and a black teenager had been murdered in a white ethnic Brooklyn neighborhood. In the polarized atmosphere of the summer of 1989, Dinkins emerged as a peacemaker. His image as an avuncular, deliberative leader seemed a welcome balm to New Yorkers. To appear cool and unflappable in the summer heat, Dinkins had his aides carry three or four identical linen suits, allowing for quick changes.

In Bensonhurst, where black community leaders had organized a march to protest the killing of Yusef Hawkins in August, Dinkins faced an angry crowd that booed his arrival. He managed to quiet the boos and obtain his audience's respect. According to an account by Todd Purdum in the *New York Times,* he approached it this way: "Let's be clear on something. There's no need for you to agree with me. You have every right to prefer someone else. But understand this also. There will come a November 7 and then there'll be a November 8, and the people will have spoken. And after they've spoken, I'm equally confident that you're going to obey and abide by that judgment.''

Such moments of eloquence were rare for Dinkins. Even his supporters joked about his wooden speaking style. On the eve of the general election, in a televised candidate's debate, he was given 60 seconds to explain why he should be mayor. To do this he needed to read aloud from a prepared text. For months on the campaign trail, reporters' eyes would glaze over when he repeated, for the umpteenth time, his vision of the city's ethnic diversity as ''a gorgeous mosaic.'' He deviated little from his script.

Dinkins's two main campaign hurdles were civil rights leader Jesse Jackson and his own personal finances. Dinkins's association with Jackson, whose private pronouncement of New York as ''Hymietown'' still infuriated many, limited Dinkins's support among Jewish voters. The mayoral candidate's campaign strategists, however, were able to convince a plurality of Jewish voters that Dinkins was his own man and solidly within the Democratic party tradition.

A second obstacle was the integrity issue. Dinkins paid no income taxes from 1969 through 1972, although he later paid back taxes in full with interest. He referred to the omission as an oversight. He also came under a cloud for his perceived unethical handling of his stock portfolio; he had transferred ownership to his son and substantially underreported its cash worth. Dinkins spent much time in the latter part of the campaign addressing those issues, often with visible reluctance and resentment.

Attended Howard University

Dinkins was born in Trenton, New Jersey, in 1927. His family had come from the South the previous year after pulling up roots in Newport News, Virginia. During Dinkins's early childhood, his parents separated, and he and his younger sister went with their mother to start a new life in Harlem. He returned to Trenton to attend high school, then went on to Howard University. His studies were interrupted by World War II, during which he served in the Marines. ''Dink'' was recalled by classmates as a fine student; media interviews with those classmates depict a young man with strong social skills, popular with one and all, and involved in a fraternity. It was at Howard that Dinkins met Joyce Burrows, a campus queen of a rival fraternity. The two eventually became engaged.

While strongly involved in social life at Howard—a primarily black college in Washington, D.C.—as an undergraduate, Dinkins occasionally ventured off campus to see movies in the Washington area. The capital was very much a segregated city at that time. An inveterate movie buff, Dinkins would don a turban and fake a foreign accent in order to enter movie theaters off limits to blacks. The episodes apparently did not stir any racial bitterness in the young man.

Soon after graduation Dinkins married his fiance in an Episcopalian church in Harlem, where the couple then set up housekeeping. Mrs. Dinkins had grown up in a very political family—her father was Daniel Burrows, former assemblyman and district leader—and provided strong encouragement for the young man to consider a political career. In 1953 Dinkins enrolled at Brooklyn Law School, entertaining the possibility of launching a political career. The young family soon moved to a state-subsidized, middle-class housing project in Harlem, where they raised two children.

Dinkins eventually complied with the wishes of his wife's parents. Introduced to J. Raymond Jones, the so-called ''Harlem Fox,'' Dinkins became a cog in the powerful Harlem political machine, the Carver Club. The organization trained generations of young black business and political leaders and was well entrenched within the city's power structure. Dinkins took on the grunt work that is part of every campaign, awakening at dawn to hang posters at Harlem subway stops. He worked long and hard without complaint, and his dedication was duly noted. Within the Carver Club, racial rhetoric was rare, congeniality the byword. Dinkins mixed easily with politicos from all walks of life. Among his peers and cronies were Basil Paterson, Charles Rangel, and Percy Sutton, all of whom were to emerge as three of the city's most powerful black politicians. As Dinkins grew older and took on more responsibility, his associations came to include a number of the city's movers and shakers. He played tennis with them at the River Club, visited their estates in South Hampton, and vacationed in Europe at their expense.

None of this endeared Dinkins to black community leaders or younger, more activist voters. Yet as the momentum of his campaign grew, and it became clear he had a very real chance to become the city's first black mayor, misgivings gave way to racial pride. Blacks sporting ''Dinkins'' buttons on their lapels began turning up all over town. When his chauffeured car pulled into a black neighborhood, the excitement became palpable. A *Newsday* editorial writer asked Dinkins whether he feared his image was that of an Uncle Tom. He answered, ''*Au contraire.* What I do is provide hope.''

Elected Manhattan Borough President

In 1965 Dinkins ran for his first elective office, representing his district in the New York State Assembly, and won. At the end of his two-year term, however, his district was redrawn, and he chose not to run again. He bided his time handling local political tasks. When Mayor Abraham Beame offered him a post in his administration as deputy mayor, Dinkins accepted—then withdrew in the midst of a media hoopla over his unpaid taxes. Dinkins paid his taxes and, still very much in the party's good graces, was hastily appointed city clerk. His responsibilities mainly involved signing marriage certificates; his salary was $71,000.

In 1977 Percy Sutton resigned as Manhattan borough president and anointed Dinkins to run for the office. Dinkins did, but lost by a wide margin. Four years later he ran again, losing once more in a landslide. In 1985 he vied a third time and was elected. The post he took over included a staff of more than 100 and an annual budget of nearly $5 million.

As borough president, Dinkins did little to upset the apple cart. He put together task forces on a range of urban issues, from pedestrian safety to school decentralization. Perhaps his strongest stance was in support of community-based AIDS services.

Neil Barsky wrote in the *Wall Street Journal,* "By most accounts he made little of the post, and was best known among city politicians for his problems making up his mind" on budget and land-use matters. Dinkins earned a reputation as a procrastinator, withholding his opinion or his vote until he could hold lengthy, detailed briefings with aides and consultants. To the public he was deliberate, cool-headed, and rather vague, as evidenced by an answer given to *New York Times* reporter Todd Purdum in response to a question on streamlining the city's bureaucracy: "I cannot now set forth a specific blueprint and guarantee that we can do everything in one stop. All I'm saying is there must exist the ingenuity among us if we start off with the assumption that it's a desirable goal."

Shattering of the "Gorgeous Mosaic"

Early in his tenure, Dinkins experienced firsthand the glaring difference between a candidate who can promise the sky and an office-holder who cannot, to the dismay of some constituents, deliver all things to all people. The city Dinkins inherited, in the eyes of many political pundits, was looking more ungovernable with each passing day, presenting a string of concrete challenges to the idealism that had drawn the electorate to him during the campaign. The budget deficit was running at $1.8 billion, a national recession was robbing the city of jobs and cutting revenues, and crime continued to claim victims in cases that made the national news and further enhanced the image of New York as an archetype of urban decay.

In addition, it was by no means helpful that at a time when New Yorkers were in need of greater government services, federal aid to cities across the country had been given the budgetary ax. After being criticized for initially wavering on New York finances, Dinkins bit the bullet, avoiding deficit spending by cutting the city's work force and dramatically scaling back health, education, housing, and other social programs. These moves, while praised as fiscally prudent, had a political cost. Some claimed Dinkins hadn't done enough, particularly with the downsizing of government, and others maintained he had alienated those constituents in the labor and African American communities who had been among his most strident supporters. "I sort of get it from both sides," Dinkins was quoted as saying in *Emerge.* "You can't make political judgments about actions you take. You really need to make a judgment that's consistent with the correct thing to do and what's good for all people. When it comes to 'my constituency' so-called—I frankly see everyone as my constituency."

In addition to facing attacks on his financial handling of the city, Dinkins began to see the further shattering of his beloved "gorgeous mosaic." In 1991 violent protests erupted after a car in the entourage of a Brooklyn Jewish leader struck and killed a black youth in Queens. Dinkins appealed to both sides to follow the light of reason rather than cave in to emotion, stereotypes, and hate and was credited with having brokered a peace, albeit a fragile one.

A more rigorous test of his healing powers was delivered in 1992, when riots ravaged cities throughout the country in the wake of the not guilty verdict in the controversial Rodney King case, which involved the question of brutality inflicted by white police officers on a black citizen. Visiting neighborhoods most vulnerable to violent explosion, Dinkins again succeeded in deactivating a racial time bomb and earned, at least temporarily, a respite from his critics. "This was defining moment for him," state Democratic Chairman John A. Marino was quoted as saying in the *New York Times.* "He showed why he was elected, in a sense. I'm hearing a lot of good things about David N. Dinkins from people who a few weeks ago didn't have anything good to say about him."

Dinkins continued to have good luck in 1992, as the city prepared for the lucrative Democratic National Convention—a feather in the mayor's political cap. An unexpected budget surplus was discovered, and the Internal Revenue Service (IRS) ruled in May that the mayor had not violated federal tax rules in the 1986 stock transaction with his son. A July 2, 1992, poll indicated New Yorkers had a 41 percent favorable opinion of him, not the number of a universally loved politician, but 12 points higher than it had been in March.

Dinkins has learned, however, that luck is as fleeting in politics as it is in other fields, perhaps more so. As the 1993 election approached, Dinkins was facing a steady stream of criticism that he has hired incompetent workers to top municipal posts, that he acts reactively rather than proactively, and that, while displaying a talent for pacifying, he lacks the consistently strong leadership and stalwart vision that the city's multifaceted problems demand.

Still, Dinkins continued trumpeting the populist, idealistic themes that carried him through the 1989 election and that he hoped would serve him well in 1993, when he faced challenges from Giuliani and George Marlin, Conservative and Right to Life Parties. "I came into government hearing the voices of those in need, and I will never stop listening," the *New York Times* quoted the mayor as saying in his 1992 state-of-the-city speech. "There is more hope in this city than there are street corners." Nonetheless, Giuliani defeated him by a narrow margin and Dinkins became the first black mayor of a major American city who was not reelected to office.

Further Reading

Black Enterprise, November 1989.

Detroit Free Press, January 5, 1992.

Economist, November 11, 1989.

Emerge, November 1991.

Jet, August 28, 1995, p. 6.

Newsday, October 28, 1989.

Newsweek, May 28, 1990.

New York, November 5, 1990; November 11, 1991; May 25, 1992.

New Yorker, July 20, 1992; November 15, 1993, pp. 52-59.

New York Times, September 13, 1989; September 14, 1989; October 20, 1989; October 26, 1989; October 28, 1989; November 2, 1989; November 8, 1989; January 2, 1990; September 13, 1990; January 9, 1991; February 4, 1991; April 7, 1991; May 11, 1991; June 24, 1991 January 3, 1992; May 6, 1992; May 11, 1992, December 23, 1995, p. 29.

Wall Street Journal, October 28, 1989. ☐

Walter Elias Disney

An American filmmaker and entrepreneur, Walter Elias Disney (1901-1966) created a new kind of popular culture in feature-length animated cartoons and live-action "family" films.

Walter Elias Disney was born in Chicago, Illinois, on December 5, 1901, the fourth of five children born to a Canadian farmer and a mother from Ohio. He was raised on a Midwestern farm in Marceline, Missouri, and in Kansas City, where he was able to acquire some rudimentary art instruction from correspondence courses and Saturday museum classes. He would later use many of the animals and characters that he knew from that Missouri farm in his cartoons.

He dropped out of high school at 17 to serve in World War I. After serving briefly overseas as an ambulance driver, Disney returned in 1919 to Kansas City for an apprenticeship as a commercial illustrator and later made primitive animated advertising cartoons. By 1922, he had set up his own shop in association with Ub Iwerks, whose drawing ability and technical inventiveness were prime factors in Disney's eventual success.

Initial failure sent Disney to Hollywood in 1923, where in partnership with his loyal elder brother Roy, he managed to resume cartoon production. His first success came with the creation of Mickey Mouse in *Steamboat Willie. Steamboat Willie* was the first fully synchronized sound cartoon and featured Disney as the voice of a character first called "Mortimer Mouse." Disney's wife, Lillian, suggested that Mickey sounded better and Disney agreed.

Living frugally, he reinvested profits to make better pictures. His insistence on technical perfection and his unsurpassed gifts as story editor quickly pushed his firm ahead. The invention of such cartoon characters as Mickey Mouse, Donald Duck, Minnie, and Goofy combined with the daring and innovative use of music, sound, and folk material (as in *The Three Little Pigs*) made the Disney shorts of the 1930s a phenomenon of worldwide success. This success led to the establishment of immensely profitable, Disney-controlled sidelines in advertising, publishing, and franchised goods, which helped shape popular taste for nearly 40 years.

Disney rapidly expanded his studio facilities to include a training school where a whole new generation of animators developed and made possible the production of the first feature-length cartoon, *Snow White* (1937). Other costly animated features followed, including *Pinocchio, Bambi,* and the celebrated musical experiment *Fantasia.* With *Seal Island* (1948), wildlife films became an additional source of income, and in 1950 his use of blocked funds in

England to make pictures like *Treasure Island* led to what became the studio's major product, live-action films, which practically cornered the traditional "family" market. Eventually the Disney formula emphasized slick production techniques. It included, as in his biggest hit, *Mary Poppins,* occasional animation to project wholesome, exciting stories heavily laced with sentiment and, often, music.

In 1954, Disney successfully invaded television, and by the time of his death, the Disney studio's output amounted to 21 full-length animated films, 493 short subjects, 47 live-action films, seven True-Life Adventure features, 330 hours of Mickey Mouse Club television programs, 78 half-hour *Zorro* television adventures, and 280 other television shows.

On July 18, 1957, Disney opened Disneyland, a gigantic projection of his personal fantasies in Anaheim, California, which has proved the most successful amusement park in history with 6.7 million people visiting it by 1966. The idea for the park came to him after taking his children to other amusement parks and watching them have fun on amusement rides. He decided to build a park where the entire family could have fun together. In 1971, Disney World, in Orlando, Florida, opened. Since then, Disney theme parks have opened in Tokyo and Paris.

Disney had also dreamed of developing a city of the future, a dream realized in 1982 with the opening of EPCOT, which stands for Experimental Prototype Community of Tomorrow. EPCOT, which cost an initial $900 million, was conceived of as a real-life community of the future with the very latest in high technology. The two principle areas of EPCOT are Future World and World Showcase, both of which were designed to appeal to adults rather than children.

In addition to his theme parks, Disney created and endowed a new university, the California Institute of the Arts, known as Cal Arts. He thought of this as the ultimate in education for the arts, where people in many different disciplines could work together, dream and develop, and create the mixture of arts needed for the future. Disney once commented: "It's the principle thing I hope to leave when I move on to greener pastures. If I can help provide a place to develop the talent of the future, I think I will have accomplished something."

Disney's parks continue to grow with the creation of the Disney-MGM Studios, Animal Kingdom, and a extensive sports complex in Orlando. The Disney Corporation has also branched out into other types of films with the creation of Touchstone Films, into music with Hollywood Records, and even vacationing with its Disney Cruise Lines. In all, the Disney name now lends itself to a multi-billion dollar enterprise, with multiple undertakings all over the world.

In 1939, Disney received an honorary Academy Award and in 1954 he received four Academy Awards. In 1965, President Lyndon B. Johnson presented Disney with the Presidential Medal of Freedom and in the same year Disney was awarded the Freedom Foundation Award.

Happily married for 41 years, this moody, deliberately "ordinary" man was moving ahead with his plans for gigantic new outdoor recreational facilities when he died of circulatory problems on December 15, 1966, at St. Joseph's Hospital in Los Angeles, CA. At the time of his death, his enterprises had garnered him respect, admiration, and a business empire worth over $100 million-a-year, but Disney was still remembered primarily as the man who had created Mickey Mouse over two decades before.

Further Reading

The best book on Disney is Richard Schickel, *The Disney Version: The Life, Times, Art, and Commerce of Walt Disney* (1968). A useful source of technical information is Robert D. Feild, *The Art of Walt Disney* (1942). For an accurate study of the humanitarian and business aspects of Disney, see Steven Watts, *The Magic Kingdom: Walt Disney and the American Way of Life* (1998). The most intimate portrait of Disney is by his daughter, Diane Disney Miller, *The Story of Walt Disney* (1957). Biographies of Disney appear in both the 1952 and 1967 issues of *Current Biography*. Disney's obituary appears in the December 16, 1966, issue of *New York Times*. □

Father Divine

Father Divine (ca. 1877-1965) founded a cultish religious movement known as the Peace Mission. He served as its director from 1915 to 1965.

Father Divine is one of the more perplexing figures in twentieth-century African American history. The founder of a cultish religious movement whose mem-

bers regarded him as God, Father Divine was also an untiring champion of equal rights for all Americans regardless of color or creed, as well as a very practical businessman whose many retail and farming establishments flourished in the midst of the Great Depression. Regarded by many members of the traditional black church as an imposter or even a lunatic, Divine was praised by other observers as a powerful agent of social change, alone among the many cult leaders in Depression-era New York in providing tangible economic benefits for thousands of his disciples.

The early biography of the man who later called himself Father Divine is little more than a patchwork of guesses: Divine was apparently unwilling to discuss his life except in its "spiritual" aspects. Believing himself to be God incarnate, he felt the details of his worldly existence were unimportant; the result is that historians are not certain even of his original name or place of birth. Most agree, however, that Father Divine was probably born ten to twenty years after the end of the Civil War, somewhere in the Deep South, and that his given name was George Baker.

As betrayed by the accent and colloquialisms of his speaking style, Baker seemed to have grown up in the rural South, no doubt in a family of farmers struggling to survive under the twin burdens of economic exploitation and racially discriminatory Jim Crow laws. At an early age, Baker escaped the drudgery of farm work by becoming a traveling preacher, gradually working his way north to Baltimore, Maryland, in the year 1899.

The Messenger

In Baltimore, Baker worked as a gardener, restricting his preaching to an occasional turn at the Baptist church's Wednesday night prayer meeting, where his powerful speaking style was much encouraged by his fellow churchgoers. Though a man of stubby proportions with a high-pitched voice, Baker enthralled listeners with his fluid storytelling and highly emotional delivery, typical of the sermons given at the rural southern churches where he grew up.

But Baker was also a restless man of independent opinions, and it was not long before he felt compelled to resume the life of a traveling preacher. He returned to the South with two specific goals: to combat the spread of Jim Crow segregation and to offer an alternative to the otherworldly emphasis of most established churches. Such a crusade was not likely to meet with much success—indeed, Baker was fortunate not to be lynched—yet it reflected a concern for social issues that would remain constant throughout the long career of Father Divine.

Baker returned to Baltimore around 1906 and there fell under the influence of an eccentric preacher named Samuel Morris. Morris had been thrown out of numerous churches for proclaiming himself to be God, a belief he derived from a passage in St Paul's First Letter to the Corinthians which asks, "Know ye not that . . . the spirit of God dwelleth in you?" This teaching provided Baker with a religious foundation for his social activism: if God lived within every human being, all were therefore divine and hence equal. Baker became Morris's staunch supporter and disciple. Morris took to calling himself "Father Jehovia," while his prophet Baker adopted the appropriate title of "The Messenger." It was not long before The Messenger again felt the need to spread his gospel southward, and in 1912 Baker set off for the backwoods of Georgia.

At some point in his travels Baker apparently realized that if Samuel Morris were God, so too was he, and he henceforth referred to himself as the living incarnation of the Lord God Almighty. Such a claim was naturally alarming to the pastors of the churches where Baker stopped to preach, and in 1914 he was arrested in Valdosta, Georgia, as a public nuisance who was possibly "insane." The court recorded his name as "John Doe, alias God," but with the help of a local writer who took an interest in The Messenger's strange story, Baker was released and told to leave the state of Georgia. Instead, he was promptly rearrested in a nearby town and sent to the state insane asylum, whereupon his benefactor once again freed him after a short time.

Though Baker's theology was no doubt peculiar, he impressed most people as a man of sound mind and deep moral commitment. "I remember," his attorney later told the *New Yorker,* "that there was about the man an unmistakable quiet power that manifested itself to anyone who came in contact with him."

The Making of a Cult

Baker soon tired of his troubles in Georgia and in 1915 made his way to New York City, bringing with him a handful of disciples he had picked up along the way. With these followers, Baker set up a communal household in which income was shared and a life of chastity and abstinence was encouraged, all under the direction of "Major J. Devine," as Baker was then styling himself. Major Devine preached the doctrine of God within each individual, but there was never any doubt among his followers as to who was the actual incarnation of the deity—only Devine, or "Divine," as the name inevitably came to be spelled, could claim that honor. Divine helped his disciples find work, and they in turn entrusted him with the management of the group's finances as well as its spiritual well-being. By living simply and pooling their resources, Divine's movement was able to purchase a house in suburban Sayville, New York, in 1919, by which time Divine had also taken as his wife a disciple named Pinninnah.

In contrast to his earlier, public preaching, which had often expressed the need for racial equality and justice, Divine's spiritual work was now confined to the salvation of his followers and was based on harmony within and between individuals. To the outside world, Father Divine was a quiet, well-respected member of the Sayville community (otherwise all-white) who ran an employment agency for the many African American men and women staying at his house on Macon Street. Divine excelled at both of his professions. As his church grew by leaps and bounds, the preacher—also a shrewd businessman—not only found work for his disciples but oversaw the investment of their common earnings with the talent of a natural entrepreneur. Divine taught his followers the virtues of hard work, honesty, and service in their business dealings, exhorting them to achieve economic security in this world as preparation for salvation in the next. Under the guidance of Divine's leadership, his disciples gained a reputation as excellent employees and the operators of honest, efficient businesses.

Divine's "Peace Mission," as he called his following, remained relatively unknown until the start of the Great Depression in 1929. New York was full of such cult organizations, each boasting its own charismatic preacher and offering to the thousands of recently arrived black southern emigrants an emotional brand of religion similar to what they had known in their hometowns. With the advent of the Depression, however, desperate economic conditions made the Peace Mission's generosity all the more striking.

Each Sunday at the Sayville residence was set aside for an all-day banquet, free of charge and open to anyone who cared to attend. Father Divine would accept no payment for these feasts, nor did he take charitable contributions; he asked only that everyone who sat down to dinner behave in a Christian manner and abstain from the consumption of alcohol. Word quickly spread of Divine's "miraculous" bounty, and by the early 1930s his Sunday dinners were attracting hundreds of hungry poor people—mostly black but not exclusively so—to the house in Sayville. Disturbed by this eruption of black power in their midst, residents of Sayville had Divine arrested as a public nuisance. A thorough police investigation uncovered no signs of financial or moral improprieties at the Peace Mission, but Divine was nevertheless sentenced to one year in prison by a judge who considered him a dangerous fraud. When the judge promptly died three days later, Divine's reputation as a divine Christian being was enhanced: like Jesus, he had been wrongly accused, and now his persecutor was paid back in full. Divine was set free on bail, his conviction later overturned, and the Peace Mission attracted new followers by the thousands.

Peace Mission Flourished

Divine's success in the 1930s was indeed nothing short of "miraculous." After moving his headquarters to Harlem, the center of black artistic and cultural life in New York and the nation, his Peace Mission rapidly added scores of affiliated branches elsewhere in New York, in New Jersey, and as far away as California. About 85 percent of Peace Mission disciples were black, and at least 75 percent were female, many drawn as much by the electrifying person of Father Divine as by his social or theological message.

Since full-fledged disciples (known as "Angels") were required to donate all of their worldly possessions to the Mission, Father Divine was soon overseeing an organization of considerable financial size. By all accounts, he did so honestly and skillfully, helping his followers to find jobs, start innumerable small businesses, and after 1935 settle on farmland purchased by the Mission in upstate New York— all of this in the midst of the worst depression in the history of the United States. Divine did allow himself a few luxuries: he lived in the finest of the Mission's many Harlem properties, was chauffeured in a Rolls Royce, and was rarely seen in anything but a fashionable three-piece business suit.

Father Divine never advocated the virtues of poverty: his followers had all too much of that as it was. In his preaching, Divine combined an almost fanatical faith with strict adherence to the ethics of American life, urging his followers to rise from poverty by old-fashioned thrift, hard work, and scrupulous honesty. To work, in his eyes, was to serve God. Divine was especially wary of the dangers of borrowing money, and all of the Mission's business was conducted in cash, even real estate being paid for in cash and in advance. The flaunting of large amounts of money naturally drew the attention of the Internal Revenue Service, which never found any irregularities in the dealings of Father Divine or the Peace Mission. On the contrary, on many occasions his disciples startled former employers or tradesmen by repaying long forgotten debts; in one instance, this involved the sum of 66 cents for a train ride taken 40 years before.

Father Divine saw economic independence as a stepping stone toward his overall goal of racial equality. He was unequivocally opposed to any form of racial discrimination, or even to the recognition of racial difference. For Divine, all human beings partook of the divine essence, and all Americans were due the rights granted them by the Constitution. He therefore purposely bought many pieces of property in all-white areas, including most notably an estate on the Hudson River opposite the home of President Franklin D. Roosevelt, as well as a beachfront hotel near Atlantic City, New Jersey, and extensive tracts of farmland in upstate New York. When challenged by segregationists for such moves, Divine would often speak of the American way of life, as in an article published in *New Day*, a Mission

newspaper: "My co-workers and followers are endeavoring to express our citizenry and enact the Bill of Rights in every activity and even in every community . . . to enjoy life, liberty and the reality of happiness."

Divine's Retirement

The end of the Depression also witnessed the gradual retirement of Father Divine. Already in his sixties, Divine was shaken by a lawsuit filed in 1937 by a former disciple who sought repayment of money she had given to the Peace Mission over the years. A long series of legal maneuvers eventually resulted in the incorporation of the Peace Mission and Father Divine's move to Philadelphia, beyond the reach of New York State law. Of greater fundamental importance to the Peace Mission was the advent of war in 1939, when the American economy snapped out of its long depression and jobs became plentiful. The Peace Mission's style of frugal collective living lost much of its appeal in a booming economic climate, and the organization stagnated, with Father Divine gradually retiring to a life of quiet wealth outside Philadelphia.

In 1946 Divine married his second wife, a 21-year-old white disciple named Edna Rose Ritchings—a move that required all of his rhetorical skill to explain as the act of a celibate divinity. Ritchings nevertheless went on to become de facto head of the Mission, known first by her cult name of "Sweet Angel" and later simply as Mother Divine.

Father Divine lived until 1965, little seen and not active in the few remaining Mission projects. However, he did remain a powerful symbol of hope for racial unity and a role model for later generations of people of color. Divine is probably best remembered as a man who, in his own peculiar way, acted in his own interest while skillfully advancing the cause of thousands of inner city African Americans.

Further Reading

The African-American Almanac, edited by Kenneth Estell, Gale, 1994.

Dictionary of American Negro Biography, edited by Rayford W. Logan and Michael R. Winston, Norton, 1982.

Harris, Sara, *Father Divine,* Collier Books, 1971.

Parker, Robert Allerton, *The Incredible Messiah: The Deification of Father Divine,* Little, Brown, 1937.

Weisbrot, Robert, *Father Divine and the Struggle for Racial Equality,* University of Illinois Press, 1983.

Nation, February 6, 1935.

New Day (Peace Mission publication), various issues, 1936.

New Yorker, June 13, 1936; June 20, 1936; June 27, 1936.

New York Times, September 11, 1965, p. 1.

Spoken Word (Peace Mission publication), various issues, 1934-37. □

Robert J. Dole

Robert J. Dole (born 1923) of Kansas represented that state in the Senate from 1968 until 1996. He served as Republican National Committee chair under President Richard Nixon and was Gerald Ford's running mate in 1976. As

Senate majority leader during the second administration of President Ronald Reagan and again from 1994 to 1996, Dole was an articulate spokesperson for Republican policies. Dole won the Republican presidential nomination in 1996, but lost the general election to the incumbent president, Bill Clinton.

B orn in a one bedroom home in the small Kansas town of Russell on July 22, 1923, Robert J. Dole knew the hard scrabble life of Plains states' folks at first hand. Doran, his father, ran a grain elevator while his mother, Tina (Talbott), sold sewing machines. Dole and his three siblings grew up in a larger, more comfortable home than he had been born in, but his parents rented the upper floor to earn extra income.

His childhood was the commonplace one of a farmtown boy: Methodist church meetings, Boy Scouts, public schools, a strict loving home life, and a penchant for work. An honor secondary school student, Dole was extremely ambitious, at one time entertaining the dream of medical school. He had a passion for sports and won letters in running, football, and basketball. At the University of Kansas (Lawrence) he enrolled in a pre-med course and continued his athletics, becoming a star quarter-miler.

Life Threatened in War

In 1943, Dole's studies were interrupted by World War II and he began training in various military specialties at schools around the country, completing his training as an infantry second lieutenant at Fort Benning (Georgia) Officer Candidate School. Assigned as a platoon leader to the 10th

Mountain Division in Italy in early 1945, he saw action against German units in March. A month later—on April 14, 1945—he received a wound which kept him hospitalized for more than three years and left him with a permanently disabled right arm.

For a while there was no guarantee he would live, since the shell hit his shoulder and spine, paralyzing all his limbs. When the European war ended less than four weeks after he was injured, Dole's private war with deadly infection, experimental drugs, grueling therapy, and many operations had just begun. These tested his spirit and courage deeply and sharpened two qualities which characterized him later: optimism and tenacity.

In 1948, while in the hospital, he met and married Phyllis Holden, by whom he had his only child, Robin. Phyllis was a physical therapist who aided him in his return to school. He took up his education again, this time at Washburn University (Topeka) where he earned bachelor's and law degrees.

Political Career Led to Washington

Dole discarded medicine as a career in favor of politics, and even before he had earned his law degree he ran for and won a seat in the Kansas House of Representatives. After a single term as state lawmaker (1951-1953), Dole ran for Russell County prosecutor, a post he held for seven years until his successful 1960 race for the U.S. House of Representatives.

Dole served as a member of the six-person Kansas House delegation for one term, survived the 1960 reapportionment—which cost the state one seat—in his second race, and was re-elected twice more. During his eight years as a House member (1961-1969) Dole came across as a combative, rural-oriented, conservative Republican opposed on principle to much of the Great Society's program. In 1964, for example, he voted to prohibit the Supreme Court from interfering in reapportionment cases involving state legislatures, voted against the Economic Opportunity Act, and opposed the Urban Mass Transportation Act. He did support the Civil Rights Act of that year, however, and backed similar legislation throughout his career. In 1968 he took advantage of the retirement of a Republican incumbent and won the nomination as the Republican Party's candidate for the Senate. In the general election he defeated moderate Democrat William Robinson decisively, winning more than 60 percent of the popular vote.

Dole emerged in the Senate of the 91st Congress (1969-1971) as a powerful national figure. Service on the Senate Agriculture and Forestry Committee gave him the opportunity to keep fences mended at home. He also gave a good deal of time on party matters, devoting himself to the Nixon Administration's efforts to build a new national Republican coalition. Resented by some party liberals, he nevertheless became Nixon's choice for chair of the Republican National Committee and won high praise from the president for his part in the stunning victory of 1972.

Untouched by Watergate, Dole continued his growth in the Senate, winning a second term in 1974 and climbing the seniority ladder. His conservative voting record helped him win the nomination as President Gerald Ford's vice presidential candidate at the Kansas City (Missouri) Republican convention in August, 1976. The selection was viewed as a means of placating party conservatives, angry over Ford's choice of Nelson Rockefeller as his first vice president. Dole won the support of Western and Midwestern voters but was widely criticized as Ford's "hatchet man." He and Governor Jimmy Carter's vice presidential candidate, Senator Walter Mondale, participated in the explosive and precedent-setting first vice presidential debate at Houston, Texas, in October. Both Dole and Mondale emerged from the 1976 election as national figures. Dole returned to the Senate floor, Mondale mounted to the chair of president of the Senate.

Dole's life's work was also his hobby and all consuming interest: he lived politics every working hour. Meanwhile, he had experienced upheaval in his personal life. His marriage to Phyllis Holden ended in divorce in 1972, and three years later, on December 6, 1975, he married a brilliant Harvard-educated activist lawyer named Elizabeth (Liddy) Hanford. The couple became one of Washington's most powerful teams as Senator Dole won election as majority leader of the Republican-controlled Senate in January 1985; Elizabeth Dole had already been confirmed as President Reagan's Secretary of Transportation. Among numerous other posts, she also served as Secretary of Labor and director of the American Red Cross. She also assisted her husband in creating the Dole Foundation, which raised millions of dollars to assist disabled Americans.

Recurring Candidate for the Presidency

Dole made a very brief run for the presidential nomination in 1980, but he was overwhelmed by Ronald Reagan. His disappointment over his early poor showing was tempered somewhat by the fact that the Republicans gained control of the Senate as well as the Presidency. Dole became chair of the Finance Committee with an important role in ushering President Reagan's economic policies through Congress. He became majority leader of the Senate in late 1984 and helped craft a comprehensive deficit reduction bill in 1985.

In November of 1986, the Democrats regained the Senate, and Dole was demoted to leading the minority party. As the two terms of the Reagan Administration drew to a close, Dole decided once again to seek the presidency, this time with more organization, stature, and money than he had had in 1980. He battled early and often with George Bush, Reagan's vice president, who ultimately won the 1988 Republican nomination and the election.

Dole seemed to receive a new lease on life when Democratic candidate Bill Clinton was elected President in 1992. With the Presidency no longer in Republican hands, Dole became the nation's head Republican. Early in the Clinton Administration, Dole became a fixture on television news shows, positioning himself as the chief spokesperson against the president's policies. He led Senate Republicans in filibusters against Clinton's legislation, and he forced Clinton to scale back an economic stimulus bill the President tried to steer through Congress early in the Administra-

tion. Already in 1993, Dole was visiting the early presidential primary states of Iowa and New Hampshire.

In 1994, Republicans won the House for the first time in four decades, and they regained control of the Senate where Dole once again became majority leader. As the Republicans worked to fulfill the "Contract with America" with which they had won in '94, Dole planned his third attempt for presidential office.

Loses to Bill Clinton in 1996

The first primaries early in 1996 went badly. Candidate Steve Forbes made Dole the target of some $25 million in negative advertising, and Dole lost races to Forbes and Patrick Buchanan. With the Republican party establishment rallying to his defense, Dole locked up the nomination in March. He initially tried to remain majority leader while campaigning for the presidency. However, the Democrats frustrated his legislative efforts so successfully that he was forced to leave the Senate. In June of 1996, he ended his 35-year congressional career by resigning both as Senator from Kansas as well as majority leader.

Dole spent the next four months crisscrossing the country on the campaign trail. Even before the contest was over, many Republicans criticized Dole for doing a poor job of delivering the party's messages. Polls showed that the two televised presidential candidates debates in October helped Clinton and hurt Dole. In election day exit polls, seven out of ten voters said they did not believe Dole's promise to cut taxes by fifteen percent, the key theme of his campaign. It traditionally has been difficult to defeat an incumbent president during times of peace and economic prosperity. However, a *New York Times* analysis concluded that Dole's "third run for the presidency was plagued by missteps, indecision, and strategic blunders so fundamental that they bordered on amateurish."

Clinton won handily in an election marked by the lowest voter turnout in 72 years. Clinton took 49 percent of those voting and carried 31 states. Dole received 41 percent of the popular vote and won 19 states. (Reform Party candidate Ross Perot took another eight percent of the vote.) Yet the election was hardly a rout for the Republicans. The GOP maintained majority control of both the House and Senate and elected a majority of the nation's governors.

After the election, the Doles remained in Washington, D. C., where Elizabeth Dole served as president of the American Red Cross. Robert Dole joined the law firm of Verner, Liipfert, Bernhard, McPherson & Hand. A major lobbying concern, Verner Liipfert represented foreign nations as well as some of the largest business corporations in the U.S. and abroad. Dole became the senior Republican among the firm's lobbyists, whose roster included three former Democratic governors and two former Democratic senators.

Altogether—including their earnings from pensions, product endorsements, speaking fees and Elizabeth Dole's Red Cross salary—the Doles enjoyed an income well in excess of $1 million in 1997. No longer under intense public scrutiny, the former Senator traded in his 1987 Chevrolet Celebrity on a brand new Cadillac. Dole also advanced the $300,000 House Speaker Newt Gingrich owed as a penalty for violating ethics rules, giving Gingrich eight years to pay at 10 percent interest.

Dole was part of negotiations for a NATO peace agreement with Serbian officials in March of 1999 over their plans to force ethnic Albanians from the Yugoslav province of Kosovo.

Further Reading

Bob Dole is referred to in the memoirs of the principal figures of his day. Former President Gerald Ford's autobiography, *A Time to Heal* (1979), for example, has insightful observations on Dole's part in the 1976 campaign. Martin Schram's *Running for President 1976* (1977) treats the same subject in less detail.

Cramer, Richard, *Bob Dole* (Random House, 1995). Dole, Bob and Elizabeth Dole, *Unlimited Partners: Our American Story* (Simon & Schuster, 1996). Dole, Bob and Jack Kemp, *Trusting the People: The Dole-Kemp Plan to Free the Economy & Create a Better America* (HarperCollins, 1996). Hilton, Stanley, *Senator for Sale* (Saint Martin's, 1996). Margolis, Jon, *The Quotable Bob Dole: Witty, Wise & Otherwise* (Avon Books, 1996). McCurry, Michael and John Buckley "Inside Story," *New Yorker*, November 18, 1996, pages 44-60. "Masters of the Message," *Time*, November 18, 1996, pages 76-96. □

John Roderigo Dos Passos

The reputation of the American novelist John Roderigo Dos Passos (1896-1970) is based chiefly on his early work, especially the trilogy "U.S.A."

John Dos Passos was born in Chicago on Jan. 14, 1896, the illegitimate son of a noted New York lawyer, John Randolph Dos Passos, and a wealthy Virginian, Lucy Addison Sprigg. His father did not acknowledge paternity until a year before his death, when the young Dos Passos was 20. As a boy, Dos Passos lived principally on the Virginia farm of his mother's family, and he also traveled frequently with his mother to Mexico, Belgium, and England.

Dos Passos attended Choate School under the name John Roderigo Madison. He graduated from Harvard in 1916, meanwhile publishing stories, verse, and reviews in the Harvard *Monthly*.

In 1917 Dos Passos was in Spain, studying Spanish culture. During World War I he enlisted in the Norton-Harjes Ambulance Unit and served in Spain and Italy. In 1918 he became a private in the U.S. Medical Corps, serving in France. Demobilized in 1919, he remained in Europe to finish two novels: *One Man's Initiation—1917* (1920) and *Three Soldiers* (1921). During the 1920s Dos Passos worked as a newspaper correspondent and traveled extensively but, as an increasingly successful author, he lived chiefly in New York.

First Novels

One Man's Initiation—1917, based on Dos Passos' experiences as an ambulance corpsman, is poignantly antiwar. It also foreshadows a more pervasive theme of his work: contemporary technological society's crippling effects on its inhabitants.

Dos Passos' first significant novel, *Three Soldiers,* (1921) is a bitterly ironic commentary on the professed ideals for which World War I was fought and, more deeply, on the "values" by which modern, mechanized man lives. Dos Passos sees the real enemy as the army itself, which by exacerbating the ordinary weaknesses and inner conflicts of its members causes irreparable harm. His three major characters are entirely broken by army life. *Three Soldiers* is part of an anti-World War I literary tradition that includes works by Ernest Hemingway, Robert Graves, E. E. Cummings, William Faulkner, and Erich Maria Remarque.

Literary Experiment

Manhattan Transfer (1925) is Dos Passos' first major experimental novel. Set in New York, it is a panoramic view of the frustrations and defeats of contemporary urban life. Frequently shifting focus among its marginally related characters, the novel details an oppressive picture of human calamity and defeat; fires, accidents, brawls, crimes, and suicides abound, and unhappiness is pervasive. The novel is uneven; it is contrived in its plotting and confusing in its use of time but interesting and especially noteworthy for its development of formal devices that would be better employed in *U.S.A.*

Dos Passos' 1920s output also included a volume of free verse, *A Pushcart at the Curb* (1922); two impressionistic travel books, *Rosinante to the Road Again* (1922) and *Orient Express* (1927); a novel, *Streets of Night* (1923);

two plays; and a tract in defense of the anarchists Sacco and Vanzetti, *Facing the Chair* (1927).

Politics and Reportage

The political implications of Dos Passos' early writings are clearly socialist, and in 1926 he helped found the *New Masses,* a Marxist political and cultural journal, to which he contributed until the early 1930s. In 1927 he was jailed in Boston for picketing on behalf of Sacco and Vanzetti. In 1928 he visited the Soviet Union. Returning to the United States in 1929, he married Katherine F. Smith.

As a political reporter for the *New Republic* and other journals during the early 1930s, Dos Passos covered labor flareups, political conventions, the Depression, and the New Deal. His fundamental distrust of organized society extended to organizations as well, and despite his sympathy with many Communist causes he was always a maverick rather than a party radical. In 1934 an overt rift developed between Dos Passos and the Communist movement, and it marked the beginning of a long shift to the right in his political sympathies.

After a one-man show of his sketches in 1937, Dos Passos went to Spain to help Hemingway and Joris Ivens make a film documentary of the Spanish Civil War, *The Spanish Earth.* Dos Passos and Hemingway, who had earlier survived an auto accident together, were good friends until Dos Passos' sympathies with the anarchist faction estranged Hemingway, who was partial to the main Loyalist forces.

In 1940 Dos Passos became active in behalf of political refugees, and during World War II did a good deal of war writing, principally for *Harper's* and *Life* magazines, for whom he later covered the postwar Nuremberg trials.

Major Work

U.S.A. (1937), Dos Passos' masterpiece, is a trilogy made up of *The 42nd Parallel* (1930), *Nineteen-Nineteen* (1932), and *The Big Money* (1936). To solve the time problem that flawed *Manhattan Transfer,* Dos Passos employed three unusual devices: "The Camera Eye," autobiographical episodes rendered in a Joycean stream of consciousness; "Newsreel," a Dada-like pastiche of mass culture, combining fragments of pop songs, newspaper headlines, and political speeches; and short biographies, impressionistic sketches of some of the prominent figures of the 1900-1930 time span—Henry Ford, William Randolph Hearst, Thomas A. Edison, Charles Steinmetz, and others. These sections serve as time guides and also as markers separating the narrative chapters that constitute the bulk of the trilogy and are concerned with a cross section of American social types. Among these are Mac McCreary, a poor boy who grows to a class consciousness and revolutionary commitment so strong that he deserts his family to serve the revolution in Mexico; Eleanor Stoddard, a New York interior decorator, whose gentility and estheticism are pitiably empty responses to her sordid childhood; Evaline Hutchins, an aspiring artist with little talent whose boredom with her habit of failure leads her to suicide; J. Ward Morehouse, a self-made millionaire publicist and labor politician and a prototype of the ruthless opportunist; Richard Savage, a Harvard esthete

and idealist who ultimately succumbs to the enticements of big business and becomes a Morehouse employee; Mary French, an idealistic union official who becomes disillusioned with the radical movement when her Communist fiancé marries someone of the party's choice; and Charley Anderson, a likable inventor who makes a fortune in the airplane business.

The characters' lives cross briefly and futilely. All are seen in dual perspective: publicly, as they relate to the class struggle between labor and industry; and privately, as they suffer frustration and a gnawing sense of unfulfillment. Though they are closely observed, the characters rarely get beyond social typology, so that the predominant narrative sections, ironically, are less compelling than the "device" sections. However, its scope and daring give *U.S.A.* distinction, and it had a powerful impact on the social novel in America.

Later Life and Work

In a 1947 auto accident Dos Passos lost an eye and his wife was killed. In 1950 he married Elizabeth H. Holdridge; their daughter was Dos Passos' only child. After 1949 he lived principally on his family farm in Westmoreland, Va. Dos Passos died on Sept. 28, 1970, in Baltimore.

Always prolific, after the war Dos Passos divided his writing between reportage and fiction. His later novels tend toward moodiness and romantic despair. *District of Columbia* (1952) is a trilogy consisting of *Adventures of a Young Man* (1939), *Number One* (1943), and *The Grand Design* (1949). A chronicle of the Spotswood family, it takes as its theme the destruction of individuals by a complex, mechanistic, industrial society. Critics were generally displeased with the trilogy.

Chosen Country (1951), an autobiographical novel; *Most Likely to Succeed* (1954), a novel of leftist infighting; and *The Great Days* (1958), a semiautobiographical novel, add up to little more than an anti-Communist warning to the effect that the end never justifies the means. This is also the substance and weakness of *State of the Nation* (1944), *Tour of Duty* (1946), the General Mills-commissioned *The Prospect before Us* (1950), and *The Theme Is Freedom* (1956).

Among Dos Passos' other nonfiction titles are *The Ground We Stand On* (1941), a historical survey of Anglo-American democracy; *The Head and Heart of Thomas Jefferson* (1954), a biography; *Prospects of a Golden Age* (1959), a composite biographical account of early American culture; and *The Portugal Story* (1969), a historical study.

Further Reading

Dos Passos' *The Best Times* (1966) is a fragmentary autobiography, ranging from 1896 to 1936 but focused mainly on the 1920s; it offers an especially interesting account of his literary friendships. John H. Wrenn, *John Dos Passos* (1962), is a good critical biography. Excellent critical evaluations of Dos Passos may be found in Malcolm Cowley, *Exile's Return* (1934; new ed. 1951); Joseph Warren Beach, *American Fiction, 1920-1940* (1941); Maxwell Geismar, *Writers in Crisis: The American Novel between Two Wars* (1942); Alfred Kazin, *On Na-*

tive Grounds: An Interpretation of Modern American Prose Literature (1942; abr. ed. 1956); and Jean-Paul Sartre, *Literary and Philosophical Essays* (1955).

Additional Sources

Carr, Virginia Spencer, *Dos Passos: a life,* Garden City, N.Y.: Doubleday, 1984.

Knox, George Albert, *Dos Passos and "the revolting playwrights",* Philadelphia: R. West, 1977.

Ludington, Townsend, *John Dos Passos: a twentieth century odyssey,* New York: Dutton, 1980. □

Stephen Arnold Douglas

U.S. senator Stephen Arnold Douglas (1813-1861), the foremost leader of the Democratic party in the decade preceding the Civil War, was Lincoln's political rival for the presidency.

Stephen A. Douglas was born in Brandon, Vt., on April 23, 1813. His father's early death meant Stephen's dependence on a bachelor uncle and later, a detested apprenticeship as a cabinetmaker. When his mother remarried and went to Canandaigua, N.Y., Stephen followed. He attended the academy there, developed a formidable talent as a debater, and became an ardent follower of Andrew Jackson.

Douglas made up for his short stature (5 feet 4 inches) in aggressiveness, audacity, and consuming political ambition. When he said farewell to his mother at 20, he promised to return "on his way to Congress," a prediction he made good 10 years later. He settled in Illinois, where he became a teacher. He taught himself law with borrowed books, became active in the Democratic party, and at 27 was a member of the Illinois State Supreme Court, the youngest ever to attain that office. He was called Judge Douglas thereafter.

Career in Congress

Elected to the House of Representatives in 1843 and to the Senate in 1847, Douglas became a power in all legislation having to do with territories in the West. Known as the "Little Giant" because of his massive head, heavy brown hair, broad shoulders, and booming voice, he soon won the reputation of being the most formidable legislative pugilist in Washington. His enemies called him ruthless; his admirers strove to make him president.

In 1847 Douglas married Martha Denny Martin. The following year she inherited a Mississippi plantation with 150 slaves; by the terms of his father-in-law's will, Douglas was made manager. Though he always denied ownership of any slaves himself, he did manage the plantation up to his death, and there is little doubt that he looked upon his own marriage as symbolic of a successful bridging of North and South. When his wife, after having two sons, died in childbirth, he became depressed and turned for a time to liquor. A tour abroad rejuvenated his spirits, and in 1856 he married the beautiful Adèle Cutts, another Southern woman.

Though privately Douglas held slavery to be "a curse beyond computation," publicly he pronounced it a matter "of climate, of political economy, of self-interest, not a question of legislation." It was good for Louisiana, he said, but bad for Illinois. Essentially proslavery in his legislation, he voted against abolition petitions, favored the annexation of Texas, helped Henry Clay push through the Compromise of 1850, and encouraged the purchase of Cuba to make a new slave state.

Doctrine of "Squatter Sovereignty"

Douglas's failure to reckon with the enormity of the slavery evil, and the growing Northern resentment against it, led him to devise in 1854 what modern historian Allan Nevins called "the worst Pandora's box in our history." In planning for two new states, Kansas and Nebraska, he insisted that the slavery issue be resolved by the settlers themselves rather than by Congress, thus repudiating the 20-year-old Missouri Compromise. Southern extremists saw in this "squatter sovereignty" doctrine an opportunity to make Kansas a slave state, though a majority of the actual settlers were against slavery. Missourians crossed the border at election time to overwhelm the polls and vote in a proslavery government. The antislavery majority set up a rival government in Topeka, and soon there was a small but bloody civil war in Kansas. Douglas was denounced by the abolitionists. Charles Sumner in the Senate called him the squire of slavery, "ready to do all its humiliating offices."

When President James Buchanan recognized the proslavery government in Kansas, Douglas, angered by the misuse of his popular-sovereignty doctrine, denounced the President in 1857, thereby alienating his friends in the South and damaging his presidential chances. But his Kansas-Nebraska Bill had also alienated his antislavery followers in illinois, who charged him with conniving with railroad speculators. In 1858 he went home to face a difficult reelection battle, with Abraham Lincoln as his opponent.

Debates with Lincoln

In his famous debates with Lincoln, Douglas opposed African American citizenship in any form and attacked as "monstrous heresy" Lincoln's insistence that "the Negro and the white man are made equal by the Declaration of Independence and by Divine Providence." Douglas held that African Americans "belong to an inferior race and must always occupy an inferior position." Lincoln denounced Douglas's popular-sovereignty idea as "a mere deceitful pretense for the benefit of slavery" and emphasized the callousness of Douglas's statement: "When the struggle is between the white man and the Negro, I am for the white man; when it is between the Negro and the crocodile, I am for the Negro."

Douglas barely won the senatorial election, but the debates won national recognition for his rival. In 1860, when Lincoln was nominated for president on the Republican ticket, Douglas said of him to Republicans, "Gentlemen, you have nominated a very able and a very honest man."

Presidential Candidate

Douglas expected to be nominated for president in the Democratic convention in Charleston, but a block of Southerners bolted the party, nominating instead John C. Breckinridge. The remaining Democrats nominated Douglas at a second convention in Baltimore. A fourth convention, organized by the Constitutional Union party, nominated John Bell. Douglas suspected that the four-candidate election would ensure Lincoln's victory but nevertheless campaigned vigorously, urging support for the Union he loved. "I wish to God," he said in New York City, "that we had an Old Hickory now alive in order that he might hang Northern and Southern traitors on the same gallows." In the South he deplored secession, which he said would make it necessary for his children to obtain a passport to visit the graves of their ancestors.

A Douglas feared, Lincoln's victory brought the immediate secession of South Carolina from the Union, and other states quickly followed. Douglas still labored for compromises to restore the Union, and he urged Lincoln to support a projected 13th Amendment which would guarantee that slavery would never be tampered with in the slave states. The firing on Ft. Sumter on Jan. 9, 1861, by Confederate forces ended his compromise efforts. He now swung behind Lincoln, urging a vigorous war effort and rallying Northern Democrats to the cause of the Union.

Douglas contracted typhoid fever and died June 3, 1861. Thus Lincoln lost his ablest rival at precisely the moment in history when he was most needed.

Further Reading

The bulk of Douglas's papers are at the University of Chicago, with additional letters in the illinois State Historical Society Library and the Chicago Historical Society. The brief *Autobiography of Stephen A. Douglas* (1913) and a volume of his letters, *The Letters of Stephen A. Douglas,* edited by Robert W. Johannsen (1961), are good source materials. The earliest good biography is Allen Johnson, *Stephen A. Douglas: A Study in American Politics* (1908). George Fort Milton in *The Eve of Conflict: Stephen A. Douglas and the Needless War* (1934) proves to be the most sympathetic of all the biographers and contends that, had Douglas been elected president in 1860, he would have prevented the Civil War. The same thesis in echoed in Gerald M. Capers, *Stephen A. Douglas: Defender of the Union,* edited by Oscar Handlin (1959). Historians are more critical of Douglas than these laudatory biographers. □

William Orville Douglas

William Orville Douglas (1898-1980) was one of the most liberal and activist justices of the U.S. Supreme Court and a vigorous and controversial writer.

William Orville Douglas was born on October 16, 1898, in Maine, Minnesota, where his father, a Nova Scotian missionary, had moved as an itinerant preacher. At the age of 4 William was stricken with polio; to strengthen his spindly legs he began the hiking and later the mountain climbing that became one of his characteristic signatures. When he was 6 his father died, leaving his mother and the three children to make their way on very little, so they moved in with relatives in Yakima, Washington. There William and his two siblings worked their respective ways through school in odd chores and farming jobs. William got a scholarship to Whitman College in Walla Walla, Washington, and upon graduating spent 2 years teaching English and Latin in his hometown high school.

But Douglas's aim was the law. He arrived at Columbia University Law School in 1922 almost penniless, and had to once again work his way through school doing tutoring and research for a law textbook. He was befriended by Dean Harlan Stone and deeply influenced by Professor Underhill Moore, who had a new approach to the legal sociology of corporate business, which became Douglas' focus while at Columbia. This was also the period of the creative jurisprudence on the U.S. Supreme Court of Justice Louis D. Brandeis, and this "People's Attorney" and iconoclastic judge became one of Douglas's heroes. After graduating second highest in his class and editor of Columbia's law journal, Douglas worked for Cravath, DeGersdorff, Swaine & Wood, a huge Wall Street law firm in 1925, and practiced for a year in Yakima. He was admitted to the bar in 1926. He joined the faculty at Columbia Law School in 1927 but resigned in protest against the appointment of a new dean without faculty consultation a year later. A chance meeting with Dean Robert M. Hutchins of the Yale Law School led to Douglas's appointment to a professorship there at the age of 32, and just over a year later he was made Sterling Professor of Law.

Douglas's life was transformed by President Franklin Roosevelt's New Deal, with its sense of social urgency and unparalleled opportunity for reform. In 1934 the newly created Securities and Exchange Commission asked the young law professor for a memorandum on the abuses of corporate reorganization and how these could be remedied. Douglas's reply was an eight-volume report that led to his appointment in 1936 as a member of the Commission and in 1937 he became its chairman. He prodded the stock exchanges into reorganizing themselves and also developed the Commission's surveillance of the prospectuses for new security issues, which did much to stabilize the exchanges.

When Justice Brandeis retired from the Commission, President Franklin Roosevelt turned to Douglas, despite his youth. Justice Douglas took his seat on April 17, 1939. There was talk of Douglas's resigning for high political office on two occasions during the intervening years. One time was in 1944, when Roosevelt sent two names to the Democratic Convention managers as his preferences for vice-presidential running mate—Douglas and Harry Truman. The choice fell to Truman, partly because political moguls mistrusted Douglas just as business moguls did. The second occasion was in 1948, when President Truman, needing a strong, liberal running mate, offered the place to Douglas, who turned it down.

As a justice, Douglas was one of the hardcore liberal "activists," in the sense that he believed that judicial neutrality was a myth and that judges could not rely on constitutional precedent or hard-and-fast constitutional texts to give them the judicial answers. Douglas believed that judicial

statesmanship must keep up with social change and that a judge has the duty actively to shape the law in the desired social direction. Placed for a time in a dissenting minority with Justice Hugo Black, he later found himself part of a liberal majority, as Roosevelt's appointees gradually took over the Court. He went on the defensive again in the conservative Frederick Vinson court of the cold war period but again was part of the liberal majority of the Earl Warren court.

Douglas took a strong role in desegregation cases, in the assurance of fair governmental procedures for the accused, in the freedom of religion cases, and in the cases concerning the right of access to birth-control information. In the obscenity cases he took a firm stand for the absolute freedoms guaranteed against censorship of any sort by the 1st Amendment, which to some made him a proponent of smut and "un-American" values.

Douglas's continuous record of militant judicial liberalism was bound to awaken hostility. There were rumblings about impeaching Douglas when he granted a brief stay of execution to Julius and Ethel Rosenberg, who had been convicted of spying on American atomic bomb technology. Anti-Douglas sentiments were fed by his three divorces and by his judicial opinions in religion-in-the-schools and obscenity cases. To a growing number of people he had offended God, the home, and the purity of the printed word. His book, *Points of Revolution* (1970), compared the current American Establishment with George III's, saying that unless it accepted the pressures for nonviolent revolutionary change, it would be overthrown by violence; this also stirred ire.

The impeachment movement this time gained considerable strength in the House of Representatives, fed mainly by tensions of the era and partisan politics, and a committee looking into his affairs was formed. Gerald Ford, while still in Congress, was the leading voice against Douglas. The impeachment-mongerers had their opening in Douglas's association with the Parvin fund, whose purposes were impeccable but whose money, it turned out, came from sources tainted with gambling. He collected a small fee that, despite being negligible, he still paid income taxes on, which his attackers claimed caused a conflict of interest, despite many of the other justices and government officials having received similar compensations. The impeachment attempts were all inconclusive, but persisted until Douglas retired from the Court in 1975.

An indomitable traveler, naturalist, mountain climber, lecturer, and writer, as well as teacher, administrator, and judge, Douglas reasserted the possibility of a many-faceted Renaissance existence as against a specialized, limited life. His career covered 4 decades of stormy American experience, from the early New Deal days to the tensions of the Vietnam War and the student confrontations of the late 1960s and early 1970s. He brought to these years of turmoil legal and financial skills, a passion for individual freedom, and a plain-spoken brusqueness. He will be remembered as one of the few public figures who dared challenge convention and the Establishment during the middle of the 20th century. He died on January 19, 1980.

Further Reading

William Douglas wrote multiple books, though they are more centered around either law, political philosophy, or nature than himself. However, he did write a few autobiographies, including *Go East, Young Man: The Early Years* (1974) and *The Court Years* (1980). A biographical sketch and a selection of Douglas's judicial opinions are in Vern Countryman, ed., *Douglas of the Supreme Court: A Selection of His Opinions* (1959). Douglas and the Supreme Court are also discussed in John Paul Frank, *The Warren Court* (1964); Leo Pfeffer, *This Honorable Court: A History of the United States Supreme Court* (1965); and Henry Julian Abraham, *Freedom and the Court: Civil Rights and Liberties in the United States* (1967). See also the chapter "William O. Douglas: Diogenes on Wall Street" in Max Lerner, *Ideas Are Weapons: The History and Uses of Ideas* (1939). □

Frederick Douglass

The foremost African American abolitionist in antebellum America, Frederick Douglass (ca. 1817-1895) was the first African American leader of national stature in United States history.

Frederick Douglass was born, as can best be determined, in February 1817 (he took the 14th as his birthday) on the eastern shore of Maryland. His mother, from whom he was separated at an early age, was a slave named Harriet Bailey. She named her son Frederick Augustus Washington Bailey; he never knew or saw his father. (Frederick adopted the name Douglass much later.) Douglass's childhood, though he judged it in his autobiography as being no more cruel than that of scores of others caught in similar conditions, appears to have been extraordinarily deprived of personal warmth. The lack of familial attachments, hard work, and sights of incredible inhumanity fill the text of his early remembrances of the main plantation of Col. Edward Lloyd. In 1825 his masters decided to send him to Baltimore to live with Hugh Auld.

Mrs. Auld, Douglass's new mistress and a Northerner unacquainted with the disciplinary techniques Southern slaveholders used to preserve docility in their slaves, treated young Douglass well. She taught him the rudiments of reading and writing until her husband stopped her. With this basic background he began his self-education.

Escape to Freedom

After numerous ownership disputes and after attempting to escape from a professional slave breaker, Douglass was put to work in the Baltimore shipyards. There in 1838 he borrowed a African American sailor's protection papers and by impersonating him escaped to New York. He adopted the name Douglass and married a free African American woman from the South. They settled in New Bedford, Mass., where several of their children were born.

Douglass quickly became involved in the antislavery movement, which was gaining impetus in the North. In 1841, at an abolitionist meeting in Nantucket, Mass., he delivered a moving speech about his experiences as a slave and was immediately hired as a lecturer by the Massachu-

setts Antislavery Society. By all accounts he was a forceful and even eloquent speaker. His self-taught prose and manner of speaking so inspired some Harvard students that they persuaded him to write his autobiography. *The Narrative of the Life of Frederick Douglass* was published in 1845. (Ten years later an enlarged autobiography, *My Bondage and My Freedom,* appeared. His third autobiography, *Life and Times of Frederick Douglass,* was published in 1881 and enlarged in 1892.) The 1845 publication, of course, meant exile for Douglass, a fugitive slave.

Fearing capture, Douglass fled to Britain, staying from 1845 to 1847 to speak on behalf of abolition and to earn enough money to purchase his freedom when he returned to America. Upon his return Douglass settled in Rochester, N.Y., and started publishing his newspaper, *North Star* (which continued to be published under various names until 1863).

In 1858, as a consequence of his fame and as unofficial spokesman for African Americans, Douglass was sought out by John Brown as a recruit for his planned attack on the Harpers Ferry arsenal. But Douglass could see no benefit from what he considered a futile plan and refused to lend his support.

Civil War and Reconstruction

The Civil War, beginning in 1861, raised several issues, not the least of which was what role the black man would play in his own liberation—since one of the main objectives of the war was emancipation of the slaves. Douglass kept this issue alive. In 1863, as a result of his continued insistence (as well as of political and military expediency), President Abraham Lincoln asked him to recruit African American soldiers for the Union Army. As the war proceeded, Douglass had two meetings with Lincoln to discuss the use and treatment of African American soldiers by the Union forces. In consequence, the role of African American soldiers was upgraded each time and their military effectiveness thereby increased.

The Reconstruction period laid serious responsibilities on Douglass. Politicians differed on the question of race and its corresponding problems, and as legislative battles were waged to establish the constitutional integrity of the slaves' emancipation, Douglass was the one African American with stature enough to make suggestions.

In 1870 Douglass and his sons began publishing the *New National Era* newspaper in Washington, D.C. In 1877 he was appointed by President Rutherford B. Hayes to the post of U.S. marshal for the District of Columbia. From this time until approximately 2 years before his death Douglass held a succession of offices, including that of recorder of deeds for the District of Columbia and minister-resident and consul-general to the Republic of Haiti, as well as chargé d'affaires to Santo Domingo. He resigned his assignments in Haiti and Santo Domingo when he discovered that American businessmen were taking advantage of his position in their dealings with the Haitian government. He died in Washington, D.C., on Feb. 20, 1895.

Further Reading

Douglass's writings can be found in *The Life and Writings of Frederick Douglass*, edited by Philip S. Foner (4 vols., 1950-1955). *Frederick Douglass*, edited by Benjamin Quarles (1968), contains excerpts from Douglass's writings, portrayals of him by his contemporaries, and appraisals by later historians.

Benjamin Quarles, *Frederick Douglass* (1948), is a well-written, scholarly biography. See also Philip S. Foner, *Frederick Douglass: A Biography* (1964), and Arna Bontemps, *Free at Last: The Life of Frederick Douglass* (1971). There is a biographical sketch of Douglass in William J. Simmons, *Men of Mark: Eminent, Progressive and Rising* (1887; repr. 1968). Works that discuss Douglass at length are John Hope Franklin, *From Slavery to Freedom: A History of American Negroes* (1947; 3d ed. 1967); Louis Filler, *The Crusade against Slavery, 1830-1860* (1960); and Martin Duberman, ed., *The Antislavery Vanguard: New Essays on the Abolitionists* (1965). □

Herman Theodore Dreiser

American novelist Herman Theodore Dreiser (1871-1945) projected a vitality and an honesty that established several of his novels as classics of world literature.

Like other naturalistic novelists of the 1890s Theodore Dreiser believed in evolutionary and materialistic determinism and gave these ideas powerful expression. Preoccupied with sex, he demanded the freedom to write about it as he saw fit. His hard-won victories over narrow-minded censorship marked a turning point in the history of the American novel.

Dreiser was born Aug. 27, 1871, in Terre Haute, Ind., one of 12 children of a German Catholic immigrant and an Ohio woman who gave up her Mennonite religion and her family's good opinion to marry him. Theodore was a sickly child with an almost sightless right eye; he seemed at first to have less chance of survival than the three brothers who had died before him in infancy.

Growing Up Poor

For the elder Dreiser, making a living for his large family was difficult. In 1867 he had moved them to Sullivan, Ind., where, by going deeply into debt, he bought a woolen mill that seemed promising. But in 1869 fire destroyed Dreiser's mill, leaving him even more deeply in debt. This burden was to weigh heavily upon all members of the family for years. Theodore was 7 in 1878, when his parents decided that breaking up their home was necessary for economic survival. The older children followed their father in search of jobs. The younger three, including Theodore, moved with their mother to Vincennes and then back to Sullivan. There one of the older daughters rejoined them; she was pregnant by a man who refused to marry her. When the baby was still-born in April 1878, they buried it secretly.

The family's years in Sullivan were hard for young Dreiser. He was sent home from parochial school because he had no shoes. The family was so poor that his mother took in washing (Dreiser was to remember having to deliver the bundles to affluent homes), and the boys gathered coal from the railroad tracks to keep the fire going. Dreiser's father descended upon the house-hold occasionally to rail about the children's failings in religion and morality.

The year 1881, however, brought a melodramatic reversal for the family. Paul, one of the older brothers, unexpectedly appeared, beaming with good humor and opulence. He had begun to establish his reputation as a songwriter (he would later win fame with such songs as "My Gal Sal" and "On the Banks of the Wabash"; for the latter Theodore supplied the words of the first stanza and chorus). Paul settled his mother with the younger children in a cozy home in Evansville and himself in the town's most spendid brothel, which was kept by Sallie Walker—his "Gal Sal." Food, clothing, and coal were now no problem, but Paul's flagrant life of sin troubled the religious Theodore. Paul's turbulent romance with the beautiful madam ended in 1884; he left town to seek work elsewhere. Dreiser's mother took her family to Chicago, where Theodore got a job in a dry goods store, but he was miserable and soon quit. His father rejoined the family, also out of work. Without Paul's help the Dreisers ran quickly into debt again, and soon they fled the bill collectors to Warsaw, Ind.

The nuns who had been Dreiser's teachers up to that time had made him fear school. In Warsaw he entered the public schools. A young woman teacher encouraged the shy boy to read: he fell in love with her and with the books she recommended. Again older sisters stirred town gossip: one ran off with a bar cashier who had stolen $3,500 from the bar's safe, and another had an affair with the son of a wealthy family that ended in pregnancy. These events would later provide materials for Dreiser's fiction, but at 15 he felt them only as humiliating. He left school and went to Chicago to work as a dishwasher and then a stock clerk.

In 1888 one of Dreiser's Warsaw teachers found him in Chicago and sent him to the University of Indiana the next year. College lasted only a year for him, but it was an important year. As a result of his exposure to college girls, his consciousness of the power of sex, the great theme of his fiction, became acute—and acutely painful. He returned home in 1890 to work and help care for his mother, who died that November. When a Bavarian priest refused her a funeral Mass because she had not received the last rites of the Church, Dreiser lost whatever remained of his father's religion.

Journalistic Career

Before his twenty-first birthday Dreiser had found a job on the staff of the *Chicago Globe*. Progressing rapidly in newspaper work, he moved to the *St. Louis Globe-Democrat*. In 1893 the *St. Louis Republic* sent him to the World's Columbian Exposition in Chicago as leader of a group of schoolteachers, one of whom was a pretty redhead named Sara Osborne White, called "Jug." Dreiser was then having an affair with his landlady and was romantically involved with some other women, but Jug would 6 years later become his wife. To fulfill his dream of quick success, and perhaps also to try to escape Jug, Dreiser quit his job and traveled east, taking a job on the *Pittsburgh Dispatch*. There he saw the injustices of industrial society in sharp focus, yet

his editors stopped his stories about them, explaining, "The big steel men just about own the place."

If he could not write, Dreiser could read: Honoré de Balzac shaped his conception of the novel, and T.H. Huxley and Herbert Spencer gave him a new philosophy. Spencer, Dreiser reported later, "took every shred of belief away from me; showed me that I was a chemical atom in a whirl of unknown forces. . . ." In that frame of mind he moved to New York in 1894 and found work on the *World*. But the shy young man, very tall, very thin, his bad eye partially hidden by his gold-rimmed glasses, neither looked nor acted the part of the brash metropolitan reporter. If he had not quit, he would surely have been fired.

Almost destitute, Dreiser convinced his brother Paul and two other songwriters to let him edit a magazine that would give their work wider audience. Dreiser titled it *Ev'ry Month,* and filled it with popular poetry, stories, and essays, as well as the songs; he also published Stephen Crane's "A Mystery of Heroism," some other pieces of literary interest, and many of his own serious articles. He left this magazine in 1897 but found work on other magazines, for which he interviewed Thomas A. Edison, Andrew Carnegie, William Dean Howells, Marshall Field, and other celebrities, writing of their rise to success. For the first time he had money—and no further excuse for postponing marriage to the eager Jug; it took place in December 1898.

For more than a dozen years Dreiser continued his successful journalistic career in New York. He wrote features for the *Daily News;* edited dime novels; and served as editor of *Smith's Magazine, Broadway Magazine,* and three magazines published to encourage women to buy Butterick dress patterns, including the *Delineator.* He raised the *Delineator's* circulation dramatically by anticipating the responses of its female readers. (In 1908 he secured H.L. Mencken as a contributor—the beginning of a long, important friendship.) Dreiser was one of the best-paid editors in the country in 1910, when the enraged mother of an 18-year-old girl with whom he was in love got him fired by threatening to make public the sordid history of his philandering. His marriage also suffered: his wife went home to her family in Missouri. She returned now and again, but in 1914 their separation became permanent, although neither sought a divorce.

Career as Novelist

Dreiser had begun experimenting with fiction in 1899. His first important novel, *Sister Carrie,* occupied him for about 4 months in 1899-1900. Jug helped with the grammar, and literary friends reduced the manuscript by 40,000 words after Dreiser had finished it; although Dreiser required help in polishing the surface of his work, the profundities of the novel's conceptions and characterizations prove that he was from the beginning a master of the essentials of fiction. The novel's heroine, Carrie Meeber, goes to Chicago to live with her sister and seek work but finds working conditions terrible and pay small. She becomes the mistress of a salesman but turns subsequently to Hurstwood, manager of an elegant bar. Hurstwood, whose marriage is breaking up, is tempted to steal money from the bar's safe, which he finds open. He removes the money, then decides to return it to the safe, but the safe door accidently closes and locks: chance has made him a thief. Chance operates again and again in the lives of Hurstwood and Carrie (with whom he runs away), bringing one to suicide and the other to an ungratifying success as a musical comedy star. The novel is far from explicit in its treatment of sex, but in its failure to give virtue and vice their appropriate rewards it constituted an affront to the official moral standards of the day. One publisher turned it down; but at Doubleday, Page and Company, it received a warm reception from Frank Norris, who was reader for the firm. Doubleday contracted to publish *Carrie,* but when Frank Doubleday and his wife read it, they had second thoughts. Dreiser held the firm to their contract, however, and they published the book in 1901 but did not advertise it. Norris tried hard to publicize it, but the final tally showed 456 copies sold, giving the author a royalty of $68.40. Not until 1907, when another publisher reissued it, did *Sister Carrie* attract notice and sell.

The initial failure of *Sister Carrie* drove Dreiser to a nervous and physical breakdown, but with Paul's help he recovered and turned back to his editorial work. When he lost his job at Butterick in 1910, he went to work on the other novels he had begun after *Sister Carrie.* Now he finished *Jennie Gerhardt.* Published in 1911, it received critical acclaim and sales success, in part because, without compromising his principles, Dreiser avoided affronting public morals this time: Jennie, also drawn from Dreiser's wayward sisters, does not prosper from her sins. Encouraged by the novel's success, Dreiser pressed ahead on *The Financier,* which was based on the sensational career of Charles T. Yerkes (named Frank Algernon Cowperwood in the novel), who made a fortune in Philadelphia, went to prison for embezzlement, and made another fortune after his release, while scoring almost as many romantic triumphs as business coups. *The Titan* (1914) and *The Stoic* (1947) continue with the same character.

A trip to Europe in 1911 provided material for *A Traveler at Forty* (1913), but Dreiser devoted his best efforts to fiction. *The Genius* (1915) is his most autobiographical novel. The romance with the young girl that had ended Dreiser's career at Butterick constitutes a principal incident, but the artist-hero's philosophic calm at the story's end is more wish-fulfillment fantasy than autobiography. Some critics expressed moral outrage. The New York Society for the Suppression of Vice got the book banned for over a year; yet out of the storm a critical consensus was emerging: whatever the moral or literary failings of *The Genius,* it was the work of an artist who possessed elements of genius himself.

An American Tragedy

In the following year Dreiser published several volumes of nonfiction, notably *Twelve Men* (1919). That same year he met his charming 25-year-old cousin Helen Richardson, who was fleeing an unhappy marriage. They moved to Los Angeles together, where she contributed to their household expenses by taking supporting parts in films. In nearly 3 years in California, Dreiser wrote several volumes

of sketches, some bad poetry, and the first 20 chapters of his greatest novel. Based on the highly publicized 1906 murder trial of a young New York man, *An American Tragedy* (2 vols., 1925) shows Clyde Griffiths, impoverished son of a street evangelist, working in his rich uncle's shirt factory and falling in love with a girl of beauty, wealth, and position. Only one thing blocks their marriage: Clyde has made a factory girl pregnant. Alone with the pregnant girl in a boat on a lake, he plots to murder her but loses his nerve; nevertheless, there is an accident, she drowns, and he later pays with his life. The book is genuinely tragic: Clyde is not villain but victim. If there is a villain, it is society with its conventionalism, its economic injustice, and its hypocrisy about sex. The book was a triumph: Joseph Wood Krutch spoke for most critics when he called it "the greatest American novel of our generation." The first 2 weeks' royalty check was for $11,872.02.

That splendid success was the last of Dreiser's novels to appear in his lifetime (two inferior pieces, *The Bulwark,* 1946, and *The Stoic,* 1947, appeared after his death). In 1926 he traveled with Richardson to Europe; in 1927 his trip to the Soviet Union resulted in *Dreiser Looks at Russia* (1928). In 1929 he and Richardson settled near Mount Kisco, N.Y. In 1942 Dreiser's wife died, and in 1944 he married Richardson. Travel, political activity, and a surprising turn toward mysticism occupied his late years. When he died of a heart attack in Hollywood, Calif., on Dec. 28, 1945, he was already well established in the history of world literature. Distinguished films were made in 1951 of *An American Tragedy* (under the title *A Place in the Sun*) and *Sister Carrie.*

Further Reading

Dreiser's autobiographical works include *A Hoosier Holiday* (1916), *A Book about Myself* (1922), and *Dawn* (1931). W.A. Swanberg's admirable *Dreiser* (1965) is the standard biography, but Robert H. Elias, *Theodore Dreiser: Apostle of Nature* (1949), remains valuable for its critical emphasis. Charles Shapiro, *Theodore Dreiser: Our Bitter Patriot* (1962); John J. McAleer, *Theodore Dreiser: An Introduction and Interpretation* (1968); and Ellen Moers, *Two Dreisers* (1969), are full-length discussions of the novels. Larzer Ziff, *The American 1890s: Life and Times of a Lost Generation* (1966), contains a brilliant assessment of Dreiser's accomplishments and relation to his period. □

Charles Richard Drew

African American surgeon Charles Richard Drew (1904-1950) was a pioneer in developing the blood bank and was an outstanding leader in the training of surgeons.

Charles R. Drew was born in Washington, D.C., on June 3, 1904, the eldest of five children. The close-knit family lived in modest circumstances and was highly respected.

Drew was educated in the Washington public schools. He earned a bachelor of arts degree from Amherst College (1926) and his doctor of medicine and master of surgery degrees from McGill University in Canada (1933). Having

their training under him became board-certified and did significant work all over the world.

Drew published 19 papers, the first 13 dealing with blood therapy. The last 6 reflected broadening interests, one posthumous title being "Negro Scholars in Scientific Research."

During 6 years as chairman of the surgical section of the National Medical Association, Drew brought new vigor and standards to the group. He was in demand as a speaker, and he served on numerous boards with a wide spectrum of interests, including the 12th Street Branch of the YMCA in Washington.

Most of Drew's achievements were promptly recognized. He received the Spingarn Medal of the NAACP (1943) and honorary doctor of science degrees from Virginia State College (1945) and Amherst College (1947). In 1946 he became a fellow of the International College of Surgeons and served in 1949 as surgical consultant to the surgeon general, U.S. Army. Drew's radiant geniality and warm sense of humor endeared him to patients. He married Minnie Lenore Robbins on Sept. 23, 1939, and the couple had four children. He was killed in an automobile accident on April 1, 1950.

In 1959 the Sigma Pi Phi fraternity presented an oil portrait of Dr. Drew to the American National Red Cross. In Los Angeles the Charles R. Drew Medical Society and the Charles R. Drew Postgraduate Medical School of the Martin Luther King Jr. Hospital perpetuate his name. A health center in Brooklyn and the Harlem Hospital Center blood bank in New York City are named for him. The surgical section of the National Medical Association has an annual Charles R. Drew Forum for the presentation of original surgical research, and about 20 public schools in America have been named for him.

Further Reading

Three full-length studies of Drew are Richard Hardwick, *Charles Richard Drew: Pioneer in Blood Research* (1967); Robert Lichello, *Pioneer in Blood Plasma: Dr. Charles Richard Drew* (1968) and Roland Bertol, *Charles Drew* (1970). There are sections devoted to Drew in Ben Richardson, *Great American Negroes* (1945; rev. ed. 1956); Emma Gelders Steme, *Blood Brothers: Four Men of Science* (1959); and Louis Haber, *Black Pioneers of Science and Invention* (1970). □

decided upon a career in surgery, he went to Howard University in Washington, D.C., in 1935. After the next year as a surgical resident, he was sent by Howard for 2 years of advanced study under a General Education Board fellowship to Columbia University, which awarded him the doctor of medical science degree (1940).

At Columbia, under the direction of John Scudder, Drew completed his pioneering and definitive thesis *Banked Blood* (1940). The Blood Transfusion Betterment Association in New York funded various programs of research; one of these, on blood plasma, was conducted by Scudder and Drew. In 1940, during World War II, Scudder suggested that the association ship dried plasma to France and England. The association appointed Drew director of its "Blood for Britain" project in September 1940.

In 1941 Drew was appointed director of the first American Red Cross Bank and assistant director of blood procurement for the National Research Council, in charge of blood for use by the U.S. Army and Navy. He criticized the policy of segregating blood racially as having no scientific basis.

In October 1941 Drew returned to Howard as head of the department of surgery and was made an examiner for the American Board of Surgery. Chief of staff of Freedmen's Hospital from 1944 to 1946, he was appointed medical director of the hospital for 1946-1947. At Howard, Drew firmly established a progressive modern surgery program. He was a dynamic and inspirational teacher. While he was still alive, eight of his residents became diplomates of the American Board of Surgery, and many more who started

William Edward Burghardt Du Bois

William Edward Burghardt Du Bois (1868-1963) was a major African American scholar, an early leader in the 20th-century African American protest movement, and an advocate of pan-Africanism.

On Feb. 23, 1868, W. E. B. Du Bois was born in Great Barrington, Mass., where he grew up. During his youth he did some newspaper reporting. In 1884 he graduated as valedictorian from high school. He got his bachelor of arts from Fisk University in Nashville,

of scholars and professionals. Du Bois founded and edited the *Moon* (1906) and the *Horizon* (1907-1910) as organs for the Niagara movement. In 1909 Du Bois was among the founders of the National Association for the Advancement of Colored People (NAACP) and from 1910 to 1934 served it as director of publicity and research, a member of the board of directors, and editor of the *Crisis,* its monthly magazine.

In the *Crisis,* Du Bois directed a constant stream of agitation—often bitter and sarcastic—at white Americans while serving as a source of information and pride to African Americans. The magazine always published young African American writers. Racial protest during the decade following World War I focused on securing antilynching legislation. During this period the NAACP was the leading protest organization and Du Bois its leading figure.

In 1934 Du Bois resigned from the NAACP board and from the *Crisis* because of his new advocacy of an African American nationalist strategy: African American controlled institutions, schools, and economic cooperatives. This approach opposed the NAACP's commitment to integration. However, he returned to the NAACP as director of special research from 1944 to 1948. During this period he was active in placing the grievances of African Americans before the United Nations, serving as a consultant to the UN founding convention (1945) and writing the famous "An Appeal to the World" (1947).

Du Bois was a member of the Socialist party from 1910 to 1912 and always considered himself a Socialist. In 1948 he was cochairman of the Council on African Affairs; in 1949 he attended the New York, Paris, and Moscow peace congresses; in 1950 he served as chairman of the Peace Information Center and ran for the U.S. Senate on the American Labor party ticket in New York. In 1950-1951 Du Bois was tried and acquitted as an agent of a foreign power in one of the most ludicrous actions ever taken by the American government. Du Bois traveled widely throughout Russia and China in 1958-1959 and in 1961 joined the Communist party of the United States. He also took up residence in Ghana, Africa, in 1961.

Pan-Africanism

Du Bois was also active in behalf of pan-Africanism and concerned with the conditions of people of African descent wherever they lived. In 1900 he attended the First Pan-African Conference held in London, was elected a vice president, and wrote the "Address to the Nations of the World." The Niagara movement included a "pan-African department." In 1911 Du Bois attended the First Universal Races Congress in London along with black intellectuals from Africa and the West Indies.

Du Bois organized a series of pan-African congresses around the world, in 1919, 1921, 1923, and 1927. The delegations comprised intellectuals from Africa, the West Indies, and the United States. Though resolutions condemning colonialism and calling for alleviation of the oppression of Africans were passed, little concrete action was taken. The Fifth Congress (1945, Manchester, England) elected Du Bois as chairman, but the power was clearly in the hands of younger activists, such as George Padmore and

Tenn., in 1888, having spent summers teaching in African American schools in Nashville's rural areas. In 1888 he entered Harvard University as a junior, took a bachelor of arts *cum laude* in 1890, and was one of six commencement speakers. From 1892 to 1894 he pursued graduate studies in history and economics at the University of Berlin on a Slater Fund fellowship. He served for 2 years as professor of Greek and Latin at Wilberforce University in Ohio.

In 1891 Du Bois got his master of arts and in 1895 his doctorate in history from Harvard. His dissertation, *The Suppression of the African Slave Trade to the United States of America, 1638-1870,* was published as No. 1 in the Harvard Historical Series. This important work has yet to be surpassed. In 1896 he married Nina Gomer, and they had two children.

In 1896-1897 Du Bois became assistant instructor in sociology at the University of Pennsylvania. There he conducted the pioneering sociological study of an urban community, published as *The Philadelphia Negro: A Social Study* (1899). These first two works assured Du Bois's place among America's leading scholars.

Du Bois's life and work were an inseparable mixture of scholarship, protest activity, and polemics. All of his efforts were geared toward gaining equal treatment for black people in a world dominated by whites and toward marshaling and presenting evidence to refute the myths of racial inferiority.

As Racial Activist

In 1905 Du Bois was a founder and general secretary of the Niagara movement, an African American protest group

Kwame Nkrumah, who later became significant in the independence movements of their respective countries. Du Bois's final pan-African gesture was to take up citizenship in Ghana in 1961 at the request of President Kwame Nkrumah and to begin work as director of the *Encyclopedia Africana.*

As Scholar

Du Bois's most lasting contribution is his writing. As poet, playwright, novelist, essayist, sociologist, historian, and journalist, he wrote 21 books, edited 15 more, and published over 100 essays and articles. Only a few of his most significant works will be mentioned here.

From 1897 to 1910 Du Bois served as professor of economics and history at Atlanta University, where he organized conferences titled the Atlanta University Studies of the Negro Problem and edited or coedited 16 of the annual publications, on such topics as *The Negro in Business* (1899), *The Negro Artisan* (1902), *The Negro Church* (1903), *Economic Cooperation among Negro Americans* (1907), and *The Negro American Family* (1908). Other significant publications were *The Souls of Black Folk: Essays and Sketches* (1903), one of the outstanding collections of essays in American letters, and *John Brown* (1909), a sympathetic portrayal published in the American Crisis Biographies series.

Du Bois also wrote two novels, *The Quest of the Silver Fleece* (1911) and *Dark Princess: A Romance* (1928); a book of essays and poetry, *Darkwater: Voices from within the Veil* (1920); and two histories of black people, *The Negro* (1915) and *The Gift of Black Folk: Negroes in the Making of America* (1924).

From 1934 to 1944 Du Bois was chairman of the department of sociology at Atlanta University. In 1940 he founded *Phylon,* a social science quarterly. *Black Reconstruction in America, 1860-1880* (1935), perhaps his most significant historical work, details the role of African Americans in American society, specifically during the Reconstruction period. The book was criticized for its use of Marxist concepts and for its attacks on the racist character of much of American historiography. However, it remains the best single source on its subject.

Black Folk, Then and Now (1939) is an elaboration of the history of black people in Africa and the New World. *Color and Democracy: Colonies and Peace* (1945) is a brief call for the granting of independence to Africans, and *The World and Africa: An Inquiry into the Part Which Africa Has Played in World History* (1947; enlarged ed. 1965) is a major work anticipating many later scholarly conclusions regarding the significance and complexity of African history and culture. A trilogy of novels, collectively entitled *The Black Flame* (1957, 1959, 1961), and a selection of his writings, *An ABC of Color* (1963), are also worthy.

Du Bois received many honorary degrees, was a fellow and life member of the American Association for the Advancement of Science, and a member of the National Institute of Arts and Letters. He was the outstanding African American intellectual of his period in America.

Du Bois died in Ghana on Aug. 27, 1963, on the eve of the civil rights march in Washington, D.C. He was given a state funeral, at which Kwame Nkrumah remarked that he was "a phenomenon."

Further Reading

Indispensable starting points for an understanding of Du Bois's life are his autobiographical writings (the dates are of the most recent editions): *The Autobiography of W. E. B. Du Bois: A Soliloquy on Viewing My Life from the Last Decades of Its First Century* (1968); *Dusk of Dawn: An Essay toward an Autobiography of a Race Concept* (1968); *Darkwater: Voices from within the Veil* (1969); and *The Souls of Black Folk* (1969). Two critical biographies are Francis L. Broderick, *W. E. B. Du Bois: Negro Leader in a Time of Crisis* (1959), and Elliott M. Rudwick, *W. E. B. Du Bois: A Study of Minority Group Leadership* (1960; 1968). Also of importance is the W. E. B. Du Bois memorial issue of *Freedomways* magazine (vol. 5, no. 1, 1965). This was expanded and published in book form as *Black Titan: W. E. B. Du Bois* (1970). Arna Bontemps, *100 Years of Negro Freedom* (1963), has a biographical sketch. Meyer Weinberg, Walter Wilson, Julius Lester, and Andrew G. Paschal edited Du Bois readers. Philip S. Foner edited *W. E. B. Du Bois Speaks* (1970), two volumes of speeches and addresses. ☐

John Foster Dulles

John Foster Dulles (1888-1959), American diplomat, was secretary of state under Eisenhower. He strove to create a United States policy of "containing" communism.

John Foster Dulles was born in Washington, D.C., on Feb. 25, 1888. His grandfather, John W. Foster, had been secretary of state under Benjamin Harrison, and his uncle, Robert Lansing, had been secretary of state under Woodrow Wilson. Educated at Princeton and the law school of George Washington University, Dulles joined the international law firm of Sullivan and Cromwell in 1911, became a partner in 1920, and was head of the firm in 1927. He was eminent in his field.

Dulles's interest in foreign affairs was of long standing; at the age of 31, he had attended the 1919 Paris Peace Conference as legal counsel to the American delegation. In 1945 he was appointed legal adviser to the United States delegation at the San Francisco conference which drew up the Charter of the United Nations.

A Republican, Dulles served in the U.S. Senate in 1949-1950. In 1951, as ambassador-at-large, he negotiated a peace treaty with Japan acquitting himself brilliantly in overcoming Soviet opposition and other difficulties.

In 1952 Dulles was an ardent partisan of Dwight D. Eisenhower for president and was rewarded the next year with the office of secretary of state, which he held until his death. In his first months in office Dulles brought about an armistice in the Korean War, probably by the threat of the resumption of the war if the negotiations did not succeed. Less successful was his effort to roll back the Iron Curtain: in the East German revolt of 1953 and the Hungarian revolt of

1956 the United States was unable to offer any support to the rebels.

Dulles was a firm supporter of the North Atlantic Treaty Organization and supported the proposal for an international defense force in Europe. This project failed, however, and it was Anthony Eden, rather than Dulles, who played the leading role in forging a new treaty that invigorated the European alliance and admitted Germany to full membership.

In 1955 came the Big Four Conference at Geneva, attended by the four heads of government— Eden of England, Edgar Faure of France, N. A. Bulganin of the U.S.S.R., and Eisenhower of the United States—with a view to bettering understanding with the Soviet Union. Dulles had a part in the proceedings, but little was accomplished. As a matter of fact, from the outset the secretary of state had regarded the project with pessimism.

In 1956 came one of the most serious crises of Dulles's career. In the summer of that year Gamal Abdel Nasser, the Egyptian dictator, seized and nationalized the Suez Canal, creating great resentment in France and Britain. Dulles labored manfully to find a peaceful solution of the problem, but in December the British and the French, using an Israeli attack on Egypt as a pretext, landed forces in the canal zone. With great courage Dulles protested this violation of the peace and brought the situation before the United Nations. As a result, the invaders were compelled to withdraw.

Dulles's activities were by no means confined to Europe. The United States played a part in the overthrow of a Communist regime in Guatemala. In the Far East, Dulles played a leading role in the formation of the Southeast Asia Treaty Organization, an alliance of the United States, Britain, France, Australia, New Zealand, the Philippines, Thailand and Pakistan. This alliance did not explicitly call for armed action, but it bound the signatories to consult whenever the integrity of any country in Southeast Asia was menaced. Importantly, it marked the extension of United States commitments in this area. Dulles also signed a defense treaty with the Chinese Nationalist government on Taiwan (Formosa) and twice thwarted hostile attacks by the (Communist) Chinese People's Republic on the Nationalists' island of Quemoy. Dulles's attempt to bring together some of the countries of the Middle East in opposition to communism resulted in an alliance that soon disintegrated.

A believer in keeping firm opposition to the Communist menace, Dulles based his diplomacy on strong ideology. He was ready to use force or the threat of force (as in the Formosa Strait) when he believed that such action would balk aggression. His diplomacy was highly personal. He was not a great administrator, but he was a dedicated public servant. In the last year of his life he suffered from cancer, which he bore with real heroism. He died on May 24, 1959.

Further Reading

Louis L. Gerson, *John Foster Dulles*, vol. 17 in Samuel F. Bemis and Robert H. Ferrell, eds., *The American Secretaries of State and Their Diplomacy* (1967), is recommended. See also John Robinson Beal, *John Foster Dulles* (1957); Roscoe Drummond and Gaston Coblentz, *Duel at the Brink: John Foster Dulles Command of American Power* (1960); and Richard Goold-Adams, *John Foster Dulles: A Reappraisal* (1962). □

Paul Laurence Dunbar

Paul Laurence Dunbar (1872-1906), poet and novelist, was the first African American author to gain national recognition and a wide popular audience.

Born June 27, 1872, the son of a former slave in Dayton, Ohio, Paul Laurence Dunbar achieved a formal education through high school, graduating in 1891. He had served as editor of the school paper and as class poet. Unable to go to college, Dunbar worked as an elevator operator. He published his first book of poems, *Oak and Ivy,* in 1893 at his own expense, and his second, *Majors and Minors,* 2 years later. Seeing the second book, William Dean Howells, then one of America's most distinguished literary critics, urged the young poet to concentrate on dialect verse.

With the 1896 publication of *Lyrics of Lowly Life,* for which Howells wrote a laudatory preface, Dunbar's professional career got an auspicious start. Demand for his work was soon sufficient to enable him to earn his living as a writer. He took Howell's advice to study the "moods and traits of his own race in its own accents of our English," so that his art was best shown in those "pieces which . . . described the range between appetite and emotion . . . which is the range of the race." (This was Howells's limited view of African Americans.)

Dunbar wanted to satisfy the popular taste for the light, romantic, comic, and sentimental. His short stories, which began appearing in popular magazines in the 1890s, usually depict African American folk characters, Southern scenes, and humorous situations. His first novel, *The Uncalled* (1898), like two of the three that followed—*The Love of Landry* (1900) and *The Fanatics* (1901)—is a sentimental tale about white people. These novels are competent but undistinguished. His last long fiction, *The Sport of the Gods* (1902), is notable only for his failure to realize the potential in the story of an agrarian African American family's urbanization.

In 1898 Dunbar married Alice Moore; the marriage was unhappy, and the couple separated in 1901, when Dunbar went to Washington, D.C., as a consultant to the Library of Congress. He was unhappy with his writing too. At about this time he confided to a friend, "I see now very clearly that Mr. Howells has done me irrevocable harm in the dictum he laid down regarding my dialect verse."

Dunbar had contracted tuberculosis and tried all the "cures"; alcohol brought temporary relief, and he became addicted. He continued to turn out short stories and poems. Sick, and discouraged by the lukewarm reception of *The Heart of Happy Hollow* (1904), a collection of short stories, and of *Lyrics of Love and Sunshine* (1905), which contains some of his best verses in pure English, he returned to Dayton, where he died on Feb. 9, 1906. The *Complete Poems of Paul Laurence Dunbar* (1913; still in print) shows how well he succeeded in capturing many aspects of African American life.

Further Reading

Two full-length biographies of Dunbar are Benjamin Brawley, *Paul Laurence Dunbar: Poet of His People* (1936), and the better-balanced *Paul Laurence Dunbar and His Song* (1947) by Virginia Cunningham. Jean Gould, *That Dunbar Boy* (1958), is for children. Dunbar gets brief treatment in Sterling A. Brown, Arthur P. Davis, and Ulysses Lee, *Negro Caravan* (1941); Hugh M. Gloster, *Negro Voices in American Fiction* (1948); and James A. Emanuel and Theodore L. Gross, *Dark Symphony* (1968). □

William Crapo Durant

The American industrialist William Crapo Durant (1861-1947) was the founder of General Motors, an automobile manufacturing company.

William C. Durant was born in Boston, Mass., on Dec. 8, 1861. He grew up in Flint, Mich., where he became a leading carriage manufacturer. In 1886 he organized the Durant-Dort Company and helped to make Flint the carriage capital of the nation.

Durant acquired control of the Buick Motor Car Company in 1904 and revived it; by 1908 Buick was one of the four leading automobile companies. Durant had a vision of the boundless possibilities of the automobile, particularly the moderate-priced car, and attempted to capitalize on these possibilities by establishing a large-scale enterprise based on volume production. He intended that his company would be well financed, market a variety of automobiles, and produce many of its own parts.

After an attempt to buy Ford Motor Company in 1907 failed because Henry Ford wanted to be paid in cash, Durant established the General Motors Company the next year. He began with the Buick and added Cadillac, Oldsmobile, Oakland (Pontiac), and other lesser companies. Durant overextended himself, and by 1910 General Motors needed the intervention of a bankers' syndicate to lift the burden of debt. Durant returned to the automobile business in 1911 with the Chevrolet car. In 1916, with the backing of the Du Pont family, he recovered control of General Motors.

In 1919 General Motors was one of the largest American industrial enterprises, but Durant exercised little control over its operation; General Motors was too decentralized to be effective. When the Panic of 1920 occurred, Durant was overcommitted in the stock market. He tried unsuccessfully to support the price of General Motors stock; he was forced out of the company in 1920 by the Du Ponts, who wanted to protect their sizable investment.

The remainder of Durant's life was anticlimactic. In 1921 he started Durant Motors, which failed to become a major automobile producer. Durant Motors was already shaky when the 1929 crash occurred; the Depression then sharply reduced automobile sales and resulted in 1933 in dissolution of the firm. Durant was bankrupt by 1935. During his remaining years he engaged in a variety of business enterprises but without marked success. He died in New York City on March 18, 1947.

Durant was a pioneer in the automotive industry, and his most notable creation, General Motors, has dominated the automobile market since. Some of his chance ideas, such as the entry of General Motors into the manufacture of refrigerators, were highly successful. However, Durant never succeeded in organizing and administrative structure adequate for the giant enterprise he founded, and the task of converting General Motors into an enduring monument was left to his successors.

Further Reading

John B. Rae, *The American Automobile: A Brief History* (1965), places Durant in the context of his times and industry. Alfred D. Chandler, Jr., *Strategy and Structure: Chapters in the History of the Industrial Enterprise* (1962), has a chapter which analyzes Durant's administrative strategy. Carl Crow, *The City of Flint Grows Up: The Success Story of an American Community* (1945), includes a brief account of Durant's early years.

Additional Sources

Weisberger, Bernard A., *The dream maker: William C. Durant, founder of General Motors,* Boston: Little, Brown, 1979. □

Bob Dylan

Throughout a career that has seen the better part of three decades, Bob Dylan (born 1941) has been pop music's master poet and an ever-changing performer.

In the early 1960s Bob Dylan was heralded as the spokesman for his generation, writing and singing folk songs that were as deep and moving as those of any artist since his idol, Woody Guthrie. At the 1965 Newport Folk Festival Dylan shocked his following by going electric and venturing into rock and roll. He proved to be equally superior in that field also and by 1968 he was trying his hand at folk-rock, creating an impact that touched even the Beatles and the Rolling Stones. As the 1980s came around Dylan was undergoing a spiritual rebirth and his writing reflected a religious conviction that was truly heartfelt.

Began Exploring Folk Music

Born Robert Zimmerman in Duluth, Minnesota, Dylan was raised in the northern mining town of Hibbing from the age of six. His earliest musical influences, Hank Williams, Muddy Waters, Jimmy Reed, Howlin' Wolf and John Lee Hooker, were brought to him via the airwaves of a Shreveport, Louisiana, radio station. He played in a variety of bands during high school, including the Golden Chords, before enrolling at the University of Minnesota in 1959. It was at college that he changed his name to Dylan (probably after the poet Dylan Thomas) and began creating his own mythological background, which made him out to be everything from an Indian to a hobo to Bobby Vee. After hearing the Kingston Trio and Odetta he began to explore folk music, learning older tunes and sitting in at local coffeehouses around campus.

Just one year into college, Dylan dropped out and hitchhiked to New York to meet legendary singer Woody Guthrie, who was in an East Coast hospital suffering from Huntington's disease. "Guthrie was my last idol," Dylan said in *Rock 100.* "My future idols will be myself." Obviously in little need of self-confidence, by April 1961 he was gigging at Gerde's Folk City in New York's Greenwich Village. With the folk scene booming, Columbia executive and talent scout John Hammond had just signed Pete Seeger; Dylan followed soon after.

His debut LP, *Bob Dylan,* was released in March 1962. Recorded for a mere $402, the album featured acoustic reinterpretations of old folk songs, but also included two Dylan originals, "Song for Woody" and "Talking New York." Within a year his second LP, *The Freewheelin' Bob Dylan*—containing self-penned compositions only—was released. Protest tunes like "A Hard Rain's a-Gonna Fall," "Masters of War," and "Don't Think Twice, It's Alright" were making listeners more conscious and aware, both politically and personally. The trio of Peter, Paul & Mary recorded a version of "Blowin' in the Wind" from the LP that helped put the spotlight on Dylan. In July of that year at the Newport Folk Festival he was crowned leader of the folk movement with Joan Baez as the reigning queen. The new voice of youth, "Dylan's albums were listened to as if they were seismic readings from an impending apocalypse," reported *Rock 100.*

Unique Phrasing

The Times They Are a-Changin', with its title track and "The Lonesome Death of Hattie Carroll," broke in the new year of 1964. Imitators of his guitar/harmonica rig and odd singing (talking?) voice were sprouting up everywhere. "It's phrasing," Dylan told *Rolling Stone*, "I think I've phrased everything in a way that it's never been phrased before." In addition to his unique voice, lyrics, and meter, Dylan's physical image was just as intriguing with his wild conk of hair, stovepipe legs, and facial scowl. As much as the public and critics adored him, they also were frustrated as attempts to gain insight were met with toying word games and sometimes downright humiliation. Dylan began to question his role as guru on his fourth LP, *Another Side of Bob Dylan*, moving away from political themes and towards personal love songs. "My Back Pages" and "It Ain't Me Babe" signalled that a different Dylan had now arrived.

Bringing It All Back Home (1965) was a half-acoustic, half-electric outing that featured Dylan classics "Subterranean Homesick Blues," "Maggie's Farm," "Mr. Tambourine Man," and "It's Alright Ma (I'm Only Bleeding)." Dylan's first step into rock was also his first million-seller. Even so, his die-hard fans were not prepared for Dylan's performance at the 1965 Newport Folk Festival, when he appeared onstage backed by the electric Paul Butterfield Blues Band. Cries of "sell-out" and "gone commercial" filled the air as he was booed off the stage only to return for a final acoustic number, "It's All Over Now, Baby Blue." Anyone who doubted his commitment only needed to check out the next LP, *Highway 61 Revisited*, which was

able to leap off the turntable courtesy of Michael Bloomfield's stinging guitar lines. The album featured the songs "Desolation Row," "Just Like Tom Thumb's Blues," "Queen Jane Approximately," and perhaps Dylan's most popular tune yet, "Like a Rolling Stone" (which went all the way to number two).

1966's Masterpiece *Blond on Blonde*

His masterpiece, *Blond on Blonde* (1966), is considered by some to be the finest rock album in history. A double LP recorded with Nashville session men, it is filled with an amazing display of Dylan's songwriting abilities: "Sad Eyed Lady of the Lowlands," "Absolutely Sweet Marie," "Rainy Day Women No. 12 & 35," "Memphis Blues Again," "I Want You," and others that firmly established Dylan as the most prolific stylist of all time. Just when it seemed he was in full force, Dylan was seriously injured in a motorcycle accident on July 29, 1966. He would spend the next year and a half recuperating from a broken neck in upstate New York. He recorded tracks with his backup group, the Band, but they would not be released until 1975 as *The Basement Tapes* (an LP that was bootlegged endlessly during the nine-year delay).

After flirting with death, Dylan's comeback album, *John Wesley Harding*, relied more on religious themes and a mellower country flavor. "All Along the Watchtower" became a hit shortly after for Jimi Hendrix while the entire mood of *JWH* sent an influential wave out that touched other artists of the time. Dylan carried the country style even further on *Nashville Skyline*, recording a duet with Johnny Cash, and the easy-going "Lay Lady Lay." His next release, however, was a commercial and critical disappointment. *Self-Portrait* was a double album consisting mainly of non-originals that seemed to be almost intentionally bad. *New Morning*, also from 1970, did not fare much better; Dylan's talent seemed to have peaked.

In 1973 Dylan's Columbia contract expired and he signed with Asylum just after releasing his soundtrack to the movie *Pat Garrett and Billy the Kid*, which included one of his biggest hits, "Knockin' on Heaven's Door." (Dylan also played the part of Alias in the film. Actor Sam Shepard told Rolling Stone that Dylan "knows how to play a part. He and Billy Graham are the two greatest actors in the world.") As if in retaliation for his leaving, Columbia released *Dylan*, a collection of studio outtakes and cover tunes that accomplished little more than embarrassing Dylan. His two Asylum LPs, *Planet Waves* and *Before the Flood*, were both recorded with the Band, the first being a studio album and the second featuring live recordings of the ensuing tour in early 1974.

Recordings Reflected Religious Beliefs

In 1975 Dylan re-signed with Columbia and recorded one of his best records yet, *Blood on the Tracks*, which seemed to harken back to his earlier style. "Tangled up in Blue," "Idiot Wind," "Shelter From the Storm," "Meet Me in the Morning," and "Buckets of Rain" amongst others had critics gushing with joy over yet another Dylan comeback. He then hit the road with a musically varied ensemble called the Rolling Thunder Revue: Mick Ronson, Joan Baez, T-Bone Burnett, Roger McGuinn, Ramblin' Jack Elliott, and David Mansfield, all blasting off on Dylan classics and material from his newest LP, *Desire*. That album topped both the British and U.S. charts riding a crest of popularity created by "Hurricane," Dylan's thumping plea for the release of the imprisoned boxer Ruben "Hurricane" Carter. In 1976 the live *Hard Rain* album captured the revue on vinyl. Two years later he would release another fine studio effort, *Street Legal*, featuring "Where Are You Tonight," "Baby Stop Crying," and "Changing of the Guards."

Dylan's next phase can be summed up in three albums, *Slow Train Coming, Saved*, and *Shot of Love*, and one word: Christianity. In 1979 he became "born-again," as writers coined it, studying the Bible at the Vineyard Christian Fellowship school in California. Although raised a Jew, Dylan took his new-found belief to the point of righteousness. "Dylan hadn't simply found Jesus but seemed to imply that he had His home phone number as well," wrote Kurt Loder in his *Rolling Stone* review of *Slow Train Coming*. The LP revolved around Dylan's beliefs, but it also rocked with the aid of Dire Straits guitarist Mark Knopfler. Critics and the public were split over the newest Dylan. Jann Wenner explained his view of this period in *Rolling Stone*: "Dylan created so many images and expectations that he narrowed his room for maneuverability and finally became unsure of his own instincts."

Made MTV *Unplugged* Appearance

A rejuvenated Dylan appeared in 1983 on *Infidels*, produced by Knopfler with ex-Rolling Stone Mick Taylor on guitar. Dylan had joined an ultra-Orthodox Jewish sect, Lubavitcher Hasidim, and the songs reflected the move (although more subtly than during his Christian phase). In the mid-1980s Dylan continued to record and toured with Tom Petty and the Heartbreakers and the Grateful Dead as his backup bands. In 1988 he appeared as one of the Traveling Wilburys alongside Jeff Lynne, Tom Petty, George Harrison,

and the late Roy Orbison. More changes can probably be expected from this master of the unexpected; Dylan has stayed on top by keeping ahead of the pack, knowing where his audience wants to be next, and then delivering.

Another important year for Dylan was 1995, as he reemerged as "the bard who matters most," according to the *Boston Globe*. The rock legend embarked on a U.S. tour, released an *MTV Unplugged* album, and a new CD-ROM entitled *Bob Dylan: Highway 61 Interactive*, all to favorable reviews.

Further Reading

Christgau, Robert, *Christgau's Record Guide*, Ticknor & Fields, 1981.

Dalton, David, and Lenny Kaye, *Rock 100*, Grosset & Dunlap, 1977.

Dylan, Bob, *Tarantula*, Macmillan, 1970.

Bob Dylan: The Illustrated Record, Harmony, 1978.

The Illustrated Encyclopedia of Rock, compiled by Nick Logan and Bob Woffinden, Harmony, 1977.

The Rolling Stone Illustrated History of Rock and Roll, edited by Jim Miller, Random House/Rolling Stone Press, 1976.

The Rolling Stone Record Guide, edited by Dave Marsh with John Swenson, Random House/Rolling Stone Press, 1979.

Shepard, Sam, *Rolling Thunder Logbook*, Viking Press, 1977.

Spitz, Bob, *Dylan, A Biography*, McGraw, 1989.

What's That Sound?, edited by Ben Fong-Torres, Anchor, 1976.

Boston Globe, December 8, 1995; February 9, 1995.

Detroit News, July 9, 1989.

Musician, September 1986.

New York Times, April 30, 1995.

Oakland Press, July 2, 1989.

Rolling Stone, March 11, 1976; September 21, 1978; November 16, 1978; July 12, 1979; September 20, 1979; September 18, 1980; June 21, 1984; Summer 1986; College Papers, Number 3.

USA Today, May 5, 1995.

Washington Post, May 17, 1995; February 8, 1995. □

NAME INDEX

Name Index

OCCUPATION INDEX

Occupation Index

Occupation Index

Occupation Index

Occupation Index

President (continued)

Roosevelt, Franklin Delano
Volume IV: 857

Roosevelt, Theodore
Volume IV: 860

Taft, William Howard
Volume IV: 949

Taylor, Zachary
Volume IV: 953

Truman, Harry S
Volume IV: 972

Tyler, John
Volume IV: 983

Van Buren, Martin
Volume IV: 990

Washington, George
Volume IV: 1009

Wilson, Thomas Woodrow
Volume IV: 1043

Psychologist

Skinner, Burrhus Frederic
Volume IV: 918

Publisher

Hearst, William Randolph
Volume II: 426

Johnson, John Harold
Volume II: 514

Luce, Henry Robinson
Volume III: 630

Religious Leader

Bernardin, Joseph Cardinal
Volume I: 69

Black Elk, Nicholas
Volume I: 80

Divine, Father
Volume I: 255

Graham, William Franklin Jr.
Volume II: 383

Handsome Lake
Volume II: 411

Heschel, Abraham Joshua
Volume II: 444

Mather, Cotton
Volume III: 654

Muhammad, Elijah
Volume III: 719

Perry, Harold Robert
Volume III: 774

Robertson, Pat
Volume IV: 840

Sheen, Fulton J.
Volume IV: 900

Smith, Joseph
Volume IV: 921

Smohalla
Volume IV: 922

Turner, Henry McNeal
Volume IV: 976

Williams, Roger
Volume IV: 1038

Wovoka
Volume IV: 1051

Young, Brigham
Volume IV: 1064

Scholar

Sequoyah
Volume IV: 894

Scientist

Kinsey, Alfred C.
Volume III: 561

Sculptor

Barthe, Richmond
Volume I: 54

Noguchi, Isamu
Volume III: 740

Occupation Index